The Genocide against the Tutsi, and the Rwandan Churches

Between Grief and Denial

JAMES CURREY series information:
RELIGION IN TRANSFORMING AFRICA
ISSN 2398-8673

Series Editors
Barbara Bompani, Joseph Hellweg, Ousmane Kane and **Emma Wild-Wood**

Editorial Reading Panel
Robert Baum (Dartmouth College)
Dianna Bell (University of Cape Town)
Ezra Chitando (University of Zimbabwe)
Martha Frederiks (Utrecht University)
Paul Gifford (SOAS)
David M. Gordon (Bowdoin College)
Jörg Haustein (University of Cambridge)
Paul Lubeck (Johns Hopkins University-SAIS)
Philomena Mwaura (Kenyatta University, Nairobi)
Hassan Ndzovu (Moi University)
Ebenezer Obadare (University of Kansas)
Abdulkader I. Tayob (University of Cape Town)
M. Sani Umar (Northwestern University)
Stephen Wooten (University of Oregon)

Series description
The series is open to submissions that examine local or regional realities on the complexities of religion and spirituality in Africa. Religion in Transforming Africa will showcase cutting-edge research into continent-wide issues on Christianity, Islam and other religions of Africa; Traditional beliefs and witchcraft; Religion, culture & society; History of religion, politics and power; Global networks and new missions; Religion in conflict and peace-building processes; Religion and development; Religious rituals and texts and their role in shaping religious ideologies and theologies. Innovative, and challenging current perspectives, the series provides an indispensable resource on this key area of African Studies for academics, students, international policy-makers and development practitioners.

Please contact the Series Editors with an outline or download the proposal form at www.jamescurrey.com.

Dr Barbara Bompani, Reader in Africa and International Development, University of Edinburgh: b.bompani@ed.ac.uk
Dr Joseph Hellweg, Associate Professor of Religion, Department of Religion, Florida State University: jhellweg@fsu.edu
Professor Ousmane Kane, Prince Alwaleed Bin Talal Professor of Contemporary Islamic Religion & Society, Harvard Divinity School: okane@hds.harvard.edu
Dr Emma Wild-Wood, Senior Lecturer, African Christianity and African Indigenous Religions, University of Edinburgh: emma.wildwood@ed.ac.uk

Previously published titles in the series are listed at the back of this volume.

The Genocide against the Tutsi, and the Rwandan Churches

Between Grief and Denial

Philippe Denis

www.fountainpublishers.co.ug

James Currey
is an imprint of
Boydell & Brewer Ltd
PO Box 9, Woodbridge
Suffolk IP12 3DF (GB)
www.jamescurrey.com
and of
Boydell & Brewer Inc.
668 Mt Hope Avenue
Rochester, NY 14620-2731 (US)
www.boydellandbrewer.com

© Philippe Denis, 2022
Paperback edition 2024
First published in 2022

First published in Uganda and Rwanda in 2022 by Fountain Publishers Ltd
Plot 55 Nkrumah Rd
P. O. Box 488 Kampala
Tel: +256 414 259163 | +256 312 263041 | +256 414 543443
publishing@fountainpublishers.co.ug | www.fountainpublishers.co.ug

The right of Philippe Denis to be identified as
the author of this work has been asserted in accordance with
sections 77 and 78 of the Copyright, Designs and Patents Act 1988

All Rights Reserved. Except as permitted under current legislation
no part of this work may be photocopied, stored in a retrieval system,
published, performed in public, adapted, broadcast, transmitted,
recorded or reproduced in any form or by any means, without the
prior permission of the copyright owner

The publisher has no responsibility for the continued existence or accuracy of URLs for
external or third-party internet websites referred to in this book, and does not guarantee
that any content on such websites is, or will remain, accurate or appropriate

British Library Cataloguing in Publication Data
A catalogue record for this book is available from the British Library

A catalogue record for this book is available from the British Library

ISBN 978-1-84701-290-6 (James Currey hardback)
ISBN 978-1-84701-378-1 (Paperback)
ISBN 978-9970-19-662-3 (Fountain Publishers paperback)

To Lorie, Lucas, Aquilin and Kuelo

Contents

Addenda	viii
Acknowledgements	ix
List of Abbreviations	xi
Map of Rwanda, 1994	xiv
Introduction	1
1 The burden of the past	22
2 The run-up to the genocide	45
3 Religion in the midst of the genocide	69
4 The Catholic Church in the aftermath of the genocide	101
5 The Presbyterian Church's confession of guilt	127
6 The Missionaries of Africa's response to the genocide	158
7 Church and state relations after the genocide	187
8 A case of two narratives: Gabriel Maindron, a hero made and unmade	221
9 Remembering 1994 in Congo-Nil	249
10 The quest for forgiveness and reconciliation	275
Conclusion	304
Select Bibliography	313
Index	327

Addenda: note on genocide figures and their interpretation, and alleged 'crimes of the RPF'

To avoid misunderstanding and for the sake of clarification the author brings the following to the attention of the reader:

1. Number of victims of the genocide against the Tutsi

The estimate of the number of Tutsi victims depends on the manner of its assessment. As Note 5 of the Introduction explains, one method is to use as a starting point the number of Tutsi people in the 1991 Rwandan population census, adjusting it in view of the fact that some Tutsi were counted as Hutu and subtracting from it the number of genocide survivors. Using this method, 'the approximate number of deaths in the genocide could be placed at between 800,000 and 850,000, a loss of about 11% of the population' (G. Prunier, *The Rwanda Crisis: History of a Genocide* (New York: Columbia University Press, 1995, 265)). However, a house survey conducted throughout Rwanda in July 2002 by 1,825 censor agents appointed and trained by the Ministry of Local Governance and Social Affairs, found that 1,074,017 people were declared victims of the genocide against the Tutsi but 934,218 was a more accurate number given the possibility of errors of memory or omissions. This took into consideration people killed between October 1990 and December 1994 because they were Tutsi, looked like Tutsi, were friends to Tutsi or had political opinions vigorously opposed to the divisionist ideology. (Ministry of Local Governance and Social Affairs, *Dénombrement des victimes du génocide. Rapport final* [Enumeration of the victims of the genocide. Final report], Kigali, April 2004: https://cnlg.gov.rw/fileadmin/templates/Publications/denombrement_des_victimes_du_genocide_perpetre_contre_les_tutsi_avril_2004.pdf.

2. Alleged 'crimes of the RPF' (Rwandan Patriotic Front)

There is an abundant literature on the alleged 'crimes of the RPF'. This book discusses this, but readers should note that while the book uses the phrase 'alleged crimes of the RPF' when referring to the issue (pp. 170, 241, 287), this does not mean that the author endorses any suggestion that such crimes were in fact committed. That a certain number of Hutu people were killed before, during and after the genocide against the Tutsi by elements of the RPF as a result of war or for various other reasons is widely recognised, but there is no consensus on the number of victims, which genocide denialists tend grossly to exaggerate. Likewise, there is no evidence that the leadership of the RPF as a political-military organisation was involved in any criminal acts against the Hutu population. Any suggestion that there has been more than one genocide, as defined by the 1948 United Nations' Convention on the Prevention and Punishment of the Crime of Genocide, in Rwanda deserves to be rejected with vigour.

Acknowledgements

It is customary to include a note of gratitude in a book of this kind. Because of the gravity of the subject, the intensity of the emotions involved and the quality of the relationships developed with the research participants as the project moved on, I am at a loss for words. Working on the history of the genocide against the Tutsi has been a challenging experience. I feel humbled by the trust put in me by the men and women who shared their stories with me and who gave access to their archives. I hope that this book, however imperfect it may be, will advance the cause of peace and reconciliation in Rwanda.

I cannot mention the names of all the people who assisted me. I should at least thank the staff of the National Commission for the Fight against Genocide (CNLG) in Kigali, and in particular Jean-Damascène Bizimana and Jean-Damascène Gasanabo, for their willingness to engage in a partnership with me. I express gratitude to the archivists of the Missionaries of Africa in Rome, Brussels and Kigali, the Dominican Missionary Sisters in Namur, the archives of the *Dialogue* Christian journal in Brussels and *La contemporaine* documentation centre at Paris Nanterre University for their help. I also thank the custodians of the archives of the episcopal conference of Rwanda, of the Head Office of the Presbyterian Church in Rwanda, of the Society of Jesus, of the Centre de Formation et de Documentation (CFD), of the Centre de Documentation et de Pastorale (CEDOREP) and the Parliament Library in Kigali for their cooperation.

During the course of this research, I never ceased to exchange views with colleagues sharing the same interests. They helped me to correct misjudged views and identify new sources of information. Some of them agreed to comment upon draft chapters. In some way, this ongoing process of consultation gives this book the character of a collective enterprise, even though I am the only one to take responsibility for it. Marcel Kabanda, Paul Rutayisire and Simon Gasibirege are the first ones I would like to mention because of their ongoing support and engagement during the past six years. I also benefitted from the comments and advice of Hélène Dumas, Remi Korman, Gerard van 't Spijker, Tharcisse Gatwa, Emmanuel Ntakarutimana and Guy Theunis.

As mentioned earlier, the Dominican brothers from Kigali not only hosted me on regular occasions but provided me with a pastoral and intellectual platform from which I could conduct this research in the best possible conditions. They proposed the research assistant who helped me during the first phase of the project. Equally important was the guidance of Émilienne Mukansoro, my second research assistant. By sharing her reflections on her own experience and introducing me to a vast network of genocide survivors, she played a critical role in the research.

I also express my gratitude to the National Research Foundation of South Africa, which funded the project, and to the University of KwaZulu-Natal, which granted me a sabbatical to complete the writing of this book.

Lastly, I would like to thank James Currey – an academic publisher specialising in African Studies, now an imprint of Boydell & Brewer – for accepting my manuscript for publication and steering with courtesy and professionalism the process that ultimately led to the production of this book.

I dedicate this book to Lorie, Lucas, Aquilin and Kuelo. They are some of the children I got to know and appreciate when travelling in Rwanda for this research. May this new generation be spared the sufferings of the previous one and grow in a country that confidently looks forward to the future.

Abbreviations

AACC	All Africa Conference of Churches
ACEAC	Association of Episcopal Conferences of Central Africa
ACIST	Community African Initiatives Support
ACN	Aid to the Church in Need
ACT	Agence de Coopération Technique
ADFL	Alliance of Democratic Forces for the Liberation of Congo
ADL	Association for the Defence of the Rights of the Person and the Public Liberties
AEE	African Evangelistic Enterprise
AHA	African Humanitarian Action
AIDR	International Association of Rural Development
AMA	Archives of the Missionaries of Africa
AMECEA	Association of Member Episcopal Conferences in Eastern Africa
ANB-BIA	*African News Bulletin – Bulletin d'Information Africaine*
APRERWA	Assembly of the Rwandan Priests
ARBED	Association Rwandaise pour le Bien-Être Familial
ARDHO	Rwandan Association for the Defence of Human Rights
ASF	Amour Sans Frontière
ASUMA	Association of Major Superiors of Rwanda
AVP	Association des Volontaires de la Paix
CDI	Christian Democrat International
CDR	Coalition for the Defence of the Republic
CEDOREP	Centre de Documentation et de Pastorale
CFD	Centre de Formation et de Documentation

CIM	Comité des Instituts Missionnaires
CLIIR	Centre de lutte contre l'impunité et l'injustice au Rwanda
CMGM	Commission for the Memorial of the Genocide and the Massacres
CNLG	National Commission for the Fight against Genocide
CPR	Protestant Council of Rwanda
CRAP	Comité de Relance des Activités Pastorales [Commission for the Revival of Pastoral Activities]
CVP	Christelijke Volkspartij
DAMI	Détachement d'Assistance Militaire et d'Instruction
DRC	Democratic Republic of Congo
EPR	Église presbytérienne au Rwanda
ESI	School of Nursing Sciences
FAR	Forces Armées Rwandaises
ICA	Institut catéchétique africain
ICTR	International Criminal Tribunal for Rwanda
IFHIM	Montreal Institute of Integration and Formation
IHOM	Institute for the Healing of Memories
IPK	Kirinda Presbyterian Institute
IRST	Scientific and Technological Research Institute
JAC	Association of Young Catholic Farmers
MDR	Mouvement Démocratique Républicain
MOUCECORE	Christian Movement for Evangelisation, Counselling and Reconciliation
MRND	National Revolutionary Movement for Development
MSF	Médecins Sans Frontières
NGO	Non-governmental organisation
NURC	National Commission for Unity and Reconciliation
ONAPO	Office National de la Population
Parmehutu	Party of the Hutu Emancipation Movement
PL	Liberal Party
PSC	Parti Social Chrétien
RADER	Rassemblement Démocratique Rwandais
RDR	Rassemblement pour le Retour de la Démocratie au Rwanda

RFI	Radio France Internationale
RICM	Régiment d'infanterie et de chars de marine
RPA	Rwandan Patriotic Army
RPF	Rwandan Patriotic Front
RTLM	Radio Télévision des Mille Collines
SAT	Service d'Animation Théologique
SBMPC	Belgian Society of Protestant Missions in Congo
TRC	Truth and Reconciliation Commission
UN	United Nations
UNAR	Union Nationale Rwandaise
UNESCO	United Nations Educational, Scientific and Cultural Organization
VEM	United Evangelical Mission
WCC	World Council of Churches

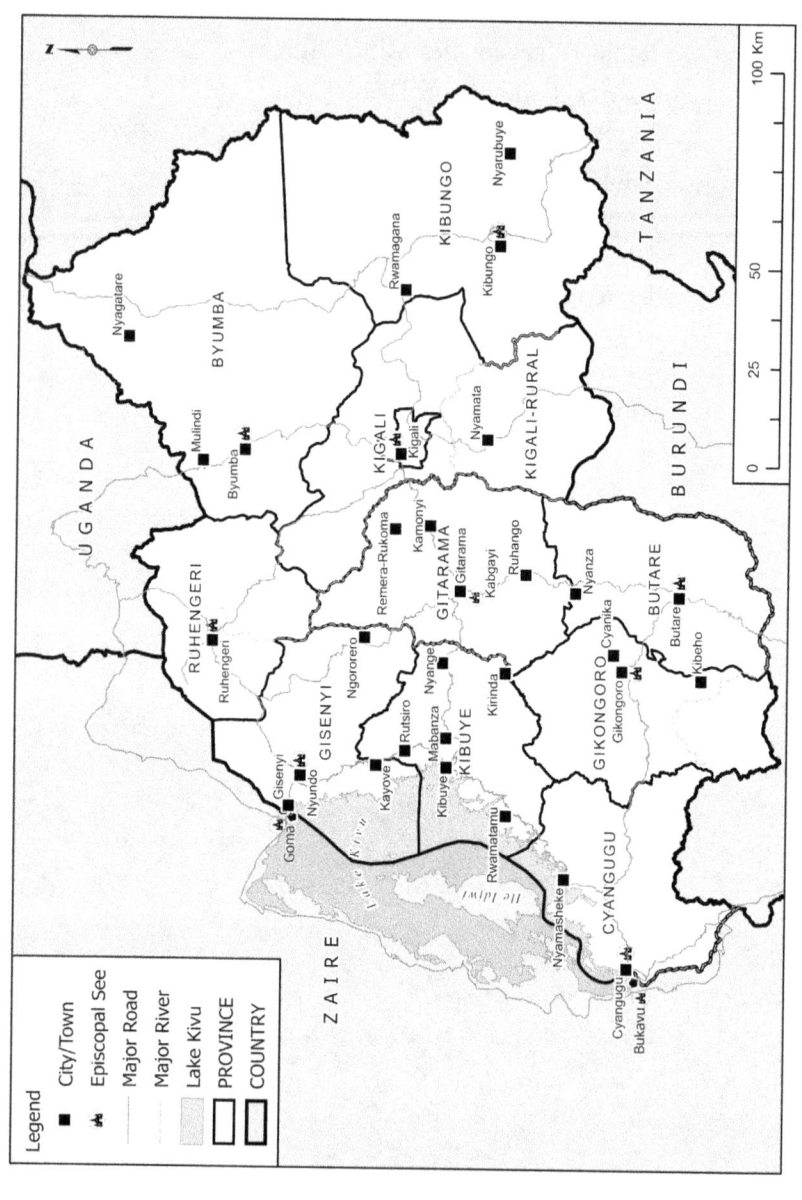

Rwanda, 1994, showing the towns and localities mentioned in the book. Brice Gijsbertsen, University of KwaZulu-Natal.

Introduction

On 6 April 1994, when the plane of President Juvénal Habyarimana was shot down in Kigali, an attack which triggered the genocide against the Tutsi, I was in South Africa, holding my breath, like all my friends and colleagues, for the upcoming democratic elections, which we hoped would turn the page of apartheid but could be derailed at any moment through political violence. I missed the genocide. Three years later, I experienced first-hand the upheaval that had hit the Great Lakes Region in the 1990s when, after a journey by road from Kigali to Bujumbura, I facilitated a conflict resolution workshop for Hutu and Tutsi Dominicans from Rwanda and Burundi, to whose congregation I also belong. I made three more trips in the area during this period. What I saw and heard then is the seed of the research, initiated fifteen years later, that gave rise to this book.

I rapidly discovered that there are different and sometimes conflicting ways of envisaging the genocide against the Tutsi – and the episodes of mass violence affecting Burundi and Eastern Congo, which will not be discussed here – and that the debate on the memory of the genocide does not spare the churches. In fact, the attitudes of the churches, which were at the same time victims, opponents and participants in the genocide, are among the most contested aspects of that history.

This work with the Dominican brothers from the Great Lake Region brought back memories of my first trip to Rwanda in August 1974, when I spent a few days as a young man in Collège Christ-Roi in Nyanza at the invitation of Canon Eugène Ernotte, a priest from my home diocese of Liège, Belgium, who was a friend of my parents. I remember him proudly citing the names of his former pupils who had become cabinet ministers. He mentioned the massacres of Tutsi that had occurred the year before, but I was too ignorant of Rwandan history to understand what he was saying. Much later, I became uneasy when I found reports – inaccurate as they turned out to be – that Ernotte was one of the authors of the Bahutu Manifesto, the document that prepared the way for the 1959 Rwandan

Social Revolution and the anti-Tutsi violence that followed.[1] Also upsetting was the information, spread on the Internet, that shortly before his death on 27 August 1994 in Liège, Ernotte had received a visit from the former gendarmery commander Pierre Célestin Rwagafirita – a leading figure of the genocide in Kibungo and one of Ernotte's former students. This episode illustrates what this book is about. The history of the genocide against the Tutsi, and of the events that preceded and followed it, is clouded by rumours and gossip, attacks and counter-attacks. Complex emotions are involved. It is also very politicised. I like to believe that the work of the historian has the potential to dissipate, at least in part, the confusion that surrounds these contested events and put to rest unverified and sometimes malicious assertions. A critical historical investigation based on a wide array of written and oral sources, with due consideration to the cultural, political and religious biases that the situatedness of the researcher necessarily entails,[2] opens the door to a more serene and fruitful debate about the past. Well-conducted historical research can be an instrument of peace and reconciliation.

The question of Ernotte's relationship to the ethnist ideology reigning in the church in his time is a case in point. During the course of my research, Jean Ndorimana, a victim of the anti-Tutsi pogroms of 1973 who later served as vicar general of the Catholic Diocese of Cyangugu, told me that Ernotte had gone out of his way to reintegrate him into Collège Christ-Roi after the massacres, in spite of the absence of the required police clearance.[3] He was not the pro-Hutu ideologue that some people claimed he was, but there is no doubt that he supported the 1959 Social Revolution. His background, which a recent thesis has brought to light, explains why. If he promoted the enrolment of Hutu learners, at that stage largely excluded from secondary education, it was because he

---

[1] The source of this information is Ian Linden, *Church and Revolution in Rwanda* (Manchester: Manchester University Press, 1977), 249. See Léon Saur, 'Catholiques belges et Rwanda, 1950–1965. Les pièges de l'évidence', unpublished PhD thesis, Université Paris I, 2013, 693.

[2] I developed this point in 'On teaching Christian history in the postmodern world', *HTS. Theological Studies*, 75/1 (2019), a5210.

[3] Jean Ndorimana, *De la région des Grands Lacs au Vatican. Intrigues, scandales et idéologie du génocide au sein de la hiérarchie catholique* (Kigali: Imprimerie Prograph, 2008), 50–4. On Eugène Ernotte's response to the massacres in 1973, see also Jean-Paul Kimonyo, *Un génocide populaire* (Paris: Karthala, 2008), 80.

had in mind the working-class children he had been teaching in Seraing, an industrial area near Liège, in the 1940s.[4]

Remembering the genocide against the Tutsi

This study explores in what way and at which point of their history the Rwandan churches preserved and processed – or not – the memory of the genocide against the Tutsi. Two churches whose memory practices stand in stark contrast with each other, the Catholic Church and the Presbyterian Church, will receive special attention. The focus will be on the period 1994–2000, during which these two churches re-envisioned themselves in a context profoundly affected by the genocide and its aftermath.

Between April and July 1994, under the guise of fighting the 'accomplices' of the Rwandan Patriotic Front (RPF) (an armed movement of Tutsi refugees which had invaded Rwanda in October 1990 with the intention of gaining access to the country), Hutu militia and crowds of ordinary people exterminated an estimated 800,000 (mostly Tutsi) men, women and children, with the logistical support of local and national authorities.[5] In a mere three months, three-quarters of the Tutsi population residing in Rwanda as of April 1994 were assassinated in schools, churches, municipal halls or open fields.[6] It was not only the (assuredly enormous) number of Tutsi victims which mattered, but the message, administered with the most extreme cruelty, that these people were no longer fellow human beings and that, for this reason, they did not deserve to exist. Most of the Hutu

---

[4] Saur, 'Catholiques belges et Rwanda, 1950–1965', 1565–68. Ernotte's editorship of the *Churchill Gazette*, a clandestine antifascist and antiracist newspaper during the Second World War, gives another clue on his political opinions prior to his arrival in Rwanda in 1956.

[5] The estimate of the number of Tutsi victims depends on the manner of adjusting the ratio of Hutu and Tutsi people in the 1991 Rwandan population census, considering the fact that a certain number of Tutsi had been counted as Hutu. Using this method, Gérard Prunier considered that 'the approximate number of deaths in the genocide could be placed at between 800,000 and 850,000, a loss of about 11% of the population'. See G. Prunier, *The Rwanda Crisis: History of a Genocide* (New York: Columbia University Press, 1995), 265.

[6] Filip Reyntjens, 'Estimation du nombre de personnes tuées au Rwanda en 1994', in S. Marysse and F. Reyntjens (ed.), *L'Afrique des Grands Lacs. Annuaire 1996–1997* (Paris: L'Harmattan, 1997), 186.

who were also killed were targeted because they opposed the massacre of Tutsi. Under the influence of the Hamitic theory, which was rooted in colonialism, the Tutsi had been described for a while as strangers, supposedly superior in stature and intelligence but devious and power-hungry.[7] Now they had to be eliminated *en masse* for the mere reason that they were Tutsi. The genocide was not only immoral; it was also irrational. Which regime has ever won a war against an invading army by slaughtering a significant part of its own population?

Like the Holocaust, an admittedly very different episode of extreme violence,[8] the mass murder of the Tutsi claims a certain degree of exceptionalism. It is more than a war crime and even more than what international justice lawyers call a crime against humanity. It raises a daunting question for the human consciousness. This is why, in reference to the Jewish extermination programme carried out by the Nazis during the Second World War, the term 'genocide', coined by Raphael Lemkin in 1944 and adopted at the United Nations (UN) Convention on the Prevention and Punishment of the Crime of Genocide in 1948,[9] is used to describe it. The term is emotionally loaded and has political and legal implications. During the genocide, it was used for the first time by Médecins Sans Frontières (MSF) staffers on 13 April 1994.[10] Key to the notion of genocide is the intent to exterminate or grievously harm a national, ethnical, racial or religious group *as such* in whole or in part. As the international criminal law expert William Schabas put it, 'the definition of the 1948 Convention fits the Rwandan genocide like a glove'.

There used to be no word in Kinyarwanda for genocide. At first, people used the term *itsembabwoko,* which refers to the destruction of a clan or a tribe. In the aftermath of the genocide, Rwandan officials and civil society organisations commonly spoke of *itsembabwoko n'itsembatsemba,* which translates into English as 'genocide and massacres'. Along the way, the neologism *jenoside* was introduced. In official documents, the dedicated phrase currently is *jenoside yakorewe abatutsi* or 'genocide against the

---

[7] Jean-Pierre Chrétien and Marcel Kabanda, *Rwanda. Racisme et génocide. L'idéologie hamitique* (Paris: Éditions Belin, 2015).

[8] René Lemarchand, 'Disconnecting the threads: Rwanda and the Holocaust reconsidered', *Journal of Genocide Research*, 4 (2002), 499–518.

[9] Philippe Sands, *East West Street: On the Origins of Genocide and Crimes against Humanity* (London: Weidenfeld & Nicolson, 2016).

[10] Jean-Hervé Bradol and Marc Le Pape, *Génocide et crime de masse. L'expérience rwandaise de MSF 1982–1997* (Paris: CNRS Éditions, 2017), 67.

Tutsi'. This phrase omits reference to the non-Tutsi victims of state violence, an absence that some observers find problematic but which makes sense considering that there is no evidence of an intent to exterminate the Hutu group as such in the Great Lakes Region in the 1990s. This is the term I use in this study.[11]

The memory of the genocide against the Tutsi is contested. We have what Rwandan historian Paul Rutayisire calls a conflict of memory.[12] The debate started when the genocide was in full swing and is still active today. It affects the churches – inside and outside Rwanda – as much as any other sector of society.

This debate is two-fold. It concerns the genocide as a historical event and the politics of memory in post-genocide Rwanda. We shall not dwell on the first aspect of the debate here, except in the chapter that deals with religion in the midst of the genocide. All our attention will be devoted to the question of whether or not the churches remembered and commemorated the genocide against the Tutsi during the period under review.

Few people squarely deny the reality of the genocide against the Tutsi. There are, however, more subtle forms of denialism. One consists in saying that the genocide was merely an episode in the conflict initiated by the RPF when it invaded Rwanda in October 1990. A variation of this argument is that more Hutu than Tutsi died not only before the genocide, in the war fought in the north, or after the genocide, in Rwanda itself and in Zaire after the dismantlement of the refugee camps, but during the genocide, when the RPF was making headway from the north-east towards the south of Rwanda.[13] The RPF itself admits that its soldiers committed crimes

---

[11] On this question of terminology, see Timothy Longman, *Memory and Justice in Post-Genocide Rwanda* (Cambridge: Cambridge University Press, 2017), 245–6. The political scientist Filip Reyntjens, a known critic of the RPF government, used the phrase *génocide des Tutsi* (genocide against the Tutsi) in the title of a recent book: F. Reyntjens, *Le genocide des Tutsi* (Paris: Presses Universitaires de France, 2017).

[12] Paul Rutayisire, 'Le conflit des mémoires', in Roland Junod and Paul Rutayisire (ed.), *Citoyenneté et réconciliation au Rwanda* (Geneva: Éditions ies, 2015), 77.

[13] Jean-Pierre Chrétien, *Le défi de l'ethnisme. Rwanda et Burundi*, 2nd edn (Paris: Karthala, 2012), 65–79; Hélène Dumas, 'L'histoire des vaincus. Négationnisme du génocide des Tutsi au Rwanda', *Revue d'histoire de la Shoah*, 190 (January–June 2009), 299–347.

against Hutu civilians during this period. What is in dispute is the scale of these crimes, their motives and the level of commandment involved.[14]

Many aspects of the genocide are in discussion. First, there is the vexed question of who shot down the president's plane on Wednesday, 6 April 1994 at about 8:30pm. Other debated issues include the degree of preparation of the onslaught, the nature of the involvement of the government ministers, prefects, burgomasters and gendarmery commanders in the genocide, the number of Tutsi who lost their lives, the extent of the participation of ordinary Hutu people in the killings, the level of anti-Tutsi hatred in the population and the proportion of Hutu people who resisted the militiamen and sheltered Tutsi refugees.

The politics of memory in post-genocide Rwanda

Tzvetan Todorov made the point that there is a difference between the *recovery* of the past and its subsequent *use*. Each of these procedures has its own characteristics and paradoxes.[15] He did not refer to the Rwandan situation, but he could have done so. As much as it is necessary to document the history of the genocide, we should equally pay attention to the use that is made of that history.

According to Paul Ricoeur's typology, the use of memory encounters three types of challenges. First, memory can be pathologically 'blocked'.[16] Genocide survivors know how painful and difficult it is to remember what has happened and how risky it is to share their memories with an outsider. The memory of the genocide is very traumatic, not only at an individual level but also at a social level. The genocide deeply affected Rwandan society's sense of identity.[17] Time heals, but, even after many years, the memories of the genocide remain wounded. If we do not keep this factor

---

[14] Alison Des Forges, *Leave None to Tell the Story: Genocide in Rwanda* (New York: Human Rights Watch, 1999), 701–33; Jean-Paul Kimonyo, *Rwanda demain! Une longue marche vers la transformation* (Paris: Karthala, 2017), 151–7.

[15] Tzvetan Todorov, 'The uses and abuses of memory', in Howard Marchitello (ed.), *What Happens to History: The Renewal of Ethics in Contemporary Thought* (London and New York: Routledge, 2001), 12.

[16] Paul Ricoeur, *Memory, History, Forgetting* (Chicago: Chicago University Press, 2002), 69.

[17] Jeffrey Alexander, *Trauma: A Social Theory* (Cambridge, UK/Malden, MA: Polity Press, 2012).

in consideration, we cannot understand otherwise incomprehensible psychosocial and even political reactions.

Second, memory can be 'manipulated'. It happens, explains Ricoeur, when the confrontation with the other is felt to be a threat.[18] Memory is associated with power and ideology. Systems of authority – in our case, the Rwandan state and the forces that try to undermine or topple it – select or omit components of collective memory in order to strengthen their legitimacy.[19] Like any institution, churches can also manipulate memory to consolidate their authority. Any form of collective memory is susceptible to abuse.

Lastly, memory can be 'summoned abusively', when the injunction to remember is heard as 'an invitation to short-circuit history'. There is then a strong temptation to transform the duty to remember into 'a claim on behalf of memory in opposition to history'.[20]

In Rwanda and abroad, numerous 'agencies of articulation of memory', to use the language of Timothy Ashplant and his colleagues,[21] have developed a discourse about the genocide. In this, they include the state, the survivor organisations, the churches, the human rights organisations, the academia, the organisations of Rwandans in exile and the opposition parties. The task in this study is to identify these agencies of articulation of memory, look at their background, examine the narratives they produce and confront these narratives with those of other social actors.

The genocide-memory activists in Rwanda and their associates in the rest of the world insist on the duty to remember. They claim that it is necessary to put on display the horrors of the genocide in order to avoid their repetition in the future. Other role-players cast suspicion on the duty of memory, claiming that the memorialisation of the genocide, the annual genocide commemorations and the development of genocide memorials,

---

[18] Ricoeur, *Memory, History, Forgetting*, 80–1.
[19] *Ibid.*, 82–3.
[20] *Ibid.*, 86–7.
[21] T. G. Ashplant, Graham Dawson and Michael Roper (ed.), *The Politics of War Memory and Commemoration* (London and New York: Routledge, 2000).

for example,[22] are a ploy of the RPF government to entrench its power.[23] When looking at the manner in which the churches confronted the memory of the genocide, we must keep in mind that for them memory is also a site of struggle.

That the genocide is the object of a conflict of memory should not come as a surprise. Unlike the Nazi regime, which suffered a terminal military defeat in May 1945, the government and the army that promoted the genocide against the Tutsi took refuge in camps on the other side of the Zairian border in July 1994 with the firm intention of coming back and winning the 'war'. The former leaders never admitted any guilt, let alone expressed remorse. Two years later, the refugee camps in Tanzania and Zaire were dismantled – some violently – but incursions of former Interahamwe (Hutu militiamen) continued for several years – not without the use of great force against the Hutu assailants and the local population which sheltered them on the part of the army of the Tutsi-led Rwandan government. In a way, the genocide never came to an end. There has not been a political

---

[22] There is a growing body of literature on genocide commemorations and genocide memorials in post-genocide Rwanda. See Claudine Vidal, 'La commémoration du génocide au Rwanda. Violence symbolique, mémorisation forcée et histoire officielle', *Cahiers des études africaines*, 175/3 (2004), 575–92; Hélène Dumas and Remi Korman, 'Espaces de la mémoire du génocide au Rwanda', *Afrique contemporaine*, 238 (2011), 11–27; Erin Jessee, *Promoting Reconciliation through Exhuming and Identifying Victims in the 1994 Rwandan Genocide*, Africa Initiative Discussion Papers, 4 (2012); D. Gishoma and C. Kanazayire, 'Les commémorations du génocide au Rwanda: un espace transitionnel pour métaboliser le passé qui ne passe pas,' in J.-L. Brackelaire, M. Cornejo and J. Kinable, *Violence politique et traumatisme. Processus d'élaboration et de création* (Louvain-la-Neuve: Academia-L'Harmattan, 2013), 316–38; Remi Korman, 'Les mémoriaux du génocide: lieux de transmission de l'histoire?', in Virginie Brinker, Catherine Coquio, Alexandre Dauge-Roth, Éric Hoppenot, Nathan Réra and François Robinet (ed.), *Rwanda 1994–2014. Récits, constructions mémorielles et écritures de l'histoire* (Dijon: Les Presses du Réel, 2017), 49–60; Longman, *Memory and Justice*, 65–90; Florence Rasmont, 'Commémorer sur les collines. Lieux et acteurs de la mémoire du génocide tutsi au Rwanda', unpublished PhD thesis, Université Libre de Bruxelles, 2019; Remi Korman, 'Commémorer sur les ruines. L'État rwandais face à la mort de masse dans l'après-coup du génocide (1994–2003)', unpublished PhD thesis, Paris, École des hautes études en sciences sociales, 2020.

[23] Filip Reyntjens, 'Rwanda, ten years on: from genocide to dictatorship', *African Affairs* (2004), 199–200.

compromise followed by joint constitutional arrangement as in South Africa, for example. In that country, the April 1994 democratic elections symbolically signified the decision of the nation, Black and White citizens alike, to turn its back on apartheid. Some of the worst perpetrators, like the police commander Eugene de Kock, expressed genuine remorse for their actions at the Truth and Reconciliation Commission (TRC).[24] Nothing of that nature has happened since the genocide against the Tutsi.[25]

This sense of 'unfinished business' has great repercussions on the politics of memory in Rwanda. The various forms of genocide denialism that find expression overtly around the world or more discreetly in Rwanda exacerbate the problem. They revive the wounds of the survivors and create frustration among those who believe that lessons should be drawn from the history of this apex of ethnic violence. The absence of a genuine consensus, internationally and nationally, about the reality of the genocide against the Tutsi explains, at least in part, why the Rwandan government and the genocide survivor organisations put so much effort into memorialising the genocide with the help of international partners such as the Aegis Trust. Genocide memory is a national cause in Rwanda, benefitting from the full support of the state.[26] The ongoing debate in the international media and in academic publications on governance in Rwanda also explains why, by reaction and not without causing controversy, so little is said in public on the other victims of mass violence in the 1990s. Where does one draw a line between too much and too little memory? Which aspects of the past can be legitimately forgotten?

The fact that history and memory are sensitive issues in Rwanda with legal implications[27] affects the manner of conducting research in the country. One has to seek advice from the best sources and reflect on how to

---

[24] Pumla Gobodo-Madikizela, *A Human Being Died That Night: A South African Story of Forgiveness* (Boston: Houghton Miffin, 2003).

[25] I developed the comparison between post-Second World War Germany, post-apartheid South Africa and post-genocide Rwanda in 'Germany, South Africa and Rwanda: three manners for a Church to confess its guilt', *Studia Historiae Ecclesiasticae*, 43/2 (2017), 1–20.

[26] Longman, *Memory and Justice*, 65–90. On this theme, see also Johan Pottier, *Re-imagining Rwanda: Conflict, Survival and Disinformation in the Late Twentieth Century* (Cambridge: Cambridge University Press, 2002); Erin Jessee, *Negotiating Genocide in Rwanda: The Politics of History* (London: Palgrave Macmillan, 2017).

[27] In 2008 and in 2013, laws were promulgated to sanction the crime of genocide ideology and other related offences in Rwanda.

navigate in a difficult terrain.[28] At the same time, Rwanda attracts young researchers more than ever. In some way, the ideological war outside and inside the country is less acute today than it was immediately after the genocide. The International Criminal Tribunal for Rwanda (ICTR) has judged and sentenced some of the main instigators of the genocide. An active policy of reconciliation has been implemented in Rwanda. There is still tension about the past, but arguably less than before.

The centrality of the genocide against the Tutsi

The genocide, in the words of André Karamaga, the president of the Presbyterian Church in Rwanda in the late 1990s, is an 'inescapable starting point', not only because it has been recognised by the international community as 'a crime that does not disappear' but because it was something that had a deep impact on everybody.[29] He was responding to fellow Presbyterians, at the time refugees in Zaire, who were 'putting a question mark after the word genocide', according to a report.[30]

This conversation captures the essence of the debate on the genocide since 1994. Was it only a war or something fundamentally different? The fact is that Rwanda will never be the same as it was before the genocide. The neighbouring areas, Burundi and the Eastern Congo in particular, were also greatly affected by it. The genocide has compelled many role-players, not least in the churches, to rethink the ethnic question in the Great Lakes Region by showing to what unthinkable degrees of monstrosity a policy based on ethnic differentiation and discrimination can lead. On the negative side, unprecedented levels of mass violence have been attained. 'It is', the Belgian journalist Colette Braeckman wrote in 2003, 'as if the paroxysm violence has reached in Rwanda has spread into the entire region, lifted all taboos and authorised all enterprises of dehumanisation'.[31] In that

---

[28] I elaborated on this theme in 'Difficult navigation: dealing with divided memories in post-genocide Rwanda', *Oral History*, 39 (2021), 104–14.

[29] 'Rencontre des Presbytériens de l'intérieur et de l'extérieur du Rwanda, à Windhoek du 22 au 26/9/96. Texte présenté par André Karamaga' (Munyaneza Papers).

[30] L. R. Krol, 'Rencontre des Presbytériens de l'extérieur et de l'intérieur du Rwanda D.D. 22 au 26 septembre 1996 à Windhoek en Namibie', 8 (Munyaneza Papers). On this episode, see Chapter 5.

[31] Colette Braeckman, *Les nouveaux prédateurs. Politique des puissances en Afrique centrale* (Paris: Fayard, 2003), 163.

sense, one can speak of the centrality of the genocide against the Tutsi in the history of Rwanda and its neighbours.

It is true, as Longman pointed out, that the notion of the centrality of the genocide is key to the 'official historical narrative' promoted by the Rwandan government since 1994 and that constraints are imposed on the historical debate in the country.[32] The matter deserves discussion, but one would be mistaken to believe that this is a unique Rwandan problem, as the South African example illustrates. In the much-celebrated rainbow nation, there is also a powerful and ever-present official historical narrative that highlights the glorious role of the African National Congress in the struggle against apartheid and silences or minimises the contribution of other social movements. On the other side of the political spectrum, a controversy erupted when the names of the white soldiers who had fought in Namibia and Angola in the 1980s were excluded from the Freedom Park's Wall of Names in Pretoria.[33]

An over-debated but under-researched subject

Rwanda was a latecomer on the African missionary scene. The Missionaries of Africa, also known as White Fathers, only arrived there in 1900, and the Lutheran Missionary Society of Bethel, the first Protestant missionary body, in 1907. However, Rwanda rapidly became an evangelisation success story. The church's good fortune continued after the 1959 Social Revolution, which vast sectors of the Catholic Church wholeheartedly supported. While refusing to discriminate against Protestants, President Juvénal Habyarimana was a staunch Catholic. The Archbishop of Kigali, Vincent Nsengiyumva, had direct access to his family. The Catholic Church and, to a lesser degree, the other churches were intimately connected with the Rwandan state.

The genocide had a profoundly destabilising effect on the churches. They lost numerous members, part of their workforce and a good deal of their infrastructure. Above all, they lost credibility because of the inability of their leadership to denounce the genocide as genocide and because a certain number of bishops, priests, religious brothers and sisters, pastors and

---

[32] Longman, *Memory and Justice*, 52–6, 60–4.
[33] Sarah Nuttall and Carli Coetzee (ed.), *Negotiating the Past: the Making of Memory in South Africa* (Cape Town: Oxford University Press, 1998); Gary Baines, 'Sites of struggle: the Freedom Park fracas and the divisive legacy of South Africa's border war/liberation struggle', *Social Dynamics*, 35 (2009), 330–44.

elders had ambiguous relationships with the local authorities that organised the genocide. Some actively cooperated with the killers. After the genocide, all churches found themselves in a state of profound division, with part of the flock and the clergy in refugee camps in Tanzania and Zaire and the rest trying to rebuild the church in Rwanda in trying circumstances.

The scene was set for the churches to have a complicated relationship with the memory of the genocide against the Tutsi, which is the object of this study. Rapidly, Christians and non-Christians inside and outside Rwanda blamed the churches for their silence during the genocide, an accusation that was partly unfounded since the church leaders had issued pastoral statements between April and June 1994, yet these were very ambivalent. Some believers, including priests and pastors, plainly recognised the failures of their institution. Others denied any wrongdoing and counter-attacked by blaming the new Rwandan government for bad governance and human rights abuses. The debate since then has never ceased. The blogosphere is replete with texts attacking the churches, especially the Catholic Church, for their role during the genocide or unilaterally taking their defence.

Only parts of that history have been the object of critical investigation. There is no shortage of well-documented studies on the earlier periods, in respect of the Catholic Church[34] and the Presbyterian Church[35] in particular. Concerning the post-genocide period, there is a contrast between the masses of personal testimonies, polemical texts and grey literature, interesting for their documentary value but limited in many ways, that are available in the form of books or brochures[36] or in an electronic format, and the scarcity of scholarly research.

---

[34] Paul Rutayisire, *La christianisation du Rwanda (1900–1945). Méthode missionnaire et politique selon Mgr Classe* (Fribourg: Éditions universitaires, 1987); Ian Linden, *Christianisme et pouvoir au Rwanda (1990–1990)* (Paris: Karthala, 1999); Saur, 'Catholiques belges et Rwanda, 1950–1965'; James Carney, *Rwanda before the Genocide: Catholic Politics and Ethnic Discourse in the Late Colonial Era* (New York: Oxford University Press, 2014).

[35] Michel Twagirayesu and Jan van Butselaar, *Ce don que nous avons reçu. Histoire de l'Église presbytérienne au Rwanda (1907–1982)* (Kigali: Église presbytérienne au Rwanda, 1982); Tharcisse Gatwa and André Karamanga, *Les autres Chrétiens rwandais. La présence protestante* (Kigali: Éditions Urwego, 1990); Gerard van 't Spijker, *L'Église chrétienne au Rwanda pré et post-génocide* (Paris: L'Harmattan, 2011).

[36] For a first inventory which includes several ecclesiastical documents, see Jean-Pierre Chrétien, 'Interprétations du génocide de 1994 dans l'histoire contemporaine du Rwanda', *Clio en Afrique*, 2 (Summer 1997), 92–9.

Three studies can be singled out for the value of their contribution to scholarship. In the first one, the Rwandan journalist and theologian Tharcisse Gatwa analyses the Rwandan churches' dealings with ethnic ideology up to the post-genocide period when they tackled issues of guilt, healing and reconciliation.[37] The second is by the American political scientist Timothy Longman, who conducted fieldwork in Rwanda in 1992 and 1993, returned to the country in 1995 and 1996 as a researcher for Human Rights Watch and subsequently published a book on Rwandan Christianity that contains a detailed history of two Presbyterian missions, Kirinda and Biguhu, before and during the genocide.[38] The third is by the Rwandan historian Paul Rutayisire, who contributed a substantial chapter to a collective book on Rwandan Christian history in which he discussed, on the basis of documentary evidence, the relationship of the Catholic Church of Rwanda to power and ethnicity, from its origins to the post-genocide period.[39] While not being a historical study *per se*, the collection of essays published in 2004 under the title *Genocide in Rwanda: Complicity of the Churches?* deserves mention because it contains valuable material on aspects of the churches' responses to the genocide against the Tutsi.[40] Also of interest are Spyridon Loumakis' essay on genocide and religion in Rwanda in the 1990s[41] and Remi Korman's article on the memoriali-

---

[37] Tharcisse Gatwa, *Rwanda: Églises, victimes ou coupables? Les Églises et l'idéologie ethnique au Rwanda 1900–1994* (Yaoundé: Éditions CLÉ, 2001); *The Churches and Ethnic Ideology in the Rwandan Crises 1900–1994* (Oxford: Regnum Books International, 2005).

[38] Timothy Longman, *Christianity and Genocide in Rwanda* (Cambridge: Cambridge University Press, 2009).

[39] Paul Rutayisire, 'Le catholicisme rwandais: un regard interrogateur', in Tharcisse Gatwa and Laurent Rutinduka (ed.), *Histoire du christianisme au Rwanda. Des origines à nos jours* (Yaoundé: Éditions CLÉ, 2014), 251–343. The other chapters provide information on the Rwandan churches' pastoral achievements and challenges in history but say little on their respective responses to the genocide against the Tutsi. Note two studies on the Anglican Church of Rwanda during this period: Phillip Cantrell, 'The Anglican Church of Rwanda: domestic agendas and international linkages', *Journal of Modern African Studies*, 45 (2007), 333–54; Henry Settimba, *The Anglican Church Role in the Process of Reconciliation in Rwanda* (Cambridge: Perfect Publishers, 2009).

[40] Carol Rittner, John K. Roth and Wendy Whitworth (ed.), *Genocide in Rwanda: Complicity of the Churches?* (St Paul, Minnesota: Paragon House, 2004).

[41] Spyridon Loumakis, 'Genocide and religion in the 1990s', in André Gagné,

sation of churches in post-genocide Rwanda.[42] Lastly, we should mention Jean-Pierre Chrétien's book on 'ethnism' (*ethnisme*) in Rwanda and Burundi, which does not deal with the history of the churches in particular but cites a wide range of ecclesiastical sources.[43]

Public and private archives

Between December 2014 and March 2020, I made eight trips of two to four weeks to Rwanda in connection with this project. Hosted by the Dominican brothers in Kacyiru, in proximity to CEDOREP, which is arguably Kigali's best-furnished library on Rwandan history, I crisscrossed the city and the rest of the country in search of written material and oral testimonies on the churches' response to the genocide. I also travelled to Burundi, the Democratic Republic of Congo (DRC), France, Belgium, Italy, the United Kingdom and the Netherlands. There is no wall, in research, between written and oral sources. On numerous occasions, interviewees informed me of the existence of an archival collection and introduced me to its custodian. Conversely, written documents have drawn my attention to a witness whom I then sought to interview.

Public archives in Rwanda are still in the process of being classified and made accessible to the public. For the purpose of this research, the most important public archive repositories have been the CNLG in Kigali, which preserves the archives of the *gacaca* courts, and the Parliament Library. I also consulted church archives, in particular those of the Head Office of the Presbyterian Church in Rwanda, the episcopal conference of Rwanda, the CFD and CEDOREP in Kigali, the Missionaries of Africa in Rome, Brussels and Kigali and the Dominican Missionary Sisters of Namur. The third category of archives to which I resorted is that of private papers. I made great use of the archives that Father André Bouillot, S.J.

Spyridon Loumakis and Calogero Miceli (ed.), *The Global Impact of Religious Violence* (Eugene, Oregon: Wipf & Stock, 2016), 47–83.

[42] Remi Korman, 'Espaces sacrés et sites de massacre après le génocide des Tutsi. Les enjeux de la patrimonialisation des églises au Rwanda', *Vingtième siècle. Revue d'histoire*, 137 (2019), 155–67.

[43] Jean-Pierre Chrétien, *Le défi de l'ethnisme. Rwanda et Burundi*, 2nd edn (Paris: Karthala, 2012). The French word *ethnisme*, translated in English as 'ethnism', is commonly used in Rwanda to designate the ethnicist ideology which emphasises the intrinsic difference between Hutu and Tutsi identities in the history of the country.

in Kigali, Pastor Malachie Munyaneza in the United Kingdom and Pastor Gerard van 't Spijker in the Netherlands graciously allowed me to consult, of those of the Brussels-based now-closed Christian journal *Dialogue* and of the Hervé Deguine papers in the La Contemporaine documentation centre at Paris Nanterre University.

Oral history interviews

I interviewed ninety-two people for the purpose of this research. My intention was to conduct semi-structured thematic interviews, but, in a few instances, the interviewees chose to start the story early in their lives and the interviews ended up becoming life history interviews. Most interviews lasted between one and two hours, but some lasted as long as four or five hours. I developed a friendly relationship with some of the interviewees and met them again formally or informally after the first encounter. This led, in about twenty cases, to one or several follow-up interviews. I did not keep a record of the interviewing time, but the total probably exceeds two hundred and fifty hours.

All witnesses were interviewed individually, with the exception of two retired missionaries in Belgium, two Rwandan seminarians studying in South Africa and two ex-prisoners in Rwanda, who chose to be interviewed in pairs. The majority of interviews were conducted in French, with only a few in English. Some of the genocide survivors and a few other local witnesses were interviewed in Kinyarwanda with the help of an interpreter. Fifty-four interviews were conducted in Rwanda. The others took place in Belgium, France, the Netherlands, Italy, the United Kingdom, Burundi, the DRC and South Africa.

Categorising the interviewees is difficult, because certain categories overlap. I call ordinary Tutsi targeted during the genocide who somehow managed to escape death 'genocide survivors'. Those who have served a jail sentence for their participation in the genocide, I call 'perpetrators'. I created distinct categories for the priests, bishops, religious sisters, seminarians, involved lay persons and missionaries (all Catholics except one Protestant missionary) and pastors (all Protestants, mostly Presbyterians), knowing that some of them are also genocide survivors and could have been categorised as such. I distinguished between academics, government officials and journalists, three categories that sometimes also overlap.

Table 1. Categories of interviewees

Grassroots genocide survivors	16
Perpetrators	2
Bishops	3
Secular and regular priests	19
Religious sisters	3
Missionaries	10
Pastors	10
Seminarians	3
Involved laypersons	5
Academics	8
Officials	6
Journalists	2
Other community members	5
Total	92

Given the prominent position of the Catholic Church in Rwanda, it should not come as a surprise that a substantial part of the sample – 42 interviewees – includes Catholic bishops, priests, religious sisters, seminarians and laypeople involved in the life of the church. A further 13 – 10 pastors, 2 genocide perpetrators and a retired missionary in the Netherlands – were Protestant. Tutsi, mostly genocide survivors, constitute about half of the sample – 50 interviewees – but the point of view of the Hutu, in Rwanda or in the diaspora, is also represented, with 24 interviewees. Some Hutu people resisted the genocide and can be described as victims. Only one missionary was interviewed in Rwanda; all the others were in their country of birth or another mission field. The two journalists and all except two of the academics were interviewed in Europe.

Conducting research in a post-conflict situation

Because of the high levels of emotion involved and the complexity of the memory politics, doing research in post-genocide Rwanda presents challenges. The first, as in all research projects of that nature, was to minimise the risk of harm to research participants. In order to obtain ethical clearance from the research ethics committee of my university, I thoroughly engaged with colleagues on this matter, a procedure that satisfied the Ministry of Education in Rwanda when I subsequently applied for a research permit.

The biggest risk of harm to research participants is emotional distress and retraumatisation. This of course concerns the genocide survivors, many of whom had narrowly escaped death and lost numerous family members, but also the people who have suffered other forms of violence in Rwanda and the neighbouring countries. Some interviewees cried when narrating the horrific events in which they had taken part.[44] The stories of the genocide survivors are not necessarily depressing; they also include moments of resilience and success. The mere fact of having survived is something to celebrate. However, many of these stories have a dark side. The genocide survivors suffer from loneliness after having lost all or nearly all of their family members. Telling the story revives the pain. More than in any other oral history project, empathetic listening is essential, combined with an attitude of respect and the willingness to allow the interviewees to withdraw from the interview at any time if they choose to do so. During my stays in Rwanda, I regularly took advice from a friend who is a psychologist. His analysis of the emotions that continue to affect Rwandan people twenty-five years after the genocide – fear, sadness and anger in particular – was of great help.

Another challenge was the perplexity or, better said, the confusion I felt when listening to radically different interpretations of the same events. The experiences of the priests, pastors, genocide survivors, non-governmental organisation (NGO) workers and academics I interviewed affected their understanding not only of the genocide but of the manner in which Rwanda is governed today. An easy solution would have been to pretend to be neutral and simply compile a document with divergent opinions side by side. This was not, however, what my Rwandan interlocutors and the academic community expected from me. I had to face the challenge and try to document the recent history of Rwanda in all its complexity.

Methodological choices

When foreign researchers undertake fieldwork in Rwanda, there is a great risk of them being labelled as pro-Hutu or pro-Tutsi, with the result being that the people on the 'other side' dismiss their findings on the grounds

---

[44] On dealing with emotions during oral history interviews, see Sean Field, '"What can I do when the interviewee cries?" Oral history strategies for containment and regeneration', in Philippe Denis and Radikobo Ntsimane (ed.), *Oral History in a Wounded Country: Interactive Interviewing in South Africa* (Pietermaritzburg: University of KwaZulu-Natal Press, 2008), 144–68.

that they have already chosen their camp. They also incur the risk of being unwittingly involved in ideological wars because of an insufficient knowledge of the local context. Given the uneasiness that reigns in Rwanda on account of past experiences with foreigners, people scrutinise whom you speak to, whom you visit and to whom you refer in the conversation. They look for signals that indicate which side of the political divide you belong in. One sometimes encounters resistance when investigating matters related to the genocide. People remain silent or ostensibly give researchers the answer they expect without really engaging with them on the matter in discussion. It takes time to build trust. Research on the genocide in Rwanda requires a high level of sensitivity.

For this reason, I had to be strategic about my methodology. My first decision, and the most important one, was to interview people from all backgrounds and all political persuasions, inside and outside Rwanda. This meant, in practice, interviewing genocide survivors and people associated with the RPF government but also proponents of the double genocide theory and people who had fled the country after the genocide for fear of persecution. To understand what happened in the refugee camps in Zaire between 1994 and 1996, I made a trip to Goma and interviewed a few people there. I interviewed people who would have never dreamt of talking to each other. I crossed the ideological divides and crossed them again.

To create trust, I paid particular attention to the manner of introducing myself when approaching somebody for an interview. I would never solicit an interview without a recommendation. A missionary, for example, wanted to know which other missionaries I knew and a Hutu priest in exile, which other Hutu priests in exile I had already interviewed. The members of a religious order in Rwanda introduced me to confrères from other religious congregations. French colleagues who had been in the field longer than I helped me to establish connection with government officials.

The difficulty, of course, was to initiate this process. One has to start somewhere. The members of the Dominican Order, the religious order to which I belong, helped me a lot in this regard. As already mentioned, I had done some mediation work with them in the late 1990s. They guided my first steps into the complex world of the Catholic Church in Rwanda. To establish contact with members of the Presbyterian Church in Rwanda, I relied on the recommendation of a colleague from South Africa. The first Protestant interviewee recommended me to a second one, and so on.

All along, I had to reflect on how to position myself in the interview process. My dual nationality – Belgian and South African – was, from that point of view, an advantage. For some people the fact of being South African appeared reassuring. Unlike France, Belgium or the United States,

South Africa played no role in the genocide. In other contexts – among Belgian missionaries, in particular – my Belgian roots were of help. Coming from a similar environment, we could connect easily, irrespective of the differences of opinion we might have about the genocide itself or any other subject. In the same way, I played on the two sides of my social life: academic in a state university and church member. Depending on the circumstances, I would introduce myself as one or the other. My approach was essentially pragmatic.

Social scientists are aware of the respective advantages and disadvantages of the insider and outsider positions in research. With regard to the Rwandan culture and language, I am definitely an outsider. I have to rely on friends and colleagues to understand the local language, and the little I can make of the Rwandan culture is by association with that of KwaZulu-Natal, South Africa, where I have spent half of my adult life. Being an outsider is not necessarily a problem. It is sometimes easier for outsiders than insiders to maintain a critical distance from the subject of enquiry. They do not have to render accounts to a constituency. From the point of view of the church, which is the subject matter of this study, I rather come out as an insider, being a member of the Dominican Order, which is present in Rwanda and has been affected by the genocide against the Tutsi like all church groups. In this respect, I face the opposite problem. I have to disentangle my reflection from emotional connections and experiences that might cloud my judgement in some way.

The fact that I was born in Belgium, Rwanda's former colonial power, may have been perceived as an obstacle. In fact, I never had this impression. The Belgian academics and journalists who write on the Rwandan genocide are diverse. Some consider the efforts of the current Rwandan government to reconstruct the country favourably. Others are more critical.

I conducted about two-thirds of the interviews alone. When interviewing Kinyarwanda-speaking people, I had to rely on a research assistant. During my first two trips, I worked with a theological student who was still a child during the genocide. He knew the Catholic clergy of his home region well, a familiarity which opened many doors. However, he would not fit in all situations. My second research assistant, a genocide survivor active in a local NGO, initiated a host of other contacts, in Kigali and in the places where she grew up, where she had married and where she now resides. In different ways, my two research assistants shaped important aspects of my research.

At the beginning of the very first interview for this project in February 2015, the interviewee asked me not to use a tape recorder. He was afraid that the recording might be used against him. I took notes on a piece of paper as comprehensively as I could. Reflecting on this experience, I decided to abstain from using a tape recorder for the rest of the project and rather take notes on my laptop in shorthand, always with the consent of the interviewee.[45] Taping conversations on matters concerning the genocide can easily be seen as threatening. With the agreement of my university's research ethics committee, I also abstained from asking the interviewees to sign a written consent form. I only sought verbal consent.

From the general to the particular

The first three chapters of the book set the scene. They respectively describe the history of the ethnic question in Rwanda from the time of the colonial conquest to that of the Second Republic, in the period following the October 1990 RPF invasion and during the three months of the genocide. They show the continuity of the response of the church leaders, Catholic first then Protestant as well, to anti-Tutsi violence. They also signal the internal diversity of the churches in matters of politics and ethnicity. Many missionaries and many Rwandan priests and pastors unreservedly adhered to the ideology of the government of the day, but not all. This became evident during the genocide: there were Christians among those who fell victims to, participated in and resisted the killings.

The following four chapters look at different 'agencies of articulation of memory' as defined above. The fourth chapter examines what Rwandan Catholics, inside and outside the country, said, wrote and did in respect of the genocide against the Tutsi during the period immediately following the event. The fifth chapter does the same for the Presbyterian Church in Rwanda. The sixth chapter zooms in on the Missionaries of Africa, the most ancient and, until 1994, the most influential missionary congregation in Rwanda. It shows how their attitude and their discourse in ethnic and political matters evolved during and after the genocide. The seventh chapter discusses church and state relations after the genocide. It considers the Holy See's response to the genocide, the work of the mixed church–state commission, the prosecution of priests, brothers, sisters and pastors for crimes of genocide and the widely publicised trial of Bishop Augustin Misago in 1999 and 2000.

The eighth and ninth chapters present a case study. I dedicated it to Gabriel Maindron – a French priest who remained in his parish of Congo-Nil

---

[45] I reckon that I captured in transcription, on average, between 60 and 80 per cent of what the interviewees said.

in Western Rwanda during the genocide – rather than well-known church figures such as Wenceslas Munyeshyaka, a Rwandan priest long accused of having sided with the Interahamwe, Athanase Seromba, a priest convicted of genocide by the ICTR, or the Sovu sisters, condemned for genocide complicity in Belgium, for three reasons.

The first is that Maindron is a good representative of the group of clerics who sit somewhere between innocence and guilt on the line of genocide complicity. It was his ambiguity and his ambivalence that deserved attention.

Secondly, it is a case of two narratives about the past. Maindron himself and the people who support him speak of a man who saved Tutsi lives in very trying circumstances. The survivors who had relations with him before and during the genocide in Congo-Nil claim that if he did provide shelter and food to Tutsi people in his parish, that was never for long, and most of them perished afterwards. They stress the fact that he had close connections with the local authorities and some militiamen and that he never tried to use his authority as a pastor to stop the killings. They also point out that, on the ideological level, he had affinities with the Hutu extremists who engineered the genocide.

The third reason is that these two strands of memory are well documented. Maindron kept a diary during the first two months of the genocide, which was subsequently published. He told his story to Nicolas Poincaré, a French journalist, in a book published in early 1995. He was interviewed twice on French national television. The point of view of the genocide survivors is also well recorded. They were interviewed at length by Christian Terras, the editor of the French Catholic magazine *Golias* in 1996 and by the Swiss anthropologist André Grieder around 2010. Between 2016 and 2020, I also interviewed them. In addition, we have access to the proceedings of Maindron's *gacaca* appeal trial of 2010.

The tenth chapter describes the attempts made by the Christian churches to promote forgiveness and reconciliation after the genocide. Special attention is given to the Detmold Confession in December 1996 and to the reconciliation drive born of it, to the Christian *gacaca* held alongside the official *gacaca* and to the confession of guilt made by the Catholic Church during the 2000 Jubilee celebration.

CHAPTER 1

The burden of the past

The extreme polarisation of ethnic identities that produced the genocide against the Tutsi did not disappear with the RPF's conquest of Rwanda in July 1994. In spite of the RPF government's efforts to forge an ethnicity-free sense of national belonging, to this day it continues to affect social and political life in the country to various degrees. The contestation of memories that characterises post-genocide Rwanda is the result of a long history of separate experiences and separate perceptions. The original sin, to use a theological metaphor, was the development of a binary pattern of ethnic identities, joined to a protracted process of crystallisation and essentialisation of these identities. It is to the early history of this process that this chapter is dedicated.[1]

We shall see that the Christian churches have a part, for better and for worse, in this history. From the time of their arrival in Rwanda in 1900, they played a major role in the development and consolidation of a binary system of ethnic identities. The first form of identity, that of the Hutu, was attached to people deemed to be physically, socially and culturally inferior and who were seen, at a later stage of their history, as quintessential victims. The second one, that of the Tutsi, was attached to people presented as being born to command and who, as a result, were considered the natural oppressors of the members of the first group. The Hutu were said to form

---

[1] On the genesis and the contested meanings of ethnic categories in Rwanda, see Catharine Newbury, 'Ethnicity and the politics of history in Rwanda', *Africa Today*, 45 (1998), 7–24; Jean-Pierre Chrétien, 'Hutu et Tutsi au Rwanda et au Burundi', in Jean Loup Amselle (ed.), *Au cœur de l'ethnie. Ethnies, tribalisme et État en Afrique* (Paris: La Découverte, 2005), 129–65; Léon Saur, '"Hutu" et "Tutsi": des mots pour quoi dire?', *Histoire, monde et cultures religieuses*, 30 (2014), 119–38; James Carney, *Rwanda before the Genocide: Catholic Politics and Ethnic Discourse in the Late Colonial Era* (New York: Oxford University Press, 2014), 10–15.

a natural 'majority', in contrast to the Tutsi 'minority' that was not genuinely Rwandan and had violently 'conquered' the native population.

This rigid pseudo-scientific anthropology ignored or misinterpreted phenomena such as the transition from one group to another or mixed marriages. Likewise, it did not account for the fact that the majority of rural Tutsi were just as poor as their Hutu counterparts. It confused the upper-class Tutsi with a biologically distinct group. Lastly, it overlooked the regional factor, which played an essential role during the Second Republic (1973–94), with the Hutu from the south, who had been influential under President Kayibanda, losing power and prestige under President Habyarimana, a man from the north.

If the responsibility of colonial administrators and missionaries in the polarisation of Rwandan society along ethnic lines is indubitable, it is also true that the indigenous elites, Tutsi as well as Hutu, uncritically appropriated this polarisation during and after the colonial era. Some Tutsi, those linked to the aristocracy in particular, saw themselves as superior and taught their children to show their distinction through their attire and their behaviour. Particularly influential in this matter was the widely respected Tutsi priest and historian Alexis Kagame, who legitimised the colonial stereotypes by manipulating the oral traditions circulating at the Mwami's court.

A good example is the institution of pastoral clientship (*ubuhake*). Traditionally devoid of any reference to an economic transaction, it was transformed in colonial times into a contractual relationship between a patron who owned a cow and a client who received the use of it in return for a form of labour.[2] The Belgian administrators superimposed the feudal categories of the European Middle Ages with which they were familiar over an institution that they did not understand. This created, quite understandably, resentment among the people categorised as Hutu, who felt treated like slaves. The fact that poor Tutsi also became the client did not change that perception. Artificially constructed and yet pervasive complexes of superiority and inferiority developed, mutually reinforcing each other.

The history of Christianity in colonial and independent Rwanda until the time of the genocide is relatively well known, thanks to a range of archive-based studies.[3] The first generation of Catholic missionaries, joined

---

[2] Saur, '"Hutu" et "Tutsi"', 128–9.

[3] Alison Des Forges, 'Kings without Crowns: the White Fathers in Ruanda', in Daniel McCall, Norman Bennett and Jeffrey Butler (ed.), *Eastern African History* (London: Praeger, 1969), 176–207; Paul Rutayisire, *La*

a few years later by Protestant missionaries, soon made Hutu converts. In the late 1920s and early 1930s, the vicar apostolic Léon Classe managed to co-opt the Tutsi monarchy, provoking a 'tornado' of conversions. It was during this period, in 1926, that the colonial authority introduced a system of ethnic identity cards to differentiate between Hutu and Tutsi. This measure strongly entrenched ethnic polarisation in the country. In the late 1950s, the younger generations of missionaries and André Perraudin, the newly appointed vicar apostolic of Kabgayi, changed tack and shifted their support to the Hutu elites in the name of social justice.

It would not be fair to accuse the colonial administrators, German or Belgian, and the missionaries of having 'invented' the categories of Hutu, Tutsi and Twa, a third group making up about 1 per cent of the population. They existed in pre-colonial Rwanda, as mentioned in the relations of the first travellers and missionaries. But they were fluid and ever-changing. They did not designate a 'race', as Perraudin wrote in his famous pastoral letter of February 1959, or an ethnic group, as we would say today. They referred to a variety of ill-defined socio-economic, tribal or kinship groups.

The Hamitic theory

Economic factors such as the recession experienced in Rwanda in the late 1980s and political factors such as the institution of multiparty democracy reluctantly approved by President Habyarimana in 1991 explain, in part, the genocide against the Tutsi. The RPF's October 1990 invasion also played a role in the heightening of tensions. But poverty, interparty competition and civil war do not sufficiently explain a genocide which entails the systematic extermination of three-quarters or more of

---

christianisation du Rwanda (1940–1945). Méthode missionnaire et politique selon Mgr Classe (Fribourg: Éditions universitaires, 1987); Ian Linden, *Christianisme et pouvoir au Rwanda, 1900–1990* (Paris: Karthala, 1999); Tharcisse Gatwa, *The Churches and Ethnic Ideology in the Rwandan Crises 1900–1994* (Oxford: Regnum Books International, 2005); Timothy Longman, *Christianity and Genocide in Rwanda* (Cambridge: Cambridge University Press, 2011), 1–197; Léon Saur, 'Catholiques belges et Rwanda, 1950–1965'. Les pièges de l'évidence', unpublished PhD thesis, Université Paris I, 2013; Carney, *Rwanda before the Genocide*; Tharcisse Gatwa and Laurent Rutinduka (ed.), *Histoire du christianisme au Rwanda. Des origines à nos jours* (Yaoundé: Éditions CLÉ, 2014); Stefaan Minnaert, *Histoire de l'évangélisation au Rwanda. Recueil d'articles et de documents* (Kigali: Imprimu, 2017).

an ethnic group in a mere three months.⁴ The key determinant in the Rwandan case was ideology.

For the purpose of this study, this is an important consideration. The churches can more or less credibly claim that they do not have a major influence on economic development and politics. This argument falls flat when it comes to ideology. This is their area of expertise. When preparing church members to sacraments, when preaching, when training candidates for ministry and when issuing pastoral letters, they refer to a system of values. They say what is right and wrong. We need, therefore, to scrutinise the manner in which the Rwandan churches shaped, or responded to, the production of ideology in Rwanda.

At the core of the ideology that triggered the genocide was the so-called Hamitic theory, whose roots can be traced to the nineteenth century. During this period, French, German and British geographers, anthropologists and explorers came to believe that in the scale of races from the least to the most civilised, there must have been an intermediary one, halfway between the Negro and the Caucasian, whose prototype was Cham, one of Noah's sons. Depending on the authors, the representatives of this 'race' were from a Jewish, Egyptian or Ethiopian background. They were said to live in the interlacustrine region of East Africa or even further afield.⁵ In his *Journal of the Discovery of the Source of the Nile* in 1863, the British explorer John Hanning Speke expressed the conviction that 'judging from their appearance,' the Wahuma – a tribe akin to the Batutsi that he had met in Uganda – could not be 'of any other race than the semi-Shem Hamitic of Ethiopia'.⁶ Unlike the surrounding tribes, he argued, the Wahuma were pastoralists. 'In these countries,' he went on, 'the government is in the hands of foreigners, who had invaded and taken possession of them, leaving the agricultural aborigines to till the ground, whilst the junior

---

⁴ According to Filip Reyntjens, who tends to underestimate the number of Tutsi killed during the genocide rather than the opposite, the figure of three-quarters of the Tutsi population 'does not rely on an empirical basis but is plausible in the light of a certain number of samples at municipal and family levels'; see 'Estimation du nombre de personnes tuées au Rwanda en 1994', *Annuaire des Grands Lacs 1996–1997* (Paris: L'Harmattan, 1997), 86.

⁵ Jean-Pierre Chrétien and Marcel Kabanda, *Rwanda. Racisme et génocide. L'idéologie hamitique* (Paris: Éditions Belin, 2015), 45–79. See also Danielle de Lame, *A Hill among a Thousand: Transformation and Ruptures in Rural Rwanda* (Madison: University of Wisconsin Press, 2005), 3–12.

⁶ John Hanning Speke, *Journal of the Discovery of the Source of the Nile* (London: William Blackwood and Sons, 1863), 246.

members of the usurping clans herded cattle.'[7] While he was at the court of Kamurasi, the king of Bunyoro, he showed him a Bible and assured him that he was a descendant of Zerah the Cushite, who is mentioned in the Book of Chronicles.[8]

Speke's self-styled 'theory of conquest of inferior by superior races'[9] was destined for greatness. Generations of colonial agents and missionaries sincerely believed that the 'Hamites' were the 'carriers of a superior civilisation' and that they had subjugated the 'inferior races' of the Great Lakes Region. The only thing they had in common with the 'Bantu' races was the colour of their skin. There were indeed variations in the theory. The White Father Albert Pagès, author of *Un royaume hamite au coeur de l'Afrique*[10] [A Hamite kingdom in the heart of Africa] in 1930, speculated that the Tutsi descended from the ancient Egyptians. Louis de Lacger, a French priest, spoke of Asia Minor. In 1931, the governor general of the Belgian Congo, Pierre Ryckmans, wrote that 'the Batutsi are meant to reign' and that 'their fine presence is in itself enough to give them a great prestige vis-à-vis the inferior races which surround them'.[11] All described the 'Hamites' as mainly pastoralists and the 'Bantu' as essentially farmers.

Through their internal policies, their interaction with the monarchy and their attempts at developing an anthropology of the people they wanted to convert, the Catholic missionaries contributed in a significant way to the entrenchment of the Hutu–Tutsi divide. In 1935, Léon Classe, the strongman of the Catholic mission, wrote in the White Father's journal *Grands Lacs* that 'the Tutsi are not Bantu; they are, if you will, Negroids – they are the African people who display the strongest Hamitic indications'.[12] The American historian and theologian James Carney pointed out that if Classe practised discrimination in education by giving precedence to Tutsi children, he did not oppose Hutu advancement in the church, as proved by the fact that he appointed Hutu priests and catechists to lead missions and appointed a Hutu, Gallican Bushishi, as professor in the major seminary

---

[7] *Ibid.*, 247.
[8] *Ibid.*, 546–7. See Chrétien and Kabanda, *Rwanda. Racisme et génocide*, 64.
[9] *Ibid.*, 246.
[10] Albert Pagès, *Un royaume hamite au cœur de l'Afrique* (Brussels: Hayez, 1933).
[11] Pierre Ryckmans, *Dominer pour servir* (Brussels: Albert Dewit, 1931), 26. From the same author see also 'Des gens de haute taille', *Grands Lacs*, 52, 5–6 (1936), 279–80.
[12] Léon Classe, 'Un pays et trois races', *Grands Lacs*, 51, 5–6, 138, quoted in Carney, *Rwanda before the Genocide*, 34.

of Kabgayi. He is remembered, however, as the man who promoted ethnic stratification within the Catholic Church.[13]

In the early 1960s, the Belgian anthropologist Marcel d'Hertefelt continued to describe the Tutsi as an 'Ethiopian race'.[14] In the 1970s and 1980s, however, scholars such as Catharine and David Newbury, Claudine Vidal and Emmanuel Ntezimana began to question the assumptions upon which the Hamitic theory had been based. It has now lost all credibility in academic circles, but it continues to have a popular appeal. Meanwhile, as Danielle de Lame observed, in rural Rwanda ethnic terms were used with flexibility until the eve of the genocide. One of her older informants indiscriminately called all teachers Tutsi because of their lifestyle, setting them apart from manual workers.[15]

Perraudin's pastoral letter

1959 is no doubt a turning point in Rwandan history. In the interviews with convicted *génocidaires* and genocide survivors which Erin Jessee,[16] Amélie Faucheux[17] and I conducted, it becomes evident again and again. The *génocidaires* describe 1959 as the year when Hutu were 'liberated' and entered into an era of peace and harmony; the survivors, on the contrary, see it as the start of a period of regular massacres and ongoing discrimination. The October 1990 RPF invasion was motivated by the desire of (mostly Tutsi) people who had lived in exile since 1959 to return to their country. The Hutu extremist propaganda used the fear of a return to the pre-1959 'feudal slavery' to legitimise the genocide against the Tutsi. Both sides made abundant use of the memory of 1959 to justify their actions, but in opposite ways.

The history of the Christian response to the Rwandan Social Revolution is documented in the work of two historians, James Carney and Léon Saur, who respectively made use of the missionary and colonial archives. They

---

[13] Carney, *Rwanda before the Genocide*, 33–6.
[14] Marcel d'Hertefelt, *Les anciens royaumes de la zone interlacustre méridionale Rwanda, Burundi, Buha* (Tervuren, Belgium: Musée Royal de l'Afrique Centrale, 1962), 18, quoted in Carney, *Rwanda before the Genocide,* 12.
[15] De Lame, *A Hill among a Thousand*, 96.
[16] Erin Jessee, *Negotiating Genocide in Rwanda: The Politics of History* (London: Palgrave Macmillan, 2017).
[17] Amélie Faucheux, 'Massacrer dans l'intimité. La question de la rupture des liens sociaux et familiaux dans le cas du génocide des Tutsi du Rwanda de 1994', unpublished PhD thesis, Paris, École pratique des hautes études, 2019.

pointed out that until the mid-1950s, the Hutu–Tutsi question was rarely evoked in public. More prominent were the questions of democratisation and communism. When a group of mission-trained *évolués* started to promote the Hutu cause in 1956, the vicar apostolic André Perraudin and the provincial of the Belgian White Fathers, Guy Mosmans, refrained from making any public statement.[18] There is no evidence that the Bahutu Manifesto of March 1957, which articulated the Hutu people's grievances in terms similar to those of the Hutu extremist propagandists in the 1990s, was drafted by one of the Belgian missionaries or by the vicar apostolic, but its proponents all had links with the Catholic missionary establishment. Two served as editors of the Catholic magazine *Kinyamateka*, one worked as Perraudin's personal secretary and three were former seminarians.

Meanwhile, Perraudin's pastoral letter of 11 February 1959, entitled '*Super omnia caritas*' [Charity above all], had considerable repercussions. It is true that the Swiss bishop's aim was to apply the social teaching of the Catholic Church to the Rwandan situation in the spirit of social justice. However, by declaring that 'race' was the country's main problem and that 'in Rwanda the social differences and inequalities [were] for a large part related to racial differences',[19] he gave the Hutu educated elite's argumentation a forum it did not have before. He contributed to the entrenchment of the binary system of ethnic identities to which I referred at the beginning of this chapter.

There was indeed a social problem in Rwanda, which revolved around the privileges of the aristocratic group educated at the Centre scolaire d'Astrida, not far from the royal court. Instead of pleading the cause of the *rubanda rugufi* (small people), Perraudin became the advocate of the *rubanda nyamwinshi* (majority people). The 'racial' issue took centre stage, and this was to remain until the genocide and beyond.

Saur convincingly demonstrated that Perraudin, who arrived in Rwanda in 1950 and only saw the country through the eyes of a seminary rector and a bishop, had a superficial understanding of Rwandan society and did not anticipate the political impact of his pastoral letter. Using a deductive method, Perraudin wanted to offer guidance to the church in a time of transition and to preserve its influence in the political landscape that would

---

[18] Carney, *Rwanda before the Genocide*, 78–80; Saur, 'Catholiques belges et Rwanda, 1950–1965', 692–3.

[19] André Perraudin, '*Super omnia caritas*', in Vénuste Linguyeneza (ed.), *Vérité, justice, charité. Lettres pastorales et autres déclarations des évêques catholiques du Rwanda, 1956–1962* (Waterloo, Belgium, 2001), 28.

arise after independence.[20] Even his Tutsi colleague, Aloys Bigirumwami, the bishop of Nyundo, who had argued in an article published the year before that the Rwandan problem was social and economic rather than racial and ethnic,[21] found the pastoral letter acceptable and had it read in the parishes of his diocese.

But it was the time when pro-Hutu and pro-Tutsi social movements, some radical, others moderate and ethnically diverse, were transforming into political parties in preparation for elections which were to set the country on the path to independence. The suspicious death of Mwami Mutara Rudahigwa in July 1959 added to the uncertainty. Rumours that the Tutsi traditionalists, who would soon found the Union Nationale Rwandaise (UNAR) party, had communist connections exacerbated the tensions. In this heated atmosphere, Perraudin's discourse acted as a detonator.[22] He died in 2003. Shortly before his death, he vehemently defended his actions in a volume of memoirs.[23] This did not prevent him from being the object of an enduring controversy in post-genocide Rwanda. For some, he was an advocate of social justice; for others, he was the cleric who made the genocide possible.

The Rwandan Social Revolution

The Rwandan Social Revolution of 1959 is, in some ways, a misnomer.[24] A few hundred people died in the upsurge of violence and destruction that hit Rwanda on 1 November 1959 – hence the term 'Rwandan All Saints Day' – but the protest did not have a clear political aim. The victims were Tutsi chiefs and innocent bystanders. The insurgents burned houses and slaughtered cattle. Many chiefs fled to Uganda and other neighbouring countries with their families.[25]

---

[20] Saur, 'Catholiques belges et Rwanda, 1950–1965,' 626–32. Linguyeneza adopts a similar point of view in the introduction to the collection of Rwandan episcopal documents he published in 2001.

[21] Aloys Bigirumwami, 'Le problème des Hutu, Tutsi et Twa', *Témoignage chrétien* (Belgian edition), 5 September 1958.

[22] Saur, 'Catholiques belges et Rwanda, 1950–1965', 631–63.

[23] André Perraudin, *Un évêque au Rwanda: 'Par-dessus tout la charité': les six premières années de mon épiscopat (1956–1962)* (Saint-Maurice, Suisse: Éditions Saint-Augustin, 2003).

[24] On the various interpretations of the Rwandan Social Revolution, see Newbury, 'Ethnicity and the politics of history in Rwanda', 9–10.

[25] Jean Hubert, *La Toussaint rwandaise et sa répression* (Bruxelles: Académie royale des sciences d'outremer, 1965).

It was the colonial power, and more precisely Guy Logiest, the Belgian special military resident and high representative, who effected the revolution. He took it upon himself to replace the thousands of exiled Tutsi chiefs with Hutu teachers, businesspeople, merchants and catechists. By late December, 158 of Rwanda's 478 *sous-chefferies* [sub-chieftaincies] and 24 of Rwanda's 49 *chefferies* [chieftaincies] had changed hands.[26] On 28 January 1960, 2,873 of the 3,125 burgomasters abolished the monarchy in what has been termed the 'Gitarama coup d'état', but here again Logiest was involved. He had been approached beforehand by the leader of the Party of the Hutu Emancipation Movement (Parmehutu) and future president Grégoire Kayibanda and he ratified the new political order in only four days.[27] On its part, Parmehutu had called in October 1959 for 'the end of Tutsi colonialism' and of the 'feudal' regime dominated by the Tutsi.[28] The downfall of the monarchy was a joint operation of the Belgian coloniser and the radical Hutu movement.

This 'revolution' has left a deep mark in the memories of the genocide survivors and the returnees, because it inaugurated a long list of anti-Tutsi pogroms in Rwanda. In late 1960 and early 1961, 3,000 houses were destroyed in response to attacks by Tutsi activists and 22,000 people were forced into exile. On 26 and 27 March 1962, following a raid that had caused the death of Belgian tourists and attacks on local officials, Hutu militia killed between 1,000 and 2,000 Tutsi men, women and children in the northern town of Byumba.[29] Then, on 21 December 1963, a few hundred Tutsi activists crossed the Burundian border and went as far as Nyamata in the vicinity of Kigali. On the faith of a probably forged document found on the dead body of a Congolese soldier, the government arrested and executed twenty internal members of UNAR and the Rassemblement Démocratique Rwandais (RADER), another opposition party.[30] On 23 December, Tutsi civilians were murdered in Cyangugu and Kibungo. In the following days, between 8,000 and 14,000 Tutsi suffered the same fate in the Gikongoro area.[31]

---

[26] Carney, *Rwanda before the Genocide*, 127.
[27] *Ibid.*, 155–6.
[28] *Ibid.*, 109.
[29] *Ibid.*, 156–7. On the Byumba massacre, see also René Lemarchand, *Rwanda and Burundi* (New York: Praeger, 1970), 217–19; Paul Rutayisire, 'Les mécanismes de l'exclusion des Tutsi', *Africa Review of Books* (September 2005), 20.
[30] Carney, *Rwanda before the Genocide*, 177.
[31] *Ibid.*, 178.

The pattern of Tutsi civilians being designated as 'accomplices' of armed troops of exiles invading the country and being killed as a result in large numbers – a pattern which characterised the 1994 genocide – was already in play thirty years before. In 1964, critics of the Rwandan government were already using the term genocide. The alarm was rung by a Swiss UNESCO (UN Educational, Scientific and Cultural Organization) volunteer in Butare by the name of Denis-Gilles Vuillemin who visited the missions of Cyanika, Kaduha and Kibeho in January 1964 and collected information on the massacres that had been perpetrated before his arrival.[32] The French daily *Le Monde* echoed his testimony.[33] Even Radio Vatican broadcast the news, probably tipped by two Tutsi exiles: Michel Kayihura, the brother of the bishop of Butare Jean-Baptiste Gahamanyi; and Jean-Bosco Kayonga, a monk from the Trappist monastery of Mokoto in North Kivu.[34] The Belgian anthropologist Luc De Heusch, who denounced the 1963 massacre to the Belgian League of Human Rights,[35] and the British philosopher Bertrand Russell, who described it as 'the most horrible and systematic massacre we have had occasion to witness since the extermination of the Jews by the Nazis',[36] are also on record for having taken a public stand on the slaughter.

Nine years later, in the aftermath of a massacre of Hutu teachers, priests, pastors and businesspeople in Burundi which was also described as a genocide, the Rwandan Tutsi suffered another attack, comparatively less costly in terms of human lives but with far-reaching psychological consequences for the survivors. In late 1972, Tutsi students were forcibly removed from the Catholic schools of Byimana, Save and Nyamasheke. The purge spread

---

[32] Marcel Kabanda, 'Rwanda, les massacres de 1963. Le témoignage de G. D. Vuillemin', in Christine Deslaurier et Dominique Juhé-Beaulaton (ed.), *Afrique, terre d'histoire. Au coeur de la recherche avec Jean-Pierre Chrétien* (Paris: Karthala, 2007), 415–34.

[33] 'L'extermination des Tutsis. Les massacres du Ruanda sont la manifestation d'une haine raciale soigneusement entretenue', *Le Monde*, 4 February 1964.

[34] Lemarchand, *Rwanda and Burundi*, 224; Linden, *Christianisme et pouvoirs au Rwanda (1900–1990)* (Paris: Karthala, 1999), 362. A list of the grievances addressed by Kayihura and Kayonga to the Holy See and the responses given to them by a group of missionaries are included in Perraudin, *Un évêque au Rwanda*, 355–413.

[35] Luc De Heusch, 'Responsibilities for a Genocide', *Anthropology Today*, 11/4 (August 1995), 7.

[36] Quoted in Stanley Meisler, 'Holocaust in Burundi', in Willem Adriaan Veehoven (ed.), *Case Studies on Human Rights and Fundamental Freedoms* (The Hague: Martinus Nijhoff, 1976), 229.

to the National University of Rwanda in Butare in February–March 1973 under the pretext – false, according to Paul Rutayisire[37] – that the Tutsi students were overrepresented. Tutsi civil servants were also affected. Several hundred people, including two Josephite brothers, were killed during this period.[38]

Racist for a good cause, but racist all the same

Another pattern in the period under review is that of the church authorities' response to the violence against the Tutsi. As this chapter and the following one will show, there are striking similarities between the response of bishops and high-ranking missionaries in 1959 and the subsequent years, in the period following the 1990 RPF invasion and during the three months of the genocide against the Tutsi. Each time, the church authorities only denounced the violence in general terms, explained it in terms of popular anger and apportioned an equal blame to the armed forces and Hutu militia involved in the massacres of Tutsi on one side and the Tutsi troops forcing their way into the country on the other side. In all three cases, isolated priests and pastors dissociated themselves from the church authorities and denounced specific occurrences of violence committed by state agents against Tutsi civilians.

In the introduction to his monumental thesis on Belgian Catholics and Rwanda, Saur related a conversation between Jules Fafchamps, a Belgian Christian Worker activist sent to Rwanda to develop Christian trade unions, with Grégoire Kayibanda in July 1959. The future president refused to include the Batutsi in the movement because, he said, 'they would use it as a springboard to occupy posts of command'. Instead, he asked his Belgian interlocutor to help the Bahutu 'obtain the promotion of a race which is still considered by the smallest of the Batutsi as a vanquished race'. Finding this conversation unsettling, Fafchamps consulted André Perraudin, the vicar apostolic of Kabgayi. He described the meeting in a letter to Jean Brück, the leader of the Belgian Christian trade unions, in the following terms:

> After these conversations, I went to see Mgr Perraudin and, with him, tried to discover the Christian moral justifications one could give to organising

---

[37] Rutayisire, 'Les mécanismes de l'exclusion des Tutsi', 22.
[38] Filip Reyntjens, *Pouvoir et droit au Rwanda: droit public et évolution politique, 1916–1973* (Tervuren, Belgium: Musée Royal de l'Afrique Centrale, 1985), 501–4; Carney, *Rwanda before the Genocide*, 189.

or supporting a movement that was racist (in the good sense of the term) but racist nevertheless. He did not see any objection to us honouring Kayibanda's claims.[39]

Racist for a good cause, but racist all the same: this is how Fafchamps understood Perraudin's position. The implication was that, for moral rather than political reasons, the vicar apostolic had become an unqualified supporter of the Hutu cause. It was, for him, an imperative of justice. Many – though not all – Catholic missionaries made the same choice. A Belgian member of the Missionaries of Africa, who started the ministry in Rwanda in 1963, was reportedly told by his superiors on his arrival: 'The White Fathers are here for the Hutu'.[40]

Neither Perraudin nor the missionaries who shared his opinions measured the long-term consequences of this partisan position. Aloys Bigirumwami, the bishop of Nyundo, did so, but he became increasingly isolated. He publicly broke with the White Fathers in 1960 for attributing all the responsibility of Rwanda's social ills to the UNAR, and he clashed with Perraudin the following year on the dismissal of a group of Tutsi candidates for the priesthood from Nyakibanda Major Seminary.[41]

The vicar apostolic's simplistic view of the Rwandan situation, with Tutsi oppressors on one side and Hutu victims on the other side, explains his reluctance to admit that his protégés had committed serious human rights abuse in 1959 and the following years. He was genuinely shocked by the violence affecting the country but showed himself incapable of analysing it properly. His misgivings about UNAR, which he regularly accused in the diocesan bulletin *Trait d'Union* of being under the influence of the international communist movement,[42] prevented him from

---

[39] Jules Fafchamps to Jean Brück, 30 July 1959, in Jules Fafchamps, *La C.S.C. et le M.O.C. dans le Kivu, le Rwanda et le Burundi de 1958 à 1961. Échange de lettres entre Jean Brück et Jules Fafchamps, dirigeants syndicaux* (Brussels: CARHOP, 2009), 70–2, quoted in Saur, 'Catholiques belges et Rwanda, 1950–1965', 8.

[40] Interview conducted on 9 June 2016 in Brussels.

[41] Carney, *Rwanda before the Genocide*, 155, 168–9. On Aloys Bigirumwami's background, see Saur, 'Catholiques belges et Rwanda, 1950–1965', 282–99.

[42] Carney, *Rwanda before the Genocide*, 159. See in particular 'Le communisme: danger mortel en Afrique', *Trait d'Union*, January–February 1961, in Linguyeneza, *Verité, justice, charité*, Document 44. In an international context dominated by the Cold War, the communist countries offered funding and diplomatic backing to UNAR in the UN Trusteeship in 1959. However, there is no evidence that the UNAR leaders had a communist programme of

understanding the plight of the Tutsi refugees and from displaying empathy for the Tutsi civilians scapegoated by Parmehutu and the newly independent Rwandan government.

In a 16 April 1994 interview with the journalist Gert Van Langendonck, the Flemish White Father Walter Aelvoet, who was heading the minor seminary of Kabgayi at the time, described the contradictory feelings that the violence which erupted in November 1959 evoked in him, when the Hutu revolted against the 'feudal regime of the Tutsi monarchy'. Other missionaries and the vicar apostolic could have said the same thing. Asked how he experienced the Hutu rebellion, Aelvoet responded:

> As something very painful. Since there were corpses, that was very hard. But deep down I was happy. Something historical was happening: the liberation of a people. [...] I buried the first Tutsi chiefs in Gitarama. The Hutu were dancing all over with their machetes, shouting: 'They must go back to Abyssinia. Good riddance!' They were not sad. They were saying: 'Father, come back tomorrow. We shall bring you a few more.'[43]

The Catholic hierarchy's reaction to the massacres of Tutsi

In the pastoral letter he delivered on 21 November 1959 with the title 'The hour of charity', Perraudin adopted a pietistic tone, asking the faithful to pray for peace and return to work. He expressed gratitude to the missions who had sheltered refugees and invited the Christian communities to rebuild the houses that had been destroyed during the violence. He remained non-committal on the political events that had caused the violence.[44] In a private correspondence, however, he blamed UNAR for starting the troubles and claimed that its actions had 'pushed the Hutu over the edge'.[45] By contrast, in *Civitas Mariae*, the bulletin of the diocese of Nyundo, Bigirumwami gave a detailed account of the violence, regretted

---

government. See Gérard Prunier, *The Rwanda Crisis: History of a Genocide* (New York: Columbia University Press, 1995), 47.

[43] Gert Van Langendonck, 'Nu worden we wel een klein landje', *De Morgen*, 16 April 1994. A French translation of this text is included in Colette Braeckman, *Rwanda. Histoire d'un génocide* (Paris: Fayard, 1994), 42.

[44] André Perraudin, 'L'heure de la charité', 21 November 1959, in Linguyeneza, *Vérité, justice, charité*, Document 25, quoted in Carney, *Rwanda before the Genocide*, 131.

[45] *Ibid.*, 131.

the 'massive destitution of chefs and sous-chefs' and declared that 'racial hatred is incompatible with the religion of Christ'.[46]

The 'pressing and anguished call' which Perraudin launched on 14 March 1960 after a new wave of attacks was more explicit in its denunciation of the pillages, depredations and murders that happened, even though, unlike Bigirumwami, he did not speak of racial hatred.[47] For his part, the newly appointed bishop of Ruhengeri, Joseph Sibomana, took a step in that direction. In a radio message broadcast in the aftermath of the massacre of Byumba in late March 1962, he condemned not only the attacks of the Tutsi assailants but the 'terrible and inhuman reactions' that followed.[48] Interestingly, Sibomana was a Hutu. By contrast, Jean-Baptiste Gahamanyi, the new bishop of Butare, who was a Tutsi, put all the blame on the *Inyenzi* (derogatory term to designate the Tutsi) in his subsequent statements.[49]

Perraudin's reaction to the execution of political opponents in response to the December 1963 UNAR attack was also sharp. 'Certain people can be tempted, in the midst of the current difficulties, to harm others and even kill innocents', he declared in his Christmas sermon. 'My dear brothers, these thoughts are not Christian and can only draw divine condemnation on our country.'[50] The tone changed, however, a week later. In their New Year's Day address, Perraudin and the other Rwandan bishops condemned the 'armed incursion of terrorists' and accused the exiles of 'knowing very well the incalculable evils resulting from their machinations'. They described the Gikongoro massacres as a 'rage of violent reactions which have not always spared the innocent'. They attributed the violence to popular passions, noting that even if such passions could 'attenuate guilt',

---

[46] 'A propos des troubles', *Civitas Mariae*, 21 (1959), in Linguyeneza, *Vérité, justice, charité*, Document 26.

[47] 'Appel pressant et angoissé', 21 March 1960, in Linguyeneza, *Vérité, justice, charité*, Document 35. See Carney, *Rwanda before the Genocide*, 148.

[48] 'Allocution radiodiffusée de Son Excellence Monseigneur Joseph Sibomana, Évêque de Ruhengeri', n.d. [late March–early April 1962], ibid., 162–3. I express my gratitude to Fr Guy Theunis M.Afr., who drew my attention to this document.

[49] *Kinyamateka*, 32/9 (March 1964), 35/1 (January 1967), 1, quoted in Antoine Mugusera, 'Kinyamateka, les Inyenzi et les complices', *Dialogue*, 189 (November 2009), 46–7, 50–1.

[50] 'Message de Noël 1963', quoted in Carney, *Rwanda before the Genocide*, 178.

the violence was 'no less condemnable'.⁵¹ The role of the local authorities in the massacres was simply ignored.

In the diocesan bulletin *Trait d'Union*, Perraudin went further. He blamed the victims for their own misfortune, as Carney put it,⁵² and reaffirmed his absolute loyalty to the Kayibanda government:

> If there is not in all the inhabitants of this country a loyalty and good respect with regard to the institutions put in place by the referendum of 1961 – which does not stop the existence of a healthy opposition – there will never be serious peace. Without mixing ourselves in one or other partisan politics, we should be realistic about the choices facing us. We do not have the right by an equivocal attitude, of exposing the country to much greater evil than that we have known.⁵³

The kaleidoscope of the Catholic Church in Rwanda

While considering, after Carney, that Perraudin and the missionary hierarchy supported the Hutu cause in the years of the Rwandan Social Revolution, Saur points out that in the 1950s and 1960s the Rwandan clergy was far from speaking with one voice. There were differences among diocesan priests and missionaries and among the missionaries themselves, along generational, political, national and ethnic lines. The Catholic Church of Rwanda, he suggests, was like a kaleidoscope which projected a variety of colours and shades on social reality.⁵⁴

This is particularly true of the White Fathers, whom post-genocide controversialists often present as systematically pro-Hutu. The generation factor needs to be taken into account. The missionaries who arrived in Rwanda before the Second World War tended to have more sympathy for the Tutsi priests and converts than their younger confrères. But there could be differences of opinion among missionaries of the same age and even of the same family, like Jules Gyssens, who was pro-Hutu, and his brother Gustaaf, who was pro-Tutsi, in the late 1950s. In his thesis, Saur gives the

---

[51] 'Message des évêques du Rwanda à l'occasion de la nouvelle année', 1 January 1964, in *Trait d'Union*, 36 (1964), 15–16, quoted in Carney, *Rwanda before the Genocide*, 307.

[52] Carney, *Rwanda before the Genocide*, 180.

[53] 'Lettre de S. E. Monseigneur Perraudin Archevêque de Kabgayi', 1 January 1964, in *Trait d'union*, 36 (1964), 7, quoted in Carney, *Rwanda before the Genocide*, 180.

[54] Saur, 'Catholiques belges et Rwanda, 1950–1965', 1348.

name of six White Fathers – Gustaaf Gyssens, Emmanuel De Schrevel, Gerard Van Overschelde, Henri Bazot, Paul Bourgois and Jean Hochedel – who were sympathetic to the UNAR.[55]

In my interviews with Tutsi priests and pastors and in publications on Rwandan history, the names of missionaries who saved lives during the massacres of late 1963 and early 1964 and exposed the complicity of the local authorities were regularly mentioned. One who is often cited is Stanislas de Jamblinne, parish priest of Cyanika, near Gikongoro, at the time. According to Paul Rutayisire, he is remembered for having said: 'The massacre seems to have been organised by the government of the Republic itself and may have been the most sinister page of the Kayibanda government.'[56] The Anglican priest Michel Kayitaba, a survivor from the Gikongoro area who founded the Christian NGO 'Moucecore' after the genocide, spoke of de Jamblinne as a man who 'saved people who were in danger, healed them, fed them and put in writing what had happened.'[57] Jean-Damascène Bizimana also praised his behaviour, as well as that of his confrère Robert Defalque, during the massacres.[58]

The journalist Laurent Larcher recently unearthed an 'Appeal to European Christianity by a group of Missionaries in Rwanda', which was drafted by another White Father, Henri Bazot, with a view to drawing the attention of the public to the Gikongoro massacres.[59] Published in *Le Monde*, it provoked the ire of Perraudin and a few other White Fathers who presented the accusations levelled against the Rwandan government as a conspiracy.[60] The signatories accused the Rwandan Social Revolution of having fostered racial hatred and provoked the 'genocide organised at Christmas 1963 which caused nearly 10,000 deaths'. The 'stupid' attitude of the Tutsi exiles who 'did not want to admit the legitimacy of the Hutu government in place' did not justify the 'bloody repression that targeted without mercy an ethnic minority'. Bazot and his confrères found the silence of the international media scandalous. 'We, Catholics, shall we be the last ones to refuse this conspiracy of silence which made us passive accomplices of this genocide?' The most horrible, they lamented, was to

---

[55] *Ibid.*, 695.
[56] Paul Rutayisire, 'Les mécanismes de l'exclusion des Tutsi', 21.
[57] Michel Kayitaba, interview conducted on 16 March 2017 in Kigali.
[58] Jean-Damascène Bizimana, *L'Eglise et le génocide au Rwanda. Les Pères Blancs et le Négationnisme* (Paris: L'Harmattan, 2001), 27.
[59] Laurent Larcher, *Rwanda, ils parlent. Témoignage pour l'histoire* (Paris: Seuil, 2019), 27–8, 213–18, 238–44.
[60] Carney, *Rwanda before the Genocide*, 183–4.

see that most killers were 'Christians and sometimes Christian leaders, teachers and even members of Catholic Action.'[61]

Mention should also be made of the Swiss White Father Hansjörg Gyr, who worked in Nyamasheke near Cyangugu. He sent a report about the massacres he had witnessed to the Lucerne-based Catholic newspaper *Der Vaterland* but, as he explained to the Swiss Dominican Reginald Kessler, his superiors put pressure on the editor for the article to be withdrawn.[62] Kessler himself, who had ministered to the Tutsi refugees in Bukavu in the early 1960s and by then was stationed in Zurich, sent to *Le Monde* a letter of support for Denis-Gilles Vuillemin, the Swiss UNESCO volunteer who had denounced the massacres of Gikongoro.[63]

The Protestant Churches' political apathy

Tharcisse Gatwa described the political attitude of the Protestant churches before and after the Social Revolution in terms of apathy.[64] Founded by Belgian, Swiss, British, Danish, American and Swedish missionaries, respectively, the Lutheran, Adventist, Anglican, Baptist, Methodist and Pentecostal churches had faced stark opposition from the Belgian government and the White Fathers in the colonial era.[65] In the early years, only the Belgian Society of Protestant Missions in Congo (SBMPC), which gave rise to the Presbyterian Church in Rwanda in 1959, received subsidies from the government. Hoping to gain favour from the authorities, the Protestant leaders pledged them allegiance and embraced their ideology in matters of ethnicity. Joe Church, a prominent Anglican missionary in Eastern Rwanda who significantly contributed to the birth of the East African Revival in the

---

[61] Henri Bazot *et al.*, 'Un appel à la Chrétienté Européenne par un groupe de Missionnaires au Rwanda, 15 January 1964', in Henri Bazot, 'Ma vie de missionnaire au Liban, au Rwanda, au Burundi, au Zaïre et en France', unpublished manuscript, General Archives of the Missionaries of Africa, Rome, 2006. See Carney, *Rwanda before the Genocide*, 307.

[62] Kabanda, 'Rwanda, les massacres de 1963', 429.

[63] 'A propos des massacres du Ruanda', *Le Monde*, 4 March 1964.

[64] Gatwa, *The Churches and Ethnic Ideology*, 101.

[65] On the history of the Protestant churches in Rwanda, see Tharcisse Gatwa and André Karamaga, *Les autres Chrétiens rwandais. La présence protestante* (Kigali: Éditions Urwego, 1990); Gatwa and Rutinduka (ed.), *Histoire du christianisme au Rwanda*, 63–249.

1930s, was known for his support of the Hamitic theory.⁶⁶ There is no doubt that the other Protestant missionaries followed suit.

Snubbed by Guy Logiest, the Belgian military resident, the Protestant leaders played no role in the Rwandan Social Revolution, but they conformed to the state's policies after the independence of Rwanda as they had done in colonial times. In 1959, the Anglican Mission of Rwanda provided shelter to Tutsi refugees fleeing political violence and facilitated their transfer to Uganda,⁶⁷ but they did so for humanitarian reasons, not as a principled opposition to ethnic violence.⁶⁸ In subsequent years, the Anglican Church aligned itself with the pro-Hutu positions of the Rwandan government. The hierarchy was exclusively Hutu and promotion opportunities were severely hampered for Tutsi clergy.⁶⁹ The pietistic tradition of the Anglican Church and of the church bodies that participated in the East African Revival did not allow for a critical reflection on the discriminatory policies of the Rwandan government.⁷⁰ The newly established Presbyterian Church, which was still under the control of the missionaries, similarly failed to condemn the violence which the Belgian authorities 'appeared to allow, if not actually support', as an observer noted.⁷¹

The queen who used the bodies of Hutu babies as a stool

The memories of 1959 haunt all Rwandans, though in different ways. Not all the people who experienced the genocide had a direct experience of what happened during this period. The young adults who took an active part in the genocide, fell victims to it or were innocent bystanders based their judgement on stories transmitted by family members. For this section, I rely upon the interviews that Erin Jessee, Amélie Faucheux and I

---

[66] Joe Church, *Quest for the Highest: An Autobiographical Account of the East African Revival* (Carlisle: Paternoster Press, 1981), 33–4, quoted in Roger Bowen, 'Genocide in Rwanda 1994: an Anglican perspective', in Carol Rittner, John K. Roth and Wendy Whitworth, *Genocide in Rwanda. Complicity of the Churches?* (St Paul, Minnesota: Paragon House, 2004), 39.

[67] Thaddée Ntininyuzwa, 'Le réveil africain et les relations Église-État', in Gatwa and Rutinduka (ed.), *Histoire du christianisme au Rwanda*, 357.

[68] Gatwa and Karamaga, *Les autres Chrétiens rwandais*, 101.

[69] Bowen, 'Genocide in Rwanda 1994', 41.

[70] *Ibid.*, 40.

[71] H. H. Osborn, *Fire in the Hills: The Revival which Spread from Rwanda* (Crowborough: Highland Books, 1991), 187, quoted in Gatwa, *The Churches and Ethnic Ideology*, 103.

conducted, knowing that many other testimonies were recorded by journalists, anthropologists and historians.[72]

Predictably, an analysis of these interviews brings to light contrasting experiences and emotions: for some, 1959 was a 'liberation'; for others, it was the first of a long series of attacks on the lives and the property of people dear to them. Likewise, to some informants the 1990 October RPF attack was a sign of hope and to others it was bad news. As Jessee warned us, however, we should beware of single stories.[73] All have an element of complexity. Neither the Hutu nor the Tutsi experiences can be reduced to a single pattern. We must also take into account the fact that some interviewees were children of mixed marriages and that quite a few had gone into exile before or after 1994. All this had an impact on the manner in which the genocide against the Tutsi was remembered and commemorated.

The stories about the 'enslavement' of the Hutu population before 1959 told by the convicted *génocidaires* in prison tell us more about the present than the past of their authors. They draw from oral traditions transmitted from generation to generation. As David Cohen pointed out in the 1980s, oral traditions, useful as they are to gather information on the past which otherwise would be irremediably lost, should not be reified. They invite us, he wrote, 'to see individuals making and holding historical knowledge in all their complexity and individuality – considerably concerned with interests, objectives, recreation and esteem, rather less concerned with performing history according to some cultural design'.[74] Along the same lines, Liisa Malkki forged the term 'mythico-histories' to describe the stories she collected from Hutu refugees in Tanzania. Designed to make sense of the refugees' lives before and after the 1972 genocide in Burundi, they constituted 'not only a description of the past, not even merely an evaluation of the past, but a subversive recasting and reinterpretation of it in fundamentally moral terms'.[75]

---

[72] For example, Catherine Gilbert, *From Surviving to Living: Voice, Trauma and Witness in Rwandan Women's Writing* (Montpellier: Presses universitaires de la Méditerranée, 2018).

[73] Erin Jessee, 'The danger of a single story: iconic stories in the aftermath of the 1994 Rwandan genocide', *Memory Studies*, 10/2 (2017), 144–63.

[74] David William Cohen, 'The undefining of oral tradition', *Ethnohistory*, 36/1 (1989), 18.

[75] Liisa Malkki, *Purity and Exile: Violence, Memory and National Cosmology among Hutu Refugees in Tanzania* (Chicago: Chicago University Press, 1995), 55.

Jessee, who interviewed several convicted *génocidaires* in detention, commented that they demonised the Tutsi monarchy for enslaving the Hutu masses and subjecting them to a range of human rights abuses. A former history teacher and a former official, respectively codenamed Philippe and Martin, claimed that one of the Tutsi queens had the habit of keeping Hutu babies around her wherever she sat, stabbing them with a sword as they supported her weight on a stool. In a variant of that story, shared by a former salesman codenamed Michel, it was the king who planted his spear in the bodies of Hutu children to support himself. Stories about the *ubuhake*, this client–patron relationship that the convicted *génocidaires* interpreted as forced labour, abounded. By giving a Hutu neighbour a cow, Michel explained, the Tutsi patron ensured that in future he would be able to call upon that man to give him a share of his crop, cattle or any other wealth he might acquire, as well as labour. In this way, the Tutsi would become wealthy without having to do any manual labour.[76]

Faucheux, for her part, interviewed *génocidaires* old enough to have remembered humiliating experiences suffered by their parents. Simon Bikindi, a Hutu songwriter convicted for incitement to genocide in 2009 in the ICTR, declared that he had seen the chief for whom his father was working drag his naked father out of bed to do a chore for him. This type of humiliation, he commented, would take generations to be forgiven.[77] Gaspard Kanyarukiga, an affluent businessman from Kibuye, born in 1937, who was convicted for participating in the bulldozing of the Nyange church where Tutsi refugees had found shelter, gave the following testimony:

> The Hutu carried the Tutsi, the chefs and the sous-chefs. They would put them on our shoulders to be transported. In fact, we did the same with white people who worked in different areas. Yes, we were considered as slaves. I could see that the Hutu were suffering. I saw it in my family. They were only allowed to raise small animals, I mean, sheep and goats. The cows, they were for the Tutsi. And the fields also. Everything belonged to them, the crops and the flocks, because us, we did not have enough space to graze our livestock, just like we did not have space to grow potatoes and sorgho.[78]

---

[76] Jessee, *Negotiating Genocide in Rwanda*, 155–7. See also Erin Jessee and Sarah Watkins, 'Good kings, bloody tyrants and everything in between: representations of the monarchy in post-genocide Rwanda,' *History in Africa*, 41 (2014), 50–5.
[77] Faucheux, 'Massacrer dans l'intimité', 1177.
[78] *Ibid.*, 163.

Some of Faucheux's informants had memories of 1959. Ezéchiel, an Interahamwe leader detained in Ruhengeri who at that time was in Grade 3 at school, recounted his participation in the looting of Tutsi houses:

> We burned the houses of the Tutsi. Me too, with my family, we took part in it. We were roaming around to take things. We looted the Tutsi houses. Already for me, the Tutsi counted for nothing. I was small, but I would put tools, eggs, food in my pockets. I was raised with that in mind. Everything was for the Hutu. He was the one who worked the land of the country. He had been building it, He was the deserving one.[79]

A culture of violence and discrimination

Among the Tutsi, conversely, it was the memories of the massacres punctuating the First and the Second Republics, of the impunity granted to the perpetrators and of the policies preventing young people from pursuing education that were kept alive in the families. Few of the genocide survivors and of the returnees Jessee interviewed had direct experiences of the violence inflicted on Tutsi people during the Rwandan Social Revolution and the first years of independence. What emerged from their narratives, she noted, were 'pervasive accounts of structural violence that invaded their everyday lives and which they associated very clearly with the Kayibanda leadership'.[80] Anti-Tutsi violence increasingly became politically and culturally acceptable.

In the interviews I conducted, the victim of the 1963–4 violence that came up most often was the priest Modeste Mungwarareba, one of the founders of the Comité de Relance des Activités Pastorales [Commission for the Revival of Pastoral Activities] (CRAP) in the diocese of Butare after the genocide and subsequently the general secretary of the Conference of Catholic Bishops of Rwanda. He was twelve years old at the time. He narrowly escaped death for a second time during the genocide. He is remembered not only as a victim of anti-Tutsi violence but as a man who refused hatred and campaigned for interethnic reconciliation.

It was at school, he recounted in an article published in 1997, that people addressed him for the first time as a Tutsi. 'It meant', he commented, 'bad, arrogant, dominating, deceitful. It was at that moment that the first racial complex developed in me, made of fear, mistrust and hidden revolt'.[81]

---

[79] *Ibid.*, 870.

[80] Jessee, *Negotiating Genocide in Rwanda*, 126.

[81] Modeste Mungwarareba, 'Le pardon, guérison et chemin pour vivre', *Dialogue*, 197 (March–April 1997), 64.

The family hut was looted and destroyed in 1959. Instead of the promised social revolution it was, he discovered, an ethnic revolution. Then during the holidays of December 1963, in reprisal for the attack of the Tutsi refugees, he fell victim to an assault and nearly died:

> Beaten to death by a band of adult men, most of them known because they were living in the area, I felt unconscious in a coma and was left as dead. I was woken up by the rain at about four in the afternoon. From a distance, a Christian, M. Berchmans Kanyabujinja, had observed everything without being able to do anything against those fanatics. When he saw me standing on my feet, he came to collect me and hid me in his house, at great risk to himself.[82]

Other church ministers were among the victims. Antoine Rutayisire, an Anglican priest who served as vice-president of the National Commission for Unity and Reconciliation (NURC) after the genocide, lost his father to ethnic violence in 1963.[83] Jérôme Masinzo, a Catholic priest from the diocese of Butare who was a baby at the time heard from his parents that his family had found shelter in the parish church of Kaduha while countless people were being killed around them.[84] The massacres were restricted to certain areas, but all Tutsi people knew of them and were afraid of suffering the same fate one day.

Equally traumatic were the expulsions of Tutsi school pupils and university students in late 1972 and early 1973 and the subsequent killings. Ubald Rugirangoga, a Catholic priest who, like Rutayisire and Masinzo, promoted reconciliation after the genocide, was forced to leave Rwanda with his family, as he related in an autobiographical sketch posted on his website:

> In 1973, while I was doing my studies in the St Pius X Minor Seminary in the diocese of Nyundo, Hutu seminarians chased us from this seminary because we were Tutsi. There was insecurity everywhere in the country, Tutsi people were threatened by death, my paternal uncle who was a teacher was unfairly sent to jail, the threat of death was imminent for all Tutsi people and I was forced to take refuge in Burundi.[85]

Ignace-Marie Uwimana, a sixty-four-year-old genocide survivor interviewed by Amélie Faucheux, had already experienced ethnic violence in

---

[82] *Ibid.*, 65.
[83] Antoine Rutayisire, interview conducted on 15 March 2017 in Kigali.
[84] Jérôme Masinzo, interview conducted on 29 March 2017 in Nyumba.
[85] 'Information sur la Pastorale de pardon et réconciliation dans la Paroisse de Mushaka', n.d. <htpps://frubald.files.wordpress.com.2013/04>.

1959 and 1973. According to her, each episode was worse than the previous one. In 1959, there was 'still friendship' and people respected the cross. In 1973, it was similar but worse:

> Where I lived near Butare, there had again been something like reprisals. Men armed with machetes and clubs went to the schools and, I remember well, they entered the seminary where I worked with the Bernardine Sisters in Kansi and we ran away. They beat many children and it went on for a week. I went to Burundi, for the time for things to calm down. On my return, I went to the family. I had a small sister who studied in Rwaza. She had been badly beaten. I also had a small brother whom I found in the hospital in Kabgayi. My sister could not go back to school because the people who had beaten her were children of the same hill. They had studied with her.[86]

The children were not the only ones to be exposed to harassment, Uwimana explained. The quota system was applied arbitrarily. In the government department where she was working, on certain days in the morning, they would find the names of Tutsi people displayed on the door. On those days and the days that followed, access was refused to them. The same happened at the university. She was forced to walk a long distance on foot to get another job. People thought that the Tutsi were so clever that nobody else could find employment. 'It was strange', she commented, 'to be demonised in this way and at the same time to be exalted.'[87]

By 1990, when the RPF invaded Rwanda, the relations between Tutsi and Hutu were generally friendly, as witnessed by the important number of intermarriages, especially in the south of Rwanda. The members of the two groups shared beer and their children played together. Yet, this apparent harmony was superficial. A battery of rules and regulations, at school, in the administration, reminded the Tutsi, overtly or covertly, that they did not fully belong to the country. Apart from bribing officials to change the ethnic designation on their identity cards, they were defenceless in the face of discrimination and spoliation. Everybody knew who was who. At the end of the day, a Tutsi was simultaneously somebody one wanted to emulate and an *inyenzi* (cockroach) that one profoundly despised.

---

[86] Faucheux, 'Massacrer dans l'intimité', 685.
[87] *Ibid.*, 685–6.

CHAPTER 2

The run-up to the genocide

On 1 October 1990, four hundred combatants of the Rwandan Patriotic Army (RPA), the armed wing of the Rwandan Patriotic Front (RPF), invaded Rwanda from Uganda to allow the return of the hundreds of thousands of Tutsi refugees scattered in the neighbouring countries and create an alternative to the pro-Hutu government of Juvénal Habyarimana. The Rwandan army soon repelled the invaders with the support of Zairian, Belgian and French troops. The RPA commander, Fred Rwigema, was killed on the second day. On 30 October, the Rwandan government announced that the war was over.[1]

Under the leadership of Paul Kagame, however, the RPA restructured itself sufficiently to occupy a stretch of territory in the north of Rwanda and launch an attack on Ruhengeri in January 1991 and on Ruhengeri and Byumba in February 1993. Massive population displacements occurred as a result, and many people died during the military engagements. During the same period, using the RPF attack as a pretext, soldiers and armed groups close to the Habyarimana government and enjoying its support massacred an estimated two thousand Tutsi civilians in the north-west of the country and in the Bugesera.[2] Many of them were Bagogwe, an essentially rural ethnic group that had been isolated from mainstream Rwandan politics for more than a century but was nevertheless considered Tutsi. Philip Verwimp has argued that these massacres, which human rights activists described as early as 1993 as a genocide, were part of a strategy aiming to turn land that was used for pasture into agricultural land through the *paysannat* settlement scheme.[3]

---

[1] Gérard Prunier, *The Rwanda Crisis: History of a Genocide* (New York: Columbia University Press, 1995), 93–6.
[2] Philip Verwimp, 'The 1990–92 massacres in Rwanda: a case of spatial and social engineering', *Journal of Agrarian Change*, 11 (2011), 396.
[3] *Ibid.*, 400–2.

The periodisation of Rwandan history is contested. The current Rwandan government and an important body of researchers consider that, given its amplitude, the particular nature of mass violence it deployed and the profoundly destabilising effect it had on the country itself and the neighbouring areas, the genocide is a central event in Rwandan history. Intellectuals linked to the opposition and a certain number of academics claim, on the contrary, that the turning point was the October 1990 RPF invasion, which ended a virtuous cycle of economic development and social harmony and initiated a series of violent episodes that led to the genocide and further destabilisation in the region. As we shall see in chapters 4, 5 and 6, several Rwandan clerics and missionaries adopted this position.

In fact, recent studies show that the Rwandan crisis preceded the RPF October 1990 attack. The invasion exacerbated it rather than provoked the crisis. A year before this, Marie-France Cros, the *La Libre Belgique* African correspondent, had published an article under the title 'Atmosphère fin de règne à Kigali' [End of an era atmosphere in Kigali].[4] Antoine Jouan, Peter Uvin and Jean-Paul Kimonyo have shown that in the mid-1980s, Rwanda, which development agencies and international organisations commonly hailed as a success story, entered into a severe agricultural and financial crisis, caused by a fall in the price of tea, coffee and cassiterite, which affected all social groups. The living conditions of the rural population deteriorated to unprecedented levels. Life expectancy plummeted. Only members of the elite managed to maintain wealth and status, thanks to party and family connections.[5] For a long time, Rwanda had the image of a country less corrupt than its neighbours. A series of scandals revealed that this was no longer the case. In 1989, the editor of the Catholic bi-weekly *Kinyamateka* – André Sibomana, to whom we shall return in Chapter 4 – was arrested for revealing that a minister of finance had embezzled 30 million Rwandan francs. He also irritated the government by publishing articles on the drought that devastated a large part of Rwanda.[6] The grip that the National Revolutionary Movement for

---

[4] Marie-France Cros, 'Atmosphère fin de siècle à Kigali', *La Libre Belgique*, 31 October–1 November 1989, quoted in Jean-Paul Kimonyo, *Rwanda, un génocide populaire* (Paris: Karthala, 2008), 102.

[5] Antoine Jouan, 'Rwanda, octobre 1990–avril 1994: Les errances de la gestion d'un conflit', *Relations internationales et stratégiques*, 23 (Autumn 1996), 132–4, 139–41; Peter Uvin, *Aiding Violence: The Development Enterprise in Rwanda* (West Hartford, Connecticut: Kumarian Press, 1998), 53–9; Kimonyo, *Rwanda, un génocide populaire*, 92–102.

[6] Longman, *Christianity and Genocide*, 129–31.

Development (MRND – the single party created by Juvénal Habyarimana after the July 1973 coup) had on the population started to loosen, especially in the south of the country, which benefitted less from the president's largesse than the northern prefectures of Gisenyi and Ruhengeri, from which he and his allies originated.

In its early years, the Habyarimana regime was characterised by a relative relaxation of ethnic tension. Many interviewees made note of it. Things started to change in the late 1980s. In an interview, Servilien Nzakamwita, the current bishop of Byumba, referred to the attacks launched on the Tutsi in the minor seminary of Rwesero, north of Kigali, in 1989. He left his post of rector soon afterwards to pursue studies in Belgium. He often wonders today whether he would still be alive if he had stayed.[7] The Belgian anthropologist Danielle de Lame, who was doing fieldwork in the south of Rwanda at the time, made a similar observation:

> The multiplication of violence at the local level against the background of increased inequalities in the access to money and land took marked ethnic tonalities as early as 1989 and it became manifest in 1990 through the publication of well-known pamphlets circulated, through the intermediary of low-key officials and businesspeople, in the most remote hills.[8]

The stated purpose of the RPF October 1990 invasion was to allow the return of the Tutsi refugees scattered in neighbouring countries; the Rwandan government estimated there were 200,000 refugees, but in reality there were probably three times that number.[9] In Uganda, their first place of exile, they never ceased to be considered strangers, despite their significant contribution to overturning the Obote regime.[10] After initially refusing any possibility of return, in February 1989 Habyarimana created a Special Commission on the Problems of Migrants, and in July 1990 the Commission recommended that 85,000 eligible refugees be given the opportunity to return to the country.[11] Critics of the RPF, including the

---

[7] Mgr Servilien Nzakamwita, interview conducted on 20 March 2019 in Kigali.

[8] Danielle de Lame, 'L'histoire se fait aussi "par le bas"', *Afrique & Histoire*, 2 (1994), 290.

[9] André Guichaoua, *Le problème des réfugiés rwandais et des populations banyarwanda dans la région des Grands Lacs africains* (Geneva: UN High Commissioner for Refugees, 1992), 22–3.

[10] Jinmi Adisa, *The Comfort of Strangers: The Impact of Rwandan Refugees in Neighbouring Countries* (Ibadan: IFRA, 1996), 39–45.

[11] *Ibid.*, 31.

White Father Serge Desouter, argue that on this basis the Tutsi refugees could have returned to Rwanda without a war and that, since they did not, the only reason they invaded Rwanda was the conquest of power.[12] This point deserves discussion. First, the refugees were considerably more than 85,000 and there was no guarantee at all that all those who wanted to return would have been allowed to do so. Secondly, the Rwandan government only opened the door for the return of refugees because it was a request from the international community. As Gérard Prunier heard from a Rwandan diplomat in 1993, the Kigali government envoys who were supposed to have gone to Uganda during the summer of 1990 to select 'a representative group of refugees' to launch the repatriation process were told 'not to hurry'.[13]

The expatriates' open letter

On 22 October 1990, the Belgian daily *Le Soir* published an open letter from 101 expatriates in Rwanda, who assured that, despite rebel attacks in the north-east and a few gunshots in Kigali, the situation was under control. They blamed the international media for relaying information from Rwandans abroad who were 'accomplices of the rebels'. These media acted as 'objective enemies of Rwanda' by creating panic in the population. The signatories vigorously defended the Habyarimana government, which they praised for bringing stability to the country. They dismissed the criticisms levelled against it. The problem of the refugees was complex, and the government had created a commission to resolve it. There was indeed corruption but less than in other African countries. For reasons that outsiders were unable to understand, there were indeed ethnic tensions in Rwanda, but the situation had improved since 1973.[14]

More than half the signatories (63) were Belgian. The others were from Canada (11), Poland (9), Switzerland (9), France (5) and a few other countries. The list published in *Le Soir* only provided information on the Belgian expatriates. According to another list, disclosed a day earlier, almost half the signatories registered by then (29 out of 63) were missionaries.[15] The final proportion must have been similar. At least ten were Missionaries

---

[12] Serge Desouter, *Rwanda: Le procès du RPF. Mise au point du RPF* (Paris: L'Harmattan, 2007), 9.
[13] Prunier, *The Rwanda Crisis*, 99.
[14] 'Rwanda: 101 expatriés témoignent', *Le Soir*, 22 October 1990.
[15] Missionaries of Africa, 'Informations diffusées par la Région du Rwanda 1990–1994', compiled by Jef Vleugels, Brussels, December 2005, 229–30.

of Africa. The others were Salesians, Pallottines, Dominicans, diocesan priests and sisters from various female congregations. The second-largest group of expatriates comprised medical doctors: twelve from Belgium and probably a few others from other countries.

This document shows that many missionaries, and White Fathers in particular, adopted a position of unqualified loyalty to the Habyarimana government from the start.[16] At the time, the Missionaries of Africa from Rwanda numbered about ninety, down from nearly two hundred thirty years before.[17] As they aged, they were gradually handing over their parishes to the Rwandan clergy, except in the northern dioceses of Ruhengeri and Byumba, which still experienced a shortage of priests.

The idea of the open letter came from a group of twenty-six development workers and medical professionals, most of whom were Belgian, and not from the White Father Guy Theunis, as has been reported.[18] The first version of the document, dated 17 October 1990,[19] was longer than the one published in *Le Soir* and did not include any missionaries.

Meanwhile, in Belgium, various Catholic organisations expressed support for the embattled Rwandan government. In November a group of Flemish NGOs praised the Habyarimana regime's 'success in matters of development, democracy and respect of human rights', while noting, not without contradicting themselves, its 'totalitarian' character.[20] Writing in *Le Soir* on 6 November 1990, the Belgian Jesuit Fernand Boedts, chairperson of the Brussels-based Comité des Instituts Missionnaires (CIM), denounced the lack of objectivity of the media and highlighted the 'diplomatic skills of the Tutsi, heirs of a brilliant culture of royal courtship'.[21]

---

[16] According to a French White Father present in Rwanda from 1972 to 1994, who chose to remain anonymous, during a meeting with French Ambassador Georges Martres that had been arranged by Colonel René Galinié in 1991, Archbishop André Perraudin, who was retired at the time, emphatically said, 'We must support Habyarimana'. See Laurent Larcher, *Rwanda, ils parlent. Témoignage pour l'histoire* (Paris: Seuil, 2019), 223.

[17] General Archives of the Missionaries of Africa (AMA), Assemblée précapitulaire, 22–26 October 1991, Rapport du régional.

[18] Jean-Damascène Bizimana, 'Les attaques médiatiques du Père Theunis contre le Rwanda ou la poursuite de la stratégie génocidaire et négationniste,' *Rwanda News*, 29 March 2012.

[19] A copy of this document is kept in the library of the CEDOREP in Kigali.

[20] Jean-Pierre Chrétien, *Le défi de l'ethnisme, Rwanda et Burundi, 1990–1996*, 1st edn (Paris: Karthala, 1997), 76–7.

[21] *Le Soir*, 6 November 1990, quoted in Missionaries of Africa, 'Informations diffusées par la Région du Rwanda', 255–6.

Then Joseph-Marie Devulder, a White Father, wrote to the director of the French television channel TF1 that the RPF had invaded Rwanda not to create space for the Tutsi refugees but to re-establish the 'royal power' they had lost in 1959.[22]

The signatories of the open letter to *Le Soir* and the Belgian Catholics who defended the Rwandan government accused the international media of bias towards the RPF. They were, however, selective themselves. They denied something that the human rights organisations rapidly understood: that the gunshots allegedly fired by 'accomplices' of the RPF in early October[23] were, in fact, a fake attack staged by the Rwandan government to justify the arrest of political opponents. But they could not have ignored the consequences of this dubious strategy. No fewer than 13,000 members of the opposition spent time in jail without charge in Kigali and elsewhere in the country. Many were tortured and dozens died. More than 90 per cent of the detainees were Tutsi.[24] Among them were eight priests and religious brothers who – as the Minister of Justice Théoneste Mujyanama declared in a letter to Pax Christi Switzerland – had 'actively participated as accomplices in the attack on the country'.[25]

The expatriates' open letter claimed that 'there [had] not been, at this point, pogroms nor attempts at a systematic liquidation of the Tutsi'.[26] Yet Jef Vleugels, the regional superior of the Missionaries of Africa and one of the signatories, said the opposite in a report sent by fax – the second in a long list – to the Generalate in Rome and the provincial

---

[22] Jean-Damascène Bizimana, *L'Eglise et le génocide au Rwanda. Les Pères Blancs et le Négationnisme* (L'Harmattan, 2001), 32.

[23] 'Rwanda: 101 expatriés témoignent', *Le Soir*, 22 October 1990.

[24] For the figure of 13,000, see Des Forges, *Leave None to Tell the Story*, 49. Tharcisse Gatwa speaks of 'more than 10,000 persons' in T. Gatwa, *The Churches and Ethnic Ideology in the Rwandan Crises 1990–1994* (Oxford: Regnum Books International, 2005), 124.

[25] The names of the eight priests and brothers are mentioned in a fax sent by Jef Vleugels on 26 December 1990 (Missionaries of Africa, 'Informations diffusées par la Région du Rwanda', 43). The last five to be released are listed in Théoneste Mujyanama's letter to Pax Christi Switzerland, Kigali, 3 December 1990 (Centre Dominicain de Recherche et de Pastorale, Kigali). One of them was Modeste Mungwarareba, who was to play a major role in the reconstruction of the church in Butare after the genocide. According to Mujyanama, Mungwarareba was arrested because he had 'hosted in his house meetings during which the invasion was planned'.

[26] 'Rwanda: 101 expatriés témoignent', *Le Soir*, 22 October 1990.

superior in Brussels on 19 October, three days before the publication of the open letter in *Le Soir*:

> What we feared from the beginning of the hostilities eventually happened, though only in one area. In the commune of Kibilira in the prefecture of Gisenyi, sous-prefecture of Ngororero, bands of Hutu burned dozens of houses belonging to Tutsi. There seems to have been dozens of deaths and many injured people. The authorities reacted late but strongly. The sub-prefect and the burgomaster are in jail.[27]

As a report of the Association rwandaise pour la Défense des Droits de la Personne et des Libertés publiques (ADL) documented a year later, 357 Bagogwe were killed and many were injured or lost property between 11 and 13 October 1990 in Kibilira.[28] The attackers were led by teachers, councillors and civil servants. The massacre stopped after a young priest of the local parish of Muhororo alerted the Belgian and French embassies and the apostolic nunciature in Kigali. The prefect of Gisenyi instructed the people who had found refuge in the church to return home 'because they attracted journalists'. If they did not comply, they would be treated as Inkotanyi (RPF members) and treated as such.[29]

Even if Vleugels' claim that the sub-prefect and the burgomaster were sent to jail is correct, they were not there for long. According to Human Rights Watch, no one, neither official nor ordinary citizen, was ever convicted of any crime in connection with these massacres. Some suspected assailants were arrested after the Kibilira massacre but released several weeks later.[30] The witnesses interviewed by ADL in 1992 expressed the belief that the killings had been 'teleguided'.[31]

'Balancing' the information

ADL, the human rights organisation mentioned in the previous section, was founded in September 1991 by a group of concerned people including three clerics, André Sibomana, a diocesan priest; Guy Theunis, a White Father; and Tharcisse Gatwa, the director of the Rwandan Bible Society

---

[27] Jef Vleugels, fax of 19 October 1990, in Missionaries of Africa, 'Informations diffusées par la Région du Rwanda', 35.
[28] ADL, *Rapport sur les droits de l'homme, septembre 1991–septembre 1992* (Kigali: ADL, 1992), 109–16.
[29] *Ibid.*, 101–2.
[30] Des Forges, *Leave None to Tell the Story*, 73.
[31] ADL, *Rapport sur les droits de l'homme*, 101.

and a former general secretary of the Presbyterian Church.[32] ADL published two voluminous reports in December 1992 and December 1993, respectively, that contained information collected by the organisation's fieldworkers and other human rights organisations on the state of human rights in Rwanda. Theunis was in charge of the organisation's publications in the French language and, judging from what he said on 28 April 1998 to the French Parliamentary Commission on Rwanda, he was the main compiler of the two reports.[33]

The first report, which covered the period from September 1991 to September 1992, gave a detailed account of the massacres and other forms of discrimination suffered by the Tutsi throughout Rwanda, often with the complicity of state officials. ADL reported on the massacres of Kibilira in October 1990, as we have seen, and on those perpetrated against the Bagogwe the following year by the security forces in the prefectures of Ruhengeri and Gisenyi in reprisal against the short-lived RPF attack of Ruhengeri on 22 and 23 January 1991. The authors did not hesitate to speak of the 'genocide of the Bagogwe'.[34] They also documented massacres committed in Murambi, Rusumo, Gitarama, Rwamatamu and the Bugesera in 1991 and 1992.

But what about the RPF? ADL did not have much information on the crimes allegedly committed by the rebel army in the areas it occupied in the north of the country. This is where Vleugels, the regional superior, probably in consultation with Theunis, stepped in. On 14 September 1991, he shared with the communities of missionaries in the country his concern about the 'disinformation' in the media regarding Rwanda. Various lists of Tutsi victims, he pointed out, some with hundreds of names, were circulated by the RPF and its allies in Europe, but that was only one side of the picture:

> The RPF which – it is the least one could say – has provoked this tragedy comes out unscathed, with clean hands. It is therefore urgent to balance this information and show in the media, especially abroad, an aspect that is never spoken about: the civilian victims of these attacks and these infiltrations.[35]

---

[32] Longman, *Christianity and Genocide*, 142.
[33] Audition of Father Guy Theunis, 28 April 1998, in 'Mission d'information sur le Rwanda, Sommaire des comptes rendus du 24 mars 1998 au 5 mai 1998', Assemblée Nationale, Archives de la XIe Législature.
[34] ADL, *Rapport sur les droits de l'homme*, 117.
[35] *Ibid.*, 67–8.

In order to fight this 'disinformation', Vleugels asked the missionaries working in the dioceses of Ruhengeri and Byumba to list the civilian victims of the RPF attacks. The December 1992 ADL report included 790 names collected in this fashion.[36] The methodology used for the compilation of the lists was not specified. In the introductory section of the report, Vleugels admitted that 'the list [did] not always differentiate between the names of people killed by the RPF and the Rwandan army'.[37] In fact, the authors of the survey lumped together the civilians enrolled and armed by the Rwandan army, the collateral victims of combats and the civilians summarily executed by the RPF on the suspicion, founded or not, that they represented a threat.

Information on the crimes allegedly committed by the RPF in the north of the country before the genocide is hard to find.[38] Vleugels' faxes and the report he compiled for ADL are among the only sources we have on the war casualties during the period 1991–2. The faxes describe many skirmishes that resulted in the death of civilians. One of the victims was Renée Poppa, an eighty-five-year-old Oblate Sister of the Assumption still practising as a medical doctor, who was killed on 25 February 1992 in Rushaki in the diocese of Byumba.[39] Whether the local people carried weapons provided by the government – something that often happened according to Servilien Nzakamwita, who served as a priest in the diocese of Byumba before the genocide[40] – is not clear. There had no doubt been senseless killings, like those of the elders and handicapped people reportedly murdered in the Tovu valley in December 1990.[41] It was a dirty war! On 12 February 1992, sixteen priests of the Mutara deanery in the diocese of Byumba, including thirteen White Fathers, lamented that rather than 'battles between two armies', they witnessed 'terrorism against peaceful

---

[36] *Ibid.*, 69–90.

[37] *Ibid.*, 68.

[38] Nigel Eltringham, *Accounting for Horror: Post-Genocide Debates in Rwanda* (London: Pluto Press, 2004), 101.

[39] Marcel Neusch, 'Soeur Guido Poppa, médecin, victime de la guerre civile', *La Croix*, 28 February 1992.

[40] Mgr Servilien Nzakamwita, interviewed conducted in Kigali on 20 March 2019. In an interview, Giovanni Nsengiyumva, a convicted killer, confirmed that weapons were distributed to the local authorities before the genocide. See Félicité Lyamukuru, *L'ouragan a frappé Nyundo* (Mons: Cerisier, 2018), 86–7.

[41] Jef Vleugels, fax of 26 December 1990, in Missionaries of Africa, 'Informations diffusées par la Région du Rwanda', 41.

populations'.[42] What compounded the problem was the fact, mentioned in one of the faxes, that 'it was not the habit, neither on one side nor on the other, to take prisoners'.[43]

Vleugels declared that the figures he had compiled included 'as many civilians killed by a stray bullet or blown up by a mine as those, and they are many, who were massacred in cold blood'.[44] How common the latter were is pure guesswork. The regional superior, who did not hide his opposition to the RPF 'terrorists', believed that they were a frequent occurrence. Less disputed is the fact that the RPF attack on Ruhengeri in February 1993, in the period leading to the signing of the Arusha Agreement, had a heavy toll on civilians. The government accused the RPF of having killed 'several tens of thousands of citizens'. According to Africa Watch, such estimates were not credible. There was reliable evidence, according to them, that the RPF killed more than one hundred civilians.[45] According to Prunier, this bloodshed shocked the moderate Hutu who had supported the cause of the Tutsi refugees until then.[46]

The main consequence of the war was the exodus of an estimated 350,000 (mostly Hutu) refugees to camps – first in the north-east, then closer to Kigali – where they lived in appalling conditions. Some fled because of their experience of the war, others out of intense fear of an enemy that the government propaganda had systematically demonised.[47] A certain number of displaced people joined the ranks of the Interahamwe and played an active role in the genocide. Tens of thousands fled to Zaire in July 1994.

---

[42] Missionaries of Africa, 'Informations diffusées par la Région du Rwanda', 71.

[43] Jef Vleugels, fax of 29 March 1991, in Missionaries of Africa, 'Informations diffusées par la Région du Rwanda', 51.

[44] Jef Vleugels, fax of 1 February 1992, in Missionaries of Africa, 'Informations diffusées par la Région du Rwanda', 67.

[45] Africa Watch, 'Beyond the rhetoric: continuing human rights abuses in Rwanda', *News from Africa Watch*, 5/7 (June 1993), 22.

[46] Prunier, *The Rwanda Crisis*, 180. See also Des Forges, *Leave None to Tell the Story*, 701.

[47] François, a confessed *génocidaire* from Rubengera who spent several years in jail, declared, in an interview conducted on 7 December 2018, that in 1993 he had met people from Byumba in Kigali who said that the Inkontanyi had killed many people.

The Church authorities' ambiguous response to ethnic violence

The churches' delayed and ambiguous response to the Habyarimana regime's victimisation of the Tutsi minority after the October 1990 RPF invasion deserves scrutiny, because it prefigures their response to the genocide against the Tutsi four years later and lays the foundation for an enduring battle of memory on what the churches should have done during this tragedy. We have seen that using the pretext of a fake attack in Kigali, the security forces arrested an estimated 13,000 (mostly Tutsi) people a few days after the invasion. Throughout the country, the authorities organised mock funerals of the deceased RPF commander, Fred Rwigema, with banana trees as substitutes for his body. The Tutsi were forced to attend this humiliating ceremony and cheer with the others.[48] In response to the RPF attack, the government made the deliberate choice to fuel ethnic hatred in order to regain the initiative.

The church authorities' response to the crisis – Catholic as well as Protestant – was judged severely by Timothy Longman. 'Ultimately,' he wrote, 'church officials, fearing the loss of their own power, offered tacit support to the policy that state officials used to regain the political initiative – scapegoating of Tutsi – a policy that finally culminated in the genocide.'[49] Tharcisse Gatwa, a Christian activist at the time, concurred. For him, the root of the problem was the imbrication of church structures in the state organs. Until Rome asked him to withdraw from political involvement in 1985, the Catholic archbishop of Kigali, Vincent Nsengiyumva, was a member of the central committee of the ruling party.[50] He also served as chairperson of the influential Commission of Social Affairs. From its creation in 1986, Michel Twagirayesu, the president of the Presbyterian Church, chaired the Association Rwandaise pour le Bien-Être Familial (ARBED), which dealt with family planning. Members of the clergy participated in prefectural and communal development

---

[48] Jean-Paul Kimonyo, *Rwanda demain! Une longue marche vers la transformation* (Paris: Karthala, 2017), 119. In C. Habonimana, *Le dernier des Tutsi* (Paris: Plon, 2019), 17–20, the genocide survivor Charles Habonimana described the 'funeral of banana trees' in which he was asked to participate in Muyunzwe when he was eight years old. A similar ritual took place in the Catholic major seminary of Nyakibanda. See Jean-Baptiste Hategeka, 'Mgr J.B. Misago coincé contre les esprits et les rescapés de Bufundu-Nyaraguru', *Kinyamateka* (July 1999).

[49] Longman, *Christianity and Genocide*, 117.

[50] Vincent Nsengiyumva was from the same region as the president. See Rutayisire, 'Un regard interrogateur', 288.

committees. All church institutions, including schools, hospitals, convents and charity organisations were considered cells of the party and the priests or ministers in charge were *de facto* associated with the MRND.[51]

As we shall see in Chapter 7, however, the position of the church authorities evolved during the four-year period leading to the genocide. In 1990 and 1991, they considered the RPF an enemy and pledged total support to the Habyarimana government. The adoption of the multiparty system in June 1991, the formation of an interim coalition government that included members of the opposition in March 1992 and the signing of the Arusha Agreement in August 1993, which paved the way for the participation of the RPF in the affairs of the country, modified the context. The creation of the Comité de Contacts dates from this period. An informal ecumenical body including most church leaders, the Comité attempted to play a mediating role in the period immediately preceding the genocide.

On the cover of a compilation of pastoral letters from the period 1990–4 he published in 2000,[52] Joseph Ngomanzungu inserted this quotation from the bishop of Kabgayi, Thaddée Nsengiyumva, one of the clerics assassinated by RPF soldiers on 5 June 1994: 'Politicians did not want to listen to us.' This view of history is all but disingenuous. Nsengiyumva was an atypical bishop. Before the genocide, he and Wenceslas Kalibushi, his colleague from Nyundo, were the only prelates who publicly distanced themselves, on certain occasions, from the regime. During the genocide, because they remained in the sphere of influence of the government or because they did not want to appear to favour the RPF, the Rwandan bishops as a group failed to condemn the attacks by the MRND and its allies on the Tutsi as a form of murder and violence targeting a specific ethnic group. The war offered no justification for these horrible deeds. The bishops did not remain silent. They spoke out against ethnic violence. The problem is that they did so in general terms. Critics of the church authorities make the point that, had they used their moral authority to condemn the killing of people not for what they said, did or possessed but for what they were, there might have been less popular support for the genocide against the Tutsi in April 1994.

---

[51] Guy Theunis, 'Le rôle de l'Église catholique dans les événements récents', in André Guichaoua (ed.), *Les crises politiques au Rwanda et au Burundi 1993–1994. Analyses, faits et documents* (Lille: Université des Sciences et Technologie, 1995), 291; Gatwa, *The Churches and Ethnic Division*, 126–9.

[52] Joseph Ngomanzungu, *L'Église et la crise rwandaise de 1990–1994. Essai de chronologie* (Kigali: Palloti Press, 2000).

In preparation for Pope John Paul II's visit, which took place from 7 to 9 September 1990, less than a month before the RPF attack, the bishops published a pastoral letter in three parts that was entitled 'Christ, our unity'. The first part, issued on 28 February 1990, blamed the Rwandans who 'continue[d] to support ethnic rivalries through all sorts of speeches and manoeuvres' and proclaimed that 'the Twa, the Hutu, the Tutsi, the foreign guest, all of us are children of God and we possess exactly the same father: God'.[53] The second, issued on 6 May 1990, denounced, with special emphasis, nepotism, favouritism and bribery in the administration, the schools and the providers of employment. No reference was made, however, to the practice of ethnic quotas. As Longman pointed out, while the bishops acknowledged the existence of corruption, nepotism and human rights abuse in Rwanda, they maintained their support for the regime. They praised it, on the contrary, for supporting human rights treatises and making efforts to apply them.[54] The third part of the pastoral letter, issued on 14 August, essentially spoke of the need for justice and peace. It also invited the faithful to exercise caution with regard to the apparitions of the Virgin Mary in Kibeho, which were interpreted in some quarters as an incitement to fear, discord and hatred.[55]

The letter issued by Vincent Nsengiyumva, the archbishop of Kigali, on behalf of the episcopal conference on 18 October made no reference to the massacres of Kibilira, despite the fact that a local priest had reported them to the authorities and to several foreign embassies.[56] The bishops did not protest against the arbitrary detention of eight Catholic priests and brothers, implicitly validating the government's claim that they were 'accomplices' of the RPF. They merely called for a rapid judgement of the people detained *en masse* in the aftermath of the 1 October attack. Like the

---

[53] *Recueil des lettres et messages de la Conférence des Évêques catholiques du Rwanda publiées pendant la période de guerre* (Kigali: Secrétariat général de la Conférence des Évêques catholiques du Rwanda, 1995), quoted in Longman, *Christianity and Genocide*, 148. See also Ngomanzungu, *L'Église et la crise rwandaise*, 5–6.

[54] *Recueil*, quoted in Longman, *Christianity and Genocide*, 149–50. See also Ngomanzungu, *L'Église et la crise rwandaise*, 6–7.

[55] *Recueil*, quoted in Longman, *Christianity and Genocide*, 150. See also Ngomanzungu, *L'Église et la crise rwandaise*, 7.

[56] Ngomanzungu, *L'Église et la crise rwandaise*, 10. Vincent Nsengiyumva had already made a statement on 12 October 1990, in which he encouraged the faithful to 'love the homeland' (*aimer la patrie*).

expatriates in their open letter to *Le Soir*, they blamed the foreign media for adopting the position of the rebel movement:

> The Bishops invite the faithful and all people of good will to beware of rumours and lies on the past and current situation of Rwanda. [...] [They] regret the disinformation that is organised and invite the mass media agents to remain faithful to their professional deontology and to be artisans of peace rather than division and war.[57]

In the section of the pastoral letter addressed to the authorities, the bishops justified on biblical and theological grounds their unqualified support for the Habyarimana regime in the war it waged against the RPF:

> Since the attack on our country, we have greatly appreciated the efforts displayed, with great sacrifice, to assure security and peace to our population. [...] Knowing that all authority emanated from God (Rom 13:1–2), we entrust you to that same God so that he helps you with heavy responsibilities. Providence has entrusted you with the charge of watching over Common Good of our Nation. [...] We assure you of our close collaboration.

In the pastoral letter they published on 31 May 1991 under the title 'The truth will make you free', the bishops spoke in positive terms of the transition to democracy that was taking place at the time and incited the faithful to choose parties with a programme compatible with evangelical teaching. Yet, they remained silent on the massacres perpetrated by the security forces against the Bagogwe during the same period in the prefectures of Ruhengeri and Gisenyi. They merely advised, in broad terms, that the authorities abstain from 'duplicity, intolerance, contempt and ethnic, regional or religious exclusion'.[58]

The tonality of the statements issued during this period by the Presbyterian Church in Rwanda, the most longstanding Protestant denomination in the country, was no different. In a message sent to President Habyarimana on 25 July 1986, the leadership expressed its 'support and solidarity for the valuable efforts with which [he] conduct[ed] the Rwandan people united under the MRND, for their harmonious development in peace and unity'.[59] Like the Catholic bishops, the Presbyterian leaders quoted Romans 13 to justify their allegiance to the regime. In an article published in *Dialogue*, the German missionary Helmut Keiner

---

[57] *Ibid.*
[58] Ngomanzungu, *L'Église et la crise rwandaise*, 20–1; *Recueil*, quoted in Longman, *Christianity and Genocide*, 152–3.
[59] Gatwa, *The Churches and Ethnic Ideology*, 139.

warned, with reference to the Confessing Church's reluctance to condemn the oppression of the communists and the Jews in Nazi Germany, that the church might end up facing persecution itself if it did not stand for justice.[60] He was not heard. In July 1988, the General Synod of the Presbyterian Church wrote to the 'Father of the Nation' that they 'rejoiced because of the supreme decision taken by the 6th Congress of the MRND to re-elect [him] as president of the MRND'.[61] Five years later, the synod congratulated the president for the signing of the Arusha Agreement and, in a language reminiscent of previous statements, submitted its 'testimony of unfailing support'.[62]

Alternative voices

The first Christian-based public denunciation of the state's contribution to the growing climate of violence and of the inadequacy of the church's response came from the presbyterium of the diocese of Kabgayi, headed by Bishop Thaddée Nsengiyumva, on 1 December 1991. The main driver of the initiative was apparently André Sibomana, the editor of the church bi-weekly *Kinyamateka*.[63] Entitled 'Twivugurure tubane mu mahoro' [Let us convert to live together in peace], the letter had 'a bomb effect', according to Augustin Misago, the newly appointed bishop of Gikongoro, in a speech delivered shortly afterwards.[64] It broke with the politically correct tone of the other church documents:

> Rwandan society currently knows a recrudescence of theft, armed aggression, and other reprehensible acts that are not prosecuted in the justice system. One would think that the people qualified to create respect for the law have resigned or that they are accomplices of their partners. The agents of the state no longer do their work conscientiously.[65]

---

[60] [Helmut Keiner], 'Sectes et esprit protestant', *Dialogue*, 129 (1988), 117–21, quoted in Gatwa, *The Churches and Ethnic Ideology*, 140.
[61] Gatwa, *The Churches and Ethnic Ideology*, 141.
[62] *Ibid.*, 142.
[63] Des Forges, *Leave None to Tell the Story*, 52.
[64] Augustin Misago, 'L'Église au Rwanda et son clergé vu par la presse', in *Le prêtre diocésain dans la société rwandaise en mutation. Actes de la Session des prêtres diocésains, Nyakibanda (7–11/9/1992) Kabgayi (21–25/9/1992)* (Kigali, 1992), 43.
[65] [*Recueil*], quoted in Longman, *Christianity and Genocide*, 154–5. See also Ngomanzungu, *L'Église et la crise rwandaise*, 26–7. The Catholic magazine

The letter described the Catholic Church as a 'giant with feet of clay' that had failed to respond to the social and political problems of Rwanda and claimed that its credibility was compromised. 'The Church', it read, 'lives in a continual lie, because its submission to temporal powers impedes it from being critical towards this power and from denouncing the numerous violations of human rights'. In conclusion, the priests of Kabgayi demanded a negotiated termination of the war and a rapid move towards democratic rule.[66]

One of the reasons for the letter's impact was that the bishop himself and Sibomana, who was a priest of the diocese, were Hutu. More than ever, the Catholic Church was divided along ethnic lines, with the Tutsi priests being in the majority, partly because the ethnic quota policy had deprived them of other job opportunities. Criticisms of the church's hierarchy on the part of the Tutsi priests were not uncommon.

The forced demission of Félicien Muvara in April 1989 on the trumped-up charge that he had fathered a child had scandalised his Tutsi confrères; the Tutsi auxiliary bishop-elect of Butare had been appointed just four months earlier and his resignation came two days before his installation. The archbishop of Kigali and the nuncio, present during an audience with a high-ranking prelate, had pressurised Muvara to present his letter of resignation, allegedly on the direct instructions of the Rwandan president. Jean-Baptiste Gahamanyi, the bishop of Butare, was the only one to believe in his good faith.[67] On hearing the news, a group of priests from Kibuye had denounced the 'lack of transparency of the church of Rwanda' in a letter to the Episcopal Council.[68]

In April 1990, a few months before the pope's visit, another group of Tutsi priests, this time from Nyundo, had produced a document that was widely circulated, which criticised the bishops' February 1990 pastoral letter for being aligned to the government's position in ethnic matters:

Dialogue published a one-page summary of the document in its February 1992 issue.

[66] *Ibid.*

[67] Longman, *Christianity and Genocide*, 96. See Muvara's letter of resignation, Butare, 20 April 1989, in Jean Ndorimana, *De la région des Grands Lacs au Vatican. Intrigues, scandales et idéologie du génocide au sein de la hiérarchie catholique* (Kigali: Imprimerie Prograph, 2008), 287–8.

[68] Quoted in Misago, 'L'Église au Rwanda et son clergé vu par la presse', 26; African Rights, *Rwanda: Death, Despair and Defiance*, 2nd edn (London: African Rights, 1995), 870; Longman, *Christianity and Genocide*, 153–4.

It is regrettable that in their letter the bishops take as their point of departure political slogans. [...] The church should dare to say to the Rwandan state that it should agree to consider citizens applying considerations of ethnicity or region. The maintenance of this discrimination gives rise to many problems and casts doubt upon the most beautiful speech concerning unity. A nation in search of unity cannot continue to base everything on ethnic and regional identity. If the church was committed to supporting to the letter the policy of the country, but was prepared to dare to suggest firmly to the state the true principles of social justice, then it would have assumed its prophetic mission. But alas![69]

Another illustration of the Catholic Church's internal diversity is the session for diocesan priests held at Nyakibanda Major Seminary in September 1992. Four bishops and seventy-one priests were present. One of the speakers was none other than Félicien Muvara, who denounced the 'Constantinian model in Rwanda' and its legacy after independence.[70] Another was Smaragde Mbonyintege, the future bishop of Kabgayi, who traced the history of ethnic divisions in the church from the time of the Rwandan Social Revolution to the Muvara affair.[71] He described the ethnic issue as a taboo. 'It is shameful to describe oneself as ethnist among priests.' According to Mbonyintege, one had to look at the underlying causes of the problem. Ethnic tensions, he suggested, were the result of a 'wrong conception of power in the church'.[72]

Dissatisfaction with the institutional church's inability to deal with the crisis in the country preceded the October 1990 RPF attack. In February of the same year, in preparation for the pope's visit, Sibomana had published in *Kinyamateka* the results of a survey conducted in the diocese of Kabgayi. The respondents, he reported, found that many priests lacked apostolic zeal. They behaved like 'princes' (*abatware*), with little concern for the poor and the oppressed. Some religious congregations were accused of privileging the recruitment of Tutsi candidates for the priesthood.[73]

---

[69] Quoted in Longman, *Christianity and Genocide*, 154; African Rights, *Rwanda: Death, Despair and Defiance*, 870. See Misago, 'L'Église au Rwanda et son clergé vu par la presse', 25.

[70] Félicien Muvara, 'L'Église et la politique au Rwanda', in *Le prêtre diocésain dans la société rwandaise en mutation*, 10–20.

[71] Smaragde Mbonyintege, 'Le problème ethnique dans le clergé rwandais', in *Le prêtre diocésain dans la société rwandaise en mutation*, 49–55.

[72] *Ibid.*, 54.

[73] 'Papa naza mu Rwanda azavuga ibibazo by'abiyeguriyimana' [When the pope comes to Rwanda, he will have to face the problems regarding the

The criticisms did not go away. During his stay in Rwanda as a doctoral candidate in 1992 and 1993, Longman heard many people complaining about the church leaders' conservatism. Some voted with their feet and moved to another church or dropped out of active participation in any church. Yet, he observed, many people continued to see in the church the institution most capable of influencing the state and providing support through its material and spiritual resources in difficult times.[74]

From government supporter to mediator

In 1992 the Catholic Church and the Protestant churches moved from a position of unequivocal support of the MRND government to one of mediator between the embattled government, the opposition parties and the RPF. Several factors account for this change of direction. On the Catholic side, the 1 December 1991 letter from the presbyterium of the diocese of Kabgayi seems to have played a role. According to Misago,[75] it incited the bishops, like the priests of Kabgayi, to support the idea of negotiations between the government and the RPF in a national conference and to recommend the prompt return of the Tutsi refugees from exile. On these matters, their message for the New Year 1991 marked a departure from the previous episcopal statements.[76] 'Unbelievable!', the RPF-sponsored magazine *Kanguka* wrote, 'Even the priests want a sovereign national conference!'[77] There are indications that the newly appointed nuncio, Giuseppe Bertello, later reviled by the Hutu extremists for having established contact with the RPF leadership in Mulindi, encouraged the Rwandan bishops to press for a national conference.[78] On 8 January 1992, a delegation of bishops had an audience with the president. They asked him to form a government of transition with representatives of all the political parties and to initiate negotiations to put an end to the war.[79]

On the Protestant side, the impulse for a more sustained action came from the All Africa Conference of Churches (AACC), which organised a

---

consecrated people], *Kinyamateka*, 131 (February 1990), 3, quoted in Misago, 'L'Église au Rwanda et son clergé vu par la presse', 29.

[74] Longman, *Christianity and Genocide*, 146.
[75] Misago, 'L'Église au Rwanda et son clergé vu par la presse', 44.
[76] *Recueil*, quoted in Longman, *Christianity and Genocide*, 135; Ngomanzungu, *L'Église et la crise rwandaise*, 29–31.
[77] Misago, 'L'Église au Rwanda et son clergé vu par la presse', 45.
[78] Longman, *Christianity and Genocide*, 154–5.
[79] Ngomanzungu, *L'Église et la crise rwandaise*, 33.

conference on peace and reconciliation in Rwanda from 19 to 22 August 1991 in Nairobi, in partnership with the World Council of Churches (WCC). Representatives from the Anglican, Methodist, Presbyterian and Baptist churches of Rwanda, the Protestant Council of Rwanda, the Catholic Church in Rwanda and various church bodies from Zaire, Burundi, Tanzania and Uganda were present. The Rwandan government was represented by the Rwandan embassy in Nairobi and a Rwandan official and Rwandan refugees, by two refugees from Burundi and one from Switzerland.[80] The outcome of the Nairobi conference was the constitution, on 22 January 1992, of a 'Comité de Contacts' which included bishops or general secretaries from the Catholic, Anglican, Methodist, Presbyterian, Pentecostal and Adventist churches.[81] In an article published in 1995, André Karamaga, AACC staff worker and future president of the Presbyterian Church in Rwanda, soberly commented that one of the church leaders' motivations was the hope of becoming the president of the national conference and working with other senior clergy in the rest of Africa.[82]

The Comité's brief was to facilitate a dialogue between the political movements, the Rwandan government and the RPF. Joseph Ngomanzungu gave a detailed account of all its achievements.[83] They lobbied for the installation of a multiparty government, developed contacts with the RPF in Nairobi and Bujumbura and encouraged the stakeholders to participate in the meetings that eventually led to the signing of the Arusha Agreement in August 1993.

In January 1992 a twelve-member commission appointed by the Synodal Council of the Presbyterian Church denounced regionalism and ethnocentrism and pleaded in favour of a national conference.[84] Two months later, the Catholic bishops and the Protestant leaders condemned, in a joint communiqué, 'those who appropriate by force the property of

---

[80] Joseph Ngomanzungu, *Efforts de médiation œcuménique des Églises dans la crise rwandaise: Le Comité de contacts (1991–1994)* ([Kigali: Pallotti Press], 2003), 9–15.

[81] *Ibid.*, 4–8, 13–14; Gatwa, *The Churches and Ethnic Ideology*, 206.

[82] André Karamaga, 'Les Églises protestantes et la crise rwandaise', in André Guichaoua (ed.), *Les crises politiques au Burundi et au Rwanda (1993–1994). Analyses, faits et documents* (Lille: Université des Sciences et Technologies, 1995), 301.

[83] Ngomanzungu, *Efforts de médiation*, 17–61.

[84] EPR, *Ukuri kubaka igihugu* (Kigali: Urwego, March 1992), quoted in Gatwa, *The Churches and Ethnic Ideology*, 214–15.

the state and of particulars, those who resort to acts of provocation and to lies and those who burn houses and destroy human lives'.[85] No more than the Catholic bishops in their previous pastoral letters, however, did the signatories highlight the responsibility of the security forces and of the militia trained and armed by the ruling party in these violent acts. They simply affirmed the principle that 'all Rwandans are brothers and enjoy the same dignity. Hutu, Tutsi and Twa all have the right to live in peace, in perfect harmony and in mutual love and respect'.[86]

The problem with the Comité de Contacts was the Rwandan churches' long history of allegiance to the Rwandan state. The church leaders had modelled their lifestyle on that of the government officials, sometimes resorting to corruption to secure an election and driving in luxury cars, when priests and pastors on the ground had just enough to live.[87] As Longman argued, they could not credibly appear neutral in the civil war that was tearing apart the fabric of Rwandan society:

> The role of neutral arbiter is a classic position for churches to take. This approach assumes that churches lack substantial political interests of their own and are above the political fray and that they can therefore help mediate between divided parties. While seeking a negotiated peace is a commendable goal, in the Rwandan case, this approach was problematic because the churches were *not* in fact politically neutral. The church leaders had clearly allied their institutions with the ruling regime and had an interest in preserving the existing structure of power, and thus in seeking a compromise with those opposed to the regime, they made no effort to assess the real sources of the conflict.[88]

It is worth noting in this regard that the Catholic bishops did not raise their voice when François Cardinal was murdered by soldiers on 29 November 1992; Cardinal, a Canadian brother in charge of an agricultural training centre south of Kigali, had denounced the embezzlement of aid funding by people close to the president.[89] Nor did they protest when, on 10 March 1992, members of the presidential guard assassinated an Italian Catholic volunteer by the name of Antonia Locatelli, who had defended Tutsi refugees in the Bugesera and reported a massacre on Radio France Internationale (RFI). Amnesty International demanded a formal

---

[85] Ngomanzungu, *Efforts de médiation*, 22.
[86] *Ibid.*, 22.
[87] Karamaga, 'Les Églises protestantes et la crise rwandaise', 302.
[88] Longman, *Christianity and Genocide*, 159.
[89] *Ibid.*, 174; Jean-Damascène Bizimana, *L'Église et le génocide au Rwanda*, 41.

investigation of her murder. Under the RPF government, she was hailed as the first victim of the genocide.[90]

The only priests who publicly distanced themselves from state-sponsored violence were those of Nyundo, many of whom were Tutsi. We have already mentioned the February 1990 letter from the priests of Nyundo and the fact that, in October 1990, a priest, described as young, had alerted the government and the main embassies about the massacres committed in Kibilira with the support of the authorities. In 1991, when hundreds of Bagogwe were killed by the security forces and thousands chased away from their homes, the clergy was divided. The European Sisters and Brothers of Christian Instruction assisted refugees, and the bishop of Nyundo, Wenceslas Kalibushi, personally intervened with the authorities to save lives.[91] On the other hand, a priest by the name of Wenceslas Karuta allegedly refused to open his church to Tutsi refugees at Busogo mission in the diocese of Ruhengeri. A survivor heard him saying that the 'house of God could not shelter *Inyenzi*'.[92] In December 1993, the bishop and the priests from the diocese of Nyundo published a letter criticising the Rwandan government for distributing weapons to the citizens.[93] They knew that a genocide was in the making. Many of them succumbed to it in April 1994.

Marching for peace

In 1993 and early 1994, as one after the other the political parties split into moderate and extremist wings and unprecedented levels of public violence hit the country, the conference of bishops only published two

---

[90] On the murder of Antonia Locatelli, see also 'The danger of a single story: iconic stories in the aftermath of the 1994 Rwandan genocide', *Memory Studies*, 10/2 (2017), 154–5.

[91] Diogène Bideri, *Le massacre des Bagogwe, un prélude au génocide des Tutsi. Rwanda (1990–1993)* (Paris: L'Harmattan, 2008), 72, 86, 96.

[92] Testimony of a woman who survived the Kinigi massacre in the parish of Busogo, *ibid.*, 71. There is a similar accusation in Jean-Damascène Bizimana, 'L'Église catholique et le génocide des Tutsi: de l'idéologie à la négation', *La Nuit rwandaise*, 2 (7 April 2008), 252. Wenceslas Karuta currently serves as a priest in the diocese of San Miniato in Italy.

[93] René Degni-Segui, 'Extraits de rapports 1994–1995 sur la situation des droits de l'Homme au Rwanda', in Raymond Verdier, Emmanuel Decaux, Jean-Pierre Chrétien (ed.), *Rwanda: Un génocide au XXe siècle* (Paris: L'Harmattan, 1995), 67.

pastoral letters, one for Lent and one for Advent, which received little attention.[94] Individual bishops and groups of Christians, meanwhile, multiplied peace initiatives, often on an ecumenical basis. Rather than confronting the growing Hutu extremist movement, the politicians supporting the Arusha Agreement, and the RPF on the political terrain, they shifted the emphasis to the moral terrain, prefiguring the response the church authorities would give to the genocide against the Tutsi in April 1994 and the following months. One of the most vocal campaigners for peace was Laurien Ntezimana, a lay theologian trained in Belgium. In February 1993, he invited the RPF and the Forces Armées Rwandaises (FAR) to 'put away their artillery' and condemned those who 'call defence of the homeland the extermination of innocent people'.[95]

The White Fathers took part in this movement. At the regional superior's instigation, the assembly held in Kigali after the general chapter of the Missionaries of Africa in 1992 recommended that all the communities be 'sensitised to active non-violence'.[96] The White Fathers spearheaded the establishment of a Rwandan branch of the international movement Pax Christi, which organised several sessions on non-violence in February 1994.[97] The religious communities also tried to address the challenge of ethnicity. In March and April 1993, the Association of Major Superiors (ASUMA) organised a series of sessions to deal with ethnic tensions within the male and female communities. The participants were invited to reflect on the impact of ethnicity in their personal and community lives and overcome mutual conflicts through dialogue and reconciliation.[98]

The most important initiative was the movement *Duharanire amahoro* [Let us struggle for peace], as part of which prayer vigils and peace marches – organised by Pax Christi, ADL, the African Evangelistic Enterprise (AEE) and a few other bodies – were to be held in Kigali and various provincial cities on 1 January 1994, with the participation of Catholic and Protestant personalities. The first planning meeting was held on 26

---

[94] Longman, *Christianity and Genocide*, 184.

[95] Laurien Ntezimana, 'Message de paix des chrétiens catholiques de Butare lors de la marche de paix du 28/02/1993', in *Ma guerre à la guerre. Libres paroles d'un théologien rwandais dans la tourmente rwandaise (1990–1995)* (Paris: Édilivre, 2017), 84–5, 87.

[96] AMA, Rome, Rapport de l'Assemblée post-capitulaire, 16–22 novembre 1992, 6.

[97] Missionaries of Africa, 'Informations diffusées par la Région du Rwanda', 147–8.

[98] ASUMA, 'Réflexion sur la réconciliation inter-ethnique dans la vie religieuse. Rencontre de mars-avril 1993'.

November 1993. An estimated 30,000 people took part in these marches. In the following weeks, prayer groups were held and petitions were sent to the authorities.[99]

Asked in a January 1995 interview to explain why, in his opinion, the church had not been able to stop the 'madness' of the genocide, André Sibomana made reference to the peace marches:

> My reflection has the form of a question mark. The social role of the Church, was it really perceived as an action in favour of the people? I would be inclined to respond: not sufficiently. The peace marches, of the organisation in which I participated, did they not come too late? Probably. Were not the clergy and the hierarchy above the people instead of being in its midst? It is possible.[100]

Conclusion

The question of the church's 'silence' is a recurrent one in post-genocide Rwanda. The following chapter will assess what the churches said and did – or did not say and did not do – during the three months of the genocide against the Tutsi. In this chapter and the previous one, we have focused on the preceding periods. My argument is that the churches' responses to the genocide mimicked in a number of ways those provided in 1959, 1960, 1963–4, 1972–3 and 1990–4. It would have been unrealistic to expect a sudden change of heart from the church authorities, Catholic as well as Protestant, in April 1994.

Key to the comprehension of this problem is what I termed the ideological factor – that is, the pervasive influence of the Hamitic theory, in its 'hard' version of a country divided between Tutsi strangers and local Hutu, which continued to circulate among Hutu extremists until the genocide; or in its 'soft' version, which consisted in seeing all Tutsi, and the RPF by extension, as potentially deceitful and dominating. As they were intimately linked to the Habyarimana regime, which had built its power on an ethnic and regional foundation, the churches never went beyond pious and self-indulgent calls to ethnic reconciliation. For the church authorities,

---

[99] Guy Theunis, 'Les marches pour la paix', *Dialogue*, 173 (February 1994), 63–5; Gatwa, *The Churches and Ethnic Ideology*, 216–17; Gerard van 't Spijker, *L'Église chrétienne au Rwanda pré et post-génocide* (Paris: L'Harmattan, 2011), 108–9.

[100] 'Rwanda: l'urgence de la justice et du pardon. Une interview du Père André Sibomana, prêtre et journaliste', *L'Actualité religieuse dans le monde*, 129 (15 January 1995), 13.

UNAR and its successor, the RPF, were not an enemy like any other. They personified a return to a situation that was too horrible to contemplate. Hence the decision – practical more than theoretical – to condone the massacres of Tutsi which punctuated the history of the period. Recognising that the Rwandan government had committed atrocities, André Perraudin wrote on 1 January 1964, would expose the country 'to much greater evil than those we have known'. The Catholic bishops' reluctance to denounce the massacres of Tutsi as Tutsi in 1990 and the following years had the same roots. The Protestant leaders, who were just as much linked to the regime, did not think otherwise.

The problem was not that the church leaders remained silent. They produced numerous statements, some of them produced on an ecumenical basis. They denounced ethnic rivalries and discrimination. They denounced ethnic violence. The flaw was that they only denounced ethnic violence in broad terms. They never took the risk of condemning the complicity of the Rwandan government or its militia, whether under Kayibanda or Habyarimana, in the massacre of innocent civilians. Instead, they blamed the Tutsi invaders as if the strategic decisions they had made justified in any way the massacre of their brothers and sisters who had remained in the country. It is this silence that is the problem, not silence in general.

Another aspect of the churches' response to ethnic violence is their tendency to 'balance' information, as Jef Vleugels put it in the letter he sent in September 1991 to the Missionaries of Africa asking them to collect information on human rights abuses committed by the RPF in the prefectures of Byumba and Ruhengeri. Many church leaders followed this approach in the period leading to the genocide, anticipating the 'double genocide' theory developed during and after the genocide. This balancing act is problematic because it puts war crimes on the same level as the killing of people for belonging to a certain ethnic group.

Léon Saur spoke of the Catholic Church of the late 1950s and early 1960s as a kaleidoscope. This comment is valid for the other periods, including that of the genocide. The Catholic Church of Rwanda never spoke in one voice. In the 1990s, the priests of Nyundo and Kabgayi played the role that Stanislas de Jamblinne, Robert Defalque, Henri Bazot and Hansjörg Gyr assumed in the 1960s. The bishops themselves had disagreements. André Perraudin did not measure the danger of a binary and therefore exclusionary discourse. Aloys Bigirumwami did. In the early 1990s, Wenceslas Kalibushi and Thaddée Nsengiyumva were able, in their personal capacity, to challenge the authorities of the country. The other bishops did not. As the next chapter will indicate, similar fractures appeared during the genocide itself.

CHAPTER 3

Religion in the midst of the genocide

In *Une initiation*, Stéphane Audoin-Rouzeau suggested that the genocide against the Tutsi was to be seen not only as a phenomenon that negatively affected church life and religious practice but as a religious phenomenon in its own right.[1] Put differently, we should ask ourselves whether the fact that numerous massacres took place in churches and that about a quarter of the church personnel were massacred by fellow believers was incidental or, on the contrary, central to the comprehension of the dynamics of the genocide. It is to this question that this chapter is dedicated.

The first task is to establish what happened. The subsequent debates on the role of the church in the genocide, with a flurry of attacks by genocide-memory activists and counter-attacks by church apologists, somewhat cloud the analysis. Using the typology of agents, victims and opponents of oppression elaborated by the authors of the South African TRC's report on the faith communities hearing,[2] we shall examine how the bishops, priests, pastors, religious brothers or sisters and ordinary church members positioned themselves during the three months of the genocide. The churches were agents, victims and opponents. They contributed to the genocide, fell victims of it and opposed it. Sometimes, one should note, these categories overlapped. There are examples of genocide perpetrators who, strangely enough, saved Tutsi lives. In the last section of this chapter, we shall consider, with the oral and written sources at our disposal, what use the perpetrators and the survivors made of religious symbols and beliefs during this dark period of Rwandan history.

---

[1] Stéphane Audoin-Rouzeau, *Une initiation. Rwanda (1994–2016)* (Paris: Seuil, 2017), 111.
[2] 'TRC Faith Communities Hearing Report', in James Cochrane, John de Gruchy and Steven Martin (ed.), *Facing the Truth. South African Faith Communities and the Truth and Reconciliation Commission* (Cape Town: David Philip, 1999), 16.

The story of St Vincent Minor Seminary in Ndera, east of Kigali, which César Murangira – a twenty-year-old Tutsi student who fled there with his family and hundreds of other Tutsi refugees on 9 April 1994 – narrated in a book significantly entitled *Un sachet d'hosties pour cinq* [A pack of altar bread for five],³ shows the diversity of Catholic clergy responses to the genocide. Six priests resided in the school, by then nearly empty because the students were on holiday: Alexis Havugimana, the rector; Ananie Rugasira, the bursar; Patrice Munyentwali, a recently ordained Hutu priest; Jean-Bosco Ntagungira and Jean-Baptiste Murengeranka, two young Tutsi priests; and Tito Oggioni Macagnino, a sixty-four-year-old missionary from Lecce in southern Italy. Rugasira, who was Hutu, was shot dead after he refused to hand over the keys of the seminary to the Interahamwe. The rector, who also resisted, was hit on the chest and lost two fingers. The Italian priest, whom the survivors described as compassionate, soon boarded a plane to Italy with Antonietta Stasi, an Italian volunteer. From his hiding place within the seminary, Murangira observed with amazement Munyentwali walking around with Stanislas Mbonampeka, a former cabinet minister known for having taken over leadership of the Hutu extremist wing of the Liberal Party in 1993, who was directing the killers. Munyentwali volunteered to put at Mbonampeka's disposal three hundred machetes used to cut wood for the kitchen ovens.⁴ He later escaped to Italy, where he works today as a priest. He was never questioned about his role in the genocide.

The loss of church personnel

Lists of Catholic bishops, priests, brothers, sisters and consecrated laity killed during the genocide started to circulate in May 1994 and were regularly updated afterwards.⁵ Between April and July 1994, 3 bishops, 100 diocesan priests, 3 Jesuits, 2 White Fathers, 40 brothers and 55 sisters

---

³ César Murangira, *Un sachet d'hosties pour cinq. Récit d'un rescapé du génocide des Tutsi commis en 1994 au Rwanda* (Nantes: Éditions Amalthée, 2016), 74. The altar bread helped the survivors hiding in the bush to resist hunger before the RPF's arrival in late April.
⁴ *Ibid.*, 74.
⁵ *Dialogue*, 117 (August–September 1994), 123–35; *Kinyamateka*, 1414 (December 1994); Neno Contran, *They Are a Target: 200 African Priests Killed* (Nairobi: Paulines Publications Africa, 1996), 65–123; Joseph Ngomanzungu, *La souffrance de l'Eglise à travers son personnel* (Kigali: Pallotti Press, 2002); 'Le martyrologe de l'Eglise du Rwanda en 1994', Fides Service, Rome, 2004.

were reported as having been killed.[6] These lists are difficult to interpret, because they do not differentiate between the Tutsi victims, the Hutu killed because they refused to betray Tutsi people and the Hutu killed by the RPF. As we shall see, the third category accounted for about a tenth of the total.

What is significant is that about a quarter of the locally born Catholic priests serving the church before the genocide were massacred. According to Paul Rutayisire, there were four hundred ordained priests, without counting the missionaries, on the eve of the genocide.[7] The proportion of religious brothers and sisters cannot be determined with precision, but it was also high. Most victims were Tutsi. Such lists do not seem to exist for the Protestant churches. We can safely assume that the same proportion – a quarter of all Rwandan pastors – was reached in the Presbyterian Church and probably in the Seventh Day Adventist Church as well. We do not have figures for the other churches. The majority of these priests and pastors were designated as 'accomplices' of the RPF and killed for that reason.

Some priests and pastors were targeted because they had tried to resist ethnic violence before the genocide. On 7 April 1994, hours after President Habyarimana was shot, the leaders of three prominent Christian organisations were killed in a move which had all the appearances of having been planned beforehand. Around 9:00pm, Rwandan soldiers murdered 3 Jesuits, 4 diocesan priests, 8 young women from the Christian organisation Vita et Pax and 2 more people at the Centre Christus in Remera, an area of Kigali that the RPF would occupy later in the same day. Only a Hutu priest, Juvénal Rutumbu, and a woman from Vita et Pax, whose accents betrayed their Northern Rwandan origin, were spared. It soon became clear that the main target was Chrysologue Mahame, the oldest Rwandan Jesuit and the founder of the Association des Volontaires de la Paix (AVP).[8] The others were killed because of their association with

---

[6] Ngomanzungu, *La souffrance de l'Eglise*, 30.

[7] Paul Rutayisire, 'Silences et compromissions de la hiérarchie de l'Église catholique du Rwanda', *Au cœur de l'Afrique*, 61, 2–3 (1995), 414. The figure of 400 is obtained by adding together 103 priests, including three bishops, who were killed during the genocide, 183 who took refuge in Zaire and 114 who remained in Rwanda.

[8] Victor Bourdeau, 'Une semaine d'horreur à Kigali', *Dialogue*, 177 (August–September 1994), 4–14; Jean-Baptiste Ganza, 'Trois grains posés en terre rwandaise', *Promotio Iustitiae*, 117 (2015), 19–21. Informed of the massacre, Peter-Hans Kolvenbach, the superior general of the Society of Jesus, correctly noted that the three Jesuits had been killed 'because their evangelical

him. The Emmanuel Community, a Catholic charismatic organisation that had also campaigned for peace, lost its founders, Cyprien and Daphrose Rugamba, the same morning. Another community leader, Jean-Marie Twambazemungu, a Hutu married to a Tutsi woman, narrowly escaped death, as did François-Xavier Ngarambe and his wife Solange, who were lucky enough to board a plane for Nairobi.[9] At about the same time, Israel Havugimana, the team leader of the AEE – a South African organisation also active in the field of peace building and reconciliation – was killed at his home. His colleague, Malachie Munyaneza, a Presbyterian pastor classified as Hutu who looked like a Tutsi because of his high stature, had miraculously escaped earlier attempts on his life and managed to leave Kigali in mid-May.[10]

Likewise, it was clear that the Rwandan army and the Interahamwe deliberately targeted the clergy of Nyundo, who had denounced the anti-Tutsi pogroms in the diocese since 1990. No fewer than 30 priests, 27 religious brothers and sisters, 11 consecrated women and 4 seminarians lost their lives in the diocese. Before the genocide, the priests numbered 59. The killings started in the Nyundo Minor Seminary and in Busasamana, north-east of Gisenyi, on 7 April. They continued unabated during the whole of April. The bishop's house and the cathedral of Nyundo became the scene of two horrific massacres on 9 April and 1 May 1994, respectively. The bishop, Wenceslas Kalibushi, a Tutsi, was undressed and lined up in front of a grave when an order from the military commander enjoined the killers to spare him. The bishop and the few Tutsi priests who survived managed to find shelter in Gisenyi and, later in June, in Goma.[11]

---

hospitality did not please the extremists', but he completely misjudged the situation: 'This by no way exceptional event on the African continent reminds us to pray for the woes of Africa: tribal wars and wars or religion, various forms of racial discrimination and Muslim fundamentalism, AIDS and famine, economic underdevelopment and political corruption' (P.-H. Kolvenbach to the major superiors, Rome, 12 April 1994. Copy in André Bouillot Papers).

[9] Yvonne-Solange Kagoyire, François-Xavier Ngarambe and Jean-Marie Twambamezungu, *Rescapés de Kigali. Témoignage* (Paris: Éditions de l'Emmanuel, 2014).

[10] Malachie Munyaneza, 'La tragédie rwandaise et la survie de la vie', unpublished document, August 1994.

[11] 'Des rescapés du diocèse de Nyundo témoignent', *Dialogue*, 177 (August–September 1994), 59–68.

There are other examples of Catholic priests, brothers and sisters killed in joint operations. On 26 April, 5 sisters, 2 diocesan priests and 2 brothers were murdered in Birambo, in the southern part of the diocese of Nyundo. 'People say that the burgomasters call the shots', the regional superior of the Assumption Sisters wrote on 25 May, 'and that they wanted to take revenge on the Church.' She was shocked to hear that the Interahamwe had 'sorted out' (*trié*) the sisters.[12] On 22 May, 13 Good Shepherd professed sisters, novices and postulants fleeing from Kigali were killed in Kamonyi, on the road to Butare.[13] On 7 June, the Josephites suffered an attack in Nyamirambo, a sector of Kigali, which resulted in the death of seven brothers.[14]

More famously, on 24 May, the army and the Interahamwe raided Kabgayi Major Seminary (also called Philosophicum), arrested 4 diocesan priests, 4 Josephite brothers, 3 Marist brothers, 1 Mwenebikira sister and 4 lay people, all Tutsi, and gunned them down in nearby Bukomero. According to Hildebrand Karangwa, a seminarian at the time, Vincent Nsengiyumva, the archbishop of Kigali, then residing in Kabgayi, was seen the same morning in conversation with an unknown person at the gate of the seminary.[15] During the raid, as a source in Burundi wrote to the White Fathers Vleugels and Theunis in Brussels, 'four soldiers and five civilians [took] the time to explain to the archbishop that they had proof of these people's complicity with the enemy'.[16] A Human Rights Watch source also noted that the archbishop of Kigali stood aside and allowed the squad to

[12] Sr Clare Teresa to the Assumptionist Sisters, Paris, 25 May 1994 (André Bouillot Papers).

[13] 'Liste des prêtres, religieux, religieuses et laïcs consacrés tués au Rwanda', *Dialogue*, 177 (August–September 1994), 134.

[14] 'Diary of the horror. Notes from Otto Mayer, a White Father in Rwanda, translated by John O'Donohue', unpublished document, Cologne, 1994. An eighth Josephite brother by the name of Pierre Gacamumakuba was killed on 10 June in Nyamirambo. Two of the victims were in ministry, two were students and the others were retired. See Bernardin Muzungu, 'Un documentaire historique sur la Congrégation des Frères Joséphites du Rwanda', *Cahiers Lumière et Société*, 56 (February 2017), 29.

[15] Hildebrand Karangwa, *Quelques témoignages des rescapés de Kabgayi (le 2 juin 1994)*, s.d. [2001], 116. Karangwa was a key witness at the trial of Emmanuel Rukundo, a military chaplain found guilty of genocide and sentenced to twenty-five years in prison. See ICTR, The Prosecutor vs Emmanuel Rukundo, Judgement, 27 February 2009. The Chamber exonerated Rukundo from any implication in the 24 May 1994 massacre.

[16] Jef Vleugels and Guy Theunis, Fax No. 16, Brussels, 2 June 1994 in

search the rooms.[17] Joseph Ngomanzungu claimed in a report that Thaddée Nsengiyumva, the bishop of Kabgayi, subsequently sent a letter of protest to the government.[18] However, when Françoise Boucher-Saulnier visited Kabgayi shortly after the genocide, she heard from André Sibomana, by then the apostolic administrator of the diocese, that when priests like himself had asked Bishop Nsengiyumva to use his influence with the authorities to stop the massacres, he had refused. He had only obtained that the executions should be perpetrated outside the diocesan buildings.[19]

The Protestant churches also suffered heavy losses of personnel, as will be discussed in the fifth chapter. According to a document compiled by Gédéon Gakindi, the general secretary of the Presbyterian Church, and Donat Nyilinkindi, the general treasurer, in August 1994 16 pastors and delegate pastors – out of 95, missionaries included, in April 1994 – and 'a big number of evangelists' were killed during the genocide.[20] The biggest massacre took place on 14 April 1994 in Kirinda, an important Presbyterian centre in west-central Rwanda.[21] In the early days of the genocide, a group of Tutsi pastors led by Édouard Gafaringa, the president of the Kigali region, took refuge in the Remera-Rukoma parish near Gitarama with their families. On 23 May, their hiding place was discovered and all, including the Hutu pastor who had sheltered them, were slaughtered. According to Jérôme Bizimana – the current pastor of Remera-Rukoma – 6 pastors from

---

Missionaries of Africa, 'Informations diffusées par la Région du Rwanda, 1990–1994', compiled by Jef Vleugels, Brussels, December 2005, 192.

[17] Interview conducted on 29 August 1994, quoted in Alison Des Forges, *Leave None to Tell the Story: Genocide in Rwanda* (New York: Human Rights Watch, 1999), 247.

[18] Joseph Ngomanzungu, *L'Église et la crise rwandaise de 1990–1994. Essai de chronologie* (Kigali: Pallotti Press, 2000), 124.

[19] Françoise Boucher-Saulnier and Frédéric Laffont, *Maudits soient les yeux fermés* (Paris: Éditions J. C. Lattès, 1995), 89–90.

[20] Donat Nyilinkindi and Gédéon Gakindi, 'Église presbytérienne au Rwanda. Programme de redressement', 25 August 1994, 1, 3 (Munyaneza Papers). In an open letter to the Assembly of the WCC in Harare, African Rights also spoke of sixteen pastors murdered in Remera-Rukoma ('The Protestant Churches and the Genocide', December 2018, 13). The names of the five pastors killed in Remera-Rukoma are mentioned in Gerard van 't Spijker, *L'Église chrétienne au Rwanda pré et post-génocide* (Paris: L'Harmattan, 2011), 25.

[21] Timothy Longman, *Christianity and Genocide in Rwanda* (Cambridge: Cambridge University Press, 2011), 268–300.

the region, 11 pastors from other regions, 7 lay people and 29 children are buried in his parish.[22]

The involvement of a prominent Seventh Day Adventist Church leader, Elizaphan Ntakirutimana, in a massacre perpetrated in Mugonero near Kibuye on 16 April 1994 was given worldwide publicity in a book by the American journalist Philip Gourevitch in 1998.[23] The ICTR declared him and his son Gérard guilty of genocide in 2003. Seven Adventist pastors died in Mugonero.[24] They wrote the letter whose opening sentence gave Gourevitch's book its title: 'We wish to inform you that tomorrow we shall be killed with our families'. A similar massacre took place in the Adventist University of Central Africa in Gitwe near Nyanza in southern Rwanda. Lecturers and students were killed with the Tutsi people who had taken refuge in the university.[25] In total, according to Jérôme Birikunzira, about a hundred Adventist pastors and workers such as teachers and nurses, not to mention their wives and children, were killed during the genocide.[26]

The priests and bishops killed by the RPF

The fact that RPF soldiers killed several priests in the Byumba prefecture in late April 1994 and a group of bishops, priests and lay people in the Josephite novitiate in Gakurazo on 5 June 1994 is well attested. The respected genocide researcher Alison Des Forges raised the issue in a section of her 1999 Human Rights Watch report.[27] Yet, more research is necessary to establish the scale and the intention of the crimes allegedly committed by the RPF during and after the genocide. The highly politicised nature of the topic, its instrumentalisation by opposition politicians, journalists and academics in Europe and North America, the lack of cooperation from the current Rwandan government and the involvement of high-ranking RPF dissidents with dubious agendas in the debate all render

---

[22] Jérôme Bizimana, interview conducted on 22 March 2017 in Remera-Rukoma.
[23] Philip Gourevitch, *We Wish to Inform You that Tomorrow We Will Be Killed with Our Families* (New York: Picador, 1998).
[24] *Ibid.*, 28.
[25] Jérôme Birikunzira, 'L'Eglise adventiste du 7ᵉ jour au Rwanda (1919–2000)', in Tharcisse Gatwa and Laurent Rutinduka (ed.), *Histoire du christianisme au Rwanda des origines à nos jours* (Yaoundé: Éditions CLÉ, 2014), 113.
[26] Jérôme Birikunzira, 'Implantation and growth of the Seventh-Day Adventist Church in Rwanda (1919–2000)', unpublished master's dissertation, University of South Africa, 2008, 116.
[27] Des Forges, *Leave None to Tell the Story*, 711, 714.

a fair and honest assessment difficult. Here we shall only talk about the Catholic priests and bishops killed by RPF soldiers.

The sources that I have managed to retrieve so far show a double phenomenon: a high level of violence on the part of the RPF army in the territories conquered during the genocide and a systematic pattern of retaliation. The context must be taken into account. The RPF soldiers and their local supporters were traumatised and infuriated by the horrendous accounts of Tutsi extermination brought back in mid-April by refugees from Kigali and other places. In a sinister tit-for-tat phenomenon, each RPF-led massacre of civilians responded to a genocide event. Both sides committed what many observers considered to be serious crimes, but their motives were different. The Rwandan army and the Interahamwe claimed that they would end the war and restore the security of the country by killing all the Tutsi, under the pretence that any Tutsi person, even a child, was in essence a RPF 'accomplice'. The RPF army, continually reinforced by angry genocide survivors, retaliated with excessive use of force. The fact that the Habyarimana government had armed the population before the genocide and incited all able men to fight the RPF doubtless contributed to the latter army's grievous tendency to consider anyone suspicious a hidden member of the Interahamwe, and kill them for that reason.

The RPF arrived in the Giti area, south of the Byumba prefecture, on 16 April and in Byumba itself on 17 April. A church worker who kept a diary during this period described the horror that the stories told by the refugees from Kigali caused among the people assisting them in Byumba:

> We speak to the group of refugees or, rather, it is they who speak to us because they are dying to find people to whom they can narrate what they have experienced, horrors really. One must be strong to listen to all these stories, each more gruesome than the previous one. One gets the impression that Kigali has become a heap of mutilated bodies. The families are decimated. The survivors tremble and a phrase often comes up: 'We thought that it was the end of the world!'[28]

Another entry describes the climate of violence that developed in Byumba:

> The sad thing is that the government soldiers had distributed weapons to the population, especially those who held some authority. They disappeared

---

[28] Byumba, 25 April 2019. A copy of the diary was entrusted to the author in April 2019. According to this source, the FAR and the local authorities left Byumba late at night on 16 April and the RPF arrived the following day in the afternoon.

without claiming back the weapons and the owners pay the price of this 'collaboration'. There are also arbitrary denunciations on the part of the population and the sanctions do not wait for other forms of investigation. Among the newcomers, there is such an obsession about the Interahamwe, the government militia, that anybody who is accused of being part of them is shot down straight away.[29]

The circumstances of the disappearance and death of two Rwandan priests, Célestin Muhayimana and Augustin Mashyendeli, in the parish of Nyinawimana outside Byumba on 21 April are not known. On 27 April, four days after a massacre in the Byumba Stadium that claimed several hundred lives, according to Human Rights Watch,[30] Joseph Hitimana and Fidèle Mulinda, two priests from Byumba; Faustin Mulindwa, a priest who happened to be visiting the city; and Joachim Vallmajo, a Spanish White Father who worked in nearby Kageyo, were taken away and killed.[31] According to Armand Duval, Vallmajo's biographer, the most likely reason for these senseless murders is that the priests, or some of them, had requested explanations for the killings perpetrated during the previous days.[32]

Meanwhile, on 23 April in the southern part of the Byumba prefecture, three priests from Rwesero Minor Seminary (including the former rector Christian Nkiliyehe) and other staff members were killed in the Karusha camp where they had found shelter after an alert. An elderly priest, Gaspard Mudashimwa, and a sister were killed a month later, on 21 May, while travelling to Byumba.[33] In a book published in 2002, Léonard Nduwayo, a medical doctor residing in France, described the massacres perpetrated by the RPF in the Giti commune, which includes Rwesero, with the help of lists of victims compiled in Tanzanian and Zairian refugee camps after the genocide. He correctly pointed out that, thanks to the wisdom and the generosity of the burgomaster Édouard Subushumba, Giti was one of the few Rwandan communes not to be affected by the genocide.[34] The reasons for the RPF soldiers' animosity against the Catholic Church must be found elsewhere. In an article on the 'historical consciousness' manifested

---

[29] Byumba, 20 April 2019. Same document.
[30] Des Forges, *Leave None to Tell the Story*, 16.
[31] *Ibid.*, 545.
[32] Armand Duval, *L'évangile de Quim* (Paris: Mediaspaul, 1998), 104.
[33] Léonard Nduwayo, *Giti et le génocide Rwandais* (Paris: L'Harmattan, 2002), 172–7.
[34] *Ibid.*, 10–12.

in Giti, the American anthropologist John Janzen pointed out that in the adjacent commune of Muhura the Tutsi had serious grievances against the Catholic priests, with the exception of the Italian Barnabite Mario Falconi, whom they considered a saint. One of Janzen's informants made the following statement:

> The Church is dead in Giti. In 1990, I was in the bush for weeks, and my family was displaced. The priests didn't help at all. The Rwandan priest even ordered machetes. When he heard the RPF was coming, he fled to Muhura and was killed by the RPF. The Spanish priest didn't support the Tutsi. He was in Burundi during the Bagaza era. Coming here, he was against the Tutsi. He is in Spain now.[35]

On the evening of 5 June 1994, three days after the RPF's arrival in Kabgayi, 4 soldiers shot dead Vincent Nsengiyumva, the archbishop of Kigali; Thaddée Nsengiyumva, the bishop of Kabgayi; Joseph Ruzindana, the bishop of Byumba; Jean-Baptiste Nsinga, the general superior of the Josephite brothers; 9 priests mostly from the diocese of Kabgayi and 2 children in the dining room of the Josephites' novitiate house in Gakurazo, not far from Kabgayi. This violent event would have lasting consequences on the relations between church and state in post-genocide Rwanda. It caused the three White Fathers who, against all odds, had remained in their parish of Nyabitimbo in the diocese of Cyangugu during the genocide to flee to Burundi. It dominated the visit of Cardinal Etchegaray, the pope's envoy, in late June.

Thanks to the testimonies of Emmanuel Dukuzemungu, a priest present during the killings who managed to escape,[36] and to Vénuste Linguyeneza,

---

[35] John Janzen, 'Historical consciousness and a "prise de conscience" in genocidal Rwanda', *Journal of African Cultural Studies*, 13 (2000), 161. The Spanish priest mentioned in Janzen's article appears to be Juan José Mancebo, who was expelled from Burundi in 1985 and worked in the parish of Rwamiko north of Giti until 1994. In the early 1990s he took care of the Hutu refugees fleeing the RPF, which may explain why he was perceived as anti-RPF. In a documentary, Mancebo claimed that he and his Spanish confrères also provided support to the Tutsi during the genocide. See Laura Daniele, 'Los misionarios mercedarios lleven al cine el genocidio de Ruanda', *ABC*, 2 April 2019.

[36] 'Rwanda: Assassinat à Gakurazo de quinze civils dont treize ecclésiastiques et deux jeunes gens. Témoignage d'Emmanuel Dukuzemungu, l'unique rescapé', 5 June 2000. <www.musabyimana.net›uploads›2015/08›Gakurazo> [accessed 5 November 2019].

the rector of the Philosophicum in Kabgayi who subsequently buried the victims,[37] the facts are well known. The matter has been investigated by the ICTR in Arusha, which handed over the case to the Rwandan government in 2008. Meanwhile, four officers had been arrested in 2004 in Rwanda and two of them sentenced to eight years of imprisonment, later reduced to five years. This trial, however, did not put an end to the controversy surrounding the motives of the Gakurazo massacre and the chain of command that led to it.[38] The personality of the archbishop of Kigali, widely believed to be on the side of the *génocidaires*,[39] probably played a role in the massacre. Another reason for the RPF soldiers' animosity against the Catholic Church was the perception among the Tutsi that had taken refuge in neighbouring areas since 1959 of having been let down by the church of their home country.[40] This sentiment had fuelled the conviction that the Catholic Church of Rwanda was biased in favour of the Hutu.

Those who opposed the genocide

According to Filip Reyntjens, an author who tends to underestimate the number of Tutsi victims of the genocide, three-quarters of the Tutsi population residing in Rwanda by April 1994 were killed during the genocide.[41] This means that between 150,000 and 200,000 Tutsi, depending on the estimate of genocide victims, survived. All the survivors' stories, whether put in print or collected by way of oral history interviews, show that, at one point or another, these survivors found Hutu people along the way who provided them with shelter, or at least food, and thereby accepted the

---

[37] Vénuste Linguyeneza, '5 juin 1994: trois évêques assassinés', *Dialogue*, 213 (November–December 1999), 79–88. In the testimony quoted above, Dukuzemengu claimed that RPF soldiers also killed two Josephite brothers, Balthazar Ntibagendeza and Vivens Mugwiza, in Kinazi in the Bugesera on 23 July 1994.

[38] André Guichaoua, *Rwanda. De la guerre au génocide. Les politiques criminelles au Rwanda (1990–1994)* (Paris: La Découverte, 2010), 563.

[39] See Chapter 7.

[40] This does not mean that the Catholic Church gave no support to the Tutsi refugees in Uganda. A case in point is Barnabas Halem'Imana, the bishop of Kabale in Uganda, who gave open support to the Tutsi 'rebels' in October 1990. See Moses Talemwa, 'Activist Bishop Halem'Imana bids farewell', *The Observer*, Kampala, 13 January 2016.

[41] Filip Reyntjens, 'Estimation du nombre de personnes tuées au Rwanda en 1994', in S. Marysse and F. Reyntjens (ed.), *L'Afrique des Grands Lacs. Annuaire 1996–1997* (Paris: L'Harmattan, 1997), 186.

risk of being considered RPF 'accomplices' and being killed themselves. Otherwise, the survivors would not have been there to tell their story. As much as the genocide project found support in the population, with the support of relentless media campaigns and the encouragement, tacit or explicit, of the authorities, it did also encounter resistance, although the assisting of genocide survivors did tend to decrease over time. Meanwhile, for reasons difficult to grasp, Interahamwe leaders sometimes saved Tutsi lives, as Sebuhuku, the saviour of Charles Habonimana, did in Mayunzwe.[42]

There is no doubt that Christians supported fellow Christians during the genocide. Even though the genocide had great popular support, with neighbours betraying or even killing neighbours,[43] many Hutu people took risks to save other human beings' lives.[44] The majority of them never gained recognition. Some of them were priests or pastors. They are called Justs, in reference to the non-Jews who risked their lives for the Jews during the Holocaust. The names of Ananie Rugasira, who lost his life in Ndera for refusing to open the minor seminary to the killers, and Mario Falconi, the Italian missionary who chose to remain in Rwanda during the genocide and saved lives in the Muhura parish, have already been mentioned. The same spirit animated Joseph Gatare and Jean-Bosco Munyaneza, Tutsi and Hutu, respectively, who refused to betray their flock in Mukarange in the diocese of Kibungo,[45] and Dorothée Mukandanga, the director of a nursing school in Kabgayi who was killed for refusing to hand over Tutsi female students to soldiers that wanted to rape them.[46] Nine priests and a seminarian – six Hutu and four Tutsi – who risked their lives to confront the *génocidaires* are featured in the French magazine *Golias*.[47]

---

[42] Charles Habonimana, *Moi, le dernier Tutsi* (Paris: Plon, 2019). Mayunzwe (not to be confused with Muyunzwe) is situated near Mugina, south-east of Muhanga (formerly Gitarama).

[43] Jean-Paul Kimonyo, *Rwanda. Un génocide populaire* (Paris: Karthala, 2008).

[44] Daniel-Ange, *Rwanda. Au fond de l'enfer, le ciel ouvert* (Paris: Éditions Béatitude, 2019).

[45] African Rights, *Rwanda: Death, Despair and Defiance*, 2nd edn (London: African Rights, 1995), 884; Bertrand Jouanno, 'Dossier', *La Croix*, 6 April 2004.

[46] Boniface Musoni, 'Holocause noir (extraits)', *Dialogue*, 177 (August–September 1994), 88.

[47] 'Ils ont sauvé l'honneur de l'Eglise au Rwanda', *Golias*, 48–9 (Summer 1996), 122. Reproduced in *La Nouvelle Relève*, 392 (October 1999), 10. These priests

More widely known is the story of Felicitas Niyitegeka, an Auxiliary of the Apostolate from Gisenyi whose heroism is celebrated in various publications.[48] In the first days of the genocide, she refused to follow the advice of her brother, who was a colonel in the Rwandan army, and flee. Instead, she helped dozens of Tutsi refugees to cross the border to Zaire. On 21 April, the Interahamwe came to fetch her as well as six other Auxiliaries of the Apostolate and twenty or so Tutsi refugees. She was given a last chance to withdraw her support to her Tutsi sisters, but she declined and was shot dead.

Equally brave was Stanislas Urbaniak, a Polish Pallotine who, from his own testimony, was 'forgotten' in mid-April when the soldiers of the UN Peacekeeping Force were scouting for expatriates all over the country with a view to sending them abroad for their security.[49] He lived in Ruhango where he had founded, in association with the Emmanuel Community, the Centre Jésus Miséricordieux, a place of spiritual healing and contemplation, in the early 1990s. When the Interahamwe came to fetch a Tutsi priest and a group of refugees, he brandished an image of the Virgin Mary and said: 'Kill me first if you want to kill them!' He then lay down on the ground, his arms and his body forming a cross. The killers moved back. Urbaniak protected the Tutsi refugees until the end of the genocide.[50]

Under this heading, we should also mention the parishes, Catholic as well as Protestant, that provided shelter to Tutsi refugees. As we know, many church buildings were violated and became the scene of horrific massacres. Not all though. The Sainte-Famille parish in Kigali and various church buildings in Kabgayi hosted refugees until the arrival of the

---

are Oscar Nkundayezu (Hutu), Félicien Bahizi (Hutu), Baudouin Busunyu (Hutu), Joseph Boneza (Tutsi), Pierre Ngoga (Hutu), Joseph Niyomugabo (Tutsi), Célestin Hazikimana (Hutu), Ananie Rusagira (Hutu), Augustin Nkezabera (Hutu), Evode Mwanangu (Tutsi).

[48] See, in particular, Jean d'Amour Dusengumuremyi, *Félicité Niyitegeka. Une lumière dans la nuit rwandaise. Agir face à l'inacceptable* (Kampala: Angel Agencies Ltd, 2012). English translation: *No Greater Love. Testimonies on the Life and Death of Felicitas Niyitegeka* (Lake Oswego, Oregon: Dignity Press, 2015).

[49] Information provided on 16 October 2019 in Paris by Aleksander Edelman, who held it from conversations with Stanislas Urbaniak in Poland.

[50] Cassien Kalisa, genocide survivor, interview conducted on 23 May 2008 in Ruhango. On Stanislas Urbaniak, see also Wojciech Tochman, *Aujourd'hui, nous allons dessiner la mort* (Lausanne: Les Éditions Noir sur Blanc, 2014), 103–5.

RPF. Proportionally, fewer Tutsi died in Kigali than in the other parts of the country. This form of opposition to the genocide, however, was all but ambiguous. Wenceslas Munyeshyaka, the priest in charge of the Sainte-Famille during the genocide, is a case in point. He did indeed shelter Tutsi refugees in his parish, but genocide survivors accused him of having betrayed refugees to the Interahamwe, with whom he appeared to have entertained a cordial relationship.[51] In 2015, after years of litigation, a French judge ruled that Munyeshyaka's friendly relations with the authorities implicated in the genocide were not sufficient to establish that he had participated in the crime of genocide.

The Catholic Church hosted and fed 20,000 refugees in Kabgayi. Some were Hutu people from Northern Rwanda who had left their homes on the arrival of the RPF in the early 1990s. The majority were Tutsi. Sheltering so many refugees raised huge logistical problems, which the church authorities tried to resolve with the help of external funding agencies.[52] Many Tutsi refugees survived, but not all. As we have seen, the Interahamwe regularly came with lists of alleged accomplices of the RPF. The church authorities only obtained from them that the executions should take place outside the diocesan property.[53]

The implication of priests and pastors in the genocide

The number of priests and pastors who played an active role in the genocide against the Tutsi will never be known with precision. The first reason is that, when confronted, these clerics deny all responsibility, sometimes despite evidence to the contrary. Often, they receive the support of their hierarchies, who refuse to believe in their culpability. If indeed they are guilty, admitting this would require an enormous amount of faith and courage on the part of these priests and pastors.

The second reason is the impossibility, despite all the efforts made by genocide-memory activists in Rwanda and other countries since 1994, of tracking down all the clerics who absorbed the Hutu extremist ideology

---

[51] The French magazine *Golias* published twelve testimonies of genocide survivors who accused Munyeshyaka, who was always heavily armed, of having refused to intercede in their favour when the Interahamwe raided the parish – see supplement to *Golias*, 43 (July–August 1995).

[52] Thaddée Nsengiyumva to Henri Hamus, Kabgayi, 15 May 1994 (Malachie Munyaneza Papers).

[53] Françoise Boucher-Saulnier and Frédéric Laffont, *Maudits soient les yeux fermés* (Paris: Éditions J. C. Lattès, 1995), 90.

and acted accordingly. Quite a few remained under the radar, like the above-mentioned Patrice Munyentwali,[54] whose story only came to light in 2016 and whose culpability was never tested in court. A former member of a female congregation told me, in tears, the story of two young sisters who in May 1994 had notified the local burgomaster of the presence in the convent of a woman and two children, aged twelve and ten, who had escaped a prior massacre. The three refugees were taken away and shot. The two sisters in question have never been denounced.

The case of Étienne Kabera is different. He fled to Zaire after the genocide and was killed with six other priests by rebel soldiers in the refugee camp of Kalima on 25 February 1997.[55] Had he remained alive, he would probably have faced trial. His complete lack of remorse and his identification with the Hutu extremist ideology shocked the French journalists who met him in Butare in June 1994. 'The Tutsi were preparing to kill us,' he told Laurent Bijard. 'They had lists. We were ahead of them by some days.'[56] During the same period, he declared to a completely astounded Nicolas Poincaré and Laurent Grzybowski, Poincaré's Catholic colleague, 'As I said today at Mass, we must complete the work. We must finish off the children.'[57] Cyril Musoni, who worked at the mission warehouse La Procure in Butare, explained to Jean Damascène Bizimana – a Missionary of Africa student who subsequently left religious life – that Kabera took an active part in the massacres of children and teachers in the Butare school where he worked as a chaplain. Every night he met the Interahamwe and offered them beer he had collected for them at the Procure.[58]

Several bishops, priests and pastors have been prosecuted for genocide. Out of a total of 96 persons indicted by the ICTR for genocide, 5 were clerics: an Anglican bishop (Samuel Musabyimana), three Catholic priests (Athanase Seromba, Emmanuel Rukundo and Hormisdas Nsengimana) and an Adventist pastor (Elizaphan Ntakirutimana). Musabyimana died in jail before being tried and Nsengimana was acquitted. A few clerics were tried in the Western countries in which they had taken refuge, including Wenceslas Munyeshyaka, whose case was dismissed in 2015

---

[54] See above p. 70.
[55] Ngomanzungu, *La souffrance de l'Église*, 22.
[56] Laurent Bijard, 'Turquoise, l'Opération sans boussole', *Le Nouvel Observateur*, 20 June 1994, quoted in African Rights, *Rwanda: Death, Despair and Defiance*, 915.
[57] Nicolas Poincaré, interview conducted on 21 April 2018 in Paris.
[58] Jean-Damascène Bizimana, *L'Église et le génocide au Rwanda* (Paris: L'Harmattan, 2001), 64.

by a French court after a lengthy procedure, and two Benedictine sisters, Consolata Mukagango and Julienne Mukabutera, who were sentenced to fifteen and twelve years of imprisonment, respectively, by a Belgian court in 2001. In addition, the Rwandan tribunals and the *gacaca* courts sentenced a few dozen priests, pastors, brothers and sisters to various pains of imprisonment, though these sentences were sometimes dropped on appeal and some prisoners were released without trial after spending time in jail.[59] Among the Catholic priests sentenced for genocide or suspected of genocide complicity, a large proportion were Hutu priests ordained in the five years preceding the genocide.[60] This suggests that this generation of priests was particularly vulnerable to the Hutu extremist propaganda. The participation of some of them in a pro-Hutu student association called Komite Ngarukiragihugu [Committee for the defence of the country] when they trained for the priesthood at Nyakibanda Major Seminary in the early 1990s was mentioned by a young priest by the name of Aimé Rutaremara during the trial of Bishop Augustin Misago in 2000.[61]

Virtually all these cases, even those which were handled by the ICTR, have been contested, despite overwhelming evidence in some instances. There does not seem to be a single case of a church leader who admitted his or her guilt. As will be discussed in Chapter 7, all we can say is that there has been a continuum between indubitable genocide complicity and less obvious forms of support of the genocide. To use the language of the South African TRC, there have been acts of omission and commission. It is a fact that some clerics have been unfairly detained or condemned since 1994. This, however, does not remove the fact that, if only by their silence, a non-negligible number of priests, pastors, brothers and sisters have played a role in the genocide. In many places, their silence persisted after the killings. Angélique Umugwaneza, a twelve-year-old child at the time, found the first Mass she attended after the atrocities, in June 1994 in the Gikongoro area, 'cold and sad'. 'The priest did not say a word about

---

[59] For an overview of the Catholic priests, brothers and sisters detained and condemned for acts of genocide between 1994 and 1999, see Ngomanzungu, *La souffrance de l'Église*, 34–54.

[60] Étienne Kabera (ord. 1990), Aimé Mategeko (ord. 1990), Jean-Baptiste Ntamugabumwe (ord. 1990), Wenceslas Munyeshyaka (ord. 1991), Emmanuel Rukundo (ord. 1991), Joseph Ndagijimana (ord. 1991), Athanase Nyandwi (ord. 1991), François Kayiranga (ord. 1992), Patrice Munyentwali (ord. 1993), Athanase Seromba (ord. 1993).

[61] Tribunal of 1st Instance of Kigali, Trial of Augustin Misago, audience of 29 February 2000.

what had taken place,' she recalled. 'Everything was done as if nothing had happened. Before it was always nice to be in church. This time, it looked weird, horrible even. Were there not murderers in the assembly? And there were lots of innocent children wearing beautiful clothes looted from others.'[62]

A war or a genocide?

The genocide against the Tutsi started hours after the shooting down of President Habyarimana's plane and not after the evacuation of the expatriates around 12 April, as some authors have claimed. As early as 7 April, Tutsi people were hunted down and massacred in Rukoma near Kibungo,[63] as well as in Nyundo and the nearby village of Busasamana.[64] On 8 April, it was the turn of Nyamirambo (a parish held by the White Fathers in Kigali),[65] Ndera,[66] Gikongoro[67] and a few other places. The following day hundreds of Tutsi were massacred in the church of Gikondo in front of the Polish Pallottine missionaries who were running the parish.[68] By 11 April, an estimated 20,000 (mostly Tutsi) people had already been murdered.[69]

How long did it take for the priests, the pastors and the bishops to realise that the Tutsi were being targeted as Tutsi on a massive scale and that a genocide – a term first used in a report from Doctors Without Borders[70] and, simultaneously, in the Belgian daily *La Libre Belgique* on 13 April, but which only became familiar to the Rwandan people later – was taking place? Different answers are given to this question. Malachie Munyaneza,

[62] Angélique Umugwaneza and Peder Fuglsang, *Les enfants du Rwanda* (Gaïa: Montfort-en-Chalosse, 2014), 37–8.
[63] 'La tragédie d'avril 1994 dans le diocèse de Kibungo', *Stella Matutina. Bulletin du Diocèse de Kibungo*, 112 (1995), 6.
[64] 'Des rescapés du diocèse de Nyundo témoignent', 59–64.
[65] Otto Mayer, 'Trois mois d'enfer au jour le jour', *Dialogue*, 177 (August–September 1994), 23.
[66] Murangira, *Un sachet d'hosties pour cinq*, 74.
[67] Madeleine Raffin, *Rwanda: un autre regard* (Lille: Éditions Sources du Nil, 2012), 87.
[68] Florent Piton, 'Tueurs, Ibitero et notabilités génocidaires au Rwanda (avril 1994)', *Le Vingtième Siècle*, 138 (2018), 129–31. As Piton pointed out, 'the killings perpetrated between 7 and 11 April invalidate the thesis according to which the genocide only started on 12 April' (*ibid.*, 128).
[69] Des Forges, *Leave None to Tell the Story*, 201.
[70] Jean-Hervé Bradol and Marc Le Pape, *Génocide et crimes de masse. L'expérience rwandaise de MSF 1982–1997* (Paris: CNRS Éditions, 2017), 57.

who remained in Kigali until mid-May, understood that a sinister plan was in operation on 19 April, when he heard the interim president, Théodore Sindikubwabo, on Radio Rwanda, inviting the population to 'work' after the sacking of a prefect who had refused to carry out the genocide.[71] Marc François, who had witnessed, powerless, the massacre of part of his flock in Nyamitimbo near Cyangugu, stated that the incessant calls to murder on Radio Télévision des Mille Collines (RTLM) showed without doubt that a genocide was taking place.[72]

This begs the question of why if some clerics understood that a genocide was happening, others – church leaders in particular – did not come to the same realisation. Part of the answer is that three among the most influential of them – Vincent Nsengiyumva (the archbishop of Kigali), Joseph Ruzindana (the bishop of Byumba) and Thaddée Nsengiyumva (the bishop of Kabgayi and president of the episcopal conference) – chose to stay in the latter's residence, a short distance from the interim government's headquarters in Gitarama. The first two arrived under military escort from Kigali on 12 April 1994, their cars brandishing episcopal flags, as a witness later testified at the trial of Bishop Misago.[73] Geographically but also symbolically, the leadership of the Catholic Church was in close proximity to the interim government, the latter of which started to encourage the population to practise self-defence (a euphemism for killing the Tutsi) as soon as it arrived in Gitarama. On 18 April, Frédéric Rubwejanga, the bishop of Kibungo, received an invitation from Augustin Bizimungu, the chief of staff of the Rwandan army, to rejoin his fellow bishops in Kabgayi with two soldiers in escort. Significantly, Rubwejanga elected to return to his diocese almost immediately, against the advice of the authorities and at his own peril, since he was a Tutsi.[74]

Between April and June 1994, the Catholic bishops issued, collectively or individually, eight statements. Under the umbrella of the revived

---

[71] Malachie Munyaneza, interview conducted on 8 October 2019 in Wolverhampton. On this speech, see Jean-Pierre Chrétien (ed.), *Rwanda. Les médias du génocide* (Paris: Karthala, 2002), 192.

[72] Marc François, interview conducted on 11 December 2017 in Kigali.

[73] Testimony of Dominique Rwigamba at the trial of Bishop Augustin Misago, Tribunal of 1st Instance of Kigali, 9th audience, 27 October 1999. From Kabgayi, Rubwejanga delivered a speech on radio for the Christians of his diocese, resisting the pressure of the minister of information, who wanted him to specifically ask the RPF to disarm.

[74] Emeritus Bishop Frédéric Rubwejanga, interview conducted on 27 February 2017 in Chimay, Belgium.

Comité de Contacts, the Catholic bishops and the Anglican, Presbyterian and Methodist church leaders issued two statements on 16 May and 20 June 1994, respectively. On 22 April, a statement was jointly signed by the Catholic and Anglican bishops of Byumba.[75] These statements were similar to those of the preceding period. They condemned violence and called for peace but did not question, except in broad terms, the responsibility of the Rwandan government. All they did was denounce the effects of the war between the RPF and the Rwandan government and exhort Hutu and Tutsi to live in harmony. They never referred, even in an oblique way, to the fact that the government had encouraged the population to 'work' for the extermination of the Tutsi people and that, throughout the country, the army, the police and the local authorities had passively authorised or actively supported the genocide. The church leaders' statements did not refute the widely broadcast argument that all Tutsi were 'accomplices' of the RPF and therefore deserved to be killed. The church leaders pretended to be presented with a conventional war, as if a country attacked by external forces had ever won a war by turning against itself and slaughtering a massive part of its own population.

Typical of this attitude is the letter Thaddée Nsengiyumva, the archbishop of Kabgayi, sent on 15 May 1994 to a Luxemburger missionary in Bujumbura to request financial support for the refugees in his diocese. As showed by the courageous statement he published jointly with the presbyterium of Kabgayi in December 1991,[76] Nsengiyumva was, compared to his colleagues, a rather enlightened bishop. Yet, six weeks after the beginning of the massacres, he persisted in analysing the situation in terms of war, *de facto* denying the reality of the genocide against the Tutsi:

> The war continues in Kigali and in the eastern part of the country. Uganda supports the RPF rebels and Burundi (a Tutsi military regime) also wants to participate in order to support the RPF. There are many massacres and we denounce them. We demand the end of the war and negotiations. In Kabgayi 20,000 refugees of all ethnic groups. Not enough food. Chemical products for the war are lacking, as a result no water for four days. We must draw water from the springs [...] for so many people. There is no security,

---

[75] Extracts of these statements have been published by Joseph Ngomanzungu in *L'Église et la crise rwandaise*, 111–55. Ngomanzungu occupied the function of assistant general secretary of the Catholic Bishops' Conference before and during the genocide.

[76] See Chapter 2.

everybody is afraid of isolated murders, which remain unpunished. All bishops are alive but several priests have been killed.[77]

The first episcopal statement, dated 9 April and published in the 11–12 April issue of the *Osservatore Romano,* set the tone. Writing in his capacity as president of the episcopal conference, Thaddée Nsengiyumva denounced 'those who, under the effect of anger and grief act in a spirit of vengeance and go on looting, which brings them to abundantly shed the blood of other Rwandans, with no respect for the leaders and compassion for the small children'. He then expressed gratitude to the FAR for 'taking to heart the problems of security' and pledged support to the new government.[78] In their joint statement of 13 May, the Catholic and Protestant church leaders denounced the massacres in the same way and called for a negotiated settlement of the conflict.[79] The closest to a denunciation of the genocide is found in a letter from Thaddée Nsengiyumva to 'the friends of Rwanda' on 16 May. 'It is clear', he wrote, 'that there are too many political ambitions at play and a certain refusal to share power with the opposition. I would say that we are witnessing a political and even sometimes ethnic policy, though not often admitted as such.'[80] A few days before their death in Gakurazo, the bishops of Kabgayi, Kigali and Byumba tried to suggest the idea of a security zone around Kabgayi, a project that the *Osservatore Romano* mentioned in its 4 June issue.[81]

The most problematic statement was the one jointly issued on 16 June by the Catholic bishops of Gikongoro and Cyangugu, the administrator of the archdiocese of Kabgayi, three Anglican bishops, one Methodist bishop and the president of the Presbyterian Church under the heading 'Memorandum of the representatives of the Catholic and Protestant churches to the Rwandan Government, the Rwandan Patriotic Front and

---

[77] Thaddée Nsengiyumva to Henri Hamus, Gitarama, 15 May 1994 (Malachie Munyaneza Papers). In the letter he sent to 'the White Fathers, friends of Rwanda' on 16 May 1994 (Archives of the Dominican Missionary Sisters of Namur), the bishop of Kabgayi similarly focused all the attention on the war between the 'belligerents' without saying a word on the genocide against the Tutsi.

[78] 'Communicato dei Vescovi cattolici del Rwanda', *Osservatore Romano,* 11–12 April 1994, 2. The document is not dated. The date of 9 April is mentioned in Ngomanzungu, *L'Église et la crise rwandaise,* 111.

[79] Ngomanzungu, *L'Église et la crise rwandaise,* 121–2.

[80] *Ibid.,* 122.

[81] *Ibid.,* 125. See *Osservatore Romano,* 4 June 1994, 1–2.

the international community in an attempt to seek peace'.[82] The document squarely put the responsibility of the crisis on the RPF, which had 'started the war on 1 October 1990 with the support of Uganda'. In a section on the 'roots of the Rwandan evil', they noted that 'until 1959 Rwanda knew a feodo-monarchical regime dominated by the minority Tutsi ethnic group'. As in the previous documents, the signatories called for a ceasefire and asked the international community to intervene. They made no reference whatsoever to the genocide.

As was common in Rwanda under Habyarimana, priests, pastors and bishops had regular contact with the local authorities. This continued during the genocide in places like Kibungo, Cyangugu and Kabgayi. With good reason, these meetings are today considered suspicious. Yet, the clerics concerned may have attended them to obtain protection for the refugees under their care or to mitigate the effects of the violence. We know of one such meeting that gave a bishop – Thaddée Ntihinyurwa, the Catholic bishop of Cyangugu – the opportunity to challenge the logic of the genocide. He did so, however, privately. His lucidity did not prevent the allegations of genocidal complicity made against him at a *gacaca* court in 2005,[83] despite these being refuted by Tutsi priests who had worked closely with him at the time.[84] According to a diary compiled by a priest named Modeste Kajyibwami during the genocide,[85] at a meeting of government officials on 21 April in Cyangagu, which Ntihinyurwa and two priests took part in, the bishop distanced himself from the anti-Tutsi rhetoric of the authorities in the following terms:

> None of the speakers lamented the innocent death of the Tutsi, except the bishop of Cyangugu, His Excellency Thaddée Ntihinyurwa, who stood up to say that he felt like a mother who saw nearly all her children perish in front of her eyes, and that the authorities should at least commit themselves to protecting the survivors. As to the fact that they may be accomplices of

---

[82] Extract in Ngomanzungu, *L'Église et la crise rwandaise*, 127–8. Full copy in the archives of *Dialogue* magazine in Brussels.

[83] *The New Times*, Kigali, 20 July 2005.

[84] Testimonies of Ubald Rugirangoga and Apollinaire Ntamabyariro, *Kinyamateka*, 1516 (May 1999), translated into French in Jean Ndorimana, *Rwanda. Idéologie, méthodes et négationnisme du génocide des Tutsi à lumière de la chronique de la région de Cyangugu* (Rome: Edizioni Vivere In, 2003), 207–8.

[85] Jean Ndorimana, interview conducted on 4 December 2018 in Kigali. Extracts of this diary are published in Ndorimana, *Rwanda. Idéologie, méthodes et négationnisme*.

the RPF, this culpability must be proven by the courts in all transparency and the dead people who lie everywhere on the ground should be buried with dignity.[86]

Rome and the genocide

Did Rome have any influence on the events that unfolded in Rwanda? The Catholic Church is a highly centralised body with the pope at the top, assisted by the secretary of state and the cardinal prefect of the Congregation for the Propagation of the Faith. In practice, however, the pope and the Curia depend on the information provided to them by their envoys on the ground. On 7 April, the nuncio was Giuseppe Bertello, a man who had never given unqualified support to the Habyarimana government and who had established contact with the RPF prior to the genocide for the sake of peace. He was evacuated to Bujumbura on 11 April and returned to Rome on 25 April.[87]

Pope John Paul II made a brief statement on the Rwandan situation on 8 April, on the eve of the synod of bishops for Africa,[88] then a more significant one, from his hospital bed in Gemelli Hospital in Rome, on 27 April. On this occasion, he famously became the first head of state to use the word genocide in a public statement. Boutros Boutros-Ghali, the general secretary of the UN, only did so on 4 May. 'I invite', the pope said, 'those who hold responsibility to act generously and efficiently in order to stop this genocide. It is the hour of fraternity! It is the hour of reconciliation!'[89] During his stay in Bujumbura, Bertello may have met the Doctors Without Borders team, which, like Oxfam, was pressing its leadership in Europe to publicly denounce the genocide in Rwanda. It is very likely that it was he, on his return to Rome or by fax in the preceding days, who explained to the pope that a genocide was taking place. Yet, John Paul II spoke of a genocide in general terms without specifying who the victims were and why they were killed. He made a similar statement on 15 May. 'It is purely

---

[86] *Ibid.*, 77–8.
[87] André Guichaoua, *Les Crises politiques au Burundi et au Rwanda* (Lille: Université des Sciences et Technologies, 1995), 525, 528.
[88] *Osservatore Romano*, 10 April 1994, 1; Joseph Ngomanzungu, *Sa Sainteté le pape Jean-Paul II et le Rwanda. 25 ans de pontificat (1978–2003)* (Kigali: Pallotti Press, 2000), 121.
[89] *Osservatore Romano*, 28 April 1994, 1; Ngomanzungu, *Sa Sainteté le pape Jean-Paul II et le Rwanda*, 122.

and simply a genocide', he then declared, 'for which Catholics are also unfortunately responsible.'[90] These two speeches, however, were isolated events. Neither the pope, nor Henryk Hoser, Bertello's substitute at the nunciature in Kigali, nor the Rwandan bishops mentioned the word genocide again in a public statement until April 1995.

Critical to the understanding of Rome's position regarding the genocide is the trip Roger Etchegaray made to Rwanda in late June at the pope's request. The president of the Pontifical Commission for Justice and Peace, this French cardinal, widely appreciated for his commitment to social justice, had already visited the country in May 1993. Against the government's advice, he had paid a visit to the RPF leadership in the northern area of Rubaya, which the movement was occupying at the time.[91] His second mission to Rwanda is narrated in an autobiographical book published in 2007.[92] He arrived in Bujumbura on 21 June. From there he travelled to Butare on 23 June, Gikongoro, Kibuye and Gisenyi on 25 June, Goma in Zaire on 26 June, Byumba via Uganda on 27 June and Kabgayi on 28 June. He flew back to Rome from Bujumbura on 29 June.

The speech that Etchegaray delivered in Gisenyi and, in exactly the same terms, in Byumba – which was later published in the *Osservatore Romano* – was in line with the Rwandan bishops' statement of the previous weeks:

> It is not enough to say: I want peace (I hear that all the time among you), one also needs to make peace by paying the price for it which is very high in Rwanda. Before all this senseless war should stop. It won't stop on its own. I implore the political and military authorities to meet again, agree on a ceasefire and keep to it at all cost.[93]

Like the Rwandan bishops, the cardinal castigated the 'odious massacres' perpetrated in the country and the transformation of churches into 'slaughterhouses'. He did not mention the fact, however, that the majority of victims were Tutsi people and that they had been killed because they were Tutsi. Intentionally or not, he ignored the ethnic nature of the conflict. The word genocide, which the pope had used two months before,

---

[90] *Osservatore Romano*, 17 May 1994, 1; Ngomanzungu, *Sa Sainteté le pape Jean-Paul II et le Rwanda*, 123.

[91] On this visit, see Guy Theunis, 'Le cardinal Etchegaray au Rwanda', *Dialogue*, 168 (July 1993), 108–14 ; Roger Etchegaray, *J'ai senti battre le cœur du monde. Conversation avec Bernard Lecompte* (Paris: Fayard, 2017), 238.

[92] *Ibid.*, 241–4.

[93] *Osservatore Romano*, 3 July 1994, 1.

was absent from his discourse. The cardinal spoke as a diplomat whose mission was to bring two warring parties together and pressurise them to make peace.

In view of this, one wonders what Etchegaray saw and understood during his trip. In Butare, he met the bishop Jean-Baptiste Gahamanyi, a Tutsi whose life was at risk, and he heard Augustin Misago, the bishop of Gikongoro, requesting help for the priests whose lives were threatened. He also heard government officials delivering lenifying discourses. He discovered later, though he did not say when, that the authorities had assassinated Tutsi prisoners a few hours after his departure.[94]

In Kibuye, the prefect, Clément Kayishema, a redoubtable man later convicted of genocide by the ICTR, took charge of Etchegaray's visit. As Marie Julianne Farrington, the superior general of the sisters of St Mary of Namur, revealed later, he arranged that the cardinal would stay in a guesthouse near the lake and not in the sisters' convent, as initially planned. 'That evening,' she wrote, 'there was a tightly controlled public meeting and the Sisters had no opportunity to talk privately or freely to the Cardinal.'[95] The latter did, however, meet a group of diocesan priests led by the French priest Gabriel Maindron, who handed him a letter conveying the Hutu extremist point of view on the conflict.[96] The same happened in Gisenyi, where Phocas Nikwigize, the bishop of Ruhengeri, advised him, in language reminiscent of the Hutu extremist propaganda, not to focus on the massacres of Tutsi. 'Only considering the Tutsi', he said, 'will merely reactivate ethnic hatred and vengeance. People express compassion for the unfortunate of today and overlook the wretched of always.'[97]

---

[94] Etchegaray, *J'ai senti battre le cœur du monde*, 242; Raffin, *Rwanda: un autre regard*, 112.

[95] Marie Julianne Farrington, 'Rwanda – 100 Days – 1994: one perspective', in Carol Rittner, John K. Roth and Wendy Whitworth, *Genocide in Rwanda. Complicity of the Churches?* (St Paul, Minnesota: Paragon House, 2004), 106.

[96] See Chapter 7.

[97] Phocas Nikwigize, speech to Cardinal Etchegaray, Gisenyi, 26 June 1994, in Simon Habyarimana, *Phocas Nikwigize. Le Pacifique Pacificateur* (Lille: Éditions Sources du Nil, 2016), 141–2. On 29 June, five priests (mostly Tutsi) who had survived the genocide, also addressed a letter to Cardinal Etchegaray, but it is doubtful that he ever received it. See Jean-Baptiste Hategeka, *Raisins verts pour dents agacées* ([Modena: Golinelli Industrie Graphiche], 1994), 140–6.

Etchegaray heard the RPF's point of view on the conflict in Byumba, but he was also told – furtively, as a source indicated – that several priests had been killed by RPF soldiers two months before. On the way to Kabgayi, he was shocked to see long lines of people that the advancing army was displacing to the north so that they would not be caught in the crossfire of an impending battle.[98] His most traumatic experience was the Mass celebrated with a handful of people in the Kabgayi cathedral for the three bishops killed by RPF soldiers three weeks earlier whose bodies had been hastily buried nearby.[99] The last part of Etchegaray's trip did little to give him a positive impression of the RPF, which would complete the conquest of Rwanda soon afterwards. This may have contributed to the negative stance Rome would take towards the RPF in the following years. Did Etchegaray understand that a genocide and not only a war was taking place? It is difficult to say. Privat Rutazibwa, a former priest from North Kivu who escorted the prelate from Byumba to Kabgayi at the RPF's request, remembered him as a man who positioned himself as a mediator. He had come to Rwanda as a diplomat.[100]

The instrumentalisation of religion

The genocide against the Tutsi cannot be described as a religious war, because the conflict was not about religion. However, it had a religious dimension, as Audoin-Rouzeau suggested. The fact that fifty places of worship became massacre sites, according to a list compiled by the Commission for the Memorial of the Genocide and the Massacres in Rwanda (CMGM) in 1996,[101] and that an estimated 12 per cent of all victims died inside a church building speaks for itself. The testimonies of the witnesses and the transcripts of the messages broadcast on radio show that the use of religious symbols, far from being anecdotal, was systematic. The organisers and the executants of the genocide claimed again and again that God was on their side and that he had abandoned the Tutsi. Also mobilised were Jesus, the Virgin Mary and the Bible. As noted by Malachie Munyaneza,

---

[98] Etchegaray, *J'ai senti battre le cœur du monde*, 244.
[99] *Ibid.*, 244.
[100] Privat Rutazibwa, interview conducted on 8 December 2017 in Kigali.
[101] CNLG, Archives of the CMGM in Rwanda: 'Amaguye abantu benshi mu itsembabokwo n'itsembatsemba hakwiye kuba urwibibutso. I. Amasengero n'ibigo by'abihaye Imana uko hitwa', n.d. [February 1996].

the interim government called itself *Leta y'Abatabazi* [Government of the Saviours] in reference to Jesus *Umutabazi* [the Saviour].[102]

In May 1994, Valérie Bemeriki, a particularly violent radio presenter on RTLM, put across the religious message of the *génocidaires* in the following terms:

> If somebody takes arms and shoots you, you will not say: I shall pray, that's it. Well, God helps the one who helps himself. It means that each time we shall ask for it, each time we shall stand up, God will always be with us, Jesus will be behind us and, as a result, we shall lead and win the war.[103]

According to her, the Virgin Mary also took part in the fight against the Tutsi:

> In fact, the Virgin Mary is with us and we are with her. She knows that we are innocent victims. Because she knows that we are innocent victims, she shall encourage us.[104]

In the diary he kept during the genocide, Gabriel Maindron, a French priest in Congo-Nil near Kibuye, told the story of a killer who was sporting a rosary around his neck. A sister asked him: 'Why do you carry this rosary?' He responded: 'The Virgin Mary helps me to find the hidden enemies.'[105] According to Valérie Bemeriki, Valentine Nyiramukiza, one of the girls who saw the Virgin Mary appearing in Kibeho in the 1980s, had asked Our Lady whether God's children would continue the fight. 'The Virgin in person', Bemeriki declared, 'did not hesitate to respond, "Only the vanquished will stop fighting."'[106]

The Bible was also instrumentalised. In 1990, the Hutu extremist newspaper *Kangura* published 'ten commandments' modelled on the ten commandments entrusted by God to Moses on Mount Sinai, which reproduced the stereotypes of the power-hungry and deceitful Tutsi and incited the

---

[102] Malachie Munyaneza, 'Violence as institution, an African religious experience: the case of Rwanda', *Contagion: Journal of Violence, Mimesis, and Culture*, 8 (2001), 57.

[103] Chrétien (ed.), *Les médias du génocide*, 330.

[104] Amélie Faucheux, 'Massacrer dans l'intimité. La question de la rupture des liens sociaux et familiaux dans le cas du génocide des Tutsi du Rwanda de 1994', unpublished PhD thesis, Paris, École pratique des hautes études, 2019, 417.

[105] Gabriel Maindron, 'Rwanda: l'horreur', *Dialogue*, 177 (August–September 1994), 54.

[106] Chrétien (ed.), *Les médias du génocide*, 330.

Hutu to distrust them at all times.[107] According to a witness at the ICTR, in May 1994 Jean-Baptiste Ruzindaza, the president of the Court of First Instance in Butare, held the Bible and said that the people who would fight the enemy with success would be rewarded by God. On another occasion, he urged the Hutu people to leave behind no traces, quoting Jesus' words that all things secrets would be brought into the open (Luke 8:17).[108] Justin Mugenzi, the minister of trade and industry in the interim government, reminded those who did not fight the RPF of Isaiah's warning that the people who neglected their duties would face misfortune.[109] Donat, a convicted *génocidaire* interviewed by Amélie Faucheux, believed that killing was a normal thing. Even Longinus, the Roman soldier who had pierced Jesus' heart, he argued, had been allowed to do so.[110]

Of all the manipulations of the Bible, the most shocking is the one Emmanuel Mwezi, a genocide survivor from Muhazi in north-east Rwanda, attributed to a Presbyterian pastor of the area in an interview:

> There was a pastor that one could see on the shore [of Muhazi Lake], a churchman. I heard him saying when we were hiding, that he had read the Old Testament and the New Testament and that he had not found in the holy pages that killing a Tutsi was a sin. He explained that only the Book counted and that, in it, it was always question of 'humans'. Who had written in the Bible that Tutsi were humans? The term Tutsi did not appear in it. Therefore, no wrong had been committed. The Bible did not mention the word Hutu either, but the absence of the word Tutsi was enough, since the Hutu were humans.[111]

An important theme in the religious discourse of the *génocidaires* was that God had abandoned the Tutsi. In Ndera, an Interahamwe told César Murangira: 'You, the Tutsi, you claim to know the Lord? He abandoned you, the Lord!'[112] In Mugonero, one of the survivors testified that Elizaphan Ntakirutimana, the chief pastor, had declared to his Tutsi colleagues before

---

[107] *Kangura*, 6 (December 1990), 6–8, quoted in Chrétien (ed.), *Les medias du génocide*, 141–2.

[108] Spyridon Loumakis, 'Genocide and religion in the 1990s', in André Gagné, Spyridon Loumakis and Calogero Miceli (ed.), *The Global Impact of Religious Violence* (Eugene, Oregon: Wipf & Stock, 2016), 60.

[109] *Ibid.*, 61.

[110] Faucheux, 'Massacrer dans l'intimité', 990.

[111] *Ibid.*, 679.

[112] Murangira, *Un sachet d'hosties pour cinq*, 49.

they were killed: 'You must be eliminated. God no longer wants you.'[113] In an interview, Damas Gisimba, the director of an orphanage in Kigali, described an extraordinary scene of sacrilege and murder in the church of St André College in Nyamirambo. The killers, he explained, wanted to convince themselves that God was on their side and that the Tutsi had nobody to turn to:

> At St André College, they killed more than 40,000 people who had taken refuge there. Even in the church because the killers came to kill in the sanctuary. I saw it. Some dressed as priests and used the chalices of the parish to put beer in them and drink it. Even in the stoups. That was to say, they claimed, that God himself accepted what they were doing by killing the Tutsi. When killing them, they would say: 'Even God, abandoned you.' I also heard them say: 'You look like Jesus, with your nose [...] But Jesus saw that you are traitors, and then he gave us the right to kill you.'[114]

In the same manner, Emmanuel Murangira, a genocide survivor from Nyarusiza near Gikongoro, recounted that the burgomaster and the councillors of Nyamagabe came to tell the crowd: 'Go and destroy the houses of the Tutsi! Kill them! God has abandoned them.' During the first attacks on 11 April 1994, the Hutu killers blew their whistles and chanted: 'The God of Tutsi is no longer around', and 'The God of the Hutu is the only one that remains.'[115] Jean-Marie Twambazemungu, a lay leader of the Emmanuel Community in Kigali, wrote that on the first day of the genocide an Interahamwe leader, finding a crucifix in his house, remained silent for a moment and then said: 'You say that you are not an accomplice and you pray to Jesus who is a Tutsi!'[116]

This suggests that, in the mind of the *génocidaires*, the inherent division between Hutu and Tutsi inherited from the Hamitic theory had an equivalent in heaven. There were also two Gods, face to face: the God of the Tutsi, brought to Rwanda by the missionaries, and the God of the Hutu, who replaced his rival during the Rwandan Social Revolution and was now claiming final victory over him. Likewise, they were two Jesus': a Tutsi one, characterised by his beauty, and a Hutu one, who now supplanted his Tutsi counterpart.

---

[113] Gourevitch, *We Wish to Inform You*, 28.
[114] Faucheux, 'Massacrer dans l'intimité', 1186.
[115] Samuel Totten and Ubaldo Rifiki (ed.), *We Cannot Forget: Interviews with Survivors of the 1994 Genocide in Rwanda* (New Brunswick, NJ: Rutgers University Press, 2011), 85.
[116] Yvonne-Solange Kagoyire *et al.*, *Rescapés de Kigali*, 75.

This would explain why, throughout Rwanda, the Interahamwe and the mobs following them engaged in acts of iconoclasm. Numerous cases of attacks on statues have been reported. A beautiful Christ was a Tutsi Christ and therefore had to disappear, just like his human followers. In the Centre Saint-Paul in Kigali, the Interahamwe tried to break the neck of a wooden Christ with their machetes. He was, they said, 'the God of the Tutsi'.[117] The same happened in Nyamasheke near Cyangugu, where they broke the leg of Christ in one of the statues.[118] The Virgin Mary was also accused of being Tutsi in Kibeho, where the Interahamwe cut off her hands.[119] In Nyange, they smashed her hands and nose, saying: 'See how ugly you will become now and even your God will no longer be your God!'[120] The Centre Christus in Kigali now displays a wooden Christ with the arms and nose cut off, which was found in Gisenyi after the genocide.

The spirituality of the survivors

The instrumentalisation of religion in the genocide alongside the silence and, in some cases, complicity of the priests and pastors tested the faith of the survivors to the extreme. Several of them subsequently changed their church affiliation or ceased all religious practice, like Albert Nsengimana, a child survivor from the Kabarondo district in the Kibungo prefecture who, once the genocide was over, felt that 'he could no longer enter any place of worship'.[121] For some, on the other hand, the trials of the genocide triggered a spiritual journey of great depth. Here are two examples.

Yolande Mukagasana, author, in 1997, of one of the first genocide survivor testimonies, described her revolt against the Christian religion when a friend suggested that she should pray. 'Praying?' she said to herself, 'I am fed up with the Christian religion. I have lost my husband and I do not know where my children are. And they ask me to pray!'[122] Later on, she had a 'moment of fervour' for Emmanuelle, a Christian woman who had helped her, but it was an 'atheistic fervour'. 'I pray to the goddess Fate, born straight away from my imagination, that she protects the

---

[117] Yolande Mukagasana, *La mort ne veut pas de moi* (Paris: Fixot, 1997), 239.
[118] Ndorimana, *Rwanda: idéologie, méthode et négationnisme*, 41.
[119] Audoin-Rouzeau, *L'initiation*, 114.
[120] Faucheux, 'Massacrer dans l'intimité', 1003.
[121] Albert Nsengimana, *Ma mère m'a tué. Survivre au génocide des Tutsi au Rwanda* (Paris: Hugo Doc, 2019), 78.
[122] Mukagasana, *La mort ne veut pas de moi*, 121.

one who risked her life to save me. [...] Christ? He was unable to save my husband Joseph. And where did he hide my children?'[123] After a long run, she reached the parish in Nyamirambo ministered to by two White Fathers, Henri Blanchard and Otto Mayer. She took part in a Mass that she described as sad and declined to go for communion. Yet, her mood was changing. 'I feel one instant that I am becoming a Christian again. Two weeks of manhunt made me become pagan but of a paganism full of admiration for the image of the man who gave himself for the salvation of his fellow human beings.' Then she addressed herself to one of the priests: 'Thank you, Father. You just brought me faith.'[124]

The Presbyterian pastor Malachie Munyaneza was at risk, because before the genocide he had denounced on Christian grounds, at public meetings and on radio, the climate of violence that had engulfed the country. He lost several family members and a few good friends, though, fortunately, no members of his immediate family. The most severe attack happened near his house in Gikondo on 11 April 1994. In May, he managed to reach his birthplace near Gitarama, where he found his children. In an interview, he described the prayer he addressed to God during this period. He acutely felt the loss of his friends Alphonse and Béatrice and his neighbour Olivier as well as his family, and found it unbearable. All were slaughtered in front of him in Gikondo.

> I was wondering why I was still alive. On 11 April, I had made this prayer: 'Lord, will you do a miracle for me? I see that you are not saving me.' Later on, seeing that He was not responding, I made a second prayer: 'Shall I become God for one minute? I would like to overturn the earth and make it like the moon.' But He still did not respond. Eventually, I made a third prayer: 'Lord, will you allow me to go where I was before I was born?' I was looking for protection. I wanted to leave this life. I wanted to return to where I was before I was born. Ephesians, chapter 1, verse 3: 'Before the creation of the world...' I then heard a response. I immersed myself in the thought of the God of the origins, in the mystery of having been with Him before the creation of the world but also of having been on earth through His will. If I return there, nobody will be able to kill me. I shall be in God.'[125]

---

[123] *Ibid.*, 159.
[124] *Ibid.*, 160.
[125] Malachie Munyaneza, interview conducted on 30 March 2019 in Wolverhampton.

Conclusion

The genocide was an act of collective madness. It is true that the RPF attack represented a threat to the Habyarimana regime. It is also true that the RPF waged a brutal war and killed many people, including priests and bishops, who resisted them or were suspected of being hostile to them. This, however, in no way justified the plan, executed with the support of state officials, to exterminate all Tutsi people for the simple reason that they were Tutsi.

The churches paid a heavy price for the genocide. The Catholic, Presbyterian and Adventist churches, probably the other churches as well, lost about a quarter of their workforce, not to mention the desecration of churches and the destruction of property. Individual Christians, and among them a certain number of priests, pastors, brothers and sisters, took risks to save the lives of their Tutsi neighbours and died as a result.

Some clerical voices have denounced the massacres. The Catholic and Protestant church leaders made several statements to that effect, and so did Cardinal Etchegaray, the pope's envoy. None of these church leaders, however, publicly contradicted the specious argument, broadcast day after day on radio and repeated, in a euphemistic language that everybody understood, that in order to win the war the people who loved their country had to eliminate the 'accomplices': in other words, their Tutsi neighbours and, in some cases, the members of their own family. Apart from Thaddée Ntihinyurwa, the Catholic bishop of Cyangugu, who only spoke in the privacy of an officials' meeting, nobody declared that the people suspected of being 'accomplices' of the RPF should be tried instead of being summarily executed. The church leaders never publicly refuted the fallacy that their Tutsi priests and pastors were secret agents of the RPF and deserved to die for that reason. As two priests from the diocese of Kabgayi told a French journalist in early May 1994, 'the bishops made a few speeches, but they had no prophetic commitment. If they had spoken out, the massacres might have stopped.'[126]

This silence has been, and still is today, resented by the genocide survivors. A contributing problem is the fact that the majority of missionaries from Europe and North America left Rwanda in the days that followed the first massacres. Only a small number of them remained, including eight White Fathers from Belgium, France, Canada and Germany, one Franciscan from Bosnia, one Pallotine from Poland, one Barnabite from

---

[126] Jean Chatain, 'Deux prêtres témoignent sur les atrocités au Rwanda', L'Humanité, 3 May 1994.

Italy, one Holy Cross Missionary from Canada, five diocesan priests from Belgium and France incardinated in the diocese of Nyundo, a diocesan priest from Belgium incardinated in the diocese of Kabgayi and three Dominican sisters from Belgium. The presence of a larger number of missionaries might have reduced the intensity of the genocide.

Commentators such as Gabriel Maindron, to whom we shall return in Chapter 8, Luc De Hovre (a Belgian bishop who visited Rwanda in October 1994)[127] and the charismatic leader Daniel-Ange argued that the genocide against the Tutsi was inexplicable and that it must have been the work of the devil.[128] Others echoed the Hutu extremist propagandists' argument that the perpetrators were young 'rascals', angry at the death of their president. These explanations obscure the main cause of the genocide, which was ideological. Without the stereotype, born out of the Hamitic theory, of the arrogant, deceitful and power-hungry Tutsi, the argument that the survival of the 'Hutu majority' was under threat and the notion that one should 'understand' the anger of the Hutu people, there might have been political violence, as in other parts of Africa, but not a genocide. The debate on the churches' responsibility in the catastrophe must integrate this dimension, since, intentionally or not, many bishops, priests and pastors have contributed to the stock of ideas that made the genocide possible.

---

[127] 'Visite de Mgr Luk [Luc] de Hovre à l'Eglise du Rwanda', 24 October 1994 (Archives *Dialogue*, Brussels).
[128] Maindron, 'Rwanda: l'horreur', 52; Daniel-Ange, *Rwanda. Au fond de l'enfer, le ciel ouvert*.

CHAPTER 4

The Catholic Church in the aftermath of the genocide

In July 1994 and subsequent months, Rwanda showed a landscape of devastation. The infrastructure was destroyed, mutilated bodies were lying in the open, genocide survivors were wandering around in search of relatives and thousands of orphans were in need of care. Two million people had fled to Tanzania and Zaire and four hundred thousand 'old refugees' from Uganda and Burundi had returned, occupying the houses abandoned by those who had left even temporarily. To add to the confusion, the former regime's army, defeated but not disarmed, still remained a threat in nearby Kivu. Rumours of counter-attacks abounded. From the beginning of 1995, the prefectures of Gisenyi, Kibuye and Cyangugu increasingly became the scene of raids and infiltration. All over the country, lone Interahamwe militiamen continued to kill Tutsi people.

The biggest problem was the absence of a judicial system able to prosecute the genocide perpetrators according to the rule of law. There were only a handful of judges and procurators and they had no means at their disposal. The once-disciplined RPF army, now filled with angry survivors and opportunists, either proceeded to extra-judiciary executions or sent suspects to jail on the basis of unverified denunciations. In this atmosphere of rage, greed and paranoia, every Hutu was a suspect, even those who had taken risks to rescue Tutsi people during the genocide. As Jean-Paul Kimonyo pointed out, 'the experience of the massive participation [of the local population] in the genocide produced among the survivors the conviction that the Hutu were collectively guilty'.[1]

This chaotic situation could be interpreted in two manners. It could be regarded as proof that the new regime was as culpable of human rights abuse and as ethnically biased as its predecessor, or it could be seen, conversely,

---

[1] Jean-Paul Kimonyo, *Rwanda demain! Une longue marche vers la transfomation* (Paris: Karthala, 2017), 132.

as the result of the trauma generated by the genocide. Collective trauma, also called cultural trauma, occurs, according to Jeffrey Alexander, when 'members of a collectivity feel they have been subjected to a horrendous event that leaves indelible marks upon their group consciousness, marking their memories forever and changing their future identity in fundamental and irrevocable ways'.[2] Collective trauma alters the way people respond to crisis. One can argue that the trauma of the genocide produced severe stress among the victims and the people associated with them and generated new forms of violence which, through a vicious cycle, increased the chaos, preventing the rest of the population from fully accepting the reality of the genocide. This is an important consideration for this study, since after 1994 many church people, overly preoccupied by the situation of the refugees in Tanzania and Zaire, tended to minimise the significance of the genocide in Rwandan history and, as a result, resisted its memorialisation.

The fact that, in the areas controlled by the RPF during the genocide and in the rest of Rwanda afterwards, innocents have been thrown to jail, people have disappeared and massacres of civilians have been perpetrated by the army cannot be denied. What is in dispute is the scale and the intention of these human rights abuses. Some of them were grossly exaggerated or even fabricated by propagandists of the old regime in the refugee camps from Tanzania and Zaire. We do not know to what extent the higher echelons of command in the army were able to control its subordinates on the ground; ultimately, it is not clear who bears the responsibility of these abuses.

The first allegations of RFP crimes appear in reports from Doctors Without Borders and Human Rights Watch from May 1994.[3] In the same month, on his return from a journey in the Byumba and Kibungo prefectures, Jan de Bekker, a Dutch White Father, declared to his confrères that the RPF 'was busy eliminating its enemies in a more discreet manner than the militia of the Hutu extremists'.[4] Such reports increased in number in the second half of 1994 and in subsequent years; in particular, there have been allegations of massacres of civilians in the Gitarama and Butare areas.

---

[2] Jeffrey Alexander, *Trauma: A Social Theory* (Cambridge, UK/Malden, MA: Polity Press, 2012), 6.

[3] Jean-Hervé Bradol et Marc Le Pape, *Génocide et crimes de masse. L'expérience rwandaise de MSF 1982–1997* (Paris: CNRS Éditions, 2017), 70–3; Alison Des Forges, *Leave None to Tell the Story: Genocide in Rwanda* (New York: Human Rights Watch, 1999), 705.

[4] Jan de Bekker, 'Aide humanitaire au Rwanda', *Petit Écho des Missionnaires d'Afrique*, 854 (August 1994), 371.

It is interesting to note, however, that the first authors who raised the alarm were careful not to blame the leadership of the RPF. In September 1994 Christophe Munzihirwa, the archbishop of Bukavu, while regretting that some of the Rwandan refugees who had chosen to return were summarily executed, acknowledged that the authorities in Kigali did not deny these exactions but attributed them to the lack of administrative and judiciary structures.[5] The political scientist Filip Reyntjens, who visited Rwanda between 15 and 22 October 1994, pointed out that it was not possible to establish whether the murders of civilians were systematic and at which level they were coordinated by order of the RPF army.[6] In December 1994 Vénuste Linguyeneza, who by then was teaching at Nyakibanda Major Seminary, denounced the practice of accusing people of genocide complicity without proof, but he added that it would be unfair to blame the authorities for it.[7]

A weakened and divided church

When the genocide violence came to an end in July 1994, the Catholic Church was – like the other churches – in a state of extreme confusion and disorder. About a hundred diocesan priests and a similar number of religious priests, brothers and sisters had been killed. Most missionaries had returned home. The archbishop of Kigali and the bishops of Kabgayi and Byumba had been assassinated. The bishop of Ruhengeri had fled to Zaire. The bishops of Nyundo, Butare and Kibungo had been under threat and were recovering from trauma. Those of Cyangugu and Gikongoro were starting to face, rightly or wrongly, the questions of some survivors about their attitude during the genocide. Numerous parishes were without priests and a considerable number of church buildings had been ransacked or destroyed.

Despite these challenges, the church leadership rapidly reconstituted itself, formally at least. The episcopal conference had its first post-genocide meeting on 5 September 1994 in Butare, with bishops present from Burundi

---

[5] Joseph Ngomanzungu, *L'Église et la crise rwandaise de 1990 à 1994. Essai de chronologie* (Kigali: Pallotti Press, 2001), 142. Later on, Archbishop Munzihirwa became very critical of the RPF.
[6] Filip Reyntjens, 'Sujets d'inquiétude au Rwanda en octobre 1994', *Dialogue*, 179 (November–December 1994), 7.
[7] Vénuste Linguyeneza, 'Justice et réconciliation au Rwanda', *Urunana. Revue des Grands Séminaristes*, 81 (February 1995), 23.

and Zaire.[8] In November, Rome appointed five apostolic administrators: three to replace the deceased bishops, one to replace Augustin Misago, the bishop of Gikongoro, who had gone overseas for medical treatment, and one to replace Phocas Nikwigize, who had taken refuge in Goma. Collectively or individually, the bishops resumed the practice of issuing pastoral letters.

On 6 December 1994, Thaddée Ntihinyurwa, the vice-president of the Rwandan episcopal conference, presented to his colleagues of the Association of Episcopal Conferences of Central Africa (ACEAC) a sombre description of his church. Of the 128 parishes functioning before the genocide, he wrote, about 50 were about to restart. Only two diocesan houses – Cyangugu and Gikongoro – were intact. Of the 400 diocesan priests incardinated in Rwanda, 103 had died, 114 were still in the country, 80 had taken refuge in Zaire and the rest were in Europe to study or exercise the ministry. About one-third of the 150 missionaries active before the genocide had come back to Rwanda, and 7 of them had died. About 150 seminarians had fled to Zaire, leaving only 59 in Rwanda.[9]

The biggest challenge was the division of the church, a problem to which we shall return. The priests, religious people and seminarians living in refugee camps in Zaire, or many of them, at least, were separated not only geographically from the church in Rwanda but also ideologically. They were incapable or unwilling to distance themselves from the Hutu extremist propaganda, which continued to circulate in the camps. Both sides – the church inside Rwanda and the one outside – claimed legitimacy. There were few points of communication between the two.

Another cause of tension was the arrest of priests and religious sisters accused of genocide complicity. The first two suspects, priests Denis Sekamana and Thaddée Rusingizandekwe, were arrested in October 1994, followed in November of the same year by two Franciscan sisters, Bénédicte Mukanyangezi and Bernadette Mukarusine.[10] Many would follow. Also traumatic were the murders, allegedly at the hands of RPF soldiers, of Claude Simard de Roberval, a Canadian priest of the

---

[8] Ngomanzungu, *L'Église et la crise rwandaise*, 140–1.

[9] Thaddée Ntihinyurwa, 'Brève présentation de la situation de l'Église catholique au Rwanda avant et après le drame rwandais. Á l'occasion de l'Assemblée plénière de l'ACEAC (Kinshasa, 9–10/12/1994)', Kigali, 6 December 1994 (Archives *Dialogue*, Brussels).

[10] Joseph Ngomanzungu, *La souffrance de l'Église à travers son personnel: massacres, emprisonnements et expulsions d'ouvriers apostoliques (1990–2002)* (Kigali: Pallotti Press, 2002), 34–40, 49.

Order of Sainte-Croix, on 18 October 1994 in Ruyenzi near Butare; Pio Ntahobali, a Rwandan diocesan priest, on 1 October 1995 in Kamonyi near Gitarama; and Guy Pinard, a Canadian White Father, on 2 February 1997, in Kampanga near Ruhengeri.[11]

The episcopal statements

The episcopal statements issued in the aftermath of the genocide suffered from the same ambiguity as those from the preceding periods. The bishops responded with outrage to the accusations of complicity or silence levelled against the Catholic Church by the genocide survivors and the government. Unlike a certain number of priests and lay people, they did not accept any form of responsibility for the disaster. Rather, they denounced, more and more vocally, the revenge killings committed by soldiers and survivors, the detentions without trial of genocide suspects and the illegal occupation of properties belonging to people having fled the country. This refusal to confront the past lasted until the time of the preparation of the extraordinary synod on ethnocentrism in 1998.[12]

It was not until 30 March 1995 that the bishops employed the term 'genocide' – coupled, as was commonly done at the time, with the term 'massacres' – for the first time. The word appeared, almost incidentally, at the end of the document:

> We condemn and disapprove of the acts of massacres and genocide (*les actes de massacres et de génocide*) which marked the last year. We ask all those who love peace to refuse for themselves and combat any idea of restarting such a tragedy.[13]

---

[11] *Ibid.*, 20–1; André Sibomana, *Gardons l'espoir pour le Rwanda. Entretiens avec Laure Guibert et Hervé Deguine*, 2nd edn (Paris: L'Harmattan, 2008), 166–7.

[12] The only author who covered, though briefly, this period of the history of the Catholic Church in Rwanda is Paul Rutayisire. See his essay, 'Église catholique dans la société rwandaise: un regard interrogateur', in Tharcisse Gatwa and Laurent Rutinduka (ed.), *Histoire du christianisme au Rwanda des origines à nos jours* (Yaoundé: Éditions CLÉ, 2014), 299–304.

[13] 'Message des évêques catholiques du Rwanda à l'occasion du jour anniversaire en mémoire des victimes de la guerre et des massacres', Kigali, 30 March 1995. Text in *African News Bulletin – Bulletin d'Information Africaine*, Brussels, Missionaries of Africa, 7 April 1995.

This was their fourth statement since the end of the genocide. The first, very short, was issued on 5 September 1994, when the bishops met as a group in Butare and had a brief encounter with Pie Mugabo, a representative of the RPF government.[14] The second, more substantial, was the pastoral letter *'Aime ton frère'* [Love your brother], published for Christmas on 21 December 1994.[15] The document mentioned the people 'ignominiously massacred' because of 'their ethnic group, their region or their political ideas' and the 'bad spirit of ethnic and regional segregation' but failed to acknowledge the genocide as such. The third was a document entitled 'Pastoral priorities of the after-war period' and dated 13 January 1995, which promoted reconciliation and justice and called for the return of the refugees.[16] During the same period, the bishops issued a document entitled 'Concerns of the members of the Conference of Catholic Bishops from Rwanda addressed to the Rwandan authorities' which denounced, quite vigorously, the insecurity in the country, the arrests based on simple denunciation and the disappearances of political opponents.[17]

The omission of any mention of the genocide was intentional. To understand why, let us consider the 'Brief presentation of the situation of the Catholic Church in Rwanda before and after the Rwandan tragedy' that Thaddée Ntihinyurwa wrote on 6 December 1994 in his capacity as vice-president of the Bishops' Conference of Rwanda, in preparation for the ACEAC meeting. This document spoke, in a language reminiscent of the episcopal statements issued during the genocide, of the 'two power-hungry warring parties (RPF and Rwandan armed forces)' and declared that the accusation that the Catholic Church was subservient to the old regime and that it did not sufficiently protect the Tutsi refugees was 'unjustified'.[18] Meanwhile, the declaration signed by the thirty participating bishops from

---

[14] Ngomanzungu, *L'Église et la crise rwandaise*, 140.

[15] 'Aime ton prochain', 21 December 1994, in *La Documentation catholique*, 2113 (2 April 1995), 336–40. Extracts in Ngomanzungu, *L'Église et la crise rwandaise*, 151–2.

[16] 'Priorités pastorales pour la période de l'après-guerre', 13 January 1995, in *La Documentation catholique*, 2113 (2 April 1995), 340–3. Extracts in Joseph Ngomanzungu, 'Messages et lettres pastorales des Évêques Catholiques pendant la période 1994–2004', *Urunana. Revue des Grands Séminaristes*, 108 (January 2004), 7–8.

[17] 'Préoccupations des Membres de la Conférence des Évêques Catholiques du Rwanda adressées aux autorités rwandaises', 12 January 1995. Summary in Ngomanzungu, 'Messages et lettres pastorales', 7.

[18] Thaddée Ntihinyurwa, 'Brève présentation de la situation de l'Église

Zaire, Rwanda and Burundi, including the two representatives from the Bishops' Conference of Rwanda, did mention the term 'genocide' in a paragraph denouncing 'ethnic integralism' (*intégrisme ethnique*), the 'Manichean heresy of the twentieth century'. The lack of leadership, the document read, 'led, in our region in general [Central Africa] and in Rwanda and Burundi in particular, to massacres of population and acts of genocide (*actes génocidaires*) aiming at the physical destruction of human lives on the basis of ethnic and political identity'.[19]

If the joint document spoke of a genocide, why did the Rwandan bishops refuse to use the term in their presentation? A document from the same period shows that this omission was deliberate. In a letter to a group of Catholics from Butare in January 1995, the White Father Wolfgang Schöneke, secretary of the Association of Member Episcopal Conferences in Eastern Africa (AMECEA), explained why the word genocide had been omitted in the message that the Eastern African bishops representing AMECEA had addressed to the Rwandan government on 21 November 1994 after a visit to the country. 'If the bishops did not use this word,' he wrote, 'that was out of respect for their host bishops who did not use the word either in their descriptions of the tragic events nor in their last message to the Rwandan government. [...] They wanted to respect the sensitivities of their brother bishops and not judge or interpret the events.'[20] According to Schöneke, the Eastern African bishops would have lacked 'respect' for their Rwandan colleagues if they had spoken of a genocide. This statement is rather perplexing. What would the Rwandan bishops have lost by hearing that a genocide had taken place in their country? Were they afraid of alienating the refugees in Tanzania and Zaire, who refused, in many instances, to recognise the genocide as genocide and instead blamed the RPF for their misfortune?

The harshest denunciation on the part of the Catholic hierarchy of the abuses allegedly committed by the government came from Henryk Hoser,

---

catholique au Rwanda avant et après le drame rwandais', 6 December 1994 (Archives *Dialogue*, Brussels).

[19] Association des Conférences Épiscopales de l'Afrique Centrale, 'Message des Évêques au Peuple de Dieu qui est au Burundi, au Rwanda et au Zaïre', Kinshasa, 10 December 1994 (Archives *Dialogue*, Brussels).

[20] Wolfgang Schöneke to a member of the CRAP, 20 January 1995, quoted in 'Rwanda: Préoccupations sur l'attitude de l'Église catholique', in Privat Rutazibwa, *Contre l'ethnisme* (Kigali: Éditions du CRID, 2017), 161.

the apostolic visitor of Alphonse Marie Nkubito, the minister of justice, on 9 January 1995.'[21] We shall return to this episode in Chapter 7.

Grief and penance

Being reluctant to acknowledge the existence of a genocide does not mean denying the reality of the massacres. In the months following the installation of the new government, one of the main tasks of the priests and bishops who had remained in the country was to bury the dead. They also had to deal, pastorally and liturgically, with the presence among the faithful of a considerable number of murderers. They had to rethink the ways in which they ran the church with a view to preventing the errors of the past. As we shall see, three dioceses, those of Butare, Kigali and Nyundo, took interesting initiatives in this respect.

In all dioceses, discussion took place on whether or not, in view of the massive number of murders and sacrileges committed by members of the Christian communities, the celebration of sacraments should be suspended. Thaddée Ntihinyurwa, the bishop of Cyangugu, raised the matter in his pastoral letter of 23 September 1994, the first to be issued after the genocide. He announced that a six-week programme of reconciliation would be organised in the diocese and that no Eucharist would be celebrated on Sunday, 2 October, the first day of the programme. He also declared that looters would have to give back the goods they had stolen before being admitted to the Holy Communion.[22] In its second bulletin, dated 26 September, the Commission for the Revival of Pastoral Activities of Butare recommended that drums and dances be banned, that the weekday Masses be replaced by Bible sharing on the recent events and that the communities draw up a 'list of our dead', erect a monument and choose a date of commemoration.[23] On 2 November, André Sibomana, the newly appointed apostolic administrator of the diocese of Kabgayi, announced that a structured programme of conversion would be proposed to the faithful and that the celebration of baptism, first communion, confirmation and marriage should be suspended until the completion of the programme. Sibomana also decreed that no Mass should be celebrated in the churches

---

[21] Henryk Hoser and Pierre Nguyên Van Tôt to Alphonse Marie Nkubito, 9 January 1995 (Archives *Dialogue*, Brussels).
[22] Ngomanzungu, *L'Église et la crise rwandaise*, 143.
[23] *Fécondité de la crise rwandaise. Jalons pour une nouvelle évangélisation au Rwanda. Recueil de douze documents publiés par la Commission de Relance des Activités Pastorales* (Butare: Diocèse catholique de Butare, 1996), 16–17.

where people had been killed until a ceremony of liturgical rehabilitation had taken place.[24]

Only one diocese, that of Nyundo, decided to suspend the celebration of masses altogether and replace them with penitential services.[25] In the diocese of Butare, the Commission felt that this would be going too far:

> As to the sanctions to take, for example the suspension of Eucharistic celebrations, the Commission finds the measure excessive. First, this measure seems artificial because it comes without warning, from outside and indiscriminately on everybody. Further, one cannot do the Church without the Eucharist. It is the moment, if there is one, to celebrate the death of the innocent and proclaim his resurrection in order to fortify the weakening hope and straighten the bending knees.[26]

André Sibomana, the administrator of the Kabgayi diocese, also found that it would be unfair to deprive meritorious Christians from the sacraments:

> Contrary to the recommendation of some Christians who spoke in favour of systematically interrupting the administration of all sacraments including the Eucharist, we cannot ignore that those who behaved in a really Christian way found their strength in the sacraments. It was in this way that God gave them the strength to resist evil. As a result we cannot decide to systematically interrupt the administration of sacraments for everybody.[27]

At a meeting held on 30 January 1995, the pastoral commission of the archdiocese of Kigali echoed this sentiment. If the celebration of sacraments could be delayed on some occasions, they declared, it was for pastoral and pedagogical reasons 'and not in order to punish'. The victims find strength in the sacrament. Given the shortage of priests, however, the end of mourning ceremonies should be prepared by lay people and not include Mass.[28]

---

[24] 'Convertissez vous et croyez à la bonne nouvelle. Message de l'abbé administrateur diocésain adressé à tous les chrétiens du diocèse de Kabgayi', Kabgayi, 2 November 1994 (Archives *Dialogue*, Brussels). On this programme of conversion and penance, see Corine Lesnes, 'L'Église rwandaise fait ses comptes et reprend vie', *Le Monde*, 21 January 1995; André Sibomana, *Gardons l'espoir pour le Rwanda*, 167–9.

[25] Fabien Rwakareke, interview conducted on 28 May 2018 in Nyundo.

[26] *Fécondité de la crise rwandaise*, 13 (Bulletin 1, 21 September 1994).

[27] 'Convertissez-vous et croyez à la bonne nouvelle', 8.

[28] Minutes of the first meeting of the Pastoral Commission of the Archdiocese of Kigali, 30 January 1995 (Archives *Dialogue*, Brussels).

Loyal appraisal

Particularly significant was the work of the Commission pour la relance de l'activité pastorale (Commission for the Revival of Pastoral Activities - CRAP) which Jean-Baptiste Gahamanyi instituted in the diocese of Butare on 17 August 1994, soon after his return from Bukavu, where he had taken refuge at the end of the genocide.[29] Its aim was to re-establish the church in the diocese, which was one of the most affected by the genocide and also one where revenge killings and other forms of injustice were taking place at the time. The Commission was placed under the responsibility of Félicien Mubiligi, the vicar general. It also included Laurien Ntezimana, a lay theologian trained at the University of Louvain in the 1980s, and Modeste Mungwarareba, a Tutsi priest who had narrowly escaped death during the 1963 anti-Tutsi violence, spent several months in jail without trial in 1990–1 and been targeted by the Hutu extremist media during the genocide.

Heir to the Service d'Animation Théologique (Service of Theological Training) or SAT, a lay education programme established before the genocide, the Commission adopted the position, from the beginning, that given the trauma caused by the genocide, it would not make sense to think in terms of 'business as usual'. A new way of being a church had to be invented, one that was less reliant on clergy, big parishes and church-based institutions. Lay educators should receive leadership training and be deployed in the various sectors of the church. Priests should work closely with them.

While he was not actively involved in the project, Gahamanyi gave it his full support. Within a year, 22 men and 16 women had been trained as lay educators and ministered to their local communities under the Commission's supervision.[30] The parish priests, who resented the credit given to the lay educators and criticised the lack of preparation in the liturgies that some of them were leading, were less enthusiastic. The provocative tone of the Commission's bulletins annoyed more than a few.

In 1997, Mungwarareba was appointed general secretary of the Bishops' Conference in Kigali and a new bishop, less supportive of the Commission, was installed in Butare. The project lost some of its initial coherence and eventually ceased to exist. To this day, Ntezimana regularly writes articles in church journals and magazines on theological, pastoral and ethical matters; until his untimely death in 1999, Mungwarareba did the same.

---

[29] Ngomanzungu, *L'Église et la crise rwandaise*, 138.

[30] *Fécondité de la crise rwandaise*, 72 (Bulletin 10, 25 December 1995).

The Commission produced twelve well-disseminated bulletins between September 1994 and December 1995. The Commission was among the few church initiatives of the post-genocide period that gained approval across the spectrum of political and ideological opinions. It was mentioned with praise by Paul Rutayisire, a Catholic historian critical of his church's 'silences and compromises',[31] by the French left-wing Catholic magazine *Golias,* which campaigned for the recognition of the Catholic Church's complicity in the genocide,[32] and in the above-mentioned memorandum to Pope John Paul II.[33] Extracts of the Commission's bulletins were even reproduced in *Dialogue,* a Brussels-based journal which gave a forum to the Hutu in exile and regularly denounced the exactions allegedly committed by the RPF government.[34] Church documents from all quarters referred favourably to the bulletins.

The first bulletin, published on 21 September 1994, set the tone. In a *constat loyal* (loyal appraisal), it evoked the 'contradictory feelings' of the Tutsi, 'who were meant to die' but survived and in a number of cases wanted vengeance, and of the Hutu, 'who were not meant to die' and took part 'more or less or not at all' in the massacres. There was an 'unanimous consensus', it further observed, on the fact that 'Christians, from all walks of life, had not been up to the mark, except for a few who stayed faithful to love which is stronger than death'. The first task was to analyse the reasons of the *la débandade chrétienne* (Christian hurry-scurry) and put an end to it with an evangelisation resolutely more in tune with the Gospel. 'The Commission insists on the fact that an important part of the responsibility lies with the church authorities (clergy, religious) who did not succeed in integrating the reforms of Vatican II.'[35]

The theme of the 'loyal appraisal' – that is, of the necessity of acknowledging the reality of the genocide and of the post-genocide period's social ills – ran through all the bulletins. The 'ideal evangelist', the November 1994 issue read, should be somebody who 'has combated the genocide and continues to combat any form of murder, proving that he situates himself above what divides the sons and daughters of this nation'.[36] Another recur-

---

[31] Paul Rutayisire, 'Silences et compromissions de la hiérarchie de l'Église catholique au Rwanda,' *Au cœur de l'Afrique,* 61 (1995), 436.
[32] *Golias,* 43 (July–August 1995) and 48–9 (July–August 1996).
[33] 'Rwanda: Préoccupations sur l'attitude de l'Église catholique', in Rutazibwa, *Contre l'ethnisme,* 161.
[34] *Dialogue,* 178 (October 1994), 55–7, and 181 (March 1995), 54–6.
[35] *Fécondité de la crise rwandaise,* 10–14 (Bulletin 1, 21 September 1994).
[36] *Fécondité de la crise rwandaise,* 27 (Bulletin 4, 11 November 1994).

rent theme in the Commission's bulletins was that of the 'good power' (*bonne puissance*), which Ntezimana had developed in his pre-dissertation work after reading the work of the French theologian Maurice Bellet and familiarising himself with Eastern spirituality. The 'good power' implies a spiritually grounded sense of inner security, the ability to develop resilience in challenging situations and an unconditional acceptance of people other than oneself.[37] It is what allowed a certain number of Rwandans to adopt the right attitude during the genocide, and what would help them to find their way in the post-genocide situation.

The Commission's bulletins chronicled the events of the day – for example, the arrest of two priests and two sisters in October and November 1994, the first anniversary of the genocide in April 1995 and the parliamentary debate about the funeral of Vincent Nsengiyumva, the controversial archbishop of Kigali, in July 1995. The Commission did not hesitate to criticise the Catholic bishops' reluctance to use the term genocide. In reference to the message that the AMECEA delegation addressed to the Rwandan government on 21 November 1994, the fifth bulletin commented:

> When one starts a document with the words 'The recent war and massacres left us...,' an attentive ear immediately picks up that the essential components of the current situation are occulted. The word 'genocide' and the sad reality it designates embarrass so many people that one prefers to maintain upon everything an imprudent silence.[38]

Questions about the church

In the months following the genocide, various initiatives aiming at dealing with the situation sprung up in the Roman Catholic Archdiocese of Kigali. Many were characterised – to use the Commission's language – by an honest appraisal of the trauma. One of the most pressing problems was the huge number of orphans and children in search of their parents.

---

[37] Laurien Ntezimana, *Libres paroles d'un théologien rwandais. Joyeux propos de bonne puissance* (Paris: Karthala, 1998). See also Laurien Ntezimana, 'La bonne puissance à l'œuvre dans l'histoire du Rwanda', in Bernard Van Meenen (ed.), *Intelligence de la foi et engagement social* (Brussels: Presses de l'Université Saint-Louis, 2010), 29–66.

[38] *Fécondité de la crise rwandaise*, 35–6 (Bulletin 5, Christmas 1994).

The archdiocese's Urban Social Bureau collected funds and launched an innovative programme to respond to their material and emotional needs.[39]

On 14 November 1994, at the initiative of the bishop, a group of priests from Kigali met to discuss the situation.[40] The meeting was chaired by Bernardin Muzungu, a Rwandan Dominican established in Burundi who had lost many family members in the genocide and had returned to Rwanda in July 1994. Disagreement soon emerged on the opportuneness of questioning the attitude of the Catholic Church during the genocide. One of the more reluctant to do so was Henri Blanchard, a White Father who had remained in his Nyamirambo parish during the genocide. As he explained to a French journalist, he felt that one should rather insist on the 'solidarity and cohesion' of the priests from Kigali, including Wenceslas Munyeshyaka, during the 'catastrophe' and he objected to the 'repeated attacks against the church'.[41]

The other members of the group continued to meet at regular intervals. In 1995 they published a booklet entitled '*Des prêtres rwandais s'interrogent*' [Rwandan priests are interrogating themselves]. 'The question that is being asked here,' they wrote, 'is whether Christians really committed faults, directly and consciously. All agree that unfortunately the response is positive. Given our numbers in this country, the crisis would have been impossible if no Christians had taken part in it.'[42] During the following fifteen years, Muzungu and his colleagues published reflection papers on ecclesiastical, historical and cultural matters in a series called *Cahiers Évangile et Société* [*Gospel and Society Bulletin*], later renamed *Cahiers Lumière et Société* [*Light and Society Bulletin*].

On the whole, the priests adopted a less defensive attitude in matters concerning the genocide than those regarding the episcopal hierarchy. The proceedings of a meeting held from 29 May to 1 June 1995 at the Christus Centre in Kigali bear witness to this. Eighty-three Rwandan priests from all over the country took part in the session. Four bishops were present, but they did not make any statement. There were no missionaries. That speakers such as Oreste Incimata, a priest of the Kibungo diocese, would invite the participants to take the accusations levelled against the Church 'as a

---

[39] Julia Spry-Leverton, 'Lessons in survival for children of war', *Child and Youth Care*, 14/7 (July 1996), 11–12.

[40] Ngomanzungu, *L'Église et la crise rwandaise*, 148.

[41] Henri Blanchard, 'Réponses à quelques questions par une journaliste de La Vie', Kigali, 7 August 1997 (Paris-Nanterre University, La Contemporaine: Fonds Hervé Deguine, Affaire Sibomana, Carton 3).

[42] *Des prêtres rwandais s'interrogent* (Bujumbura: Centre Lavigerie, 1995), 39.

point of departure for a constructive reflection'[43] or that a man like the Jesuit Octave Ugirashebuja would insist on the 'duty of intellectual lucidity'[44] did not come as a surprise. More unexpected were the declarations of the participants that were recorded – anonymously – in the proceedings. The church's collision with the temporal power was denounced, for example, as well as the exploitation of the ethnic problem within the church and the lack of discernment when evil forces started to manifest themselves. 'On many occasions,' a small group reported, 'the church under-estimated the danger of an emerging institution, of an ongoing diabolic idea or project such as the parties Parmehutu and CDR or Radio RTLM.'[45] Also questioned, in one of the small groups, was 'the timidity and inefficiency of [the church's] interventions'. 'The bishops', they said, 'rarely take a personal stand on local situations and sometimes give the impression of sheltering themselves behind the decisions of the Conference of Bishops.' 'The church statements', another small group reported, 'used to come too late and did not address the real issues.'[46] This group of priests, which came to be known as the Assembly of the Rwandan Priests (APRERWA), continued to meet after this.[47]

The same frankness was expressed in the essays a group of 125 trainee teachers, college students and final-year high school students from the Lycée Notre-Dame de Cîteaux in Kigali submitted in late 1994 at the invitation of their religion teacher. 'Nobody ignores', one wrote, 'that many Christians took part in the massacres. They did not only do it to kill, but to induce in error those who followed the right path.' 'I have noticed that many Christians and many religious participated in the genocide,' another one declared. 'Priests, sisters, pastors did not give to their flock the example of love. On the contrary, they hightlighted the distinctions of race.' 'At the beginning,' a third one said, 'those who claimed to be Christian were not really Christians because they had not received the strength from

---

[43] Oreste Incimatata, 'Isura ya Kiliziya Gatolika muri iki gihe', in *Rôle du prêtre rwandais dans l'édification de l'Église et la réconciliation nationale. Session des prêtres rwandais tenu du 29 mai au 1er juin au Centre Christus Remera/Kigali* (Butare: Imprimerie Euthymia, 1995), 18.

[44] Octave Ugirashebuya, 'Les défis lancés aux prêtres rwandais après le génocide et les massacres de 1994', *ibid.*, 23.

[45] 'Travail en groupe et mise en commun', *ibid.*, 14.

[46] 'Travail en groupe et mise en commun', *ibid.*, 27.

[47] Testimony of Jérôme Masinzo, in Fulgence Rubawiza, *Guérir le Rwanda de la violence. La Confession de Detmold, un premier pas* (Paris: L'Harmattan, 1998), 68.

Above which is the Spirit of God, which could have made them reject evil. For a long time they fooled themselves by believing they were Christian while they were about to deny their faith.'[48]

The Nyundo memorial

As mentioned in the previous chapter, the diocese of Nyundo paid a heavy price for the genocide against the Tutsi: it lost 30 priests, 27 religious brothers and sisters, 11 consecrated women and 4 seminarians. Bishop Wenceslas Kalibushi, who had narrowly escaped death, and five priests, whose lives were at risk, managed to find refuge in Gisenyi and then in Goma and subsequently in a house belonging to the Emmanuel Community in Helvoirt in the Netherlands. One of them published his testimony a few months after the genocide.[49] Some of the other priests, including Athanase Seromba, who was found guilty by the ICTR, were ideologically close to Hutu Power.[50] They fled to Zaire in July 1994.

The bishop and the priest-survivors spent three months in the Netherlands to recover. On their return, they implemented a revival plan similar to the one the Commission was busy launching in the diocese of Butare. At one point, Laurien Ntezimana came to give a talk to the pastoral team of the diocese.[51] Fabien Rwakareke, who was appointed vicar general on his return from the Netherlands, coordinated the implementation of the pastoral plan. At first, he recalled, there was good will among the faithful because the memories of the genocide were still fresh:

> When we arrived in the diocese after all the things that had happened, the spirit was strong. All the parishes had a leader, a layperson who was recognised by the others and led the prayers. [...] We brought the people together and reflected with them. We helped them to think otherwise. They should not remain stuck in the politics that had demolished them. We tried to reflect on the meaning of being human and on the gospel.

---

[48] Marius Dion, 'Des étudiants parlent de leur foi, de leur Église, de leurs peines, de leurs attentes', *Dialogue*, 175 (November–December 1994), 47–66.
[49] Jean-Baptiste Hategeka, *Raisins verts pour dents agacées. Cri contre les nazis Noirs du Rwanda* (Formigine, Modena: Golinelli, 1994).
[50] For a discussion of the crimes for which Athanase Seromba was convicted at the ICTR, see Timothée Brunet-Lefèvre, *Le père Seromba. Destructeur de l'Église de Nyange (Rwanda, 1994)* (Paris: Éditions Hoosch, 2021).
[51] *Fécondité de la crise rwandaise*, 55 (Bulletin 7, February 1995).

It was in this context that, as mentioned earlier, the priests decided a moratorium on the celebration of sacraments:

> We said that we could not continue to administer the sacraments before the people had taken the time to reflect on what had happened. It was different from the other dioceses. Even in Butare, they administered the sacraments. We, the priests, did not want it. Until Lent 96, we celebrated penitential services. We confessed our sins together. We have all sinned in some way because there have been people who wanted to kill but the victims were perhaps thinking that, if they could, they would do to the others all the evil they were doing to them.[52]

The cathedral of Nyundo was one of the first churches, if not the first, in Rwanda to have a memorial of the genocide. The initiative came from the Christian community and not from the Rwandan state, as would happen later in other parts of the country. The cathedral had witnessed several massacres, and people were afraid of entering it. They would only pray in front of the cathedral. In 1995, the bishop performed an exorcism and, on this occasion, three wooden panels with the following messages were placed on the main door:

> IBUKA. Remember the genocide perpetrated against the Tutsi. More than five hundred people brutally lost their lives here. 09.04.1994 – 01.05.1994.

> UGAYE. Feel indignant at this wickedness and at what caused it. A house can be rebuilt and the bricks and stone. Shed blood cannot be retrieved.

> USABE. Pray God that this does not happen again and remember that it is complete opposition to the custom that we are bound to respect.[53]

On 19 May 1996, the diocese organised a ceremony of purification of the cathedral of Nyundo to which the minister of higher education, Joseph Nsengimana, and representatives of civil society were invited. Until then, Mass had been celebrated in front of the building. This ritual was a manner of publicly recognising that the massacres committed in the cathedral constituted a sacrilege.[54]

---

[52] Fabien Rwakareke, interview conducted on 28 May 2018 in Nyundo.

[53] The text in Kinyarwanda of the first two panels with a French translation is reproduced in Félicité Lyamukuru, *L'ouragan a frappé Nyundo* (Cuesmes, Belgium: Éditions du Cerisier, 2018), 151–2.

[54] CNLG, Archives of the Commission for the Memorial of the Genocide and the Massacres: Wenceslas Kalibushi to the Minister of Higher Education and Scientific Research, Gisenyi, 6 May 1994. See Hélène Dumas and Rémi

Further south, in Nyamagumba (previously known as Gitwa), an outstation of the Congo-Nil parish, Mathias Abimana – a former chairperson of the parish council who had lost his wife and two children during the genocide – had become the burgomaster of the commune of Mabanza in September 1994. Abimana obtained from the bishop of Nyundo, Wenceslas Kalibushi, that the site of a school chapel where several hundred Tutsi had been massacred be donated by the church to the people of Mabanza, to be transformed into a genocide memorial. The first commemoration took place in April 1995.[55]

According to Rwakareke, the atmosphere changed in the diocese after the return of the refugees from Zaire in late 1996. More politicised, they were reluctant to admit the reality of the genocide. Another destabilising factor was the so-called *Abacengezi* War [Infiltrators' War] waged by insurgents nostalgic about the old regime in north-west Rwanda and accompanied by violent state repression. This low-intensity conflict, which devastated the area until 1999, severely hampered the reconstruction of the church.[56]

The Sibomana affair

On 11 August 1994, Henryk Hoser, the pope's representative in Rwanda, appointed André Sibomana as apostolic administrator of the diocese of Kabgayi. He remained in this position until the installation of Bishop Anastase Mutabazi in March 1996. Before the genocide, this native priest from Muyunzwe near Kabgayi, who took on the functions of editor of the Catholic bi-monthly newspaper *Kinyamateka* and vice-president of the ADL, was an important figure in the Catholic Church. As mentioned in Chapter 2, he is credited for having incited his bishop, Thaddée

---

Korman, 'Espaces de la mémoire du genocide des Tutsis au Rwanda. Mémoriaux et lieux de mémoire', *Afrique contemporaine*, 238 (2011), 239. For a discussion of the theological and cultural dimensions of the purification of churches desecrated by the genocide, see François Lumbala Kabasele, *La Lettre des Grands Lacs,* Kinshasa, 4–5 (April–May 1996).

[55] Mathias Abimana, interview conducted on 4 March 2020 in Rubengera. On the genocide in Congo-Nil, see chapters 8 and 9. Gitwa was renamed Nyamagumba in reference to a site of the same name near Ruhengeri where Tutsi had been massacred in December 1973. See CMGM, 'Rapport préliminaire d'identification des sites du génocide et des massacres d'avril-juillet 1994 au Rwanda', February 1996, 158.

[56] Fabien Rwakareke, interview conducted on 28 May 2018 in Nyundo.

Nsengiyumva, and the priests of his diocese to distance themselves from the Habyarimana government in a statement issued in December 1991. Sibomana contributed to the 1992 and 1993 ADL reports that denounced the army and local authorities' exactions against Tutsi civilians.

After the genocide, he soon rose to prominence in the church. By then, he was wearing three hats: as apostolic administrator of the Kabgayi diocese, as editor of *Kinyamateka* and as ADL president. Meanwhile, his work as an independent journalist had earned him international recognition, as evidenced by the fact that the advocacy organisation Reporters Without Borders awarded him its annual prize in Paris in December 1994.

Yet, voices arose among genocide survivors to criticise the anti-Tutsi stance Sibomana had allegedly taken before and during the genocide. This led to the controversial insertion of his name in a list of twenty-five 'priests and pastors who assassinated or encouraged assassinations' in the widely disseminated issue 'La machette et le goupillon' [The machete and the sprinkler] of the French left-wing Catholic magazine *Golias* in July 1995.[57] Many names had already been mentioned in the *Death, Defiance and Despair* report of the London-based human rights organisation African Rights in 1994, but not Sibomana's. *Golias*'s source was a note from Eugène Twagira Mutabazi, special reporter to Rwanda, based on interviews with genocide survivors.[58] Rakiya Omaar, the editor of African Rights, had also collected information on Sibomana during a stay in Rwanda in early 1995, but she had found that the case against him was not strong enough and, as a result, decided not to mention his name in the second edition of *Death, Defiance and Despair*, which came out in August 1995.[59]

Sibomana's main accuser was a former *Kinyamateka* journalist by the name of Gaspard Gasasira, who had been in conflict with him around professional issues in 1989 and 1990.[60] He told Omaar and Mutabazi that, up to 1993, Sibomana had meetings with Froduald Karamira and Donat

---

[57] 'Prêtres ou pasteurs qui ont assassiné ou encouragé des assassinats', *Golias*, 43 (July–August 1995), 50–1. On *Golias* and its editor, Christian Terras, see Chapter 8.

[58] Eugène Mutabazi, Report to the editor of *Golias*, Kigali, 10 May 1995 (Paris-Nanterre University, La Contemporaine: Fonds Deguine, Affaire Sibomana, Carton 4).

[59] Rakiya Omaar to Robert Menard, London, 26 July 1995 (Paris-Nanterre University, La Contemporaine: Fonds Deguine, Affaire Sibomana, Carton 3).

[60] André Sibomana to Gaspard Gasasira, Kigali, 31 August 1989, 28 February

Murego, two Mouvement Démocratique Républicain (MDR) leaders who joined the Hutu Power branch of the party during this period and played a role in the genocide.[61] Genocide survivors reported to Mutabazi that Sibomana had anti-Tutsi biases before the genocide. They also mentioned that he had failed to protect Tutsi refugees at the Centre Saint-Paul in Kigali before he fled to Gitarama on 9 April and after this date in his home parish of Muyunzwe.[62]

Sibomana's mention in the *Golias* dossier caused a commotion in journalists' and human rights activists' circles. Many, especially those with Catholic connections, found it outrageous that he should be accused of genocide complicity. They claimed that, in Rwanda's volatile post-genocide climate, this accusation might put his life at risk. Others, like the journalist Jean-François Dupaquier and the historian Jean-Pierre Chrétien, were more guarded, while dissociating themselves from the article and encouraging Christian Terras, the editor of *Golias*, to withdraw it.

In August 1995, Reporters Without Borders sued *Golias* for defamation on behalf of Sibomana. To their dismay, the tribunal dismissed the case on the grounds that the complainant had been mentioned in the document in his capacity as a priest and not as a journalist and that, since there was evidence of a controversy in Rwanda about his role during the genocide, the article was not 'deliberately and evidently' defamatory.[63] Hervé Deguine's decision to publish an interview-book on Sibomana as a way of restoring his good name[64] was a direct result of this affair.

The debate around Sibomana's role during the genocide is puzzling. ADL, the human rights organisation to which he actively contributed, publicised the massacres of Tutsi perpetrated during the last years of the Habyarimana government. According to Alison Des Forges, senior adviser at Human Rights Watch, after his flight from Kigali where his life was under threat, Sibomana met with Fidèle Uwizeye, the prefect of Gitarama,

---

and 1 June 1990 (Paris-Nanterre University, La Contemporaine: Fonds Deguine, Affaire Sibomana, Carton 3).

[61] Mutabazi, Report; Omaar to Menard, 26 July 1995.

[62] Mutabazi, Report; Hildebrand Karangwa, *Le génocide au centre du Rwanda. Quelques témoignages des rescapés de Kabgayi* (n.p., 2001), 42–3.

[63] 'Ordonnance de référé, Tribunal de Grande Instance de Lyon, 11 Septembre 1995', *Golias*, 44 (September 1995), 9.

[64] André Sibomana, *Gardons l'espoir pour le Rwanda. Entretiens avec Laure Guibert et Hervé Deguine*, 2nd edn (Paris: Desclée de Brouwer, 2008). The first edition came out in 1997.

and encouraged him to resist the killings.[65] While in Muyunzwe, he tried to save lives.[66] Unlike Bishop Thaddée Ntihinyurwa, for example, in his December 1994 message to the ACEAC, Sibomana referred to the genocide by name in an editorial published in *Kinyamateka* the same month.[67]

In his analysis of the Rwandan genocide and of the events leading to it, Gérard Prunier pointed out that 'the game was not two-sided [...] but in fact three-sided, between the Habyarimana regime jockeying for survival, the internal opposition struggling to achieve recognition, and the Tutsi exiles trying to make some sort of comeback'.[68] This applies to Sibomana who, as a man from the south, had an affinity to the MDR – a revived version of Grégoire Kayibanda's Parmehutu – without formally belonging to it. He belonged to the so-called Hutu moderates and, for this reason, could have been killed by the Interahamwe during the genocide. But, as he unashamedly acknowledged in his interview-book, he had no sympathy at all for the RPF, which he accused of having destabilised Rwanda by invading the country in October 1990.[69]

After the genocide, Sibomana became the voice of the internal opposition. He used his position as editor of *Kinyamateka* to remind the new government of its duty to restore security in the country, to put an end to the arbitrary detentions of suspects and to investigate political murders. On 4 January 1995, he took the drastic step of dissociating himself, in his capacity as ADL president, from a comprehensive report on the human rights abuses committed in Kigali during the genocide period on the grounds that it had been doctored to add or remove names of suspects.[70] During the

---

[65] Des Forges, *Leave None to Tell the Story*, 272.
[66] Sibomana, *Gardons l'espoir pour le Rwanda*, 96.
[67] *Kinyamateka*, 1414 (December 1994), 1.
[68] Gérard Prunier, *The Rwanda Crisis: History of a Genocide* (New York: Columbia University Press, 1995), 99.
[69] Sibomana, *Gardons l'espoir pour le Rwanda*, 67. For a critique of Sibomana's position after the genocide from an author close to the RPF, see Privat Rutazibwa, 'Ibaruwa Ifunguye kuri Myr Andereya Sibomana, umuyobozi wa Kinyamateka' (Open letter to Mgr André Sibomana, director of Kinyamateka), June 1997, in *Rwanda. Contre l'ethnisme*, 194–209.
[70] *Rapport de l'enquête sur les violations massives des droits de l'homme commises au Rwanda à partir du 06 avril 1994*, Kigali, December 1994. See the letters exchanged between André Sibomana and François-Xavier Nsanzuwera, president of CLADHO, an umbrella body of human rights organisations in Rwanda, 3 and 16 January 1995 (Paris-Nanterre University, La Contemporaine: Fonds Hervé Deguine, Affaire Sibomana, Carton 4). See also Sibomana, *Gardons l'espoir pour le Rwanda*, 152–3; Françoise

same period, he investigated the massacres perpetrated by RPF soldiers in June and July 1994 in the Gitarama area.[71] On 21 January 1995, he reported at a meeting of the bishops of Rwanda and Burundi that 216 people had been killed by RPF soldiers in July and August 1994 and that 2,000 had disappeared in the commune of Masango, near Gitarama, alone.[72]

There is no evidence that the security forces ever planned to assassinate Sibomana, but he felt that it might be the case and therefore lived in fear. The ensuing stress may have contributed to the disease that caused his death in March 1998. What we know for sure is that his criticisms of the post-genocide governance irritated those who thought that the church's duty was to help the government to reconstruct the country. They felt that he used his contacts abroad to bring bad publicity to Rwanda.[73] At the meeting of priests of May 1995 in Kigali, the Jesuit Octave Ugirashebuya blamed him without mentioning his name. '*Kinyamateka*', he said, 'which is for the moment the only official organ of the Church, cannot be left to the whims of a single man: a fully responsible editorial committee must be put in place without any delay.'[74] Sibomana was a man of controversies. He contributed to the atmosphere of confrontation between church and state that prevailed in the aftermath of the genocide.

Genocide denialism in the refugee camps

The mood was quite different in the refugee camps of South and North Kivu, where an estimated 1,300,000 people – then gradually less until the Rwandan army and the Alliance of Democratic Forces for the Liberation of Congo (ADFL) rebels forcefully closed the camps in October and November 1996 – gathered under the supervision of the UN Refugee Agency. The defeated army, which was never disarmed, and the former government reconstituted themselves, and the Rwandan administrative apparatus with cells, sectors, municipalities and prefectures was recreated.

Boucher-Saulnier and Frédéric Laffont, *Maudits soient les yeux fermés* (Paris: Éditions J. C. Lattès, 1995), 111–12.

[71] These massacres were also reported by Human Rights Watch. See Nigel Eltringham, *Accounting for Horror: Post-Genocide Debates in Rwanda* (London: Pluto Press, 2004), 103.

[72] 'Communications d'informations sur le diocèse de Kabgayi à la réunion des Conférences des évêques du Rwanda et du Burundi à Kigali le 21 janvier 1995' (Archives *Dialogue*, Brussels).

[73] Rutazibwa, 'Ibaruwa Ifunguye kuri Myr Andereya Sibomana'.

[74] *Rôle du prêtre rwandais dans l'édification de l'Église*, 25.

The proportion of genocide perpetrators in the refugee population is difficult to establish,[75] but it is clear that they held sway over the thousands of ordinary people who had fled the country in panic, stirred up by the RTLM propaganda, when the RPF had seized power. These people were discouraged by the *génocidaires*, sometimes under threat of death, from returning to the country. Rumours about the atrocities committed by the RPF army in Rwanda, partly true but grossly exaggerated, abounded.[76]

For the ex-FAR and the Interahamwe, Rwanda had gone through a war, not a genocide. They entertained the hope, at least until 1995, that they could fight back and re-establish their rule. There was no question of recognising that a genocide had taken place. At a meeting held in Goma in September 1994, the High Command of the FAR described as a strategic 'weakness' the fact that 'the Government [was] the object of accusations of genocide by the RPF and certain countries and international organisations favourable to the RPF'.[77]

Eighty Catholic priests and more than a hundred seminarians, according to the Conference of Rwandan Bishops, took refuge in Zaire.[78] Like the government in exile, the church recreated in the camps, as effectively as it could, the ecclesiastical structures that were in place in Rwanda before the exile. Each camp had 'parishes' served by a certain number of

---

[75] According to an international evaluation task force, 'between 10 to 15 per cent of the refugees in the camps (adult and adolescent) are alleged to have participated directly in mass killing'. See Joint Evaluation of the Emergency Assistance to Rwanda, 'the international response to conflict and genocide: lessons from the Rwanda experience. Synthesis report', March 1996, 39. However, according to a UN report quoted in 'Goma-Bukavu: témoignage direct novembre 96-janvier 97', *Dialogue*, 196 (February 1997), 53.7 per cent of the refugees had taken part in the massacres.

[76] Jean-Pierre Godding, 'L'insécurité dans les camps de réfugiés de Goma et l'attitude des ONG', *Dialogue*, 179 (November–December 1994), 20–4; Filip Reyntjens, *The Great African War: Congo and Regional Geopolitics, 1996–2006* (Cambridge: Cambridge University Press, 2009), 19; Eltringham, *Accounting for Horror*, 121–2; Bradol and Le Pape, *Génocide et crimes de masse*, 90–119.

[77] 'Rapport de la réunion du Haut Commandement des Forces Rwandaises et des membres des commissions tenue à Goma du 02 au 08 septembre 1994', 30. Copy ICTR, 12 December 2006.

[78] 'Brève présentation de l'Église catholique au Rwanda avant et après le drame rwandais', 1.

priests. Church buildings had been put at their disposal by the UN Refugee Agency in the biggest camps.[79]

The symbiotic relationship between church and state that had characterised the Habyarimana regime reproduced itself in the refugee camps. At its September 1994 meeting, the High Command of the FAR made it clear that they regarded the clergy as an ally. 'The Ministry of External Relations and Cooperation', the report reads, 'should facilitate the movements of our clergy in order to let people understand our cause.'[80] According to the diary of Pauline Nyiramasuhuko, the Minister for Family in the interim government, the church representatives had several meetings with the political authorities in the camps during the second half of 1994.[81] On their part, the Catholic priests – and the Protestant pastors[82] – tended to be ideologically close to the Hutu extremist position, which the authorities in the camps continued to promote. This was the case, in particular, of the bishop of Ruhengeri, Phocas Nikwigize, and of his vicar general, Simon Habyarimana, who oversaw the pastoral activities in the refugee camps in the Goma diocese.[83]

Typical from that point of view was the letter that twenty-nine priests from Goma addressed to Pope John Paul II on 2 August 1994. The problem, for them, was not the genocide, about which they hardly said a word, but a 'vast anti-Catholic movement fed, unfortunately, by some priests who actively participated in the subversive manoeuvres of the RPF'. They accused the RPF of numerous atrocities and described the security situation in the country as apocalyptic. This explained, they argued, *le courroux du peuple* [the anger of the people], including 'some of our best

---

[79] Jérôme Karimumuryango, *Les réfugiés rwandais dans la région de Bukavu Congo RDC. La survie du réfugié dans les camps de secours d'urgence* (Paris: Karthala, 2000), 26.

[80] 'Rapport de la réunion du Haut Commandement des Forces Rwandaises', 23.

[81] André Guichaoua, *Rwanda 1994. Les politiques du génocide à Butare* (Paris: Karthala, 2005), 437–43.

[82] See Chapter 5. When the executive secretary for Africa of the United Evangelical Mission visited Goma in August 1994, the Presbyterian pastors staying there told him that as many Hutu had been killed as Tutsi and that, for that reason, 'the term genocide does not describe the situation in a realist or accurate manner'. See Kakule Molo, 'Rapport de la visite à Goma et Bukavu', Wuppertal, 5 September 1994 (Van 't Spijker Papers).

[83] Simon Habyarimana, *Phocas Nikwigize, le Pacifique Pacificateur, Evêque émérite du Diocèse de Ruhengeri, Rwanda* (Lille: Éditions Sources du Nil, 2016).

Christians'. As a condition for their return to Rwanda, they demanded that the RPF ceased to 'fill Kigali with elements foreign to this city' and that one should stop 'speaking of an international tribunal where the criminals would be at the same time the accusers and the judges'.[84]

We do not know who drafted the letter and canvassed the signatories.[85] Some of these, in fact, did not sign by hand, and there are indications they did not endorse the letter. Seventeen of the priests who supported the initiative – more than half of the total – were from the diocese of Ruhengeri, an area where few people had had a direct experience of the genocide because only a small number of Tutsi lived there at the time. The priests from Ruhengeri had seen, on the other hand, the chaos reigning in the camps of Hutu refugees fleeing the advance of the RPF between 1990 and 1994.

On the attitude of the Hutu priests in exile, the diary of Pierre Cariou, a French priest who had worked in North Kivu as a missionary in the mid-1980s and who had returned to Goma in August 1995 for two weeks at the invitation of Faustin Ngabu, the local bishop, provides precious first-hand information. He had no sympathy for the RPF but was unwavering in his condemnation of the genocide. During a one-day visit to Kigali at the end of his stay, he found the time to visit the genocide sites of Nyamata and Ntarama and came back from there in shock.[86] He found the sketch of Rwandan history that Phocas Nikwigize, the bishop of Ruhengeri, gave him one day 'reductionist' (*réducteur*): Nikwigize did not even mention the massacres suffered by the Tutsi population in 1959 and in subsequent years.[87] On 6 August 1995, during a visit of the refugee camp of Katale in Nikwigize's company, he entered the following comment in his diary: 'Regarding the tragedy of last year, I expected expressions of regret or remorse. Nothing of that kind! It was the Tutsi who started it, they said.

---

[84] 'Lettre des prêtres des diocèses du Rwanda réfugiés Goma (Zaïre) adressée au Très Saint Père le Pape Jean-Paul', Goma, 2 August 1994, in Jean Ndorimana, *Rwanda: L'Église catholique dans le malaise* (Rome: Edizioni Vivere In, 2001). See also African Rights, *Rwanda: Death, Despair and Defiance* (London: African Rights, 1995), 906–8.

[85] Simon Habyarimana typed the letter on his electronic machine, but he did not initiate the project. See Simon Habyarimana, interview conducted on 6 October 2017 in San Miniato.

[86] Pierre Cariou, *De la Soufrière au Nyiragongo* (Saint-Derrien: Librairie S. P. Rance, 1996), 251–2.

[87] *Ibid.*, 215.

They want all the power.'⁸⁸ Hyacinthe Vulliez, another French priest who visited the camps in 1996, also found that some of the priests were heavily politicised. 'It is not easy [for the priests],' he observed, 'or at least for some of them, to escape from the straightjacket of ethnic rivalries and from the hold of party politics.'⁸⁹

One should not conclude from these testimonies that all priests in exile shared the views of the Hutu extremists. Another group of priests from Goma – some of them, perhaps, signatories of the letter to the pope – wrote on 4 September 1994 that they did not want to be instrumentalised. The church, they argued, 'should avoid the danger of subjecting itself to any political regime or getting bogged in the meanders of international decision-makers who choose one way or another according to their interests and at the cost of truth.'⁹⁰

In a letter addressed to the bishops of Rwanda on 29 November, the priests from the Bukavu refugee camps also adopted a moderate tone. The refugees, they commented, are 'like sheep without shepherds' and would welcome a visit from their bishops. 'Who speaks of reconciliation to the Rwandan people should not forget that the clergy itself must practice self-criticism in the light of the gospel so that the church of Rwanda no longer loses face in front of people and, worse still, in front of God.' More controversially, however, they requested a share of the funds sent by Rome for the training of seminarians.⁹¹ They were claiming for themselves a share of the Rwandan church's resources, thereby entrenching its division into two separate entities.

The reports of the reflection group La Chandelle (The Candle), which met at regular intervals in the refugee camps around Goma from March 1995 to September 1996, show, among the refugees who took part in them, an evolution from an attitude of anger and denial to a recognition of the horror of the genocide and an availability for reconciliation. This explains, at least in part, why the return of about 600,000 refugees to Rwanda in November 1996 after the closure of the camps took place in a much more orderly and peaceful manner than expected.

---

⁸⁸ *Ibid.*, 232–3.
⁸⁹ Jean-Pierre Godding, *Réfugiés rwandais au Zaïre. Sommes-nous encore des hommes? Documents des groupes de réflexion dans les camps* (Paris: L'Harmattan, 1997), 23.
⁹⁰ Ngomanzungu, *L'Église et la crise rwandaise*, 142.
⁹¹ 'Lettre des prêtres rwandais à leurs évêques', Bukavu, 19 November 1994, in Philippe de Dorlodot (ed.), *Les réfugiés rwandais à Bukavu au Zaïre. De nouveaux Palestiniens?* (Paris: L'Harmattan, 1996), 152–3.

In a letter to their relatives and friends in Rwanda on the occasion of the New Year in 1996, the members of La Chandelle and another eight organisations asked whether peace had been restored in the country so that they might return. 'We regret and lament the horrible massacres of men, women and children perpetrated by sons and daughters of Rwanda,' they wrote. 'We can understand the terrible suffering of the survivors and ask them to forgive us so that we could rebuild something together.'[92]

Towards the end of 1995, a Christian woman declared in public, quoting the Book of Daniel, that 'one should not wait until the new authorities in Rwanda acknowledge the evil they have committed before denouncing and regretting all the evil committed by one's own group, even if one personally did nothing wrong.' The refugee camp leaders, an observer commented, found this totally unacceptable.[93]

Conclusion

The discourse of the missionaries, which will be the object of a subsequent chapter, and the official statements of the church authorities may give the impression that the Catholic Church of Rwanda as a whole was fixed, after 1994, in a defensive anti-RPF position and refused to acknowledge its responsibility, albeit indirect, in the ethnic polarisation that had produced the genocide. This attitude has existed, and still exists today, but is not the only one – far from it. The examples we have given here, drawn from the dioceses of Butare, Kigali and Nyundo, show a different picture. Even in the refugee camps in Zaire, some people came to acknowledge the full reality of the genocide after a year or so. This being said, the Catholic took much longer than the Presbyterian Church, to which we shall turn in the next chapter, to recognise its guilt and ask for forgiveness.

---

[92] 'Souhaits de Nouvel An à la population restée au Rwanda', Goma, 1 January 1996, in Godding, *Réfugiés rwandais au Zaïre*, 146.
[93] *Ibid.*, 194–5.

CHAPTER 5

The Presbyterian Church's confession of guilt

The Presbyterian Church in Rwanda (Église presbytérienne au Rwanda or EPR) is the second-oldest church in Rwanda. Established in 1907 by Ernst Johanssen and Gerhard Ruccius, two missionaries of the German-based Lutheran Missionary Society of Bethel, it was handed over to the Belgian Society of Protestant Missions in Congo in 1921, before being granted independence in 1959 under the name of the Evangelical Presbyterian Church in Rwanda. Held in suspicion and marginalised by the Catholic missionaries and the first generation of post-independence Rwandan leaders, it gained a certain form of recognition after Juvénal Habyarimana became president in 1973, which explains why many Presbyterian church leaders, including the president, Michel Twagirayesu, showed unfettered loyalty to the regime before and during the genocide.[1]

Like the Catholic Church, the Presbyterian Church emerged from the genocide bruised and disoriented with nearly 20 per cent of its pastors assassinated, its infrastructure damaged or destroyed and about a quarter of its members in refugee camps in Zaire or elsewhere. However, the manner in which the church reconstructed itself after the tragedy differs from that of the Catholic Church in several respects. The Catholic Church in Rwanda, because of its size and its incorporation into a centralised international body, retained its structure and its integrity after the genocide despite the assassination of three bishops in June 1994. The priests who

[1] Michel Twagirayesu and Jan van Butselaar, *Ce don que nous avons reçu. Histoire de l'Église presbytérienne au Rwanda (1907–1982)* (Kigali: Église presbytérienne au Rwanda, 1982); Tharcisse Gatwa and André Karamaga, *Les autres Chrétiens rwandais. La présence protestante* (Kigali: Éditions Urwego, 1990); Tharcisse Gatwa, 'L'Église presbytérienne au Rwanda', in Tharcisse Gatwa and Laurent Rutinduka (ed.), *Histoire du christianisme au Rwanda des origines à nos jours* (Yaoundé: Éditions CLÉ, 2014), 63–96.

took refuge in Goma or further afield in July 1994 rapidly lost influence. The bishops remained in Rwanda with the exception of Phocas Nikwigize, who left Ruhengeri for Goma in July 1994 and was allegedly killed by the RPF two years later at the border.[2] Meanwhile, the Catholic Church in Rwanda was divided on the issue of genocide, with some openly recognising the church's failure to denounce the systematic extermination of the Tutsi people and others adopting a defensive attitude and focusing all their attention on the shortcomings of the new government. As we shall see in subsequent chapters, the two groups found some common ground in the late 1990s, but the uneasiness with regard to the genocide against the Tutsi remains up to this day.

The Presbyterian Church was also divided. The difference was that, out of fear of the RPF, an important part of its leadership fled to Bukavu with the intention of continuing to govern the church from there. Its refusal to plainly admit the reality of the genocide against the Tutsi and its closeness to the former Rwandan government, as well as the news that Presbyterian pastors and officials had been implicated in the massacres committed in the mission station of Kirinda, rapidly provoked a crisis of confidence. In February 1995 new leaders were elected in Rwanda, and in December 1996 the General Synod took the unprecedented step of publicly confessing its guilt for having not done enough to stop the genocide. It is to that story that this chapter is dedicated.

The waning leadership of Michel Twagirayesu

Unlike the Catholic Church, which follows a monarchical model of ecclesiastical government, the Presbyterian Church in Rwanda is characterised, in the words of Tharcisse Gatwa, by an 'ecclesiology of consensus'.[3] The president of the church is accountable to the Synodal Council and to the General Synod. As a result of the genocide, however, the cohesion of the church came under threat, with the result that the figure of the president – Michel Twagirayesu until February 1995 and André Karamaga after this – became more prominent and more visible.

A native of Kirinda – one of the most ancient mission stations in western Rwanda and the strategic centre of the EPR alongside Kigali and

---

[2] The source on the circumstances of Bishop Nikwigize's death is the former priest and opposition politician Thomas Nahimana. See Simon Habyarimana, *Phocas Nikwigize, le Pacifique Pacificateur, Évêque émérite du Diocèse de Ruhengeri, Rwanda* (Lille: Éditions Sources du Nil, 2016), 146–56.

[3] Gatwa, 'L'Église presbytérienne au Rwanda', 91.

Remera-Rukoma near Gitarama – Michel Twagirayesu became the second president of the church in 1977, at a time when the term of office was four years and renewable without a specified limit.[4]

In church circles, Twagirayesu was influential. He was one of the main drivers of the Comité de Contacts, the ecumenical group which offered a mediation between the Rwandan governments, the opposition parties and the RPF in 1992 and 1993 and which was resurrected when representatives of the Catholic and Protestant churches met to issue joint statements during the genocide, first on 13 May 1994[5] and then on 20 June.[6] He was also a member of the Executive Committee, and at one point the deputy chairperson, of the WCC in Geneva.[7] Socially, Twagirayesu was also a well-known figure. A member of the MRND Executive Committee in Kibuye since his appointment as president of the Presbyterian Church,[8] he was a staunch supporter of President Habyarimana. Like Archbishop Vincent Nsengiyumva but with different views on birth control, he was a member of the Office National de la Population (ONAPO), a state organ created to deal with the problem of overpopulation. In 1991, he participated in the state commission mandated to write a new constitution.[9]

In Kirinda, an isolated rural locality with a hospital, a secondary school, an advanced nursing school and a women's programme run by the Presbyterian Church, not to mention several church offices, he was a powerful local figure. Several of his relatives held positions in church-sponsored institutions or in businesses linked to the church. When opposition parties became authorised in the early 1990s, popular protest erupted after a ring of corruption scandals and occurrences of maladministration, and the MDR started to gain adherents in the area. Meanwhile, the burgomaster and the heads of the church-sponsored institutions continued to support the Habyarimana regime. In September 1992, they became

---

[4] Twagirayesu and van Butselaar, *Ce don que nous avons reçu*, 154.
[5] Comité de Contacts – Conférence des Évêques catholiques du Rwanda – Conseil Protestant du Rwanda, 'Communiqué des Églises catholique et protestantes du Rwanda', 13 May 1994 (Archives Dialogue, Brussels).
[6] The joint statement issued by the Catholic and Protestant church leaders on 20 June 1994 did not make reference to the Comité de Contacts. On these documents, see Chapter 2.
[7] *APS News Features and Bulletin*, 20 February 1995, 5.
[8] Timothy Longman, *Christianity and Genocide in Rwanda* (Cambridge: Cambridge University Press, 2011), 89.
[9] Gerard van 't Spijker, *Indicible Rwanda. Expériences et réflexions d'un pasteur missionnaire* (Yaoundé: Éditions CLÉ, 2007), 20.

part of a 'security committee' whose brief was to fight local gangsters but which rapidly developed an anti-RPF and anti-Tutsi rhetoric.[10] According to Aaron Mugemera, a pastor serving in a neighbouring parish who owned a house in Kirinda, Twagirayesu had relations with the security committee and was often seen sharing beers with Tharcisse Kabasha – the burgomaster of Bwakira, the commune of which Kirinda was part – and other members of the committee.[11]

Twagirayesu left Kirinda on 3 July with his family. He arrived in Bukavu two weeks later with the funds, the vehicles and the office equipment of the church, a move destined, in his eyes, to preserve the church's assets but for which he was later criticised by the Presbyterians who remained in Rwanda.[12] There he found Antoine Kamanzi, the director of Kirinda Hospital; Fidèle Ntawirukanayo, the director of Kirinda Presbyterian Institute (IPK); Marcellin Nsengiyumva, the director of the School of Nursing Sciences (ESI); Tharcisse Kabasha; and about a dozen Presbyterian pastors and evangelists.[13] Most of them subsequently moved to Muku, a refugee camp some distance from Bukavu, where they remained until the RPF army dismantled the camps in October 1996.

In discussions with members of partner organisations visiting Bukavu and in letters sent to them all over Europe, Twagirayesu continued to speak as president of the EPR, despite his new status as a refugee in Zaire. He provided information on his role during the genocide without, however, ever using the word. He would rather speak, as in a letter to the partners of late August, of 'the war of October 1990 which resumed its hostilities on 6 April 1994'. 'Despite the sad and ignominious events that we have condemned in the powerlessness and silence imposed on the Church during the past few months,' he wrote in the same letter, 'we render grace to God for the Christians and the pastors who survived the war up to this day.'[14]

Emmanuel Nkusi, the general secretary of the Protestant Council of Rwanda (CPR) (the coordinating body of the Protestant churches in Rwanda); Samuel Musabyimana, the Anglican bishop of Shyogwe;[15] and

---

[10] Longman, *Christianity and Genocide*, 231.
[11] Aaron Mugemera, interview conducted on 28 February 2020 in Kigali.
[12] Michel Twagirayesu to [Phares] Kakule Molo, Bukavu, 25 August 1994 (Munyaneza Papers).
[13] All signed the letter that Michel Twagirayesu sent to the partners of the EPR in late July 1994 (Munyaneza Papers).
[14] Twagirayesu to Kakule Molo, 25 August 1994.
[15] Bishop Samuel Musabyimana was indicted by the ICTR for genocide in 2011. He died in jail before the trial could take place.

representatives of the Free Methodist, Baptist and Pentecostal churches also fled to Bukavu. When Patricia Nickson, a Church Missionary Society missionary working for Community African Initiatives Support (ACIST), met them from 5 to 8 August, they explained 'how they had talked to the then government (interim government of 9 April) to ask them to stop the massacres'. 'Promises were made,' they said, 'but no apparent steps were taken. They then approached the RPF, and had no reply – except in the murder of the Roman Catholic archbishop, bishops and clergy'.[16]

The correspondence exchanged between Twagirayesu and the German, Dutch, Belgian and Swiss partner organisations of the EPR shows a man who had no doubt regarding his capacity to lead the Presbyterian Church from outside the country. He tried to convince the partner organisations that the church was still up and running and that all that was needed was funds to organise a meeting – in Nairobi or in Goma – between the Presbyterians remaining in Rwanda and those in exile. Initially, José Chipenda (the general secretary of the AACC in Nairobi) and some international partners gave their support. On 12 August, the church leaders in exile decided to open a CPR liaison office in Nairobi and on 16 August Nkusi moved there with his family.[17]

On two occasions – firstly on 25 August in a letter to Phares Kakule Molo, the executive secretary for Africa of the Wuppertal-based United Evangelical Mission (VEM), and secondly in a letter to his Dutch, Swiss, Belgian and German correspondents on 28 September – Twagirayesu described, probably in response to questions raised by genocide survivors and echoed by the partner organisations, his role during the massacres. He claimed to have interceded with the authorities for refugees threatened by the Interahamwe in the EPR guesthouse in Kigali; organised food assistance for the refugees of the Kugituntu parish; brought the body of Athanase Rwamuhizi (the pastor of Kugituntu) back to Kirinda and buried him after his assassination on 11 April; and evacuated a group of pastors gathered in Kirinda for a church meeting to Gitarama for their safety. He also explained how he helped a man by the name of Mathias and his family to escape from a crowd of 'fifty youngsters, enraged like drug addicts and armed with white weapons', who had attacked the local school. Neither the gendarmes nor the prefect of Kibuye, he said, were prepared to intervene. On 14 April, the day of a massacre in the hospital and the nursing

---

[16] Dr Patricia Nickson, Second visit to Bukavu and Rwanda, 11 August 1994 (Munyaneza Papers).
[17] Emmanuel Nkusi to the partner organisations, Nairobi, 30 August (Munyaneza Papers).

school that claimed more than a hundred lives,[18] he declared to Pastor Aaron Mugemera and to Géras Mutimura, an agronomist employed by the church in the neighbouring parish of Biguhu, that he could not guarantee their security and that of their families and was prepared to put vehicles at their disposal. They did not believe that the danger was imminent, he wrote, and did not follow his advice.[19] On 16 May, following a meeting of the Comité de Contacts during which the Catholic and Protestant churches issued a joint statement, Twagirayesu went to see Jean Kambanda, the prime minister of the interim government, in Gitarama to request protection for five Tutsi pastors in danger of death in the nearby Remera-Rukoma parish and confirmed the request in writing two days later.[20]

The EPR partners' change of mind

Faced with the contradictory claims of the Presbyterians who remained in Rwanda and those in exile, the Belgian, Dutch, German and Swiss partners met on 13 September 1994 in Brussels to coordinate their actions and prepare a mission of exploration to the country. Désiré Rutaganda – a pastor who had lost his wife and his son during the genocide – and Phares Kakule Molo were present. The verbal report of Burkhard Bartel, a pastor from the Evangelical Church of Germany who visited what was left of the EPR in Kigali, Kabgayi and Kirinda in August, seems to have instilled doubt in the mind of the partners on the credibility of Twagirayesu and his colleagues from Bukavu. This is what he said:

> The authorities of the EPR apparently took their personal belongings, those of the church and those of Pastor Gafaranga as well as all the vehicles of the EPR, twelve in total, and transported everything to Bukavu. From there Michel Twagirayesu is said to have sent trucks to collect the money and the belongings of the Centre Béthanie. He seems to have emptied the bank of the EPR because the bank is also in Bukavu.

---

[18] Arrêt de la Cour d'appel de Ruhengeri, 4 avril 2004, in Avocats Sans Frontières, *Recueil de jurisprudence, contentieux du génocide*, vol. 7 (Brussels : n.p., 2006), 212.
[19] Michel Twagirayesu to [Phares] Kakule Molo, Bukavu, 25 August 1994 and Michel Twagirayesu to Rob Krol, Jean Ramoni, [Phares] Kakule Molo and Theo Stevens, 28 September 1994 (Munyaneza Papers).
[20] Twagirayesu to Kakule Molo, 25 August 1994. A copy of Twagirayesu's letter to Kabanda is included in the letter he sent to Gédéon Gakindi on 13 September 1994 (Munyaneza Papers).

Worse, Bartel discovered that senior members of the EPR had been involved in the genocide in Kirinda:

> An eyewitness tells how Amani, a nephew of Michel Twagirayesu, accompanied by other killers, had to break a wall to be able to kill the family of Pastor Aaron Mugemera, starting with the children, then their mother. Many Christians are said to have been transported in EPR vehicles on the Kirinda bridge and thrown away into the river. Some survived and are prepared to testify.

Bartel could not be accused of bias in favour of the RPF, since he also echoed stories of disappearances and mass execution allegedly committed by the Tutsi-led army during this period. This did not prevent him from raising the question of Twagirayesu's integrity:

> According to the testimonies received by Mr Burkhard, Michel Twagirayesu and his family are those who bear responsibility for the massacres in the EPR throughout the country. The houses of the pastors, sometimes stained with blood, have been looted. Corpses are buried in the gardens.[21]

The purpose of the Brussels meeting was to prepare an exploratory mission to Rwanda and the refugee camps in Zaire that was to take place in October. In the meantime, the partners resolved to suspend assistance to the Bukavu group 'because there [were] too many questions about them'. If the church exile were to receive aid, the minutes read, Bukavu might become a 'Gaza'.[22]

The October mission, led by Rob Krol, the general secretary of the Mission of the Reformed Churches in the Netherlands, confirmed and strengthened the line of conduct adopted in Brussels. While having no qualms, like Bartel, about questioning the RPF's records in matters of human rights, Krol was unambiguous in his denunciation of the EPR's involvement in the genocide in Kirinda. 'Dozens of people', he reported, 'have been deliberately killed, with EPR members, even leaders, taking part in the preparation and the execution of the massacres.' One realises, he noted, that 'a church that leaves such people undisturbed in their functions loses all credibility'.[23]

---

[21] Minutes of the meeting held in Brussels on 13 September 1994, 3 (Munyaneza Papers)
[22] *Ibid.*, 5.
[23] L. R. Krol, 'Rapport abrégé de la visite au Rwanda en octobre 1994', Leusden, 28 October 1994, 1.

Krol was 'impressed' by the vitality of the EPR communities he found in post-genocide Rwanda. His assessment of the EPR in Bukavu and Muku was less positive. Behind the 'ideological smoke screen', he wrote, it was difficult to distinguish between lies and the truth. Twagirayesu, with whom he had an hour-long discussion, refused to acknowledge the legitimacy of the new structures the Presbyterians who remained in Rwanda were putting in place and, instead, requested money for a reconciliation programme to be managed by the church in exile.

Krol then mentioned the 'well-known document of 6 June'. Embarrassed, Twagirayesu contended that he had been influenced by the political context when he wrote it. They were referring to a document entitled 'La tragédie du pouvoir au Rwanda' [The tragedy of power in Rwanda], which the EPR president had sent to the EPR's partners during the genocide. It reproduced, word for word, the discourse of the interim government. Apart from a brief mention of the 'hunting of the RPF's accomplices and their families', the document ignored the fact that the majority of victims were Tutsi. Rather, it explained that supporters of the 'Tutsi monarchy' had been preparing a revenge for 'more than thirty years' and accused the RPF of having 'programmed the extermination of the Hutu elites'. 'Brigades' had been sent throughout the country to bury the victims. This 'war of interethnic extermination and vengeance' had decimated 'the innocent and the guilty' – a subtle but unambiguous justification of the slaughtering of the RPF 'accomplices'. The interim government, Twagirayesu further wrote, had wanted to put an end of the war, but the RFP and its Ugandan allies had refused to do so.[24]

The partner organisations, already taken aback by the absence of any mention of the genocide against the Tutsi in the church leaders' statement of 13 May 1994,[25] reacted to Twagirayesu's letter of 6 June with surprise. Jacques and Hélène Küng, two Swiss missionaries, shared the news that André Karamaga, then in Nairobi, had found the EPR president's position hard to understand and wondered why 'the church leaders in Rwanda did not officially denounce the propaganda of the [extremist Hutu party] CDR and the Radio Télévision des Mille Collines, something they should have done months ago.'[26] Memories of the partners' discomfort resur-

---

[24] Michel Twagirayesu, 'La tragédie du pouvoir au Rwanda', 6 June 1994 (Van 't Spijker Papers).

[25] Gerard van 't Spijker, *Indicible Rwanda*, 12–13. On this statement, see Chapter 3.

[26] Jacques and Hélène Küng to the members of the 'Rwanda Group', Lausanne, 23 June 1999 (Van 't Spijker Papers).

faced in 2001 when Jan Greven, the editor of the daily newspaper *Trouw* reviewed a book of Gerard van 't Spijker, a Dutch Reformed pastor and anthropologist who had worked in Rwanda between 1973 and 1982 and again between 1995 and 1999. Van 't Spijker and his colleagues, he commented, had found it strange that Twagirayesu, a man for whom they had respect, hardly said a word about the genocide against the Tutsi, which by then was in full swing. After his flight to Bukavu, he 'never expressed regret, let alone asked for forgiveness'.[27]

In any event, Twagirayesu failed to convince Krol. In his report, the Dutch pastor recommended that the partners 'block all the previous commitments that have been contracted with the ecclesiastical structures of the EPR'. The mode of cooperation, both with the Presbyterians in the country and those in the refugee camps, would have to be reconsidered when new structures were instituted. By April 1995, when Tharcisse Gatwa (the director of the Biblical Society of Rwanda, who had gone to Edinburgh to study) visited Rwanda, the European churches' *gel de la cooperation financière* [moratorium on financial cooperation] with the EPR was still in place.[28] The $20,000 grant for the relaunch of the church's activities – which the partner organisation had decided to make at a meeting held on 27 February in Wuppertal – must have been awarded soon afterwards.[29]

The genocide in Kirinda remembered

In a letter to Gédéon Gakindi, the general secretary of the EPR in Kigali, Twagirayesu defended himself against the accusation of having betrayed the five pastors who were massacred in Remera-Rukoma on 23 May 1994. As proof, he included a copy of the letter he had written to Prime Minister Jean Kambanda on 18 May, in which he requested protection for his colleagues. As we shall see, the matter was discussed at a meeting between the two groups of Rwandan Presbyterians in September 1996 in Windhoek. There is no proof, judging from the sources consulted so

---

[27] Jan Greven, 'Zengingspijn na de Rwandese genocide', *Trouw*, 10 April 2001. The article gave a review of *Zijn daar nog woorden voor? Overwegingen bij het drama van Rwanda* (Kampen: Kok, 2001), the Dutch version of a book subsequently published by Gerard van 't Spijker in French under the title *Indicible Rwanda* (see note 25).

[28] Tharcisse Gatwa, 'Impressions d'un passage au pays', *Dialogue*, 185 (September 1995), 60.

[29] 'Rencontre des partenaires européens de l'Église presbytérienne au Rwanda', Wuppertal, 27 February 1995 (Van 't Spijker Papers).

far, that Twagirayesu was instrumental in the Remera-Rukoma massacre. According to Jérôme Bizimana, the current pastor, they were killed after an Interahamwe accidently discovered that somebody was bringing food to their hiding place.[30]

More problematic was Twagirayesu's attitude during the genocide in Kirinda. The majority of victims were assassinated on 14 April in Kirinda Hospital and, an hour later, in a dormitory of the ESI where Tutsi families had taken refuge. As mentioned earlier, more than a hundred people were murdered on that day.[31] Others lost their lives in the following days at roadblocks staffed by community members.

Even though neither Twagirayesu nor the directors of the EPR-sponsored institutions of Kirinda were brought to court except *in absentia* during a *gacaca* trial in February 2007,[32] this episode is relatively well known thanks to the work of Timothy Longman, who, after a research campaign in the area in 1992 and 1993, interviewed genocide survivors in 1995 and 1996.[33] Three reports of the London-based organisation African Rights, based on interviews conducted in 1996 and after the 2007 *gacaca* trial, complete the documentation.[34] I myself interviewed one of the survivors, Aaron Mugemera, on two occasions.[35] There is no reason to doubt the authenticity of these oral testimonies, which are concordant and consistent over time.

In his account of the role he played in Kirinda during the genocide, Twagirayesu raised two arguments: his powerlessness and the fact that the massacres were perpetrated by a crowd of 'enraged' youths who were completely out of control. In his letter to Kakule Molo, he intimated

---

[30] Jérôme Bizimana, interview conducted on 22 March 2017 in Remera-Rukoma.

[31] This figure does not include the Tutsi who were massacred in the communal hall of Bwakira, the commune that included Kirinda. They are estimated to have been at least a thousand.

[32] The public prosecutor listed them as defendants at a trial in the Tribunal of 1st Instance of Kibuye in 1999 but did not charge them because they were absent. See Avocats Sans Frontières, *Recueil de jurisprudence*, vol. 7, 211–12.

[33] Longman, *Christianity and Genocide*, 268–300.

[34] African Rights, *The African Church and the Genocide: An Appeal to the World Council of Churches' Meeting in Harare* (London: African Rights, 1998), 13–17; *The Nairobi Communiqué and the ex-FAR/Interahamwe*, December 2007, 72–4; *Summary of Information to African Rights on Genocide Suspects Submitted to the Government of Zambia*, April 2010, 3–6.

[35] Aaron Mugemera, interview conducted on 14 March 2019 and 28 February 2020 in Kigali.

that the orders to kill the Tutsi were coming as if from nowhere. 'The resumption of the combat and the civil disobedience took advantage of the well-known bandits of our areas,' he wrote. 'One could not really identify the local authorities who orchestrated "the hunt against the accomplices" (*la chasse aux complices*).'[36]

Both claims are contradicted by the survivors. The crowds in question were summoned and manipulated by the local authorities, starting with the burgomaster, Tharcisse Kabasha, whom Twagirayesu knew very well. As Longman noted, 'there appears to have been careful coordination among community leaders who planned the attacks according to a pattern followed throughout much of the country'.[37] In Kirinda, many of the people involved in the genocide were either family members of Twagirayesu or EPR officials or both. Amani Nyilingabo, a local businessman with close connections to the church who played a leading role in the killings, was a cousin of Twagirayesu by marriage[38] and a brother-in-law of Renate Ndayisaba, the head of the church's women's department, one of the first women to be ordained in the EPR.[39] Silas Kubwimana, a businessman from Taba who, according to African Rights, was widely regarded as the man whose arrival in Kirinda on 8 April ignited the massacres of Tutsi in the area,[40] was also a relative of Twagirayesu. They were connected, as shown by the fact that the EPR president lent him a car belonging to the church for a week in April, during the early days of the genocide.[41]

Also involved in the genocide were the directors of the institutions funded and supported by the EPR: Antoine Kamanzi, the director of the Kirinda Hospital; Marcellin Nsengiyumva, the director of the ESI; and, reportedly to a lesser degree, Fidèle Ntawirukanayo, the director of the

---

[36] Twagirayesu to Kakule Molo, 25 August 1994.
[37] Longman, *Christianity and Genocide*, 284.
[38] Aaron Mugemera, interview conducted on 28 February 2020 in Kigali. On Amani Nyilingabo, see Timothy Longman, 'Empowering the weak and protecting the powerful: the contradictory nature of churches in Central Africa', *African Studies Review*, 41 (1998), 63–4. In a letter to Gerard van 't Spijker (see note 49), Tharcisse Mulfinger, Michel Twagirayesu's son, downplayed his father's closeness to Nyilingabo, but Longman's biographical sketch of the Interahamwe leader, based on first-hand information, gives a different image of their relations.
[39] Longman, *Christianity and Genocide*, 220.
[40] African Rights, *The Nairobi Communiqué*, 72.
[41] Michel Twagirayesu to Gédéon Gikindi, 13 septembre 1994 (Munyaneza Papers).

IPK. Kamanzi and Ntawirukanayo, along with Nyilingabo, were members of the Kirinda 'security committee' when it started to mobilise the population against the 'RPF accomplices' on 11 April 1994. They supplied the youth gang, now organised as a militia, with arms.[42] Edouard, a confessed killer who testified at the *gacaca* in February 1997, declared that it was Kamanzi, armed with a Kalashnikov, who invited him to join the murderers in the hospital. A genocide survivor known as Gisèle said that he had opened the doors for the militiamen to enter the rooms and kill the people inside.[43]

Several EPR pastors, most notably Renate Ndayisaba, assisted the killers. Born of Burundian parents, she was related through her late husband to Kabasha and Nyilingabo. The survivors described her as vehemently anti-Tutsi. During a trip to Kirinda with a visitor from the Netherlands in August 1994, Aaron Mugemera found blood on the walls and the armchairs in her house.[44] In a court document, Léonidas Ntibimenya, the president of the Kirinda region of the EPR, admitted to having staffed the roadblocks destined to prevent the Tutsi refugees from fleeing but denied having killed anybody.[45] Longman also mentioned a relative of Twagirayesu employed as head of a church department in Kigali who organised the night patrols in Kirinda after the 14 April massacres.[46]

What about Michel Twagirayesu himself? When Kakule Molo visited the EPR in exile in Goma in August 1994, he was told that Twagirayesu had tried to protect the Tutsi during the genocide.[47] His former colleague Gerard van 't Spijker expressed in an interview that he believed in his integrity. He pointed out that the Comité de Contacts, of which Twagirayesu was a key member, tried to mediate between the Habyarimana government and the RFP in 1993.[48] For his part, Tharcisse Mulfinger, Twagirayesu's son, described his father, in a letter to van 't, as a man '[with] human kindness and caring for all' who deeply regretted the genocide. 'He was not successful [in] protecting [the Tutsi refugees],' he commented, 'but

[42] Longman, *Christianity and Genocide*, 285.
[43] African Rights, *Summary of Information*, 4–5.
[44] Mugemera, same interview.
[45] Avocats Sans Frontières, *Recueil de jurisprudence*, vol. 7, 239.
[46] Longman, *Christianity and Genocide*, 292.
[47] Kakule Molo, 'Rapport de la visite à Goma et à Bukavu', Wuppertal, 5 September 1994, 2 (Van 't Spijker Papers).
[48] Gerard van 't Spijker, interview conducted on 22 January 2018 in Eindhoven.

he did everything in his power as a churchman to protect them against the government and armed militia'.⁴⁹

Aaron Mugemera, who miraculously survived the massacre in the dormitory of the ESI in Kirinda but not without seeing the killers, led by Amani Nyilingabo, butchering his wife and his children, however, disagreed. When telling the story – to McCullum,⁵⁰ to Longman,⁵¹ to Rakiya Omaar⁵² and to me⁵³ – he explained that he had come from Biguhu, the nearby parish he pastored, to Kirinda, where he had a house, in the belief that Twagirayesu, whom everybody respected, would protect him. On 13 April, Twagirayesu, Kamanzi, Nsengiyumva and a few others came to take their names, which he found suspicious. On the morning of the 14th, Twagirayesu invited him and his friend Géras Mutimura to travel to Gitarama with church vehicles for safety. They did not decline the offer because they underestimated the danger, as Twagirayesu later claimed, but because they were afraid of the roadblocks manned by Nyilingabo's militiamen.

What Mugemera found most disturbing was the fact that Twagirayesu and his family were present, in the same building, when Nyilingabo and his men broke the door of the dormitory where they were hiding and started murdering all the people inside:

> During this massacre, Twagirayesu was near us, in his room. He did not say anything. He did not even hide a child, something he was able to do. Twagirayesu held authority in Kirinda. He was the president of the EPR and, as a result, controlled the hospital, the ESI, the IPK, because they belonged to the EPR. It was people who worked there who killed my family.⁵⁴

Was Twagirayesu as powerless as he claimed he was? The involvement of his relatives and of senior members of the EPR – the director of Kirinda Hospital in particular – is difficult to deny. 'During the genocide all the family of Twagirayesu were devils', a survivor told Longman in 1996.⁵⁵ Such a statement may have to be qualified but is nevertheless quite telling. One of Longman's sources claimed that he mobilised the community

---

⁴⁹ Tharcisse Mulfinger to Gerard van 't Spijker [c. 2018] (Van 't Spijker Papers).
⁵⁰ Hugh McCullum, *The Angels Have Left Us: The Rwanda Tragedy and the Churches* (Geneva: WCC, [1995]), 74–5.
⁵¹ Longman, *Christianity and Genocide,* 287–90.
⁵² African Rights, *Les Églises et le génocide,* 13–15.
⁵³ Mugemera, same interview.
⁵⁴ African Rights, *Les Églises et le génocide,* 14.
⁵⁵ Longman, *Christianity and Genocide,* 292.

with help from members of his family in the run-up to the 14 April massacre.⁵⁶ As the Canadian journalist Hugh McCullum reported, some people accused him of having incited people to murder.⁵⁷ These are just allegations. His silence, on the other hand, is striking. One could accept that he was afraid of confronting an angry crowd. It is possible, as he claimed, that he tried to alert the political authorities when tension was mounting up.⁵⁸ But what did he do during the Kirinda massacre to reason with his colleagues in the EPR, the members of his family and people he knew well, such as Tharcisse Kabasha (the burgomaster of Bwakira) and Amani Nyilingabo, who led the band of killers in Kirinda? He never distanced himself from them in subsequent statements. After the genocide, he spent time with them in Muku near Bukavu, where the EPR had reconstituted itself under Kabasha's watchful eye, without any apparent difficulty.⁵⁹

Twagirayesu's involvement in the Kirinda massacre was never investigated in a court of law. More research would be necessary to arrive at a conclusion. What we know for sure is that he uncritically followed the standpoint of the interim government which orchestrated the massacres. Until his dying day, he refused to recognise the reality of the genocide against the Tutsi, arguing, instead, that it was nothing other than an ugly war started by the RPF. The 6 June 1994 document whose existence Rob Krol reminded him of during a tense meeting in Muku is proof of this. As the Dutch pastor commented, 'Twagirayesu's position as impartial president of the EPR [was] seriously compromised'.⁶⁰

Re-establishing the church on a new basis

The enormity of the involvement of EPR ministers and officials in the Kirinda massacres and the leadership in exile's reluctance to recognise the reality of the genocide are arguably the main reasons for the decision,

---

⁵⁶ *Ibid.*, 285.

⁵⁷ Hugh McCullum, 'Postface à l'édition française', in *Dieu était-il au Rwanda? La faillite des Églises* (Paris: L'Harmattan, 1996), 218. This information is not included in *The Angels Have Left Us* (see note 50).

⁵⁸ Mulfinger to van 't Spijker [c. 2018].

⁵⁹ Danielle de Lame, *A Hill among a Thousand: Transformations and Ruptures in Rural Rwanda* (Madison: University of Wisconsin Press, 2005), 460. De Lame visited Muku in 1995 as a researcher with the Steering Committee of the Joint Evaluation of Emergency Assistance to Rwanda.

⁶⁰ Krol, 'Rapport abrégé de la visite au Rwanda en octobre 1994', 2.

accepted by the partner organisations,[61] to re-establish the church on a new basis and to publicly confess the church's complicity in the genocide.

On 20 July 1994, four pastors – including Naasson Hitimana (Twagirayesu's predecessor as EPR president) and Aaron Mugemera – the widows of two pastors killed during the genocide, three elders, a deacon and an evangelist created an informal body whose task was to carry out the reconstruction of the EPR and named it the Presbyterian Rehabilitation Committee.[62] André Karamaga, a Rwandan pastor who headed the AACC theology and interfaith desk in Nairobi at the time, supported them through frequent visits to Rwanda. He too had lost family members to the genocide, his father in particular.[63] According to McCullum, who met the members of the committee, they also called themselves the Surviving Church and the Repentant Church. Their first move was to send a call for help entitled 'SOS pour les Presbytériens rescapés du génocide au Rwanda' [SOS for the Presbyterian survivors of the genocide].[64]

The members of the Rehabilitation Committee met José Chipenda and Burkhard Bartel during their visit to Rwanda in August[65] and Rob Krol when he came on an exploration mission in October.[66] They told the latter that their goal was to establish a 'Confessing Church' – in reference to the German Christians who chose to dissociate themselves from the churches that supported the Nazi regime in the 1930s – and that they felt that a complete renewal of the church was the only option. They were highly critical of the previous leadership and, according to Krol, 'from time to time [used] a language influenced by the RFP'.[67]

Alongside this committee, the members of the EPR's Executive Committee who had remained in Rwanda also tried to relaunch the church, but with due attention to the church's constitution and with the support

---

[61] 'Rencontre des partenaires européens de l'Eglise presbytérienne du Rwanda', Wuppertal, 27 February 1996 (Van 't Spijker Papers).
[62] For the date, see Michel Twagirayesu, 'Visite de la délégation des partenaires missionnaires de l'Église presbytérienne au Rwanda du 1 au 15 octobre 1994. Aide-mémoire' [Visit of the delegation of missionary partners of the Presbyterian Church in Rwanda from 1 to 15 October 1995. Aide-memoire], Bukavu, 12 octobre 1994 (Munyaneza Papers).
[63] Aaron Mugemera, interview conducted on 28 February 2020 in Kigali.
[64] Hugh McCullum, *The Angels Have Left Us*, 71–2.
[65] Minutes of the meeting held in Brussels on 13 September 1994, 3. See also McCullum, *The Angels Have Left Us*, 75.
[66] Krol, 'Rapport abrégé de la visite au Rwanda en octobre 1994', 3.
[67] Ibid., 3.

of the local, regional and national councils that were still in place. Of the 20 members of the Synodal Council who had been appointed before the genocide, 9 were still in Rwanda. Five had been killed, 1 was in jail and 5 had fled the country.[68] Before April 1994, the church employed 95 pastors, including a few missionaries. Out of those, 16 had been killed during the genocide, 38 had gone into exile and only 41 had remained in Rwanda.[69] The Rehabilitation Committee and the EPR Executive Committee, Krol observed, followed different methodologies but they worked in good accord.[70]

Like Twagirayesu in Bukavu, Gédéon Gakindi, the general secretary of the EPR, and Donat Nyilinkindi, the general treasurer – two officials who remained in the country – turned to the church partner organisations to obtain funding for the rehabilitation of the church's buildings, the provision of material support to the bereaved families and the reorganisation of the parishes. In a document entitled 'Programme de redressement' [Uplifting programme], they argued that the church could no longer function under the authority of the president because he was out of the country and that new ways had to be found to resolve the crisis. In a veiled attack on the pastors who had supported the interim government during the genocide, they pointed out that some pastors had been involved in political activities in contravention of the church's constitution. They also criticised the leadership of the church for having taken the church's funds, vehicles and office equipment to Bukavu.[71] Predictably, when a copy of the document ended up in his hands, Twagirayesu vehemently protested.[72]

The extraordinary synod of February 1995

In January 1995 the reconstruction programme shifted to a higher gear when the Presbyterian Rehabilitation Committee, in concertation with the EPR Executive Committee and the Synodal Council, invited a wide range

[68] Gerard van 't Spijker, *L'Église chrétienne au Rwanda pré et post-génocide* (Paris: L'Harmattan, 2011), 31. According to a preparatory document of the February 1995 synod (Munyaneza Papers), only six Synodal Council members were still in the country in early 1995.

[69] Donat Nyilinkindi and Gédéon Gakindi, 'Église presbytérienne au Rwanda: Programme de redressement', 25 August 1994, 4 (Munyaneza Papers).

[70] Krol, 'Rapport abrégé de la visite au Rwanda en octobre 1994', 4.

[71] Nyilinkindi and Gakindi, 'Programme de redressement'.

[72] Michel Twagirayesu to Gédéon Gakindi, Bukavu, 13 September 1994 (Munyaneza Papers).

of stakeholders – pastors, evangelists, theology students, staff members and partners – to a meeting with the purpose of evaluating the situation of the church and launching a rehabilitation programme. No fewer than two hundred people attended the event. The meeting took place between 30 January and 3 February 1995 in Kigali.

Van 't Spijker heard of the plan to hold this meeting during a visit to Rwanda in early January 1995 and encouraged the church's partners to fund it on his return to Europe. The drivers of the project, he reported, were Naasson Hitimana, the former president; Siméon Nzabahimana, a Hutu pastor who had saved Tutsi lives during the massacres; and André Karamaga, who was in Rwanda at the time.[73] 'One could see', van 't Spijker commented, 'that even though they did not speak of an ethnic equilibrium at that point, all components of the population were represented in the leadership of the Church.'[74]

Karamaga had arrived from Nairobi with his wife after Hutu refugees had issued threats against him and his family, causing one of his sons to be sent to jail on a false pretext.[75] A man reputed for his theological insights, Karamaga had been working for the AACC since the late 1980s. Prior to that, he had experienced tensions with Hutu colleagues who believed he should not be promoted because he was Tutsi.[76] 'One feels ashamed to mention it,' he wrote in a book edited by the French political scientist André Guichaoua in 1994, 'but the ethnic discrimination that characterised the practice of government [in Rwanda], also existed in the church. [...] Any appointment or any promotion to a position of ecclesiastical responsibility was subjected to ethnic criteria, admittedly with a discretion skilfully dissimulated under the sweet language familiar to ecclesiastical circles.'[77]

Rob Krol, who took part in the Kigali meeting, described the atmosphere reigning in it in the following terms:

---

[73] Van 't Spijker, *Indicible Rwanda*, 38–9.

[74] Van 't Spijker, *Indicible Rwanda*, 40.

[75] *Ibid.*, 38. The information about the threats against Karamaga in Nairobi was omitted in the revised version of van 't Spijker's book, which came out under the title *L'Église chrétienne au Rwanda pré et post-génocide* (Paris: L'Harmattan, 2011).

[76] Longman, *Christianity and Genocide*, 96; Jan van Butselaar, 'Timothy Longman's Christianity and genocide', *Social Sciences and Missions*, 26/2–3 (2013), 264.

[77] André Karamaga, 'Les Églises protestantes et la crise rwandaise', in André Guichaoua, *Les crises politiques au Burundi et au Rwanda (1993–1994)* (Lille: Université des Sciences et Technologies, 1994), 302.

One felt the joy of the reunion, the sadness because of the dead, the encouragement provided by the prayers, the songs and the dances but also fear and shame for what had happened in the church and in society in Rwanda.[78]

'André Karamaga', Gerard van 't Spijker noted, 'is a man who has clear ideas for the future.'[79] In Kigali he rapidly displayed the leadership qualities that were to illustrate this tenure as EPR president in the following years. In a bold move, the delegates constituted themselves in an extraordinary synod for the reason that the president, Michel Twagirayesu, was no longer in a position to lead the church and that the majority of Synodal Council members were either dead or outside the country. They elected Karamaga as president, Hitimana as vice-president and Malachie Munyaneza as general secretary. A tall man who was often mistaken for a Tutsi despite being officially classified as Hutu, Munyaneza had publicly denounced the ethnic divisions in the country before the genocide while working for the AEE. In April 1994, he had witnessed the murder of friends and neighbours in his Gikondo home and narrowly escaped death himself before going to his village of birth near Gitarama. After the war, he had followed his wife Julienne to London, where she had taken a post at the World Association for Christian Communication before the genocide. He agreed to come back to Rwanda for a year on Karamaga's insistence.[80]

The extraordinary synod resolved that the church should engage in a two-year transition period during which a new constitution would be drafted. The structures of the church would be 'profoundly changed to adapt to the teaching of the gospel and conform to the Presbyterian model that gives priority to the active participation of the entire people of God

---

[78] Van 't Spijker, *Indicible Rwanda*, 40.

[79] *Ibid.*, 38.

[80] Malachie Munyaneza described his ordeal in July 1994 in a seventeen-page handwritten document entitled 'La tragédie rwandaise et la survie de la vie' (Munyaneza Papers). See below, p. 98. The reflection papers he published after the genocide include 'Violence as institution in African religious experience', *Contagion. Journal of Violence, Mimesis and Culture*, 8, 2001, 39–68, and 'Genocide in the name of "salvation": the combined contribution of biblical translation/interpretation and indigenous myth to the 1994 Rwandan genocide', in Jonneke Bekkenkamp and Yvonne Sherwood (ed.), *Sanctified Agression: Legacies of Biblical and Post Biblical Vocabularies of Violence* (London and New York: T & T Clark International, 2003), 60–75. His wife also took the pen to describe her experience in the genocide. See Julienne Munyaneza, *Grace in the Midst of the Genocide* (Exeter: Onwards and Upwards Publishers, 2017).

in the life of the Church'. The terms of office would be shortened and the participation of the laity, women in particular, would be encouraged. The accounts would be audited at all levels of the church. The faculty of theology at Butare would be reopened. New conventions would be signed with the partner churches in Europe.[81]

The meeting did not shy away from addressing the issue of the genocide at a time when the Catholic bishops, as noted in the last chapter, deliberately avoided using the term in public statements. The synod expressed the wish that the genocide survivors should 'heal from their traumatism and regain their dignity', that 'the people involved in the genocide and the massacres be brought to repentance as a way to forgiveness' and that the prisoners be visited and comforted. In reference to the 'extremists', the synod reaffirmed that 'the blood of Christ made of all people brothers and sisters created in the image of God' and that 'those who remain blocked in their ethnic identities mock the blood of Jesus Christ shed on the cross to make of all brothers and sisters'.[82]

Lastly, the synod recognised 'with sadness' that Rwandans lived in exile in 'miserable conditions' and that among them were members of the Presbyterian Church. It called for their return 'so as the Body of Christ be one again'.[83]

The ecumenical movement supported the EPR's decision of holding an extraordinary synod and of opening a two-year transition period. Its support for the victims of the genocide against the Tutsi was in line with the concern for human rights that the WCC and the AACC had manifested in the early 1990s.[84] On 7 March 1995, *Ecumenical News International*, an ecumenical newsletter funded by the WCC and three other international church bodies, hailed the election of Karamaga as president and wished him success in the 'difficult' task of rebuilding the EPR. Providing support to Karamaga was, in fact, all but evident. Until 1994, Twagirayesu had been a member of the WCC Central Committee. It fell to José Chipenda, the AACC general secretary in Nairobi, to describe, in a fine balancing act, Twagirayesu as an 'outstanding leader' and Karamaga as a 'very sound leader'. Nevertheless, the article quoted Sam Isaac, a WCC official, as

---

[81] 'Résolutions du Synode général extraordinaire réuni à Kigali le 3 février 1995' (Munyaneza Papers).
[82] *Ibid.*, 3.
[83] *Ibid.*, 3.
[84] Tharcisse Gatwa, *The Churches and Ethnic Ideology in the Rwandan Crises 1900–1994* (Oxford: Regnum Books International, 2005), 202–6.

having said that 'the churches in Rwanda had been discredited by aligning themselves far too closely with the former Hutu-dominated regime'.[85]

The opposition to the synod

In the refugee camps in Zaire, Twagirayesu and his colleagues reacted with dismay to the news that an extraordinary General Synod had elected a new leadership. In a letter addressed to the president of the General Synod of the EPR on 24 February, the self-styled 'members of the Presbyterian Church in Rwanda in South-Kivu' castigated the 'fury of certain malicious people, power hungry and full of a divisionist spirit, to pretend bringing together people who are still living in the anguish of seeing their dear homeland divided with the aim of swallowing them into their errors and maintaining them in an intimidation that makes them forget the love of their neighbour and of God our heavenly Father who put them aside'. They declared the synod unconstitutional and condemned as manipulative and intimidating the election of the new president by a show of hands 'under the vigilant eye of the single candidate'. They also denounced the decision of electing Naasson Hitimana – who had retired for health reasons – as vice-president and president of a region. There was no reason, according to them, to hold this synod. The Executive Committee of the Synodal Council was still operational, and the information circulated well between the Rwandans from inside the country and those from outside.[86]

A group of Rwandan Presbyterians from North Kivu sent a similar letter to the president of the General Synod a few days later, but to no avail. The tenants of the old leadership in Zaire had lost the battle for recognition. Their refusal to accept the reality of the genocide against the Tutsi in all its horror had disqualified them. Their attacks on the RPF, accusing them of perpetrating a genocide against the Hutu, did not suffice to restore their image in the ecumenical world.

Later in the same year, in a conversation with the journalist Hugh McCullum in Nairobi, Twagirayesu reiterated that the synod had been invalidly constituted and that he was still the legal representative of the EPR.[87] A section of the community of Hutu refugees in Nairobi vehemently

---

[85] 'New leader elected for Rwandan Church', *Ecumenical News International*, 7 March 1995.

[86] Membres de l'Église Presbytérienne au Rwanda Sud-Kivu au Président au Synode Général de l'Église Presbytérienne au Rwanda, Bukavu, 24 février 1994 (Van 't Spijker Papers).

[87] McCullum, 'Postface', 219.

opposed the new Rwandan government and refused to accept any form of responsibility for the genocide. On 14 November 1995, Karamaga and two other church leaders – Samuel Rugambage and Éraste Iyamuremye, legal representatives of the Union of the Baptist Churches and the Free Methodist Church, respectively – took Emmanuel Nkusi, the general secretary of the Protestant Council of Rwanda, to task for maintaining links with the milieus of Hutu extremists in Nairobi. They accused him of having endorsed, in his official capacity, a negationist document penned by the Free Methodist Church bishop Aaron Ruhumuliza in Nairobi under the title 'The point of view of the Protestant Church on the Rwandese crisis'.[88] For this reason and due to alleged financial irregularities, Karamaga and his colleagues called for his immediate resignation.[89] Nkusi denied any wrongdoing, claiming that all he had done was to attend meetings with Rwandans from inside and outside the country that had been organised by the AACC in Nairobi.[90] This incident revealed the nervousness of the Protestant church leaders in Rwanda regarding genocide denialism. Eighteen months after the end of the genocide, the relations between the church members who remained in Rwanda and those in exile remained tense.

A new beginning

Meanwhile, the new leadership of the EPR set out to implement the rehabilitation programme agreed upon during the February synod. On 9 July 1995, in a ceremony destined to show that the church was now governed from the bottom up according to the Presbyterian ecclesiology, the elders of the Kigali parish, representing those of the entire church, witnessed the consecration of the officials in charge of the four new programmes. With focuses on evangelisation, formation and information; human and material resources; rehabilitation and reconstruction; and service to the poor,

---

[88] Extracts of this document are included in *The African Church and the Genocide: An Appeal to the World Council of Churches' Meeting in Harare* (London: African Rights, 1998), 21–2. Genocide survivors accused Bishop Aaron Ruhumuliza of having been actively involved in the Gikondo massacre on 9 April 1994.
[89] Samuel Rugambage, André Karamaga and Éraste Iyamuremye to Emmanuel Nkusi, [Kigali], 14 November 1995 (Munyaneza Papers).
[90] Emmanuel Nkusi to André Karamaga, Samuel Rugambabe and Éraste Iyamuremye, Kigali, 16 November (Munyaneza Papers).

these programmes aimed to make the EPR functional again at a time when Rwanda itself was busy reconstructing itself.[91]

The first achievement was the reopening of the Faculty of Protestant Theology of Butare on 6 November 1995.[92] The last dean, Faustin Rwagacuzi, had been murdered with his family during the genocide after refusing to kill his Tutsi wife. The buildings of the faculty had been completely ransacked. This interdenominational institution, established in 1970, was administered by the EPR. Because of the desperate need for ordained pastors in the church, Karamaga and his colleagues decided to fast track the training of theological students, limiting the course to two years instead of four and no longer sanctioning it by a government-accredited diploma. The first intake comprised 45 Presbyterian, Anglican, Methodist, Baptist and Pentecostal students, including 15 women. This special programme was rolled out three times, until 2001. In subsequent years, the students who had followed it took complementary courses in order to obtain a diploma. At Karamaga's request, Élisée Musamekweli, a Rwandan pastor who was busy completing a doctoral degree in Brussels, came back to teach in the faculty in the company of Jacques and Hélène Küng – a missionary couple from Switzerland – and Gerard van 't Spijker, who coordinated a programme for the laity.[93]

In a society traumatised by the death of numerous people, faced with thousands of needy widows and orphans and confronted with acts of vengeance, undocumented detentions, illegal house occupations and other forms of post-genocidal violence, everything had to be reinvented. One of the most pressing tasks of the pastors was to bury the dead in dignity. The liturgy had to be adapted to the new situation. To be reassured, some people asked to be baptised by immersion rather than by aspersion. The EPR authorised those who wanted it to follow the new rite.[94] Novel interpretations of the Bible were proposed, with an emphasis, for example, on Jeremiah and Ezekiel's theology of reconstruction. Sin, repentance and

---

[91] 'Lancement de nouveaux programmes de l'EPR', *Bâtissons*, 1 (August 1995), 1–4.

[92] 'La faculté de Théologie Protestante de Butare a réouvert ses portes', *Bâtissons*, 4 (November–December 1995), 6.

[93] Van 't Spijker, *Indicible Rwanda*, 53–6.

[94] 'Réunion du Conseil synodal de l'EPR', *Bâtissons*, 3 (October 1995), 2–3. See Van 't Spijker, *Indicible Rwanda*, 46. Unlike other churches in Rwanda, the EPR refused to administer a second baptism to people who wanted to be reassured about their spiritual status.

reconciliation became dominant themes. Years later, Malachie Munyaneza remembered the message he and his colleagues were trying to convey:

> When Jesus rose from the dead, he did not say, 'You dogs, you abandoned me!' He said, 'I give you my peace.' Jesus absorbed the violence of the world. People have to understand that violence is not a solution to their problems. What will happen on judgment day? How can you take the life of somebody whom you did not create, who did not ask to be Hutu or Tutsi, from the north or from the south? He is a gift of life. Our theology and our reflection must free us from our ethnic and regional bonds.[95]

The first time Munyaneza addressed a congregation after the genocide, people were clapping hands. 'You should rather cry,' he told them. 'We are empty. Something is missing in us.' As he explained, this was a difficult experience:

> People were not only in denial, they were ignorant. [...] I could no longer, as a pastor, celebrate the Lord's Supper during the year that I was there. I kept asking myself: Do we have the right to share the cup and the bread? One day someone asked me to celebrate the wedding of a soldier. I told him: After this event, this tragedy, do I have the courage to marry people? Are they crazy? Are they serious? Then he told me: Even in the camps people get married. He went on: This soldier will marry a girl he has protected during the war. I then said: I shall do it. We need time, we Rwandans, to think about ourselves, reflect and find a new direction. We have to help the widows and orphans, pay the school fees, repair the houses, feed the hungry, support the initiatives of the parishioners. All this is a step towards the reconstruction.[96]

The newsletter *Bâtissons* [Let us build], launched by the EPR in August 1995,[97] became a forum on the matter of reconciliation. In the October 1995 issue, a genocide survivor by the name of Justin Hakizimana argued that repentance should precede reconciliation. Preachers, he wrote, should think twice before speaking of reconciliation. They should rather call people to repentance. 'The Christians must apologise for the beastlike

---

[95] Malachie Munyaneza, interview conducted on 30 March 2019 in Wolverhampton.
[96] Munyaneza, same interview.
[97] An edition in Kinyarwanda was published concurrently under the name *Twubake*.

behaviour of some among their midsts during the genocide. Then the fruits of repentance will lead to reconciliation.'[98]

A response, backed up by an impressive list of biblical quotations, was penned by Charles Karagwa, a staff member of the AEE, in the following issue. Hakizimana should first reconcile himself with God, he wrote, and consider that God himself reconciled with humankind. If God asks him to forgive the murderers outside or inside the country, he should do so in the name of Jesus. It is sad, he concluded, that people oppose reconciliation. It is the road to peace.[99]

Naasson Hitimana, the vice-president of the EPR, then intervened. 'In my distress,' he shared, 'I continued to read the word of God and I discovered that reconciliation has a special place in the Bible.' The genocide perpetrators should be judged according to the law, but that is not enough. In a statement that can be read as a comment on post-genocide Rwanda's difficulty to put in place an equitable judicial system, he outlined what was, according to him, the Christian understanding of justice:

> When justice is administered in a just manner, it plays an important role in reconciliation. Justice only functions well when everybody helps the judges to find the truth about what happened. If everybody was saying the truth and abstained from accusing neighbours unjustly or exonerating from guilt those who did wrong, if guilty people confessed their guilt, repented and asked for forgiveness, justice would render equitable judgments. If that happened, we would be on the way to repentance, forgiveness and reconciliation.[100]

The Windhoek meeting

Meetings between genocide survivors and people involved in the reconstruction of Rwanda, on the one side, and Rwandans in exile, on the other, have been, and still are, a rare occurrence. Channels of communication between the two groups hardly exist. Thanks to the ecumenical movement and the partner organisations, the EPR, which was as politically divided as the rest of the Rwandan nation, benefitted from such an opportunity. The meeting between the Presbyterians from inside and outside the country, which Twagirayesu and his colleagues from Bukavu had been calling for since August 1994, was held, after a long preparatory period, in Windhoek,

---

[98] *Bâtissons*, 3 (October 1995), 3–4.
[99] *Bâtissons*, 4 (November–December 1995), 4–5.
[100] *Bâtissons*, 5 (January 1996), 3–4

Namibia, between 22 and 26 September 1996. It would be illusory to say that the two sides found common ground, but the fact that the meeting took place at all can be hailed as an achievement. As Samuel Cyuma, a member of the delegation of Presbyterians in exile in Nairobi, put it, 'a time of dialogue occurred that nobody had expected'.[101]

The AACC team facilitated the meeting. Desmond Tutu, president of the AACC at the time, also played a role by obtaining, at the last minute, permission for the meeting to take place in Namibia and not, as initially planned, in Botswana, where the administrative hurdles proved insurmountable. Rob Krol, who compiled a report, represented the partner organisations.[102] The participants included 10 Presbyterians from Rwanda, 3 from Nairobi, 3 from Zaire, 3 AACC officials and Krol. Twagirayesu, the former president, and Karamaga, his successor, were both present.

The Windhoek meeting's main purpose was to permit a dialogue between the Presbyterians who remained in Rwanda and those in exile. It is of interest for the purpose of this study, since it revealed with particular clarity the difference of opinion between the Presbyterians inside and outside Rwanda on the significance of the genocide. If the former insisted on the centrality of the genocide in recent Rwandan history, the latter, or at least some of them, underplayed its importance. The two points of view moved closer together but remained different.

Twagirayesu explained that the Presbyterians in Goma and Bukavu felt abandoned by the church and by the partners. He and his colleagues had come to Windhoek to renew contacts. They wanted 'a structure for the EPR without borders' and were keen to 'organise, together with the church from inside a programme for the promotion of forgiveness and reconciliation'. They pointed out that 'in the camps people speak of forgiveness and reconciliation and that there are people who, in private, confess what they have done'. They were not prepared to return to Rwanda because stories of unjust arrests and overcrowded prisons abounded.[103]

For the Presbyterians who remained in the country, any suggestion of a semi-permanent structure outside the borders was unacceptable. They

---

[101] Samuel Cyuma, *Picking Up the Pieces: The Church and Conflict Resolution in South Africa and Rwanda* (Oxford: Regnum Books International, 2012), 226.

[102] L. R. Krol, 'Rencontre des Presbytériens de l'extérieur et de l'intérieur du Rwanda D.D. 22 au 26 septembre 1996 à Windhoek en Namibie' (Munyaneza Papers). On the Windhoek meeting, see also Van 't Spijker, *Indicible Rwanda*, 61–3.

[103] *Bâtissons*, 5 (January 1996), 6–7.

agreed that the judicial system in Rwanda was not perfect, but said that progress was being made and the refugees should be encouraged to return.

The main issue was the interpretation of the genocide. Karamaga started by saying that even though some of them '[did] not want to hear the word or pronounce it', the genocide was an 'inescapable starting point' not only because it had been recognised by the international community as 'a crime that does not disappear' but also because it was something that had a deep impact on everybody. All were touched, 'whether they lost their dear ones, committed murder or witnessed from near of far way this human savagery'. The Presbyterian Church, he went on, 'had an undeniable responsibility in the 1994 genocide'. Where were the Christians in Kirinda, Remera and Rubengera? The crimes committed there cannot simply be forgotten. 'The crisis of the genocide', he concluded, 'resembles the crisis of the cross.' The early disciples of Jesus were ashamed of the cross at first and then became proud of it. 'The blood of the martyrs is the seed of the Church.'[104]

In his report, Krol vividly captured the essential difference between the Rwandans in exile and the genocide survivors. As Karamaga had observed, the former were reluctant to speak of a genocide; the latter insisted that it was a prerequisite to reconciliation:

> The participants from outside the country spoke explicitly of their failure and of their hope in God's grace. At the same time, they put a question mark after the word genocide. What happened in 1994 should be best qualified as killings. And those killings were the result of an unplanned popular insurrection. [...] Mrs Thérèse Gasenge and Mr Zacharie Habiyakare [two members of the delegation from Rwanda] violently reacted. 'We experienced it ourselves. We won't get anywhere unless there is a confession of the genocide as genocide.'[105]

A key moment was the exchange about Twagirayesu's alleged participation in the genocide. He emotionally brandished two letters that the genocide survivors claimed were proof of his culpability. In the first, dated 6 March 1994, he requested a gun from the minister of defence to protect the EPR premises in Remera; in the second, dated 18 May 1994, he asked, as we saw earlier, the prime minister of the interim government,

---

[104] 'Rencontre des Presbytériens de l''intérieur et de l'extérieur du Rwanda, à Windhoek du 22 au 26/9/96. Texte présenté par André Karamaga' (Munyaneza Papers). Karamaga's speech was subsequently published in *Echos d'outremer*, the newsletter of the Département missionnaire des Églises protestantes de Suisse romande based in Lausanne.

[105] Krol, 'Rencontre', 8.

Jean Kambanda, to provide protection to the Tutsi refugees in Remera. He denounced the accusations levelled against him. Mugemera then said: 'You could have protected me and my family from where you were.' 'Each project of rescue I put in place fell through,' Twagirayesu responded. 'I was completely powerless.'[106]

The expected reconciliation did not take place. Mugemera refused to greet Twagirayesu.[107] Later, as van 't Spijker recounted in his memoir, Karamaga told him how 'deeply disappointed' he had been by the manner in which, according to witnesses, Twagirayesu had described the Windhoek meeting in Bukavu:

> In the presence of high-ranking officers, he would have triumphantly said: 'We got them!' A. Karamaga declared that, after that, there was no point in pursuing contacts.'[108]

In a private correspondence with van 't Spijker, Twagirayesu denied having made this statement. The passage is omitted in the second edition of the Dutch missionary's book.[109] Whatever happened in Bukavu, the episode shows that mutual distrust continued to prevail after the Windhoek meeting. More discussion might have happened if the refugee camps in Tanzania and Zaire had not been closed two or three months later, but that did not happen. Twagirayesu never returned to Rwanda. He eventually migrated to the United States, where he died in 2010.[110]

Confessing the church's guilt

Unlike the post-Second World War German churches with the October 1945 Stuttgart Declaration and the post-apartheid South African churches with the November 1990 Rustenburg Confession, the Rwandan churches have long been reluctant to confess their guilt as churches for their ambivalence or their silence in the face of massive human rights abuses.[111] Some, like the Catholic and Anglican churches, made a step in that direction in

---

[106] *Ibid.*, 9.
[107] Mugemera, same interview.
[108] Van 't Spijker, *Indicible Rwanda*, 62–3.
[109] Van 't Spijker, same interview.
[110] Van Butselaar, review of Longman's *Christianity and Genocide*, 254.
[111] Philippe Denis, 'Germany, South Africa, Rwanda: Three manners for a church to confess its guilt', *Studia Historiae Ecclesiasticae*, 43/2 (2017), 1–20.

the twenty-five years following the genocide, but internally the debate on the need for the church to confess its guilt never abated.

The first church that made such a confession was the EPR at the General Synod it held in Kigali from 10 to 15 December 1996. It was the first synod since February 1995, when a new leadership was elected and a programme of rehabilitation adopted. As scheduled, the delegates approved a new constitution that limited the term of office of the president to four years, renewable only once, and made provision for women to comprise half of the laypeople at all levels of church government.[112]

Several resolutions dealt with the consequences of the genocide. Significantly, the synod encouraged the church members to provide assistance not only to the genocide survivors but also to the refugees from 1994, who had returned from Tanzania and Zaire in big numbers after the closure of the camps in October and November. Church members were invited to befriend them and show them the love of Christ. 'All must learn that it is necessary for all to live together in the same country', one of the resolutions read. 'One must dedicate oneself to the building up of a new Rwanda.' The houses that had been occupied since the end of the genocide had to be returned to their original owners.[113]

On the need to repent for acts of genocide, the synod was uncompromising. 'All must understand and be conscious of the fact', it resolved, 'that the one who committed a sin must bear the consequences.' The synod called for the arrest of the people who 'became extremists on the basis of ethnicity' and asked that justice played its role. This concerned the pastors who had been found guilty of genocide. 'It is necessary', a resolution read, 'that those who worked for the EPR and behaved badly should be suspended from their functions.' The pastors and evangelists known for having been implicated in the genocide were banned, and those who had left the country in 1994 and decided to return were told to manifest themselves before the end of 1997 if they wanted to reintegrate into the ministry.[114] This was a wide-reaching decision. The Catholic Church, for example, never did anything similar when priests and seminarians returned from Zaire.

Even more momentous was the church's confession of guilt.[115] The synod asked for forgiveness not only – like the Catholic Church would do in 2000 – for those of its members who had erred, but for itself:

[112] *Bâtissons*, 9 (January–February 1997), 5–6.
[113] EPR, Resolutions of the General Synod held in Kigali, 10–15 December 1995.
[114] Aaron Mugemera, interview conducted on 28 February 2020 in Kigali.
[115] Gatwa, *The Churches and Ethnic Ideology*, 227–8; Van 't Spijker, *Indicible*

Dear Rwandans and Christians, the time has come to proceed with self-criticism because the Church of God is ashamed of having been incapable of opposing or denouncing the planning and execution of the genocide. As God's servant Nehemiah did (Neh. 1.5-11), so we, the Synod, in the name of the members of the Presbyterian Church of Rwanda, repent and ask forgiveness before God and nation for the weakness and lack of courage when these were needed. The Synod asks the people of Rwanda and the worldwide Christian family to oppose every rejection of God's will for His creatures, to denounce and resist strongly ethnicism, regionalism and religious divisions. For God, there is no Jew, Greek, Hutu, Tutsi nor Twa. We are all one in Christ.[116]

In March 1997 the CPR, then presided over by Naasson Hitimana, held a three-day seminar on the theme 'The Church before, during and after the Genocide' with the participation of José Chipenda, Modeste Mungwarareba, the general secretary of the Conference of Catholic bishops and a few international guests. The resolution adopted at the end of the meeting was in tune with the EPR's confession of guilt. 'After the genocide,' it read, 'the Church continued to act as if nothing had happened. [...] The genocide is a major failure not only for the Church in Rwanda but for the universal Church.'[117] The CPR itself published during the same period a 'Message of the member churches of the Protestant Council of Rwanda to all Rwandans', which condemned the 'horrible penchant towards the genocide and other crimes of blood' and called for repentance, without, however, confessing the guilt of the churches, as the EPR had done.[118]

Rwanda, 48. For a discussion of the EPR's December 1996 confession of guilt in light of Dietrich Bonhoeffer's theology, see Pascal Bataringaya, *Versöhnung nach dem Genozid. Impulse der Friedensethik Dietrich Bonhoeffers für Kirche und Gesellschaft in Ruanda* (Kamen: Verlag Hartmut Spener, 2012).

[116] The original document was published in the January–February 1997 issue of *Twubake*, the Kinyarwanda version of *Bâtissons*. I quote Tharcisse Gatwa's English translation of the document (*The Churches and Ethnic Ideology*, 227–8).

[117] *Bâtissons*, 9 (January–February 1997), 2.

[118] 'Message des Églises membres du Conseil Protestant du Rwanda (CPR) à tous les Rwandais', *Bâtissons*, 11 (March–April 1997), 3.

Conclusion

How do we explain the EPR's single-handed and wholehearted decision to confess its guilt two years after the genocide? Of all the Rwandan churches, it is the only one which, almost from the start, has consistently denounced the genocide as genocide and stigmatised the 'ethnist' ideology that led to it. We have seen that the most outspoken Presbyterians in exile disagreed with this view. They would rather speak of the genocide 'with a question mark', as they said in Windhoek. In different ways, the Dutch Protestant missionaries – Kees Overdulve, who unreservedly embraced the double genocide theory;[119] Jan van Butselaar, who made a point of defending the church from before the genocide;[120] and Gerard van 't Spijker, who tended to consider the EPR leadership's insistence on the centrality of the genocide an alignment on the RPF's ideology[121] – distanced themselves from the church's line of conduct. The confession of guilt emanated from the Presbyterians of the interior, Hutu as well as Tutsi.

Several factors explain the originality of the EPR's position. The first is the quality of its leadership. The role of the Presbyterian Rehabilitation Committee, a body avowedly inspired by the Confessing Church in Nazi Germany, which started its work on 20 July 1994, a few days after the RPF had put an end to the genocide, should not be underestimated. Equally important was André Karamaga's contribution. It was he who persuaded Malachie Munyaneza, Élisée Musamekweli, Gerard van 't Spijker and others to participate in the reconstruction of the EPR. As his speech in Windhoek demonstrated, he had clear views on the centrality of the genocide in recent Rwanda history and on the need for the church to unambiguously condemn it.

The polarisation of the EPR, stronger than that of the Catholic Church, with one part of the church leadership sharing the views of the ex-Rwandan government in exile, paradoxically helped the new leadership of the church to radically distance itself from the genocide ethos. As Rob Krol put it in a report, Michel Twagirayesu's position as impartial president of the EPR was 'seriously compromised'. The implication of some EPR pastors

---

[119] C. M. Overdulve, *Rwanda. Un peuple avec une histoire* (Paris: L'Harmattan, 1997), 69–75.

[120] See Jan van Butselaar's reviews of Hugh McCullum's *The Angels Have Left Us* ('Kerk in Rwanda: geen partij maar vrede stichten', *Trouw*, 17 May 1995) and of Timothy Longman's *Christianity and Genocide* (*Social Sciences and Missions*), 26/2–3, 2013, 253–74).

[121] In *Indicible Rwanda*, 43 and *passim*.

and officials in the Kirinda massacres could not be denied. The attitude of Twagirayesu, who never condemned those of his colleagues and relatives who had been involved in the killings, was a cause for concern. The ecumenical movement and the EPR's organisations had no other option than to accept his replacement by Karamaga in the extraordinary synod of February 1995. In the battle for credibility, Twagiresu and his friends were on the losing side.

CHAPTER 6

The Missionaries of Africa's response to the genocide

In the 15 June 1998 issue of *La Nouvelle Relève*, a quasi-official Rwandan publication, thirty prominent people, including members of Parliament and cabinet ministers, suggested to the general chapter of the Missionaries of Africa, then meeting in Rome, that they should 'momentarily withdraw from the country'. They might come back later, they added, 'with staff who would have never been involved in the Rwandan tragedy'.[1] Two weeks later, Privat Rutazibwa, a former Catholic priest from North Kivu who had joined the RPF in 1992 when it was still fighting the Habyarimana regime and who was now heading the Rwandan Information Agency, made the same claim in an article entitled 'Missionnaires de l'évangile ou apôtres de la haine' [Missionaries of the gospel or apostles of hatred]. The article took the form of an open letter to the heads of the male and female branches of ASUMA, Jan Lenssen, the regional superior of the Missionaries of Africa, and Frieda Schaubroeck, a Bernardine sister.[2]

Since their return to Rwanda after the genocide against the Tutsi, the Missionaries of Africa, the congregation that had initiated the evangelisation of Rwanda in 1900 and had been a dominant force in the ecclesial, social and political life of the country ever since, had kept a relatively low profile. Why, then, this attack from people linked to the RPF government?

Two episodes, mentioned in Rutazibwa's article, give the reason. The first was the publication by ASUMA, on 7 April 1998, of a text entitled 'Situation de notre pays et des communautés' [Situation of our country and of the communities], which pledged solidarity for the 'suffering of so many men, women and children victims, for about eight years, of a

---

[1] *La Nouvelle Relève*, 361 (15 June 1998), 5.
[2] Privat Rutazibwa, 'Missionnaires de l'Evangile ou apôtres de la haine. Lettre ouverte aux responsables de l'ASUMA/Rwanda', *La Nouvelle Relève*, 362 (30 June 1998), 12–16, reprinted in Privat Rutazibwa, *Contre l'ethnisme* (Kigali: Éditions du CRID, 2017), 210–35.

conflict over which they have no control'.³ For the signatories of the article in *La Nouvelle Relève,* this was nothing short of a provocation. On 7 April 1998, Rwanda celebrated the fourth anniversary of the beginning of the genocide which had claimed the lives of close to a million people, mostly of Tutsi origin. Speaking of eight years, as the religious leaders did in their memorandum, meant that all the trouble started in 1990 when the RPF invaded Rwanda to resolve the decade-long problem of Tutsi refugees in camps outside the country. No mention was made of the genocide which was commemorated all over the country on the same day. If the ASUMA leadership had wanted to show that the genocide was of minor importance in their eyes, they would not have expressed themselves differently.

The second episode that triggered the reaction of the Rwandan officials was a sermon preached by the German White Father Otto Mayer in the Nyamirambo parish in Kigali on Sunday, 24 April 1998. Two days earlier, twenty-two presumed genocide perpetrators had been publicly executed in various parts of the city. Three men and a woman had been put to death in the Nyamirambo stadium, not far from the parish.⁴ The venue had not been chosen at random. On 13 June 1994, two hundred Tutsi refugees had been massacred by the Interahamwe in the Nyamirambo parish, despite the pleas for clemency made by the same Otto Mayer and his confrère Henri Blanchard, two of the few European priests who had remained in Kigali during the genocide.⁵ A few parishioners, presumably genocide survivors, had gone to see the executions and reportedly cheered at the sound of the bullets. In his sermon on the following Sunday, Mayer had castigated them for rejoicing at the death of fellow human beings. The parishioners had angrily responded that he was protecting criminals and left the church.⁶

---

³ Rutazibwa, *Contre l'ethnisme*, 232; Jean-Damascène Bizimana, *L'Église et le génocide au Rwanda. Les Pères Blancs et le Négationnisme* (Paris: L'Harmattan, 2001), 71.

⁴ *Dialogue*, 204 (May–June 1998), 76. Two priests from Nyundo, Jean Emmanuel François Kayiranga and Edouard Nturiye, were condemned to death by the tribunal of Kibuye on 17 April 1998, one week before the public executions, but they were acquitted on 25 October 2000 in Ruhengeri. Later on, Nturiye was condemned to life imprisonment, while Nayiranga went into exile. See Joseph Ngomanzungu, *La souffrance de l'Église à travers son personnel* (Kigali: Pallotti Press, 2002), 43, 45.

⁵ Otto Mayer, 'Trois mois d'enfer au jour le jour', *Dialogue*, 177 (August–September 1994), 23–30.

⁶ Rutazibwa, *Contre l'ethnisme*, 232; Bizimana, *L'Église et le génocide au Rwanda*, 79.

The question of the Missionaries of Africa's response to the genocide against the Tutsi is disputed. Did they underplay it for various reasons, as the two episodes recalled here seem to suggest? Or did they recognise its unique character and draw lessons from it? The matter was never the object of a critical enquiry. Instead, attacks and counter-attacks have prevailed in newspaper articles, written publications and Internet blogs from the time of the genocide to this day. What exactly the White Fathers said and did has never been properly documented. Reference was made to their attitude in the run-up to the genocide in the second chapter of this book. The purpose of this chapter is to examine their position during and after the genocide against the Tutsi. Special attention will be paid to the variations of their position over time and to the differences of opinion within the congregation itself on the genocide and its aftermath.

Solidarity with the oppressed

As mentioned in the first chapter, the White Fathers did not speak with one voice in post-independence Rwanda. Some of them publicly denounced the massacres of Tutsi perpetrated with the tacit support of the government in late 1963 and early 1964. Meanwhile, the majority of missionaries saw the granting of unqualified support to the Hutu cause as an imperative of social justice. 'When I came to Rwanda, I was told that we were on the side of the Hutu,' a Belgian White Father who arrived in 1963 candidly admitted in an interview. To various degrees, they embraced the stereotypes of the arrogant and devious Tutsi and of the Hutu being always at risk of returning to their 'slave' status. This did not prevent them from developing friendships with Tutsi with the understanding that these particular men and women were the exception to the rule. Few paid attention to the nefarious consequences of this binary view of Rwandan society in the long term.

In 2008 Lisa Brille, a master's history student at the University of Ghent, interviewed four Flemish White Fathers who had worked as missionaries in Rwanda for her dissertation on 'the shifting mentality of the White Fathers on the Rwandese "dual colonialism" 1900–1962'. The verbatim transcriptions (in Dutch) of the interviews are included in the thesis.[7] This small sample, which certainly cannot claim to be representative of the congregation, illustrates the views common among the Missionaries of Africa on the Hutu–Tutsi distinction in Rwanda.

---

[7] Lisa Brille, 'Etnische breuklijnen in Rwanda: De verschuivende mentaliteit van de Witte Paters in het Rwandese "Dual Colonialism", 1900–1962', unpublished master's thesis, University of Ghent, 2008, 82–118.

The first interviewee, a missionary by the name of Jean Van der Meersch who worked in the southern part of Rwanda from 1962 to 1992 mostly as a teacher in a catechetical school, said he had no *voorkeur* [preference] for Hutu or Tutsi. He did not know of any White Father who had declared that the Tutsi should be killed, but he acknowledged that some of his confrères had 'a little preference for a group or another'. He expressed compassion for the Tutsi who had been killed in Cyanika in 1963.[8]

The contrast between Van der Meersch and the second interviewee, a Flemish White Father who chose to remain anonymous, could not be greater. In response to a question on the Catholic Church's attitude towards the Tutsi during the colonial period, he made a statement entirely in line with the Hamitic theory. The Tutsi, he declared, 'are not a people (*volk*) like the other blacks. They come from Ethiopia. […] They always give a good impression. They can manipulate the whites. […] I arrived in Rwanda in 1958, in the bush, ten months before the revolution started. And it was a great time, but not for me.' When the Tutsi came to Rwanda with their cattle 'five centuries ago', he continued, they said to the Hutu that if they wanted milk and cattle, they had to work for them. 'That is how they colonised them.' During the Social Revolution, he added, the Tutsi were thrown out of Rwanda, but they will come back, not with cattle this time, but with '*belles filles*' (beautiful girls).[9]

The third interviewee, a White Father by the name of Philippe De Vestele who worked in Rwanda from 1961 to 1994, also subscribed to the stereotype of the domineering Tutsi, though in a less demeaning language than his anonymous confrère. Before the Rwandan Social Revolution, he explained, the missionaries believed that the Tutsi were 'born to command'. How could the church, which taught the love of the neighbour, accept such a thing? De Vestele admitted that the Hamitic theory was not 'hundred per cent sure', but for him the 'typical characteristics' of the Tutsi were a clear indication of its validity. The Tutsi were among the peoples who migrated westwards from Abyssinia and the Nile region.[10]

Desouter, the RPF's archenemy

The fourth interviewee, Serge Desouter, was a much higher-profile person. A loner, he has been living in the margins of the congregation for a long time and certainly cannot be described as a representative of it. By the

[8] *Ibid.*, 85–7.
[9] *Ibid.*, 90.
[10] *Ibid.*, 97–100.

time of the interview, he had published books on the history of Rwanda,[11] on the situation arisen from the genocide[12] and on the RPF.[13] In late 1994, he had taken part in a Belgian-led political initiative aiming, as we shall see later in this chapter (p. 179), to consolidate the Hutu opposition to the RPF-led government installed in Rwanda after the genocide. Born in 1939 in Antwerp, he made his missionary oath in 1967 and arrived in Rwanda the following year. Posted to a rural parish in the diocese of Ruhengeri, he developed an interest in aviculture that in 1974 led him to become the director of a youth rural training centre in Butamwa, south of Kigali.[14] Back in Belgium, he trained as a veterinarian at the Tropical Institute in Antwerp, while working for the International Association of Rural Development (AIDR) in Brussels for several years. Apart from a three-year stint as an AIDR representative in Kigali between 1980 and 1983, he never stayed again in Rwanda. He supervised development projects in Niger and in Madagascar among other countries. In 1986, he co-founded the Agence de Coopération Technique (ACT) with Rika De Backer – a former senator and cabinet minister of the Christelijke Volkspartij (CVP). The ACT was a development organisation closely linked to the CVP which funded projects in various African countries, including Rwanda.[15]

Desouter's first book on Rwanda, *De gebroken lans* [The broken spear] was jointly published by the Vlaams Rwandese Vereeniging [Flemish Rwandan Association] and the ACT in 1992 with a foreword by Rika De Backer praising the publication of a study on Rwanda in the Dutch language. The book gave an account of Rwanda's pre-colonial and colonial history essentially based on authors from the colonial time such as Louis de Lacger, Albert Pagès and Alexis Kagame. The works of more recent scholars such as Jan Vansina, René Lemarchand, Alison Des Forges, Catharine Newbury and Emmanuel Ntezimana, who critically examined the oral traditions collected by missionaries and Tutsi intellectuals among

---

[11] Serge Desouter, *De gebroken lans* (Brussels: Vlaams Rwandeze Vereeniging and ACT, 1992).

[12] Serge Desouter and François Nzabahimana, *Rwanda. Achtergronden van een tragedie* (Brussels: ACT, 1994); *Clés pour un retour à la paix* (Brussels: ACT, 1995).

[13] Serge Desouter, *Rwanda: Le procès du RPF. Mise au point historique* (Paris: L'Harmattan, 2007).

[14] Ian Linden, *Christianisme et pouvoirs au Rwanda (1900–1990)* (Paris: Karthala, 1999), 391.

[15] Serge Desouter, Curriculum Vitae submitted to the ICTR, 3 April 2006. In 2001 the CVP was renamed Christen-Democratisch en Vlaams (CD&V).

people visiting the *mwami*'s court or the missions, were cited in passing but never discussed in detail. While distancing himself from the Hamitic theory,[16] the Flemish missionary attributed an absolute power over the region to the *mwami* and the Tutsi 'military caste', a vision that is disputed today.[17] He established a sharp distinction between the 'culture of hunters and gatherers' (Twa), the 'culture of the granary' (Hutu) and the 'culture of the spear' (Tutsi) as if these 'cultures' were hermetically closed realities that did not evolve over time. Traditionally, he argued, 'the power of the king is almost absolute. He has full control over the lives and the properties of his subjects.'[18] Oppression, according to him, continued until the end of the colonial period. 'Slowly but surely the Hutu started to be fed up with this situation. They saw the Tutsi domination everywhere and felt systematically humiliated (*systematisch vernederd*).'[19]

Desouter's interview with Lisa Brille puts across the same message as the book. Asked if he came to Rwanda for the Hutu, he responded: 'I did not come for the Hutu, I came for justice.'[20] For him, the fight for the Hutu people was a fight for justice. The situation Richard Kandt, the first German resident in Rwanda, found on his arrival in Kigali in 1908, he explained, resembled the one experienced by the Flemish people since the sixteenth century:

> It is clear that [Kandt] had a sort of sympathy for the oppressed. On the other hand, an oppressed people (*onderdrukt volk*) is an oppressed people in the sense that it has little power to resist. This is what we had in Flanders. We lost our elite in the sixteenth century, the seventeenth century. [...] Thus, an oppressed people has very little power to resist. This is what we see now again. The RPF is in power and the people cannot open their mouth, they cannot do anything.[21]

Of the four interviewees, Desouter was the only one who analysed the Rwandan situation in Belgian party-political terms. In the interview he did not disguise his antipathy for the 'freemasons' and Jean Gol, the leader of the Belgian Liberal Party, in particular. Gol was said to have mocked, in reference to Rwanda, 'la république des nonnes et des bons pères'

---

[16] Desouter, *De gebroken lans*, 39.
[17] Danielle de Lame, *A Hill among a Thousand. Transformation and Ruptures in Rural Rwanda* (Madison: University of Wisconsin Press, 2005), 44–7.
[18] Desouter, *De gebroken lans*, 71.
[19] *Ibid.*, 327.
[20] Brille, 'Etnische breuklijnen in Rwanda', 112.
[21] *Ibid.*, 104.

[the republic of nuns and good fathers]. In Desouter's eyes, the Belgian liberals' support for the RPF 'rebels' in the early 1990s and the Kagame government later was a ploy to undermine the influence of the Catholic Church in Rwanda.[22]

Léon Saur, a former staffer of the Parti Social Chrétien (PSC) – the French-speaking branch of the Belgian Christian Democrat party – wrote a book describing the involvement of Christian Democrat International (CDI – a Brussels-based organisation coordinating the various Christian democrat parties in the world) – in the affairs of Rwanda before and after the genocide.[23] Juvénal Habyarimana's MRND party was a CDI affiliate. Through his links with Rika De Backer, the president of the ACT, Desouter had contacts not only with the CVP but with CDI. All saw the RPF as a threat to a regime with which they had a long association in matters of rural development.

The Missionaries of Africa during the genocide

On the eve of the genocide, the Missionaries of Africa in Rwanda numbered eighty-one, not including an intern and a few students outside the country. All but two were Europeans or North Americans. Half (40) were Belgian and, in most cases, Flemish. The French were the second-largest group (16). The others were Canadian (7), Italian (6), German (4), Dutch (3), Spanish (2), Swiss (2), Congolese (1) and Tanzanian (1).[24]

Like the bulk of the UN's peacekeeping forces and virtually all expatriates, 'all or almost all' of the Missionaries of Africa left Rwanda soon after the shooting down of President Habyarimana's plane on the evening of Wednesday, 6 April 1994.[25] They left Rwanda by road via Butare and the Burundian border or on planes chartered by the French, Belgian or Italian governments when Kigali airport was still open. Because of the anger directed at Belgium in the population under the influence of the Hutu extremist media, the troops from that country put particular pressure

---

[22] *Ibid.*, 113.

[23] Léon Saur, *Influences parallèles. L'internationale démocrate chrétienne au Rwanda* (Brussels: Éditions Luc Pire, 1998).

[24] Missionaries of Africa, 'Informations diffusées par la Région du Rwanda, 1990–1994. Présentation et annotation par le père Jef Vleugels, M.Afr. Régional du Rwanda du 01/07/1988 au 30/06/1994', typewritten document, Brussels, 2005, 5–7.

[25] André Sibomana, *Gardons l'espoir pour le Rwanda. Entretiens avec Laure Guibert et Hervé Deguine*, 2nd edn (Paris: L'Harmattan, 2008), 164.

on their compatriots, church workers included, who were reluctant to leave Rwanda. Nobody could blame the missionaries for accepting evacuation more or less willingly, but their swift departure raised questions for those who stayed behind, especially the Tutsi civilians who were murdered in large numbers. They felt that the missionaries did not act differently from the other expatriates whose exodus left a space wide open for the Hutu extremists' killing programme.

This being said, some White Fathers were part of the group of missionaries who chose not to leave. In late April, they still numbered twenty-one, according to Belgian journalist François Janne d'Othée.[26] Henri Blanchard and Otto Mayer remained in their parish of Nyamirambo in Kigali until 6 June, when they witnessed, powerlessly, the murder of two hundred Tutsi who had taken refuge in the church premises. Marc François, Alain Coeffic and Armand Poulin, who also witnessed a massacre in their parish of Nyabitimbo in the south-west, left the place in mid-June when they heard that the bishops of Kigali, Kabgayi and Byumba had been murdered by RPF soldiers in Gakurazo near Gitarama. Three missionaries, Léo Bossuyt, Alphonse Calozet and Jean-Marie Luca, stayed in Nyagahanga in the zone occupied by the RPF in the diocese of Byumba until the end of the genocide.

As pointed out in the third chapter, two white Fathers, André Caloone and Joachim Vallmajo, lost their lives at the beginning of the genocide period. Informed by the faxes that Vleugels and Theunis sent from Kigali between 7 and 10 April 1994,[27] the General Council of the Missionaries of Africa in Rome was quite understandably worried about the security of its members.[28] Somehow, these faxes, which were meant to brief the congregation about the situation of the confrères in Rwanda and were not destined for publication, became controversial. On reading them, the genocide survivors and some academics found it surprising that so little was said about the systematic killing of the Tutsi, which had already started on a major scale by the time they were sent.

In addition to the news of the confrères, the faxes gave a factual description of the situation on the ground. Theunis, the main author of the faxes, depended on ecclesiastical sources for his information. Neither he nor his sources seemed to understand the nature of the tragedy that was unfolding

---

[26] François Janne d'Othée, 'Dieu était à leurs côtés', *Le Vif L'Express*, 29 April 1994, 105–7.
[27] Missionaries of Africa, 'Informations diffusées par la Région du Rwanda', 153–66.
[28] AMA, Rome, General Council, April–June 1994.

before their eyes. Only one fax, sent on 8 April at noon, mentioned that the victims of the Rwandan soldiers – in Nyamirambo and in Masaka near Kigali – were Tutsi.[29] In a fax sent the same day in the evening, Theunis observed that 'the massacres [had] spread throughout the country and the city of Kigali'. No indication was given of the fact that, almost from the start, the overwhelming majority of victims were targeted for the simple reason that they were Tutsi. It is true that a fair amount of Hutu personalities described as 'moderates' lost their lives in the first two or three days, but many more Tutsi were killed in Gikondo, Ndera, Nyundo, Gikongoro, Nyamasheke and Congo-Nil, for example, as many survivors reported.[30] The faxes' factual tone struck the French historian Gérard Prunier, the author of the first academic study of the genocide in 1995. 'One has almost the impression', he wrote, 'of reading a trade union or diplomatic list, where only the welfare of the insiders is of concern. Violence is described as "happening" but the perpetrators are never identified. One has the surrealistic impression of reading about murders being committed by armies of ghosts whose faces are forever blurred.'[31]

One of the members of the General Council, the Spaniard Pedro Sala, happened to be visiting Kigali when the president's plane was shot down. He stayed in Kanombe Airport with Guy Theunis at the request of Johan Swinnen, the Belgian ambassador, until 14 April.[32] Back in Rome, he became the main source of information on Rwanda, where he had ministered for some time before being appointed to the General Council. He reported on the Rwandan situation to his fellow councillors on 17 April. The discussion essentially revolved around the repatriation of the confrères. 'As a first step,' the minutes read, 'the General Council decides to contact the provincials who have confrères repatriated from Rwanda and ask them to pay attention to their psychological and human needs and explore how to help them "detoxify" from the climate of violence and hatred they witnessed in recent times.'[33] At a subsequent meeting, on 30 May 1994, Jean-Claude Ceillier, a French councillor, reported on a meeting of about forty Belgian,

---

[29] Missionaries of Africa, 'Informations diffusées par la Région du Rwanda', 157.
[30] See Chapter 3.
[31] Gérard Prunier, *The Rwanda Crisis 1959–1994* (New York: Columbia University Press, 1995), 250–1.
[32] Missionaries of Africa, 'Informations diffusées par la Région du Rwanda', 146.
[33] AMA, General Council, 17 April 1994.

French, Dutch, German and Spanish missionaries repatriated from Rwanda that had been held in Antwerp two weeks before.[34]

The first sign of a greater awareness of the complexity of the genocide situation on the part of the General Council – there will be others – appears in the minutes of the meeting held on 1 June 1994. 'The General Council', they read, 'asks Father Sala to draw the attention of the regional [Jef Vleugels] on some of their statements which lack objectivity and that they should be careful not take sides.'[35] From this succinct record, we can infer that the General Council was concerned about the partisan stance taken by some Belgian White Fathers who tended to side with the interim government and see the RPF as the enemy.

Early responses to the genocide

On hearing about mass massacres in Rwanda, some White Fathers arrived at the conclusion that something had gone wrong with the evangelisation of the country. Clément Forestier, a French missionary who had signed the expatriates' letter complaining about the disinformation in the media in October 1990 but who was also known, according to Jean-Damascène Bizimana, for having objected to the discrimination against Tutsi during the Habyarimana regime,[36] expressed disillusion after his return to France in April 1994. 'My biggest disappointment,' he declared to a Belgian journalist, 'is to realise that this religion was superficial. We did outside painting but no in-depth work. As long as the churches were full, we were happy. Now they are full of corpses.'[37] He did not deny the fact that Christians had been involved in the genocide. 'Deep in my heart,' he told a group of Catholic students in October 1994, 'I blame all the friends I have [in Rwanda] who have killed. I cannot forgive them.'[38] Otto Mayer, an eyewitness of the genocide, also realised that the church had to do a

---

[34] AMA, General Council, 30 May 1994. See also Missionaries of Africa, 'Informations diffusées par la Région du Rwanda', 186.

[35] AMA, General Council, 1 June 1994.

[36] Jean-Damascène Bizimana, 'Les attaques médiatiques du Père Theunis contre le Rwanda ou la poursuite de la stratégie génocidaire et négationniste', *Rwanda News*, 29 March 2012.

[37] Janne d'Othée, 'Dieu était à leurs côtés'.

[38] *Chrétiens dans l'enfer du Rwanda*, video produced by Chrétiens en Grandes Écoles – Mission étudiante catholique – Île de France, 24 October 1994, quoted in Jean-Paul Gouteux, *Un génocide sans importance. La France et le Vatican au Rwanda*, rev. edn (Lyon: Tahin Party, 2007), 46.

self-critique. 'I do not believe the theory of the popular anger', he said in an interview with the French Catholic newspaper *La Croix*. 'Too many people lied: the government, the opposition and even the church. [...] It was in cahoots with the state.'[39]

How many White Fathers shared these views is not known. They probably represented a minority. Both outside and inside Rwanda there has been great resistance, not least in church circles, to accepting the reality of the genocide. The fact that many White Fathers refused to use the term until mid-1995 is a clear indication of this attitude. It was much easier to speak of 'ethnic violence' and 'widespread massacres' than of a deliberate attempt to exterminate an entire population group. To account for the genocide, many missionaries, especially in the older generation, fell back on the familiar ethnic-based explanation. For them, the scale of the massacres did not change the fact that, even after thirty years of Hutu rule, the Tutsi were the oppressors and the Hutu their victims. By invading Rwanda in October 1990, so the argument went, the Tutsi army had caused havoc in the country. Ultimately, they, and nobody else, were responsible for the genocide.

One of the first to speak along those lines – in the 16 April 1994 issue of the Belgian Dutch-language newspaper *De Morgen* – was Walter Aelvoet, a Flemish White Father who had worked in Rwanda since 1952. In 1959, he told the journalist, he had found the killings of Tutsi he had witnessed in Kabgayi, where he directed a Catholic school at the time, sad but comprehensible. The Hutu had suffered 'for centuries' under the 'feudal regime of the Tutsi monarchy'. They were a peaceful people but, in recent weeks, they had listened to the propaganda of the Hutu extremists and had become angry. The Tutsi, for their part, were people who could control their anger. They had waited for thirty years before taking their revenge.[40]

In May 1994, *African News Bulletin – Bulletin d'Information Africaine* (*ANB-BIA*), a newsletter compiled by the Missionaries of Africa in Brussels, published, as a 'point of view which may help to understand what is happening in Rwanda', an unsigned article of 25 April 1994 entitled '*Le chaudron de l'Afrique centrale*' [The cauldron of Central Africa]. The author – in whom one is tempted to recognise the anonymous White Father interviewed by Lisa Brille in 2008 – made a vitriolic attack on the European media that, according to him, were 'passionate about the

---

[39] *La Croix*, 6 July 1994, quoted in Sophie Pontzeele, 'Burundi 1972/Rwanda 1994. L'"efficacité" dramatique d'une reconstruction du passé par la presse', unpublished PhD thesis, University of Lille, 2004, 202.

[40] *De Morgen*, 16 April 1994, 17–18. On this statement, see Chapter 1.

defence of the minorities but uninterested in the extermination of the majorities'. Massive disinformation, he argued in a language reminiscent of the interview quoted above, was taking place. Tutsi priests had managed to secure influence in Radio Vatican. 'Beautiful Tutsi women have infiltrated the humanitarian organisations and made use of their charms to conquer the ground.' Amazingly, when one considers that by then dozens of Tutsi priests had been killed in the diocese of Nyundo and in other parts of Rwanda, this paranoid article seemingly enjoyed the support of the White Fathers. The editor of *ANB-BIA* backed up the argument by referring, between brackets, to an earlier article that blamed an international human rights commission for dedicating ninety-five pages to human rights abuses committed by the Rwandan government in 1993 and only four to those committed by the RPF.[41]

In Switzerland, André Perraudin, the bishop emeritus of Kabgayi, gave interviews to various Swiss French-language newspapers during the genocide period. On 18 April 1994, for example, in *Le Journal de Genève* he echoed the opinion Aelvoet had expressed two days before in the Flemish newspaper *De Morgen*. 'I condemn [the authors of the killings],' he said, 'but I try to understand them. They act out of anger and fear. Out of anger against the murder of their president Juvénal Habyarimana on 6 April. And out of fear of returning into slavery because, if the press says today that it is the Hutu who are massacring the Tutsi, looting and creating havoc, we must remember that, for centuries, Tutsi believed in their natural right to command and dominate. It was the institution of serfdom, an institution of pride and domination of a race over another.'[42]

The testimony of Jean-Damascène Bizimana, a Tutsi White Father seminarian who was on holiday in Switzerland during the genocide, gives a hint, limited of course, of the discourse his confrères were holding during that period in the European communities. Bizimana, who hailed from Cyanika in southern Rwanda, lost many family members during the genocide. In a text entitled 'Grande est ma souffrance, infinie mon espérance' [Huge is my suffering, infinite my hope], which the *Petit Écho*

---

[41] *ANB-BIA*, 254, 1 May 1994, 4–5. The article referred to by the editor of *ANB-BIA* had been published by Omer d'Hoe in the July 1993 issue of the Dutch language missionary magazine *Wereldwijd*.

[42] Roger de Diesbach, 'L'ancien archevêque suisse du Rwanda crie son angoisse', *Journal de Genève*, 18 April 1994. See Jean-Pierre Chrétien, *Le défi de l'ethnisme. Rwanda et Burundi*, 2nd edn (Paris: Karthala 2012), 165. Perraudin also expressed his views on Rwanda in the 21 May 1994 issue of *Gazette de Lausanne* and in the 13 June 1994 issue of *Journal de Genève*.

des Missionnaires d'Afrique published in February 1995, he expressed his indignation at hearing consecrated people justifying the war and the massacres.[43] One of them, he reported in a book a few years later, a Swiss brother by the name of Léon Seuret who had worked in Rwanda from 1950 to 1981, told him one day: 'Jean Damascène, I condemn this barbarism. It is diabolical! But I understand the Hutu's anger. You always considered yourself superior to them. It is normal that they rebelled.'[44] Bizimana had the same experience in Toulouse, where he went later the same year to further his studies. He could not bear 'hearing again and again priests who were denying the genocide, minimising it or, even worse, justifying it'.[45]

The emergence of the double genocide theory

As we have seen, the term genocide, which had been used in Rwanda in 1964, in Burundi in 1972 and again in Rwanda in 1993, reappeared – simultaneously in the Belgian newspaper *La Libre Belgique* and in an internal report of Doctors Without Borders – a week after the start of the massacres following the shooting of President Habyarimana's plane.[46] Hardly a month later, after the first acts of vengeance by RPF soldiers became known and reports of RPF atrocities, which Human Rights Watch did not judge as credible at the time, started to filter down from camps of Hutu refugees in Tanzania,[47] the term 'double genocide' also became part of the political vocabulary. On 16 May 1994, for example, the French conservative newspaper *Le Figaro* ran as a headline: 'Rwanda: double genocide'.[48]

Missionaries of Africa were among the first – along with French military commanders such as General Christian Quesnot – to accredit the idea that, though less visible, the crimes of the RPF equalled those of the Hutu militias in size and cruelty. As we shall see, the first Missionary of Africa who used the term double genocide was Philippe de Dorlodot in July 1994, but some of his confrères had started to disseminate the same idea before this date, at a time when the genocide against the Tutsi was still in full swing.

In May 1994, Jan de Bekker, a Dutch White Father who had worked in the diocese of Byumba until the genocide and returned to the Netherlands

---

[43] *Petit Écho des Missionnaires d'Afrique*, 858 (1995/2), 86.
[44] Bizimana, *L'Église et le génocide au Rwanda*, 38.
[45] *Ibid.*, 74.
[46] See Chapter 3.
[47] *Human Rights Watch*, 6/4, May 1994.
[48] Chrétien, *Le défi de l'ethnisme*, 95.

soon afterwards, made a six-day trip to the prefectures of Byumba and Kibungo, then under the control of the RPF, at the request of the Dutch Caritas. In an article published in the August 1994 issue of the *Petit Écho*, he claimed to have seen an empty country. He acknowledged that the RPF had gathered the people in camps because of the presence of Hutu militias in the area, and he certainly knew that more than 300,000 people had fled to Tanzania at the end of April. For him, though, this was not a satisfactory explanation. 'In reality, he wrote, the RPF is busy eliminating all its enemies in a manner more discreet than the militia of Hutu extremists. They enquire about the political past of the people and all those (in particular the elites) who supported the MRND are eliminated without mercy.'[49]

De Bekker referred to the murder of three Hutu priests in Byumba, an information mentioned in other reports of the crimes committed by the RPF in this area in April 1994.[50] One wonders, though, how he could have assessed the nature and the scale of the RPF's crimes in the entire country after a trip of only six days. We do not know how many Missionaries of Africa read his article. It is possible that it contributed to their negative attitude towards the RPF after the genocide.

Meanwhile, in Belgium the news of the genocide created anxiety in the political parties and development agencies that had supported the Habyarimana for many years. This prompted Rika De Backer to ask her long-time friend Serge Desouter in June 1994, when the genocide was still on, to write a piece on the Rwandan situation. Under the title *Rwanda. Achtergronden van een tragedie* [Rwanda: Background to a tragedy], it was published in the form of a book by the ACT in July 1994, together with a Dutch translation of an article by François Nzabahimana, a former Rwandan minister in exile, about the events that led to the genocide.[51]

Desouter did not deny that massacres had taken place. In a letter to Jean-Paul Gouteux, a French activist associated with the magazine *Golias*, he pointed out that in his capacity as chairperson of the CIM he had published a statement on the matter as early as 8 April 1994 and that, together with Protestant organisations, he had organised a prayer vigil to put an

---

[49] *Petit Écho*, 854 (1994/8), 371.
[50] Alison Des Forges, *Leave None to Tell the Story: Genocide in Rwanda* (New York: Human Rights Watch, 1999), 711–12; André Guichaoua, *Rwanda. De la guerre au génocide. Les politiques criminelles au Rwanda (1990–1994)* (Paris: La Découverte, 2010), 563. On the murder of priests by the RFP in April 1994 in Byumba, see Chapter 3.
[51] Serge Desouter and François Nzabahimana, *Rwanda. Achtergronden van een tragedie* (Brussels: ACT, 1994).

end to the killings on 23 April 1994 at St Michael and St Gudula Cathedral in Brussels.[52] In *Rwanda. Achtergronden van een tragedie,* he mentioned the 'pogroms' against the Tutsi who took refuge in the churches and the murder of three Jesuits at the Centre Christus in Kigali. However, in a manner that seemed to justify the Hutu extremist propaganda, he attributed the latter's killings to 'the contacts of their provincial and later of the Rwandan fathers with the RPF'.[53] He was adamant that the October 1990 RPF invasion was the main cause of the 'anarchy' that had developed in Rwanda. Using a language akin to that of the double genocide theory, he insinuated that the RPF might well have killed more people than the Hutu militias. 'One does not know how many people – Hutu and Tutsi – have died,' he claimed. 'Everybody talks about corpses: we have so many! So the one who scores the highest has right on his side. This is the attitude one often finds in the RPF. But we do not always know what happens in their "liberated zones".'[54]

'Rejoining the Rwandans where they are'

The question of the return to Rwanda of the Missionaries of Africa who had left the country in April 1994 was raised as soon as the RPF had completed its conquest of the country in mid-July, forcing the former Rwandan government to take refuge in Zaire and ending the massacres of the Tutsi despite pockets of Interahamwe resistance. In early August, a second Dutch White Father, Kees Maas, visited the dioceses of Byumba and Kibungo and the refugee camps in Tanzania at the request of the Dutch Caritas. A few days later, Antonio Martinez, a Spanish confrère, made a trip to Butare, Kabgayi, Kigali and Nyagahanga. On 24 August, Pedro Sala, a member of the General Council in Rome, and Jan Lenssen, the newly appointed regional superior of Rwanda, went on a mission to Rwanda at the request of the General Council.[55]

---

[52] Paris-Nanterre University, La Contemporaine: Fonds Hervé Deguine, Affaire Sibomana, Carton 3: Serge Desouter to Jean-Pierre [Jean-Paul] Gouteux, Brussels, 7 August 1995. On Desouter's activism in April 1994, see also Brille, 'Etnische breuklijnen in Rwanda', 114.

[53] Desouter and Nzabahimana, *Rwanda. Achtergronden van een tragedie,* 32–3.

[54] *Ibid.,* 43.

[55] Missionaries of Africa, 'Informations diffusées par la Région du Rwanda', 212.

On 12 September, Sala reported to the General Council that the church would welcome a return of the Missionaries of Africa and that the new government had 'expressed the need for missionaries to reconstruct the country'. However, 'on our side', the minutes of the meeting read, 'it won't be possible to resume all the commitments we had before'. On the same day, according to Sala, the Regional Council of Rwanda, which comprised the missionaries who had fled the country, was meeting in Brussels. It decided to reinforce its presence in Nyagahanga in the diocese of Byumba, where three White Fathers had stayed during the genocide, in Kigali and in places like Ruhengeri and Gikongoro that were without priests. One of the criteria for sending missionaries back to Rwanda, the General Council resolved, was to 'intervene where there [was] hope of reconciliation'.

There would always be the risk, they added, 'of being accused on both sides, that is, of being pro-RPF in Rwanda and pro-Hutu in the refugee camps of Goma and Bukavu. In a tone very different from that of many White Fathers previously active in Rwanda, the General Council had a discussion on the ideological dimension of the Rwandan conflict. 'The question "Tutsi-Hutu" needs clarification,' they pointed out. 'For some it is a false problem; for others there is a problem, it seems. There is also an ethnic problem in the [diocesan] clergy and in the religious congregation. In the current circumstances, we must realise that we cannot return and work exactly as we used to do before.'[56]

On 30 September, Jan Lenssen, the regional superior, went to Rome for a meeting with the General Council. He expressed the view that the Missionaries of Africa should 'commit themselves to the Rwandese people and the Church in Rwanda where they are, in the refugee camps and inside the country'. He reported that three White Fathers – Léopold Greindl, Jef Vleugels, the former regional superior, and Guy Theunis – had been declared undesirable by the Rwandan government and should be assigned to other duties.[57]

A passage of the minutes of this meeting suggests that the General Council may have been reluctant to put the genocide and the acts of violence attributed to the RPF on the same footing, as some White Fathers were inclined to do. At an international conference on human rights and reconciliation in Rwanda on 16 and 17 September in The Hague, Theunis had implied an equivalence between the two 'sides' – the interim government and the RPF – involved in the 'genocide and the massacres'. There

---

[56] AMA, General Council, 12 September 1994.
[57] *Ibid.*, 30 September 1994.

ought to be, he had said, 'a direct dialogue between the two belligerents and a trial of those responsible for the genocide and the massacres on both sides'.[58] Lenssen, who shared this analysis, had asked the General Council for permission to reproduce Theunis' paper in the *Petit Écho*, the internal bulletin of the congregation. Remarkably, the General Council declined to publish it 'first because of the use of certain phrases and because it presents views on the policy of the Society by Fr Theunis who is not even a regional superior'. Instead, with Lenssen's consent they amended the text and published it as a 'Letter of the General Council' in the September 1994 issue of *the Petit Écho*. In the revised document, the paragraph devoted to the political situation in Rwanda read: 'Today, the arms are silent, but we must say that a certain logic of war remains: thousands of refugees are still outside the country and everything should be done to establish a real dialogue between the forces in presence.'[59]

Meanwhile, volunteers were returning to Rwanda. By September, there were only 16 White Fathers in Rwandan communities: 3 in Kigali, 3 in Nyagahanga and the rest in the refugee camps of Tanzania, Burundi and Zaire.[60] The first to come back to Rwanda on a permanent basis, on 3 September 1994, was Henri Blanchard, who had left Kigali in June.[61] Otto Mayer and Marc François arrived on 1 October. Others were too old or too traumatised to envisage a return to Rwanda or felt that they could not work in a country ruled by the RPF. On 8 December, Lenssen reopened the provincial house in Kigali. On 31 December 1994, he proudly announced, in an article entitled 'The region is alive again' in the *Petit Écho*, that nineteen confrères were now working in Rwanda and eleven in the refugee camps.[62]

The ideological debate

The question of whether the new regime should be given a chance and be assisted in its enterprise of reconstruction or, on the contrary, be vigorously opposed because of its exactions against the Hutu population never ceased to be debated within the congregation. Despite some misgivings, those who chose to return to Rwanda generally opted for the first option,

---

[58] Chrétien, *Le défi de l'ethnisme*, 128; Rutazibwa, *Contre l'ethnisme*, 216–17.
[59] *Petit Écho* (1994/9), 418–19.
[60] *Petit Écho* (1994/9), 418.
[61] 'Le Père Blanchard repart à Kigali', *Voix d'Afrique. Revue des Missionnaires d'Afrique*, 23 September 1994, 9.
[62] *Petit Écho* (1995/4), 173–4.

with the support of the General Council in Rome. Those who remained in Europe, and especially in Belgium, and those who worked in the refugee camps in Tanzania and Zaire until they closed in 1996, tended to take a hard line against the RPF government. The debate was internal and external. When journalists in Catholic as well as secular media wanted information on Rwanda, they often came to the White Fathers, the best-known missionary congregation in Rwanda.[63]

While deploring the acts of vengeance committed by RPF soldiers, by the Tutsi refugees who had returned to the country and by some genocide survivors, the White Fathers who returned to Rwanda plainly recognised the reality of the genocide and expressed sympathy for the survivors. Clément Forestier, who came back in February 1995, found that the testimonies of the survivors 'were horrific and beyond imagination'. He also felt that most newcomers had come with a spirit of vengeance and that 'their arrogance was hard to bear'. 'I came here', he shared, 'at the service of a traumatised church which tries to find its way. Having ceased to be as powerful as before, it rediscovers humility in service'.[64] Along the same lines, Henri Blanchard wrote in 1997 that 'a lot of energy and a lot of courage [would] be necessary to rebuild something' and that 'all the moral forces of the country should help the people to recognise, accept and welcome each other'. He refused, however, to blame the churches, whom he knew were accused in various quarters of collusion with the interim government. 'Let us not discredit too quickly the churches,' he said in the same letter, 'even though they must do a revision of life'.[65] In a written response to the questions of a journalist, he vigorously took the defence of the Kigali priests, Wenceslas Munyeshyaka included, who, according to him, supported each other during the genocide, whether they were Hutu or Tutsi, and provided shelter to the people seeking protection.[66] The tone was different in the writings of the Missionaries of Africa who worked

---

[63] In February 1997, a young White Father by the name of Laurent Balas, who was based in North Kivu, gained some fame by reporting, anonymously at first, the massacres of Hutu refugees fleeing the camps in late 1996 to the French media. See Gérard Prunier, *Africa's World War. Congo, the Rwandan Genocide and the Making of a Continental Catastrophe* (Oxford and New York: Oxford University Press, 2009), 124–5; François Robinet, 'Les conflits africains au regard des médias français', unpublished PhD thesis, University of Saint-Quentin-en-Yvelines, 2012, 246, 249.

[64] *Petit Écho*, 864 (1995/8), 395–6.

[65] *Petit Écho*, 881 (1997/5), 233.

[66] Paris-Nanterre University, La Contemporaine: Fonds Hervé Deguine,

in the refugee camps or remained in Europe. Yves Vermeire, a Belgian White Father who did reconciliation work in the refugee camps of Benaco in Tanzania, is one of the few who acknowledged, admittedly in a veiled way, that some of the refugees had taken part in the genocide. Their heart, he wrote in a report of 20 December 1994, can be 'tortured by feelings of [...] shame at the recollection of the horrible scenes which they witnessed or in which they unwittingly took part'.[67]

By contrast, most testimonies of missionaries and development workers present in the camps of Bukavu or Goma during this period downplayed or even denied the possibility that refugees might have been involved in the genocide. Typical from that point of view was the report the Belgian White Father Philippe de Dorlodot wrote on return from a visit of the refugee camps around Goma, then battling with cholera, on 26 July 1994. Based in Bukavu at the time, he was one of the first to speak explicitly of 'two genocides', one perpetrated by 'certain authorities, the military and the Interahamwe' against the Tutsi, and the genocide 'of which nobody talks', committed by the RPF against the Hutu in the occupied zones. 'We know', he commented, 'that there have been massive massacres and the testimonies that were missing are starting to emerge'.[68] In a further section of the document, he described as 'a genocide' the afflux of a million refugees in Goma panicked by the RPF who wanted to empty the north-west [of Rwanda] to avoid having to manage a hostile population'. He only described as a 'crime' the calls made by the interim government and the Hutu extremist-led RTLM to run away from the RPF and escape to Zaire. The only solution, he concluded, was to return to the pre-1990 situation when the respective rights of the Hutu and of the Tutsi, who represented 85 per cent and 15 per cent of the population, were protected.[69]

Equally virulent was Léopold Greindl, a Belgian White Father who had directed a pedagogical institute in the north of Rwanda before the genocide. In November 1994 he wrote in the French Christian magazine *Missi* that on 7 April 1994 the RPF 'knew that something was cooking' and that he used this opportunity to establish a 'Pol Pot-type system'.[70] He was interrogated by the Belgian Senate on 29 May 1997 because he happened

---

Affaire Sibomana, Carton 3: Henri Blanchard, 'Réponses à quelques questions posées par un journaliste de La Vie', Nyamirambo, 7 August 1995.

[67] *Petit Écho*, 869 (1995/4), 175.

[68] Philippe de Dorlodot (ed.), *Les réfugiés rwandais à Bukavu au Zaïre. De nouveaux Palestiniens?* (Paris: L'Harmattan, 1996), 88.

[69] *Ibid.*, 89.

[70] Chrétien, *Le défi de l'ethnisme*, 102.

to have been on his way to Kigali airport when President Habyarimana's plane was shot down on the evening of 6 April 1994. The liberal and socialist senators grilled him on his activities in the north of Rwanda before the genocide, on the advisory role he played when the Belgian prime minister Wilfried Martens visited Rwanda in early 1994 and on his links with Rika De Backer. Greindl candidly admitted that his superiors had asked him to restrain himself. 'They asked me to stay in Europe to calm down but it has not happened', he declared before adding, rather oddly, 'I do not think that the White Fathers have devised a Machiavellian plan to exterminate the Tutsi.'[71]

The Bukavu meeting

As already mentioned, the most resolute enemy of the RPF among the Missionaries of Africa was Serge Desouter. His deep-seated animosity towards the new government of Rwanda had several roots. The first was his proximity to the CVP, a Flemish Christian democrat party campaigning for the rights of both the Flemish nation and the Catholic Church. The CVP had strong links with the Habyarimana regime. Many Flemish politicians and opinion-makers saw counterparts in the Hutu people who, like them, had long suffered oppression from a dominant ethnic group. Also important was the clerical/anticlerical divide. Belgium is often described as a country that is 'pillarised' – that is, divided from the bottom to the top of the social structure, including health, education and culture – between two antagonistic 'pillars', one Catholic and the other liberal and anticlerical. Desouter regularly accused the Belgian Liberal Party of indiscriminately supporting the RPF.[72]

The second reason for Desouter's animosity was his development work in Rwanda in the 1970s and in various other countries afterwards. He felt bitter towards the RPF who, according to him, had destroyed, by its ill-considered decision to attack Rwanda, a country that was on the road to development. He would have disagreed, of course, with authors such as

---

[71] Belgian Senate, Parliamentary Commission concerning the events in Rwanda, Analytical transcription of the auditions, Wednesday, 28 May 1997.
[72] Brille, 'Etnische breuklijnen in Rwanda', 113; Serge Desouter, *In Gods linkerhand. Herdenkingsboek van een missionaris* (Soest: Boekscout, 2014), 366–7. The French and Dutch equivalents of 'pillarisation' are, respectively, *pilarisation* and *verzuiling*.

Peter Uvin[73] or Jean-Paul Kimonyo,[74] who argued that the international development agencies which heavily invested in Rwanda in the 1980s had failed to secure sustainable economic development, had favoured nepotism and had hardly opposed the ethnic violence affecting the country prior to the genocide.

The third reason was more personal. Desouter's first posting, soon after his ordination, was to the parish of Muyanza, in the diocese of Ruhengeri, from 1968 to 1974. It was there that he developed an interest in aviculture and started to study Rwandan history. In 1972 he wrote a piece entitled 'Cailloux, pierres et roches sacrés. Réflexions à propos de l'autel de Muyanza' [Sacred pebbles, stones and rocks: Reflections about Muyanza's altar].[75] In 1994, he was very distressed to hear from people he knew that, on 22 April, eight hundred people had been killed in Muyanza by RPF soldiers.[76] This crime, which was never investigated, is mentioned on various anti-RPF websites. It certainly reinforced Desouter's determination to denounce as widely as possible the alleged exactions of the RPF.

As we have seen, when the genocide started to be reported in the media, Rika De Backer turned to Desouter for advice. The genocide was potentially damaging for Flemish Catholic interests in Rwanda. This led to the publication, by Desouter and François Nzabahimana, of *Rwanda. Achtergronden van een tragedie* in July 1994.[77] A revised and augmented version of this book was published in Dutch in December 1994[78] and, with a somewhat different structure, in French in February 1995.[79] These books gave the point of view of the exiled Hutu elites on the recent developments in Rwanda. The authors argued that the responsibility for the disaster that had struck Rwanda lay entirely with the RPF. It was true that a genocide had happened, but the RPF crimes were even worse. The only solution was

---

[73] Peter Uvin, *Aiding Violence: The Development Enterprise in Rwanda* (West Hartford, Connecticut: Kumarian Press, 1998).

[74] Jean-Paul Kimonyo, *Rwanda demain! Une longue marche vers la transformation* (Paris: Karthala, 2017).

[75] Serge Desouter, Curriculum Vitae submitted to the ICTR, 3 April 2006.

[76] Desouter, *In Gods linkerhand*, 355.

[77] Serge Desouter and François Nzabahimana, *Rwanda. Achtergronden van een tragedie* (Brussels: ACT, 1994). The section of the book authored by Desouter is dated 30 June 1994.

[78] Serge Desouter and François Nzabahimana, *Bouwstenen voor de toekomst* (Brussels: ACT, 1994).

[79] Serge Desouter and François Nzabahimana, *Clés pour un retour à la paix* (Brussels: ACT, 1995).

to apply a revised version of the Arusha Agreement and prevent the RPF from ruling Rwanda alone.

Desouter was part of a delegation of European politicians, including Rika De Backer and the former CDI counsellor Alain de Brouwer, who tried to put in place a political solution for Rwanda along those lines at a meeting held between 23 and 25 October 1994 in Bukavu. Refugee representatives from Kenya, Tanzania, Burundi and Zaire and members of the four major political parties present in Rwanda before the genocide were present.[80] In April 1995, this led to the creation, under the direction of François Nzabahimana, of the Rassemblement pour le Retour de la Démocratie au Rwanda (RDR), a Hutu opposition party which petered out when the refugee camps started to be dismantled.[81]

The Bukavu meeting adopted a 'Charter for the rapid and peaceful return of the Rwandan refugees', which proposed the creation of an international tribunal for all crimes committed since October 1990 and the relaunch of the process of democratic pluralism in line with the Arusha Agreement.[82] In his memoirs, Desouter recalled having 'worked hard' at the drafting of this document.[83]

In the preface to the book that presented the charter, Rika De Backer mentioned that the organisers of the Bukavu meeting did not invite 'anybody who had been associated in any way with the massacres of April and May 1994'.[84] If this was the case, one does not see why François Nzabahimana suggested in the same volume[85] that Théodore Sindikubwabo, the man who, in his capacity as interim president of Rwanda, had incited the Butare population to join the killing campaigns against the Tutsi on 19 April 1994,[86] should remain in the same position in a post-genocide settlement by virtue of the 1991 Constitution. This contradiction shows that the organisers of the Bukavu meeting had a very restrictive view of the genocide. They had no qualms about developing links with the leaders of the former Rwandan government and the commandment of the ex-FAR,

---

[80] *Ibid.*, 8.
[81] Saur, *Influences parallèles*, 95–9; Jean-Pierre Chrétien and Marcel Kabanda. *Rwanda. Racisme et génocide. L'idéologie hamitique* (Paris: Éditions Belin, 2015), 310–11.
[82] Desouter and Nzabahimana, *Clés pour un retour à la paix*, 64–6.
[83] Desouter, *In Gods linkerhand*, 360.
[84] Desouter and Nzabahimana, *Clés pour un retour à la paix*, 8.
[85] *Ibid.* 45–6.
[86] Des Forges, *Leave None to Tell the Story*, 459–60.

both of whom had played a major role in the genocide, as the ICTR later established. No wonder the RPF ignored their proposal.

Back home, Desouter continued along the same lines. In June 1995, he published a report entitled *Rwanda: Les violations des droits de l'homme par le RPF/APR. Plaidoyer pour une enquête approfondie* [Rwanda: The RPF/APR's human rights violations. Plea for a comprehensive investigation] in association with Filip Reyntjens, a political scientist of the University of Antwerp who had served as President Habyarimana's adviser on constitutional matters and who shared the Flemish missionary's abhorrence of the RPF.[87] Both had been in Rwanda after the genocide: Reyntjens for one week in mid-October 1994[88] and Desouter in transit on the way from Bujumbura to Bukavu during the same period. This was not enough to compile a report on the exactions attributed to the RPF. For their June 1995 compilation, they relied on reports from Human Rights Watch and a Spanish human rights organisation and on testimonies from Rwandans in exile.

In March 2006, Desouter was one of the exonerating witnesses at the trial of Aloys Ntabakuze, a military commander charged with genocide crimes, crimes against humanity and war crimes at the ICTR in Arusha. Ntabakuze was declared guilty and sentenced to life imprisonment. Desouter did not mention the defendant's name in his ninety-page long 'expert report'.[89] Instead, he testified against the RPF, which according to him was seeking power at all costs, and endeavoured to demonstrate that the genocide had not been planned. An expanded version of the report, complemented by appendices, was published the following year under the title *Rwanda: Le procès du RPF. Mise au point historique* [Rwanda: The trial of the RPF. Historical clarification].[90]

---

[87] Serge Desouter and Filip Reyntjens, 'Rwanda. Les violations des droits de l'homme par le FPR/APR. Plaidoyer pour une enquête approfondie', University of Antwerp, Institute of Development Policy and Management, Working Paper, June 1995, 49 pages.

[88] Filip Reyntjens, 'Sujet d'inquiétude au Rwanda, en octobre 1994', *Dialogue*, 179 (November–December 1994), 3–14.

[89] 'Expert report presented by Serge A. Desouter before ICTR in the case of the Prosecutor versus Aloys Ntabakuze, No ICTR-98-41-T', March 2006, 94 pages.

[90] Serge Desouter, *Rwanda: Le procès du RPF. Mise au point historique* (Paris: L'Harmattan, 2007).

Guy Theunis' media activism

After the genocide, the White Father the most active in the French-speaking media on matters concerning Rwanda was Guy Theunis. Many erroneously believed that he was the spokesperson of his congregation. His analytical tone and his sense of nuance were somewhat reassuring, but this does not mean he was neutral – far from it. It would be hard to find anything positive written about the new government of Rwanda in his name. Without going as far as Desouter or de Dorlodot in his denunciation of a double genocide, he always made a point of balancing the genocide, which he agreed was tragic, with the equally execrable crimes his numerous contacts in the Hutu community in exile attributed to the RPF.

An active member of ADL in the early 1990s, as mentioned earlier, he often presented himself as a human rights activist after the genocide, a title which gave him credibility in the media world. It is a fact that, alongside Rwandan people such as André Sibomana, he had criticised the abuses of the Habyarimana government. Presenting him as pro-Hutu would be incorrect. He had as many Tutsi friends as Hutu ones. During his first pastoral posting in Cyanika near Gikongoro, he had heard from his confrère Stanislas de Jamblinne the stories of the crimes committed against the Tutsi in the area in 1963 and 1964 and witnessed *de visu* violence between Hutu and Tutsi.[91] If he became controversial in some circles after the genocide – and received applause in others – it was because of his political positioning. He was resolutely, and without any concession, a critic of the RPF.

Theunis had worked in Rwanda since 1970. After his time in Cyanika, he worked in various parishes while teaching in schools and in the major seminary.[92] He was never formally trained as a journalist. He learned on the job as editor of the Christian information and reflection journal *Dialogue* in Kigali from 1989 to 1992, as compiler of a review of the Rwandan press afterwards and as a presenter on the Rwandan Catholic radio once a week. He was good at drafting reports and sending news bulletins. As we have seen, from April to August 1994, in association with Jef Vleugels, he sent faxes to his religious superiors with news of the Rwandan situation that were read far beyond the confines of his congregation.

---

[91] Guy Theunis, 'Mon point de vue sur l'histoire du Rwanda', 1. Document kindly communicated by Guy Theunis to the author.
[92] Colette Braeckman, 'Le Rwanda était toute la vie de Guy Theunis', *Le Soir*, 13 September 2005.

One of the first tasks Theunis completed on his return to Belgium in April 1994 was to prepare the issue of the journal *Dialogue* that should have come out in Kigali the same month for publication. Most articles had been submitted to the editor before the genocide. The only later addition was an article by Antoine Mugesera, a member of the editorial committee of *Dialogue* in the 1980s who had joined the RPF in the meantime. He gave the point of view of his movement on the recent events in Rwanda and responded to the accusations of human rights abuse levelled against the RPF at the time.[93] Theunis remained the editor of *Dialogue* until 1995. François Nzabahimana was a member of the editorial committee in Brussels until he took on leadership of the RDR. The August–September 1994 issue of *Dialogue* included a remarkable collection of first-hand accounts of the genocide. The 'Belgian' *Dialogue* – as opposed to the 'Rwandan' *Dialogue* that has been published in Kigali since 2004[94] – appeared until 2009. It gradually became the mouthpiece of the Hutu community in exile, containing numerous articles that were critical of the RPF government.

Radio Amahoro, which Theunis administered on his return to Belgium, played a similar role. It had programmes in Kinyarwanda for Rwandans around the world, including in the refugee camps in Tanzania and Zaire. Its mission, according to its original charter, was to 'provide Rwanda and neighbouring countries with credible information allowing the Rwandese to obtain elements of information which the current Rwandese radios never mention'.[95]

In 1996, Theunis was assigned to other pastoral duties by his congregation. Journalists and conference organisers, however, continued to call on him. He was interrogated in June 1997 by the Belgian Senate and in April 1998 by the French National Assembly on matters related to the genocide in Rwanda.

Theunis did not deny in any way the reality of the genocide. In a talk he gave on 24 September 1995 in Brussels, for example, he mentioned the 'planned massacre of the Tutsi'. He also observed that some people had 'not yet accepted the reality of what happened either because they deny

---

[93] Antoine Mugesera, 'Réflexions d'un membre du RPF.' *Dialogue*, 176 (June–July 1994), 39–48.

[94] Antoine Mugesera, 'Entretien avec l'auteur', in *Rwanda 1896–1959. La désintégration d'une nation. Anthologie*, vol. 1 (Kigali: Izuba Éditions, 2017), 303–7.

[95] Quoted in Antoine Mugesera, 'Du Père Guy Theunis: Un damné non condamné', *Umuvugizi*, 2 August <https://umuvugizi.wordpress.com/2013/08/02/du-pere-guy-theunis-383444> [accessed 27 July 2018].

the reality of the genocide or because personally they have been deeply traumatised'.⁹⁶ Nor did he come out as an unconditional defender of the Catholic Church. In an essay written at the invitation of the French sociologist André Guichaoua in July 1994, he did not hesitate to speak of the 'marriage' between the church and the state in Rwanda and of the church's fear of making pronouncements on matters of justice, peace and development because of its links to the state.⁹⁷ Lastly, unlike many of his Flemish confrères, he never entertained the idea that the main problem in Rwanda was the 'oppression' of the Hutu by the Tutsi.

Yet, in his public statements, Theunis so often cast suspicion on the RPF leaders' integrity in matters of human rights, always 'balancing' the genocide and the alleged crimes of the RPF, that his recognition of the reality of the genocide, though attested, became inaudible. Despite the fact that he and his friends provided support to genocide survivors in Rwanda and in Europe, he appeared as the spokesperson of the Hutu community in exile. It is a fact that he often expressed sympathy in public for their plight. Typical is this declaration to a journalist on 30 August 1995: 'Since 1990, there may not have been a genocide [against the Hutu], but there have been massacres which continue to this day. Every day we receive messages saying that killings have taken place in this or that region. [...] We should perhaps speak, as in Burundi, of a selective genocide.'⁹⁸ Elsewhere, he denounced, in language reminiscent – intentionally or not – of the Hamitic theory, 'the glaring injustice' of a 'country conquered by a people of strangers while the original inhabitants live in poverty either as refugees in a foreign land or as displaced people inside their country'.⁹⁹

Theunis' ambivalence appeared in a debate organised by the missionary magazine *Wereldwijd* in June 1997. 'The Hutu are generally peaceful,' he declared on that occasion. 'They wanted a non-violent evolution. Violence always comes from the same side. From one side!' To the journalist who asked whom he meant, he responded in reference to when, in November

---

⁹⁶ Guy Theunis, 'L'Église au Rwanda: où en est-elle aujourd'hui', unpublished paper, Brussels, 24 September 1995 (Archives *Dialogue*, Brussels).

⁹⁷ Guy Theunis, 'Le rôle de l'Église catholique dans les événements récents', in André Guichaoua (ed.), *Les crises politiques au Rwanda et au Burundi, 1993–1994. Analyses, faits et documents* (Lille: Université des Sciences et Technologies, 1995), 289–98.

⁹⁸ Guy Theunis, 'Sur le rôle de l'Église catholique au Rwanda', *Le Soir*, 30 August 1995.

⁹⁹ Guy Theunis, 'Les véritables causes du génocide et des massacres', *Incroyance et foi*, 72 (Winter 1994), 8.

1959, Dominique Mbonyumutwa was attacked by a Tutsi *sous-chef* and to the October 1990 RPF invasion: 'On the Tutsi side. It is always the Tutsi who provoke in one way or another and spoil the whole thing.' The White Father's co-debater, Colette Braeckman, then intervened, having in mind the genocide against the Tutsi. Did Theunis mean that the Tutsi always initiated violence? Realising that he was on slippery ground, the missionary changed his tune: 'This is a caricature. [...] I simply protest against the fact of opposing two categories of people. On both sides, there have always been pacifists in Rwanda. They constitute the majority.'[100]

Uneasy coexistence

In Rwanda, the relations between church and state started to improve around 1998, as will be seen in the next chapter. The missionaries, many of whom were critical of the RPF government in private, kept a low profile. Most of them, in any event, were willing to work towards the reconstruction of the country in a context marked by continuous military tension in the western prefectures in particular.

Only one White Father, a Fleming by the name of Stefaan Minnaert, departed from the common attitude of opposition to the RPF. After working as a teacher in Kigali after the genocide, he published the diary of the late-nineteenth-century missionary Jean-Joseph Hirth[101] and served as a general archivist in Rome before leaving the congregation and joining the diocese of Ghent in Belgium. He has regularly collaborated with the *Dialogue* journal based in Kigali since 2004.

In '*Missionnaires de l'évangile ou apôtres de la haine*', the June 1998 article cited at the beginning of this chapter, Rutazibwa mostly criticised the attitude of the Rwandan churches before the genocide and the attacks made on the new government from Europe after the genocide. He did not have much to say about the White Fathers in Rwanda during that period. He blamed two of them – Jan Lenssen, the regional superior, and Antonio

---

[100] Guy Goris and Marc Van Laere Goris, 'L'Église est-elle coupable au Rwanda. Un débat entre Filip Reyntjens, Colette Braeckman and Guy Theunis', *Wereldwijd*, June 1997. French translation in *ANB-BIA* 326 (15 June 1997), 15.

[101] Stefaan Minnaert (ed.), *Premier voyage de Mgr Hirth au Rwanda: de novembre 1899 à février 1990: contribution à l'étude de la fondation de l'Église catholique au Rwanda* (Kigali: Éditions rwandaises, 2006). See also Stefaan Minnaert, *Recueil d'articles et de documents concernant le cardinal Lavigerie, Mgr Hirth, le Dr Kandt, le P. Brard, le P. Classe, le P. Loupias, le chef Rukara, Mgr Perraudin, etc* (Kigali: Imprimu, 2017).

Martinez, the apostolic administrator of the diocese of Ruhengeri – for being part of an anti-government 'ideological circle'.[102] André Comblin, a Belgian White Father who had travelled to Rwanda to convince the sisters of the Benedictine monastery of Sovu to desist from accusing their prioress and a young sister of having taken part in the genocide, was briefly arrested in September 1995 but was not sent to jail. His visa was even extended by a month to January 1996 when it was eventually revoked.[103]

The response of the religious superiors to Rutazibwa's article was remarkably moderate. At an extraordinary meeting of the ASUMA Committee, to which Jean-Damascène Ndayambaje, the superior of the Josephite brothers of Rwanda, a largely Tutsi congregation which had lost many of its members during the genocide, had been invited, they discussed all the issues raised by Rutazibwa. In a statement subsequently published in *La Nouvelle Relève,* they recognised that the publication of their earlier document on 7 April 1998, the commemoration day of the genocide, had been inappropriate. They also admitted that before 1994 the church had 'not reacted to the official racist and ethnist ideology' and that it sometimes had to 'confess the sins of its children'. They invited their critics, however, to consider the past events in their context and to avoid all globalisation.[104]

The religious superiors were not the only ones to react to Rutazibwa's letter with moderation. The Commission for Religious Life of the Episcopal Conference also discussed it and sent a written response. Even more surprisingly, one of the White Fathers working in the Nyamirambo parish went to see Rutazibwa to exchange views on the role of the church in the genocide.[105]

Conclusion

It was the White Fathers, one should remember, who established the Catholic Church in Rwanda at the beginning of the twentieth century. For better or worse, they shaped, ecclesiastically but also culturally and politically, the destiny of the country. When a local church started to emerge in the second half of the century, they continued to exert influence through their capacity to raise funds among other things.

---

[102] Rutazibwa, *Contre l'ethnisme*, 144.
[103] *Ibid.*, 151–2.
[104] 'Réunion du Comité de l'ASUMA 11.7.98', *La Nouvelle Relève*, 364 (30 July 1998), 26.
[105] Rutazibwa, *Contre l'ethnisme*, 7.

During the genocide, just like in the late 1950s and early 1960s, when the first pogroms against the Tutsi occurred, some of them showed compassion and tried to save lives. The majority of the eighty or so White Fathers who ministered in Rwanda before the genocide left the country in April. Among those who came back later on a voluntary basis, a certain number acknowledged the pain of the survivors, recognised that the church had committed errors in the past and endeavoured to restart the mission on a new basis. We have seen that the General Council of the Missionaries of Africa in Rome tended to support this type of response to the genocide.

Judging from the Missionaries of Africa's declarations to the press, their publications and various conversations with them, we can say that many of them, particularly those who did not return to Rwanda, rapidly moved away from a focus on the genocide to a systematic critique of the RPF's policies and actions. Some promoted the double genocide theory.

These missionaries reacted in two different ways. The older missionaries – those who had arrived in Rwanda in the 1950s and 1970s – gave credence, in the statements they made after the genocide, to the stereotype of the cunning and deceitful Tutsi who oppress the Hutu 'majority'. No consideration was given to the fact that, in 1994, many Tutsi lived in rural areas and were just as poor as their Hutu neighbours. Some White Fathers continued to adhere, as in colonial times, to the discredited Hamitic theory. The younger missionaries, on the other hand, abstained from using overtly 'ethnist' language, but their opposition to the RPF, who were culpable in their eyes of serious human rights abuse, was no less resolute.

The best way of describing the attitude of the majority of White Fathers regarding the Rwandan question is that they have long been, and remain to this day, partisan. In September 1991, the regional superior, Jef Vleugels, invited his confrères to fight the 'disinformation' benefitting the RPF by documenting their crimes in the north of Rwanda. He wanted to 'balance' the information.[106] Something similar happened after the genocide. A sort of equivalence was made between the human rights abuses attributed to the RPF, which occupied all the attention, and the atrocity of the genocide against the Tutsi, which was gradually underplayed under the pretext that the ruling party was using it to consolidate its power. There have been White Fathers such as Henri Bazot, the former whistle blower,[107] or Stefaan Minnaert who considered the efforts of the new Rwandan government in a more positive light, but they were very few and generally marginal.

---

[106] See Chapter 2.

[107] See Chapter 1. Henri Bazot died in 2016. On his last days, see Laurent Larcher, *Rwanda, ils parlent. Témoignage pour l'histoire* (Paris: Seuil, 2019), 248–9.

CHAPTER 7

Church and state relations after the genocide

An important memory actor in post-genocide Rwanda was the Holy See, the government of the Catholic Church in Rome. Catholics like the members of the Commission for the Revival of Pastoral Activities in the diocese of Butare, the priests who met in May and November 1995 in Kigali or local bishops such as Wenceslas Kalibushi in Nyundo and Frédéric Rubwejanga in Kibungo played a significant role in the articulation of genocide memory in Rwanda, not to mention the bishops, pastors and laypeople of the other churches. The Catholic Bishops' Conference and the papal representatives who, as we shall see, dictated the conduct of the bishops in matters of genocide memory were, however, more influential because of their visibility and their particular position on the political scene. This chapter will focus on the relations between church and state in the post-genocide period and their influence on the politics of memory in the country. In this respect, the Catholic Church, the oldest and most powerful church in Rwanda, was the one that counted most. The Rwandan government had less public interaction with the leadership of the Protestant churches.

The Roman factor

Giuseppe Bertello, the nuncio in office when the president's plane was shot down, had resisted the tendency, common to many Rwandan Catholics, of uncritically aligning himself with the Habyarimana government's ideological positions. As Jean Birara, a former governor of the Bank of Rwanda who fled to Belgium in April 1994, put it in an interview, 'until 1990 Habyarimana was considered a saint or almost a saint. It was not until a new nuncio was appointed in Kigali that a new understanding of reality started to develop. The church was beginning to move.'[1] Bertello

---

[1] Jean Birara, 'Á bout portant', *Le Soir*, 7 May 1994.

is credited with having encouraged Thaddée Nsengiyumva, the bishop of Kabgayi, to endorse a pastoral letter supporting the idea of a negotiation between the then-government and the RPF in December 1991 and for having established contacts with the RPF in Mulindi.[2]

The contrast with Henryk Hoser – who arrived in Rwanda on 5 August 1994, less than a month after the end of the genocide, with the title of apostolic visitator[3] – and with Julius Janusz – who took office as nuncio in August 1995 and remained in that position until his appointment as nuncio to Mozambique in September 1998 – could not be bigger. Both were aggressively anti-RPF and adopted an adversarial approach to the Rwandan government in matters of genocide commemoration. Very different in this respect was the nuncio that followed, Salvatore Pennachio, who took office in early 1999. One of his first moves was to establish a project for genocide orphans called City of Nazareth in Kabgayi at the request of Pope John Paul II who had celebrated Mass in the area during his trip to Rwanda in September 1990.[4]

Intriguingly, Pierre Nguyên Van Tot, the chargé d'affaires appointed by the pope at the Rwandan nunciature in June 1994; Henryk Hoser, the apostolic visitator who joined him in August of the same year; and Julius Janusz, who arrived in August 1995, had in common the fact that they came from either a communist country (Vietnam) or a country which had just ceased to be communist (Poland). For Nguyên Van Tot, who had been transferred from the Vatican embassy in Kinshasa during the genocide,[5] it may have been fortuitous. The fact that two Poles were appointed at a time when the RPF had the reputation, in Catholic circles, of being a communist Trojan horse, is probably not a coincidence. Already at the time of the Rwandan Social Revolution, the UNAR, the RPF's remote predecessor, was considered a friend of Moscow.[6] The accusation resurfaced in the early 1990s. 'Is the RPF Marxist?' André Louis, the influential vice-president of CDI, wrote in an internal note on 13 April 1994. 'It is a question to which only the future will respond. What is certain, though is that the movement has assimilated and integrated the Marxist methodology of power conquest

---

[2] See Chapter 2.

[3] 'Abp Henryk Hoser: Kościół nie brał udziału w ludobójstwie' [Archbishop Henryk Hoser: The church did not participate in genocide], *Niedziela*, 6 July 2012.

[4] <https://www.nolitetimere.com/index.php/en/who-we-are/the-cite-des-jeunes-nazareth> [accessed 19 April 2020].

[5] Catholic News Service, 18 June 1994.

[6] See Chapter 1.

and that it is using it in a masterly way.'⁷ General Christian Quesnot, the chief of staff of the French army, expressed a similar sentiment on 29 April 1994 when he described the RPF, in a memorandum, as 'black Khmers'.⁸ The memory of Jean-Baptiste Bagaza, also a Tutsi, who had expelled missionaries and imposed restrictions on Catholic worship during his tenure as president of Burundi in the late 1970s and 1980s,⁹ may have also fuelled the mistrust of the RPF.

As the rest of this chapter will indicate, Hoser's attitude – and Janusz' – contributed to the worsening of the relations between the Catholic Church and the Rwandan state after 1994. At the heart of the dispute was Hoser's reluctance to recognise the genocide as genocide. From this fact, we should not conclude, however, that his appointment was political. From an ecclesiastical point of view, he was a good candidate for the post of apostolic visitator. A qualified medical doctor, he had experience in development. Though resolutely opposed to the Habyarimana government on the issue of artificial contraception,¹⁰ a stance that had endeared him to the conservative sectors of the Roman Curia, he had served – like Michel Twagirayesu, the president of the Presbyterian Church – in the ONAPO and developed in this way connections with government officials. From 1981 to 1991 he had held leadership positions in the Pallotine congregation, which, with forty-odd members, was one of the biggest male missionary congregations in Rwanda at the time. In April 1994, while being in Europe, he had attended the synod for Africa in Rome. The Rwandan bishops having been prevented from coming because of President Habyarimana's death, he was the only cleric who could speak with authority about Rwanda during the synod.¹¹

---

[7] André Louis, 'Rwanda: la stratégie du FPR', 4 April 1993 (Archives of the Dominican Missionary Sisters of Namur).

[8] Pierre Favier et Michel Martin-Roland, *La Décennie Mitterrand*, vol. 4: *Les déchirements* (Paris: Seuil, 1999), 478. See also Catherine Coquio, 'La guerre coloniale française et le génocide rwandais', in Virginie Brinker *et al.* (ed.), *Rwanda 1994–2014. Histoire, mémoires et récits* (Dijon: Les Presses du Réel, 2017), 118.

[9] James Carney, 'Christendom in crisis: the Catholic Church and postcolonial politics in Central Africa', in Elias Bongmba (ed.), *Routledge Companion to Christianity in Africa* (London and New York: Routledge, 2015), 372.

[10] Franciszek Kania, *Rwanda wczoraj i dziś: 21 lat posługi misyjnej w Rwandzie (1973–1994)* [Rwanda yesterday and today: 21 years of missionary service in Rwanda] (Ząbki: Apostolicum, 2003).

[11] Apart from a short biography published by the Polish Catholic agency KAI

Politically, Hoser was a hardliner. Did this play a role in his appointment as apostolic visitator in July 1994? It is possible. The matter will only be clarified when the archives of the Secretariat of State, the department of the Roman Curia responsible for political and diplomatic affairs, are opened to researchers. It is to the secretary of state, one should remember, that all nuncios report. Since 1991, the incumbent had been Angelo Sodano, a member of the right-wing Catholic movement Opus Dei who had developed links with the dictator Augusto Pinochet when serving as nuncio to Chile in the late 1970s and early 1980s.

The assassination of the three bishops by APR soldiers on 5 June 1994 is an important element of context. It made a deep impression on Cardinal Etchegaray, the pope's envoy, when he visited Rwanda in late June 1994. As pointed out in an earlier chapter, rather than recognising the genocide as genocide, the prelate saw the Rwandan 'war' as a power struggle between two ethnic groups. It is very likely that the report he made to John Paul II on his return to Rome strengthened the hand of those – the secretary of state and perhaps the pope himself – who were seeing in the RFP's impending accession to power a threat for the church and wanted to see a personality capable of confronting it in Kigali. Hardly a month after Etchegaray's return, Hoser was in Rwanda.

The spectre of church persecution

Nguyên Van Tot and Hoser's 9 January 1995 letter to Alphonse Marie Nkubito, the minister of justice in the first post-genocide Rwandan government, and the response of Pie Mugabo, the minister of labour and social affairs, on 27 January 1995 illustrate the tonality of the conversation between the nunciature and the RPF-led government during this period. Nkubito had been the founding president of the Rwandan Association for the Defence of Human Rights (ARDHO) and was perceived as relatively independent from the RPF. This may be the reason why the two Roman

---

on 7 July 2016, there does not seem to be any study of Henryk Hoser's life and ministry. He served as archbishop of Warszawa-Praga from 2008 to 2017. After he was accused of genocide complicity in several Polish newspapers, he granted interviews to the Polish Catholic Sunday newspaper *Niedziela* (6 July 2012) and the Catholic online newspaper *Onet* (5 May 2014). He briefly responded to the questions of the journalist Wojciech Tochman in 2010 but refused him permission to quote his responses. See Wojciech Tochman, *Aujourd'hui nous allons dessiner la mort*, trans. Margot Carlier (Lausanne: Éditions Noir sur Blanc, 2014), 92.

officials felt it would be judicious to write to him. While conceding that the new government had started to reconstruct the infrastructure of the country, they expressed 'concerns' about the arbitrary detentions, secret executions and spoliations of property that Rwanda was experiencing at the time. In this situation, the Catholic Church was the 'voice of those who do not have a voice to cry out their distress', and yet it was the object, on the national radio and in the media close to the government, of constant accusations of genocide complicity. Without saying it explicitly, they suggested in a veiled way that the regime was attacking the church to cover up its own misdeeds:

> It is not excluded that the aim of such accusations is to draw the attention away from the messages broadcast for a long time by the Catholic Hierarchy in Rwanda and elsewhere in favour of peace and reconciliation unless it is to mask the crimes committed against the Hierarchy and the ecclesiastical personnel.[12]

During the 'war and the massacres', the authors of the letter continued, three bishops, about a hundred priests, a hundred brothers and sisters and numerous lay people had been killed. 'As if it was not enough', the clergy was now the victim of numerous attacks. A priest had been assassinated, two priests and one sister had gone missing and a group of religious people had received death threats. Two priests, a seminarian and two sisters were detained without hope of a prompt judgement.[13]

In the eyes of the nunciature, the church was persecuted, a theme which some opposition media in exile would develop *ad nauseam* in subsequent years. There was no doubt that some clerics had been killed after the genocide, but not as many as Nguyên Van Tot and Hoser claimed. In a comprehensive survey of the 'sufferings' of the Catholic Church after the genocide which he compiled in 2002, Joseph Ngomanzungu, a former assistant general secretary of the Conference of Rwandan Bishops, recorded the death of only one priest – Claude Simard[14] – during the period July–December 1994. Denys Sekamana and Thaddée Rusingizandekwe, two priests from Butare and Gikongoro, respectively, arrested in September and October 1994, and Bernadette Mukarusine and Bénédicte Mukanyangezi, two sisters from Shyorongi, north of Kigali, arrested during the same period, did indeed wait a long time for their trial – because of the staggering numbers

---

[12] Pierre Nguyên Van Tot and Henryk Hoser to Alphonse Nkubito, 9 January 1995, 3 (Archives *Dialogue*, Brussels).
[13] *Ibid.*, 3–4.
[14] See Chapter 4.

of people accused of genocide-related crimes – but they were not arbitrarily detained. During the genocide, Sekamana had been seen, armed with a gun and in military uniform, manning a roadblock destined to prevent the Tutsi from escaping near the Institut catéchétique africain (ICA) in Butare, of which he was the director. Rusingizandekwe, who was a military chaplain and the son of an Interahamwe, had been accused by genocide survivors of complicity in the massacre of Tutsi in the church of Kibeho.[15] The two sisters from Shyorongi had reportedly chased away Tutsi refugees from their convent and given their names to the Interahamwe.[16]

The response from the government came on 27 January, signed by Pie Mugabo, the minister of labour and social affairs, who had church and state relations among his responsibilities.[17] A former state attorney, he was serving in the government of national unity as a member of the Liberal Party (PL), of which he was the president. His letter, addressed to Nguyên Van Tot, was courteous but firm. He had found the tone of the letter 'surprising', he wrote, as it seemed to imply that there was a conflict between the government and the church and that the latter was persecuted. All recent speeches of the president and other cabinet ministers indicated, on the contrary, that the government was counting on the church's help in its efforts of pacification and reconciliation.

Why was the nunciature speaking of persecution, Mugabo went on, when other sectors of the Catholic Church, not only priests from Kigali, Butare and Kabgayi but even the ACEAC itself, did not shy away from recognising the failings of the church? In support of this affirmation, Mugabo quoted a recent statement of the ACEAC stipulating that the church was 'taking in charge the sins of its children in the region' and that it was committed to 'correcting the deviations undermining the spirits and the human societies'.[18]

---

[15] Jean Ndorimana, 'À quand les sanctions canoniques pour le clergé rwandais coupables de génocide?', *Dialogue* (Kigali), 210 (November 2019), 240, 243.

[16] African Rights, *Rwanda: Death, Despair and Defiance*, 2nd edn (London: African Rights, 1995), 919–22.

[17] Pie Mugabo to Pierre Nguyên Van Tot, 27 January 1995 (Archives *Dialogue*, Brussels).

[18] *Ibid.*, 2. Quoted from ACEAC, 'Message des évêques au peuple de Dieu qui est au Burundi, au Rwanda et au Zaïre', Kinshasa, 10 December 1994, 2 (Archives of the Conference of Rwandan Bishops, Kigali). Two Rwandan bishops, Thaddée Ntihinyurwa and Frédéric Rubwejanga, signed the document.

The subtext was that the nunciature was alone in accusing the Rwandan government of abuse. This was only partly true. As already noted, the Rwandan bishops carefully avoided using the word genocide in their statements at the time.[19] On 12 January 1995, three days after Nguyên Vat Tot and Hoser had written to Nkubito, the Rwandan bishops issued a document entitled 'Preoccupations of the members of the Conference of Catholic bishops of Rwanda addressed to the authorities of Rwanda', which echoed the Roman officials' letter, though in a much less aggressive tone.[20] The coincidence of dates suggests that the bishops addressed their complaints to the government at the request of the nunciature or at least in concertation with it.

Mugabo acknowledged the assassination of the bishops and priests in June 1994 in Gakurazo but refused to hold the government responsible for it. According to him, the 'delinquency that everywhere accompanies moments like those we have been through' was the cause. The government was doing its best to repress it. The refugees were invited to return to the country, but they would not benefit from amnesty if they had committed crimes. The fact that priests and religious people had been arrested in Rwanda for their participation in the genocide should not deter their confrères in exile from coming back if they had nothing on their conscience.[21]

At the centre of the conflict between the nunciature – and other Catholic priests and laity, especially those in exile – and the government was the question of the centrality of the genocide. Hoser did not want to dwell on the subject. As reported in a Rome-based newsletter in January 1995, he considered that the RPF 'did not represent a sufficient number of people in order to govern' and that the former government, now in exile in Bukavu, should be included in a power-sharing deal.[22] The fact that the latter had orchestrated the genocide and never apologised for it was not an issue for him. He felt that it was time to move on. His allocution to the priests gathered at the Centre Christus in Kigali on 30 May 1995 was significant from that point of view. They should, he told them, stick to their priestly identity despite the 'unspeakable' events they had witnessed. 'The risk is

---

[19] See Chapter 4.
[20] Conférence Épiscopale du Rwanda, 'Préoccupations des membres de la Conférence des évêques catholiques du Rwanda adressées aux autorités rwandaises', Kigali, 12 January 1995 (Archives *Dialogue*, Brussels).
[21] Mugabo to Nguyên Van Tot, 27 January 1995, 5.
[22] *Agenzia Fides, Organo di informazione delle Pontifice Opere Missionarie*, 28 January 1995, quoted in Jean-Paul Kimonyo, *Rwanda demain! Une longue marche vers la transformation* (Paris: Karthala, 2017), 168.

big to be obsessed by the past.'[23] In fact, the participants did not heed to his call. The entire session was devoted to a 'loyal appraisal' of the situation born out of the genocide, as the lay theologian Laurien Ntezimana, one of the speakers, put it in his presentation.

A fax sent by Hoser to Christine de Coudray on 10 October 1995, when he was busy handing over the office to Julius Janusz in Kigali, shows that, during this period, the nunciature was locked in a siege mentality, with perceived enemies inside and outside the church. The addressee was the African project director of Aid to the Church in Need (ACN), an organisation of pontifical right founded to help Christians persecuted in the communist world which was active in the refugee camps in Zaire.[24] Hoser was worried about the future of the church in Rwanda:

> It is striking to see how a campaign launched against the Church from Europe (Golias, articles against the Caritas) finds echoes in Rwanda itself or rather coincides with the one that is conducted here. We count on your prayers for the unity of the Rwandan church. Its internal division is much bigger than the external difficulties.[25]

Anger at the church in Parliament

On two occasions, each prompted by an inconsiderate decision of the bishops, the matter of the church's involvement in the genocide and the related question of church–state relations were discussed in Parliament in an emotion-laden atmosphere.[26] This cathartic experience had no lasting

---

[23] *Rôle du prêtre rwandais dans l'édification de l'Église et la reconstruction nationale. Session des prêtres rwandais tenue du 29 mai au 1er juin 1995 au Centre Christus Remera/Kigali*, 13.

[24] Jean-Pierre Chrétien, *Le défi de l'ethnisme. Rwanda et Burundi*, 2nd edn (Paris: Karthala, 2012), 55.

[25] Fax attached to a letter from Christine de Coudray to Hervé Deguine, Königstein, 20 October 1995. Paris-Nanterre University, La Contemporaine: Fonds Hervé Deguine, Affaire Sibomana, Carton 4.

[26] For this section, I am indebted to a chapter of Remi Korman's doctoral dissertation on the church–state conflict about the sites of massacre in post-genocide Rwanda. See R. Korman, 'Commémorer sur les ruines. L'État rwandais face à la mort de masse dans l'après-coup du génocide (1994–2003)', unpublished PhD thesis, Paris, École des hautes études en sciences sociales, 2020, 497–572.

consequences on church and state relations. However, it brought to light the new situation in which the Catholic Church, the only one which really mattered in these debates, was finding itself. The time of a privileged, if not incestuous, relation with the government was over. This does not mean that the new Rwandan government had an anticlerical agenda. There were too many practising Catholics in its midst for this to happen. If Paul Kagame, the strongman of the regime, felt that the church and the state had had too many interests in common under Habyarimana, as he said in an interview in July 1994,[27] he knew that the new government needed the church to reconstruct the country.

This being said, the state expanded its zone of influence, taking responsibility, for example, for the burying of the dead, a task until then reserved for the established religions. Admittedly, the situation was confused in the chaos that followed the genocide. In some parishes, like Butare, Simbi, Cyahinda, Nyumba and Gakoma, all in the diocese of Butare, the faithful organised mass grave burials and maintained the sites afterwards.[28] Elsewhere, the authorities dug up bodies from the latrines and open fields where they had been thrown off and authoritatively transported them, sometimes by batches of twenty thousand at a time, to mass graves.[29] In October 1995, the government announced, without consultation with the churches, that the feast of All Saints, traditionally celebrated on 1 November, would no longer be a public holiday.[30] In 1996, plans were made to replace the course of religion in the schools with a course of moral instruction. They were withdrawn after an outcry from the Catholic, Protestant and Muslim religious leaders.[31]

---

[27] Quoted in Anne Gorce, 'Une Église sous les décombres', *La Croix*, 4 August 1994.
[28] *Fécondité de la crise rwandaise. Jalons pour une nouvelle évangélisation au Rwanda. Recueil de douze documents publiés par la Commission de Relance des Activités Pastorales*, Document 7, February 1995 (Butare: Diocèse catholique de Butare, 1996), 52.
[29] *Fécondité de la crise rwandaise*, Document 11 (September–October 1995), 80–1.
[30] Claudine Vidal, 'Commémoration du génocide au Rwanda', *Cahiers d'études africaines*, 175 (2004), 583.
[31] Testimony of Jérôme Masinzo, a genocide survivor who took part in the Detmold meeting in December 1996, in Fulgence Rubayiza, *Guérir le Rwanda de la violence. La Confession de Detmold, un premier pas* (Paris: L'Harmattan, 1998), 67.

The first parliamentary debate on the church arose unannounced on 29 May 1995 after the news came out that the Rwandan bishops were planning a 'grandiose' reburial ceremony of the three assassinated bishops at the Kigali cathedral the following month.[32] The personality of Vincent Nsengiyumva, the late archbishop of Kigali, was the main object of dispute. The members of Parliament, many of whom were genocide survivors, had no doubt that he was guilty of genocide complicity. He had been a member of the central committee of the MRND, the ruling party, until 1985[33] and had intimate links with Juvénal Habyarimana's family and more particularly his wife, Agathe, who was widely believed to have supported, if not initiated, the genocide.

In the morning of 7 April 1994, a few hours after the president's death, Nsengiyumva had paid a visit to his bereaved family in the presidential palace in Kanombe in the company of Sister Godelieve and Sister Télesphore, two blood sisters of the president, and Sister Salomé, the superior of the congregation of sisters attached to the archdiocese of Kigali.[34] In a document presented to the Belgian military police on 26 May 1994, Jean Birara, a former Bank of Rwanda governor and businessman who had fled to Belgium in the early days of the genocide, recounted that, on this fateful morning, Nsengiyumva had 'decided to say Mass, recommending that one should forgive everybody because Agathe H[abyarimana] had just called for the massacre of all the Tutsi'.[35]

Nobody has ever questioned the credibility of Birara: the Belgian military police considered him 'honest and serious' and the political scientist Filip Reyntjens believed he was independent from the RPF.[36] His testimony does not show in any way that Nsengiyumva was guilty of genocide, but it reveals an astonishing proximity to the family and entourage of the president – particularly Protais Mpiranya, the commander of the presidential guard that went on a killing spree the same morning. The archbishop of Kigali knew that the decision to kill all Tutsi had been mooted at the highest level. His subsequent statements remained completely silent about this obvious threat.

---

[32] *Fécondité de la crise rwandaise*, Document 9, July 1995, 66.
[33] Timothy Longman, *Christianity and Genocide in Rwanda* (Cambridge: Cambridge University Press, 2011), 154. See Chapter 2.
[34] André Guichaoua, *De la guerre au génocide* (Paris: La Découverte, 2010), Annexe 54.
[35] Guy Artiges, Audition of Jean Birara, Brussels, 26 May 1994.
[36] Filip Reyntjens, *Political Governance in Post-Genocide Rwanda* (Cambridge: Cambridge University Press, 2013), 10.

The long-time collusion between the Catholic Church and the Habyarimana regime that Nsengiyumva exemplified explains the *hargne* (rage)[37] that the evocation of the archbishop's name triggered among the members of Parliament in May 1995. Esdras Kayiranga, a PL representative from Butare, declared that the 'burial of these criminals [the three bishops] in a house of God would be an insult to God' and that 'it would be better to remove them from where they are and bring them to the hills or the banana plantations were those that they have killed are lying'. Richard Rutatina, a former refugee from Uganda, pointed out that 'each person who has taken part in the massacres loses his dignity even if he is respected by everybody'.[38] In conclusion, the National Assembly decided that Mgr Nsengiyumva would be included in the list of the people held responsible for the genocide and the massacres and that he would be judged *post mortem*. They requested the Catholic Church to abstain from holding the reburial ceremony until a judgement had been rendered.[39] The same day, the bishops announced their decision to suspend the ceremony 'for reasons independent of their will'.[40]

The second parliamentary debate on church–state relations came in response to a letter of 12 February 1996 from Thaddée Ntihinyurwa on behalf of the episcopal conference to Pie Mugabo, requesting that the Easter celebration, which fell that year on 7 April, be distinguished from the second anniversary of the genocide (which was also due to be commemorated on 7 April), 'so as to take into account the sensitivity of our people'.[41] This letter, which betrayed a noticeable lack of judgement on the side of the bishops, elicited a fierce debate which lasted three days.

This time the question of the relation between church and state was at the centre of the discussion. 'The church does not know that things have changed,' declared Laurent Nkongoli, a Tutsi lawyer from Butare, 'because in the past it had the right to make decisions for the state.' Tito Rutaremara, a RPF heavyweight, made the same point. The church had not understood the evolution of society since 1994, he pointed out, and might

---

[37] *Fécondité de la crise rwandaise*, Document 7 (July 1995), 65.
[38] Parliament of Rwanda, Compte-rendu n°067/AN/95 (26 May 1995), quoted in Remi Korman, 'Commémorer sur les ruines', 520.
[39] Communiqué of the National Assembly, quoted in James K. Gasana, *Rwanda: du parti-état à l'état-garnison* (Paris: L'Harmattan, 2010), 307–8.
[40] Joseph Ngomanzungu, 'Messages et lettres pastorales des Évêques Catholiques pendant la période 1994–2004', *Urunana*, 37 (June 2004), 9.
[41] Thaddée Ntihinyurwa to Pie Mugabo, 12 February 1996, quoted in Vidal, 'Commémoration du génocide au Rwanda', 584.

take 'forty-five years' to ask for forgiveness for its responsibility in the genocide, as had been done with the Holocaust.[42] 'Thousands of people have been killed in the churches', Emmanuel Nsabimana, a PL representative from Kibuye, also said. 'The church did not save them. The church must recognise this fact.'[43]

In the end, the two celebrations took place on the same day. The church celebrated Easter 'in churches still stained with the blood of the victims and with walls bearing the marks of bullets and gunshots', as the Belgian journalist Colette Braeckman put it.[44] The state commemorated the genocide in Gikongoro in the presence of Augustin Misago, the local bishop, who for the first time publicly faced the anger of the genocide survivors who blamed him for having done nothing to protect them.[45]

In the previous regime, the government interfered at least once – when Félicien Muvara, a Tutsi bishop-elect was forced to resign just before his installation[46] – in an episcopal appointment. No such thing happened under the new Rwandan government. The nuncio recommended for the pope's approval the appointment of two batches of bishops after the genocide, those of Kigali, Byumba and Kabgayi on 25 March 1996 and those of Nyundo, Butare and Cyangugu on 18 January 1997. As with the last batch of appointments in 1992, a mix of Hutu and Tutsi bishops made the cut. The only appointment with a political overtone was that of the bishop of Kabgayi. André Sibomana, the apostolic administrator of the diocese, was an obvious candidate, but he was a known critic of the Rwandan government.[47] The rector of Nyakibanda Major Seminary, Anastase Mutabazi, was appointed instead. There is no evidence of political pressure, however. More important is the fact that in the Roman Curia, as Sibomana himself noted in a book interview, there were officials like Cardinal Jozef Tomko,

---

[42] It was later, during a trip to Jerusalem in March 2000, that John Paul II famously asked God's forgiveness for the crimes committed by Christians against the Jews. Rutaremara seemingly referred to the institution of the Annual Day of Christian–Jewish Reflection in 1990.

[43] Parliament of Rwanda, Compte-rendu n°177/AN/96 (28 February 1996), quoted in Remi Korman, 'Commémorer sur les ruines', 524.

[44] Colette Braeckman, 'Pâques de deuil au Rwanda dans la mémoire du génocide', *Le Soir*, 9 April 1996.

[45] *Ibid.* See Vidal, 'Commémoration du génocide au Rwanda', 584.

[46] See Chapter 2.

[47] See Chapter 4.

the prefect of the Congregation for the Evangelisation of Peoples, who felt that he was too much involved in politics.[48]

The pope's statement on the genocide

The first Roman pronouncement on the genocide came out during this period.[49] The occasion was the visit of a Roman official, Paul Joseph Cordes, president of the Pontifical Council Cor Unum, the Roman aid agency, to Rwanda. It is unlikely that this visit was prompted by the parliamentary debate of February, because such events are prepared a long time in advance. Yet the message from Pope John Paul II, which Cordes delivered on his arrival in the country, constituted a response of sorts to the issue debated in Parliament. For the first time, if one makes an exception for the two short messages issued in April and May 1994, the pope mentioned as such the 'genocide which has cost the lives of thousands of persons' and expressed an opinion, which was to become a doctrinal reference in subsequent years, on the question of the church's responsibility in the genocide. He did not respond to the expectations of those who – like Tito Rutaremara during the parliamentary debate of February, or the genocide survivors – would have liked a confession of guilt on the part of the Catholic Church for its complicity, at least indirect, in the genocide. This was what the General Synod of the Presbyterian Church in Rwanda would do a few months later.[50] While recognising that it was the Rwandan state's duty to administer justice, the pope only conceded that some 'members' of the church, and not the church itself, should recognise their guilt:

> The state faces an important and difficult challenge. Its essential duty is to administer justice to all. I must also say that justice and truth must go hand in hand when it comes to bringing to light the responsibilities in the tragedy that your country has experienced. The church as such (*en tant que telle*) should not be held responsible for the faults of its members who acted against the law of the gospel. They will be called to account for their

---

[48] André Sibomana, *Gardons l'espoir pour le Rwanda*, 2nd edn (Paris: L'Harmattan, 2008), 171.
[49] Note that, intentionally or not, Pope John Paul II did not make any reference to the genocide in the speech he pronounced on 19 September 1995 in Uhuru Park, Nairobi. Referring to 'the peoples of Rwanda and Burundi', he spoke instead of 'the terrible ethnic conflict that [was] still latent after having engulfed so many innocent victims'.
[50] See Chapter 5.

acts. All the members of the church who have sinned during the genocide must have the courage to bear the consequences of the deeds they committed against God and their neighbours.[51]

The difference between this letter and that of Nguyên Van Tot and Hoser's letter to the minister of justice a year before is so obvious that it is unlikely that the nunciature – or the Secretariat of State for that matter – had anything to do with it. Until the archives of the Vatican for this period are accessible, it will be difficult to know who advised the pope on the situation in Rwanda in this instance. There seem to have been two views in Rome at the time, one frankly negationist and one more open to the reality of the genocide.

In his address to Cordes, on 19 March, Ntihinyurwa did not rise to the occasion. Unlike the pope, he did not say a word about the genocide, choosing to speak instead of the 'war'. He complained about the insecurity in the country and the church's lack of means. Without detracting from the defensive attitude that the Catholic Church had adopted since 1994, he attributed the decrease in faith observed in the church to the 'unfounded accusations against the church and its personnel'.[52]

The homily Cordes preached in Kigali before returning to Rome vividly illustrated the gap between the attitude of the Rwandan bishops – not to mention the nunciature – towards the genocide and that of the segment of Catholic opinion that he represented. The unspeakable reality of the genocide was at the centre of his message. Referring to his own German background, he recalled the 'regime of terror instituted by national-socialism with the hunting of the Jews'. He also mentioned the crimes committed in ex-Yugoslavia. If he did not designate the Tutsi by name, he alluded to their sufferings when speaking of an 'encounter with an apocalyptic terror and a distress without name'. After evoking the figure of a Benebikira sister massacred in Nyanza, he conveyed a message of support from the pope who, he noted, had 'witnessed the extermination of the Jews in his homeland of Poland'.[53]

---

[51] 'Message du Pape Jean-Paul II à Son Exc. Mgr Thaddée Ntihinyurwa, Évêque de Cyangugu, Président de la Conférence Épiscopale du Rwanda', 14 March 1996, in *Osservatore Romano*, 20–1 March 1996, 5; *La Documentation catholique*, 2138 (5 May 1996), 407–8.

[52] 'Adresse de Monseigneur Thaddée Ntihinyurwa, Vice-Président de la Conférence des Évêques catholiques du Rwanda, à son Excellence Monseigneur Paul Joseph Cordes, Président du Conseil Pontifical Cor Unum', Kigali, 19 March 1996.

[53] 'Homélie de Mgr P.- J. Cordes le 23 mars 1996 à Kigali à la cathédrale

The mixed church–state commission

On the matter of the recognition of the genocide, however, the Rwandan bishops had no option but to soften their position. A purely defensive attitude was not tenable in the long run. As will be explained in Chapter 10, the Jubilee Celebration of 2000 and the diocesan synods which preceded it marked the beginning of a change of heart. Between 1996 and 1998, the question of the transformation of churches into genocide memorials, controversial and emotional as it was, had the unintended effect of inciting the bishops to negotiate a compromise with the state and, in this manner, to participate in the memorialisation of the genocide.[54]

The idea of keeping the memory of the genocide alive and of displaying, through commemoration ceremonies and monuments, the horror of what had happened arose rapidly after the installation of the government of national unity, which included genocide survivors, Hutu who had opposed the genocide and former refugees from Uganda, Burundi and Zaire. The first national commemoration of the genocide took place in Kigali on 7 April 1995. In October of the same year, the government instituted the CMGM (in Kinyarwanda: *Komisiyo y'Urwibutso rw'Itsembabwoko n'Itsembatsemba*), which was placed under the responsibility of Joseph Nsengimana, the minister of higher education and culture; an official of his department, Louis Kanamugire, was appointed as president of the Commission. In February 1996, at the request of Prime Minister Pierre Célestin Rwigema, Nsengimana and Kanamugire compiled a list of fifty churches and temples where Tutsi people had been massacred.[55]

The establishment of this list entailed two questions: which churches should be earmarked to become memorials of the genocide, and what

---

Saint-Michel', *Dialogue*, 190 (April–May 1996), 73–6.

[54] On the discussions about the memorialisation of the genocide, see Claudine Vidal, 'La commémoration du génocide'; Hélène Dumas and Rémi Korman, 'Espaces de la mémoire du génocide des Tutsis au Rwanda', *Afrique contemporaine*, 238 (2011), 11–27; Rachel Ibreck, 'Remembering humanity: the politics of genocide memorialisation in Rwanda', unpublished PhD thesis, University of Bristol, 2009; James Smith and Carol Rittner, 'Churches as memorial sites: a photo essay', in Carol Rittner, John K. Roth and Wendy Whitworth (ed.), *Genocide in Rwanda. Complicity of the Churches* (St Paul, Minnesota: Paragon House, 2004), 181–205.

[55] CNLG, Archives of the Commission for the Mémorial of the Genocide and the Massacres in Rwanda: 'Amaguye abantu benshi mu itsembabokwo n'itsembatsemba hakwiye kuba urwibibutso. I. Amasengero n'ibigo by'abihaye Imana uko hitwa', n.d. [February 1996].

arrangements should be made with the church for the transformation of these churches into genocide memorials? For the project to succeed, church and state had to find a common ground. It was never a question, on the part of the government of Rwanda, of requisitioning churches for the purpose of forcefully transforming them into cemeteries or museums, as some opponents, inside and outside the church, claimed they intended to do. Even though there were frictions between the Catholic Church – to which the quasi-totality of the fifty churches listed by Nsengimana and Kanamugire belonged – and the political authorities, the latter were confident that they would come to an agreement with the church on the issue of the genocide memorials.

For the authorities of the church, on the other hand, this was uncharted territory. The Code of Canon Law of the Catholic Church, last revised in 1983, gave bishops the power to authorise the building of churches or to allow disaffected churches to be used 'for a secular but not unbecoming purpose'.[56] In the event of a sacred place being desecrated by 'acts done in them which are gravely injurious and give scandal to the faithful', the Code recommended that no worship should be held in them 'until the harm [was] repaired by means of a penitential rite'.[57] In theory, the bishops could have consented to the transformation of some churches into genocide memorials without referring this to Rome. In practice, however, they felt the need to consult the nuncio, who himself referred the matter to the Secretariat of State in Rome, and that is where all the problems started: on the matter of genocide memorials, the local bishops and the Roman officials had very different views.

After an initial meeting of the bishops with the prime minister on 23 December 1995 and an informal discussion between Ntihinyurwa, Nsengimana and Kanamugire during a genocide commemoration in Nyamasheke near Cyangugu on 29 April 1996, the assembly of Rwandan bishops agreed to participate in a mixed church–state commission to discuss the matter of the church genocide memorials. The first meeting was held on 6 June 1996, with representatives from all the dioceses. Three more meetings, with a smaller number of church representatives, took place on 23 September 1996, 23 October 1997 and 2 March 1998. Kanamugire attended all the meetings. Towards the end of the process, Jacques Bihozagara, the minister of youth, sports, culture and vocational

---

[56] *Codex Iuris Canonici*, canon 1222, art. 1.
[57] *Ibid.*, canon 1211.

training, replaced Nsengimana when the responsibility of church and state relations was transferred to his department.

As Dumas and Korman pointed out, 'it was not a ruthless fight'.[58] The exchanges between the bishops and the government representatives were cordial. Both sides were prepared to compromise. The personality of Modeste Mungwarareba, the general secretary of the Bishops' Conference, who attended all the meetings, was a pacifying factor. Twice a victim of anti-Tutsi violence – in 1963 and in 1994 – he was the co-author of the CRAP bulletins, which invited the Catholics of the diocese of Butare to accept in all honesty the devastating reality of the genocide.[59] The fact that both Nsengimana and Kanamugire were practising Catholics also helped.

At the first meeting of the mixed commission on 6 June 1996, the two parties agreed that there would be two categories of churches: seven – Nyamata (Kigali), Nyumba (Butare), Mugina (Kabgayi), Kibuye (Nyundo), Nyarubuye (Kibungo), Nyamasheke (Cyangugu) and Kibeho (Gikongoro) – would be turned into genocide memorials and host the remains of the victims. The churches of the second category would continue to be used as places of worship but would commemorate the genocide in some way, for example by displaying the body of one victim.[60] The English version of the minutes, compiled by Mungwarareba, mentioned that the delegation of the Catholic Church had proposed that 'another project of memorial [...] for all the victims of the war' – an allusion to the non-Tutsi victims of the conflict during and after the genocide – should be considered. The Kinyarwanda version of the minutes, written by Kanamugire, did not mention this point. The fact that it was mentioned during the meeting, however, is worthy of note.

The intervention from the nunciature

The bishops, however, soon backtracked. In a letter dated 12 June 1996 which they all signed by hand, they indicated that the churches of the first category would commemorate the genocide in a manner to be jointly discussed but would remain places of worship. In this way, they noted, 'our Christians will receive a better instruction in matters of memory'. They no

---

[58] Dumas and Korman, 'Espaces de la mémoire du génocide des Tutsis au Rwanda', 239.
[59] See Chapter 4.
[60] CNLG, Archives of the CMGM, 'Compte rendu de la rencontre de la Commission mixte Église catholique-État sur la question des églises en passe de devenir monuments commémoratifs, le 6 juin à Kacyiru.'

longer referred to two categories of churches, some being transformed into genocide memorials and others remaining open to worship but displaying exhibits of the genocide.[61]

The report Nsengiyumva sent to the first minister about his meeting with the nuncio on 24 June 1996 clearly shows that the main reason for the bishops' volte-face was an intervention from the nunciature. Never, Janusz declared to the minister, would the Catholic Church accept that the Rwandan churches cease to be places of worship. According to him and his superiors in Rome, that would be in opposition with canon law. Secondly, it would contradict the Helsinki meeting on human rights, including the freedom of worship. Using the same language as the bishops in their letter of 12 June, the nuncio asserted that 'during Mass, one does nothing else than remembering death'. For him, Nsengiyumva wrote, that was enough. 'No need to find excuses for burying [the bodies] in churches as the Christians in some areas would like.'[62]

The reference to the July 1975 Helsinki Conference on Security and Cooperation in Europe, during which the Western countries and the Soviet Union and its allies pledged to improve their relations in various matters including freedom of worship, signalled that Janusz considered the matter of genocide memorials through an anti-communist lens. According to Kanamugire, who attended the meeting, Janusz spoke forcefully and with anger. 'He located the problem', he recounted in a later document, 'in a universal communism versus capitalism and Catholicism versus atheism framework. [...] He demonstrated that the current regime in Rwanda had transgressed the statutes which linked it to the church, insinuating that it was atheistic and communist and that it wanted to transform the church buildings into amphitheatres, forgetting the long-term lease that the Rwandan state had granted to the church.'[63]

Despite this setback, the dialogue between the bishops and the members of the Memorial Commission continued, though at a slow pace. In his individual capacity, Frédéric Rubwejanga, the bishop of Kibungo, proposed that the left wing of the Nyarubuye church, where a gigantic

---

[61] Archives of the CMGM, Thaddée Ntihinyurwa and seven other bishops or representatives of bishops to Joseph Nsengiyumva, 12 June 1996. The bishop of Cyangugu was absent when the document was presented for signature.

[62] Archives of the CMGM, Joseph Nsengiyumva to Pierre-Célestin Rwigema, 24 June 1996.

[63] Louis Kanamugire, 'Les grands sites du génocide perpétré contre les Tutsi au Rwanda. Témoignages recueillis et réflexions personnelles', unpublished document, March 2012, 176.

massacre had taken place,⁶⁴ become a genocide memorial and that three classrooms of the adjacent school be transformed into a museum.⁶⁵ At the third meeting of the mixed church–state commission on 23 October 1997, the government representatives proposed that one church be transformed into a genocide memorial and a crypt erected or, if this was not possible, that other signs of the genocide be arranged in the other churches. This proposal was accepted at the fourth meeting, on 2 March 1998, pending approval from the Secretariat of State in Rome. The Nyamata church – where transformations had, in fact, already taken place – would become a genocide memorial and signs evoking the genocide would be introduced in the churches of the second category.

On 25 September 1998, Jacques Bihozagara, the minister in charge of church and state relations, sent a draft agreement to the nuncio.⁶⁶ Five months later, Thaddée Ntihinyurwa transmitted without a word of comment Rome's curt reply to the Rwandan government. The 'requisition' of the Nyamata church was considered 'a fait accompli'. Any commemorative sign should express a prayer to the dead and invite forgiveness. In the churches where human remains had already been buried, the status quo should prevail to avoid emotional reactions, but no more transfers of bones should take place.⁶⁷

The dry tone of the letter from Rome betrayed a remarkable lack of empathy for the victims of the Rwandan genocide and the people associated with them. The message was that the church should only commemorate the genocide in situations that could not be avoided. The document does not seem, however, to have been widely circulated.

This episode shows, on the part of the Rwandan bishops, a total deference to their superiors. This was not uncommon in the Catholic Church, particularly during John Paul II's pontificate. In the end, no agreement was signed. Did it matter? The answer to this is unclear. Only two churches – Nyamata and Ntarama in the outskirts of Kigali – have been integrally transformed into genocide memorials, but many others, for example in

---

⁶⁴ Privat Rutazibwa and Paul Rutayisire, *Génocide à Nyarubuye* (Kigali: Éditions rwandaises, [2007]).

⁶⁵ Archives of the CMGM, Frédéric Rubwejanga to Joseph Nsengiyumva, 24 June 1996.

⁶⁶ Archives of the CMGM, 'Protocole d'accord entre l'Église catholique et le gouvernement rwandais sur les églises-mémoriaux du génocide et des massacres de 1994', n.d.

⁶⁷ Archives of the CMGM, Thaddée Ntihinyurwa to [Anastase Gasana], minister of institutional relations, 25 February 1999.

Kibuye, in Nyarubuye or at the Sainte-Famille in Kigali, display a genocide monument on the church premises. In Kibeho, half of the church has become a genocide memorial. In Nyange, a new church has been erected next to the church that was bulldozed over the bodies of the Tutsi refugees during the genocide. In this matter, one should note the moderation of the Rwandan government. It refrained from any violent action against the church, choosing instead to reach consensus. It knew that it had much to lose in an open conflict.

The prosecution of ministers of religion for acts of genocide

Contrary to what the critics of the Rwandan government said, the personnel of the Catholic Church – or of any other church, for that matter – were not targeted because of their church affiliation when suspected, rightly or wrongly, of being involved in the genocide.[68] But they were not exonerated from prosecution for that reason either. They were treated like any other citizens. That is the point. The Catholic Church had lost the privileged position it was enjoying before the genocide, and the new rulers were determined to act independently in matters of criminal justice.

The theory of a persecution of the church does not hold water. What is true is that since 1994 a certain number of ministers of religion have been prosecuted for acts of genocide. In some cases, their culpability was evident. In others, the tribunal found the evidence weak and pronounced an acquittal unless they were simply released for lack of evidence. The decisions that created controversies were those concerning an offence – having close links with Interahamwe or officials involved in the killings and remaining silent when a public statement might have saved lives – that was open to divergent interpretations. The most disputed cases were those of priests or pastors who had been condemned to imprisonment despite the fact that genocide survivors had testified to having been rescued by them. In the minds of the judges, the possibility existed that they might

---

[68] See, for example, the document posted on the Internet by the Centre de lutte contre l'impunité et l'injustice au Rwanda (CLIIR) under the title 'La persécution contre l'Église Catholique du Rwanda par le "pouvoir occulte" des extrémistes tutsi' (30 April 1999). In *La souffrance de l'Église à travers son personnel* (Kigali: Pallotti Press, 2002), without explicitly speaking of a persecution of the church, Joseph Ngomanzungu seems to imply that all the priests and religious arrested and detained since 1994 without exception were unjustly accused and therefore innocent.

have played a role in the genocide and saved lives at the same time, as has happened for a number of *génocidaires*.

Data is available on the judicial history of thirty-six Catholic consecrated persons accused of genocide after 1994. The list may be incomplete, given the difficulty in accessing some of the records, those of the *gacaca* trials in particular.

Ministers of religion were among the vast numbers of genocide suspects arrested and detained, sometimes without any documentation and for a long time, after July 1994. By the end of 1996, close to 100,000 people were waiting in overcrowded prisons and police cells, a number that had increased to 130,000 by early 1998.

Increasingly worried about the problem of prison overcrowding, the Rwandan government tried to institute a more efficient judicial system.[69] In August 1996, it passed a legislation which divided the suspects into four (later reduced to three) categories and laid the ground for trial procedures which conformed to international norms. They also instituted special chambers to deal with cases of genocide. A total of 28 consecrated persons of the Catholic Church, 17 pastors and preachers of various Protestant churches and 2 traditional healers were included in the lists of suspects of the first category[70] published in the *Official Gazette of the Republic of Rwanda* in November 1996, December 1999 and March 2001, respectively.

A second strategy, to which we shall return in Chapter 10, was to establish popular courts called *gacaca* to judge, at the level of each local entity, the massive number of cases which the conventional courts did not have the time or resources to handle. Some clerics who had received a sentence in a conventional tribunal were tried again in a *gacaca* court.

The table below, which concerns only Catholic consecrated persons, shows a great diversity of situations.[71] Genocide suspects could be judged

---

[69] Jean-Paul Kimonyo, *Rwanda demain!*, 178–80. For an analysis of the administration of justice in post-genocide Rwanda that is well informed, though marred by a systematic anti-RPF bias which distorts the historical perspective, see Filip Reyntjens, *Political Governance in Post-Genocide Rwanda*, 212–51.

[70] The first category of offenders included the planners, instigators and organisers of the genocide or of a crime against humanity, the persons who abused positions of authority at any level in order to commit crimes, the murderers who distinguished themselves by their excessive malice and the perpetrators of sexual torture (Organic Law No. 08/96 of 30 August 1996).

[71] The main sources are the *Official Gazette of the Republic of Rwanda*, 35 (30 November 1996), 38 (31 December 1999) and 40 (21 March 2001); Joseph

in four types of courts (with the possibility of being successively judged in two or three different types of courts): a Rwandan conventional court, a *gacaca* court, an ICTR court or a court in a third country under the principle of universal jurisdiction in international criminal law. The lists published in the *Official Gazette* contain 28 names of Catholic consecrated persons: 17 in 1996,[72] 8 more in 1999 and 3 more in 2001. The *gacaca* courts judged 11 cases involving a Catholic priest or religious person, the ICTR courts 3 and the courts in a third country 3 (not including decisions on extradition requests, which were usually rejected). One should note that out of 36 suspects, only 20 were judged in Rwanda. The remaining 16, including 2 missionaries (Gabriel Maindron and Carlo Bellomi), had left the country after the genocide. Out of those, 3 were arrested outside Rwanda and referred to the ICTR (Athanase Seromba, Emmanuel Rukundo and Hormisdas Nsengimana),[73] 2 were tried in Brussels (the Sovu sisters) and 1 in France (Wenceslas Munyeshyaka).

Table 2 also shows diversity in the outcome of the judiciary procedures. In total 12 suspects, that is a third of the total, were released for lack of evidence or acquitted. The most famous acquittal is that of Augustin Misago, the bishop of Gikongoro, as discussed in the next section. One suspect (Hormisdas Nsengimana) was acquitted by an ICTR court, the others by a Rwandan court. A Belgian court condemned 2 suspects (the Sovu sisters) to pain of imprisonment and the *gacaca* courts 8. Out of those, 6 were condemned to life imprisonment (Déogratias Gakuba, Aimé Mategeko, Joseph Ndagijimana, François Nkusi, Édouard Ntuliye and Dominique Rwesero) and 2 (Laurent Ntimugura and Denis Sekamana) to fifteen or twenty years of imprisonment. Quite a few were declared suspects by the Rwandan government but never put on trial because they lived abroad.

Ngomanzungu, *La souffrance de l'Église*; Jean Ndorimana, 'À quand les sanctions canoniques'; various press releases and newspaper articles available online.

[72] Seven of these names had been mentioned by African Rights and six by *Golias*, but both publications had provided many names of genocide suspects which are not included in the *Official Gazette*. The officials who drew up the list of first-category suspects in 1996 may have used these two reports, but these were not their only sources. See African Rights, *Rwanda: Death, Despair and Defiance*, 910–22; *Golias*, 43 (July–August 1995), 50–1.

[73] On the circumstances of the arrest of Emmanuel Rukundo and Athanase Seromba by ICTR 'trackers', see Philippe Braewaeys, *Traqueurs de génocidaires. Sur les traces des tueurs rwandais* (Brussels: Renaissance du Livre), 2015, 68–74, 85–91.

Table 2. Catholic bishops, priests and religious accused of acts of genocide

Name	Status	Diocese	Timespan*	Court(s)	Outcome
Bellomi, Carlo	Priest (Italy)	Kibungo	1995–6	Rwandan Tribunal	Briefly arrested, sent back to Italy, then charged *in absentia*
Gakuba, Déogratias	Priest	Kigali	1996, 2008	Gacaca	Condemned to life imprisonment
Gashegu, Emmanuel	Seminarian	Butare	1994–2006	Gacaca	Detained until his acquittal
Hitayezu, Marcel	Priest	Nyundo	1996–2016	Rwandan Tribunal / Third Country Court	Charged *in absentia* / Extradition request rejected
Hitimana, Josaphat	Priest	Kabgayi	2009	Gacaca	Tried several times. Fled to Zaire, acquitted *in absentia*
Kabalira, Martin	Priest	Butare	2014–15	Rwandan Tribunal / Third Country Court	Charged *in absentia* / Extradition requested
Kayiranga, François	Priest	Nyundo	1996–2000	Rwandan Tribunal	Condemned, then acquitted on appeal
Maindron, Gabriel	Priest (France)	Nyundo	1996, 2010	Rwandan Tribunal / Gacaca	Charged *in absentia* / Sentenced *in absentia* to life imprisonment
Mategeko, Aimé	Priest	Cyangugu	2009	Gacaca	Condemned to life imprisonment
Misago, Augustin	Bishop	Gikongoro	1999–2000	Rwandan Tribunal	Acquitted

*Date from the arrest or the indictment to the end of the judiciary procedure.

Table 2. Catholics bishops, priests and religious accused of acts of genocide—*continued*

Name	Status	Diocese	Timespan*	Court(s)	Outcome
Mukabutera, Julienne (Marie Kisito)	Sister	Butare	2001	Belgian Tribunal	Condemned to 12-year imprisonment
Mukagango, Consolata (Gertrude)	Sister	Butare	2001	Belgian Tribunal	Condemned to 15-year imprisonment
Mukakimenyi, Jacqueline	Sister	Nyundo	1996	N/A	Detained, then released for lack of evidence
Mukanyangezi, Bénédicte	Sister	Kigali	1994–2007	Gacaca	Detained, then released for lack of evidence
Mukarusine, Bernadette	Sister	Kigali	1994–2007	Gacaca	Detained, then released for lack of evidence
Munyeshyaka, Wenceslas	Priest	Kigali	2006–2015	Rwandan Tribunal / ICTR/ Third Country Court	Sentenced to life imprisonment / Indicted ICTR / Referred to the French jurisdiction / Case dismissed
Ndagijimana, Joseph	Priest	Kabgayi	1995–2009	Rwandan Tribunal / Gacaca	Condemned to life imprisonment, appealed and condemned again

Name	Role	Location	Year	Court	Outcome
Ngirabanyiginya, Dominique	Priest	Nyundo	1995	N/A	Arrested, then released
Ngirinshuti, Thaddée	Priest	Cyangugu	1998–2001	Rwandan Tribunal	Condemned to 20-year imprisonment, acquitted on appeal
Nkusi, François	Brother	Kabgayi	2001, 2009	Rwandan Tribunal	Condemned to death, then acquitted, then condemned to life imprisonment
Nsengimana, Hormisdas	Priest	Butare	2002–9	ICTR	Arrested in Cameroon, indicted and acquitted
Ntamugabumwe, Jean-Baptiste	Priest	Nyundo	1996	Rwandan Tribunal	Charged *in absentia*
Ntihinyurwa, Thaddée	Bishop	Cyangugu	2005	Gacaca	Acquitted
Ntimugura, Laurent	Priest	Cyangugu	1997–2001	Rwandan Tribunal	Sentenced to 20-year imprisonment
Ntuliye, Edouard	Priest	Nyundo	1998–2009	Rwandan Tribunal / Gacaca	Condemned to death, then acquitted, then sentenced to life imprisonment
Rutihunza, Jean-Baptiste	Brother	Butare	1996–2013	Rwandan Tribunal	Charged *in absentia* / Extradition request rejected
Rukundo, Emmanuel	Priest	Kabgayi	2001–9	ICTR	Condemned to 25-year imprisonment
Rusingizandekwe, Thaddée	Priest	Gikongoro	1994–2005	Rwandan Tribunal	Arrested and detained Disappears before Gacaca trial
Rwamayanja, Jean-Baptiste	Priest	Ruhengeri	1994	Rwandan Tribunal	Indicted but not judged

Table 2. Catholics bishops, priests and religious accused of acts of genocide—*concluded*

Name	Status	Diocese	Timespan*	Court(s)	Outcome
Rwesero, Dominique	Brother	Kabgayi	1998–9	Rwandan Tribunal	Death sentence, commuted to life imprisonment on appeal
Sekamana, Denis	Priest	Butare	1994–8, 2008	Rwandan Tribunal / Gacaca	First sentenced to 4 years and later to 15 years of prison
Seromba, Athanase	Priest	Nyundo	2001–8	ICTR	Condemned to a 15-year imprisonment, then life on appeal
Subiza, Innocent	Deacon	Cyangugu	1995–2000	Rwandan Tribunal	Detained then released for lack of evidence
Theunis, Guy	Priest (Belg.)	N/A	2005	Gacaca / Belgium Tribunal	Detained, then transferred to Belgium and released
Twagirayezu, Urbain	Priest	Nyundo	1996	Rwandan Tribunal	Indicted *in absentia*
Uwayezu, Emmanuel	Priest	Butare	2009–10	Rwandan Tribunal / Italian Tribunal	Indicted in Rwanda, arrested in Italy Extradition request rejected

Catholic bishops, priests and religious people were not the only ministers of religion to face prosecution for acts of genocide. As already mentioned, 17 Protestant pastors and preachers were included in the lists of first-category suspects published in the *Official Gazette* in 1996, 1999 and 2001. They served in the Anglican, Presbyterian, Adventist and Pentecostal churches among others. A couple of traditional healers were also in the lists. Three Protestant church leaders – Elizaphan Ntakirutimana, the pastor of the Adventist Mugonero mission near Kibuye; Samuel Musabyimana, the bishop of Shyogwe in the Gitarama prefecture; and Jean Uwinkindi, a Pentecostal pastor based in Nyamata – were indicted by the ICTR. Ntakirutimana was condemned to twenty-five years of imprisonment.[74] Musabyimana died in custody before a trial could take place. Uwinkindi was transferred to Rwanda and sentenced to life imprisonment. About ten pastors of the Presbyterian Church, including a woman, were condemned to prison by Rwandan tribunals or a *gacaca* courts, according to oral testimonies. Some were acquitted on appeal.

The trial of Augustin Misago

The biggest crisis in the relations between the Catholic Church and the Rwandan state in the post-genocide era was the one that followed the arrest of Augustin Misago, the bishop of Gikongoro, on 14 April 1999. Never during this period, except perhaps in September 2005 when the White Father Guy Theunis was arrested while in transit at Kigali airport and detained for several weeks,[75] had the tension been so strong.

After nearly thirty audiences of an endless trial in the Kigali Tribunal of 1st Instance, Misago was acquitted on 15 May 2000.[76] This episode

---

[74] His son Gérard, a medical doctor, was also condemned for genocide at the ICTR. On the genocide in Mugenero, see Philip Gourevitch, *We Wish to Inform You That Tomorrow We Will Be Killed with Our Families* (New York: Picador, 1998), 25–43.

[75] Guy Theunis, *Mes soixante-quinze jours de prison à Kigali* (Paris: Karthala, 2012).

[76] For the history of the Misago trial, we have at our disposal two important sources. First, a detailed account of almost all the audiences by the general secretary of the Conference of Rwandan Bishops is available on the website of the Centre on Conflict, Development and Peacebuilding of the Graduate Institute of Geneva. Second, Misago's version of the events is documented in three texts published in *Dialogue*, 209 (March–April 1999), 37–85, 86–91, 93–8. See also Jean-Damascène Bizimana, *L'Église et le génocide au*

revealed a deep fracture in public opinion about the involvement of the church's hierarchy in the genocide. On one side, Misago himself, the other Rwandan bishops, the Holy See, a certain number of Rwandan Catholics and a powerful Catholic lobby abroad considered that the bishop of Gikongoro had done what he could during the trying period of the genocide and that he had been powerless in the face of criminal attacks on the Tutsi in his diocese. The RFP-led government, they felt, was using the occasion to settle political scores against the Catholic Church.[77] On the other side, the genocide survivors, part of the Rwandan political intelligentsia and a certain number of journalists and opinion-makers in the West believed that, even if Misago had not killed anybody, he had close links with the local authorities and would have mitigated the impact of the genocide if he had taken a firm stand against it.

The difficulty with the Misago case was that the lines were not clearly drawn. The bishop was neither completely innocent nor completely guilty. There were emotions on both sides: among the genocide survivors and their friends, who wanted justice done, and among the supporters of the bishops, who believed that the trial was politically motivated and that, through Misago, it was the church that the RPF regime was attacking.

The truth of the matter is that Misago's arrest had not been planned beforehand. The accusation had little time to gather evidence and address, in a convincing way, the issue at stake. From a legal point of view, the case against Misago was weak. The defence – a team of three lawyers led by Alfred Pognon, an experienced Beninese attorney – successfully argued that Misago was not directly engaged in the murders committed against the Tutsi priests and school learners in his entourage.

Pressure had been mounting on Misago for a long time. When a team from African Rights had visited Gikongoro in 1995, the survivors had told them that the bishop had refused to provide shelter to Tutsi refugees during the killings and had instead defended Thaddée Rusingizandekwe, a

---

Rwanda. Les Pères Blancs et le Négationnisme (Paris: L'Harmattan, 2001), 96–129.

[77] See, for example, Madeleine Raffin, 'Le procès de Mgr Augustin Misago, évêque de Gikongoro', *Foi et Vie. Revue de l'Archidiocèse de Toulouse*, 18 (17 October 1999): 'This trial is a political trial and not the trial of the individual Augustin Misago'. Madeleine Raffin headed the Caritas office of the diocese of Gikongoro from 1993 to 1997. Vehemently opposed to the RPF, she recounted her experience of the genocide in Gikongoro in *Rwanda: un autre regard. Trois décennies à son service* (Lille: Éditions Sources du Nil, 2012), 79–115.

priest allegedly implicated in the killings.[78] Misago had responded to these accusations in a thirty-two-page document subsequently published in the Brussels-based journal *Dialogue*.[79] The same year, survivors had publicly challenged the bishop during the second national commemoration of the genocide in Gikongoro.[80] Misago had been summoned to the Tribunal of 1st Instance of Gikongoro on 11 February 1998 and to that of Kigali on 23 February 1998 to account for his attitude during the genocide.[81]

The Misago affair started on 7 April 1999, the day of the fifth commemoration of the genocide, when a group of survivors nominally attacked the bishop during the commemoration in the presence of Pasteur Bizimungu, the president of Rwanda, during a state visit to Murambi and Kibeho, two genocide sites in the prefecture of Gikongoro. Bizimungu was very upset. 'During all my visits', the president was reported as having said, 'people speak of Misago everywhere. The bird that flies in front of me sings Misago. Misago himself did not know what to say.'[82] Informed of the incident, the public prosecutor decided to reopen the case. Misago was arrested on 14 April 1999 as he was about to attend a meeting of the Bishops' Conference in Kigali and was immediately sent to jail.

'I thought he could save us'

The charge sheet was couched in very general terms. The trial essentially evolved around accusations of non-assistance of persons in danger. The fact that Misago had taken part in meetings with political and military officials, including Prime Minister Jean Kambanda, was also held against him. His role in the public celebration of the death of Fred Rwigema, the leader of the RPF, in early November 1990, when he still was the rector of

---

[78] African Rights, *Rwanda: Death, Despair and Defiance*, 899–900.
[79] Augustin Misago, 'Réactions aux accusations d'African Rights', *Dialogue*, 209 (March–April 1999), 37–85.
[80] Colette Braeckman, 'Pâques de deuil au Rwanda dans la mémoire du génocide', *Le Soir*, 7 April 1996.
[81] Judgement of the Tribunal of 1st Instance of Kigali, 23 February 1998. See Augustin Misago, 'Je ne me suis pas tu', *Dialogue*, 209 (March–April 1999), 93–8.
[82] *Imvaho*, 47 (April 1999), 13, quoted in Jean-Baptiste Hategeka, 'Monseigneur A. Misago coincé entre les esprits et les rescapés de Bufundu-Nyaruguru', *Kinyamateka*, 1523 (1 July 1999), 7.

Nyakibanda Major Seminary, was given as proof that he had sympathy for the Hutu extremist positions.[83]

On 17 April 1994, two days after an important massacre of Tutsi in the church of Kibeho, Misago visited the site in the company of Laurent Bucyibaruta, the prefect of Gikongoro, who, as Misago said at the trial, was 'apparently afflicted by the killings'. This bishop discovered a few children who were still alive, put them in his car and brought them to the Anglican hospital of Kigeme near Gikongoro. Later on, the children were taken to a technical school still in construction in Murambi where, on 20 April, thousands of Tutsi people were killed. Producing, to everybody's surprise, one of the children from the Kibeho school who had survived the massacre of Murambi, the defence had no difficulty in showing that Misago had done nothing wrong in this instance.[84]

Another massacre took place in Cyanika on 21 April. The parish priest, Joseph Niyomugabo, who was a Tutsi, found shelter in a pharmacy, and from there he managed to phone Misago. The bishop, however, did not come to the priest's rescue, and Niyomubago was slaughtered two days later together with a nephew and a seminarian. At the trial, Misago explained that he could not have come to Cyanika because there were roadblocks, a fact that a witness confirmed to the audience. The bishop added that he had 'asked himself whether it was opportune to inform the prefect or the gendarmery commander' because of a 'crisis of confidence' he had with them. This was a significant admission, because all along Misago had apparently entertained good relations with the prefect and the gendarmery commander, with whom he had regular meetings. According to Alison Des Forges, the main instigator of the genocide in the Gikongoro prefecture was the deputy prefect, Damien Biniga, and not the prefect.[85] In fact, Misago was also in touch with Biniga. It was the deputy prefect who announced to him the death of Niyomugabo, and the bishop gave him money to bury the priest. This ongoing relationship with the authorities, ambiguous as it was, explains why the survivors believed that he could

---

[83] Augustin Misago, 'Participation aux manifestations publiques', *Dialogue*, 209 (March–April 1999), 86–91. In the testimony he gave at the 15th audience of the trial (3 February 2000), Bishop Frédéric Rubwejanga, who was a lecturer at Nyakibanda Major Seminary at the time, recounted that several seminarians, though not Misago himself, loudly rejoiced at the news of Rwigema's death.

[84] Misago trial, 5th audience, 23 September 1999; Misago, 'Réactions aux accusations d'African Rights', 53–4; Bizamana, *L'Église et le génocide*, 115.

[85] Des Forges, *Leave None to Tell the Story*, 309.

have rescued the priest if he had really tried. This was the opinion, in particular, of Jean-Bosco Gakwisi, a Tutsi seminarian later ordained to the priesthood, who took shelter in the bishop's house during the duration of the genocide and was present when Niyomugabo made a phone call.[86]

On 4 May 1999, Major Bizimungu, the gendarmery commander, accompanied by an officer of the judiciary police, came to the bishop's house to interrogate three Tutsi priests, Irénée Nyamwasa, Canisius Mulinzi and Alois Musoni, who had taken refuge there. They came back on 7 May with a warrant of arrest and drove the priests to Butare; on 15 May, the priests were brought back to the prison of Gikongoro, where they were assassinated. This tragic episode raised, once again, the issue of Misago's responsibility for the death of his priests. In response, he claimed that he had questioned the validity of the documents produced by the police to prove the three priests' affiliation to the RPF and that he had told them that, since the Arusha Agreement, it was not a crime to be a member of the RPF. In the end, however, he had let them go. According to Gakwisi, the bishop did not sufficiently insist on obtaining the liberation of the priests: 'On seeing all these authorities coming to the bishop's house, I thought that he could save us.'[87]

On 7 May 1994, eighty-two Tutsi school pupils from the Groupe Scolaire Marie-Merci of Kibeho were assassinated by the Interahamwe and some of their Hutu schoolmates. A few days before, alerted by a priest, Misago had visited the school with the prefect and the gendarmery commander. On hearing that the two groups of students had been at loggerheads for some time, the bishop had spoken to them and obtained that additional policemen would keep a watch. The problem came when a second team of policemen, who were fiercely anti-Tutsi, replaced the first one. A massacre soon followed. At the audience Théophile Zigirumugabe, a Tutsi student who had survived the massacre, accused Misago of having done nothing to save them and of having said, when he met the children at the school, that the Tutsi had to be eliminated because they were RPF accomplices. Misago vehemently denied having used this language to the audience.[88]

---

[86] Misago trial, 7th audience, 29 September 1999; Misago, 'Réactions aux accusations d'African Rights', 68–73; Bizimana, *L'Église et le génocide*, 107.
[87] Misago trial, 21st audience, 29 February 2000; Misago, 'Réactions aux accusations d'African Rights', 64–8; Bizimana, *L'Église et le génocide*, 108.
[88] Misago trial, 10th audience, 4 November 1999. Théophile Zigirumugabe gave a similar testimony to African Rights in an interview conducted on 29 June 1995. See African Rights, *Not So Innocent: When Women Become Killers* (London: African Rights, 1995).

It remains that the faith the bishop put in the police in early May, at a time when everybody knew that the security forces had been involved in dozens of massacres in the country, is hard to understand. Had he himself not admitted to having a 'crisis of confidence' in the police a few days before? When Philip Gourevitch, an American journalist who interviewed him in Gikongoro after the genocide, asked him why he had not been able to protect the children, Misago responded that he had been misinformed. 'The bishop wasn't really denying that he'd committed a major blunder at Kibeho,' Gourevitch commented. 'But he didn't think it was a crime and also although he said he was "embarrassed" to have been taken in by official propaganda, he gave no sign of remorse.'[89]

A controversial verdict

The judge, a Tutsi magistrate by the name of Jariel Rutaremara, ruled that the accusations were not supported by evidence, and Misago was acquitted. Neither the public prosecutor nor the lawyer for the civil party appealed the judgement. The law governing the prosecution of genocide crimes only permitted an appeal on questions of law and blatant errors of fact,[90] which meant that the chances of a successful appeal were minimal.

For the bishop of Gikongoro and for his supporters, that was a victory. Justice had been done. The verdict, however, failed to convince the survivors and the people who had heard their testimony. They reacted to the judgement with disbelief, some arguing that the decision not to appeal had been made at the highest level to avoid antagonising the Catholic Church.[91]

Far from developing a consensus by establishing the facts in an incontrovertible way, the Misago trial had a divisive effect on Rwandan society. Ill feelings against the bishop did not subside. Interviewed in 2017, Michel Kayitaba, the respected director of the peace-building organisation Moucecore and a survivor himself, was adamant that the bishop had betrayed his priests. He was hiding in Gikongoro at the time, he recounted, and heard from eye-witnesses that Misago had shown no inclination to rescue Joseph Niyomugabo.[92] At the trial of the Sovu sisters in April 2001 in Brussels, the journalist Colette Braeckman also distanced herself from

---

[89] Gourevitch, *We Wish to Inform You*, 139.
[90] Organic Law No. 08/96 of 30 August 1996 on the Organization of Prosecutions for Offences constituting the Crime of Genocide or Crimes against Humanity Committed since October 1 1990, article 24.
[91] Bizimana, *L'Église et le génocide*, 125–9.
[92] Michel Kayitaba, interview conducted on 16 March 2017 in Kigali.

the verdict. 'As recently as last week,' she declared, 'I have received very precise testimonies that [Misago] attended meetings, that he saw all the preparation of the genocide, that he did not object to people being drawn to the churches, to the places of worship and to the parishes, knowing that they would close up on them as in a trap and that they would be killed.'[93]

Meanwhile, in Rome the Misago affair had given weapons to those who claimed that the Catholic Church of Rwanda was suffering persecution. On 19 June 1999, in an article entitled 'Genocidio rwandese: ultimo atto' [The Rwandan genocide: the last act], an anonymous Curia official, only identified by a triple asterisk, had written that Misago was the victim of a state-driven campaign of defamation. 'Bishop Misago's arrest exactly five years after the massacres', the author said in a language akin to that of Nguyên Van Tot and Hoser's in their letter of January 1995, 'has to be considered the latest act in a Rwandan government strategy to reduce or eliminate the reconciliatory role that the Church has historically played in Rwanda's past and still plays today, by trying in every way to tarnish her image.' In reference to the recent debate on the transformation of churches into genocide memorials in Rwanda, the author, who was obviously well informed, reiterated the Holy See's position that the churches were houses of prayer for Hutu and Tutsi alike and could not be 'monopolized as charnel-houses by part of the population'. He concluded by affirming that a 'double genocide' had taken place, one in Rwanda in 1994 and another one 'in the forests of Zaire, where fleeing Hutus were massacred for months, without any protection from the international community'.[94]

Conclusion

This polemical text, which clearly emanated from the Secretariat of State in Rome, should not lead one to conclude that the Rwandan state and the Catholic Church had radically opposite views about the genocide against the Tutsi. Chapter 10 will show that, by the time of the Misago trial, the church was more conscious than ever before of the reality of the genocide and that it was searching for new ways of dealing with its consequences. The minutes of the meetings of the mixed church–state commission indicate that the church representatives, including Augustin Misago, were

[93] Assises Rwanda 2001, 'Compte rendu intégral du procès, Témoin de contexte: Colette Braeckman, journaliste'.
[94] 'Genocidio rwandese: ultimo atto', *Osservatore Romano*, 16 May 1999. The same article appeared in the French edition of the *Osservatore Romano* on 26 May 1999 and in the English edition on 2 June 1999.

willing to find a compromise with the state on the difficult question of the transformation of churches into genocide memorials.

In some sectors of the Catholic Church, however, there was resistance to the idea of cooperation with the state in matters of genocide memory. The two papal representatives, Henryk Hoser and Julius Janusz, whose declarations found an echo in the *Osservatore Romano* article, favoured a confrontational approach. In the refugee camps until November 1996 and in Europe and in North America afterwards, the Hutu priests in exile, or at least some of them – as well as a certain number of missionaries – were on the same wavelength. Why the nunciature in Kigali and the Secretariat of State in Rome adopted a systematically antagonistic attitude towards the Rwandan government in the late 1990s is not entirely clear. We have seen that the fear of communism played a role. It is also likely, even though we have no evidence for it, that the missionaries, aid workers and Rwandan priests who had resettled in Europe and rejected with outrage the idea that the church should be blamed for the genocide and believed that the RPF was the real culprit had their entries in Rome and influenced the policies of the Curia.

No archive-based study of the Rwandan state's religious policy during this period has been conducted so far. It would probably show similar internal differences. On both sides, there has been a gradual relaxation of the tension over the years. The relation between the Catholic Church and the Rwandan state after the genocide can be described as uneasy and fraught with misunderstandings, but functioning despite this.

CHAPTER 8

A case of two narratives: Gabriel Maindron, a hero made and unmade

On 30 June 1994, in Kibuye – a small town on the Rwandan side of Lake Kivu which had witnessed one of the worst massacres of Tutsi people in the genocide just two months before – a group of French journalists received a visit from a French priest by the name of Gabriel Maindron in the hotel where they were staying.[1] The majority of missionaries had left the country in April 1994. He was one of the few – together with Jean-Baptiste Mendiondo (another French priest) and three Belgian confrères, Paul Kesenne, Joseph Schmetz and Raymond Delporte, all working in the diocese of Nyundo in Western Rwanda – who had remained in the country.

Maindron had heard on RFI that the French military had established a base in Kibuye as part of Opération Turquoise, a partly humanitarian and partly geostrategic military operation of the French army in genocide-torn Rwanda that had been launched seven days before with the approval of the UN Security Council. The journalists had come to Kibuye to cover the well-publicised intervention of the French army in nearby Bisesero, an area where, as became clear later, the French army had failed to protect a group of Tutsi refugees from the Interahamwe after the latter had paid them an initial visit on 27 June.

Maindron told the journalists that he needed the assistance of the French soldiers to rescue a group of Tutsi refugees he was sheltering in his presbytery in La Crête Zaïre-Nil (also known as La Crête Congo-Nil or shortened to Congo-Nil, as the parish is called today) in the commune of Rutsiro, about forty kilometres from Kibuye on bad roads at the time. On 1 July, late at night, two military vehicles from Captain Éric Bucquet's

---

[1] Nicolas Poincaré, *Rwanda. Gabriel Maindron, un prêtre dans la tragédie* (Paris: Éditions Ouvrières, 1995), 107.

Régiment d'infanterie et de chars de marine (RICM) arrived at Maindron's parish, where they were welcomed as liberators by ten-odd Tutsi refugees and later joined by a few others who had been hiding in the bush.[2] Three journalists – François Luizet from *Le Figaro*, Nicolas Poincaré from Radio France and France Inter, and Philippe Chaffanjon from RTL – were part of the expedition. Having left his wallet in the presbytery, Chaffanjon, accompanied by Poincaré, returned to Congo-Nil the following day and rescued another two Tutsi people.[3]

Two reasons explain why Gabriel Maindron, a forty-eight-year-old Catholic priest and native of Vendée in Western France who had come to Rwanda in 1959 as a seminarian and received the ordination to the priesthood in the diocese of Nyundo seven years later, rose to a modest but persistent level of celebrity as a result of this incident. The first is that, thanks to the presence of 'embedded' journalists in Opération Turquoise, the story was soon publicised in the French media: on 4 July in *Le Figaro*,[4] on 5 July in *La Croix*[5] and on 7 July in *L'Événement du jeudi*.[6] The authors of the first two articles, François Luizet and Mathieu Castagnet, had been in Rwanda since 27 and 28 June, respectively, and had written their article in that time.[7] The third article, unsigned, had been published in France by Jean-François Dupaquier, a journalist who later became a critic of the French army's involvement in Rwanda.[8]

What made Maindron's story interesting from a journalistic point of view was that he had kept a diary for his friends and relatives of the events which had occurred in his parish from 6 April, the day President Habyarimana's plane was shot down, to 17 April 1994. During this period, several thousand Tutsi had been killed in a local clinic, in the municipal

---

[2] *Ibid.*, 107–13.

[3] Nicolas Poincaré, interview conducted on 21 April 2018 in Paris.

[4] François Luizet, 'Rwanda: "Le journal de guerre" du père Maindron', *Le Figaro*, 4 July 1994.

[5] Mathieu Castagnet, 'Le récit effaré du père Maindron', *La Croix*, 5 July 1994.

[6] [Jean-Marie Dupaquier], 'L'hallucinant témoignage d'un curé du Rwanda', *L'Événement du jeudi*, 7–13 July 1994.

[7] Sophie Pontzeele, 'Burundi 1972/Rwanda 1974: L'"efficacité" dramatique d'une reconstruction idéologique par la presse', unpublished PhD thesis, University of Lille, 2004, 237.

[8] Pascal Krop, *Le Génocide franco-africain: faut-il juger les Mitterrand?* (Paris: J. C. Lattès, 1994), quoted in Jean-Paul Gouteux, *Un génocide sans importance. La France et le Vatican au Rwanda*, rev. edn (Lyon: Tahin Party, 2007), 78.

hall, in the precincts of the presbytery and in a school chapel belonging to the parish a few kilometres away. This day-to-day narrative ended with a text entitled 'Quelques réflexions' [Some reflections] on the causes of the 'tragic events' Maindron had witnessed. Extracts from the diary were published in the three newspaper articles of early July 1994 and the full text was reviewed by the White Father Guy Theunis and a group of (mostly Hutu) Rwandans in exile in the August–September 1994 issue of *Dialogue*, published in Brussels.[9]

Subsequently, alerted by Luizet's article in *Le Figaro*, Les Éditions Ouvrières, a French Catholic publisher, asked Maindron, who had returned to France in the meantime, to expand his diary into a book. For this, the former parish priest of Congo-Nil requested the assistance of Nicolas Poincaré, the journalist he had met in Kibuye on 30 June 1994. The book appeared in early 1995 under the title *Rwanda: Gabriel Maindron, un prêtre dans la tragédie* [Rwanda: Gabriel Maindron, a priest in the tragedy].[10]

Maindron as a case study

Since 1994, numerous testimonies of the genocide against the Tutsi have come to light. If Maindron's narrative had remained unchallenged, few people would pay attention to his story today. Its significance, for a historian interested in the manner in which the memories of the genocide found expression and developed over time, is that it soon became subject to contestation. The debate on what Maindron said and did – or did not say and did not do – in Congo-Nil during the three months of the genocide illustrates the debate on the genocide in Rwanda and the affected countries in general and in the Christian churches in particular.

One can say, to simplify, that two views of Maindron's role in Congo-Nil during the genocide developed concurrently. The first, articulated in Maindron's diary itself, in the media coverage of July 1994, in Poincaré's book, in a few subsequent testimonies and in an interview that I conducted with him in February 2015, is that of a man who, despite some weaknesses, which he admitted himself, had done his best to save lives in trying circumstances.

What the Tutsi survivors who knew Maindron in Congo-Nil before and during the genocide remember is different. They shared their recollections

---

[9] Gabriel Maindron, 'Rwanda: l'horreur', *Dialogue*, 177 (August–September 1994), 41–58.
[10] Nicolas Poincaré, same interview.

about the French priest's role during the genocide with a certain number of journalists and researchers who relayed them in newspapers, websites and academic publications from 1995 to this date. This alternative narrative is that of a priest with close ties to the local authorities who failed to use the moral authority he enjoyed in a traditionally Catholic community to challenge the behaviour of his friends when they allowed the Interahamwe and the local people following them to exterminate the Tutsi and sometimes actively facilitated their work. The survivors question Maindron's claim of having saved Tutsi lives. According to them, he did indeed shelter Tutsi refugees but never for long, and many died afterwards.

Maindron cannot be said to be representative of the Rwandan clergy. As mentioned in the previous chapters, before, during and after the genocide, the church personnel and the faithful, not only in the Catholic Church but in the other churches as well, were characterised by considerable diversity in political, cultural and spiritual matters. Maindron's story is interesting, because it illustrates the complex dynamics at work in the churches in post-genocide Rwanda when they were trying to come to terms – or not – with this highly traumatic event.

The analysis of the evolving representations of Maindron's role in Congo-Nil will allow us to get a sense of who the main agents of memory are in post-genocide Rwanda and how the international scene – France, in this instance – and the Rwandan one interact when it comes to apprehending the reality of the genocide. It will also help us to understand why a quarter of a century later several narratives of the genocide against the Tutsi are running in parallel. It will highlight, through the study of one particular priest, the situation of church leaders who were neither genocide criminals nor innocent bystanders. Maindron's case was by no means unique. His ambiguities, his silences and his denials are similar to those of many clerics, Catholic as well as Protestant, during this period.

Maindron's diary

Maindron's diary gives the point of view of a priest who initially refused to believe that a large-scale massacre of Tutsi people was taking place in his parish and who had faith in the intervention of the burgomaster, Raphaël Benimana, and of the local *gendarmerie*. After a while, however, he noted, without explaining why, that they did not do anything to prevent the 'armed group' from slaughtering people in the clinic, the municipal hall and the surroundings of the presbytery. 'The response of the gendarmes is very weak and perhaps symbolic, just for the form', Maindron laconically wrote on Monday, 11 April, two days after the massacres had started in Congo-Nil and five days after the shooting down of President Habyarimana's plane.[11] 'The burgomaster looked from afar, powerless.'[12]

More than two hundred Tutsi refugees found shelter in the presbytery. Only on one occasion, according to the diary, did Maindron prevent the killers from murdering his Tutsi parishioners. 'If you take them,' he told them, 'it is I that you are attacking.' Then, he wrote in his diary, he knelt down, presented his neck to the killers and declared: 'Do your dirty job and leave my people quiet.'[13] The killers, who knew him, obeyed. That was the only act of active resistance on his part that has been recorded. The following day, he negotiated with the police commander that the Tutsi refugees would be transferred by bus to Rubengera, twenty-five kilometres away. They subsequently moved to Kibuye, where, on the instructions of the infamous prefect Clément Kayishema, the majority of them were massacred on 17 and 18 April in the town's stadium and in the parish church.

The only hint at the possible responsibility of the local authorities is made on Wednesday, 13 April. 'In the morning,' he wrote, 'we hear that an automatic gun has been stolen from a policeman. The rabble (*racaille*) grabbed it from the hand of the policeman, the burgomaster tells us. Others think that it was voluntarily given to them to facilitate the attack of Gitwa hill. In Gitwa, hundreds of Tutsi are gathered. This Wednesday the final assault is taking place.'[14] A massacre of a thousand of people, if not more, effectively took place on that day, inside and around the school chapel of Gitwa (the town known today as Nyamagumba), on a site belonging to the parish of Congo-Nil. If the gun had indeed been 'voluntarily given' to the killers, that means that the police, and presumably the burgomaster to whom they reported, were in cahoots with them. Why did the burgomaster claim that the gun had been 'stolen'? Maindron did not elaborate on that.

A few days later, Maindron used the word 'genocide' to describe the events he was witnessing:

> The manhunt continues. It is not a civil war, because most people are defenceless. They are butchered like lambs in the slaughtering house. It is a genocide, a perfect ethnic cleansing. In truth, the RPF has a great responsibility in this popular anger. But this anger is exploited by the authorities. Why take vengeance on innocents?[15]

---

[11] Maindron, 'Rwanda: l'horreur', 45.
[12] *Ibid.*, 45.
[13] *Ibid.*, 46.
[14] *Ibid.*, 49.
[15] *Ibid.*, 51.

The narrative of the events which occurred during the first ten days of the genocide is followed by a brief analysis. For most Rwandans, he explained, 'this war was an ethnic war between Hutu and Tutsi'. The RPF has 'numerous accomplices inside the country, especially among Tutsi'. Some had weapons. 'They even discovered in several areas lists of influential Hutu who were meant to be executed by the RPF and its accomplices'. After the death of President Habyarimana, 'the authorities were not able to stem the popular fury. Indeed, some approved of it and exploited it for political or personal interests'.[16]

Twenty-nine Tutsi priests from the Nyundo diocese were massacred during the first month of the genocide. Maindron explained the 'acrimony against the Catholic Church' by the fact that the Tutsi had been overrepresented in the body of priests of the diocese. Many Tutsi priests, he pointed out, 'ostensibly showed their sympathy for the RPF'. Some were 'even accused of having collaborated with them through contributions and sharing of information'.[17]

Remarkably, Maindron spoke in positive terms of the Coalition for the Defence of the Republic (CDR), a Hutu extremist party and member of Hutu Power, known for having favoured the ideology that fuelled the genocide.[18]

> The peace accord of Arusha, which gave the advantage to the RPF and its supporters, could not be implemented. The RPF refused the CDR the right to have a seat at the Assembly. The CDR party claimed to defend the interest of the people, above all the Hutu. The past events have showed that the CDR is a strong party and that its ideas have been adopted by the other parties. Why this intransigence of the RPF for a single seat and this against the opinion of the church representatives and the accredited ambassadors in the country?[19]

The contrast between the manner in which Maindron and his Belgian confrère Raymond Delporte approached this question could not be bigger. In a text written in Gisenyi on 1 July 1994, when the genocide was still ongoing, Delporte described the CDR as 'the party of the extremist Hutu who trained civil militia for planned massacres and distributed weapons in all the communes of the north'.[20]

---

[16] *Ibid.*, 56.

[17] *Ibid.*, 57.

[18] Alison Des Forges, *Leave None to Tell the Story. Genocide in Rwanda* (New York: Human Rights Watch, 1999), 137–40.

[19] Maindron, 'Rwanda: l'horreur', 55.

[20] Raymond Delporte, 'Les massacres du Rwanda, avril–mai 1994', Gisenyi,

None of the newspapers which published extracts of Maindron's diary in early July analysed the last part of the document that clearly indicated that the French priest had uncritically absorbed key elements of the Hutu Power ideology. In effect, both *Le Figaro* and *La Croix* echoed Maindron's argument that the genocide was the result of the 'popular fury', as if the interim government, the provincial and municipal authorities, the police and the army had nothing to do with it. The subtitle of Luizet's article in *Le Figaro* insisted on that point. 'Installed for 32 years in Africa,' it read, 'the pastor had never seen such "popular fury". He testifies on the diabolical relentlessness of the Hutu militia against the Tutsi.'[21]

This myopic view of the genocide was not unique to *Le Figaro* and *La Croix*. Marc Le Pape has shown that the majority of newspapers that covered the genocide in France between April and July 1994, including *Le Monde*, followed an essentially descriptive approach to the massacres. They did not pay attention to the discourse of the Rwandan authorities that presented the systematic extermination of the Tutsi as a patriotic necessity in the war against the RPF. They described the genocide as a war between two ethnic groups, each having committed human rights abuses against the members of the other group.[22]

Taken for a ride

Nicolas Poincaré's book also contributed to the image of Maindron as a priest who saved Tutsi lives. As a radio journalist, he made no fewer than four trips to Rwanda between April and July 1994. He had personally witnessed the genocide. During the second trip, he saw piles of corpses of Tutsi people spread along the roads of Nyamata in the Bugesera. He knew that the Rwandan authorities were lying to the journalists and the diplomats. Yet, he was impressed by Maindron. On his return to France, he agreed to write his story because, as he explained in an interview, he felt that he had to write something about the genocide. He did not want to keep his experiences to himself. He had noted a certain ambiguity in Maindron but found this ambiguity interesting. He liked the French priest's candidness.[23]

    1 July 1994. Copy in the archives of the Dominican Missionary Sisters of Namur, Belgium.
[21] Luizet, 'Rwanda: le "journal de guerre" du père Maindron'.
[22] Marc Le Pape, 'Des journalistes au Rwanda. L'histoire immédiate d'un génocide', *Les Temps Modernes*, 583 (July–August 1995), 161–80.
[23] Nicolas Poincaré, same interview.

The book as we know it, however, is not the one Poincaré wrote after several meetings with Maindron in the church residence rue de Vaugirard in Paris where the latter had been staying since his return to France on 28 July 1994.[24] One day, the journalist revealed in the interview, a close friend of Maindron's, Annick Nedelec, had visited him. Nedelec, a woman from Brittany, had raised funds for Maindron's development projects in Congo-Nil, visited him there a few times and accompanied him to a camp of Hutu refugees in northern Rwanda. She told him that his manuscript was a 'filthy rag' (*torchon*). Poincaré remembered her as a 'pro-Hutu French woman, unbelievably anti-Tutsi and anti-Kagame'. In some parts of the manuscripts, Nedelec lamented, Maindron had admitted to mistakes and provided details that could be exploited by the former Rwandan government's enemies. Reluctantly, Poincaré agreed to revise the manuscript. The following week Maindron came with a list of corrections compiled by Nedelec that were incorporated into the final version of the manuscript. The original document is apparently lost.[25]

The book that came off the press in early 1995 is therefore a censored work. Later on, Poincaré, who did not have the time to verify his sources on his return from Rwanda, discovered aspects of Maindron's behaviour that he had not initially picked up and that he found troubling. He distanced himself from his book in an interview with the journalist Laurent Larcher which was included in a collection of testimonies on the Rwandan genocide in 2019:

> [Poincaré] tells me how he was taken for a ride with the writing of his book *Rwanda. Gabriel Maindron, un prêtre dans la tragédie*, by this White Father.[26] He had a brief encounter with him in 1994, having seen the Tutsi girls hidden in his double ceiling… hence this book in tribute to him. Father Maindron did not dissimulate, in front of the journalist, some of his weaknesses. Except that the others, those that are hidden, Poincaré would later discover, are worse than those he had recognised. 'All this to say that I am not very proud of this book,' he went on.[27]

---

[24] Jef Vleugels and Guy Theunis, Fax No. 22, 6 August 1994, in Missionaries of Africa, 'Informations diffusées par la Région du Rwanda, 1990–1994', Brussels, 2005, 209.

[25] Nicolas Poincaré, same interview.

[26] More correctly, a secular priest from the diocese of Nyundo. Maindron was never a White Father.

[27] Laurent Larcher, *Rwanda, ils parlent. Témoignages pour l'histoire* (Paris: Seuil, 2019), 331–2.

Even censored, the book is revealing. It shows how Maindron narrated his experience of the genocide and, while doing so, betrays aspects of his ministry that, as we shall see in a subsequent section, the genocide survivors would comment upon critically.

Three of the ten chapters in the book cover the period described in the diary without differing significantly from it. They were preceded by a section on Maindron's priestly vocation, his seminary training in Rwanda, his first years of ministry and the period following the RPF's invasion of Rwanda in October 1990. The last chapter continued the story where the diary had left off.

Some parts of the narrative give interesting clues. For example, when recounting the episode of Maindron's encounter with the killers who wanted to murder the refugees from the presbytery, Poincaré wrote, surely after having heard it from the priest: 'This unreflected act [*cet acte irréfléchi*] impresses the killers.'[28] Why 'unreflected'? Why did Maindron not intentionally make the killers feel guilty in order to reduce the number of victims? This was his main act of bravery during the genocide.

In the diary, we shall remember, Maindron noted that, according to some members of the community, a gun used in the massacre of the school chapel of Gitwa had been 'voluntarily given' to the killers. The burgomaster, meanwhile, had suggested that it had been 'stolen'. Raphaël Benimana, the burgomaster, was mentioned several times in the book. He was portrayed as a close friend of Maindron, a point that the genocide survivors later confirmed. It is interesting to observe the wording of the same episode in the book: 'This morning, the gun of a policeman was stolen without any resistance. This automatic weapon, the militia need it to complete the work in the Gitwa hill.'[29] This time, the theft was presented as a fact. This may have been one of the passages censored by Annick Nedelec.

Along the same lines, the description of the massacre of the Tutsi as a 'genocide' in the diary is omitted in the book:

> Gabriel noted in his journal: 'It is not a civil war because most people are defenceless. They are killed like lambs in the slaughterhouse [...] They want to eliminate everything that is Tutsi.'[30]

---

[28] Poincaré, *Rwanda. Gabriel Maindron*, 75.
[29] *Ibid.*, 86.
[30] *Ibid.*, 101.

Did Maindron – or Nedelec – intentionally remove the word genocide, which, in the second half of 1994, had heavy connotations in the international community?

In some sections, the diary showed a willingness, on Maindron's part, to candidly relate what happened. 'Tell the whole truth,' he told Poincaré, 'but do not try to portray me as a hero. I do not want to hide anything, neither my weaknesses nor my cowardice.'[31] He admitted, for example, to having lacked judgement when on 11 April he encouraged a group of Tutsi refugees to run to Lake Kivu to escape the blows of the killers, but they were found and massacred.[32]

The book did not include the 'reflections' inserted at the end of the diary on the causes of the genocide, the reasons for the murder of Tutsi priests and the injustice allegedly suffered by the Hutu party CDR. It did not echo the accusations levelled by the Hutu extremists against the Tutsi 'accomplices'. But, anticipating what defenders of the former Rwandan regime would soon call the 'double genocide', it drew a parallel, as if they were the two sides of an equation, between the RPF and the perpetrators of the genocide against the Tutsi. He described Radio Muhabura, the radio of the RPF which broadcast a pan-African and anti-imperialist message and encouraged the return of the Tutsi,[33] and RTLM, which spread the rumour that the RPF had asked the Tutsi to dig graves to bury the Hutu, as equally 'dangerous'.[34]

In a sermon preached on Sunday, 17 April, Poincaré wrote, shortly after the massacres in Congo-Nil and on the day thousands of Tutsi were being slaughtered in nearby Kibuye, Maindron narrated to an audience of 'five hundred people' a dream he had the night before in which Hutu killers and Tutsi soldiers from Burundi killed each other before joyfully reconciling.[35] Almost certainly, some of the local killers listened to the sermon. The dream signalled that the recent wave of murders was to be put on the same level as the murders committed by the Tutsi, but since none of those had taken place near Congo-Nil, the action was located in Burundi. Without the word being pronounced, it was a formulation of the double genocide theory.

---

[31] *Ibid.*, 63.
[32] *Ibid.*, 76.
[33] Jean-Pierre Chrétien (ed.), *Rwanda. Les médias du génocide* (Paris: Karthala, 2002), 358–9.
[34] Poincaré, *Rwanda. Gabriel Maindron*, 55.
[35] *Ibid.*, 92.

Hutu priests and Tutsi priests

The three newspaper articles of July 1994 and Maindron's biography essentially had a French readership. To the public of his country, he was presented, in Poincaré's words, as a priest who 'ran a lot, tried to save lives and took conscience of his powerlessness'[36]. It was a different situation in Rwanda and, more specifically, in the Catholic diocese of Nyundo. This territory was known for being run by secular priests, Black and White, since the time of Aloys Bigirumwami, a Black bishop appointed in 1952, and not by members of missionary congregations such as the White Fathers. As Maindron correctly pointed out in his diary, there were large numbers of Tutsi priests. After the RPF's invasion of Rwanda in October 1990, the clergy of the diocese became polarised, with one group condemning the pogroms of Bagogwe and other Tutsi groups organised by the Habyarimana regime in retaliation against the attacks of the RPF and another one claiming that the Tutsi priests secretly supported the enemy. In late December 1993, Wenceslas Kalibushi, the bishop of Nyundo, and several priests from Gisenyi and Kibuye issued a letter criticising the government for distributing weapons to civilians.[37] Maindron was reported as having refused to sign the letter. For him, the arming of Hutu militia was necessary for the protection of the country against the RPF.[38] Three young Hutu priests, Urbain Twagirayezu, Athanase Seromba and Jean-Berchmans Ntihabose, all ordained after 1990, shared this detestation of the rebel movement.[39]

Unknown to the French media and to the academic world, a controversy erupted in June 1994, when the genocide was still in full swing, regarding the attitude of Maindron and the priests who shared his views on the murder of Tutsi priests that had taken place in and around Nyundo

---

[36] *Ibid.*, 10.
[37] Robert Block, 'The Tragedy or Rwanda', *The New York Review*, 20 October 1994, 4, quoted in Timothy Longman, *Christianity and Genocide in Rwanda* (Cambridge: Cambridge University Press, 2011), 64; René Degni-Segui, 'Extraits de rapports 1994–1995 sur la situation des droits de l'Homme au Rwanda, dans Raymond Verdier, Emmanuel Decaux, Jean-Pierre Chrétien (ed.), *Rwanda. Un génocide au XXe siècle* (Paris: L'Harmattan, 1995), 67.
[38] 'Les mensonges par omission de l'abbé Maindron', *Golias*, 48–9 (Summer 1996), 75. Christian Terras, the author of the article, did not quote his source in this instance. The information was probably provided by Jean-Baptiste Hategeka or Jean Kashyengo, two Tutsi priests who survived the genocide and gave their testimony to Terras.
[39] Twagirayezu was ordained in 1991, Seromba and Ntihabose in 1993.

in April. Echoes of this debate only started to filter down in 1995 and 1996. The occasion was the visit of Cardinal Roger Etchegaray, Pope John Paul II's envoy, to genocide-torn Rwanda from 23 to 29 June. He made a stop in Kibuye on Saturday 25 June, two days after the soldiers of Opération Turquoise arrived in Rwanda. He then met Maindron, his French confrère Jean-Baptiste Mendiondo and a group of seven Hutu priests during a visit that was tightly controlled by the prefect Clément Kayishema, who was unrepentant as ever about the large-scale massacre of Tutsi he had engineered in the church and the stadium of Kibuye in April 1994.[40]

The most senior priest, Jean Ntirivamunda, a man known as being kind, who must have been influenced by his young colleagues, made a speech on behalf of the local clergy, whose text, typed on Maindron's typewriter and bearing the signatures of the two French priests and their seven Rwandan colleagues, was handed to Cardinal Etchegaray.[41] The purpose of the document was to draw the prelate's attention to the shortage of priests in the diocese, the difficulty of administering sacraments to the faithful and the material destructions suffered by the church. The priests who had survived the massacres and the bishop of the diocese were implicitly blamed for having taken refuge in Goma. 'Where is the diocese of Nyundo: in Zaire or in Rwanda?' The genocide was hinted at without being named. All the blame was put on the Tutsi priests, who were accused of having supported the RPF:

> After the assassination of the President of the Rwandan Republic, Juvénal Habyalimana, the BaTutsi under threat took refuge in the churches. Unfortunately, a certain number of priests and religious were accomplices of the RPF. Some documents that were found and even weapons are testimony to it. This explains the aggressiveness of the Bahutu who attacked everything that was Tutsi, even religious people – without discernment and without paying attention to their guilt or their innocence. The priests have been attacked for their ethnic identity, especially if they had given shelter to Tutsi refugees in their parishes.

This virulent condemnation of unnamed Tutsi priests was followed by a 'political analysis' of the recent events:

---

[40] Poincaré, *Rwanda. Gabriel Maindron*, 113; Marie Julianne Farrington, 'Rwanda – 100 Days – 1994: One Perspective', in Carol Rittner, John K. Roth and Wendy Whitworth (ed.), *Genocide in Rwanda. Complicity of the Churches?* (St Paul, Minnesota: Paragon House, 2004), 106.

[41] Jean-Baptiste Hategeka, 'Le "coup d'Église" de Gabriel Maindron', *Golias*, 43 (July–August 1995), 54.

One can see that the Catholic Church has not been truthful and that it has often been an instrument of the power in place. One should have denounced and condemned the political murders and the massacres from the beginning of the hostilities from whichever side they came. In future, the Church should be more faithful to its message and less concerned about diplomacy.[42]

A copy of this letter ended up in the hands of the Tutsi priest Jean Ndorimana, who was vicar general of the diocese of Cyangugu at the time. He published it in 2001.[43]

The other diary

This episode would probably have disappeared from most memories today if one of the survivors of the massacre of Nyundo, Jean-Baptiste Hategeka, the vicar general of the diocese, had not published his diary in Italy, where he took refuge in late 1994. It was he who alerted Christian Terras, the editor of the French left-wing Catholic magazine *Golias*, opening the door to the development of a counter-memory of Maindron and a few other clerics allegedly involved in the genocide.[44] His book, which is difficult to find today, was printed in Formigine, Modena, in December 1994 under the title *Raisins verts pour dents agaçées. Cri contre les Nazis noirs du Rwanda* [Sour grapes for clenched teeth. Cry against the black Nazis of Rwanda].[45] An Italian translation appeared two years later.[46]

Hategeka was part a group of five Tutsi priests and one Hutu priest – who was Tutsi in appearance – who miraculously survived the massacres of 7–8 April 1994 in Nyundo. They first found shelter in nearby Gisenyi, in a house belonging to Bishop Wenceslas Kalibushi, a man who had

---

[42] Gabriel Maindron and eight other priests from the diocese of Nyundo to Cardinal Etchegaray, n.d. [25 June 1994], in Jean Ndorimana, *Rwanda. L'Eglise catholique dans le malaise. Symptômes et témoignages* (Rome: Edizioni Vivere In, 2001), 168–9.

[43] *Ibid.*

[44] Christian Terras, interview conducted on 10 June 2016 in Villeurbanne, Lyon.

[45] Jean-Baptiste Hategeka, *Raisins verts pour dents agacées? Cri contre les nazis Noirs du RWANDA* (Formigine, Modena: Golinelli, 1994), 66. I thank Jean Ndorimana for graciously giving me a copy of this rare book he had received from the author, who passed away in March 2016.

[46] Jean-Baptiste Hategeka, *Uva acerba che allega i denti?: grido contro i nazisti neri del Rwanda* (Formigine, Modena: Golinelli, 1996), 77.

narrowly escaped death for having gained the reputation, in the preceding months, of resisting government-sponsored violence. On 19 June, the military commander of Nyundo agreed to escort the refugees to the residence of the bishop of Goma, Faustin Ngabu, in exchange for bribe money provided by the nunciature of Bujumbura.[47] After the installation of an RPF-led government in Kigali in July, the five Tutsi priests and the bishop spent three months in a property of the Emmanuel Community in Helvoirt in the Netherlands to recover from the trauma of the genocide. Hategeka, who suffered from acute diabetes, went to Italy, where he published his diary, which he had started in May in Gisenyi.[48]

Raisins verts pour dents agaçées is the first public expression of an alternative memory of Maindron's role in Congo-Nil, although it can hardly be called public, since the book had an extremely reduced audience. The publication of Hategeka's book was nevertheless significant. The sections that referred to Maindron are of interest to us here. The rest narrated the odyssey of the surviving priests until they arrived in Europe and proposed a political and theological analysis of the genocide. Maindron was mentioned by name on one occasion and indirectly in a response to the letter to Cardinal Etchegaray on 25 June.

On 30 May 1994 – halfway through the genocide – Gabriel Maindron, Jean-Baptiste Ntamugabumwe and Jean Ntirivamunda, three priests who would sign the letter to Cardinal Etchegaray, went to see the bishop of Nyundo in his refuge of Gisenyi, with the mission, in Hategeka's words, 'to impose on Bishop Kalibushi the opening of the parishes that he had not closed'. They requested 'the pastoral appointment of Hutu priests whose only quality was to be Hutu and maintenance budgets only for these pastors'.[49] How 'cynical' it was, commented Hategeka, to signify to a bishop in great distress that life continued without him! 'Our tragedy counted for so little in their eyes: the dead were not to be grieved for but replaced and

---

[47] Hategeka, *Raisins verts*, 47. The price per head was 'between 15,000 and 50,000 Rwandan francs'.

[48] Fabien Rwakareke, interview conducted in Nyundo on 28 May 2018. Prosper Ntiyamira, the Hutu priest who shared the life of the Tutsi refugees in Gisenyi and Goma, did not go to the Netherlands.

[49] The parishioners who had chased away or killed their priests in the diocese of Cyangugu also asked their bishop to appoint new priests, preferably Hutu. See Jean Ndorimana, *Rwanda. Idéologies, méthode et négationnisme du genocide des Tutsi à la lumière de la chronique de la région de Cyangugu* (Rome: Edizioni Vivere In, 2001), 81.

forgotten.'⁵⁰ Fabien Rwakareke, one of the surviving priests in Gisenyi, also remembered the visit of Maindron and the two Hutu priests: 'They were accompanied by an Interahamwe with a black beard. For them it was as if we were already dead.'⁵¹

Hategeka and his colleagues reacted with the same indignation to the 25 June letter of Maindron, Mendiondo and seven Hutu priests to Cardinal Etchegaray when it reached Goma, where they had taken refuge in the meantime. It was too late to send a letter to the pope's envoy, who only made a brief visit to the Congolese border town on Sunday, 26 June early in the morning.⁵² Instead, the surviving priests opted for sending an open letter to their confrères on Wednesday, 29 June. A copy of the document is included in *Raisins verts pour dents agaçées*.⁵³

> Why blame the Tutsi priests, they asked, for taking refuge in Goma? We thought that the assassination of your confrères would have caused some distress in you and that you did not want the few of them who survived to suffer the same fate. [...] We are horrified to see you talking [to Cardinal Etchegaray] about the 'disarray of the priests and laity' who deplore the lack of administration without worrying about the systematic extermination of a section of the population that includes many members of the body of Christ, especially in your zone of Kibuye. [...] In the circumstances that this country is going through the most urgent needs are the distribution of sacraments and the means of transport! [...] Did you not notice among the perpetrators of the horrors that you know 'practising' Christians and even 'community leaders'?⁵⁴

The surviving priests then questioned the statement that some Tutsi priests were accomplices of the RPF. 'Did you seriously verify the sources of this information before sharing them with the whole world since your message has been read in public?'⁵⁵ In conclusion, they expressed the wish to meet their contradictors face to face. Their reaction should not be seen as a negative judgement but as a call to dialogue.

Significantly, the Tutsi survivors were not the only ones to find abhorrent the idea of replacing the priests who had been killed while the

---

⁵⁰ *Ibid.*, 49.
⁵¹ Fabien Rwakareke, interview conducted on 28 May 2018 in Nyundo.
⁵² Roger Etchegaray, *J'ai senti battre le cœur du monde. Conversations avec Bernard Lecomte* (Paris: Fayard, 2007), 243.
⁵³ Hategeka, *Raisins verts pour dents agacées*, 19–22.
⁵⁴ *Ibid.*, 19–20.
⁵⁵ *Ibid.*, 21.

massacres were still on. On 1 July 1994, Raymond Delporte made the following comment from Gisenyi:

> How should we interpret, from a Christian point of view, the urgent requests from the current Rwandan 'authorities' to put a priest in these abandoned parishes […] and where abominable massacres continue? Is it about a Hutu extremist church for parishes where human rights are constantly violated?[56]

How *Golias* discovered Maindron

Before the genocide, Maindron was mostly known – outside the diocese of Nyundo where he served as chaplain of the Association of Young Catholic Farmers (JAC) and as priest in different parishes – for his campaigns to promote the apparitions of the Virgin Mary to five teenage girls in Kibeho in southern Rwanda. This attracted the attention of President Habyarimana, a devout Catholic, to whom Maindron addressed a vibrant homage in the book he published under the title *Des apparitions à Kibeho* in 1984, three years after the first sighting of the Virgin Mary in the refectory of the local Catholic boarding school.[57]

By his own admission, Maindron was a powerful figure in Congo-Nil.[58] This mission station, founded by Aloys Bigirumwami, the first bishop of Nyundo, in the 1950s,[59] came into existence before the establishment of the commune of Rutsiro, whose offices were originally located near Murunda, further to the north.[60] 'In the villages,' Maindron explained to Nicolas

---

[56] Raymond Delporte, 'Les massacres du Rwanda, avril–mai 1994', Gisenyi, 1 July 1994. Copy in the archives of the Dominican Missionary Sisters of Namur, Belgium.

[57] Gabriel Maindron, *Des apparitions à Kibeho. Annonce de Marie au cœur de l'Afrique* (Paris: O.E.I.L, 1984), 26, quoted in Léon Saur, *Le sabre, la machette et le goupillon. Des apparitions de Fatima au génocide rwandais* (Bierges: Éditions Mols, 2004), 292.

[58] Poincaré, *Rwanda. Gabriel Maindron*, 24, 36.

[59] In an article published in the April–May 1958 issue of *Vivant Univers*, a missionary magazine, Mgr Bigirumwami evoked the possibility of erecting a Marian shrine in Congo-Nil, on the model of the one in Banneux, near Liège, Belgium, where Marian apparitions were reported to have occurred in the 1930s. See Léon Saur, 'Catholiques belges et Rwanda, 1950–1965': les pièges de l'évidence', unpublished PhD thesis, University Paris I Sorbonne, 2013, 290.

[60] Marcel Kabanda, interview conducted on 25 April 2019 in Paris.

Poincaré, 'the *curés* generally have more influence and sometimes more power than the burgomasters'.[61] In Congo-Nil, he had a good rapport with the burgomaster, Raphaël Benimana. 'The tasks are shared, but the priest has perhaps more influence and power than the burgomaster.'[62]

It is interesting to note that Maindron's name did not appear in either of the two editions of *Rwanda: Death, Despair and Defiance*, a detailed account of the genocide in Rwanda published by the London-based human rights organisation African Rights. The first edition, published in September 1994 dedicated no less than fifty-three pages to the 'attack on the Church'. It did not include a section on Kibuye, because this area was still under the interim government's control in May and June 1994 when Rakiya Omaar, the organisation's single-handed investigator, collected information in Rwanda, and it only mentioned six 'priests who killed or encouraged the killers'.[63] The revised edition, published in August 1995, did have a section on Kibuye and provides a much longer list of priests, pastors and nuns suspected of having played a role in the genocide.[64] Rakiya Omaar gained access to genocide survivors – possibly, though the matter is contested, through links with the RPF[65] – and African Rights' co-director, Alex de

---

[61] Poincaré, *Rwanda. Gabriel Maindron*, 24.

[62] *Ibid.*, 36. The burgomaster himself ranked high in pre-genocide Rwanda. See Alison Des Forges, *Leave None to Tell the Story*, 38: 'The head of the commune, the burgomaster, of course ranked below the prefect or sub-prefect, but he exercised more immediate and pervasive power over the ordinary people than did his superiors. In a style that harked back to the pre-colonial and the colonial era, the burgomaster held court one or more times a week, receiving the ordinary people who brought him their grievances or who came to give thanks for help received. [...] The ultimate authority at the local level, he was clearly and directly the president's man out on the hills. Although nominally responsible to the minister of the interior, the burgomasters were named by Habyarimana and removed by him. All were known to him and some were very close to him personally.'

[63] African Rights, *Rwanda: Death, Despair and Defiance*, 1st edn (London: African Rights, 1994), 485–532.

[64] African Rights, *Rwanda: Death, Despair and Defiance*, 2nd edn (London: African Rights, 1995), 862–930.

[65] Luc Reydams, 'NGO justice: African Rights as pseudo-prosecutor of the Rwandan genocide', *Human Rights Quarterly*, 38 (2016), 547–88. The fact that a section was dedicated to the killing of 'clergymen killed by the Rwandan Patriotic Front' in the second edition of *Death, Despair and Defiance* (pp. 893–4) shows that African Rights was not as aligned to the RPF as Reydams claimed it was. On the links between African Rights and the RPF,

Waal, processed the information in London. The silence on Maindron shows that by the first half of 1995 he had not attracted the attention of the nascent network of survivors that was trying to develop a public memory of the genocide.

Christian Terras, the editor of the magazine *Golias*, was the first Westerner to question the Congo-Nil priest's role during the genocide. 'Maindron', he declared after having heard the testimony of the genocide survivors who knew the French priest, 'was on the side of the murderers.' The story Maindron shared with Poincaré was full of gaps. He did not reveal his support for the CDR and the close links he had with the officials who supervised the massacres in Congo-Nil. He 'lied by omission'.[66]

Since 1985, the date of *Golias*' foundation, Terras, a non-conformist Christian activist trained in theology as a layman and based in Lyon, had entrusted himself with the task of tackling the shortcomings and betrayals of the institutional church, combining first-hand investigative journalism and virulent, if not tendentious, attacks on any perceived hypocrisy in the Catholic Church. By 1990, *Golias* had two thousand subscriptions and by 1995, nine thousand. Some issues – for example those regarding the right-wing Catholic organisation Opus Dei – became instant best-sellers. To this day, Terras is regularly consulted by the secular media on church matters.

Golias inaugurated its coverage of the genocide in July–August 1994 with an article by Jean Carbonare, the president of the organisation Survie, on France's responsibility in the genocide and a reflection by the Swiss Dominican René Aebischer on the 'failure' of the Gospel.[67] In the November–December 1994 issue, an article questioned the 'responsibility of the Church in the ideological justification of the genocide'.[68] The magazine also cited, for the first time, the name of Wenceslas Munyeshyaka, a young Rwandan priest accused by survivors of having close connections with the Interahamwe at the Sainte-Famille parish in Kigali during the genocide, who had been exfiltrated to France with the support of the Catholic hierarchy.[69] African Rights had mentioned his name in the first edition of

---

see Jos van Oijen, 'A totally false picture of the genocide: A critical analysis of Luc Reydams' "NGO Justice: African Rights as pseudo-prosecutor of the Rwandan genocide"', *Ravage Webzine*, June 2017.

[66] Christian Terras, 'Les mensonges par omission de l'abbé Gabriel Maindron', *Golias*, 48–9 (Summer 1996), 71.

[67] *Golias*, 37 (July–August 1994), 13–23.

[68] *Golias*, 39 (November–December 1994), 18–19.

[69] *Ibid.*, 20–1.

its report in September.[70] This prompted Terras to send a correspondent by the name of Eugène Mutabazi to Rwanda from April until June 1995.[71] The story of Munyeshyaka and of a few church people suspected of having been involved in the genocide formed the core of a special issue of *Golias* entitled '*La machette et le goupillon*' [The machete and the sprinkler]. Terras, who had a great talent for public relations, launched the issue during a well-attended press conference at the French Senate in Paris in July 1995. Journalists from the *New York Times* and Associated Press were present, giving the event an international dimension.[72] The spokesperson of the Catholic Bishops' Conference, Jean-Michel Di Falco, tried to use his connections to prevent the press conference from taking place, but he did not succeed.[73]

Meanwhile, on 24 February 1995, in an open letter addressed to Archbishop Joseph Duval, the president of the French Bishops' Conference, a group of Rwandan refugees denounced, among other things, the ideological proximity to Hutu extremist theses that Maindron's diary had revealed. 'At the moment,' they noted, 'Maindron resides and celebrates the Holy Office at the Saint-Sulpice church in Paris.'[74] It was during this period that Terras entered into contact with Jean-Baptiste Hategeka, his main source of information on Maindron, in Italy. In its July–August 1995 issue, *Golias* published a paper from the Rwandan priest entitled 'Le "coup d'Église" de Gabriel Maindron' ['Gabriel Maindron's "church coup"']. He referred to the 'pastoral plan' Maindron and his two Hutu colleagues had tried to impose on Bishop Kalibushi in Gisenyi and to their letter to Cardinal Etchegaray of 25 June 1994. He also noted that Maindron had close links

---

[70] African Rights, *Rwanda: Death, Despair and Defiance*, 1st edn, 522.
[71] University Paris-Nanterre, La Contemporaine: Fonds Hervé Deguine, Affaire Sibomana, Carton 4, Testimony of Eugène Mutabazi, special correspondent of *Golias*, Brussels, 10 August 1995.
[72] Raymond Bonner, 'Clergy in Rwanda is accused of abetting atrocity', *New York Times*, 7 July 1995; Elaine Ganley, 'Catholic Newsletter Fingers Priests, Nuns in Genocide', *Associated Press News*, 8 July 1995. On Christian Terras and *Golias*, see François Devinat, 'Terras, le pince-monseigneur', *Libération*, 10 November 1995.
[73] Christian Terras, interview conducted on 10 June 2016 in Villeurbanne, Lyon.
[74] Communauté rwandaise de France, Lettre ouverte à Monseigneur Joseph Duval, Paris, 24 February 1995, in *Golias*, 5, special edition, supplement to *Golias*, 42 (May–June 1995).

with President Habyarimana and his entourage. Hategeka passed a severe judgement on his fellow priest:

> The pastoral ministry and the ideological position [against the RPF] presented Maindron with a difficult dilemma: he still liked the minority that was being decimated but he also was deeply attached to the majority that exterminated the members of the minority. [...] For me he is nothing more than a poor opportunist who allowed himself to be tossed by the winds, even though he espoused the ideas of the MNRD/CDR without knowing to what they would lead.[75]

Terras spent two weeks in Rwanda in April 1996 to investigate Maindron's story and other cases involving the Catholic Church. He made the trip to Congo-Nil on dangerous roads to interview Tutsi survivors who had known the French priest. In July, *Golias* published another special issue on the genocide which included a sixteen-page dossier on Maindron entitled 'Les mensonges par omission de l'abbé Maindron' [The lies by omission of Abbé Maindron].[76]

The transcripts of the testimonies of three genocide survivors complemented the article. The first was from Mathias Abimana, the parish council chairman of the Congo-Nil parish in the years preceding the genocide, who was targeted by the killers and lost part of his family. The second was from Christine Nyiramana, a Tutsi refugee who had been rescued by the soldiers of Opération Turquoise at the beginning of July 1994 but claimed that Maindron had refused to protect her and the other refugees. The third was from Jean Kashyengo, a Tutsi priest who said that Maindron had admitted to sending members of his family to the school chapel of Gitwa where they were massacred.[77]

Terras also spoke to Emmanuel Uwimana, a Tutsi tradesman who had been a member of the PL before being targeted by the killers in April 1994. He heard the story of Mélane Kanyoni, a young man who had been working in one of Maindron's development projects and had observed his whereabouts during the entire period of the genocide. Back home, he received from Belgium the testimony of Clément Muteyumungu, a seminarian who had seen Maindron in the company of Clément Kayishema, the prefect of Kibuye, in the Saint-Jean churchyard shortly after the massacre that had taken place there. Were those testimonies credible? 'I did not find

---

[75] Jean-Baptiste Hategeka, 'Le "coup d'Église" de Gabriel Maindron', *Golias*, 43 (July–August 1995), 54.
[76] *Golias*, 43 (July–August 1995), 71–86.
[77] *Ibid.*, 86–7.

in those people any desire to serve the interests of the Rwandan government,' Terras responded. 'They were not seeking recognition. They were just shocked by what they had been going through.'[78]

The impact of *Golias'* dossier

Maindron is aware of the fact that *Golias* has published a dossier about him[79] but we do not know how much he has read of it. Neither he nor his friends took the trouble to write a response. At least two organisations, both very small, were cognisant of Maindron's work in Congo-Nil and provided him with support on his return from Rwanda. The most active was the Association Quintin Rwanda in Brittany, founded in 1975 by Annick Nedelec, which had funded Maindron's development projects in Congo-Nil until 1994.[80] Nedelec regularly forwarded documents to Maindron on the alleged crimes of the RPF in Rwanda and in the Congo.[81] The other organisation was Amour Sans Frontière (ASF), a Lyon-based Catholic humanitarian organisation headed, from 1997 to 2000, by Pierre Jault, a White Father who had worked in Rwanda before the genocide. Maindron collected funds for the Rwandan refugees in the Congo with the logistical support of ASF after his return to France.[82] One of the bulletins of ASF described him as a priest who had 'survived the events in Rwanda' and left the country 'in the middle of a civil war after having risked his life to save indiscriminately Tutsi and Hutu'.[83]

Golias, on the other hand, was read by the genocide-memory activists who could read French. They looked with great interest at Poincaré's biography of Maindron, which, for many of them, had escaped their attention. On 7 July 1995, following *Golias'* press conference at the French Senate, François-Xavier Verschave, the president of Survie, an NGO campaigning for a review of the links between France and corrupt African regimes, gave

---

[78] Terras, same interview.
[79] Maindron, interview conducted on 6 February 2019 in La Roche-sur-Yon, France.
[80] 'Quintin Rwanda, 40 ans de relation', *Le Télégramme*, 30 September 2015, 21.
[81] See a dossier kept in the archives of the Œuvre Pontificale Missionnaire (OPM) in Lyon. I thank Rémi Korman for having drawn my attention to this document.
[82] Poincaré, *Rwanda. Gabriel Maindron*, 120.
[83] Jean-Damascène Bizimana, *L'Église et le génocide au Rwanda. Les Pères Blancs et le Négationnisme* (Paris: L'Harmattan, 2001), 95.

his views on Maindron in an 'Open letter to Nicolas Poincaré' which was subsequently published in a supplement to *Golias:*

> Dear Sir, I have paid attention to your argumentation regarding Father Gabriel Maindron. He cannot be accused of having blood on his hands, nor be blamed for not having always been heroic. One can, however, reproach him as well as a section of the Church in Rwanda, in Belgium and in France, for a certain blindness concerning the reality and atrocity of the genocide. [...] Above all one cannot deny that, before 7 April 1994, he was a fervent supporter of the ideology of the Habyarimana clan, when the country was sliding towards the genocide. In fact, the judgment of this racist ideology and its drifting towards the 'final solution' is, in my opinion, more important than the judgment of persons.[84]

In the same line, we can quote an analysis of Poincaré's book by Jean-Pierre Chrétien, a historian of the Great Lakes Region who in April 1994 was one of the first intellectuals to denounce what he termed a 'tropical Nazism' in Rwanda.[85] It is part of a review of fifty-odd books on the genocide in Rwanda published between mid-1994 and mid-1997.[86] Like Verschave, Chrétien found 'surprising' the 'reproduction of the Habyarimana regime's ideology in the mouth of a missionary'. Certain details of the narrative puzzled him:

> The disarray of Gabriel Maindron is obvious but also the surreal or admirable character, according to the point of view, of his activity. For example, this Mass of 10 April for Hutu women while their husbands staffed the armed gangs that hunt the Tutsi hidden near the church. Or the invitations made to dying people but also terrified refugees to think about their souls before anything else and to forgive their murderers. [...] His naivety is apparent in his dealings with the gendarmes, whom he describes as 'people of good will' and upon whom he calls to evacuate by bus 200 Tutsi refugees that will end up in the Kibuye stadium where they will be exterminated on the 19th of April.'

The country where *Golias'* dossier on Maindron had the biggest impact is arguably Rwanda. On 30 November 1996, the *Official Gazette of the Republic of Rwanda* published a list of 1946 names of people suspected of having been 'planners, organizers, instigators, supervisors and leaders of

---

[84] Supplement to *Golias,* 43 (July–August 1995), 7.
[85] Jean-Pierre Chrétien, 'Un nazisme tropical', *Libération*, 26 April 1994.
[86] Jean-Pierre Chrétien, 'Interprétations du génocide de 1994 dans l'histoire contemporaine du Rwanda', *Clio en Afrique*, 2 (Summer 1997), 92–9.

the crime of genocide or of a crime against humanity'. Maindron was one of them.[87] His name appeared again on the lists published in 1999 and 2001.

Given the relative obscurity of his case, it is very likely that the officials of the Department of Justice who drew up the list picked up his name in one of the issues of *Golias*. That Terras' dossier on Maindron circulated in Rwanda is demonstrated by the fact that a summary of it appeared in the April 1998 issue of the monthly magazine *La Nouvelle Relève*, written by Jean-Baptiste Rucibigango.[88]

Terras denied having any link with the RPF.[89] There is no reason to doubt his word. But this does not mean that the RPF-dominated government and the press organs linked to it did not make use of his dossiers. There were numerous connections between the Rwandan genocide-memory activists and their counterparts in the Western world.

Maindron's trials in the *gacaca* courts

Another moment in the development and the consolidation of the collective memory of the genocide was the *gacaca* court. Apart from Hélène Dumas' classic book *Le génocide au village* [The genocide in the village],[90] not much has been written on the reliability of the *gacaca* proceedings as a historical source. Dumas made a convincing case in this respect. She attended all the sessions of the *gacaca* of Shyorongi, a genocide site north of Kigali, in 2006 and she interviewed numerous members of this community between 2008 and 2010. In total, she spent the equivalent of two years in Rwanda. This allowed her to reconstitute the unfolding of the genocide in Shyorongi, day by day, house by house, with a remarkable wealth of detail.

Most of the literature devoted to the *gacaca* courts examines them from the perspective of transitional justice. When the law instituting the *gacaca* was adopted in January 2001, it was described as an innovative form of communal justice, drawing from Rwandan ancient traditions in the context of mass violence. As time went on, analysts became more critical, citing the biases of some of the local judges, the impact of false

---

[87] *Official Gazette of the Republic of Rwanda / Journal Officiel de la République Rwandaise*, 35ᵉ année, special issue of 30 November 1996, 16 (418).

[88] Jean-Baptiste Rucibigango, 'Maindron, un missionnaire au centre des manigances génocidaires', *La Nouvelle Relève*, 358 (April 1998), 10–13.

[89] Terras, same interview.

[90] Hélène Dumas, *Le génocide au village. Le massacre des Tutsi au Rwanda* (Paris: Seuil, 2014).

testimonies on the judgements and interferences from the Rwandan government. They also regretted the fact that, even though witnesses on behalf of the accused were given the opportunity to testify, the defendants could not rely on lawyers to organise their defence.[91] Genocide survivors, on their side, expressed the fear that genocide perpetrators released too early might take revenge on them and victimise or even kill them. In a report published in 2012, the National Service of Gacaca Courts, a state organ, took note of these criticisms while stressing that there was no other way to try an exceptionally high number of suspects – there were 1,958,654 cases of genocide according to the report – in a short time. In many cases the *gacaca* courts allowed the survivors to know the identity of the people who had massacred members of their families, to interact with them and, occasionally, to forgive them after a certain lapse of time.[92]

Maindron's name was mentioned at one of the *ikusanya amakuru* (collection of information) meetings, also called pre-*gacaca*,[93] held in Congo-Nil in the early 2000s with a view to gathering data on the victims, the perpetrators, the survivors and the crimes that were committed at the level of the village (*umudugudu*) and then the cell. Pierre Setako, a Tutsi from Congo-Nil who was away from home during the genocide, attended these meetings. He noted that the majority of participants were Hutu and that, unlike during the *gacaca* sessions themselves, people spoke freely without fear of retribution. Maindron's attitude during the genocide was openly questioned by the participants. It was only later that the well-known practice of *ceceka* ('shut up' in Kinyarwanda)[94] devel-

[91] Bert Ingelaere, '"Does the truth pass across the fire without burning?" Locating the short circuit in Rwanda's Gacaca courts', *Journal of Modern African Studies,* 47 (2009), 507–28; Phil Clark, *The Gacaca Courts, Post-Genocide Justice and Reconciliation in Rwanda* (Cambridge: Cambridge University Press, 2010); Penal Reform International, *Eight Years On... A Record of Gacaca Monitoring in Rwanda* (London: Penal Reform International, 2010); Paul Christoph Bornkamm, *Rwanda's Gacaca Courts. Between Retribution and Reparation* (Oxford: Oxford University Press, 2012).

[92] National Service of Gacaca Courts, *Gacaca Courts in Rwanda* (Kigali: National Service of Gacaca Courts, 2012).

[93] On the pre-*gacaca* sessions, see Françoise Digneffe and Jacques Fierens (ed.), *Justice et gacaca. L'expérience rwandaise et le génocide* (Namur: Presses Universitaires de Namur, 2003), 106–7.

[94] On the *ceceka,* see Human Rights Watch, *Justice compromise. L'héritage des tribunaux communautaires gacaca du Rwanda* (New York: Human Rights Watch, 2011), 96; Jean-Pierre Dusingizemungu, 'Vécu du processus Gacaca par les rescapés du génocide des Tutsi: le va-et-vient entre le refus et

oped among the people who had witnessed acts of genocide, and some withdrew their testimonies.[95]

The identification sheet of Maindron's first *gacaca* trial held in Congo-Nil in August 2006 and the minutes of the *gacaca* appeal trial held in Gihango (a sector of the district of Rutsiro that includes the cell of Congo-Nil) from 13 to 18 May 2010 are kept at the CNLG in Kigali.[96] All we know of the first trial is that Maindron was accused of having joined the Hutu extremist party CDR, of having failed to protect the Tutsi refugees and of having attended a meeting chaired by Prime Minister Jean Kambanda in Kibuye.[97] In a later interview, Maindron said that his friends from Congo-Nil had told him over the phone that he had been acquitted. This may be true if he was referring to the first trial.[98] There is evidence that he was condemned *in absentia* to life imprisonment during his appeal trial.

The case was reopened in May 2010 at the request of Emmanuel Uwimana, a Tutsi tradesman and genocide survivor interviewed by Christian Terras in 1996. He argued that the court had not sufficiently taken into account the fact that Maindron had taken part in a meeting with the burgomaster of Rutsiro, Raphaël Benimana, and a few other Hutu councillors in Congo-Nil just before the killings started, that he had attended a meeting chaired by Kambanda in Kibuye and that he had escorted Tutsi refugees to the local clinic, where they were killed.

The depositions made about Maindron at the *gacaca* trials are of great value because they capture the memories of people who had not

---

l'acceptation', in Virginie Brinker, Catherine Coquio, Alexandre Dauge-Roth, Eric Hoppenot, Nathan Réra and François Robinet (ed.), *Rwanda 1994–2014. Histoire, mémoires et récits* (Dijon: Les Presses du Réel, 2017), 106.

[95] Pierre Setako, interview conducted on 14 December 2017 in Mushubati.

[96] I express my gratitude to Dr Jean-Damascène Gasanabo, the director of the CNLG Research and Documentation Centre on the Genocide, for giving me copies of all the documents related to Gabriel Maindron that he could find in the *gacaca* archives at the CNLG. I also thank Émilienne Mukansoro, who translated them into French and discussed their contents with me.

[97] The meeting held on 3 May 1994 in Kibuye during which Jean Kambanda, the prime minister of the interim government, and several cabinet ministers responded to questions of the population. See J. C MacKinley Jr, 'Ex-premier admits he led massacres in Rwanda in 1994', *New York Times*, 2 May 1998. A transcript of the speech made by Kambanda on this occasion and subsequently broadcast on Radio Rwanda has been presented as evidence at the trial of Elyézer Niyitegeka, the minister of information during the genocide, at Arusha (ICTR-96-14-T).

[98] Maindron, same interview.

read what journalists and academics were saying about the parish priest of Congo-Nil. As Dumas pointed out, people who spoke at the *gacaca* courts merely related their experience. They did not filter their statements to make them fit certain legal criteria.[99] The minutes of the *gacaca* courts read like a conversation among neighbours who agreed or disagreed on a set of controversial events that had disrupted the life of their community.

This does not mean that, in this case, that there was no bridge between the outside world and the local scene. One of the witnesses, a man by the name of André Habyarimana who described himself as a major seminarian and as a visitor, reported that he had 'done a research by using texts such as *L'Église catholique et la machette* and *Le christianisme et le pouvoir au Rwanda*'. Maindron, he added, 'was mentioned in these books'.[100] The first document can be identified as the dossier published by *Golias* in July 1995 under the title '*La machette et le goupillon*'[101] and the second as a book on the history of the Catholic Church in Rwanda published by the British writer Ian Linden.[102] The judges referred to these two books and to Jean-Baptiste Hategeka's *Raisins verts pour dents agacées* in their judgement.[103]

The *gacaca* appeal court that met in Gihango from 13 to 20 May 2010 had to assess the culpability of six people. Two were absent: Maindron (the only suspect who was eventually condemned) and a woman by the name of Veronica Nyirasafari, whom Uwimana had accused of 'having killed people in different places and attended a meeting organised by [the prime minister Jean] Kambanda at which Hutu were encouraged to kill Tutsi'.[104] Curiously, her name did not appear in the final judgement. The same applied to André Nsingaheye, a teacher who had served as vice-president of the Rutsiro branch of the CDR and who was a friend of Maindron. He had spent six years in prison, from 1995 to 2001, before being acquitted. He testified at the *gacaca* appeal court but, as with Veronica Nyirasafari,

---

[99] Dumas, *Le génocide au village*, 18.

[100] Minutes of the *gacaca* appeal trial held in Gihango from 13 to 20 May 2010, 15.

[101] *Golias*, 43 (July–August 1995).

[102] Ian Linden, *Christianisme et pouvoir au Rwanda (1990–1990)*, rev. edn, trans. Paulette Géraud (Paris: Karthala, 1999). The first edition of this book appeared in 1978 under the title *Church and Revolution in Rwanda* (New York: African Publishing Company, 1977).

[103] Minutes of the *gacaca* appeal trial held in Gihango from 13 to 20 May 2010, 21–2.

[104] Ibid., 2–3. Véronique Nyarasafari, an accountant in the Rutsiro commune, is included in the list of attendees under the number 117. See <https://umuvugizi.wordpress.com/2013/11/06/2899876/> [accessed 9 December 2019].

his name did not appear in the final judgement. The last three defendants, Joseph Humvirwumukiza, Donatile Nyirahabimana and Gaspard Maniraguha, had been accused of hiding the corpses of Tutsi genocide victims in the local clinic but were all formally acquitted.

The *gacaca* appeal court first heard Uwimana, who had requested a review of the August 2006 *gacaca* court's judgement. The debate that followed was contradictory, with statements in favour and in disfavour of the defendants. The court granted the four accused who were present the opportunity to respond, including André Nsingaheye, Maindron's friend, and Donatile Nyirahabimana, who also took Maindron's defence. Nine witnesses were then asked to testify. One of them, Stéphanie Ayingeneye, Nsingaheye's wife, flatly denied the claims made against Maindron. Others testified against the French priest, in particular Sabin Hategekimana (sometimes abbreviated as Hategeka), an Interahamwe leader who had admitted to killing hundreds of Tutsi in Murunda, Rutsiro, Gitwa, Mushubati, Rubengera and Bisesero and who had been condemned to life imprisonment for these crimes at another *gacaca* court.[105]

That some people took Maindron's defence did not prevent the judges, as already mentioned, from declaring him a category one genocide-convicted person – that is, somebody who had contributed to the planning of the genocide – and from condemning him *in absentia* to life imprisonment. They found that his proximity to the burgomaster of Rutsiro and the prefect of Kibuye as well as his participation in a meeting chaired by the prime minister in Kibuye proved beyond doubt that he was aware of the plans to exterminate the Tutsi population and did not object to them.

In the next chapter, we shall compare Maindron's version of events with the testimonies of the genocide survivors interviewed by Christian Terras in 1996 and given during Maindron's *gacaca* appeal trial in 2010. We shall also take into account the testimonies that the Swiss anthropologist Andrea Grieder collected for a thesis defended in 2012,[106] and those

---

[105] National Service of Gacaca Courts, *Gacaca Courts in Rwanda*, 217. There is no reason to suspect Hategeka of having unjustly accused Maindron in order to benefit from a lighter sentence, since he had already been judged.

[106] Andrea Grieder, *Collines des mille souvenirs. Vivre avant et après le génocide perpétré contre les Tutsi du Rwanda* (Geneva: Globethics.net, 2016). This thesis focuses on the genocide survivors' effort to deal with traumatic memories and reconstruct a normal life in totally different circumstances. She chose as terrain the hill of Nyamagumba, formerly known as Gitwa, in the Congo-Nil parish, where several hundred, perhaps a thousand, Tutsi from Rutsiro, Mabanza and other places resisted the attacks of the killers for

that I myself collected between 2016 and 2019 in Rwanda, in France and in Belgium.[107] All these testimonies show the consistency over time of the survivors' memories of Maindron's role during the genocide. They give flesh to what I propose to term the alternative narrative of his ministry in Congo-Nil.

---

five days until 13 April 1994, when most of them succumbed to the weapons of the burgomasters of Kayove, Rutsiro and Mabanza. Between 2006 and 2009, she interviewed three people who knew Maindron: Mathias Abimana, one of Terras' sources; Marthe Nyirahabimana, a teenager at the time of the genocide, who found shelter with a few others in Maindron's house after the attack on Gitwa; and Dansira (or Dancille) Mukamasabo, another parishioner of Maindron's, who survived because she had married a Hutu man and witnessed the Gitwa massacre at a short distance.

[107] I interviewed twelve genocide survivors who knew Maindron when he served as parish priest in Congo-Nil. Three of them, Mathias Abimana, Emmanuel Uwimana and Mélane Kanyoni, had already been interviewed by Christian Terras in 1996. I interviewed Josée Utomoni and Alphonsine Sillis, two women who had taken refuge in Maindron's presbytery during the genocide, and Dancille Mukamasabo, Catherine Uwimphwe and Fidèle Rurangirwa, three survivors from the massacre of Gitwa (known today as Nyamagumba). I also interviewed Béatrice Van Hoven-Ayinkamiye and Freddy Mutanguha, two survivors from neighbouring areas who had met Maindron when he visited their villages to say Mass or exercise other priestly duties. Lastly, I interviewed the historian Marcel Kabanda, who lost part of his family in Congo-Nil and had contacts with Maindron before and after the genocide, and Pierre Setako, who had left Congo-Nil to join the RPF during the genocide. He gave a testimony on the *ikusanya amakuru* process in Congo-Nil in the early 2000s.

CHAPTER 9

Remembering 1994 in Congo-Nil

The interviews that Christian Terras, Andrea Grieder and I conducted and the minutes of Maindron's *gacaca* appeal trial open a window into the survivors' memories of the French priest's role during the genocide. There were different opinions among them of course, though on certain aspects of the narrative only. I did not pick up any substantial variation in the stories of the genocide survivors who were interviewed once or more and who testified at the *gacaca* appeal court.

According to the survivors, Maindron's attitude changed after the RPF's attack in the north of Rwanda in October 1990. 'When he arrived,' Anastase Uwobibabaje, a Tutsi who later became the president of Ibuka for the Rutsiro district,[1] declared during the *gacaca* trial, 'he was a priest who helped people. When the political parties started, he wore the hat of the CDR.'[2] This Hutu extremist party was feared by the Tutsi. Mathias Abimana concurred. Abimana was a Christian believer so committed to reconciliation despite the loss of his wife and two children that he resolved, a few years after the genocide, to forgive Maindron, even though the French priest never expressed remorse for not having publicly denounced the massacres of Tutsi in Congo-Nil, as Stanislas Urbaniak, another expatriate, had done, for example. He and Maindron were very close prior to the genocide:

> When he arrived at the parish in 1985, he found me as president of the parish council. I was his right hand. [...] He visited me often. He was my confidant. Every month he would give me and my children the sacrament of confession.[3]

---

[1] Andrea Grieder, *Collines des mille souvenirs. Vivre avant et après le génocide perpétré contre les Tutsi du Rwanda* (Geneva: Globethics.net, 2016), 69.
[2] CNLG, Minutes of the *gacaca* appeal trial held in Gihango from 13 to 20 May 2010, 10.
[3] Mathias Abimana, interview conducted on 18 December 2016 in Kigali.

Maindron's attitude changed the very month of the attack, when rumours started to spread that Abimana had given money to send a member of the community to the RPF. Maindron asked his parish council chairperson to write a letter to President Habyarimana stating that he dissociated himself publicly, on behalf of all the Tutsi, from the invading army. Mathias responded that he did not have the authority to do so and that he had nothing to do with a war that was happening at the other end of Rwanda.[4]

According to Abimana, 'Maindron had a bias regarding what was happening in the country. He was on the side of the French elements who were involved in it.'[5] Every Tuesday, he recalled, Maindron would do the trip to Kigali on bad roads to meet the French ambassador to whom everybody in the parish knew he was close.[6] One of Terras' sources mentioned that he entertained good relations with Lieutenant Colonel Gilles Chollet, the commander of the Détachement d'Assistance Militaire et d'Instruction (DAMI), which provided military training to an elite battalion of the FAR in the Bigogwe Military Camp near Gisenyi. Later on, Chollet was appointed military adviser to President Habyarimana.[7]

Maindron became a supporter of the CDR when this party was founded in 1991. The genocide survivors remember him talking in favour of the Hutu extremist party and being seen in company of its affiliates. Uwimana recalled the day when Maindron provokingly put on a hat with 'CDR' written on it in the 'Chez Deo', a tavern in Congo-Nil.[8] In 1993, the opposition newspaper *Isibo* published an article with the heading: 'Incredible! A white member of the CDR'.[9] Maindron may have not been a card-carrying member of the party, but his political opinions were known to all.[10]

---

[4] *Ibid.*

[5] *Ibid.*

[6] Mathias Abimana, interview conducted on 4 March 2020 in Rubengera.

[7] Christian Terras, 'Les mensonges par omission de l'abbé Maindron', *Golias*, 48–9 (Summer 1996), 74. See the report sent by Lieutenant Colonel Gilles Chollet to Colonel Bernard Cussac, defence attaché at the French embassy, Ruhengeri on 19 August 1991 (Genocide Archives Rwanda) <http://francegenocidetutsi.org/1991-08-19CholletRuhengeri.pdf> [accessed 16 March 2018]. On Chollet's involvement in Rwanda's military operations in the early 1990s, see Gérard Prunier, *The Rwanda Crisis 1959–1994. History of a Genocide* (New York: Columbia University Press, 1995), 149; Olivier Lanotte, *La France au Rwanda (1990–1994. Entre abstention impossible et engagement ambivalent* (Brussels: P.I.E. Peter Lang, 2007), 157.

[8] Emmanuel Uwimana, interview conducted on 12 March 2017 in Kigali.

[9] Terras in 'Les mensonges par omission de l'abbé Maindron', 73.

[10] Mathias Abimana, interview conducted on 18 December 2016 in Kigali.

Béatrice Van Hoven, a genocide survivor from Murama, a village in the northern part of the Congo-Nil parish, also accused Maindron of pro-Hutu bias. A young man, son of a respected Tutsi teacher, had been killed in Murama in October 1990.[11] The Tutsi lived in fear. Béatrice could not understand the priest's lack of concern for the plight of the Tutsi:

> Maindron was coming to Murama to say Mass once a month. He used to say: 'I do not understand why people are hiding. There is nothing! You are all children of God!' It was humiliating! […] After Mass he used to hold meetings with people from the parish. When he was gone, the people were telling us: 'You are *inyenzi*. We shall kill you!'

'I am an Umumonyo'

From the survivors' testimonies emerge the picture of a man who identified almost unreservedly with the Hutu cause. He promptly believed the Hutu extremist propaganda accusing Tutsi members of the parish such as Mathias Abimana or Tutsi priests from the diocese of Nyundo of being hidden RPF activists and therefore 'enemies of the people'. Many of Maindron's friends were members of the CDR. One of them was André Nsingaheye, a teacher who was described at the *gacaca* appeal court as vice-president of the Rutsiro branch of the party.[12] This must have contributed to the priest's sympathy for the CDR without – let us make this clear again – him necessarily being a card-carrying member of the party.

According to several survivors, Maindron claimed to be an 'Umumonyo'. The Abamonyo (plural of Umumonyo) were an *umuryango* (lineage) of agriculturalists stemming from a man by the name of Kamonyo in the early twentieth century, who were based at the periphery of the parish of Congo-Nil, on the shore of Lake Kivu. Fairly prosperous, they had the reputation of being fierce Hutu. They were the first to be evangelised in this part of western Rwanda. By the time Maindron arrived in Congo-Nil, the Abamonyo had formed, all by themselves, a small Christian community.[13] Their active involvement in the parish presumably explains why

---

Pierre Setako, interview conducted on 14 December 2017 in Mushubati.
Mélane Kanyoni, interview conducted on 20 March 2019 in Mushubati.
[11] Information provided by Émilienne Mukansoro on 29 February 2020 in Kigali.
[12] See Chapter 8.
[13] Mathias Abimana, interview conducted on 4 March 2020 in Rubengera.

Maindron chose to associate himself with them despite the relatively long distance – an hour's walk – between their settlement and the mission.

After each Mass', Josée Umotoni recalled, he would say: 'I am an Umumonyo.' Maindron's Hutu colleague Prosper Ntiyamira, who nearly died during the genocide because of his Tutsi-like appearance and later was appointed parish priest in Kivumu near Gisenyi, concurred: 'Maindron wanted to be more Rwandan than the Rwandans. He claimed to be an Umumonyo. He belonged to the Abamonyo.'[14] Pierre Setako noted that one of the Abamonyo, Jean-Berchmans Ntihabose, was ordained to the priesthood in Maindron's time.[15] This vocation reinforced the link between the Abamonyo lineage and the parish priest of Congo-Nil.[16] Ntihabose was one of the signatories of the 25 June 1994 letter to Cardinal Etchegaray.[17]

Maindron's membership of the Abamonyo lineage was discussed at the *gacaca* appeal trial. It was Emmanuel Uwimana who raised the issue. 'When Maindron was baptised Umumonyo,' he declared, 'Nsingaheye was his godfather (*umubyeyi wa batisimu*).' This prompted a denial. 'Concerning the name (*izino*) given to Maindron,' Nsingaheye replied, 'it is false. Kanyamugenga [an active member of the parish] was present. He can explain why Maindron was called Umumonyo.'[18] In Kinyarwanda, *ikimonyo* means ant. Nsingaheye's argument was that Maindron received the name of Umumonyo because he was of small stature. This explanation did not convince the audience, because Umumonyo was a lineage name and not a person name. As a matter of fact, Maindron already had a Rwandan name. Since the time of his ordination, he was commonly known in the church as 'Munderere', which means 'the one who has been adopted'.[19]

Traditional baptisms existed in the Rwandan culture. Under certain circumstances, a ritual pact (*igihango*) would link the family of a neophyte

---

[14] Prosper Ntiyamira, interview conducted on 13 December 2016 in Kayove.

[15] Jean-Berchmans Ntihabose was ordained in 1993.

[16] Pierre Setako, same interview. Jean-Berchmans Ntihabose fled to the Congo after the genocide and from there to Nairobi and Spain. In October 1997 he described his odyssey in the Congolese forests in a diary entitled 'Neuf mois de tragédie à l'est du Zaïre. Mon journal' [Nine months of tragedy in Eastern Zaire: My diary] <http://www.mdrwi.org/livres/neuf%20mois%20de%20tragedie.htm> [accessed 24 July 2019].

[17] See Chapter 3.

[18] Minutes of the *gacaca* appeal trial held in Gihango from 13 to 20 May 2010, 6.

[19] Nicolas Poincaré, *Rwanda. Gabriel Maindron, un prêtre dans la tragédie* (Paris: Éditions Ouvrières, 1995), 28.

and that of his 'godfather'. It would give the latter a say in the personal matters of his 'godson' in a capacity as negotiator.[20] That a Catholic priest underwent a traditional ceremony of this nature, however, is hard to believe. At best, the word may have been used metaphorically. Another witness by the name of Kayitani hinted at something of this nature. According to him, a banana tree was planted 'in memory of Maindron's baptism'. Kanyamugenga, the priest's friend, was then asked to comment. 'I do not know the story of Maindron's baptism,' he responded. 'But I know that he was called Umumonyo. I do not know the story of the banana tree planted as a souvenir.'[21]

The burgomaster, the priest and the Bagogwe

At the *gacaca* appeal trial, Emmanuel Uwimana accused Maindron of having covered up the massacre of a group of Bagogwe in the territory of the Rutsiro commune:

> After the killings of the Bagogwe, President Habyarimana pretended to suspend the burgomaster Benimana Raphaël of all his functions. Maindron did not waste time in ensuring that Benimana resumed his functions despite the fact that he had massacred innocents.[22]

The Bagogwe were a group of Tutsi cattle raisers whose ancestors had separated themselves from the central Tutsi kingdom in pre-colonial times and had been living in isolation from the rest of the Rwandan population in remote areas of the prefectures of Ruhengeri and Gisenyi since that time. Dispossessed by the Belgian colonial government of a large part of their land, they fell victim to a succession of pogroms in the early 1960s and again in the years following the invasion of Rwanda by the RPF in October 1990.[23] From late January to mid-March 1991, Rwandan troops and Hutu militia massacred between five hundred and a thousand Bagogwe in retaliation for a RPF raid on Ruhengeri made on

---

[20] Charles Ntampaka, 'Le retour à la tradition avec le règlement des différends: le gacaca du Rwanda', *Dialogue*, 186 (October–November 1995), 98.
[21] Minutes of the *gacaca* appeal trial held in Gihango from 13 to 20 May 2010, 7.
[22] *Ibid.*, 8–9.
[23] Philip Verwimp, 'The 1990–92 Massacres in Rwanda: a case of spatial and social engineering', *Journal of Agrarian Change*, 11 (2011), 396–419.

22 and 23 January.[24] This massacre was described as a genocide by the ADL in a report published in 1993.[25]

A new wave of massacres hit the Bagogwe in December 1992 and January 1993. Among the victims were a group of at least fourteen Bagogwe from Ramba – not far from Kibilira, where a massacre had already taken place in October 1990 – who had taken refuge in the commune of Rutsiro.[26] Some may have also come from the Kayove area.[27] An international commission of enquiry visited the area in January 1993.[28] Under pressure from the international community, on 8 February 1993 the Rwandan government suspended the prefect of Gisenyi, the sub-prefects of Gisenyi and Ngororero and six burgomasters including Raphaël Benimana, the burgomaster of Rutsiro. Information on these suspensions was included in a report compiled by Jef Vleugels, the regional superior of the Missionaries of Africa.[29]

Émilienne Mukansoro, a genocide survivor from Mushubati, who was teaching in a primary school in Murunda at the time, remembered having been invited by the burgomaster, on a day she attended a teacher training session in Congo-Nil, to witness the massacre of the Bagogwe, together with other Tutsi teachers, in a nearby area. Benimana's intention, according to her, was to dissuade the Tutsi teachers from becoming

---

[24] For a detailed history of these massacres, see Diogène Bideri, *Le massacre des Bagogwe. Un prélude au génocide des Tutsi au Rwanda (1990–1993)* (Paris: L'Harmattan, 2008).

[25] Association rwandaise pour la Défense des Droits de la Personne et des Libertés publiques, *Rapport sur les droits de l'homme au Rwanda, Octobre 1992–Octobre 1993* (Kigali: ADL, 1993), 29. The massacre took place in the Muhuroro parish, which was located in the Kibilira commune, itself part of the Ngororero sub-prefecture.

[26] *Ibid.*, 161. On the Rutsiro massacre in January 1991, see Timothy Longman, *Christianity and Genocide in Rwanda* (Cambridge: Cambridge University Press, 2011), 271.

[27] Mélane Kanyoni, interview conducted on 20 March 2017 in Mushubati.

[28] Fédération Internationale des Ligues des Droits de l'Homme *et al.*, 'Rapport de la Commission internationale d'enquête sur les violations massives et systématiques des droits de l'homme depuis le 1er octobre 1990 au Rwanda', in *Lettre hebdomadaire de la FIDH*, 168, March 1993.

[29] Jef Vleugels, Fax of 15 February 1993, in Missionaries of Africa, 'Informations diffusées par la région du Rwanda, 1990–1994', Brussels, December 2005, 129.

'accomplices' of the RPF.[30] One of Christian Terras' sources testified that the Bagogwe refugees had been transported in a dump truck to the Kabana hill in the Bwiza sector, where they were pushed into a ravine and fell to their deaths.[31] Pierre Setako had heard of the incident with the dump truck but he did not think that it happened in January 1993.[32] The presence of Bagogwe refugees in Congo-Nil during this period is well attested. They were hosted in a craft skills training centre. Food was collected for them in the parish. Those who escaped the massacre of the Kabana hill came back to Congo-Nil and remained there until April 1994. Most of them then fell victims to the genocide.[33]

Maindron approved of the idea of a parish food distribution for the Bagogwe refugees. Yet, according to Mélane Kanyoni, who knew him well, the priest was 'very tense' about it and did not mention the massacre of the Bagogwe at Mass.[34] His main loyalty in this matter was to Raphaël Benimana. On 10 February 1993, two days after the burgomaster's suspension, he wrote to the minister of the interior, requesting that the measure of suspension be annulled. According to several witnesses, Maindron pressurised the Bagogwe to retract their statement against the burgomaster. A Ugandan seminarian who was staying in the parish at the time told Mathias Abimana that Maindron had asked him to distribute food to the Bagogwe refugees only on the condition that they retract their testimony against Benimana. He did so on the eve of a visit of President Juvénal Habyarimana to the commune of Rutsiro.[35] The statement Boniface Niragira, one of the few Bagogwe who survived, made to Christian Terras in 1996 corroborates Abimana's version of the event:

> Abbé Maindron asked us to sign false statements according to which our burgomaster was an innocent man, victim of calumny. We had to sign so as he could resume his position. He threatened to stop the aid he was providing to us. Under duress, we were forced to sign.[36]

---

[30] Émilienne Mukansoro, conversation held in Mushubati on 13 December 2017.
[31] Terras, 'Les mensonges par omission de l'abbé Maindron', 74.
[32] Pierre Setako, interview conducted on 27 May 2018 in Mushubati.
[33] Mélane Kanyoni, interview conducted on 20 March 2017 in Mushubati.
[34] Mélane Kanyoni, same interview.
[35] Mathias Abimana, interview conducted on 4 March 2020 in Rubengera.
[36] Terras, 'Les mensonges par omission de l'abbé Maindron', 74.

The first days of the genocide in Congo-Nil

The news of President Habyarimana's death reached the priests of the diocese who were gathered in Nyundo for a session of pastoral planning on Thursday, 7 April at about 5:00am. Maindron and his French colleague Jean-Baptiste Mendiondo immediately left for their respective parishes in the prefecture of Kibuye. Quoting the testimony of Jean-Baptiste Tuyishime, a priest from Kibuye who had attended the session, Terras claims that they were already accompanied by Interahamwe on that day.[37] To cross the roadblocks that the Hutu militia had erected on all main roads as early as April 7, the two priests only had to show their French passports. They would have been in trouble if they had been Belgian, since the Belgian army had been accused, on the radio, of having killed the president.

At the *gacaca* appeal court, Uwimana was adamant that Maindron took part in a meeting convened by the burgomaster in the Rutsiro commune's office on Friday, 8 April, during which plans were made for the genocide in Congo-Nil. His argument, repeated by the judges in the final sentence, was that the Tutsi who were working for the commune were not invited to the meeting.[38] The exclusion of the Tutsi officials was indeed problematic, but it was not sufficient to prove that Maindron had a role in the planning of the killings. In pre-genocide Rwanda it was customary to invite bishops, priests and pastors to official meetings on safety and security. Clerics as little suspected of being *génocidaires* as Frédéric Rubwejanga, the bishop of Kibungo, or Jean Ndorimana, the vicar general of the diocese of Cyangugu, took part in such meetings in their respective dioceses during the genocide period.[39] What is beyond dispute, on the other hand, is the fact that the genocide started the night of 7 April in Rutsiro. A letter from Clément Kayishema, the prefect of Kibuye, which Timothy Longman retrieved after the genocide, confirms it.[40]

---

[37] *Ibid.*, 77.

[38] Minutes of the *gacaca* appeal trial held in Gihango from 13 to 20 May 2010, 2, 21. According to Mélane Kanyoni, the Tutsi municipal officers excluded from the meeting were Boniface Gatari (judiciary police inspector), Ignace Habiyambere and Alphonse Hakamineza (assistants to the burgomaster) and Epimaque Gakuzi (tax collector). Testimony quoted in Terras, 'Les mensonges par omission de l'abbé Maindron', 77.

[39] See Chapter 3.

[40] Clément Kayishema to the government, 10 April 1994, quoted in Longman, *Christianity and Genocide*, 282: '[The] tension degenerated into an open conflict in the night of 7/4 to 8/4 in Rutsiro Commune at the commercial

More pointed was the testimony of Josée Umotoni on Maindron's attitude before the massacre of Tutsi patients in the clinic held by the Missionaries of Jesus, Mary and Joseph, a Spanish missionary congregation of sisters, in the centre of Congo-Nil. At the *gacaca* appeal trial, Uwimana simply stated that, according to some witnesses, 'there are people that Maindron took to the health centre and who have been killed'.[41] More detailed, Umotoni's testimony showed an incomprehensible blindness to the gravity of the situation on the part of the French priest. It was as if he denied the reality of the killings and, for that reason, was prepared to send his parishioners to their death.

On 8 April, Umotoni took refuge in the parish house with her parents and her brother and sister-in-law and their five children. The following day, her elder sister, who lived in Murama, was wounded by Interahamwe when walking to Congo-Nil with her four children.[42] The youngest child was also injured. Her sister went straight to the clinic and told her children to go to the parish. On hearing this, Maindron invited Umotoni to take the wounded child to the clinic and offered to give them a lift. On the way, they tried to find the young woman's sister. By then, bands of Hutu armed with machetes were roaming around. In the marketplace, a man told Umotoni that the place was dangerous and that gang members might kill her because she was a Tutsi. Maindron then drove to the health centre, a few hundred metres away. In a manner that Umotoni found shocking, he told her to come back to the parish on her own once she had found her sister and had ensured that the child received treatment at the clinic:

> When we arrived at the health centre, he just left me there and said: 'Go and find a treatment for the child. If he is hospitalised, come back. Otherwise, return with the child.' I said to the priest: 'How shall I go through this place? We have been told at the market that people are killing.' He responded: 'Everybody knows you. You do not risk anything.' I refused to stay at the health centre. I went back to the car and Maindron asked me to sit on the back seat.'[43]

---

centre of La Crête Zaïre-Nil. Currently the most affected communes are: [...] Rutsiro above all Gihango Sector and Murunda Parish. There were six recorded deaths including a priest from Murunda Parish.'

[41] Minutes of the *gacaca* appeal trial held in Gihango from 13 to 20 May 2010, 2.

[42] On his part, Longman noted that refugees from the Kayove district started to arrive in Rutsiro and Mabanza on 9 April (*Christianity and Genocide*, 282).

[43] Josée Umotoni, interview conducted on 17 December 2017 in Kigali.

Umotoni did not understand why Maindron never visited the child and his mother at the clinic. To her distress, both were killed there on Monday, 11 April in the company of several other patients.[44] She would probably have suffered the same fate if she had listened to Maindron's advice.

The attacks on the mission

Umotoni's testimony is also precious in capturing the experience of the Tutsi refugees in the parish house before they were sent to Kibuye, where most of them were massacred. By Monday, 11 April, a hundred and fifty Tutsi had taken refuge in the mission on a steep hill dominating the locality of Congo-Nil. By the following day there were two hundred.[45] Those who ventured outside the building to cook or to wash their clothes – the number is not known – fell victim, on several occasions, to the killers' blows. They stayed there until the evening of Tuesday, 12 April.

Umotoni's narrative showed, on the part of Maindron, the same apparent unwillingness to recognise that a systematic programme of extermination, executed with the support of the local authorities, was taking place before his eyes. He complied when the burgomaster asked him to count the refugees and send them to the municipal hall where, on Monday, 11 April, about a hundred refugees who had found shelter there a year before, including Bagogwe, died after the building was set on fire.

In the account of the genocide he gave to Poincaré, Maindron distinguished between the killings in Congo-Nil, which, according to him, were perpetrated by 'big mouths, traffickers, bandits and small thieves' and those in Gitwa, which were organised by Interahamwe militia coming from outside.[46] Yet, he noted in his diary that in Congo-Nil the perpetrators used grenades.[47] He did not ask himself where people who were supposedly acting spontaneously could have found such expensive and sophisticated weapons.[48]

---

[44] On this massacre, see the testimony of the Spanish sisters: Misioneras de Jesùs, María and José, *Esperanza en el infierno de Ruanda. Diario de una mission* (Madrid: Espasa Calpe, 1994), 165–82. They returned to Spain a few days later.

[45] Gabriel Maindron, 'Rwanda: l'horreur', *Dialogue*, 177 (August–September 1994), 44; Poincaré, *Rwanda. Gabriel Maindron*, 74.

[46] Poincaré, *Rwanda. Gabriel Maindron*, 86.

[47] Maindron, 'Rwanda: l'horreur', 44.

[48] *Ibid.*, 45. The number of victims of the massacre in the municipal hall, initially a hundred (*ibid.*, 45) was reduced to sixty in Poincaré's book (*Rwanda. Gabriel Maindron*, 74).

As it happened, the refugees from the mission did not go to the municipal hall on that day but it was, so to say, by mistake. Umotoni gave the following account of this episode:

> Maindron asked us to count ourselves because at the commune they wanted to know how many the refugees were in order to feed them. We gave the number to Maindron and he gave it to the burgomaster. He was with the gendarmes. After that, Benimana left the place where we were with Maindron. They were in the lounge with Maindron and after they came back they said: 'Go to the commune. We shall protect you.' Maindron confirmed it: 'You will be safe.' Some refugees said yes. Others refused: 'We cannot go to the commune because we are busy cooking. We must eat first.' Then he said: 'Stay. You will go tomorrow.'[49]

Umotoni expressed the conviction that Maindron was in cahoots with the killers. Otherwise how could one explain that they had spare keys on the day they came to murder the refugees in the mission?

> After he left, the killers came immediately as if they had spoken to each other. I think that he was aware of their plans because when they arrived, they had the keys and nobody else other than Maindron had spare keys. But some refugees had been advised to leave the keys we had in the locks. When the killers arrived, they tried to open but it did not work.[50]

The bus for Kibuye

Maindron's most controversial decision was to allow the two hundred refugees to be transported by bus to Kibuye by the authorities. According to his version of events, he and his assistant priest, Urbain Twagirayezu, expected an attack that night, and they asked the gendarmery commander to evacuate the refugees. At one o'clock in the morning, a sixty-seater bus arrived and transported the two hundred refugees to Rubengera, about twenty kilometres south of Congo-Nil. Maindron and Twagirayezu accompanied them in their respective cars.[51] Umotoni's recollection only differed on one point: she remembered having seen not one but 'two or three buses'.[52]

---

[49] Josée Umotoni, same interview.
[50] Josée Umotoni, same interview.
[51] Maindron, 'Rwanda: l'horreur', 48.
[52] Josée Umotoni, same interview.

An ambulance from the Spanish sisters' clinic also followed the convoy, packed with twenty-two refugees. The sisters' chronicle reveals that the final destination of the trip was Kibuye, the seat of the prefecture on Lake Kivu, and not Rubengera,[53] as Maindron implied in his own diary.[54] It was on the refugees' insistence that the bus driver left the majority of his passengers in this small town because they were hoping to return to Congo-Nil later.[55] They joined a group of two thousand other refugees in the local secondary school and stayed there for three days.[56] Despite being told that it was risky to continue to Kibuye that night, the sisters considered that the two places were equally dangerous and encouraged the refugees who had travelled with them to board the bus, and they arrived safely at the seat of the prefecture before dawn.[57]

Asked if Maindron knew that the refugees would be massacred in Kibuye, Umotoni responded in the affirmative: 'He was aware because he attended the meetings organised by the prefect of Kibuye.'[58] The responsibility of the prefect, Clément Kayishema, in the planning and execution of the massacre of several thousand Tutsi, including two hundred or more from Congo-Nil, between 15 and 19 April in Kibuye was recognised by the ICTR in 1999 and again, on appeal, in 2001. He was sentenced to life imprisonment.

Maindron's awareness of the fate that awaited the refugees in Kibuye and his participation in a meeting organised by the prefect were also mentioned at his *gacaca* appeal trial. A certain confusion in the chronology, however, throws doubt on the accuracy of the statements made on this point in the courtroom. One of the accusations levelled by Emmanuel Uwimana, the main witness against Maindron, was that 'he encouraged the killings of Tutsi by taking part in the meeting of [Jean] Kambanda that

---

[53] Misioneras de Jesùs, María and José, *Esperanza en el infierno de Ruanda. Diario de una mission*, 180–2.
[54] Maindron, 'Rwanda: l'horreur', 48. See also Poincaré, *Rwanda. Gabriel Maindron*, 82.
[55] Misioneras de Jesùs, María and José, *Esperanza en el infierno de Ruanda*, 181.
[56] Poincaré, *Rwanda. Gabriel Maindron*, 82. Some refugees had found shelter in the secondary school of Rubengera and others in the communal hall of Mabanza.
[57] Misioneras de Jesùs, María and José, *Esperanza en el infierno de Ruanda*, 181.
[58] Josée Umotoni, same interview.

took place in the prefecture'.⁵⁹ Gaëtan Kayihura, another witness, spoke, in relation to a suspected *génocidaire* by the name of Ildephonse Nkiriye, of a 'meeting to prepare the genocide' that 'took place in Kibuye under the chairmanship of Kambanda'.⁶⁰ In their final judgement, the judges also mentioned a meeting chaired by Jean Kambanda, the prime minister in the interim government of Rwanda, in Kibuye:

> Taking into account the minutes of the meeting held by Kambanda on the organisation of the genocide and the fact that Maindron is included in the list of those who participated in this meeting with the number 169 on the attendance list and that the witnesses say that after this meeting Maindron sent to Kibuye all the Tutsi who had taken refuge in the parish of Congo-Nil on buses knowing that he was leading them to their death.⁶¹

The problem is that if a meeting chaired by Jean Kambanda in Kibuye is well attested, it took place on 3 May 1994, long after the massacres perpetrated in the town's parish church and stadium. There is no proof that Maindron knew that the refugees he sent by bus to Kibuye would be slaughtered there. He might have suspected it because, as we shall see in the next section, a large-scale massacre of Tutsi was taking place in the school chapel of Gitwa, in his own parish, at the same time, but that is a matter of conjecture. As Mathias Abimana explained, the Interahamwe were moving southwards from one village to the next in the days following the shooting down of President Habyarimana's plane.⁶² Maindron was not necessarily aware of the fact that the killing wave affecting Congo-Nil on 8 April and the following days would spread to Rubengera and Kibuye. Dealing with a similar accusation, the ICTR admitted that one could not prove beyond reasonable doubt that Ignace Bagilishema, the burgomaster of Mabanza, knew that the Tutsi refugees he gathered in the communal office from 8 to 12 April – from Gisenyi, Kayove and other places – would be sent to their death in Kibuye.⁶³

Kambanda's speech in Kibuye was broadcast on Radio Rwanda. A French translation was made of it during his trial at the ICTR in Arusha.⁶⁴

---

⁵⁹ Minutes of the *gacaca* appeal trial held in Gihango from 13 to 20 May 2010, 8.
⁶⁰ *Ibid.*, 1.
⁶¹ *Ibid.*, 21.
⁶² Mathias Abimana, interview conducted on 14 December 2017 in Rubengera.
⁶³ ICTR 95-T. The Prosecutor versus Ignace Bagilishema. Judgement, 7 June 2001.
⁶⁴ ICTR 96-14-6: K0183686 (transcribed on 26/10/1999).

The fact that he refused to intervene in favour of orphaned children threatened with extermination in a hospital in Kibuye was held against him.[65] Neither the prime minister not the participants who asked him questions mentioned the Tutsi extermination programme by name but, reading between the lines, it is clear that they were referring to it.

The Rwandan journalist Tom Ndahiro retrieved the list of participants in the 3 May 1994 Kibuye meeting, with Prime Minister Jean Kabanda in the first position, the Kibuye prefect Clément Kayishema in the second and Maindron in the 169th, and posted it on the Internet.[66] The *gacaca* appeal court might have erred in the chronology of events, but it correctly quoted the document. Maindron never tried to distance himself from the Rwandan officials, and he would have found it normal to attend, in his capacity as parish priest of Congo-Nil, a meeting organised in his area by the prime minister. This shows a troubling proximity between the French priest and the authorities that orchestrated the genocide against the Tutsi allegedly to protect the country against the 'enemy'.

The Gitwa massacre

On Friday, 8 April, Tutsi refugees started to congregate around the school chapel of Gitwa (later known as Nyamagumba), on top of a hill dominating Lake Kivu about an hour's walk from Congo-Nil. They resisted by throwing stones at their assailants, who used planks to protect themselves. They lost the battle when, according to the genocide survivors, the burgomasters of Kayove, Rutsiro and Mabanza, each of whom had residents among the besieged, started to bring weapons. The combat lasted five days. Some refugees, like Fidèle Rurangirwa and Catherine Uwimpuhwe, managed to escape to Lake Kivu. According to Anastase Uwobibabaje, the president of the Rutsiro branch of Ibuka, nine thousand people, including children and elderly people, were killed.[67] This figure may be exaggerated.[68] Maindron, who spoke of 'at least two hundred people, perhaps many

---

[65] James McKinley, 'Ex-premier admits that he led massacres in Rwanda in 1994', *New York Times*, 2 May 1998.

[66] See https://umuvugizi.wordpress.com/2013/11/06/20001899876/ [accessed 12 December 2019].

[67] Grieder, *Colline des mille souvenirs*, 68. For its part, the CMGM gave the figure of 12,000 victims. See 'Rapport préliminaire d'identification des sites du génocide et des massacres d'avril-juillet 1994 au Rwanda', February 1996, 158.

[68] According to a house survey conducted by the genocide survivors'

more',[69] minimised, for his part, the size of the massacre. It was a horrible slaughter. The screams of the children put to death by the Interahamwe still haunts the memory of the survivors who managed to escape.

At his *gacaca* appeal trial, Maindron was condemned, among other reasons, for having 'ordered the destruction of the Gitwa chapel and numerous Tutsi who had taken refuge in it'.[70] No witnesses testified on this matter in the appeals, but since the name of Dancilla Mukamasabo, who made the same accusation in an interview,[71] appears in the identification sheet of Maindron's first *gacaca* trial in August 2006, we can assume that the judges drew their information from the minutes of this trial, which have been lost.

Another survivor from the massacre, Fidèle Rurangirwa, declared, however, that Maindron was not present in Gitwa on Wednesday, 13 April, when the refugees lost the battle against their aggressors, and that the school chapel was only pulled down to cover the bodies of the victims a week later.[72] This does not mean that the genocide survivors exonerated Maindron from all responsibility in the massacre. Jean Kashyengo (now deceased), a priest of the diocese of Nyundo who lost members of his family in Gitwa, gave the following testimony to Christian Terras in 1996:

> When I asked Maindron what he had done to protect my people, he dryly responded, a bit embarrassed: 'I did not protect the members of your family. I sent them to Gitwa with the others.' My father's wife, her six children and my aunt have all been exterminated there.[73]

---

organisation Ibuka in the late 1990s that is generally considered credible, 941 residents of Rutsiro, the commune where the parish of Congo-Nil is located, were killed during the genocide. In addition, several hundred of the 3,566 Tutsi residents of the neighbouring Mabanza commune were killed near the school chapel of Gitwa that belonged to the Congo-Nil parish. See Philip Verwimp, 'A quantitative analysis of genocide in Kibuye Prefecture, Rwanda', Centre for Economic Studies, Katholieke Universiteit Leuven, Discussions Paper Series (DPS) 01.10 (May 2001). The data collected by Ibuka do not allow one to establish the percentage of Tutsi from Rutsiro who were killed during the genocide. It was 17 per cent in the Kibuye prefecture as a whole (*ibid.*, 10).

[69] Poincaré, *Rwanda. Gabriel Maindron*, 87.
[70] Minutes of the *gacaca* appeal trial held in Gihango from 13 to 20 May 2010, 20.
[71] Dancilla Mukamasabo, interview conducted on 14 December 2017 in Mushubati.
[72] Fidèle Rurangirwa, interview conducted on 15 December 2017 in Mushubati.
[73] Jean Kashyengo, interview recorded by Christian Terras, in 'Les mensonges

Catherine Uwimpuhwe, who took part in the siege, also mentioned the existence of lists of people sent to Gitwa:

> The killers' leaders were a certain Semugeshi and [Ariel] Kanyamahanga, the councillor of the sector of Kibingo. Maindron asked these two officials to count the refugees. They told us that Maindron wanted to help us. We were making lists. Everybody wanted to be on these lists to receive aid from Maindron. Even non-Catholics wanted to be on these lists.[74]

More substantiated was the accusation that Maindron gave Ariel Kanyamahanga, the area's councillor, permission to pull down the school chapel of Gitwa as a practical way of disposing of the dead bodies of the victims after the massacre.

On this point, Maindron's version and that of the genocide survivors are in contradiction. In his diary, the French priest simply wrote: 'When will these putrefying bodies be buried?'[75] In Poincaré's book the narrative was developed. 'A few days later,' it reads, 'some peasants described to him [Maindron] the situation: dozens of corpses are decomposing, dogs and vultures are fighting for them. Just in case, he gives money to a few people of good will to perform the first burials.'[76] Fidèle Rurangirwa, who later became executive secretary of the cell of Bugina near Nyamagumba (the new name for Gitwa), had fled the site of the massacre on 13 April and only returned home on 23 August. He was, therefore, not an eyewitness. On the issue of the covering up of victims' bodies, however, he spoke with confidence:

> We have concrete information. On 13 April we lost the battle. On 20 April, Raphaël [Benimana] arrived in Gitwa with Maindron. Maindron gave the authorisation to pull down the chapel on the bodies. Nobody was alive. A week, that is a lot![77]

Mathias Abimana, who served as burgomaster in nearly Mabanza after the genocide and who coordinated the erection of a memorial on the massacre's site,[78] found in the commune's office a document stating that the Congo-Nil parish would receive a piece of land in compensation for the loss of the Gitwa school chapel. It was one of the reasons that caused Ariel

---

par omission de l'abbé Maindron', 87.
[74] Catherine Uwimpuhwe, interviewed on 14 December 2017 in Mushubati.
[75] Maindron, 'Rwanda: l'horreur', 49.
[76] Poincaré, *Rwanda. Gabriel Maindron*, 87.
[77] Rurangirwa, same interview.
[78] See Chapter 4.

Kanyamahanga to be condemned to a jail sentence.[79] This piece of land belonged, according to one of Christian Terras' sources, to a man by the name of Kabano who had been killed during the genocide.[80]

Maindron and the Interahamwe

Several genocide survivors declared that Maindron was often seen in the company of the Interahamwe, the military-trained Hutu extremists who perpetrated and coordinated the killings. During the genocide, he was known for travelling throughout the district under the escort of 'Ostrogoths', as Jean-Baptiste Hategeka described them to Christian Terras, or 'gorillas', the term used by Jean Kashyengo.[81] As we have seen, when Maindron and two Hutu priests came to see Bishop Kalibushi in Gisenyi, according to Fabien Rwakareke, another priest from the diocese of Nyundo, he was accompanied by an Interahamwe with a black beard.[82] The name of this Interahamwe, a native of Rwamatamu, was Cyriaque Bisengimana, alias Savimbi.[83]

Another testimony on Maindron's association with the Interahamwe, but one that I have not been able to verify, is that of Fidèle Rurangirwa. According to him, two Interahamwe, who were in jail at the time, had testified at the *gacaca* of Nyamagumba in 2007 that Maindron was a priest during the day but drank beers with them in a tavern in Congo-Nil at night.[84]

Sabin Hategeka (also known as Hategekimana) gave a similar testimony at Maindron's *gacaca* appeal trial. During a previous *gacaca* trial in Murunda, the same man had declared that 'he did not know the number of people he had killed because he killed so many people in so many places'. He had started to kill in Murunda and from there gone to Gitwa, Mushubati, Rubengera, Kibuye and Bisesero.[85] This time, he first accused Maindron's 'godfather', André Nsingaheye, of having taken part in the Gitwa massacre. He then described a conversation he had had with Maindron:

---

[79] Mathias Abimana, interviews conducted in Kigali on 18 December 2016 and in Rubengera on 4 March 2020.
[80] Terras, 'Les mensonges par omission de l'abbé Maindron', 82.
[81] *Ibid.*, 77, 87.
[82] Fabien Rwakareke, interview conducted on 28 May 2018 in Nyundo.
[83] Terras, 'Les mensonges par omission de l'abbé Maindron', 82, 84.
[84] Fidèle Rurangirwa, interview conducted on 15 April 2017 in Mushubati.
[85] National Service of Gacaca Courts, *Gacaca Courts in Rwanda*, 217.

I arrived at Maindron's place on the 11th [of April 1994]. I wanted to find people to kill. Maindron told us that he did not want to shed blood and that the prefect [of Kibuye] would deal with the matter.[86]

This was a damning statement! Maindron did not condemn the murders. He simply refused to be involved in them and referred the matter to Clément Kayishema, the prefect of Kibuye, who later organised the biggest massacre of Tutsi in the region.

Hategeka's testimony, like that given by the Interahamwe mentioned by Rurangirwa, must be taken with caution. People accused of genocide may have tried to compromise with people they knew in order to appear repentant and to benefit from a lighter sentence. The opposite also happened. In the *gacaca* courts, convicts sometimes put all the blame on themselves in order to protect genocide suspects. This being said, it is unlikely that Hategeka lied to the court, since he had already been sentenced. Accusing Maindron unjustly would not have changed anything.

Hategeka is our only source regarding this episode. Ultimately, whether Maindron pronounced the words attributed to him by the convicted killer will be never established with certainty. What is important is the impression of familiarity that the conversation between the two men conveyed. Judging from what we know of Maindron, it is plausible that the Interahamwe had such a discussion with the priest.

The last refugees

The stories told by the genocide survivors who tried to find refuge in the mission after the fateful bus trip to Kibuye of 13 April have one point in common: the refugees, or at least some of them, found shelter but not for long. Maindron was not prepared to take risks. The survivors that the French army found in the parish house on 1 July had only recently arrived.

One of the sources on this episode is Alphonsine Sillis, who was a seven-year-old child at the time. She ran the long distance between Murama and Congo-Nil seven times, to be told, every time, that she had to return home in Murama. She remembered that the Koko River she had to cross on the way to Congo-Nil was 'red' from the blood of victims. She nevertheless imposed her presence on the priests. She was poorly dressed and Maindron told her one day that she should rather wear her first communion dress. She did not have much to eat.

---

[86] Minutes of the *gacaca* appeal trial held in Gihango from 13 to 20 May 2010, 13.

By then – it must have been late April or May – fifteen girls were staying in the mission. They left one by one. Alphonsine believes that they have all died. After three weeks, Maindron took her to a convent of sisters in Kibuye. Later on, she found shelter in the house of an Interahamwe who, from what she understood, had decided to stop killing people. She remembered having been treated as a slave despite her young age.[87]

Béatrice Van Hoven, a teenage girl also from Murama who spent the time of the genocide in Gisenyi, mentioned, along the same lines, that her uncle, Elias Sebitama, and a few other refugees who had found shelter in the Congo-Nil mission were asked to leave in early May. All have been killed.[88]

The case of Mélane Kanyoni is interesting, because Maindron was known for appreciating this young man who was only Tutsi by his father. In the first days of the genocide he hid in various places, including in the house of his Hutu wife whom he had married only recently; together with her mother, she took great risks to dissimulate him. For a while, he remained in the bushes near the parish, only seeing Maindron at night to ask for bread. He remembered that during one of these nightly visits, Maindron told him: 'God has condemned the Tutsi. They have no chance to survive.' Kanyoni later mentioned this statement to Anastase Uwobibabaje, who repeated it at Maindron's *gacaca* appeal trial.[89] Other refugees arrived in the meantime, but they did not stay. For a few days, Kanyoni hid in a pit at the entrance of the presbytery. Nobody, not even Maindron, noticed him. He was one of the survivors the French military rescued in early July as part of Opération Turquoise. He was overjoyed. He noted, however, that some refugees were not as lucky. They were denied assistance by the French soldiers and were subsequently killed by the Interahamwe.[90]

Also eloquent was the testimony Marthe Nyirahabimana shared with Andrea Grieder on her stay in the parish house:

> I went to Maindron's place where I found many people from Murama. We remained hidden in a room and only went out at night to eat. During the meal, the burgomaster of Rutsiro would come for a chat with Abbé Maindron. We would then hide in the cook's room. We stayed there until May, when took place, in Kibuye, the meeting of political and religious

---

[87] Alphonsine Sillis, interview conducted on 17 June 2017 in Westende, Belgium.
[88] Béatrice Van Hoven, interview conducted on 22 June 2017 in Brussels.
[89] Minutes of the *gacaca* appeal trial held in Gihango from 13 to 20 May 2010, 17.
[90] Mélane Kanyoni, interview conducted on 20 March 2019 in Mushubati.

leaders in which Maindron participated. On his return, he made the following speech: 'The situation is getting more complicated than ever. Until now I have protected you, but now there is nothing else I can do. Try to find a hiding place somewhere else because if the killers found you here they would take the parish money and I would not have enough to bribe them. If you send to me those you will agree to shelter, I shall send you food. I give each of your 300 Rwandan Francs and bread.'[91]

Of all the Tutsi from Maindron's parish who survived until the end of the genocide, the most contemptuous of his attitude towards the refugees was Christine Nyiramana, a woman who found shelter in the house of some people near Gitwa hill before she heard that Maindron was prepared to welcome her. News was circulating that the French soldiers from Opération Turquoise would soon be in the region. As she explained to Christian Terras, it was a *mise en scène* to impress them:

> A few days before the arrival of the French people in Kibuye, Maindron paid people to find the Tutsi survivors in the forest. In my hiding place, we were about ten. Our first move was to refuse to go to the parish. We thought it was a trap. Tutsi have been caught that way some time before. Then Maindron sent us food to soften us in some way. We understood that he had changed his mind because before it was impossible to find refuge at his place. He was scared that his church might be destroyed or that it would be sullied in case of killings inside the building.[92]

Maindron's response

The preceding pages describe, at some length, the memories that the genocide survivors kept of Maindron's role during the genocide and that they shared with outsiders when given the opportunity to talk. To conclude this chapter, we shall examine the response – or lack of response – from Maindron and the people who supported him regarding the accusations levelled against him.

Not much can be said about the French priest's image in Rwanda outside the milieus of genocide survivors. The priests who replaced him in Congo-Nil are all from a younger generation. When asked about how the parishioners saw Maindron, they responded that, in their eyes, he

---

[91] Grieder, *Colline des mille souvenirs*, 111.
[92] Christine Nyiramana, interview transcribed by Christian Terras in 'Les mensonges par omission de l'abbé Maindron', 86.

was a good priest.[93] The matter was not probed further. While being less forthcoming about Maindron, whom he had known in the 1990s, Prosper Ntiyamira, the parish priest of Kivumu, also said that the Catholics of the area remembered him fondly.[94]

The people of Congo-Nil and further afield could not have ignored the fact that Maindron had been accused of playing a role in the genocide. He was mentioned by name on Radio Rwanda at the time of a burial ceremony of genocide victims in Rutsiro in 2004. The burgomaster, Raphaël Benimana, was described as a *génocidaire* and Maindron as a man who was working at his side.[95]

In France, Poincaré's biography of Maindron had a relatively limited readership. In a similar way, the counter-testimony presented by Christian Terras and genocide-memory activists such as Jean-Paul Gouteux[96] attracted little attention beyond the circles of *Golias* readers and the journalists or academics interested in the genocide against the Tutsi.

Occasionally, Maindron expressed his views on Rwanda in the media. In a letter to the editor of the Catholic daily *La Croix* in March 2011, he warned against the zeal of the so-called *génocidaire* hunters. 'Let us not forget that there are people paid to accuse,' he wrote. 'It is easy to confuse criminals and innocents.' For him, the main issue was the crimes committed by the RPF in Zaire. General Kagame, he went on, had been designated by 'French and Spanish judges' as the sponsor of the attack on President Habyarimana's residence in April 1994.[97]

On two occasions Maindron's story came into the open, giving him or his friends the opportunity to respond to the allegations made against him. The first was a television programme subsequent to the publication by the Rwandan government in May 2006 of a 'List of people suspected of having participated in the genocide of 1994 in Rwanda and who are abroad',[98] in which Maindron featured in good place. He was interviewed alongside Jean-Baptiste Hategeka, who spoke from Italy. The film showed

---

[93] Informal conversation held in Congo-Nil on 14 December 2016.
[94] Prosper Ntiyamira, interview conducted on 13 December 2016 in Kayove.
[95] Hirondelle News Agency, 'Rwanda: allégations de génocide contre un prêtre français', 6 July 2004.
[96] Jean-Paul Gouteux, *Un génocide sans importance. La France et le Vatican au Rwanda*, rev. edn (Lyon: Tahin Party, 2007), 76–8.
[97] *La Croix*, 4 March 2011.
[98] 'Liste des personnes suspectes d'avoir commis le crime de génocide au Rwanda en 1994 et se trouvant à l'étranger', n.d. <http://ibihwihwiswa.tripod.com/rwanda/liste_genocide_mai2006.pdf> [accessed 30 July 2019].

him responding to the interviewer's question after Mass in the Vendean church he had served since his return from Rwanda. He denied having done anything wrong. The onus was on his accusers, he declared, to demonstrate his culpability:

> I have nothing to explain. Those who put me on the list will give the explanation. I think that all Rwandans are brothers, of course the priests but even those who are not Christian, Hutu as well as Tutsi. I put my life in danger for the Tutsi during the genocide. I had a machete on my neck. I would do the same for the Hutu. Perhaps that is what disturbs some people.[99]

The documentary on France 3

Maindron was put in the dock for a second time on 23 April 2014 when, as part of the *Pièces à conviction* [Incriminating evidence] monthly programme, the French television channel France 3 broadcast a 55-minute documentary shot by the journalists Jean-Pascal Bublex and Mathieu Sarfati under the title 'Rwanda: les prêtres accusés' [Rwanda: The accused priests]. The occasion was the twentieth anniversary of the genocide. Three priests condemned *in absentia* in Rwanda for their alleged participation in the genocide and living in France were investigated: Gabriel Maindron, Wenceslas Munyeshyaka and Martin Kabalira, a former military chaplain. The documentary was distributed under the title 'La machette et le goupillon' [The machete and the sprinkler], an undisguised reference to *Golias'* July 1995 dossier. Christian Terras was asked to give his opinion on the churches' complicity in the genocide.

Unlike Munyeshyaka, who sued France Télévisions for defamation,[100] Maindron did not respond, but a few people who shared his opinions did. Cécile Hoyeau, in *La Croix*, criticised the documentary for defending the 'thesis' that 'the massacres have been stirred by a Rwandan church which had chosen its side'. She also regretted the choice to show the 'events' in Rwanda 'exclusively through the lens of the editor of *Golias*'.[101]

---

[99] AmatekaRwanda, 'Rwanda: Gabriel Maindron s'explique' (2 November 2006). Video online at <https://www.youtube.com/watch?v=DegmoXkYJrk> [accessed on 1 February 2015].

[100] Munyeshyaka won his case on the grounds that his trial – which resulted in an acquittal a year later – had not been concluded and that one had to respect the presumption of innocence.

[101] Cécile Hoyeau, 'On France 3 the malaise of the Church in Rwanda', *La Croix*, 23 April 2014.

Annick Nedelec, Maindron's long-time friend, vigorously took to his defence in a letter to the editor of *La Croix*. Presenting herself as a direct witness, she reiterated the argument that he had saved many lives:

> In the middle of the genocide I had, almost daily, telephonic conversations with Fr Gabriel Maindron and can testify that he protected Tutsi people, welcoming them in his presbytery and feeding them until the commander of the area chartered a bus, not towards the stadium of Kibuye, as is said in the documentary, but to the neighbouring commune of Mabanza. It is the ambulance of the Spanish sisters of Congo-Nil that took in charge the people who could not board the bus. Fr Maindron, unfairly accused today, really tried everything to save lives. On leaving the presbytery, people even sang hymns to thank him for what he had done for them.[102]

Hervé Cheuzeville, a humanitarian turned author as he described himself, brought the controversy to a higher level in the conservative blog *Vexilla Galliae*. For him, the testimonies from the genocide survivors were lies, extorted by agents of the Rwandan government with a view to discrediting the Catholic Church:

> How can we take seriously the statements made by people living in the Rwanda of Paul Kagame? Under the regime of terror he is imposing, a reporting of foreign journalists is not improvised. It has therefore been conducted with the benevolent collaboration of the authorities, who took it upon themselves to find the incriminating witnesses that were necessary for this work of disinformation. They even found them in prison, among life convicts who probably had nothing to lose and everything to gain from a false testimony.[103]

Maindron declined to grant an interview to the regional daily *Ouest-France*. In one of the fairest known assessments of the subject, the journalist contrasted his reputation as a widely respected priest in France with the accusations made against him in Rwanda. To document Maindron's point of view, he quoted from the short autobiographical notice Maindron had posted on the website of his Vendean parish. 'I stayed in Rwanda during these painful events,' he wrote, 'to try and save

---

[102] *La Croix*, 12 June 2014.
[103] Hervé Cheuzeville, 'Rwanda: des prêtres accusés', Vexilla Galliae, 30 April 1994. < https://www.vexilla-galliae.fr/actualites/europe-international/rwanda-des-pretres-accuses/> [accessed 16 June 2019].

what could be saved. When there was nothing else to do, and the foreigners had left the country, I also left.'[104]

Conclusion

There is indeed a gap between the memories that the genocide survivors had of Maindron's role during the genocide and his own portrayal, relayed in the French Catholic media, of his actions during the same period.

In the eyes of the genocide survivors, Maindron never took risks to save lives. He could have used his good relations with the burgomaster, the prefect and the *gendarmerie*, not to mention the French embassy and the Rwandan government in Kigali, to actively oppose the killings, but he did not. He was all but powerless. The image he projected of himself as a saviour of the Tutsi was deceitful. In effect, he showed little empathy for the victims of the genocide, choosing instead to join the ranks of those who said that the biggest problem in Rwanda after the genocide was the RPF's hunger for power.

In his diary, in his exchanges with Nicolas Poincaré and in the interview he granted me in February 2015, on the other hand, Maindron denied having done anything wrong, except lacking courage in some instances. He insisted that he had hidden Tutsi refugees in his presbytery and that, at least on one occasion, he had put his own life in the balance to prevent a massacre. As evidence, he pointed to his neck, which, according to him, the killer's machete nearly cut off on that day. He mimicked this Christ-like posture on television and on various other occasions.

It is this gap that we need to explore. During the genocide against the Tutsi – like in other mass atrocities such as the Holocaust or apartheid in South Africa – there was a continuum between unhindered involvement in the crime and active resistance to it. If Maindron had 'shed blood', to use the phrase the serial murderer Sabin Hategeka had heard him utter, the conflict of memory would probably be less acute. There would be less denial. The problem with Maindron was his long-time association with some of the killers and with the local authorities who passively witnessed and in some cases actively supported the massacres. They often met and shared the same views on Rwandan politics. Maindron did participate in a meeting of local leaders on 8 April 1994, just before the genocide started in Congo-Nil, and there is evidence that he attended the

---

[104] Bruce Dupont, 'Condamné au Rwanda, l'abbé aussi apprécié en Vendée', *Ouest-France*, 13 May 2015.

meeting chaired by Jean Kambanda, the prime minister of the interim government, in Kibuye on 3 May 1994.

This does not mean that Maindron took part in the planning and the execution of the genocide. It is true that he requested that the two hundred refugees staying in the mission be transported to Rubengera and from there to Kibuye where they were massacred. However, there is no proof that he knowingly sent them to their death. According to the genocide survivors, he allowed Councillor Ariel Kanyamahanga to pull down the school chapel of Gitwa to cover the dead bodies of the genocide victims. He did not kill them.

It is clear that Maindron was aware of the authorities' desire to put an end to the war by destroying all the RPF's 'accomplices'. He knew the situation well enough to have issued some form of public condemnation of the massacres, in the pulpit or at one of the municipal meetings, if he had wanted. Did he not explain to Poincaré, as the latter reported in his book on two occasions, that in a rural village like Congo-Nil the priest had more power and influence than the burgomaster?[105] The testimonies of the survivors depict a man who refused to believe the obvious – that his friends, those he admired for defending the Hutu cause, were providing weapons to the killers and organised their 'work'. He kept repeating to the survivors that there was no risk. His proximity to the CDR and his uncritical reception of the Hutu extremist propaganda prevented him from taking a clear stand when the Tutsi members of parish started to be hunted to death.

By the Rwandan government's standards, Maindron was a low-profile *génocidaire*. No serious attempt was made to extradite him. If an independent trial had taken place, it is unlikely that he would have been condemned. The fault that the genocide survivors accused him of having committed was moral rather than legal. They found his lack of empathy for the victims of the genocide and their families shocking. Particularly revealing was the episode of the visit to Bishop Kalibushi in May 1994 in Gisenyi, to find a replacement for the Tutsi priests murdered in April. For Maindron and his Hutu colleagues, the church had to continue its work, and from that point of view the priority was the administration of sacraments. It was business as usual! They seem to have believed that the war against the RPF could be won and that the extermination of the Tutsi would soon be forgotten.

Maindron's case, as the rest of this book shows, is emblematic. He was not the only cleric to show ambiguity in the face of the genocide. A large

---

[105] Poincaré, *Rwanda. Gabriel Maindron*, 24, 36.

section of the Catholic Church – and the same applied to the Protestant churches – had a deep loyalty to the Habyarimana regime and the Hutu cause in general. As a result, they believed in the necessity of fighting the 'enemies of the people' – the RPF – by all means. They could not and would not accept the reality of the genocide in all its horror. The scene was set for an uneasy relationship between church and state in post-genocide Rwanda.

The story narrated here is significant for another reason. Without the testimony of Jean-Baptiste Hategeka, Maindron's image would probably have remained intact, at least in Europe. But Hategeka's book, which was published in Italy, would have had no impact if Christian Terras had not relayed its message to the public in France and in the rest of the world. Without him, it is doubtful that Maindron's role in the genocide would have attracted the attention of the Rwandan government and he would not have been included in the list of suspected *génocidaires* in 1996. The construction of a public memory of Maindron's role in the genocide resulted from the interaction between memory activists from Italy, France and Rwanda.

Central in this process were the genocide survivors. In the parish of Congo-Nil, only a handful survived. There were a few thousand Tutsi in the area before the genocide. It was the genocide survivors who developed an alternative narrative of Maindron's role in the genocide. Apart from setting up the *gacaca* courts, where the genocide survivors received the opportunity to testify, the Rwandan government played no significant role in the creation of this alternative narrative.

No confrontation has ever taken place between Maindron and his critics. This is regrettable because only a forum of that nature would have allowed a meeting of memories. Implicitly in Maindron's various testimonies and explicitly in Hervé Cheuzeville's blog, the genocide survivors are accused of having made false testimonies, spontaneously or under pressure from the Rwandan government. This is an easy way of walking away from the problem. There may have been contradictions and, in a few instances, factual errors in the genocide survivors' statements. Dismissing them *en bloc*, however, does not make sense. The overwhelming impression that emerges from these testimonies is one of coherence and consistency. The stories told to Christian Terras did not vary from those I recorded twenty years or so later. There is a considerable amount of overlap in the interviews. If Maindron deserves to be heard, the genocide survivors' word must be taken seriously as well.

CHAPTER 10

The quest for forgiveness and reconciliation

Forgiveness and reconciliation have been two recurrent themes in the discourse of the Christian churches since the genocide, including the Catholic Church and the Presbyterian Church, whose histories are narrated in this book. 'The priority for Rwandans is reconciliation,' the Catholic bishops declared in their first joint message after the genocide.[1] 'Now that the genocide is over, the preachers keep talking of reconciliation,' a survivor wrote with a touch of irritation in *Bâtissons*, the newsletter of the Presbyterian Church.[2] Such emphasis is not surprising. Reconciliation, the Rwandan theologian Laurien Ntezimana pointed out, is at the centre of the Christian message. In his second epistle to the Corinthians, Paul wrote that God 'reconciled us to himself through Christ and gave us the ministry of reconciliation' (2 Cor 5:17).[3] Christians are encouraged to reconcile with those who offended them as God does with those who offended him by committing sins against him.

Forgiveness is no less a central part of the Christian message.[4] 'Forgive our trespasses as we forgive those who trespassed against us' (Mt 6:12), Jesus said in the Lord's Prayer, implying that those who want to be forgiven by God have to practise forgiveness themselves. Jesus' last utterance

---

[1] 'Message des Évêques catholiques du Rwanda', Kigali, 13 January 1995 in *La Documentation catholique*, 2133 (2 April 1995), 338.

[2] Justin Hakizimana, 'Avec qui dois-je me réconcilier?', *Bâtissons*, 3 (October 1995), 3.

[3] Laurien Ntezimana, 'La réconciliation des Rwandais, notre mission dans la jungle des passions', in Fulgence Rubayiza, *Guérir le Rwanda de la violence. La Confession de Detmold, un premier pas* (Paris: L'Harmattan, 1998), 73.

[4] Jean-Louis Brugues, 'Le Dieu des pardons', in *Le pardon. Un défi dans l'histoire. Actes du colloque qui s'est tenu à l'ICES en février 2015* (La Roche-sur-Yon: Éditions du CVRH, 2017), 77–81.

on the cross was a call to forgive those had put him to death because they did not know what they were doing (Lk 23:24). One should note, however, that if forgiveness is unconditional on the part of God and the believers who follow his example, the people who want to be forgiven are expected to admit their guilt and repent. Peter, who had betrayed Jesus three times, repented before being forgiven. The proof that Jesus did not hold a grudge against him is that he made of him the 'rock' on which the church would be built (Mt 16:18). But Peter had to admit his guilt first. Judas felt remorse but he did not repent. The Gospel suggests that he was not forgiven (Jn 17:12). It is this part of the Christian message that proved the most problematic in post-genocide Rwanda.

Reconciliation as a mutual process

The language of reconciliation and forgiveness is not without pitfalls. What does it mean to reconcile? In the context of the genocide, who should reconcile with whom and for what? How long does it take to reconcile? The related concept of forgiveness is even more problematic. Is it possible at all to forgive in the case of the genocide? Can one forgive somebody who has never admitted to having done anything wrong?[5]

Reflecting on the 'inexplicable degradation of the Rwandan social fabric,' the Commission for the Revival of Pastoral Activities of the diocese of Butare expressed the magnitude of the challenge. 'How does one explain', it wrote in September 1994, 'that a wife causes the death of her own husband, a married man executes his own spouse, a son kills his own mother or a mother slaughters her own children?'[6] A discourse on reconciliation and forgiveness which underplays the immensely destructive effect of the genocide on the victims, whose pain and anger fuelled resentment and desire for vengeance, and on the perpetrators, who experienced guilt, shame and denial, is not only vacuous but dangerous. In the Rwandan context, cheap reconciliation is tantamount to denialism.

---

[5] For a reflection on forgiveness and reconciliation from a Rwandan point of view, see Odette Mukantagara, *Rwanda. De l'horreur du génocide au pardon et à la réconciliation* (Kigali: Pallotti Press, 2018). See also Anne Kubai, *Being Church in Post-Genocide Rwanda. The Challenges of Forgiveness and Reconciliation* (Uppsala: Life and Peace Institute, 2005); Frida Umuhoza, *In the School of Resilience*, 2nd edn of *Frida, Chosen to Die, Destined to Live* (self-published, 2018).

[6] This is the question raised by Albert Nsengimana in his book *Ma mère m'a tué. Survivre au génocide des Tutsis au Rwanda* (Paris: Hugo Doc, 2019).

Before describing the efforts made by the churches in the matter of reconciliation after the genocide, we need to clarify the terms. Reconciliation is a psychosocial as much as a spiritual process. The American psychologist Ervin Staub, who has done some work in Rwanda, offers a good starting point in that respect. 'We define reconciliation', he wrote, 'as a mutual acceptance by members of formerly hostile groups of each other. Such acceptance includes positive attitudes, but also positive actions that express them as circumstances allow.'[7]

Reconciliation is a mutual process. It requires that both parties, while not ignoring their own pain, agree to recognise the pain of the other. Empathy is essential. In order to reconcile with former enemies, one must develop empathy for what they have gone through. Another condition is security, both at the social and interpersonal levels. Reconciliation was hard to achieve when lone Interahamwe continued to target Tutsi people in Rwanda just after the genocide, on the return of the refugees from Zaire in late 1996, during the Abacengezi War (*Guerre des infiltrés* in French, or Infiltrators' War in English) in north-west Rwanda in the late 1990s and during the *gacaca* trials. The refugees in Zaire who were convinced, rightly or wrongly, that the RPF would jail or kill them the moment they set foot in Rwanda were not ready for reconciliation either. For reconciliation to happen, one needs a safe and caring environment.

On the side of the victims, the biggest obstacle to reconciliation is perpetrator denial. The people who have engaged in extreme and premeditated violence, Staub observed, tend to maintain psychological distance from their own behaviour to avoid being overwhelmed by guilt and horror. To protect themselves from the emotional consequences of their actions, they blame victims and hold on to the ideology that in part motivated, and to them justified, their violence.[8]

Human science scholars have observed that although forgiveness is often interlinked with reconciliation, it can be achieved independently. As Lewis Smedes explained in a widely read book, holding a grudge imprisons, whereas forgiveness sets free. It is possible to forgive a perpetrator without expecting anything in return.[9] This is what Mathias Abimana, a

---

[7] Ervin Staub, Laurie Anne Pearlman, Alexandra Gubin and Athanase Hagengimana, 'Healing, reconciliation, forgiving and the prevention of violence after genocide or mass killing: an intervention and its experimental evaluation in Rwanda', *Journal of Social and Clinical Psychology*, 24 (2005), 301.

[8] *Ibid.*, 303.

[9] Lewis Smedes, *Forgive and Forget: Healing the Hurts We Don't Deserve* (New York: Harper Collins, 1984).

genocide survivor from Congo-Nil with strong Christian convictions, said he did in an interview. After a certain number of years, he decided to let go of his anger and forgive.[10] 'Only those who have taken the time to heal can move forward', echoed Antoine Rutayisire, an Anglican priest who became the team leader of AEE in Kigali after the genocide.[11] In a 1997 article, Modeste Mungwarareba, a genocide survivor, argued that forgiveness 'heals and gives life'. It is a question, he suggested, of 'providing support to the unjust without accepting injustice'.[12] The case of Juvénal Rutumbu also comes to mind. The Catholic theologian from Ruhengeri accused the RPF – in a book written in the late 1990s but published later – of upholding an updated version of the Hamitic theory called naturalism and cast doubt on the reality of the genocide against the Tutsi, but nevertheless advocated unconditional forgiveness on spiritual grounds.[13]

In any event, forgiving is difficult and takes time. As Paul Ricoeur put it, it is 'not easy but not impossible'.[14] If the perpetrator asks for forgiveness or at least acknowledges that the victim is willing to forgive, the process is easier, and one can envisage some form of reconciliation.

In the aftermath of the genocide, the survivor organisations and the Rwandan government were adamant that all genocide perpetrators should face trial, even though the huge number of suspects created quasi-insurmountable logistical problems. The solution it eventually found, as we shall see, was to delegate the task to popular courts called *gacaca*. The genocide survivors' and Rwandan government's insistence that the génocidaires should be punished and thus avoid impunity encountered resistance, not least in the churches, which in some instances seemed to favour reconciliation without admission of guilt, repentance and retribution.

---

[10] Mathias Abimana, interview conducted on 18 December 2016 in Kigali. See Chapters 8 and 9.

[11] Antoine Rutayisire, interview conducted on 15 March 2017 in Kigali.

[12] Modeste Mungwarareba, 'Le pardon, guérison et chemin pour vivre', *Dialogue*, 197 (March–April 1997), 63–8.

[13] Juvénal Rutumbu, Rwanda. *Les voies incontournables de la réconciliation* (Lille: Éditions Sources du Nil, 2013). Vice-rector of Nyakibanda Major Seminary before the genocide, Juvénal Rutumbu was preaching a retreat at the Centre Christus in Kigali on 7 April 1994 when the presidential guard massacred three Jesuits, four diocesan priests and a few consecrated women. He was spared because of his northern accent. See Bernard Jouanno, 'Dossier génocide', *La Croix*, 2 April 2004.

[14] Paul Ricoeur, *Memory, History, Forgetting* (Chicago: Chicago University Press, 2004), 457.

Rather than a conflict between impunity and reconciliation, however, one should speak of a tension between the two. As Ricoeur pointed out, forgiveness and the reconciliation to which forgiveness opens the door do not belong to the same domain as the judicial procedure instituted to prevent impunity. Forgiveness, he wrote, should not be institutionalised, because that would lead to impunity. It can, however, find expression in another mode, essentially in gestures that show the consideration that is due to all human beings, irrespective of their guilt.[15] In other words, the fact that the state represses the crime of genocide should not stop the two parties concerned, the perpetrators and the victims, from engaging in a process of reconciliation.

Reconciliation, one should add, was not the monopoly of the churches and non-governmental organisations. Along with national unity, the term has been used in government circles since 1994. In 1998–9, the discussions held among RPF cadres and civil society representatives at Urugwiro Village (the president's residence in Kigali) brought about the realisation that the genocide trials conducted until then had not been 'leading to reconciliation and agreement between parties but [...] rather hatred among the people'.[16] This set off the creation of the NURC in March 1999. Unlike the TRC in South Africa, this body had no binding power. It complemented rather than replaced the judiciary process. The situations were quite different. While the former apartheid government clearly renounced state violence and racial discrimination, the political and military forces implicated in the Rwandan genocide never admitted to any wrongdoing.

A related difficulty regarding forgiveness and reconciliation is the risk of balancing the crime of genocide, which aimed at exterminating an entire human group and made those who survived like 'the living dead', and the crimes imputed to the RPF, whose existence is widely acknowledged but the scale and intention of which are disputed among politicians and scholars. Some critics of the Detmold Confession, a joint admission of guilt to which we shall soon turn, accused it of balancing out the genocide and the other crimes committed in the region as if they were on the same plane. Here, too, Ricoeur's insights are valuable. Developing empathy for people who suffered during a conflict does not mean that their criminal

---

[15] *Ibid.*, 458.
[16] Office of the President of the Republic, 'Report on the reflection meetings held in the Office of the President of the Republic from May 1998 to March 1999', Kigali, August 1999, 67. On the Urugwiro Village discussions, see Jean-Paul Kimonyo, *Rwanda demain! Une longue marche vers la transformation* (Paris: Karthala, 2017), 211–21.

responsibility, if there is one, should escape retribution. The judicial and interpersonal levels are distinct. It is the pain and not the crime that counts in a process of reconciliation.

In a conflict, there are always different points of view. This is what Antoine Rutayisire, who after his time as an AEE team leader became a commissioner and vice-president of the NURC, expressed in a real-life parable. Remera, a district of Kigali close to the administrative centre where Rutayisire resided at the time, was on the frontline between the RPF army and the forces loyal to the Rwandan government. President Habyarimana's plane had been shot down the night before.

> On 7 April [1994] the militiamen came to our neighbourhood. They had massacred people here in Remera. They arrive at my door. They invade the house. Meanwhile, two RPF soldiers turn up. They shoot. Three militiamen die in front of my house. They were not equipped to fight elite troops. I said: 'Glory to God.' The son of the militiaman said: 'The RPF has killed my father!' Two stories, two perspectives.[17]

Stories of healing and reconciliation in post-genocide Rwanda

Healing and reconciliation go hand in hand after a traumatic event. In order to reconcile with their neighbours, the wounded need to heal. It is a matter of healing not only the bodies when they are injured but the minds and the memories. The survivors also need material security when they set about reconstructing their lives. Many conditions are to be met before they can focus again on the future.

In the weeks and months following the genocide, the first task was to bury the dead, take care of the orphans and reunite them with their families if possible, rebuild the infrastructure and put an end to the acts of vengeance, individual or collective, that were multiplying. Almost immediately, aid agencies arrived in the country while groups of Rwandan Christians, Catholic as well as Protestant, were trying to respond to the crisis.

It took about a year for aid agencies such as Trócaire, World Vision, Feed the Children, the Montreal Institute of Integration and Formation (IFHIM) and African Humanitarian Action (AHA), an African-based humanitarian organisation, to fully appreciate the need for psychosocial support and trauma counselling in the population. Pilot training programmes were put in place and reconciliation workshops were conducted. As a report pointed

---

[17] Rutayisire, same interview.

out, donor efforts initially concentrated on trauma counselling for children. Women, including those who had been raped by the Interahamwe, were neglected in the early phase of the reconstruction.[18]

Local Christian organisations, on their own or with the financial support of international aid agencies, contributed to the effort. Some had overtly religious motivations and borrowed heavily from the Christian language of reconciliation.

This was the case for the AEE, an organisation already working for peace before the genocide which had learnt from the British psychiatrist Rhiannon Lloyd how to run trauma counselling workshops.[19] In July 1995, the AEE organised a ten-week-long 'reconciliation mission' with the help of Michael Cassidy, the South African founder of the organisation, and Desmond Tutu, the Anglican archbishop of Cape Town. This well-planned event included a rally at the Amahoro Stadium 'with about 7000 people singing and rejoicing in the Lord',[20] as well as an encounter with prisoners in an overcrowded prison, a visit to the still-untouched genocide sites of Nyamata and Ntarama and discussions with government officials.

Less ostensibly, the Christian Movement for Evangelisation, Counselling and Reconciliation (MOUCECORE), a Protestant organisation headed by Michel Kayitaba – an Anglican priest from Gikongoro who had survived by moving from one hiding place to another during the entire genocide – organised, on an ongoing basis, biblically based evangelisation sessions. One of the organisation's objectives was to 'assist the reconciliation of the Rwandan people by relying on the Word of God'. In 1995, they hired a professional counsellor to accompany the victims of trauma.[21]

On the Catholic side, an important role-player in post-genocide Rwanda was the Charismatic Renewal Movement. Its most prominent representative in the country was the Emmanuel Community. Established in 1990 by a Christian couple, Cyprien Rugamba and Daphrose Mukansanga, this

---

[18] Krishna Kumar and David Tardif-Douglin, *Rebuilding Postwar Rwanda: The Role of the International Community,* USAID Evaluation Special Study N° 76, July 1996, viii–ix.

[19] On AEE in Rwanda see Tharcisse Gatwa, *The Churches and Ethnic Ideology in the Rwandan Crises 1900–1994* (Oxford: Regnum Books International, 2005), 213–14, 225–7.

[20] Michael Cassidy, 'Ruination and resurrection in Rwanda, being a diarised account of the African Enterprise citywide reconciliation mission in Kigali, Rwanda, 23 July–1 August 1995', unpublished document (African Enterprise, Pietermaritzburg, South Africa).

[21] *Bâtissons,* 3 (October 1995), 4.

spiritually oriented lay Catholic movement had seen a rapid development that was soon interrupted by the genocide, which cost the lives of ten of the forty or so initial members, including the two founders.[22] Quite a few fled to Zaire in July 1994 and some died when the refugee camps were forcefully closed in late 1996.

The ethnic divisions which the genocide had brought to the extreme affected the Emmanuel Community as much as the other sectors of the Catholic Church of Rwanda. This did not prevent it from doing reconciliation work between Hutu and Tutsi after the genocide in areas such as Kigali, Ruhango, Kibeho and Nyamata. In the latter, a small locality in the Bugesera, east of Kigali, thousands of Tutsi had been slaughtered. After the victory of the RPF, their place had been taken by former Tutsi refugees from Uganda who were at loggerheads with the Hutu population. Faced with a divided parish, the local priest called the Emmanuel Community to the rescue. The team members, according to a report, managed to convince the parishioners to talk to each other, and gradually the unity of the parish was restored.[23]

A similar process happened in Mutete, an area in the Byumba diocese that had witnessed the massacre of about a thousand Tutsi on 15 April 1994, with heavy reprisals against Hutu from the RPF army a week later in nearby Muyanza, the parish where Serge Desouter had worked as a missionary in the early 1970s.[24] When Servilien Nzakamwita, a seminary rector whose family had been decimated during an anti-Tutsi pogrom in October 1990, was appointed bishop of Byumba in March 1996, one of his first assignments was to bring peace to the Catholic community of Mutete. The two groups were no longer capable of worshipping together. With funds he had managed to raise, the bishop sponsored the building of thirty houses: ten for families of convicted *génocidaires*, ten for families with a husband or a father awaiting judgement in prison and ten for families of genocide survivors. Against all expectations, the former enemies developed bonds of friendship while building their houses, a Tutsi family going so far as to donate a house to a Hutu family. As a local newspaper

---

[22] Yvonne-Solange Kagoyire, François-Xavier Ngarambe and Jean-Marie Twambazemungu, *Rescapés de Kigali. Témoignage* (Paris: Éditions de l'Emmanuel, 2014).

[23] 'Voyage au Rwanda de Karel Dekempe et Jean-Luc Moens, 2 juin–17 juin 1995.' Document kindly communicated to the author by Jean-Luc Moens.

[24] See Chapter 2. On the genocide at Zoko hill, Mutete, see the testimony of Adrien Bagurijoro in *New Times*, Kigali, 10 March 2014.

put it, 'the survivors built houses for the *génocidaires*'. Similar episodes of reconciliation happened elsewhere in the diocese.[25]

Trauma facilitators from other conflict-ridden countries also intervened. A good example is Michael Lapsley, the founder of the Institute for the Healing of Memories (IHOM) in South Africa. He came to Rwanda in 1998 and again in 2004 to run Healing of Memories workshops. 'In the case of Rwanda,' he commented, 'it will take a long time for most people to fully recover, if they ever do, but I think we succeeded in providing a healing presence for those who trusted us enough to share their terrible stories.'[26]

These stories of healing and reconciliation are truly remarkable, and one could multiply the examples.[27] They should not lead to the conclusion, however, that reconciliation was a common occurrence in post-genocide Rwanda. In 2004, Oreste Incimata, the general secretary of Caritas-Rwanda, prudently noted in a report that 'nobody can determine the degree of reconciliation that has been achieved.'[28] It is one thing for two people or groups of people to listen to each other's stories and reconcile, but it is another for an entire nation to engage in a public discussion about the past and reach a common sense of identity.

The Detmold Confession

The most ambitious reconciliation attempt on the part of the churches or, rather, a group of Christians active in the churches, is the one associated with the Detmold Confession. Detmold is a small town near Hanover where a Rwandan physician by the name of Fulgence Rubayiza had moved with his family after the genocide to complete his training in obstetrics. A member of the Charismatic Renewal Movement, he was involved in an ecumenical prayer group in Hiddesen, a suburb of Detmold.

---

[25] Servilien Nzakamwita, interview conducted on 20 March 2019 in Kigali. See also Faustin Kabanza, 'Saluer le courage de Mgr Nzakamwita en 1994', *Mediapart*, 4 June 2016.

[26] Michael Lapsley, *Redeeming the Past: My Journey from Freedom Fighter to Healer* (Tyger Valley: Struik Christian Media, 2012), 226.

[27] See the case of Musha (Eastern Province), described by Benoît Guillou in *Le pardon est-il durable? Une enquête au Rwanda* (Paris: Éditions François Bourin, 2014).

[28] Oreste Incimatata, 'Perspectives d'avenir', in Commission Épiscopale Justice et Paix, *L'Eglise et la société rwandaise face au génocide et aux massacres dix ans après*, Kigali, March 2004, 198.

In October 1994, about twenty Rwandan Protestants residing in Europe and a few German aid workers had met in Saarbrücken to discuss the Rwandan situation and its significance for the churches. Rubayiza had an idea for a similar meeting, but this time for Protestants and Catholics like himself. From the start, he wanted to include Hutu, Tutsi and Europeans with a link to Rwanda in the project. Something had to be done, he wrote in a letter sent on 1 January 1995 to a few Rwandans residing in Europe, to break the 'infernal cycle of violence' that was tearing Rwanda apart. A 'spiritual combat' had to be fought not against the other but against oneself. Wounded and incapable of overcoming its divisions, the church was 'incapable of preaching a message of forgiveness and reconciliation'.[29]

From 25 to 28 May 1995, fourteen people from Germany, Belgium, Italy and Scotland, mostly Hutu and Europeans, met at his invitation for a time of prayer and discussion on forgiveness and reconciliation in the house of the Benedictine secular institute St Bonifatius in Detmold-Hiddesen. Rubayiza, Tharcisse Gatwa (a Presbyterian theologian then studying in Scotland) and Meinolf Wacker, the local pastor, made presentations. The spirituality of Chiara Lubich's Focolare Movement was one of the inspirations of the meeting.[30]

Following Rubayiza's visits to concerned people throughout Europe, a second meeting took place from 7 to 12 December 1996 in the same venue. This time, there were nine Hutu, nine Tutsi and six Europeans. Some, like Laurien Ntezimana, Modeste Mungwarareba and Jérôme Masinzo, key members of the CRAP in Butare, and Michel Kayitaba, the director of Moucecore, had flown from Rwanda.

As time went on, the programme of discussions prepared beforehand was abandoned and the participants started to share life stories informally. The exchanges became more intimate, especially at night when the participants met in a basement, playing music and drinking beers. The British trauma counsellor Rhiannon Lloyd led prayers with 'the Bible in one hand and a guitar in the other'.[31] Ntezimana described the change of mood in the following manner:

> For three or four days, we were making speeches. In the basement, there were beers, drums and a guitar. While we were playing music, we made a shift from the head to the heart.[32]

---

[29] Rubayiza, *Guérir le Rwanda de la violence*, 20.
[30] Ibid., 29–32. See Guillou, *Le pardon est-il durable?*, 194.
[31] Ibid., 195.
[32] Laurien Ntezimana, interview conducted on 25 February 2017 in Leuze, Belgium.

One evening, quite unexpectedly, one participant, then another, then everybody confessed their guilt and asked for forgiveness. The first was Nicolas Hitimana, a Hutu Adventist married to a Tutsi woman whom he had protected and cared for during the genocide but whose relatives had been involved in the killings. He had managed to flee with his family to Scotland, where he had undertaken further studies.[33] Resentful against the Tutsi because of their participation in post-genocide violence, he had been unable to grasp the depth of his wife's pain as a survivor. After a conversation with Mungwarareba, who shared his experience of having been stabbed by a Hutu before being rescued by another Hutu, he suddenly understood the gap that separated him from his wife and the Tutsi people. He stood up crying: 'Tharcisse always said that we should ask for forgiveness. I did harm to my wife!' In a typical Protestant fashion, he then confessed his guilt, in tears: 'As a Hutu I repent for the suffering I caused to the Tutsi.' Soon after, he spoke over the phone to his wife, who had remained in Scotland.[34]

Others – Hutu, Tutsi and Europeans – followed suit. A Hutu participant declared, for example: 'I have hidden Tutsi people but, I must confess, when the Tutsi refugees came back and accused me of being an Interahamwe, I started to hate the Tutsi.' A former Tutsi refugee from Uganda confessed, on his part, to having never understood the Hutu people's emotions about the hurt their ancestors had suffered at the hands of the Tutsi.[35]

The following morning, at Ntezimana's suggestion, the three groups, the Hutu, the Tutsi and the Europeans, drafted a confession of guilt in three parts. The Hutu confessed to having 'oppressed the Tutsi in various ways since 1959' and committed massacres against them 'at various periods of Rwanda history, culminating in the genocide of 1994'. The Tutsi asked the Hutu to forgive the 'repression and blind vengeance which members

---

[33] See the testimony of Jonathan Kubakundimana, Nicolas Hitimana's son, in Lillia Callum-Penso, 'Rwanda genocide survivor tells family story', *Greenville News*, 14 April 2014.

[34] Tharcisse Gatwa, interview conducted on 9 March 2017 in Butare. Laurien Ntezimana, same interview. There is a striking parallel between the processes followed by the Detmold Confession and the Rustenburg Confession during the transition to democracy period in November 1990 in South Africa. Here a Dutch Reformed theology professor by the name of Willem Jonker unexpectedly confessed on behalf of his church to not having done enough to stop apartheid and several other people or institutions did the same. See Philippe Denis, 'Germany, South Africa and Rwanda: Three manners for a church to confess its guilt', *Studia Historiae Ecclesiasticae*, 43/2 (2017), 8.

[35] Rubayiza, *Guérir le Rwanda de la violence*, 66.

of their groups [had] taken' and the 'certain arrogant and contemptuous attitude' shown to the Hutu. The Europeans expressed regret for having 'discriminated between people by generalising and judging some as good and others as bad'.[36] The same day, the text of the confession was solemnly read during an ecumenical service in one of the churches of Detmold-Hiddesen.

Who should ask for forgiveness?

Strengthened by this experience, Rubayiza, Hitimana, Mungwarareba, Ntezimana, Gatwa and a few others became champions of reconciliation in Rwanda. They published the text of the Confession of Detmold in French, German, English and Kinyarwanda with the help of the local Lutheran parish[37] and distributed it widely. The Brussels-based *Dialogue* magazine, widely seen as the mouthpiece of the Hutu in exile, and *La Nouvelle Relève*, a semi-official publication in Kigali, both reproduced it.[38]

The group, augmented by new participants, met a few times in subsequent years. After two more meetings in Brussels and in the Trappist monastery of Chimay in Southern Belgium, a delegation of twenty-two people effected a mission from 17 July to 2 August 1999 in Rwanda. They met the survivor organisations Ibuka and Avega, visited several prisons and organised – with various degrees of success – public meetings. They were also received by the newly established NURC. The prime minister, Pierre-Célestin Rwigema, sent them a letter of encouragement. The authorities of the Catholic and Protestant churches, meanwhile, did not react.[39]

The intention, expressed during the mission to Rwanda, of establishing a permanent organisation with a staff and a budget never materialised. The group met again in Detmold on 11 June 2005 and in Kigali from 10 to 16 December 2006 amid differences of opinion about the achievements of the Rwandan government. After Rubayiza moved to Ghana for work, the group gradually lost steam.[40]

---

[36] The Detmold Confession, 12 December 1996, in Gatwa, *The Churches and Ethnic Ideology*, 231–2.

[37] *Confession de Detmold, Bekenntnis von Detmold, Confession of Detmold, Intangazo Detmold* (Detmold: Landeskirchenamt der Lippischen Landeskirche, 1996), 58.

[38] *Dialogue*, 195 (January 1997), 58–60; *La Nouvelle Relève*, 334 (15 January 1997), 9.

[39] Guillou, *Le pardon est-il durable?*, 208–13.

[40] Ibid., 215–16.

If the Detmold Confession elicited interest, it also attracted criticism. The Hutu signatories faced, sometimes violently, the opposition of fellow Hutu who felt that not enough was said about the crimes of the RPF in Rwanda and in Zaire. On the Tutsi side, the accusation was that the document undermined the reality of the genocide by balancing it out with the violence suffered by the Hutu.

During the course of 1997, *Dialogue* published, in two batches, eight reactions to the Detmold Confession and four responses from participants. Some of the authors claimed the document should have declared that a double genocide had taken place. Seth Sendashonga, a former cabinet minister in the post-genocide government of national unity who was busy establishing an opposition movement in Nairobi, criticised the 'obvious minimisation of the crimes committed by the APR [the RPF army] as part of its repression campaign and blind violence perpetrated against the Hutu ethnic group in the name of the Tutsi ethnic group'.[41] Only one text, by the former priest Privat Rutazibwa, director of the Rwandan Information Agency, reflected the official Tutsi point of view. It argued that the ethnic problem was a false problem, artificially developed since 1959, and regretted the tendency to fall into 'a balancing act (*équilibrisme*) in which Hutu and Tutsi are equally guilty'.[42]

The signatories did not shy away from addressing the concerns of their critics. To a Hutu relative who had accused him of ignoring the pain of family members abused and killed in the Congolese forest, Rubayiza responded: 'Then what? Because of the wounds I have in my heart do you want me to nurture projects of vengeance? [...] If the Hutu do not recognise the pain of the Tutsi, they should not expect from the Tutsi that they recognise the pain of the Hutu.' For his part, Gatwa addressed the criticism that the Detmold Confession considered the Tutsi and the Hutu globally responsible for the crimes committed in their name:

> Did we globalise? Yes and no. [...] Do you try to convince me that anybody ignored that killing was a crime? If Rwandan society is an organic body on the sociological level and a mystical body on the spiritual level, then any fault of a member has an impact on the entire group and the disgrace only

---

[41] Seth Sendashonga, 'Pour le pardon et la justice', *Dialogue*, 197 (March–April 1997), 48.
[42] Privat Rutazibwa, 'Un pas vers la réconciliation ou piétinement vers le racisme', *ibid.*, 42.

leaves room for harmony when the evil that has been committed is regretted and a process of reparation and reconciliation undertaken.[43]

Restoring the traditional *gacaca* to bring about reconciliation[44]

Meanwhile, reflection was taking place in government circles on the manner of resolving the tensions affecting Rwandan society in the aftermath of the genocide. The result was the institution of popular courts called *gacaca* in 2001. It is a little-known fact that members of the Catholic Church, and in particular a seminary professor, future rector and bishop by the name of Smaragde Mbonyintege, played an active role in this discussion. The Catholic Church piloted its *gacaca* in the late 1990s before the state put them in place. Unlike the official *gacaca*, the Christian *gacaca* did not have the authority to impose sanctions. Their only function was to facilitate a process of reconciliation. As mentioned earlier, the Protestant churches also promoted reconciliation but in different ways.

The first Rwandan official to envisage the possibility of resorting to the traditional *gacaca* in dealing with genocide crimes was Tito Rutaremara, one of the founders of the RPF and its president from 1987 to 1993. A member of the Rwandese Alliance for National Unity, a movement of Tutsi refugees established in Nairobi in 1979 that had morphed during December 1987 into the more radical and effective RPF, he had been exposed, during a stay in Paris, to the Marxist concept of popular insurgency as practised, for example, in Latin America.[45] This made him believe that popular courts could play a role in the situation Rwanda was experiencing after the genocide.

By the time the genocide broke out in April 1994, the *gacaca* already existed in Rwanda but, as the Rwandan lawyer Charles Ntampaka pointed out, it had been evolving. The term *gacaca* means 'grass' in Kinyarwanda. Traditionally, the *gacaca* was an informal and temporary open-air procedure of conflict resolution between members of the same lineage or of different lineages. All the male members of the concerned community had to be present. The aim of the process was reconciliation. There was no reference to a code of law. Only petty crimes and property issues were

---

[43] Tharcisse Gatwa, 'Pas de globalisation', *Dialogue*, 198 (May–June 1997), 97.
[44] This section borrows from an article published by the author in the *Journal for the Study of Religion*, 32/1 (2019), 1–27 under the title 'Christian *gacaca* and official *gacaca* in post-genocide Rwanda'.
[45] Jean-Paul Kimonyo, *Rwanda demain!*, 113.

debated, not blood crimes. Similar conflict resolution mechanisms existed under different names in other African countries, including South Africa.[46] The *gacaca* that the Belgian political scientist Filip Reyntjens described in a 1990 article on the basis of fieldwork conducted in the Butare area in the late 1980s had already been transformed. It was an institution used by the families and the local authorities to arbitrate minor conflicts before referring them to a higher court if no agreement could be reached. The district tribunal served as appeal court.[47] By contrast, the traditional *gacaca* had nothing to do with a centralised, state-sponsored judicial system.

Soon after his installation as president of Rwanda in July 1994, Pasteur Bizimungu asked Rutaremara to find a way of dealing with the perpetrators of the genocide.[48] It was at the latter's instigation that an article on the need to 'restore the institution of the *agacaca* for the peaceful settlement of conflicts' was included in the action plan of the Ministry of Justice adopted on 20 August 1994.[49]

These discussions took place at Urugwiro Village. At one of the meetings, Jyoni wa Karega, an intellectual who had fled to Zaire in the 1960s at the time of the anti-Tutsi pogroms and become a professor of history there before returning to Rwanda after the genocide, was asked to collect documentation on the traditional *gacaca*. He had just been appointed dean of the Faculty of Arts at the National University of Rwanda in Butare, which was in the process of reconstructing itself after the loss of lives and property endured during the genocide.[50]

For this project, wa Karega received the support of the UN High Commissioner for Refugees, the Swiss Development Agency, the United

---

[46] Charles Ntampaka, 'Le retour à la tradition dans le règlement des différends: Le *gacaca* du Rwanda', *Dialogue*, 186 (October–November 1995), 95–104.

[47] Filip Reyntjens, 'Le *gacaca* ou la justice du gazon au Rwanda', *Politique Africaine,* 40 (1990), 31–41.

[48] Tito Rutaremara, interview conducted by Jens Meierhenrich on 8 July 2002 in Kigali, quoted in Jens Meierhenrich, 'The invention of gacaca: A logic of institutional choice', paper presented at a seminar in the Stanford Center on Democracy, Development and the Rule of Law, 16 May 2007.

[49] Ntampaka, 'Le retour à la tradition', 95; Stef Vandeginste, 'Justice, reconciliation and reparation after genocide and crimes against humanity: The proposed establishment of popular gacaca tribunals in Rwanda', paper read at the All-Africa Conference on African Principles of Conflict Resolution and Reconciliation, UN Conference Centre, Addis Ababa, 8–12 November 1999, 18.

[50] Jyoni wa Karega, interview conducted on 25 May 2018 in Kigali.

States Agency for International Development and Oxfam Quebec.[51] His first task was to build a research team. He approached four university colleagues, Déogratias Byanafashe, Aloys Muberanziza, Jean-Chrysostome Munyampirwa and Jean-Chrysostome Nkejabahizi; two members of the Scientific and Technological Research Institute (IRST), Philbert Kagabo and Ladislas Twahirwa; and Smaragde Mbonyintege, a professor of theology at the Catholic major seminary of Nyakibanda who was appointed rector of the seminary a year later and became bishop of Kabgayi in 2006. Nyakibanda was a short distance from Butare. The dean and the rector, both men of letters, used to socialise in the university town.[52] Mbonyintege was released from his teaching duties to dedicate himself to the project. He used seminary students as research assistants.[53]

This is how, at a critical moment of Rwanda's history, a partnership was established between the National University of Rwanda in Butare, an institution with close links to the new Rwandan government, and the major seminary of Nyakibanda. All team members were tasked with investigating a certain sector, including Mbonyintege, who conducted research in the area close to the seminary. Jyoni wa Karega and his colleagues presented the preliminary results of the research at a meeting held in Kigali on 13 July 1995. The report of the first phase was published in January 1996 and that of the second phase, in June of the same year. Tito Rutaremara attended the presentation of the final report. According to Mbonyintege, he engaged vigorously but sympathetically with the findings of the study.[54]

By then, the Rwandan government had not yet decided to initiate a *gacaca* process in the country, but the idea was in the air. In November 1995, Philbert Kagabo, a member of wa Karega's team, had introduced the idea of the *gacaca* at the International Genocide Conference in Kigali. Four priests, including Mbonyintege, were among the 165 attendees. The agreement was that the genocide perpetrators could not simply receive amnesty,

---

[51] *Gacaca. Le droit coutumier au Rwanda. Rapport final de la première phase d'enquête sur le terrain réalisé par les chercheurs de l'Université Nationale du Rwanda (UNR), de l'Institut de Recherche Scientifique et Technologique (IRST-Butare), du Grand Séminaire de Nyakibanda* (Kigali: Nations Unies, Haut-Commissaire aux Droits de l'Homme, Opération sur le terrain au Rwanda, January 1996). A second volume with a report on the second phase of the project was published in June 1996.

[52] Wa Karega, same interview.

[53] Smaragde Mbonyintege, interview conducted on 13 December 2016 in Kigali.

[54] Mbonyintege, same interview.

as in South Africa, for example. New forms of retribution had to be found. The conference resolved that 'in cases not involving crime against the person, customary Rwandan procedures such as the AGACACA [should] be used, or adapted, to the extent possible'.[55]

The research report of wa Karega and his colleagues revealed that, in the aftermath of the genocide, the *gacaca* method of conflict resolution had already been experimented with, or at least proposed, in various parts of the country. Philbert Kagabo, for example, described how a Wisemen Council (*Conseil des Sages*) had been instituted in Kigombe, in the Ruhengeri prefecture, to deal with land disputes and marital conflicts.[56] The report of the second phase of the project showed that various forms of *gacaca*, with or without links to the local authorities and the tribunals, had been mooted in the Kigali, Butare, Gitarama, Nyamata, Kibungo, Gikongoro, Cyangugu and Byumba areas. In all these places the informants, whether private citizens or public officials, had some knowledge of the traditional *gacaca*.

Mbonyintege's summary report, which was included in the report of the first phase of the project, discussed 'the role that Gacaca could play in the reconciliation of Rwandans'.[57] He noted that the traditional *gacaca* facilitated reconciliation but did not allow impunity. He added that the current context made things difficult because the different individuals and factions developed an understanding of peace and reconciliation that fitted their particular interests. It was the task of the tribunals, and not of the *gacaca*, to judge the murders, rapes, and thefts committed during the genocide. Where the *gacaca* could help was in establishing the truth and promoting the true values on which society could reconstruct itself. It did not help to put the Hutu on one side and the Tutsi on the other side. One should rather build associations between the two in the task of reconstruction.[58]

---

[55] *Recommendations of the conference held in Kigali from November 1st to 5th, 1995 on Genocide, Impunity and Accountability: Dialogue for a National and International Response* (Kigali: Office of the President, 1995). See William Schabas, 'Genocide trials and *gacaca* courts', *Journal of International Criminal Justice*, 3 (2005), 1–17; Paul Christoph Bornkamm, *Rwanda's Gacaca Courts: Between Retribution and Reparation* (Oxford: Oxford University Press, 2012), 25.

[56] *Gacaca, Le droit coutumier au Rwanda. Rapport final de la première phase d'enquête*, 29–30.

[57] Mboyintege, same interview.

[58] *Gacaca, Le droit coutumier au Rwanda. Rapport final de la deuxième phase d'enquête*, 35–7.

The Year 2000 Jubilee

The ideas expressed in Mbonyintege's report found expression, three years later, in the Christian *gacaca* conducted in various sectors of the Catholic Church of Rwanda during the synodal process leading to the celebration of the Year 2000 Jubilee. The Nyakibanda theologian actively contributed to the popularisation of the concept of *gacaca* in ecclesiastical circles. In August 1995, for example, he published in the Catholic magazine *Urumuri rwa Kristu* an article on the *gacaca* as an instrument for reconciliation[59] – an article that found readers not only in Rwanda but in the exile community in Europe.[60] His promotion to the rectorship of the Nyakibanda Major Seminary in April 1996 increased his influence.

In the Catholic Church, a Jubilee is a special year of forgiveness and reconciliation celebrated every twenty-five years throughout the world. The preparation for the Year 2000 Jubilee, which coincided with the advent of the third millennium, started in November 1994 with Pope John Paul II's apostolic letter *'Tertio Millenio Adveniente'*, addressed to all bishops, priests, and lay people. In 2000, the Catholic Church was also to celebrate the arrival of the first missionaries in Rwanda in Save near modern-day Butare (or Huye as it was recently renamed), 100 years earlier. By the end of 1996, the social and political situation had stabilised enough for the Rwandan bishops to apply their minds to the preparation of this double jubilee. On 12 November, they issued a pastoral letter entitled *'Let us prepare the 2000 years of Christianity and the 100 years of the arrival of the Good News in Rwanda'*.[61] By then, with the return of about 600,000 refugees to Rwanda after the dismantlement of the camps in Zaire, the polarisation between the Rwandans in exile and those remaining in the country was subsiding. The country was moving forward despite guerrilla warfare in the north-west. Gradually, a *modus vivendi* between the Rwandan state and the Catholic Church was found. The time had come for the church as an institution to recognise the reality of the genocide.

The Year 2000 Jubilee, which could have easily become a non-event, as in other countries in the world, became an occasion for the Catholic Church of Rwanda to initiate a process of self-reflection and mutual sharing on the genocide against the Tutsi. Until then, only the most progressive

---

[59] Smaragde Mbonyintege, 'Gacaca ishobora ite kongera kuba inzira y'ubwiyunge bw'abanyarwanda' [How the *gacaca* can continue to be a way of conciliation for the Rwandans], *Urumuri rwa Kristu*, 15 August 1995.

[60] Ntampaka, 'Le retour à la tradition', 96.

[61] Guillou, *Le pardon est-il durable?*, 124.

sectors of the Catholic Church had the courage to look at its moral responsibility in the genocide and examine how the work of evangelisation could be re-established on a new basis. The church leadership was reluctant to admit its close association with the former regime and its blindness to the ideological causes of the massacres. It only spoke of the Hutu priests and lay people, fairly numerous indeed, who had risked their lives to protect the Tutsi. Thanks to the insights of priests such as Smaragde Mbonyintege and Modeste Mungwarareba, the newly appointed general secretary of the Bishops' Conference, or bishops like Frédéric Rubwejanga in Kibungo, the idea started to gain currency that it did not make sense to celebrate the Jubilee without looking back at what had happened in 1994. The Catholic leadership, however, only completed half the journey. In conformity with the doctrine which Pope John Paul II had defined in a March 1996 document,[62] they recognised the failings of individual members of the church, but not of the church as a whole.

An extraordinary synod on ethnocentrism

Between 4 and 7 July 1998, a meeting of 100 priests and four bishops held at Nyakibanda Major Seminary recommended that an extraordinary synod on 'ethnocentrism' should take place. There was, one should note, ambivalence in the Catholic Church leaders' terminology at the time. The pastoral texts of this period indiscriminately spoke of 'ethnocentrism', 'ethnic racism' and 'ethnism' (*ethnisme*). The third expression, which is widely used in Rwanda today, is the best to express the ideological nature of the essentialist discourse on Hutu and Tutsi identities that eventually led to the genocide against the Tutsi. While not incorrect, the term 'ethnocentrism' is less indicative of the ideological nature of the genocide.

Yet, this was a breakthrough. For the first time, a large Catholic body declared its willingness to honestly confront the reality of ethnic division in church and society. The term 'genocide' was not used, but it was on everybody's mind. In the Presbyterian Church, a similar process, admittedly more radical, had happened two years earlier when the General Synod of the church publicly repented for its failure to oppose the genocide and the massacres.[63]

At the Nyakibanda meeting, the *gacaca* was hailed as a methodology that would allow the Christian community to come to terms with the

---

[62] See Chapter 7.
[63] See Chapter 5.

tensions born of the genocide. The findings of the wa Karega research, in which Mbonyintege, by now rector of the seminary, had participated, were presented to the delegates.[64] 'During this period of preparation for the Jubilee,' a report announced, 'each diocese will organise a synod that will proceed to the analysis of the issue of ethnic racism (*racisme ethnique*) that prevents the church from moving forward'.[65] Another report quoted the declaration that 'priority should be given to the traditional *gacaca* [...] in the preparation of the Jubilee, that is, a space where different Christian representatives meet and tell the truth'.[66]

At a meeting of the National Commission for the Jubilee held on 25 August 1998, the Rwandan bishops formally accepted the recommendations of the Nyakibanda meeting. Three months later, they announced, in the fourth preparatory letter for the Jubilee, the celebration of 'an extraordinary synod on the ethnocentrism that has provoked the sclerosis of Rwandan society'.[67] They would resort, they added, 'to the traditional culture of *gacaca*' which aimed 'at arbitrating divisions and conflicts, at punishing, counselling and reconciling'.[68] They exhorted the members of the church 'to have the courage to speak openly of the problem [of ethnocentrism] according to [their] understanding while making the effort of listening to and taking into account the opinion of others'. 'What we want', they added, 'is to incite people to share the truth in a climate of dialogue, to support each other in the sufferings they have endured, to recreate trust and to seek solutions together with the many problems they are facing'.[69]

It is worth noting that during precisely the same period, civil society representatives and people close to the government were meeting at Urugwiro Village on a weekly basis to discuss the problems facing the country. One of these was the overcrowding of prisons. On 17 October 1998, they recommended the establishment of a commission to look

---

[64] Paul Rutayisire, 'Le Catholicisme rwandais: un regard interrogateur', in Tharcisse Gatwa and Laurent Rutinduka (ed.), *Histoire du christianisme au Rwanda* (Yaoundé: Éditions CLÉ, 2014), 318.

[65] *Ihugurwa ry' abapadiri* (1998), 48, quoted in Rutayisire, 'Le Catholicisme rwandais', 308.

[66] *Kinyamateka*, 1143 (1998), 2, quoted *ibid.*, 308.

[67] Joseph Ngomanzungu, 'Messages et lettres pastorales des Évêques Catholiques pendant la période 1994–2004', *Urunana. Revue des Grands Séminaristes*, 108 (2004), 21.

[68] *Kinyamateka*, 1507 (1999), quoted in Rutayisire, 'Le Catholicisme rwandais', 309.

[69] *Ibid.*

into mechanisms that might increase popular involvement in the judicial proceedings against suspected genocide.[70] This new form of jurisdiction would be like the traditional *gacaca* but would also have the power to administer justice. The *gacaca* would become the arm of the state's judicial power at a local level. Its reconciliatory function was not abandoned, since it gave victims and perpetrators the occasion to talk to each other, but it was no longer the main feature of the institution, as in the traditional *gacaca* and the Christian *gacaca*.

On the whole, the announcement of the extraordinary synod on ethnocentrism was well received in the Catholic Church. Some sectors of the church had, in fact, anticipated the process chosen for the extraordinary synod. In 1997, Simon Gasibirege, a psychologist teaching at the National University of Rwanda in Butare, had started to run sessions for priests and religious leaders that prefigured, in some way, the Christian *gacaca* of later periods.[71] In the Rilima parish, a genocide site in the Bugesera, south-east of Kigali, a form of *gacaca* had taken place during the course of 1998.[72]

The idea of a synod on ethnocentrism also met with resistance. Jean Ndorimana, at the time vicar general of the diocese of Cyangugu, referred in an interview to a meeting of the National Commission for the Jubilee during which no consensus could be reached on the need to discuss the ethnic problem. In the end, the archbishop of Kigali, Thaddée Ntihinyurwa, arbitrated in favour of those who wanted an open discussion on this topic.[73] Some wondered if the church was ready for a debate on ethnocentrism. 'Confronting the past', the editor of the Catholic newspaper *Kinyamateka* argued, 'is problematic for people who have to relate, in words or through their example, to people who are still under the shock of the Rwandan genocide and its consequences'.[74] Félicien Mubiligi, the former vicar general of the Butare diocese, was sceptical about the church's readiness to embark on such an ambitious process.

---

[70] Vandeginste, 'Justice, reconciliation and reparation after genocide', 1; Bornkamm, *Rwanda's Gacaca Courts*, 25; Kimonyo, *Rwanda demain!*, 217–18. The Urugwiro Village meetings took place from May 1998 to March 1999.

[71] Simon Gasibirege, interview conducted on 12 December 2016 in Kigali.

[72] *Kinyamateka*, 1488 (1998), 6, quoted in Rutayisire, 'Le Catholicisme rwandais', 308.

[73] Jean Ndorimana, interview conducted on 28 March 2017 in Butare.

[74] *Kinyamateka*, 1509 (1999), 6, quoted in Rutayisire, 'Le Catholicisme rwandais', 310.

'We react to things as they come', he wrote in a church magazine, 'and we respond to emergencies, often satisfying ourselves with patching up holes. Fundamentally, we remain immobile precisely because of the paralysis that is affecting us.'[75]

The Christian *gacaca*

The synodal process opened in the diocese of Butare on 5 September 1998 – two months before the bishops ratified the choice of ethnocentrism as a theme for the extraordinary synod. The diocese of Kibungo followed on 6 December 1998. The dioceses of Nyundo and Ruhengeri, in north-west Rwanda, delayed the opening of the synod because of the guerrilla war waged by the former Interahamwe forces in this part of the country. In the diocese of Gikongoro, the process came to a halt in April 1999, when the bishop, Augustin Misago, was put in jail for his alleged participation in the genocide. He was cleared by a court fourteen months later.[76] Training sessions took place in most dioceses, facilitated by experts such as the clinical psychologist and academic Simon Gasibirege. The process ended with a synodal assembly bringing together clergy and laity.[77]

Paul Rutayisire noted the diverse approaches the nine dioceses of Rwanda took towards the synod. In his opinion, only three of them – Kigali, Cyangugu and Nyundo – seriously tackled the issue of 'ethnism' (*ethnisme*) and made use of the *gacaca* methodology in a consistent way.[78] In the Kabgayi diocese, ethnocentrism was only one theme, the others being family and education. The same applied to the Butare diocese. In dealing with the consequences of the genocide, the diocese of Kibungo tended to take a spiritualising approach.[79]

In all dioceses, except that of Ruhengeri because of the insecurity reigning there at the time, the synod started with a solemn Mass celebrated

---

[75] *Ihugurwa ry' abapadiri*, 1998, 37, quoted *ibid.*, 311.
[76] See Chapter 7.
[77] Commission Épiscopale du Clergé, *Évaluation du processus synodal: Actes de la session des prêtres, Nyakibanda du 28 Août–1er Septembre 2000* (Kigali: Commission Épiscopale du Clergé, 2000).
[78] On the Christian *gacaca* in the Catholic diocese of Kigali, see Rutayisire, 'Le Catholicisme rwandais', 316–18; Emmanuel Ngiruwonsanga, 'The shortcomings of capitalism and communism in light of John Paul II's "humanness"', unpublished master's thesis, Atlantic School of Theology, Halifax, Nova Scotia, 2013; Guillou, *Le pardon est-il durable?*, 125–6.
[79] Rutayisire, 'Le Catholicisme rwandais', 315.

by the bishop with all his priests. The objectives of the synod were then explained to the participants: 'Of all the problems faced by the Church', Anastase Mutabazi, the bishop of Kabgayi, declared, 'that of ethnism goes on for ever and is at the root of all other problems. We cannot relax and prepare the Jubilee while our society is eaten up by mistrust, suspicion, contempt, vengeance, all feelings that are dictated by ethnic differences.'[80]

In all the dioceses, structures were put in place to steer the synodal process. The first step was to organise assemblies during which experts and other knowledgeable people would give input on topics such as the history of Rwanda, trauma, healing, reconciliation, non-violence and human rights. The movement then trickled down to the parish level with the assistance of 'synod facilitators' (*abakangurambaga ba sinodi*). Audiences such as school learners, religious communities, prisoners, intellectuals and families were targeted.[81]

In the dioceses that chose to follow the *gacaca* methodology, the participants were encouraged to confess their sins to the congregation and ask for forgiveness from the people they had wronged. This applied to genocide-related crimes as well as minor offences. Forgiveness was the key. In a report published in 2003, Alice Karekezi observed that 'embedded in the Christian *gacaca* is the notion that, once an individual has confessed certain sins, it is the "divine obligation" of those personally offended or the general congregation to forgive the sinner'.[82] Stories of reconciliation in the communities, having practised the Christian *gacaca*, were not rare; however, they only concerned a relatively small number of genocide crimes.

The Charismatic movement and Father Ubald's *gacaca*

The Emmanuel Community also heeded the November 1998 bishops' call to prepare for the Jubilee with an extraordinary synod on ethnocentrism. The Community decided 'not without questions and fears', as the team

---

[80] *Ibid.*, 312.
[81] *Ibid.*, 315.
[82] Alice Karekezi, 'Juridictions gacaca: Lutte contre l'impunité et promotion de la réconciliation nationale', in E. Ntaganda (ed.), *Les juridictions gacaca et les processus de réconciliation nationale*. Cahiers du Centre de Gestion des Conflits, 3 (Butare: Université Nationale du Rwanda, 2001), 34; Philip Clark, *The Gacaca Courts, Post-Genocide Justice and Reconciliation in Rwanda* (Cambridge: Cambridge University Press, 2010), 66.

leader Jean-Luc Moens noted in a visit report,[83] to apply the *gacaca* methodology to themselves. Several meetings prepared a general assembly in July 1998 that paved the way to a *gacaca* process in four steps in all the areas where the Community had members. A final assembly closed the cycle. The Emmanuel Community developed its own interpretation of the *gacaca* in line with its spiritual tradition:

> It was clear that the objective of the Gacaca was not to seek culprits but rather to show how each one lived this situation. It consisted in hearing the teachings [of the Community] and taking part in adoration and on that basis looking at one's situation and sharing it with others, as one decided, as one wanted, in truth, as much as one felt comfortable with and in all freedom. The wisemen of the traditional Gacaca had been replaced by Jesus and the grass by the adoration. This changed the entire perspective. It was about exposing oneself to the mercy of Jesus. [...] Understood like this, the Gacaca could be a way of reconciling with oneself, with God, with the other.[84]

This methodology and this spirituality had repercussions beyond the Emmanuel Community and more particularly in the south-eastern diocese of Cyangugu. In 1998 Ubald Rugirangoga, a Tutsi priest who had tried, in vain, to prevent a massacre of refugees in his parish of Nyamasheke during the genocide before fleeing to Cyangugu and from there to Bukavu, became the secretary of the synod in the diocese of Cyangugu, while serving in the Mushaka parish where he had been sent in the meantime. He had close links with the Emmanuel Community. Like most survivors, he had lost family members to the genocide. During his ministry in Nyamasheke in the early 1990s, he had rather discreetly started a healing ministry, which he later developed in Mushaka and other areas.

In a document he subsequently posted on his website, Rugirangoga described his experience of the Christian *gacaca* in the following terms:

> I helped my parishioners to do a good synod. They openly exchanged views, debated on the problems they were facing and came to the conclusion that being part of an ethnic group was not a problem. The ethnic ideology was a political creation to manipulate the population. Our task was to

---

[83] Jean-Luc Moens, 'Voyage au Rwanda 3–17 janvier 2000'. Document kindly communicated to the author by Jean-Luc Moens.
[84] *Ibid.*

help the Christians to get out of this ideology by describing to them how the genocide against the Tutsi had been effected in the parish.[85]

Later on, when the official *gacaca* was in full swing, Rugirangoga imagined a process that resembled, in some way, that of the Emmanuel Community. It consisted in organising, according to a set schedule, separate recollections for the genocide survivors and for the people accused of having been involved in the genocide or their relatives, with a view to helping them to reconcile privately or in public, if they chose to do so. The process culminated in a joint 'feast of reconciliation' for both groups a few weeks later.[86] Subsequently, Rugirangoga organised recollections for a third group, the Hutu who had witnessed the genocide and tried to give support to the Tutsi when they were threatened by extermination.

In the same document, he explained that he had developed this method to 'calm the spirits' of his parishioners during the *gacaca* period:

> On the eve of the Gacaca trials, the convicts suspected of having perpetrated the genocide who admitted their sin were liberated in big numbers. This created a panic among the victims of the genocide against the Tutsi. Terrified, they confided to me who was their priest that they felt threatened. They thought that the *génocidaires* who had been liberated in big numbers would kill them because no witness of the genocide against the Tutsi should survive. This incited me to organise the recollections in order to calm the spirits.[87]

The celebration of the Jubilee

The Christian *gacaca* cannot be disassociated from the extraordinary synod on ethnocentrism held in preparation for the Year 2000 Jubilee. The manner in which the Jubilee was celebrated at the end of the process, in February 2000, reflected the spirit that reigned during the Christian *gacaca* sessions.

During the Jubilee celebration in Save, the site of the oldest Catholic mission station in Rwanda, the Catholic bishops made a first step towards a full confession of guilt. The Rwandan president, Pasteur Bizimungu,

---

[85] Ubald Rugirangoga, 'Information sur la pastorale de pardon et réconciliation dans la paroisse Mushaka' [2013], 2 <https://frubald.files.wordpress.com/2013/04/information-sur-la-pastorale.pdf> [accessed 9 February 2019].
[86] *Ibid.*, 4.
[87] *Ibid.*, 2.

and other dignitaries were present. In a prayer addressed to God – not to the victims, or at least not explicitly so – the bishops asked forgiveness for 'those who prepared and executed the genocide and the massacres, who deliberately shed the blood of others, who killed by vengeance, who blindly followed orders and who could not discern what was contrary to the Gospel'. They also asked forgiveness for the priests and religious leaders 'who, in moments of division, failed to be credible signs of unity and communion', for the political leaders 'who neglected their duty' and for the religious leaders 'who did not have any discernment in their relations with the powerful'.[88]

Several bishops made a confession of guilt in their individual capacities during the Jubilee celebrations. The bishop of Byumba, Servilien Nzakamwita, was particularly outspoken: 'As we celebrate the Jubilee of Evangelisation', he said, 'we feel ashamed to see that more than half of the Rwandan population that claimed to be Christian could not stop nor avoid the brutalities of the genocide and of the massacres perpetrated in this country'. Bishop Rubwejanga from Kibungo wondered, at a celebration held in Kabgayi, if the leaders of the church should not ask themselves if they had not committed 'faults similar to those for which God blamed the pastors from olden times'. He called for forgiveness in his capacity as a pastor. 'We asked for forgiveness', he said, 'for the sins committed by the priests in the care of the souls that God had entrusted to them'.[89]

As Rutayisire pointed out, these confessions of guilt have not been widely publicised.[90] In the eyes of the genocide survivors and in government circles, they were deemed insufficient. The Catholic Church, they said, only acknowledged the involvement of certain of its members in the genocide against the Tutsi and not that of the institution itself. The church did not recognise its role in the spreading of the ethnic stereotypes that contributed to the eruption of the genocide in April 1994.

That was true. However, it remains that the attitude of repentance shown by the Catholic leadership during the Jubilee celebrations was a significant departure from the defensiveness and quasi-denial adopted by many church leaders and priests in the period immediately following the genocide. Quite a few Catholics, one should remember, had been feeding the discourse on the double genocide, which *de facto* trivialised the genocide against the Tutsi and made it almost acceptable. There is no doubt that

---

[88] *Kinyamateka*, 1546 (February 2000), 7.
[89] Bulletin de la Conférence Épiscopale du Rwanda, 13–17 (1999–2000), 39, quoted in Rutayisire, 'Le Catholicisme rwandais', 322.
[90] Rutayisire, 'Le Catholicisme rwandais', 323.

the Christian *gacaca* contributed to the change of heart, at least to a certain degree, in the Catholic leadership. This extended process of sharing experiences and searching for truth during the Christian *gacaca* led to the recognition that the church had to be more overt about its responsibility for the tragedy.

Christian *gacaca* and official *gacaca*

As already mentioned, the decision to promote the Christian *gacaca* to prepare for the Jubilee and the decision to establish the official *gacaca* to resolve the problem of prison overcrowding were made during the same period, the first at a meeting held in Nyakibanda in July 1998 and the second at Urugwiro Village in October 1998. When the news filtered through that the Catholics were organising *gacaca* sessions, many people, including congregants, were wondering if the church was not competing with the state in dealing with the consequences of the genocide.

However, the two institutions had different aims. The aim of the Christian *gacaca* was to promote reconciliation in communities divided by the genocide by bringing together victims and perpetrators. That of the official *gacaca* was to judge and, if guilt was established, to punish the authors of the genocide crimes. It was also, like in the Christian *gacaca*, to restore social harmony, but only by way of a judicial process. How could these two forms of conflict resolution coexist? As the Catholic newspaper *Kinyamateka* reported, some people were saying that the *gacaca* of the church hampered the state *gacaca* because the church did not incriminate anybody and was not authorised to punish.[91]

Fortunately, channels of communication between the Catholic Church and the Rwandan government existed. Various meetings helped to clarify the misunderstandings. In October 1999, representatives of the Bishops' Conference received the opportunity to explain their position to Patrick Mazimpaka, the minister in the office of the president of the Republic. 'The bishops', they told him, 'want to say that the Christian *gacaca* is not a new instance of justice but the opportunity to get groups of Christians to debate on questions related to the life of the church as a whole and on the relations they have among themselves'.[92]

The NURC also addressed the misgivings about the role of the Christian *gacaca*. One of its tasks was to prepare the ground for the establishment

---

[91] *Kinyamateka*, 1539 (1999), 6, quoted in Rutayisire, 'Le Catholicisme rwandais', 313.
[92] *Ibid.*

of the *gacaca*. The Commission held consultations with various civil society organisations, including religious denominations.[93] During the course of the year, the president of the Commission, Jean-Népomuscène Nayinzira, a former cabinet minister, came to a synodal meeting in Kigali at which Archbishop Thaddée Ntihinyurwa was present. He echoed the government's concern that the Christian *gacaca* 'aim[ed] at uniting and reconciling but forg[o]t the objective of punishing'.[94] The archbishop responded that crime repression was the responsibility of the state and not of the church. 'The church', he argued, 'does not replace the instances responsible for punishment. It encourages people to confess and ask for forgiveness so that love returns to the place from where it had disappeared. The church is careful not to hamper the work of justice.'[95]

This work of explanation paid dividends. Gradually, the confusion dissipated. In any event, the time of the Christian *gacaca* ended after the Jubilee. Forums for survivors, perpetrators and other people concerned by the genocide carried on afterwards, as in the diocese of Cyangugu, but without the name of Christian *gacaca*.

The Catholic Church recognised the value of the official *gacaca*. While expressing concerns about the risk of false accusations, the bishops encouraged the faithful, in June 2002 and again in March 2006, to participate in the *gacaca* courts.[96] In April 2008, the Justice and Peace Commission of the Bishops' Conference published a balanced assessment of the work done so far by the *gacaca* courts. In a report based on a two-month enquiry involving 486 observers, it declared that many judges were conscientious and fair, that the witnesses felt safe and that there were very few cases of retraumatisation. The authors of the report pointed out, however, that there were instances of corruption, of intimidation of witnesses and of false testimonies.[97]

---

[93] *Rapport annuel des activités de la Commission Nationale pour l'Unité et la Réconciliation, période allant de mars 1999 à juin 2000* (Kigali: National Unity and Reconciliation Commission, 2000), 29.

[94] *Kinyamateka*, 1534 (1999), 2, quoted in Rutayisire, 'Le Catholicisme rwandais', 314.

[95] *Ibid.*

[96] Conférence Épiscopale du Rwanda, *Pour une justice qui réconcilie* (2002); *Message des évêques catholiques du Rwanda exhortant les chrétiens à prendre une part active aux juridictions gacaca* (2006).

[97] Vincent Gasana, *Rapport synthétique du monitoring des juridictions gacaca* (Kigali: Commission Justice et Paix de la Conférence Épiscopale du Rwanda, 2008). Penal Reform International, a British non-governmental

Conclusion

Reconciliation is as difficult as it is necessary. The magnitude of the trauma caused by the genocide against the Tutsi and the violent events that preceded and followed it made the challenge even bigger. How can one reconcile with a neighbour who has killed a father, a mother, a brother or a sister? If one was caught in the folly of the genocide, how does one agree to speak face to face to a survivor? In Rwanda everybody is traumatised, and not only the survivors of the genocide. There are countless people in grief and countless incomplete grief processes. As suggested in the Jean Hatzfeld novel *Un papa de sang* [A father of blood],[98] the trauma is sometimes transmitted from one generation to the next.

It is a remarkable feat that, despite all the challenges, many survivors have forgiven, many perpetrators have confessed and many scenes of reconciliation have taken place. A considerable amount of trauma counselling has been done since 1994. Non-governmental organisations and church bodies contributed to this effort. The hardest question is whether victims can forgive perpetrators who never admitted their guilt or expressed repentance. There are examples of survivors who, moved by their Christian faith or other sentiments, chose to forgive unconditionally.

This chapter has reviewed some of the achievements of the Rwandan people. Many reconciliation actors were, inevitably, not mentioned – in particular, those that fell outside the chronological framework of this study. We have described among others the work of the AEE, Moucecore, the Emmanuel Community, the group that spearheaded the Detmold Confession, Bishop Nzakamwita's Mutete project, Father Ubald Rugirangoga's healing ministry and the Christian *gacaca* in the run-up to the Catholic Church's Year 2000 Jubilee celebration.

In matters of forgiveness and reconciliation, religion is an asset, because faith in a God who forgives is a powerful encouragement to undertake this long and painful journey. There is a certain comfort in remaining closed in a posture of blame and anger. Forgiveness and reconciliation require the ability to develop empathy for the other. Those who claim to follow the Christian message are expected to put aside their pain for a moment and consider the pain of their former enemies.

---

organisation, reached similar conclusions in a report published in 2010 under the *title Eight years on... A Record of Gacaca Monitoring in Rwanda*, but they insisted more than the Justice and Peace Commission on the insufficiency of the rights of the defence.

[98] Jean Hatzfeld, *Un papa de sang* (Paris: Gallimard, 2015).

Conclusion

The genocide did not only shatter the standing of the churches, which had witnessed, powerless, the desecration of their sanctuaries and the decimation of their clergy. It shattered the image of a country dedicated to the Christian faith. Practising Christians, who knew that killing was against God's commandment, proved incapable of resisting the wave of murder that submersed Rwanda. They hunted the Tutsi to death or denounced them to the Interahamwe. It is true that not all believers participated in the genocide and that a significant number of them resisted the killers, sheltered Tutsi refugees and faced death, in some cases, to protect people in danger. On balance, however, the genocide was a terrible indictment for the churches, who had been considered exemplary agents of evangelisation for decades. Never had Christians murdered so many fellow believers in places of worship. Particularly problematic was the absence of a vigorous denunciation of the genocide against the Tutsi on the part of the church leaders. Rwanda had no Jules Saliège, who condemned the deportation of the Jews in a famous pastoral letter, and no Dietrich Bonhoeffer, who took an uncompromising position against the Nazi regime and was executed for having taken part in a conspiracy against Hitler. 'We used to think', a survivor told Anne Kubai, 'that the priests and nuns were without sin, that they played the role of God and that the church was a sacred place. But now many people realised that they are like everyone else.'[1]

This book has examined how the Rwandan churches handled the memory of the genocide against the Tutsi. Like any other sector of society, they have been the site of a conflict of memory. Faced with hard questions because of their historical connection with the Rwandan Social Revolution and the Habyarimana regime, whose actions and inactions

---

[1] Anne Kubai, *Being Church in Post-Genocide Rwanda. The Challenges of Forgiveness and Reconciliation* (Uppsala: Life and Peace Institute, 2005), 15.

had prepared the way for the genocide, they struggled to accept responsibility for their part in the tragedy.

Astoundingly, considering that the genocide reached the highest degree of horror, its true nature was never universally accepted. When it was unfolding, the perpetrators and the authorities who coordinated their 'work' pretended to wage a 'war' against invaders and their 'accomplices', women and children included. The genocide was denied at the very moment it was happening. It continued to be denied after the defeat of the Rwandan army and its flight to Kivu. In Rwanda, attempts were made to perpetuate the memory of the genocide and reconstruct the country on different principles, but there, too, the reality of the genocide was sometimes obscured. When it was not flatly denied on the basis of some conspiracy theories, its importance was minimised under the pretext that Hutu people were also killed and that other episodes of mass violence that took place in the region, well attested but of a very different nature, deserved more attention.

The research presented in this volume only concerns two churches, the Catholic Church and the Presbyterian Church, and the period immediately following the genocide. The advent of the new millennium in 2000 is the *terminus ad quem*. The picture may have been different if other churches such as the Anglican Church, the Free Methodist Church, the Adventist Church, the Union of Baptist Churches and the Church of Pentecost had been taken into consideration, yet not substantially so, from what we can judge. The debate on the genocide continued after 2000, but by then a lot of interaction had taken place between the different components of the Catholic and Presbyterian churches, the genocide survivor organisations, the state, the missionaries, the academic sphere and the media. On the whole, the positions of the various role-players had been clarified.

We have seen that for many church members, Hutu as well as Tutsi, the experience of the genocide had been so vivid and so devastating that it did not make sense to deny it. Quite a few believers openly questioned the model of evangelisation adopted in Rwanda and acknowledged the failures of the churches. The CRAP bulletins in the Catholic diocese of Butare, which were widely disseminated, illustrate this approach well. The extraordinary synod of the Presbyterian Church in February 1995, the genocide memorial erected at the cathedral of Nyundo in April 1995 and the assemblies of priests in Kigali in May and November 1995 are other examples of 'loyal appraisal'. Also significant was the participation of Smaragde Mbonyintege, a lecturer from Nyakibanda Major Seminary, and his students in the research undertaken by the National University of Rwanda in Butare on the traditional *gacaca*, a form of conflict resolution potentially applicable in the post-genocide context.

For their part, the Catholic bishops refused, initially at least, to use the word 'genocide' in their pastoral statements. As late as March 1996, Thaddée Ntihinyurwa, the president of the episcopal conference, declared that if the faith had declined in the country, it was because of the attacks launched on the church, as if it had nothing to do with the genocide. In their individual capacity, however, bishops such as Wenceslas Kalibushi of Nyundo, Frédéric Rubwejanga of Kibungo or Jean-Baptiste Gahamanyi of Butare and André Sibomana, the administrator of the diocese of Kabgayi, had no hesitation in mentioning the genocide against the Tutsi and drawing lessons from it. In 1998, as part of the preparation for the Year 2000 Jubilee, the episcopal conference launched a process of synodal discussion on 'ethnocentrism' – a euphemism for genocide. Ntihinyurwa was one of the prelates who supported the idea of holding 'Christian *gacaca*', during which genocide survivors, perpetrators and bystanders could speak to each other.

Likewise, the Missionaries of Africa did not speak with one voice. Some trivialised the genocide against the Tutsi by promoting the double genocide theory. Others chose to return to Rwanda to contribute to the reconstruction of the church and the country. A minority actively supported the government's memorialisation efforts. Even the Holy See had internal differences. Henryk Hoser, the apostolic visitor, and Julius Janusz, the nuncio, failed to recognise the nature of the genocide against the Tutsi and its effects on their flock. For them, other subjects were more important. They adopted an adversarial attitude towards the Rwandan government and its memorialisation policy, with the encouragement of the Secretariat of State in Rome. For his part, Paul Cordes, the pope's envoy, used a different language when he visited Rwanda in March 1996. In his speech, he drew a fascinating parallel between the Holocaust and the genocide against the Tutsi. Even among the refugees in Kivu, who tended to support the denialist positions of the former Rwandan government, the ex-FAR and the Interahamwe, there were church members, admittedly a small number, who recognised that awful crimes had been committed against the Tutsi and expressed regret for them.

The trajectory of the EPR was quite different. After the victory of the RPF in July 1994, it suffered a massive exodus not only of clergy and laity, like the Catholic Church, but of a substantial part of its leadership, including its president of the church, Michel Twagirayesu. The refugees in Goma, Bukavu and Nairobi tended to be politically aligned to the former Rwandan government's extremist positions. They would only speak of a genocide 'between quotation marks', as one of them said at a meeting in September 1996 in Windhoek. This prompted a reaction among the Presbyterians who had remained in the country. They elected a new leadership during the extraordinary synod of February 1995 in Kigali and, a year later, the delegates of the national synod made a confession of guilt on behalf of the church for having 'failed to oppose or denounce the planning and execution of the genocide'. The EPR's recognition of the genocide against the Tutsi could not have been clearer. It set the tone for subsequent ecumenical confessions of guilt.[2] The Catholic bishops of Rwanda also made a confession of guilt but later, in April 2000, and in more restrictive terms. They asked for forgiveness again in November 2016, on the occasion of the closure of the Jubilee Year of Mercy, but still without recognising that the church as such, and not only its sinful members, had a responsibility, even partial, in the genocide.[3] The contrast between the two approaches is noticeable.

The question of the church's guilt is an essential component of the memory debate in post-genocide Rwanda. In the EPR, the momentous December 1996 synodal declaration set the tone for all subsequent statements regarding the genocide. The church fell into line with the national memory policies. Things were less evident in the Catholic Church. Two distinct problems were discussed. The first was whether the church should ask for forgiveness as a church, as the EPR did, or only for its members who had been implicated in the genocide. The second concerned the degree of culpability of the clerics who had not taken part in the killings but had maintained close links with the authorities and failed to condemn the genocide for what it was.

A similar situation occurred in Germany after the defeat of Nazism. On 17 October 1945, eleven Protestant leaders, some part of the Confessing Church, berated themselves 'for not witnessing more courageously, for not praying more faithfully, for not believing more joyously and for not loving more ardently' in a document known as the Stuttgart Declaration.[4] They stopped short of repenting for their silence during the extermination of the Jews, an omission that would only be repaired five years later. Only a minority of Germans, however, were prepared to confess their guilt at that time.

---

[2] See in particular the Kigali Covenant, a confession of guilt adopted by representatives of various ecumenical agencies at a conference held in April 2004, on the occasion of the commemoration of the tenth anniversary of the genocide.

[3] Communiqué des Évêques catholiques du Rwanda à l'occasion de la clôture de l'Année du Jubilé extraordinaire de la Miséricorde, 20 November 2016.

[4] John Conway, 'How shall the nations repent? The Stuttgart Declaration of Guilt, October 1945', *Journal of Ecclesiastical History*, 38 (1987), 621.

It was in this context that the existentialist philosopher Karl Jaspers published an essay on the question of guilt.[5] The distinction he made between criminal, political, moral and metaphysical guilt has been applied to the South African context.[6] It is also relevant to the Rwandan situation.

Criminal guilt is the consequence of being tried and found guilty in a court of law.[7] Political guilt concerns the acts of politicians, bureaucrats and dignitaries who promote and support a criminal government policy. Judgement and guilt are pronounced on the basis of natural, common and international law.[8] Moral guilt is individual. It includes criminal, political and military actions as well as indifference and passivity. The morally guilty are those who close their eyes to criminal events or allow themselves to be intoxicated, seduced or bought with personal advantage.[9] The metaphysical guilt pertains to humanity in general. It involves a human solidarity that makes each person co-responsible for every wrong and every injustice in the world.[10]

Jaspers' typology throws light on the question of the church's guilt in Rwanda. It is not because only a small number of clerics – for example, Elizaphan Ntakirutimana, Athanase Seromba and Édouard Nturiye – were declared criminally guilty in a court of law that the churches as institutions are devoid of any culpability. The acquittal of Bishop Misago in 2000 and the dismissal of Wenceslas Munyeshyaka's case in 2015 in France after twenty years of legal wrangling did not convince the genocide survivors that church leaders like these would not have saved lives if they had openly challenged the political and military authorities with whom they were in constant contact.

The notion of moral guilt is arguably relevant for this discussion. It is exactly what the genocide survivors and the Rwandan state have in mind when they question the attitude of the bishops, priests, brothers, sisters, pastors and elders who knew what was happening and remained silent. It is a fact that the men of the cloth did not have the power to stop the massacres. As claimed by their defenders, they did not have an army. Their support for the interim government which rapidly orchestrated the genocide

---

[5] Karl Jaspers, *Die Schuldfrage* (Heidelberg: Steiner, 1946). Translated into English under the title *The German Guilt* (New York: The Dial Press, 1947).
[6] Charles Villa-Vicencio, 'The burden of moral guilt: its theological and political implications', *Journal of Church and State*, 39 (1997), 238–52.
[7] Jaspers, *The German Guilt*, 31.
[8] Ibid., 31, 63–4.
[9] Ibid., 63.
[10] Ibid., 32.

under the guise of fighting the enemy and their failure to publicly oppose the poisonous discourse of the Hutu extremist media is, however, puzzling. It is true that by 1994 only the older missionaries continued to support the discredited Hamitic theory which presented the Tutsi as strangers and justified the argument that they were the quintessential oppressors of the Hutu 'majority'. But the churches never clearly distanced themselves from the deadly ideology they had propagated for so long.

In this study, we have paid special attention to three church leaders whose behaviour during the genocide raised questions: Michel Twagirayesu, the president of the EPR, Augustin Misago, the bishop of Gikongoro, and Gabriel Maindron, the priest of Congo-Nil. Other examples could have been chosen, but these are sufficient to illustrate the problem of the church leaders' moral guilt in the sense Jaspers gave to this term. All three were respected in their community and enjoyed moral prestige. They personally knew the political leaders and the military commanders in their area. There are indications that they showed concern for Tutsi people and agreed to shelter them on occasions, which shows that they were not guilty of genocide. They did nothing, however, to prevent the massacres from happening. They are not on record for having used their moral authority, which was considerable, to challenge the criminal behaviour of the Christians involved in the killings and of the authorities who facilitated or condoned the massacres under the pretext that the Tutsi were RPF 'accomplices'. They kept silent. After the genocide, unlike the signatories of the Stuttgart Declaration and the South African church leaders at the TRC, they never apologised for their attitude during the genocide. They never expressed regret.

Linked to the refusal of the church leaders to admit any form of guilt was the pervasive attitude of denial adopted in some sectors of the churches. It was as if the detestation of the RPF, deemed guilty of all crimes, real or imagined, justified a mild judgement on the genocide against the Tutsi. Bishop Perraudin, in interviews given to the Swiss press on the onset of the genocide; Maindron, in his diary; and Twagirayesu, in a memorandum to the partners of the EPR on 6 June 1994, were representatives of this attitude. Faced with the RPF, they intimated, one had to 'understand' the angry 'crowds' that went on rampages against the Tutsi. Their visceral opposition to the RPF made them unable to admit the full reality of the genocide.

After the genocide, the tendency to balance out the genocide against the Tutsi and the crimes attributed to the RPF affected sectors of the churches, not without causing distress among genocide survivors. The opinions were starkly polarised. The troubles of the times, with warfare inside and outside Rwanda, acts of vengeance against alleged perpetrators, overcrowded prisons and a government of national unity that struggled to keep its promises, provoked a crisis of confidence among some clerics and some missionaries in the new Rwanda. They started to lend support to the opposition. Their negative sentiments had an impact on the politics of memory in the churches.

Until 1998, the date of Julius Juliusz' end of office as nuncio, the adversarial attitude of the nunciature exacerbated the tension. The news spread that the RPF-led government was persecuting the church. The restrained attitude of the authorities in the discussion on the transformation of churches into genocide memorials proved, if anybody believed otherwise, that they did not want to rock the boat. A few priests and pastors were sentenced for genocide, but neither more nor less than other categories of citizens. The persecution of the Rwandan church after the genocide is a myth. The synodal process and the confession of guilt, admittedly limited, of the Catholic bishops during the Year 2000 Jubilee celebrations brought a détente which the Misago trial did not succeed in derailing. In 2004, the participation of the prime minister and high-ranking government officials in the conference organised by the episcopal conference of Rwanda to commemorate the tenth anniversary of the genocide and the massacres illustrated the desire of both parties to work together in spite of the accusations, founded or unfounded, that had been exchanged in the previous years.[11]

If there is one thing the post-genocide Rwandan government and the churches agreed upon after 1994, that was the need for reconciliation. They used different methods, of course, and have different measures of success. While caring for the orphans and assisting the destroyed families in reconstructing their lives, the churches conducted healing and reconciliation workshops with the help of psychologists and conflict resolution professionals. Their motivation was essentially spiritual. Forgiveness was at the centre of their message. The state pursued the same aim with the difference that, from its perspective, the perpetrators had to be brought to justice in order to avoid impunity. In parallel, it ran community programmes under the auspices of the National Unity and Reconciliation Commission or other state agencies. It is significant that both the Catholic Church and the Rwandan government saw value in restoring the traditional practice of the *gacaca*. The aim of the Christian *gacaca*, when they were implemented in the late 1990s, was to reconcile the communities divided by the genocide by bringing together survivors, perpetrators and bystanders. The purpose

---

[11] *L'Église et la société rwandaise face au génocide et aux massacres dix ans après. Colloque du 29 au 31 mars 2004 au Centre Christus de Remera* (Kigali: Commission Épiscopale Justice et Paix, 2004).

of the official *gacaca* was to judge and, if guilt was established, to sanction the authors of the genocide crimes to repair the harm done and restore a sense of justice. The churches and the state had the goal of restoring social harmony in common.

History will remember that, for lack of a prophetic leadership, the Christian churches as institutions failed to give an appropriate response to the genocide against the Tutsi. At the individual level, the situations were diverse, with a mix of heroes, victims, cowards and criminals. Past the tragedy, Rwandan society tried to reconstruct itself on a new basis. Some sectors of the churches wholeheartedly embraced the work of renewal. Others adopted a defensive attitude. With time, however, their resistance to change has lessened. A new *modus vivendi* is on the cards.

There is no doubt that the religious landscape has changed in Rwanda since the genocide. The Catholic Church, once a kingmaker, has reduced in its influence. Its membership fell from 62.6 per cent of the Rwandan population on the eve of the genocide to 44 per cent in 2012.[12] It did not disintegrate, as Saskia Van Hoyweghen predicted in 1996.[13] On the contrary, it continues to attract the faithful and its seminaries are full. It loses ground, however, to the Pentecostal churches, which multiply on an exponential scale, like anywhere in sub-Saharan Africa. Because of the past controversies regarding its involvement in the genocide, the Catholic Church tends to maintain a low profile. Denominations with historical links to the erstwhile Tutsi refugee community in Uganda, such as the Anglican Church, or prominent Pentecostal churches like the Zion Temple Celebration are more prone to gain public recognition. They feature in public events under the benevolent eye of the RPF leadership. In 2005, the American evangelist Rick Warren declared Rwanda the world's first 'purpose-driven nation' with the blessing of President Kagame. There is talk of a Protestant–RPF axis that replaced the one formed between the Catholic Church and the Kayibanda and Habyarimana regimes.[14]

It is worth noting, though, that post-genocide Rwanda is a secular state. Unlike the 1991 Constitution, which opened with an invocation to God Almighty, the 2011 Constitution only refers to the 'valiant ancestors who sacrificed themselves to found Rwanda'. The RPF government never

---

[12] Andrea Mariko Grant, 'Ecumenism in question: Rwanda's contentious post-genocide religious landscape', *Journal of Southern African Studies*, 44 (2018), 227.

[13] Saskia Van Hoyweghen, 'The disintegration of the Catholic Church of Rwanda', *African Affairs*, 95 (1996), 379–401.

[14] Grant, 'Ecumenism in question', 222, 230, 231.

pursued anticlerical policies as André Louis, the vice-president of CDI, said it would in the early 1990s. It seeks the support of all civil society organisations, including the churches, to implement its nation-building programme. At the same time, it regulates and controls the activities of the churches in a centralised manner, as it does for the other sectors of public life. Between 2011 and 2013, religious institutions were invited to register with the Rwandan Governance Board to operate legally. Only 221 were approved.[15] Scores of Pentecostal churches continued to function without any legal framework. In 2018, the Rwandan government enacted draconian directives on the health and security standards of places of worship and the level of qualification of ministers of religion. About a thousand churches, most of them Pentecostal, were forced to close.[16]

The Catholic Church, the Presbyterian Church and the other mainstream churches did not protest against the new legislation. In different ways, they try to learn from their past mistakes when dealing with political authority. It would be an illusion to think that the divisions of the past are healed once and for all. The trauma of the genocide and of the episodes of mass violence that followed in Rwanda and in the neighbouring countries is too big to disappear in one generation. All Rwandans, from the bottom to the top, still have scars, and this affects the way in which the country is administered – and, indeed, some are still critical of its mode of governance.

Rwandan society shows signs of resilience and recovery. There are still tensions, but arguably fewer than before. If this book contributes, in a modest way, to a more serene appreciation of Rwanda's recent religious history and of the need to acknowledge the failures of the past in a spirit of truth, it will not have been written in vain.

---

[15] *Ibid.*, 222.

[16] Dan Ngabonziza, 'New law on religious institutions due next week', *KT Express*, 15 July 2018.

Select bibliography

Please note that this bibliography does not contain details of all references used. Additional references can be found in the footnotes.

Archival sources

African Enterprise, Pietermaritzburg
André Bouillot Papers, Kigali
Archives of the Dominican Missionary Sisters, Namur
Archives of the Episcopal Conference of Rwanda, Kigali
Archives of the Journal *Dialogue*, Brussels
Archives of the Missionaries of Africa, Generalate, Rome
—— Province of Europe, Brussels
Archives of the Presbyterian Church in Rwanda, Kigali
Archives of the Rwandan Parliament, Kigali
Centre de Documentation et de Pastorale, Kigali
Centre de Formation et de Documentation, Kigali
Gerard van 't Spijker Papers, Utrecht
Hervé Deguine Papers, La Contemporaine, Paris Nanterre University, Paris
Malachie Munyaneza Papers, Wolverhampton
National Centre for the Fight against Genocide, Kigali

Periodicals

African News Bulletin – Bulletin d'Information Africaine (ANB-BIA), Brussels
Agenzia Fides, Organo di informazione delle Pontifice Opere Missionarie, Rome
Bâtissons, Kigali
De Morgen, Brussels
Dialogue, Kigali
Dialogue, Kigali-Brussels
Golias, Lyon

Journal de Genève, Geneva
Kinyamateka, Kigali
L'Actualité religieuse dans le monde, Paris
La Croix, Paris
La Documentation catholique, Paris
La Nouvelle Relève, Kigali
La Nuit rwandaise, Paris
Le Monde, Paris
Le Soir, Brussels
Libération, Paris
Official Gazette of the Republic of Rwanda, Kigali.
Osservatore Romano, Rome
Petit Écho des Missionnaires d'Afrique, Rome
Trouw, Amsterdam
Urunana. Revue des Grands Séminaristes, Nyakibanda

Printed primary sources

African Rights, *Rwanda: Death, Despair and Defiance* (London: African Rights, 1994; rev. edn, 1995).
—— *Not So Innocent: When Women Become Killers* (London: African Rights, 1995).
—— *The African Church and the Genocide: An Appeal to the World Council of Churches' Meeting in Harare* (London: African Rights, 1998).
Association rwandaise pour la Défense des Droits de la Personne et des Libertés publiques (ADL), *Rapport sur les droits de l'homme, septembre 1991–septembre 1992* (Kigali: ADL, 1992).
—— *Rapport sur les droits de l'homme, octobre 1992–octobre 1993* (Kigali: ADL, 1993).
Audoin-Rouzeau, S., *Une initiation: Rwanda (1994–2016)* (Paris: Seuil, 2017).
Avocats Sans Frontières, *Recueil de jurisprudence, contentieux du génocide*, vol. 7 (Bruxelles: s.d. [2006]).
Bizimana, J.-D., *L'Église et le génocide au Rwanda. Les Pères Blancs et le Négationnisme* (Paris: L'Harmattan, 2001).
Boucher-Saulnier, F. and Laffont, F., *Maudits soient les yeux fermés* (Paris: Éditions J. C. Lattès, 1995).
Bradol, J.-H. and Le Pape, M., *Génocide et crime de masse. L'expérience rwandaise de MSF 1982–1997* (Paris: CNRS Éditions, 2017).
Cariou, P., *De la Soufrière au Nyiragongo* (Saint-Derrien: Librairie S. P. Rance, 1996).

Commission Épiscopale du Clergé, *Évaluation du processus synodal: Actes de la session des prêtres, Nyakibanda du 28 Août–1er Septembre 2000* (Kigali: Commission Épiscopale du Clergé, 2000).

Confession de Detmold, Bekenntnis von Detmold, Confession of Detmold, Intangazo Detmold (Detmold: Landeskirchenamt der Lippischen Landeskirche, 1996).

Contran, N., *They Are a Target: 200 African Priests Killed* (Nairobi: Paulines Publications Africa, 1996).

Cyuma, S., *Picking Up the Pieces: The Church and Conflict Resolution in South Africa and Rwanda* (Oxford: Regnum Books International, 2012).

Daniel-Ange, *Rwanda. Au fond de l'enfer, le ciel ouvert* (Paris: Éditions Béatitude, 2019).

de Dorlodot, P. (ed.), *Les réfugiés rwandais à Bukavu au Zaïre. De nouveaux Palestiniens?* (Paris: L'Harmattan, 1996).

Des Forges, A., *Leave None to Tell the Story: Genocide in Rwanda* (New York: Human Rights Watch, 1999).

Des prêtres rwandais s'interrogent (Bujumbura: Centre Lavigerie, 1995).

Desouter, S., *De gebroken lans* (Brussels: Vlaams Rwandeze Vereeniging and ACT, 1992).

—— *Rwanda: Le procès du RPF. Mise au point historique* (Paris: L'Harmattan, 2007).

—— *In Gods linkerhand. Herdenkingsboek van een missionaris* (Soest: Boekscout, 2014).

Desouter, S. and Nzabahimana, F., *Bouwstenen voor de toekomst* (Brussels: ACT, 1994).

—— *Rwanda. Achtergronden van een tragedie* (Brussels: ACT, 1994).

—— *Clés pour un retour à la paix* (Brussels: ACT, 1995).

Desouter, S. and Reyntjens, F., 'Rwanda. Les violations des droits de l'homme par le FPR/APR. Plaidoyer pour une enquête approfondie', University of Antwerp, Institute of Development Policy and Management, Working Paper, June 1995.

Dusengumuremyi, J. d'A., *No Greater Love: Testimonies on the Life and Death of Felicitas Niyitegeka* (Lake Oswego, Oregon: Dignity Press, 2015).

Duval, A., *L'évangile de Quim* (Paris: Mediaspaul, 1998).

Eltringham, N., *Accounting for Horror: Post-Genocide Debates in Rwanda* (London: Pluto Press, 2004).

Etchegaray, R., *J'ai senti battre le coeur du monde. Conversation avec Bernard Lecompte* (Paris: Fayard, 2017).

Fafchamps, J., *La C.S.C. et le M.O.C. dans le Kivu, le Rwanda et le Burundi de 1958 à 1961. Échange de lettres entre Jean Brück et Jules Fafchamps, dirigeants syndicaux* (Brussels: CARHOP, 2009).

Farrington, M. J., 'Rwanda – 100 Days – 1994: one perspective', in Carol Rittner, John K. Roth and Wendy Whitworth (ed.), *Genocide in Rwanda: Complicity of the Churches?* (St Paul, Minnesota: Paragon House, 2004), 93–110.

Fécondité de la crise rwandaise. Jalons pour une nouvelle évangélisation au Rwanda. Recueil de douze documents publiés par la Commission de Relance des Activités Pastorales (Butare: Diocèse catholique de Butare, 1996).

Fédération Internationale des Ligues des Droits de l'Homme, Africa Watch, Union Interafricaine des Droits de l'Homme et des Peuples, Centre International des Droits de la Personne et du Développement Démocratique, 'Rapport de la Commission internationale d'enquête sur les violations massives et systématiques des droits de l'homme depuis le 1er octobre 1990 au Rwanda', in *Lettre hebdomadaire de la FIDH*, 168 (March 1993).

Gacaca. Le droit coutumier au Rwanda. Rapport final de la première phase d'enquête sur le terrain réalisé par les chercheurs de l'Université Nationale du Rwanda (UNR), de l'Institut de Recherche Scientifique et Technologique (IRST-Butare), du Grand Séminaire de Nyakibanda (Kigali: Nations Unies, Haut-Commissaire aux Droits de l'Homme, Opération sur le terrain au Rwanda, June 1996).

Gacaca. Le droit coutumier au Rwanda. Rapport de la deuxième phase d'enquête sur le terrain réalisé par les chercheurs de l'Université Nationale du Rwanda (UNR), de l'Institut de Recherche Scientifique et Technologique (IRST-Butare), du Grand Séminaire de Nyakibanda (Kigali: Nations Unies, Haut-Commissaire aux Droits de l'Homme, Opération sur le terrain au Rwanda, January 1996).

Gasana, V., *Rapport synthétique du monitoring des juridictions gacaca* (Kigali: Commission Justice et Paix de la Conférence Épiscopale du Rwanda, 2008).

Gatwa, T. and Karamanga, A., *Les autres Chrétiens rwandais. La présence protestante* (Kigali: Éditions Urwego, 1990).

Godding, J.-P., *Réfugiés rwandais au Zaïre. Sommes-nous encore des hommes? Documents des groupes de réflexion dans les camps* (Paris: L'Harmattan, 1997).

Gourevitch, P., *We Wish to Inform You That Tomorrow We Will Be Killed with Our Families* (New York: Picador, 1998).

Gouteux, J.-P., *Un génocide sans importance. La France et le Vatican au Rwanda*, rev. edn (Lyon: Tahin Party, 2007).

Guichaoua, A., *Le problème des réfugiés rwandais et des populations banyarwanda dans la région des Grands Lacs africains* (Geneva: United National High Commissionner for Refugees, 1992).

Habonimana, C., *Le dernier des Tutsi* (Paris: Plon, 2019).

Habyarimana, S., *Phocas Nikwigize. Le Pacifique Pacificateur* (Lille: Éditions Sources du Nil, 2016).

Hategeka, J.-B., *Raisins verts pour dents agaçées? Cri contre les nazis Noirs au RWANDA* (Formigine: Golinelli, 1994).

—— *Uva acerba che allega i denti? Grido contro i nazisti neri del Rwanda* (Formigine: Golinelli, 1996).

Hatzfeld, J., *Un papa de sang* (Paris: Gallimard, 2015).

Hubert, J., *La Toussaint rwandaise et sa répression* (Brussels: Académie royale des sciences d'outremer, 1965).

Human Rights Watch, *Justice compromise. L'héritage des tribunaux communautaires gacaca du Rwanda* (New York: Human Rights Watch, 2011).

Kagoyire, Y.-S., Ngarambe, F.-X. and Twambamezungu, J.-M., *Rescapés de Kigali. Témoignage* (Paris: Éditions de l'Emmanuel, 2014).

Kanamugire, L., 'Les grands sites du génocide perpétré contre les Tutsi au Rwanda. Témoignages recueillis et réflexions personnelles', unpublished document, March 2012.

Kania, F., *Rwanda wczoraj i dziś: 21 lat posługi misyjnej w Rwandzie (1973–1994)* [Rwanda yesterday and today: 21 years of missionary service in Rwanda] (Ząbki: Apostolicum, 2003).

Karamaga, A., 'Les Églises protestantes et la crise rwandaise', in André Guichaoua (ed.), *Les crises politiques au Burundi et au Rwanda (1993–1994). Analyses, faits et documents* (Lille: Université des Sciences et Technologies, 1995), 299–308.

Karangwa, H., *Le génocide au centre du Rwanda. Quelques témoignages des rescapés de Kabgayi* (n.p., 2001).

Karekezi, A., 'Juridictions gacaca: Lutte contre l'impunité et promotion de la réconciliation nationale', in E. Ntaganda (ed.), *Les juridictions gacaca et les processus de réconciliation nationale*, Cahiers du Centre de Gestion des Conflits, 3 (Butare: Université Nationale du Rwanda, 2001), 9–96.

Kubai, A., *Being church in post-genocide Rwanda: The challenges of forgiveness and reconciliation* (Uppsala: Life and Peace Institute, 2005).

L'Église et la société rwandaise face au génocide et aux massacres dix ans après. Colloque du 29 au 31 mars 2004 au Centre Christus de Remera (Kigali: Commission Épiscopale 'Justice et Paix', 2004).

Lapsley, M., *Redeeming the Past: My Journey from Freedom Fighter to Healer* (Tyger Valley: Struik Christian Media, 2012).

Larcher, L., *Rwanda, ils parlent. Témoignage pour l'histoire* (Paris: Seuil, 2019).

Le prêtre diocésain dans la société rwandaise en mutation. Actes de la Session des prêtres diocésains, Nyakibanda (7–11/9/1992) Kabgayi (21–25/9/1992) [Kigali, 1992].

Linguyeneza, V. (ed.), *Vérité, justice, charité. Lettres pastorales et autres déclarations des évêques catholiques du Rwanda,1956–1962* (Waterloo, Belgium: 2001).
Lyamukuru, F., *L'ouragan a frappé Nyundo* (Cuesmes, Belgium: Éditions du Cerisier, 2018).
Maindron, G., *Des apparitions à Kibeho. Annonce de Marie au coeur de l'Afrique* (Paris: O.E.I.L, 1984).
Mbonyintege, S., 'Gacaca ishobora ite kongera kuba inzira y'ubwiyunge bw'abanyarwanda' (How the *gacaca* can continue to be a way of conciliation for the Rwandans), *Urumuri rwa Kristu*, 15 August 1995.
McCullum, H., *The Angels Have Left Us. The Rwanda Tragedy and the Churches* (Geneva: WCC, [1995]).
—— *Dieu était-il au Rwanda? La faillite des Églises* (Paris: L'Harmattan, 1996).
Misioneras de Jesùs, María and José, *Esperanza en el infierno de Ruanda. Diario de una mission* (Madrid: Espasa-Calpe, 1994).
Missionaries of Africa, 'Informations diffusées par la Région du Rwanda 1990–1994', compiled by Jef Vleugels, Brussels, December 2005.
Mugesera, A., *Rwanda 1896–1959. La désintégration d'une nation. Anthologie*, vol. 1 (Kigali: Izuba Éditions, 2017).
Mukagasana, Y., *La mort ne veut pas de moi* (Paris: Fixot, 1997).
Mukantagara, O., *Rwanda. De l'horreur du génocide au pardon et à la réconciliation* (Kigali: Pallotti Press, 2018).
Munyaneza, J., *Grace in the Midst of the Genocide* (Exeter: Onwards and Upwards Publishers, 2017).
Munyaneza, M., 'Violence as Institution in African Religious Experience', *Contagion. Journal of Violence, Mimesis and Culture*, 8, 2001, 39–68.
—— 'Genocide in the name of "salvation": the combined contribution of biblical translation/interpretation and indigenous myth to the 1994 Rwandan genocide', in Jonneke Bekkenkamp and Yvonne Sherwood (ed.), *Sanctified Agression. Legacies of Biblical and Post Biblical Vocabularies of Violence* (London and New York: T & T Clark International, 2003), 60–75.
Murangira, C., *Un sachet d'hosties pour cinq. Récit d'un rescapé du génocide des Tutsi commis en 1994 au Rwanda* (Nantes: Éditions Amalthée, 2016).
Muzungu, B., 'Un documentaire historique sur la Congrégation des Frères Joséphites du Rwanda', *Cahiers Lumière et Société*, 56 (February 2017).
National Service of Gacaca Courts, *Gacaca Courts in Rwanda* (Kigali: National Service of Gacaca Courts, 2012).
Ndorimana, J., *Rwanda: L'Église catholique dans le malaise. Symptômes et témoignages* (Rome: Edizioni Vivere In, 2001).

—— *Rwanda. Idéologie, méthodes et négationnisme du génocide des Tutsi à lumière de la chronique de la région de Cyangugu* (Rome: Edizioni Vivere In, 2003).

—— *De la région des Grands Lacs au Vatican. Intrigues, scandales et idéologie du génocide au sein de la hiérarchie catholique* (Kigali: Prograph, 2008).

Nduwayo, L., *Giti et le génocide Rwandais* (Paris: L'Harmattan, 2002).

Ngomanzungu, J., *L'Église et la crise rwandaise de 1990-1994. Essai de chronologie* (Kigali: Palloti Presse, 2000).

—— *Sa Sainteté le pape Jean-Paul II et le Rwanda. 25 ans de pontificat (1978–2003)* (Kigali: Pallotti Press, 2000).

—— *La souffrance de l'Eglise à travers son personnel* (Kigali: Pallotti Press, 2002).

—— *Efforts de médiation œcuménique des Églises dans la crise rwandaise: Le Comité de contacts (1991–1994)* ([Kigali: Pallotti Press], 2003).

—— 'Messages et Lettres Pastorales des Évêques Catholiques pendant la période 1994–2004', *Urunana*, 108 (January 2004).

Nsengimana, A., *Ma mère m'a tué. Survivre au génocide des Tutsi au Rwanda* (Paris: Hugo Doc, 2019).

Ntezimana, L. *Libres paroles d'un théologien rwandais. Joyeux propos de bonne puissance* (Paris: Karthala, 1998).

—— *Ma guerre à la guerre. Libres paroles d'un théologien rwandais dans la tourmente rwandaise (1990–1995)* (Paris: Édilivre, 2017).

Ntihabose, J.-B., 'Neuf mois de tragédie à l'est du Zaïre. Mon journal', unpublished document, Nairobi, 1997.

Overdulve, C. M., *Rwanda. Un peuple avec une histoire* (Paris: L'Harmattan, 1997).

Penal Reform International, *Eight Years On ... A Record of Gacaca Monitoring in Rwanda* (London: Penal Reform International, 2010)

Perraudin, A., *Un évêque au Rwanda: 'Par-dessus tout la charité': les six premières années de mon épiscopat (1956–1962)* (Saint-Maurice, Suisse: Éditions Saint-Augustin, 2003).

Poincaré, N., *Rwanda. Gabriel Maindron, un prêtre dans la tragédie* (Paris: Éditions Ouvrières, 1995).

Raffin, M., 'Le procès de Mgr Augustin Misago, évêque de Gikongoro', *Foi et Vie. Revue de l'Archidiocèse de Toulouse*, 18 (17 October 1999).

—— *Rwanda: un autre regard* (Lille: Éditions Sources du Nil, 2012).

Rapport annuel des activités de la Commission Nationale pour l'Unité et la Réconciliation, période allant de mars 1999 à juin 2000 (Kigali: National Unity and Reconciliation Commission, 2000).

Recueil des lettres et messages de la Conférence des Évêques catholiques du Rwanda publiées pendant la période de guerre (Kigali: Secrétariat général de la Conférence des Évêques catholiques du Rwanda, 1995).

Rôle du prêtre rwandais dans l'édification de l'Église et la réconciliation nationale. Session des prêtres rwandais tenu du 29 mai au 1er juin au Centre Christus Remera/Kigali (Butare: Imprimerie Euthymia, 1995).

Rubayiza, F., *Guérir le Rwanda de la violence* (Paris: L'Harmattan, 1998).

Rutayisire, P., 'Silences et compromissions de la hiérarchie de l'Eglise catholique du Rwanda', *Au coeur de l'Afrique*, 61/2–3 (1995), 413–41.

Rutazibwa, P., *Contre l'ethnisme* (Kigali: Éditions du CRID, 2017).

Rutumbu, J., *Rwanda. Les voies incontournables de la réconciliation* (Lille: Éditions Sources du Nil, 2013).

Saur, L., *Influences parallèles. L'internationale démocrate chrétienne au Rwanda* (Brussels: Éditions Luc Pire, 1998).

Sibomana, A., *Gardons l'espoir pour le Rwanda. Entretiens avec Laure Guibert et Hervé Deguine* (Paris: L'Harmattan, 2008).

Speke, J. H., *Journal of the Discovery of the Source of the Nile* (London: William Blackwood and Sons, 1863).

Theunis, G., 'Le rôle de l'Église catholique dans les événements récents', in A. Guichaoua (ed.), *Les crises politiques au Rwanda et au Burundi 1993–1994. Analyses, faits et documents* (Lille: Université des Sciences et Technologie, 1995), 289–98.

—— *Mes soixante-quinze jours de prison à Kigali* (Paris: Karthala, 2012).

Totten, S. and Rifiki, U. (ed.), *We Cannot Forget: Interviews with Survivors of the 1994 Genocide in Rwanda* (New Brunswick, New Jersey: Rutgers University Press, 2011).

Twagirayesu, M. and van Butselaar, J., *Ce don que nous avons reçu. Histoire de l'Église presbytérienne au Rwanda (1907–1982)* (Kigali: Église presbytérienne au Rwanda, 1982).

van 't Spijker, G., *Indicible Rwanda. Expériences et réflexions d'un pasteur missionnaire* (Yaoundé: Éditions CLÉ, 2007),

—— *L'Église chrétienne au Rwanda pré et post-génocide* (Paris: L'Harmattan, 2011).

Secondary sources

Alexander, J., *Trauma. A Social Theory* (Cambridge, UK/Malden, MA: Polity Press, 2012).

Ashplant, T. G., Dawson, G. and Roper, M. (ed.), *The Politics of War Memory and Commemoration* (London and New York: Routledge, 2000).

Baines, G., 'Sites of Struggle. The Freedom Park fracas and the divisive legacy of South Africa's border war/liberation struggle', *Social Dynamics*, 35 (2008), 330–44.

Bataringaya, P., *Versöhnung nach dem Genozid. Impulse der Friedensethik Dietrich Bonhoeffers für Kirche and Gesellschaft in Ruanda* (Kamen: Verlag Hartmut Spener, 2012).

Bideri, D., *Le massacre des Bagogwe, un prélude au génocide des Tutsi. Rwanda (1990–1993)* (Paris: L'Harmattan, 2008).

Birikunzira, J., 'L'Eglise adventiste du 7e jour au Rwanda (1919–2000)', in Tharcisse Gatwa and Laurent Rutinduka (ed.), *Histoire du christianisme au Rwanda des origines à nos jours* (Yaoundé: Éditions CIÉ, 2014), 97–116.

Bornkamm, P. C., *Rwanda's Gacaca Courts: Between Retribution and Reparation* (Oxford: Oxford University Press, 2012).

Braeckman, C., *Rwanda. Histoire d'un génocide* (Paris: Fayard, 1994).

────── *Les nouveaux prédateurs. Politique des puissances en Afrique centrale* (Paris: Fayard, 2003).

Brille, L., 'Etnische breuklijnen in Rwanda: De verschuivende mentaliteit van de Witte Paters in het Rwandese "Dual Colonialism", 1900–1962', unpublished master's thesis, University of Ghent, 2008.

Brunet-Lefèvre, T., *Le père Seromba. Destructeur de l'Église de Nyange (Rwanda, 1994)* (Paris: Éditions Hoosch, 2021).

Carney, J., *Rwanda Before the Genocide: Catholic Politics and Ethnic Discourse in the Late Colonial Era* (New York: Oxford University Press, 2014).

────── 'Christendom in crisis: The Catholic Church and postcolonial politics in Central Africa', in Elias Bongmba (ed.), *Routledge Companion to Christianity in Africa* (London and New York: Routledge, 2015), 365–84.

Chrétien, J.-P., 'Interprétations du génocide de 1994 dans l'histoire contemporaine du Rwanda', *Clio en Afrique*, 2 (Summer 1997), 92–9.

────── *Le défi de l'ethnisme. Rwanda et Burundi*, rev. edn (Paris: Karthala, 2012).

Chrétien, J.-P. (ed.), *Rwanda. Les médias du génocide* (Paris: Karthala, 2002).

Chrétien, J.-P. and Kabanda, M., *Rwanda. Racisme et génocide. L'idéologie hamitique* (Paris: Éditions Belin, 2015).

Clark, P., *The Gacaca Courts, Post-Genocide Justice and Reconciliation in Rwanda* (Cambridge: Cambridge University Press, 2010).

Conway, J., 'How shall the nations repent? The Stuttgart Declaration of Guilt, October 1945', *Journal of Ecclesiastical History*, 38 (1987), 596–622.

de Lame, D., 'L'histoire se fait aussi "par le bas"', *Afrique & Histoire*, 2 (1994), 287–93.

—— *A Hill among a Thousand. Transformation and Ruptures in Rural Rwanda* (Madison: The University of Madison Press, 2005).

Denis, P., 'Germany, South Africa and Rwanda: three manners for a Church to confess its guilt', *Studia Historiae Ecclesiasticae*, 43/2 (2017), 1–20.

—— 'Grief and denial among Rwandan Catholics in the aftermath of the genocide against the Tutsi', *Archives des sciences sociales des religions*, 183 (July–September 2018), 287–307.

—— 'Christian *gacaca* and official *gacaca* in post-genocide Rwanda', *Journal for the Study of Religion*, 32/1 (2019), 1–27.

—— 'Difficult navigation: dealing with divided memories in post-genocide Rwanda', *Oral History*, 39 (2021), 104–14.

—— 'The Missionaries of Africa and the Rwandan Genocide', *Journal of Religion in Africa*, 50/01-02 (2021), 1–28.

Des Forges, A., 'Kings without Crowns: the White Fathers in Ruanda', in Daniel McCall, Norman Bennett and Jeffrey Butler (ed.), *Eastern African History* (London: Praeger, 1969), 176–207.

Digneffe F. and Fierens, J. (ed.), *Justice et gacaca. L'expérience rwandaise et le génocide* (Namur: Presses Universitaires de Namur, 2003).

Dumas, H. and Korman, R., 'Espaces de la mémoire du génocide au Rwanda', *Afrique contemporaine*, 238 (2011), 11–27.

Dumas, H., 'L'histoire des vaincus. Négationnisme du génocide des Tutsi au Rwanda', *Revue d'histoire de la Shoah*, 190 (January–June 2009), 299–347.

—— *Le génocide au village. Le massacre des Tutsi au Rwanda* (Paris: Seuil, 2014).

Dusingizemungu, J.-P., 'Vécu du processus Gacaca par les rescapés du génocide des Tutsi: le va-et-vient entre le refus et l'acceptation', in Virginie Brinker Catherine Coquio, Alexandre Dauge-Roth, Eric Hoppenot, Nathan Réra and François Robinet (ed.), *Rwanda 1994–2014. Histoire, mémoires et récits* (Dijon, Les presses du réel, 2017), 101–7.

Faucheux, A., 'Massacrer dans l'intimité. La question de la rupture des liens sociaux et familiaux dans le cas du génocide des Tutsi du Rwanda de 1994', unpublished PhD thesis, Paris, École pratique des hautes études, 2019.

Gatwa, T., *Rwanda: Églises, victimes ou coupables? Les Églises et l'idéologie ethnique au Rwanda 1900–1994* (Yaoundé: Éditions CLÉ, 2001).

—— *The Churches and Ethnic Ideology in the Rwandan Crises 1900–1994* (Oxford: Regnum Books International, 2005).

Gatwa, T. and Denis, P., *Memory Work in Rwanda: Churches and Civil-Society Organisations Twenty Years After the Genocide Against the Tutsi* (Pietermaritzburg: Cluster Publications, 2020).

Gilbert, C., *From Surviving to Living: Voice, Trauma and Witness in Rwandan Women's Writing* (Montpellier: Presses universitaires de la Méditerranée, 2018).
Grant, A. M., 'Ecumenism in question: Rwanda's contentious post-genocide religious landscape', *Journal of Southern African Studies*, 44 (2018), 221–38.
Grieder, G., *Collines des mille souvenirs. Vivre avant et après le génocide perpétré contre les Tutsi du Rwanda* (Geneva: Globethics.net, 2016).
Guichaoua, A., *Rwanda 1994. Les politiques du génocide à Butare* (Paris: Karthala, 2005).
—— *Rwanda. De la guerre au génocide. Les politiques criminelles au Rwanda (1990–1994)* (Paris: La Découverte, 2010).
Guillou, B., *Le pardon est-il durable? Une enquête au Rwanda* (Paris: Éditions François Bourin, 2014).
Ibreck, R., 'Remembering humanity: the politics of genocide memorialisation in Rwanda', unpublished PhD thesis, University of Bristol, 2009.
Ingelaere, B., '"Does the truth pass across the fire without burning?" Locating the short circuit in Rwanda's gacaca courts', *Journal of Modern African Studies*, 47 (2009), 507–28.
Janzen, J., 'Historical consciousness and a "prise de conscience" in genocidal Rwanda, *Journal of African Cultural Studies*, 13 (2000), 153–68.
Jaspers, K., *Die Schuldfrage* (Heidelberg: Steiner, 1946). Translated into English under the title *The German Guilt* (New York: The Dial Press, 1947).
Jessee, E., 'The danger of a single story. Iconic stories in the aftermath of the 1994 Rwandan genocide', *Memory Studies*, 10/2 (2017), 144–63.
—— *Negotiating Genocide in Rwanda: The Politics of History* (London: Palgrave Macmillan, 2017).
Jessee, E. and Watkins, S, 'Good kings, bloody tyrants and everything in between: representations of the monarchy in post-genocide Rwanda,' *History in Africa*, 41 (2014), 50–5.
Kabanda, M., 'Rwanda, les massacres de 1963. Le témoignage de G. D. Vuillemin', in Christine Deslaurier and Dominique Juhé-Beaulaton (ed.), *Afrique, terre d'histoire. Au coeur de la recherche avec Jean-Pierre Chrétien* (Paris: Karthala, 2007), 415–34.
Karimumuryango, J., *Les réfugiés rwandais dans la région de Bukavu Congo RDC. La survie du réfugié dans les camps de secours d'urgence* (Paris: Karthala, 2000).
Kimonyo, J. P., *Un génocide populaire* (Paris: Karthala, 2008).
—— *Rwanda demain! Une longue marche vers la transformation* (Paris: Karthala, 2017).

Korman, R., 'Les mémoriaux du génocide: lieux de transmission de l'histoire ?' in Virginie Brinker, C. Coquio, A. Dauge-Roth, E. Hoppenot, N. Réra and F. Robinet (ed.), *Rwanda 1994–2014. Récits, constructions mémorielles et écritures de l'histoire* (Dijon: Les presses du Réel, 2017), 49–60.

—— 'Espaces sacrés et sites de massacre après le génocide des Tutsi. Les enjeux de la patrimonialisation des églises au Rwanda', *Vingtième siècle. Revue d'histoire*, 137 (2019), 155–67.

—— 'Commémorer sur les ruines. L'État rwandais face à la mort de masse dans l'après-coup du génocide (1994–2003)', unpublished PhD thesis, Paris, École des hautes études en sciences sociales, 2020.

Lanotte, O., *La France au Rwanda (1990–1994. Entre abstention impossible et engagement ambivalent)* (Bruxelles: P.I.E. Peter Lang, 2007).

Le Pape, M., 'Des journalistes au Rwanda. L'histoire immédiate d'un génocide', *Les Temps Modernes*, 583 (July–August 1995), 161–80.

Lemarchand, R., 'Disconnecting the threads: Rwanda and the Holocaust reconsidered', *Journal of Genocide Research*, 4 (2002), 499–518.

Linden, I., *Church and Revolution in Rwanda* (Manchester: Manchester University Press, 1977).

—— *Christianisme et pouvoir au Rwanda (1990–1990)* (Paris: Karthala, 1999).

Longman, T., 'Empowering the weak and protecting the powerful: the contradictory nature of churches in Central Africa', *African Studies Review*, 41 (1998), 49–72.

—— *Christianity and Genocide* (Cambridge: Cambridge University Press, 2011).

—— *Memory and Justice in Post-Genocide Rwanda* (Cambridge: Cambridge University Press, 2017).

Loumakis, S., 'Genocide and religion in the 1990s', in A. Gagné, S. Loumakis and C. Miceli (ed.), *The Global Impact of Religious Violence* (Eugene, Oregon: Wipf & Stock, 2016), 47–83.

Malkki, M., *Purity and Exile: Violence, Memory and National Cosmology Among Hutu Refugees in Tanzania* (Chicago: Chicago University Press, 1995).

Meierheinrich, J., 'The invention of gacaca: a logic of institutional choice', paper presented at a seminar in the Stanford Center on Democracy, Development and the Rule of Law, 16 May 2007.

Minnaert, S., *Histoire de l'évangélisation au Rwanda. Recueil d'articles et de documents* (Kigali: Imprimu, 2017).

Nuttall, S. and Coetzee, C., *Negotiating the Past: The Making of Memory in South Africa* (Cape Town: Oxford University Press, 1998).

Piton, F., 'Tueurs, Ibitero et notabilités génocidaires au Rwanda (avril 1994)', *Le Vingtième Siècle*, 138 (2018), 129–31.

Pontzeele, S., 'Burundi 1972/Rwanda 1994. L'"efficacité" dramatique d'une reconstruction du passé par la presse', unpublished PhD thesis, University of Lille, 2004.

Pottier, J., *Re-imagining Rwanda: Conflict, Survival and Disinformation in the Late Twentieth Century* (Cambridge: Cambridge University Press, 2002).

Prunier, G., *The Rwanda Crisis: History of a Genocide* (New York: Columbia University Press, 1995).

—— *Africa's World War: Congo, the Rwandan Genocide and the Making of a Continental Catastrophe* (Oxford and New York: Oxford University Press, 2009).

Reyntjens, F., *Pouvoir et droit au Rwanda: droit public et évolution politique, 1916–1973* (Tervuren, Belgium: Musée Royal de l'Afrique Centrale, 1985).

—— 'Le *gacaca* ou la justice du gazon au Rwanda', *Politique Africaine*, 40 (1990), 31–41.

—— 'Estimation du nombre de personnes tuées au Rwanda en 1994', *Annuaire des Grands Lacs 1996–1997* (Paris: L'Harmattan, 1997), 179–86.

—— *The Great African War: Congo and Regional Geopolitics, 1996–2006* (Cambridge: Cambridge University Press, 2009).

—— *Political Governance in Post-Genocide Rwanda* (Cambridge: Cambridge University Press, 2013).

Ricoeur, P., *Memory, History, Forgetting* (Chicago: Chicago University Press, 2002).

Rittner, C., Roth, J. K. and Whitworth, W. (ed.), *Genocide in Rwanda: Complicity of the Churches?* (St Paul, Minnesota: Paragon House, 2004).

Robinet, F., 'Les conflits africains au regard des médias français', unpublished PhD thesis, University of Saint-Quentin-en-Yvelines, 2012.

Rutayisire, P., *La christianisation du Rwanda (1900–1945). Méthode missionnaire et politique selon Mgr Classe* (Fribourg: Éditions universitaires, 1987).

—— 'Le catholicisme rwandais: un regard interrogateur', in Tharcisse Gatwa and Laurent Rutinduka (ed.), *Histoire du christianisme au Rwanda. Des origines à nos jours* (Yaoundé: Éditions CLÉ, 2014), 251–343.

—— 'Le conflit des mémoires', in Roland Junod and Paul Rutayisire (ed.), *Citoyenneté et réconciliation au Rwanda* (Geneva: Éditions ies, 2015).

Rutazibwa, P. and Rutayisire, P., *Génocide à Nyarubuye* (Kigali: Éditions rwandaises, [2007]).

Sands, P., *East West Street: On the Origins of Genocide and Crimes against Humanity* (London: Weidenfeld & Nicolson, 2016).

Saur, L., *Le sabre, la machette et le goupillon. Des apparitions de Fatima au génocide rwandais* (Bierges: Éditions Mols, 2004).
—— 'Catholiques belges et Rwanda, 1950–1965. Les pièges de l'évidence', unpublished PhD thesis, Université Paris I, 2013.
Schabas, W., 'Genocide trials and *gacaca* courts', *Journal of International Criminal Justice,* 3 (2005), 1–17.
Smedes, L., *Forgive and Forget: Healing the Hurts We Don't Deserve* (New York: Harper Collins, 1984).
Smith, J. and Rittner, C., 'Churches as memorial sites: a photo essay', in Carol Rittner, John K. Roth and Wendy Whitworth (ed.), *Genocide in Rwanda: Complicity of the Churches* (St Paul, Minnesota: Paragon House, 2004), 181–205.
Staub, E., L. A. Pearlman, A. Gubin and A. Hagengimana, 'Healing, reconciliation, forgiving and the prevention of violence after genocide or mass killing: an intervention and its experimental evaluation in Rwanda', *Journal of Social and Clinical Psychology*, 24 (2005), 297–334.
Todorov, T. 'The uses and abuses of memory', in Howard Marchitello (ed.), *What Happens to History: The Renewal of Ethics in Contemporary Thought* (London and New York: Routledge, 2001), 11–22.
Uvin, P., *Aiding Violence: The Development Enterprise in Rwanda* (West Hartford, Connecticut: Kumarian Press, 1998).
Van Hoyweghen, S., 'The disintegration of the Catholic Church of Rwanda', *African Affairs*, 95 (1996), 379–401.
Verwimp, P., 'A quantitative analysis of genocide in Kibuye Prefecture, Rwanda', Centre for Economic Studies, Katholieke Universiteit Leuven, Discussions Paper Series, 01.10, 2001.
—— 'The 1990–92 massacres in Rwanda: a case of spatial and social engineering', *Journal of Agrarian Change*, 11 (2011), 396–419.
Vidal, C., 'La commémoration du génocide au Rwanda. Violence symbolique, mémorisation forcée et histoire officielle', *Cahiers des études africaines*, 175/3 (2004), 575–92.
Villa-Vicencio, C., 'The burden of moral guilt: its theological and political implications', *Journal of Church and State*, 39 (1997), 238–52.

Index

AACC *see* All Africa Council of Churches
Abacengezi War 117, 277
Abamonyo 251–253
Abimana, Mathias 117, 240, 248–251, 255, 261, 264, 265, 277, 278
Abyssinia 34, 161
ACEAC *see* Association of Episcopal Conferences of Central Africa
ACT *see* Agence de Coopération Technique
ADFL *see* Alliance of Democratic Forces for the Liberation of Congo
ADL *see* Rwandan Association for the Defence of the Rights of the Person and the Public Liberties
Adventist Church *see* Seventh Day Adventist Church
Adventist University of Central Africa 75
Aebisher, René 238
AEE *see* African Evangelical Enterprise
Aegis Trust 9
Aelvoet, Walter 34, 168, 169
African Evangelical Enterprise (AEE) 66, 72, 144, 150, 278, 280, 281, 303
African Humanitarian Action 280
African News Bulletin – Bulletin d'Information Africaine (*ANB-BIA*) 168, 169
African Rights 60, 61, 74, 80, 83, 118, 124, 136–139, 147, 192, 208, 214–217, 237–239
Agence de Coopération Technique (ACT) 162, 164, 171, 178
Aid to the Church in Need 194
All Africa Council of Churches (AACC) 62, 63, 131, 141, 143, 145, 147, 151
Alliance of Democratic Forces for the Liberation of Congo (ADFL) 121
Amnesty International 64
Amour Sans Frontière (ASF) 241
ANB-BIA *see African News Bulletin – Bulletin d'Information Africaine*
Anglican Church 13, 37–39, 43, 63, 83, 87, 88, 130, 148, 153, 213, 216, 278, 281, 305, 311
Angola 11
Antwerp 162, 167, 180
ARBED *see* Association Rwandaise pour le Bien-Être Familial
ARDHO *see* Rwandan Association for the Defence of Human Rights
Arusha Agreement 54, 56, 59, 63, 66, 179, 217
ASF *see* Amour Sand Frontières
Association des Volontaires de la Paix 71
Association of Episcopal Conferences of Central Africa (ACEAC) 104, 106, 120, 192
Association of Genocide Widows (AVEGA) 286
Association of Major Superiors (ASUMA) 66, 158, 159, 185
Association Quintin Rwanda 241
Association Rwandaise pour le Bien-Être Familial (ARBED) 55

Astrida 28
ASUMA *see* Association of Major Superiors
AVEGA *see* Association of Genocide Widows
Ayingeneye, Stéphanie 247

Bagaza, Jean-Baptiste 78, 189
Bagogwe 45, 51, 52, 58, 65, 231, 253–255, 258
Bahutu Manifesto 1, 28
balancing 51, 68, 145, 181, 183, 279, 287, 309
Balas, Laurent 175
Bank of Rwanda 187, 196
Banneux 236
baptism 108, 252, 253
Baptist Church 38, 63, 131, 147, 148, 305
Barnabites 78, 99
Bartel, Burckhard 132, 133, 141
Bâtissons 149, 275
Bazot, Henri 37, 38, 68, 186
Belgian Society of Protestant Missions in Congo (SBMPC) 38, 127
Belgium 1, 10, 14, 15, 18, 19, 21, 23, 24, 26–333, 38, 39, 45, 47–51, 66, 84–86, 99, 100, 116, 127, 131, 132, 162, 163, 164–168, 170, 171, 175–177, 182, 184, 185, 187, 196, 198, 208, 210, 212, 221, 226, 227, 236, 240, 242, 248, 253, 256, 267, 284, 286, 289
Bellet, Maurice 112
Bellomi, Carlo 208, 209
Bemeriki, Valérie 94
Benebikira Sisters 73, 200
Benimana, Raphaël 224, 229, 237, 245, 253–255, 259, 264, 269
Bertello, Giuseppe 62, 90, 91, 187
Bible 26, 51, 93–95, 108, 148, 150, 284
 Corinthians, Letter to the 275
 Daniel, Book of 126
 Ephesians, Letter to the 98
 Isaiah, Book of 95
 John, Gospel of 276
 Luke, Gospel of 95, 276

 Matthew, Gospel of 275, 276
Bigirumwami, Aloys 29, 33, 34, 35, 68, 231, 236
Bigogwe 250
Biguhu 13, 132, 139
Bihozagara, Jacques 202, 205
Bijard, Laurent 83
Bikindi, Simon 41
Bisengimana, Cyriaque 265
Bisesero 221, 247, 265
Bizimana, Jean-Damascène 37, 83, 167, 169, 170
Bizimana, Jérôme 74, 136
Bizimungu (Major) 86, 217
Bizimungu, Pasteur 215, 289, 299
Blanchard, Henri 98, 113, 159, 165, 174–176
Boedts, Fernand 49
Bonhoeffer, Dietrich 155, 304
Bossuyt, Leo 165
Botswana 151
Boucher-Saulnier, Françoise 74
Bourgois, Paul 37
Braeckman, Colette 10, 184, 198, 218, 219
Brussels 14, 15, 26, 33, 48, 49, 51, 73, 74, 89, 100, 104, 105, 107–109, 111, 112, 121, 129, 132, 133, 141, 148, 162, 164, 168, 171–173, 178, 182, 183, 191–193, 196, 208, 215, 218, 223, 228, 239, 250, 254, 267, 286
Bublex, Jean-Pascal 270
Bucquet, Éric 221
Bugesera 45, 52, 64, 79, 227, 282, 295
Bugina 264
Bujumbura 1, 63, 87, 90, 91, 113, 180, 234
Bukavu 38, 103, 110, 122, 123, 125, 128, 130, 131–135, 138, 140–142, 146, 150, 151, 153, 173, 176, 177, 179, 180, 193, 298, 306
Burundi 1, 5, 10, 14, 15, 22, 27, 30, 31, 33, 38, 40, 43, 44, 49, 56, 63, 73, 78, 87, 90, 101, 103, 107, 113, 121, 138, 143, 164, 168, 169, 170, 174, 179, 183, 189, 192, 194, 199, 201, 222, 230

burying the dead 108, 134, 148, 195, 197, 204, 216, 230, 264, 269, 280
Bushishi, Gallican 26
Butamwa 162
Butare 31, 32, 35, 42–44, 50, 60, 66, 73, 83, 91, 92, 95, 102, 103, 105–110, 114–116, 123, 126, 145, 148, 164, 172, 179, 187, 191, 192, 195, 197, 198, 203, 209–212, 217, 276, 284, 285, 289, 290–292, 295–297, 305, 306
Bwakira 130, 136, 140
Bwiza 255
Byanafashe, Déogratias 290
Byimana 31
Byumba 30, 35, 45, 47, 49, 53, 54, 68, 75–88, 91, 93, 102, 103, 165, 170–173, 198, 282, 291, 300

Cahiers Évangile et Société 113
Cahiers Lumière et Société 73, 113
Calozet, Alphonse 165
Canada 48, 64, 99, 100, 104, 105, 140, 164
canon law 202, 204
Cape Town 281
Carbonare, Jean 238
Cardinal, François 64
Cariou, Pierre 124
Caritas 171, 172, 194, 214, 283
Cassidy, Michael 281
Castagnet, Mathieu 222
CDI *see* Christian Democrat International
CDR *see* Coalition for the Defence of the Republic
ceceka 244
Ceillier, Jean-Claude 166
Centre Christus (Kigali) 71, 97, 114, 172, 193, 194, 278, 310
Centre Saint-Paul (Kigali) 97, 119
Chaffanjon, Philippe 222
Cham 25
Charismatic Renewal Movement 72, 100, 281, 283, 297
Cheuzeville, Hervé 271, 274
Chile 190

Chimay 86, 286
Chipenda, José 131, 141, 145, 155
Chollet, Gilles 250
Chrétien, Jean-Pierre 119, 242
Christelijke Volkspartij 162, 164, 177
Christian Democrat International (CDI) 164, 179, 188, 312
church and state relations 20, 192, 194, 203, 205
Church, Joe 38, 39
Church Missionary Society 131
Church of the Pentecost 305
Comité des Instituts Missionnaires *see* CIM
City of Nazareth 188
Classe, Léon 12, 24, 26
CMGM *see* Commission for the Memorial of the Genocide and the Massacres
CNLG *see* National Commission for the Fight against Genocide
Coalition for the Defence of the Republic (CDR) 114, 134, 226, 230, 238, 240, 245, 246, 249, 250, 251, 273
cockroach 44
Coeffic, Alain 165
Collège Christ-Roi (Nyanza) 1, 2
Comblin, André 185
Comité de Contacts 56, 63, 64, 87, 129, 132, 138
Comité des Instituts Missionnaires (CIM) 49
Commission for the Memorial of the Genocide and the Massacres (CMGM) 93, 201, 204
Commission for the Revival of Pastoral Activities (CRAP) 42, 110–112, 203, 276, 284, 305
communism 28, 29, 33, 188, 194, 204, 220, 296
Community African Initiatives Support 131
Confessing Church 59, 141, 156, 307
conflict resolution 151, 289
Congo 14, 26, 30, 38, 121–123, 127, 164, 175, 235, 241, 252, 287

Congo-Nil 20, 21, 94, 117, 166, 221–274, 278, 309
Cordes, Paul 199, 200, 306
corruption 48, 57, 64, 72, 129, 302
CRAP *see* Commission for the Revival of Pastoral Activities
Cros, Marie-Françoise 46
crucifix 96
CVP *see* Christelijke Volkspartij
Cyahinda 195
Cyangugu 2, 30, 38, 78, 86, 88, 89, 97, 99, 101, 103, 104, 108, 198, 200, 202–204, 209, 211, 212, 233, 234, 256, 291, 295, 296, 298, 302
Cyuma, Samuel 151

DAMI *see* Détachement d'Assistance Militaire et d'Instruction
Daniel-Ange 80, 100
De Backer, Rika 162, 164, 171, 177, 178, 179
de Brouwer, Alain 119, 179
de Coudray, Christine 194
de Dorlodot, Philippe 125, 170, 176, 181
De Heusch, Luc 31
De Hovre, Luc 100
de Jamblinne, Stanislas 37, 68, 181
de Lacger, Louis 26, 162
De Morgen 168
De Schrevel, Emmanuel 37
De Vestele, Philippe 161
de Waal, Alex 237
defamation 119, 219, 270
defensiveness 113, 126, 128, 200, 201, 300, 311
Deguine, Hervé 15, 105, 113, 118, 119, 120, 164, 172, 175, 194, 239
Delporte, Raymond 221, 226, 236
denial 5, 9, 121, 125, 147, 149, 224, 252, 272, 276, 277, 300, 309
Denmark 38
Der Vaterland 38
Des Forges, Alison 75, 119, 162, 216
desecration 99, 117, 202, 304
Desouter, Serge 48, 161–164, 171, 172, 177–181, 282

Détachement d'Assistance Militaire et d'Instruction (DAMI) 250
Detmold Confession 21, 279, 283, 285, 286, 287, 303
development 25, 46, 49, 55, 58, 162, 164, 171, 176, 177, 178, 183, 189, 228, 240, 241
Devulder, Joseph-Marie 50
d'Hertefelt, Marcel 27
Di Falco, Jean-Michel 239
Dialogue 15, 58, 111, 122, 159, 181, 182, 184, 215, 223, 286, 287
Doctors Without Borders (MSF) 4, 85, 90, 102, 170
Dominican Missionary Sisters of Namur 14, 100
Dominicans 1, 14, 18, 19, 38, 49, 113, 238
Dukuzemungu, Emmanuel 78
Dumas, Hélène 203, 243, 246
Dupaquier, Jean-François 119, 222

East Africa 25
East African Revival 38, 39
Eastern Congo 1, 10
Éditions Ouvrières (Les) 223
Egypt 25, 26
Emmanuel Community 72, 81, 96, 115, 234, 281, 282, 297–299, 303
emotional distress 17
empathy 34, 205, 272, 273, 277, 279, 303
EPR *see* Presbyterian Church in Rwanda
Ernotte, Eugène 1–3
ESI *see* School of Nursing Sciences
Etchegaray, Roger 78, 91–93, 99, 190, 232–235, 239, 252
Ethiopia 25, 27, 161
ethnism 14, 293, 296, 297
ethnocentrism 63, 105, 293, 294, 295, 296, 297, 299, 306
Eucharist 108, 109
Evangelical Church of Germany 132
evangelisation 11, 111, 147, 158, 167, 281, 293, 304, 305

exorcism 116
Extraordinary Synod on Ethnocentrism 105, 293, 295, 297, 299

Faculty of Protestant Theology of Butare 48
Fafchamps, Jules 32, 33
Falconi, Mario 78, 80
Farrington, Marie Julianne 92
Faucheux, Amélie 39, 41, 43, 95
Feed the Children 280
feudality 23, 27, 30, 34, 168
Final Solution 242
Flanders 34, 49, 160, 161–164, 168, 169, 177, 178, 180, 183
Focolare Movement 284
Forestier, Clément 167, 175
forgiveness 9, 21, 41, 126, 135, 145, 150, 151, 154, 155, 167, 196, 198, 205, 242, 244, 249, 275–286, 292, 297, 300, 302–304, 307, 310
Formigine 115, 233
France Télévisions 270
François, Marc 86, 165, 174
Free Methodist Church 147, 305

gacaca 14, 21, 84, 89, 136, 138, 207, 208, 213, 243–247, 249, 251–253, 256, 257, 260–267, 274, 277, 278, 288–290, 291, 292, 293–299, 301, 302, 310
  Christian 21, 288, 292, 295, 296, 297, 298, 299, 301, 302, 303, 306, 310
  official 21, 288, 299, 301, 302, 311
  traditional 288, 289, 291, 294, 295, 305
Gacamumakuba, Pierre 73
Gafaringa, Édouard 74
Gahamanyi, Jean-Baptiste 31, 35, 60, 92, 110, 306
Gakindi, Gédéon 74, 132, 135, 142
Gakoma 195
Gakuba, Déogratias 208, 209
Gakurazo 75, 78, 79, 88, 165, 193

Gakwisi, Jean-Bosco 217
Galinié, René 49
Gasasira, Gaspard 118
Gasenge, Thérèse 152
Gashegu, Emmanuel 209
Gasibirege, Simon 295, 296
Gatare, Joseph 80
Gatwa, Tharcisse 13, 38, 51, 128, 135, 284, 286, 287
General Council of the Missionaries of Africa 165–167, 172–175, 186
General Synod of the Presbyterian Church in Rwanda 59, 128, 146, 154, 199, 293
genocide
  double 18, 68, 156, 170, 172, 181, 186, 219, 230, 287, 300, 306
  commemoration 188, 202
  complicity 21, 84, 103, 104, 119, 190, 191, 196
  denialism 121
  memorialisation 201
  memorials 7, 8, 117, 201, 202, 203, 204, 205, 206, 219, 220, 305, 310
  memory activists 7, 69, 82, 241, 243, 269
  sites 124, 215, 243, 281, 295
Germany 9, 24, 25, 58, 59, 99, 127, 131, 132, 141, 153, 156, 159, 163, 164, 167, 200, 284, 285, 286, 307, 308
Ghana 286
Ghent 160, 184
Gihango 245, 246, 249, 252, 253, 256, 257, 261, 263, 266, 267
Gikondo 85, 98, 144, 147, 166
Gikongoro 30, 35, 37, 38, 59, 84, 88, 91, 92, 96, 103, 104, 166, 173, 181, 191, 198, 203, 208, 209, 211, 213–218, 281, 291, 296, 309
Gisenyi 47, 51, 52, 58, 72, 81, 91, 92, 97, 101, 115, 116, 226, 231, 233–236, 239, 250, 252–254, 261, 265, 267, 273
Gitarama 30, 34, 52, 74, 80, 86, 88, 98, 102, 105, 119, 121, 129, 131, 132, 139, 144, 165, 213, 291
Giti 76–78

Gitwa   117, 225, 229, 240, 247, 248, 258, 261–265, 268, 273
Gitwe   75
Godelieve (Sister)   196
Golias   21, 80, 111, 118, 119, 171, 194, 233, 236, 238–243, 246, 269, 270
Goma   18, 72, 91, 104, 115, 122–126, 128, 131, 138, 151, 173, 176, 232, 234, 235, 306
good power   112
Good Shepherd Sisters   73
Gospel   111, 113, 238, 276, 300
Gourevitch, Philip   218
Gouteux, Jean-Paul   171
Great Lakes Region   1, 5, 10, 26, 242
Greindl, Léopold   173, 176, 177
Grieder, Andrea   21, 247, 249, 267
grief   88, 303
Groupe scolaire d'Astrida   28
Groupe Scolaire Marie-Merci (Kibeho)   217
Grzybowski, Laurent   83
guilt
  admission of   278, 279
  confession of   21, 154–156, 199, 285, 299, 300, 307, 310
  criminal   308
  metaphysical   308
  moral   308, 309, 326
  political   308
Gyr, Hansjörg   38, 68
Gyssens, Gustaaf   37
Gyssens, Jules   36

Habiyakare, Zacharie   152
Habonimana, Charles   55, 80
Habyarimana   André   246
Habyarimana, Agathe   196
Habyarimana, Juvénal   1, 11, 23, 24, 45, 47–49, 55, 56, 58, 67, 68, 71, 76, 85, 89, 90, 99, 118–120, 123, 127, 129, 138, 158, 164, 167, 169–171, 177, 180, 181, 187, 189, 195–197, 222, 225, 226, 231, 236, 237, 240, 242, 250, 253, 255, 256, 261, 269, 274, 280, 304, 311
Habyarimana, Simon   123

Hamitic theory   4, 24–27, 39, 67, 96, 100, 161, 163, 183, 186, 278, 309
Hamus, Henri   88
Hategeka, Sabin   *see* Hategikimana, Sabin
Hategeka, Jean-Baptiste   233–235, 239, 240, 246, 247, 269, 274
Hategikimana, Sabin   265, 272
Hatzfeld, Jean   303
Havugimana, Alexis   70, 72
healing   13, 81, 280, 283, 297, 298, 303, 310
Helsinki Conference   204
Helvoirt   115, 234
Hiddesen   283, 284, 286
Hirth, Jean-Joseph   184
Hitayezu, Marcel   209
Hitimana, Joseph   77
Hitimana, Naasson   141, 143, 144, 146, 150, 155
Hitimana, Nicolas   285, 286
Hochedel, Jean   37
Holocaust   4, 31, 80, 198, 272, 306
Holy Communion   108
Holy Cross Missionaries   100
Holy See   20, 31, 187, 214, 219, 306
Hoser, Henryk   91, 107, 108, 117, 188–191, 193, 194, 200, 219, 220, 306
Hoyeau, Cécile   270
Human Rights Watch   13, 51, 73, 75, 77, 102, 119, 170, 180
Humvirwumukiza, Joseph   247
Hutu moderates   120
Hutu Power   115, 119, 226, 227

Ibuka   249, 262, 263, 286
iconoclasm   97
ICTR   *see* International Criminal Tribunal for Rwanda
identity   6, 22, 24, 44, 61, 102, 107, 193, 232, 244, 283
ideology   2, 7, 9, 10, 13, 14, 18, 20, 21, 24, 25, 38, 39, 50, 58, 59, 63, 67, 82, 83, 100, 111, 134, 145, 154, 155, 156, 173, 174, 185, 187, 226, 227, 238–240, 242, 277, 281, 286, 293, 298, 299, 309

INDEX   333

Ikusanya amakuru   244, 248
impunity   42, 278, 279, 291, 310
Infiltrators' War   *see* Abacengezi War
Institute for the Healing of
  Memories   283
integralism   107
Interahamwe   8, 21, 42, 54, 70, 72, 73,
  76, 77, 80–83, 95–97, 101, 120, 122,
  131, 136, 137, 159, 172, 176, 192, 206,
  217, 221, 224, 235, 238, 247, 256–258,
  261, 263, 265–267, 277, 281, 285, 296,
  304, 306
International Association of Rural
  Development   162
International Criminal Tribunal for
  Rwanda (ICTR)   10, 21, 41, 73, 75,
  79, 83, 84, 92, 95, 115, 122, 130, 162,
  178, 180, 208, 210–213, 245, 260, 261
International Genocide
  Conference   290
Inyenzi   35, 65
IRST   *see* Scientific and Technological
  Research Institute
Isaac, Sam   145
Islam   72, 195
Itsembabwoko n'itsembatsemba   201
Iyamuremye, Éraste   147, 262

Janne d'Othée, François   165, 167
Janusz, Julius   188, 189, 194, 204, 220,
  306
Jaspers, Karl   308, 309
Jault, Pierre   241
Jessee, Erin   27, 39, 40–42
Jesuits   49, 70, 71, 114, 121, 172, 278
Jesus Christ   35, 57, 71, 93–98, 145, 149,
  150, 152, 154, 155, 235, 257, 272, 275,
  276, 298
Jews   4, 25, 31, 59, 80, 155, 198, 200,
  304, 307
Johanssen, Ernst   127
John Paul II   57, 90, 111, 123, 188, 190,
  198, 199, 205, 232, 292, 293, 296
Josephite Brothers   32, 73, 75, 78, 79,
  185
Journal de Genève   169

Jubilee Celebration of 2000   21, 201,
  292, 293–295, 297, 299–303, 306,
  307, 310
justice   4, 24, 28, 29, 33–35, 57, 59, 61,
  67, 91, 106, 108, 150, 154, 160, 163, 183,
  190, 199, 200, 206, 207, 214, 237, 243,
  287, 289, 295, 301, 302, 310, 311
Justice and Peace Commission   302,
  303

Kabalira, Martin   209, 270
Kabano   265
Kabarondo   97
Kabasha, Tharcisse   130, 137, 138, 140
Kabera, Étienne   83, 84
Kabgayi   24, 27, 32, 34, 36, 44, 56, 59,
  60–62, 68, 73, 74, 78, 79–89, 91, 93,
  99, 100, 103, 108, 109, 117–119, 121,
  132, 165, 168, 169, 172, 188, 192, 198,
  203, 209, 210–212, 290, 296, 297, 300,
  306
Kabgayi Major Seminary   73
Kaduha   31, 43
Kagabo, Philbert   290, 291
Kagame, Alexis   23, 162
Kagame, Paul   45, 164, 195, 228, 269,
  271, 311
Kageyo   77
Kajyibwami, Modeste   89
Kakule Molo, Phares   123, 130–132,
  136–138
Kalibushi, Wenceslas   56, 65, 68, 72,
  115–117, 187, 231, 233, 234, 239, 265,
  273, 306
Kalima   83
Kamanzi, Antoine   130, 137, 138, 139
Kambanda, Jean   132, 135, 153, 215,
  245, 246, 260, 261, 273
Kamonyi   73, 105
Kampanga   105
Kanamugire, Louis   201–204
Kandt, Richard   163, 184
Kangura   94, 95
Kanyabujinja, Berchmans   43
Kanyamahanga, Ariel   264, 265, 273
Kanyamugenga   252, 253

Kanyarukiga, Gaspard   41
Kanyoni, Mélane   73, 105, 240, 248, 251, 254–256, 267
Karagwa, Charles   150
Karamaga, André   10, 38, 39, 63, 64, 127, 128, 134, 141, 143–145, 147, 148, 151–153, 156, 157
Karamira, Froduald   118
Karangwa, Hildebrand   73, 119
Karekezi, Alice   297
Karuta, Wenceslas   65
Kashyengo, Jean   231, 240, 263, 265
Kayibanda, Grégoire   23, 30, 32, 33, 36, 37, 42, 68, 120, 311
Kayihura, Michel   31, 261
Kayiranga, Esdras   197
Kayiranga, François   84, 159, 209
Kayishema, Clément   92, 225, 232, 240, 256, 260, 262, 266
Kayitaba, Michel   37, 218, 281, 284
Kayonga, Jean-Bosco   31
Kayove   248, 252, 254, 257, 261, 262, 269
Keiner, Helmut   58, 59
Kesenne, Paul   221
Kessler, Reginald   38
Kibeho   31, 57, 94, 97, 192, 203, 206, 215–218, 236, 282
Kibilira   51, 52, 57, 65, 254
Kibingo   264
Kibungo   2, 30, 80, 85, 86, 89, 97, 102, 103, 113, 171, 172, 187, 203, 204, 209, 256, 291, 293, 296, 300, 306
Kibuye   41, 60, 75, 91, 92, 94, 101, 129, 131, 136, 159, 198, 203, 206, 213, 221, 223, 225, 230–232, 235, 237, 240, 242, 245, 247, 256, 258, 259, 260–263, 265, 266–268, 271, 273
Kigali   1, 2, 11, 12, 14, 19, 24, 30, 37, 38, 43, 46–57, 59, 60, 63, 64, 66, 70–74, 76, 78, 79, 81, 82, 84–91, 93, 96, 97, 103–105, 107, 108–110, 112–121, 124, 126–128, 130–132, 135, 136–138, 141, 143–145, 147, 154, 158, 159, 162–175, 177, 181, 182, 184, 187, 190, 191–194, 196, 198, 200, 201, 203, 205, 206, 209, 210, 213, 215, 218, 220, 234, 238, 243, 244, 245, 249–251, 254, 257, 265, 272, 275, 276, 278–283, 286, 289–291, 295, 296, 302, 305, 307, 310
Kigeme   216
Kimonyo, Jean-Paul   178
Kinshasa   104, 107, 117, 188, 192
Kinyamateka   28, 35, 46, 55, 59, 61, 62, 70, 89, 117, 118, 120, 121, 215, 294, 295, 300–302
Kirinda   13, 74, 128–140, 152, 157
Kirinda Hospital   130, 136–139
Kirinda Presbyterian Institute   130
Kivumu   252, 269
Kolvenbach, Peter-Hans   71, 72
Komite Ngarukiragihugu   84
Korman, Rémi   203
Krol, Rob   10, 132, 133–135, 140–143, 151, 152, 156
Kubai, Anne   304
Kubwimana, Silas   137
Kugituntu   131
Küng, Hélène   134, 148
Küng, Jacques   134, 148

La Chandelle   125, 126
La Crête Congo-Nil   *see* Congo-Nil
La Crête Zaïre-Nil   *see* Congo-Nil
La Croix   168, 227, 269–271
La Libre Belgique   46, 85, 170
La Nouvelle Relève   158, 159, 185, 243, 286
laity   15, 66, 70, 73, 75, 96, 105, 109, 110, 145, 148, 191, 193, 194, 235, 282, 292, 293, 296, 306
Lake Kivu   221, 230, 251, 260, 262
Lapsley, Michael   283
Larcher, Laurent   37, 228
Latin America   288
Le Figaro   170, 222, 223, 227
Le Monde   31, 37, 227
Le Soir   48–51, 58, 181
Lemarchand, René   162
Lemkin, Raphael   4
Lenssen, Jan   158, 172–174, 184
L'Événement du jeudi   222

Liberal Party (Belgium)   163, 177
Liberal Party (Rwanda)   70, 192
Liège   1–3, 236
Linden, Ian   246
lineage   251, 252, 288
Linguyeneza, Vénuste   28, 29, 33–35, 78, 79, 103
Lloyd, Rhiannon   281, 284
Locatelli, Antonia   64, 65
Logiest, Guy   30, 39
London   4, 6, 7, 9, 23, 25, 27, 53, 60, 80, 118, 121, 124, 136, 144, 147, 189, 192, 217, 237, 238, 244
Longinus   95
Longman, Timothy   11, 13, 55, 57, 62, 64, 136–139, 256
Louis, André   188, 189, 312
loyal appraisal   110, 111, 194, 305
Lubich, Chiara   284
Luca, Jean-Marie   165
Luizet, François   222, 223, 227
Lutheran Church   11, 38, 127, 286
Lutheran Missionary Society of Bethel   11, 127
Lycée Notre Dame de Cîteaux (Kigali)   114
Lyon   119, 167, 222, 233, 238, 239, 241, 269

Mabanza   117, 247, 248, 257, 260, 261, 262, 263, 264, 271
Macagnino, Tito Oggioni   70
Madagascar   162
Mahame, Chrysologue   71
Maindron, Gabriel   20, 21, 92, 94, 100, 208, 209, 221–274, 309
Mancebo, Juan José   78
Marist Brothers   73
Martens, Wilfred   177
Martres, Georges   49
Marxism   188, 288
Masaka   166
Masango   121
Mashyendeli, Augustin   77
Masinzo, Jérôme   43, 114, 195, 284

Mass   83, 84, 93, 98, 108, 109, 116, 188, 196, 204, 242, 248, 251, 252, 255, 270, 296
Mategeko, Aimé   84, 208, 209
Matthew, Gospel of   275, 276
Mayer, Otto   73, 85, 98, 159, 165, 167, 174
Mayunzwe   80
Mazimpaka, Patrick   301
Mbonampeka, Stanislas   70
Mbonyintege, Smaragde   61, 288, 290, 291, 292, 293, 294, 305
Mbonyumutwa, Dominique   184
McCullum, Hugh   139–141, 146
Médecins Sans Frontières (MSF)   *see* Doctors Without Borders
mediation   18, 62, 93, 129
memory   1, 3, 5–9, 12, 16, 20, 21, 27, 55, 69, 82, 187, 189, 201, 203, 220, 224, 233, 234, 238, 241, 243, 253, 263, 269, 272, 274, 304, 305, 307, 310
   abused   6, 7
   articulation of   7, 20, 187
   blocked   6
   collective   7, 243
   manipulated   7
   politics of   5, 6, 9, 187, 310
   public   238, 274
   traumatic   6, 247
Mendiondo, Jean-Baptiste   221, 232, 235, 256
Methodist Church   38, 63, 87, 88, 131, 147, 148, 305
Minnaert, Stefaan   184, 186
Misago, Augustin   20, 55, 59–62, 84, 86, 92, 104, 198, 208, 209, 213–219, 296, 308, 309, 310
Mission of the Reformed Churches in the Netherlands   133
Missionaries of Africa   11, 14, 20, 23, 28, 33, 36–38, 48–51, 53, 54, 66, 68, 70, 73, 74, 78, 85, 88, 98, 99, 105, 158–186, 228, 231, 254, 306
Missionaries of Jesus, Mary and Joseph   257, 258, 260

mixed church–state commission 20, 201, 202, 205, 219
Modena 233
Moens, Jean-Luc 282, 298
Mokoto 31
Montreal Institute of Integration and Formation 280
moral guilt 308, 309
moratorium 116, 135
Moscow 188
Mosmans, Guy 28
Moucecore 37, 218, 303
Mozambique 188
Mpiranya, Protais 196
MSF see Médecins Sans Frontières
Muberanziza, Aloys 290
Mubiligi, Félicien 110, 295
Mudashimwa, Gaspard 77
Mugabo, Pie 106, 190, 192, 193, 197
Mugina 80, 203
Mugonero 75, 95, 213
Muhayimana, Célestin 77
Muhororo 51
Muhura 78, 80
Mukabutera, Julienne 84, 210
Mukagango, Consolata 84, 210
Mukagasana, Yolande 97
Mukakimenyi, Jacqueline 210
Mukamasabo, Dancilla 248, 263
Mukandanga, Dorothée 80
Mukansanga, Daphrose 281
Mukansoro, Émilienne 254
Mukanyangezi, Bénédicte 104, 191, 210
Mukarange 80
Mukarusine, Bernadette 104, 191, 210
Muku 130, 134, 140
Mulfinger, Tharcisse 137, 138
Mulinda, Fidèle 77
Mulindwa, Faustin 77
Mulinzi, Canisius 217
Munderere 252
Mungwareba, Modeste 42, 50, 110, 155, 203, 278, 284–286, 293
Munyaneza, Jean-Bosco 80
Munyaneza, Malachie 15, 72, 85, 93, 98, 149, 156

Munyentwali, Patrice 70, 83, 84
Murama 251, 257, 266, 267
Murambi 52, 215, 216
Murangira, César 70, 85, 95
Murangira, Emmanuel 96
Murego, Donat 119
Murengeranka, Jean-Baptiste 70
Murunda 236, 247, 254, 257, 265
Musabyimana, Samuel 83, 130, 213
Mushaka 43, 298, 299
Mushubati 245, 247, 251, 254, 255, 263–265, 267
Musoni, Alois 217
Mutabazi, Anastase 117, 198, 297
Mutabazi, Eugène 118, 119, 239
Mutara 53
Mutara III Rudahigwa 29
Mutete 282, 303
Muteyumungu, Clément 240
Mutimura, Géras 132, 139
Muvara, Félicien 60, 61, 198
Muyanza 178, 282
Muyunzwe 55, 80, 117, 119, 120
Muzungu, Bernardin 73, 113
Mwami 23, 29, 163
Mwezi, Emmnanuel 95

Nairobi 63, 70, 72, 131, 134, 136, 137, 141, 143, 145–147, 151, 199, 252, 287, 288, 306
Namibia 11, 151
National Assembly (France) 182, 197
National Commission for the Fight against Genocide (CNLG) 14, 93, 116, 201, 203, 245, 249
National Commission for the Jubilee 294
National Unity and Reconciliation Commission (NURC) 43, 279, 280, 286, 301, 310
National University of Rwanda 32, 289, 290, 295, 305
Nayinzira, Jean-Népomuscène 302
Nazism 4, 8, 31, 59, 141, 156, 233, 242, 304, 307
Ndagijimana, Joseph 84, 208, 210

INDEX   337

Ndahiro, Tom   262
Ndayambaje, Jean-Damascène   185
Ndayisaba, Renate   137, 138
Ndera   70, 80, 85, 95, 166
Ndorimana, Jean   2, 233, 256, 295
Nedelec, Annick   228, 229, 230, 241, 271
Netherlands (The)   14–16, 102, 115, 131–133, 135, 138, 140, 153, 156, 160, 162, 164, 167–169, 170–172, 177, 178, 234, 285
New York Times   239, 245
Newbury, Catharine   27, 162
Newbury, David   27
Ngarambe, François-Xavier   72
Ngirabanyiginya, Dominique   211
Ngirinshuti, Thaddée   211
Ngomanzungu, Joseph   56, 63, 74, 191
Nguyên Van Tot, Pierre   188, 190, 191–193, 200, 219
Nickson, Patricia   131
Niger   162
Nikwigize, Phocas   92, 104, 123, 124, 128
Niragira, Boniface   255
Niyitegeka, Félicitas   81
Niyomugabo, Joseph   81, 216–218
Nkongoli, Laurent   197
Nkubito, Alphonse Marie   108, 190, 191, 193
Nkusi, Emmanuel   130, 131, 147
Nkusi, François   208, 211
Noah   25
non-governmental organisation   17, 279
North Kivu   31, 93, 121, 124, 146, 158, 175
Nsabimana, Emmanuel   198
Nsengimana, Albert   97, 276
Nsengimana, Hormisdas   83, 208, 211
Nsengimana, Joseph   116, 201–203
Nsengiyumva, Marcellin   130, 137
Nsengiyumva, Vincent   11, 55, 57, 73, 78, 86, 112, 129, 196, 197, 204
Nsinga, Jean-Baptiste   78
Nsingaheye, André   246, 247, 251, 252, 265

Ntabakuze, Aloys   180
Ntagungira, Jean-Bosco   70
Ntahobali, Pius   105
Ntakirutimana, Elizaphan   75, 83, 95, 213, 308
Ntampaka, Charles   288
Ntamugabumwe, Jean-Baptiste   211, 234
Ntarama   124, 205, 281
Ntawirukanayo, Fidèle   130, 137, 138
Ntezimana, Emmanuel   27, 162
Ntezimana, Laurien   66, 110, 112, 115, 194, 275, 284
Ntihabose, Jean-Baptiste   231, 252
Ntimugura, Laurent   208, 211
Ntirivamunda, Jean   232, 234
Ntiyamira, Prosper   234, 252, 269
Ntuliye, Édouard   208, 211
nunciature   51, 91, 188, 190–194, 200, 203, 204, 220, 234, 310
NURC *see* National Unity and Reconciliation Commission
Nyagahanga   165, 172–174
Nyakibanda Major Seminary   33, 55, 59, 61, 84, 103, 198, 216, 278, 290, 292–294, 296, 301, 305
Nyamagumba   117, 225, 247, 248, 262, 264, 265
Nyamasheke   31, 38, 97, 166, 202, 203, 298
Nyamata   30, 124, 203, 205, 213, 227, 281, 282, 291
Nyamirambo   73, 85, 96, 98, 113, 159, 165, 166, 176, 185
Nyamwasa, Irénée   217
Nyandwi, Athanase   84
Nyange   41, 97, 115, 206
Nyanza   1, 75, 200
Nyarubuye   203–206
Nyarusiza   96
Nyilingabo, Amani   137–140
Nyilinkindi, Donat   74, 142
Nyinawimana   77
Nyirahabimana, Donatile   247, 248, 267
Nyiramana, Christine   240, 268

Nyiramasuhuko, Pauline   123
Nyiramukiza, Valentine   94
Nyirasafari, Veronica   246
Nyumba   43, 195, 203
Nyundo   29, 33, 34, 43, 53, 56, 60, 65, 68, 72, 73, 85, 100, 103, 108, 109, 115–117, 126, 159, 166, 169, 187, 198, 203, 209–212, 221, 222, 226, 233–236, 251, 256, 263, 265, 296, 305, 306
Nzabahimana, François   162, 171, 178, 179, 182
Nzabahimana, Siméon   143
Nzakamwita, Servilien   47, 53, 282, 300, 303

Office National de la Population   129, 189
Official Gazette of the Republic of Rwanda   207, 208, 213, 242
Omaar, Rakiya   118, 119, 237
omission   84, 106, 107, 231, 238, 240, 250, 255, 256, 263, 265, 268, 307
ONAPO   *see* Office National de la Population
Opération Turquoise   221, 222, 232, 240, 267, 268
Opus Dei   190, 238
orphan care   101, 112, 148, 149, 188, 262, 280, 310
Osservatore Romano   88, 91, 220
Ouest-France   271
Overdulve, Kees   156
Oxfam   90, 290

Pagès, Albert   26, 162
Pallotines   81, 99, 189
Parmehutu   *see* Party of the Hutu Emancipation
Parti Social Chrétien (PSC)   164
Party of the Hutu Emancipation (Parmehutu)   30, 34, 114, 120
pastoral letter   24, 25, 27–29, 34, 56–58, 60, 64, 66, 104, 106, 108, 188, 292, 304
Pax Christi   50, 66

peace   2, 27, 34, 36, 57–58, 59, 63–67, 72, 87, 89–92, 105, 126, 149, 150, 183, 191, 218, 226, 281, 282, 291
peace marches   66, 67
penance   108, 109
penitential services   109, 116
Pennachio, Salvatore   188
Pentecostal churches   38, 63, 131, 148, 213, 305, 311, 312
Perraudin, André   24, 27–37, 49, 68, 169, 184, 309
persecution   18, 59, 190–192, 194, 206, 219, 310
Petit Écho des Missionnaires d'Afrique   169, 170, 171, 174
Pinard, Guy   105
Pinochet, Augusto   190
Pognon, Alfred   214
Poincaré, Nicolas   21, 83, 222, 223, 227–231, 237, 238, 241, 242, 258, 264, 269, 272, 273
Poland   48, 81, 85, 99, 188, 189, 190, 200
polarisation   22–24, 126, 156, 231, 292, 309
Pontifical Commission for Justice and Peace   91
Poulin, Armand   165
powerlessness   86, 130, 136, 139, 153, 214, 225, 231, 272, 304
Presbyterian Church in Rwanda (EPR)   3, 10, 12–14, 18, 20, 38, 39, 52, 55, 58, 59, 63, 71, 72, 74, 87, 88, 95, 98, 99, 126–156, 189, 199, 213, 275, 284, 293, 305, 306, 312
Pretoria   11
prosecution   20, 206, 213, 218
Protestant churches   11, 15, 16, 18, 20, 24, 38, 39, 55, 58, 62, 63, 66–68, 71, 74, 81, 88, 99, 123, 127, 129, 130, 132, 147, 148, 155, 156, 171, 187, 195, 207, 213, 224, 274, 280, 281, 284–286, 288, 307, 311
Protestant Council of Rwanda   130, 147, 155
Prunier, Gérard   48, 54, 120, 166

PSC   see Parti Social Chrétien
punishment   302

RADER   see Rassemblement
   Démocratique Rwandais
Radio Amahoro   182
Radio France Internationale   64
Radio Muhabura   230
Radio Rwanda   86, 245, 261, 269
Radio Télévision des Mille
   Collines   86, 94, 114, 122, 134, 176,
   230
Radio Vatican   31, 169
Rassemblement Démocratique
   Rwandais   30
Rassemblement pour le Retour de la
   Démocratie au Rwanda (RDR)   179,
   182
RDR   see Rassemblement pour le Retour
   de la Démocratie au Rwanda
reconciliation   2, 10, 13, 21, 42, 43,
   63, 66, 67, 72, 90, 106, 108, 125,
   134, 149–153, 173, 176, 191, 192, 249,
   276–283, 284, 286, 288, 289, 291, 292,
   295, 297, 299, 301, 303, 310
reconstruction   50, 117, 141, 142,
   147–150, 156, 168, 174, 184, 194, 222,
   281, 291, 306
refugee camps   5, 8, 12, 18, 77, 83, 102,
   104, 121, 123–127, 130, 133, 135, 146,
   153, 172–176, 179, 182, 194, 220, 282
Régiment d'infanterie et de chars de
   marine (RICM)   222
Rehabilitation Committee   141, 142,
   156
Remera   71, 114, 152, 153, 194, 280, 310
Remera-Rukoma   74, 75, 129, 132, 135,
   136
repentance   145, 148–150, 154, 155, 276,
   278, 285, 300, 303, 307
Reporters Without Borders   118, 119
retraumatisation   17, 302
Reyntjens, Filip   79, 103, 180, 196, 289
RICM   see Régiment d'infanterie et de
   chars de marine
Ricoeur, Paul   7, 278, 279

Roman Curia   189, 190, 198
RPA   see Rwandan Patriotic Army
RPF   see Rwandan Patriotic Front
RTLM   see Radio Télévision des Mille
   Collines
Rubayiza, Fulgence   283–287
Rubengera   54, 117, 152, 225, 247, 250,
   251, 255, 259–261, 265, 273
Rubwejanga, Frédéric   86, 187, 192,
   204, 205, 216, 256, 293, 300, 306
Ruccius, Gerhard   127
Rucibigango, Jean-Baptiste   243
Rugamba, Cyprien   281
Rugamba, Daphrose   72
Rugambage, Samuel   147
Rugasira, Ananie   70, 80
Rugirangoga   43, 89, 298, 299, 303
Ruhango   81, 282
Ruhengeri   35, 42, 45, 47, 49, 52–54,
   58, 65, 68, 92, 103, 105, 117, 123, 124,
   128, 132, 159, 162, 173, 178, 185, 211,
   250, 253, 278, 291, 296
Rukoma   85
Rukundo, Emmanuel   73, 83, 84, 208,
   211
Rurangirwa, Fidèle   248, 262–266
Rusingizandekwe, Thaddée   104, 191,
   192, 211, 214
Russell, Bertrand   31
Rustenburg Confession   153, 285
Rusumo   52
Rutaremara, Aimé   84
Rutaremara, Jariel   218
Rutaremara, Tito   197–199, 288–290
Rutatina, Richard   197
Rutayisire, Antoine   43, 278, 280
Rutayisire, Paul   5, 13, 37, 71, 111, 296
Rutazibwa, Privat   93, 158, 172, 184,
   185, 287
Rutihunza, Jean-Baptiste   211
Rutumbu, Juvénal   71, 278
Ruyenzi   105
Ruzindana, Joseph   78, 86
Ruzindaza, Jean-Baptiste   95
Rwagacuzi, Faustin   148
Rwagafirita, Pierre Célestin   2

Rwakareke, Fabien   115, 235, 265
Rwamatamu   52, 265
Rwamayanja, Jean-Baptiste   211
Rwamiko   78
Rwamuhizi, Athanase   131
Rwandan Association for the Defence of Human Rights (ARDHO)   190
Rwandan Association for the Defence of the Rights of the Person and the Public Liberties (ADL)   51–53, 66, 117–120, 181, 254
Rwandan Bible Society   51
Rwandan Patriotic Army (RPA)   45
Rwandan Patriotric Front (RPF)   3, 5, 8, 18, 20, 22, 24, 27, 32, 40, 44–58, 61–68, 70, 71, 75–80, 82, 86, 87, 89–91, 93, 95, 99, 101–104, 106, 107, 111, 120–124, 126, 128–131, 133, 134, 138, 140, 146, 156, 158, 159, 161–165, 167, 169, 170–186, 188–190, 193, 196, 197, 207, 214, 215, 217, 220, 225–227; 229–232, 234, 235, 237, 240, 241, 243, 248–251, 253, 255, 269, 272–274, 277, 278–280, 282, 287, 288, 306, 309, 310, 311
Rwandan Social Revolution   2, 11, 27, 29, 36–39, 42, 61, 96, 161, 188, 304
Rwandese Alliance for National Unity   288
Rwesero, Dominique   77, 208, 212
Rwesero Minor Seminary   47, 77
Rwigema, Fred   45, 55, 215, 216
Rwigema, Pierre Célestin   201, 204, 286
Ryckmans, Pierre   26

sacrament   25, 108, 109, 116, 232, 235, 249, 273
Sainte-Famille church (Kigali)   81, 82, 206, 238
Sala, Pedro   166, 167, 172, 173
Salesians   49
Saliège, Jules   304
Sarfati, Mathieu   270
Saur, Léon   27, 28, 32, 36, 68, 164
Save   31, 292, 299

SBMPC   *see* Belgian Society of Protestant Missions in Congo
Schaubroeck, Frieda   158
Schmetz, Joseph   221
Schöneke, Wolfgang   107
School of Nursing Sciences (ESI)   130, 136, 137, 139
Scientific and Technological Research Institute (IRST)   290
Scotland   284, 285
Sebitama, Elias   267
Sebuhuku   80
Second World War   3, 4, 9, 36, 153
Secretariat of State (Rome)   190, 200, 202, 205, 219, 220, 306
secular state   311
Sekamana, Denis   104, 191, 192, 208, 212
Semugeshi   264
Senate (Belgium)   176, 177, 182, 239, 241
Sendashonga, Seth   287
Seromba, Athanase   21, 83, 84, 115, 208, 212, 231, 308
Service d'Animation Théologique (SAT)   110
Setako, Pierre   244, 245, 248, 251, 252, 255
Seuret, Léon   170
Seventh Day Adventist Church   38, 63, 71, 75, 99, 213, 305
Shyogwe   130, 213
Shyorongi   191, 192, 243
Sibomana, André   46, 51, 59, 60, 61, 67, 74, 108, 109, 117–121, 181, 198, 306
Sibomana, Joseph   35
silence   11, 12, 37, 67, 68, 84, 97, 99, 105, 111, 112, 130, 140, 153, 224, 238, 307
Sillis, Alphonsine   248, 266, 267
Simard de Roberval, Claude   104
Simbi   195
sin   22, 95, 116, 148, 154, 185, 192, 275, 297, 299, 300, 304
Sindikubwabo, Théodore   86, 179
Smedes, Lewis   277

Sodano, Angelo   190
Sovu   21, 185, 208, 218
Spain   77, 78, 164, 167, 172, 180, 252, 257, 258, 260, 269, 271
Speke, John Hanning   25, 26
spirituality   97, 112, 284, 298
St André College (Kigali)   96
St Vincent Minor Seminary (Ndera)   70
statue   97
Staub, Ervin   277
stereotype   23, 94, 100, 160, 161, 186, 300
Stuttgart Declaration   153, 307, 309
Subiza, Innocent   212
Subushumba, Édouard   77
Survie   238, 241
Surviving Church   141
Sweden   38
Swiss Development Agency   289
Switzerland   21, 28, 31, 38, 131, 132, 134, 164, 169, 170, 238, 247, 289, 309

Taba   137
Tanzania   8, 12, 40, 63, 77, 101, 102, 107, 153, 154, 164, 170–172, 174–176, 179, 182
Télesphore (Sister)   196
Terras, Christian   21, 118, 119, 231, 233, 238–241, 243, 245, 247–250, 255, 256, 263, 265, 268–270, 274
Tertio Millenio Adveniente   292
The Hague   31, 173
theology of reconstruction   148
Theunis, Guy   49, 51, 52, 73, 165, 166, 173, 174, 181–184, 212, 213, 223
Todorov, Tzvetan   6
Tomko, Joseph   198
Toulouse   170, 214
trauma   6, 43, 93, 102–104, 110, 112, 224, 234, 247, 280, 281, 284, 297, 303, 312
trauma counselling   280, 281, 303
Trócaire   280
Trouw   135, 156
Truth and Reconciliation Commission   9, 69

Tutu, Desmond   151, 281
Twa   24, 29, 57, 64, 155, 163
Twagirayesu, Michel   55, 127–129, 130, 132–134, 138, 140, 144, 145, 146, 150, 151–153, 156, 157, 189, 306, 309
Twagirayezu, Urbain   212, 231, 259
Twahirwa, Ladislas   290
Twambazemungu, Jean-Marie   72, 96, 282
Twubake   149, 155

ubuhake   23, 41
Uganda   25, 29, 39, 45, 47, 48, 63, 79, 87, 89, 91, 101, 197, 201, 282, 285, 311
Ugirashebuja, Octave   114
Umotoni, Josée   252, 257–260
Umugwaneza, Angélique   84, 85
UNAR   *see* Union Nationale Rwandaise
UNESCO   *see* United Nations Educational, Scientific and Cultural Organisation
United Nations Educational, Scientific and Cultural Organisation (UNESCO)   31, 38
United Nations High Commissioner for Refugees   47
United Nations Refugee Agency   121
United Nations Security Council   221
Union Nationale Rwandaise   (UNAR)   29, 30, 33–35, 37, 68, 188
Union of Baptist Churches   305
United Evangelical Mission (VEM)   123, 131
United Kingdom   14, 15
United Nations   4
United States   18, 153
United States Agency for International Development (USAID)   290
Urbaniak, Stanislas   81, 249
Urugwiro Village   279, 289, 294, 295, 301
Urumuri rwa Kristu   292
Uvin, Peter   178
Uwayezu, Emmanuel   212

Uwimana, Emmanuel   240, 245–248, 250, 252, 253, 256, 257, 260
Uwimana, Ignace-Marie   43, 44
Uwimpuhwe, Catherine   262, 264
Uwizeye, Fidèle   119
Uwobibabaje, Anastase   249, 262, 267

Vallmajo, Joachim   77, 165
van Butselaar, Jan   156
Van der Meersch, Jean   161
Van Hoven, Béatrice   248, 251, 267
Van Hoyweghen, Saskia   311
Van Langendonck, Gert   34
Van Overschelde, Gerard   37
van 't Spijker, Gerard   15, 135, 138, 143, 144, 148, 153, 156
Vansina, Jan   162
Vatican   31, 111, 169, 188, 200
VEM   see United Evangelical Mission
vengeance   88, 92, 111, 134, 148, 170, 175, 225, 276, 280, 285, 287, 297, 300, 309
Vermeire, Yves   176
Verschave, François-Xavier   241, 242
Vexilla Galliae   271
Virgin Mary   57, 81, 93, 94, 97, 236
Vita et Pax   71
Vlaams Rwandese Vereniging   162
Vleugels, Jef   50, 51, 52, 53, 54, 68, 73, 165, 167, 173, 181, 186, 254
Vuillemin, Denis-Gilles   31, 38

Vulliez, Hyacinthe   125

wa Karega, Jyoni   289, 290, 291, 294
Wacker, Meinolf   284
Warren, Rick   311
WCC   see World Council of Churches
wedding   149
Wereldwijd   183
White Fathers   see Missionaries of Africa
Windhoek   10, 135, 150, 151–153, 156, 306
Wisemen Council   291
World Association for Christian Communication   144
World Council of Churches (WCC)   63, 74, 129, 136, 139, 145, 147
World Vision   280
Wuppertal   123, 131, 135, 138, 141

Young Catholic Farmers   236
Yugoslavia   200

Zaire   5, 8, 10, 12, 18, 45, 54, 63, 71, 77, 81, 83, 91, 101–104, 107, 115, 117, 122, 126, 127, 130, 133, 146, 151, 153, 154, 172, 174–176, 179, 182, 194, 201, 209, 219, 232, 252, 257, 269, 277, 282, 287, 289, 292
Zerah   26
Zigirumugabe, Théophile   217

Previously published titles in the series

Violent Conversion: Brazilian Pentecostalism and Urban Women in Mozambique, Linda Van de Kamp (2016)
Beyond Religious Tolerance: Muslim, Christian & Traditionalist Encounters in an African Town, edited by Insa Nolte, Olukoya Ogen and Rebecca Jones (2017)
Faith, Power and Family: Christianity and Social Change in French Cameroon, Charlotte Walker-Said (2018)
Contesting Catholics: Benedicto Kiwanuka and the Birth of Postcolonial Uganda, Jonathon L. Earle, J. J. Carney (2021)
Islamic Scholarship in Africa: New Directions and Global Contexts, edited by Ousmane Oumar Kane (2021)
From Rebels to Rulers: Writing Legitimacy in the Sokoto State, 1804–1837, Paul Naylor (2021)
Sacred Queer Stories: Ugandan LGBTQ+ Refugee Lives & the Bible, Adriaan van Klinken, Johanna Stiebert, Sebyala Brian and Fredrick Hudson (2021)
Labour & Christianity in the Mission: African Workers in Tanganyika & Zanzibar, 1864–1926, Michelle Liebst (2021)

Forthcoming

Competing Catholicisms: The Jesuits, the Vatican & the Making of Postcolonial French Africa, Jean Luc Enyegue, SJ (2022)

Fountain Studies in East African History

Description of the series

The series is a platform for scholarly and intellectual exchange of knowledge and information with the international community on the East African region in anthropology, culture, religion, politics and history.

#	Title	Author
1.	The East African Revival: History and Legacies	Kevin Ward & Emma Wild-Wood
2.	Battles of the Ugandan Resistance	Muhoozi Kainerugaba
3.	A History of Ankole	H.F. Morris
4.	The Roots of Ethnicity: Origins of the Acholi of Uganda	Ronald R. Atkinson
5.	A Political History of Uganda	Samwiri Rubaraza Karugire
6.	Uganda Since Independence: A Story of Unfulfilled Hopes	Phares Mutibwa
7.	Alice Lakwena and the Holy Spirits: War in Northern Uganda 1986–97	Heike Behrend
8.	Controlling Anger: The Anthropology of Gisu Violence	Suzette Heald
9.	Political Power in Pre-Colonial Buganda	Richard Reid
10.	War in Pre-Colonial Eastern Africa 1850-1999	Justin Willis
11.	A History of the Kingdom of Nkore in Western Uganda to 1896	Samwiri Karugire
12.	Not all the Kings Men: Inequality as a Political Insrument in Ankole	Martin R. Doornbos
13.	Slavery in the Great Lakes Region of East Africa	Henri Medard and Shane Doyle (eds.)
14.	Developing Uganda	Holger B. Hansen & M. Twaddle (eds.)
15.	Revealing Prophets: Prophecy in Eastern African History	D.M. Anderson & D.H. Johnson (eds.)
16.	Religion & Politics in East Africa	Holger B. Hansen & M. Twaddle (eds.)
17.	Spirit Possession, Modernity and Power in Africa	Heike Behrend & Ute Luig (eds.)
18.	The Kings of Buganda	M.S.M. Kiwanuka
19.	A History of Buganda from the Foundation of the Kingdom to 1900	M.S.M. Kiwanuka
20.	A History of Tooro in Western Uganda from the Foundation of the Kingdom to 1900	James Fergus Wilson
21.	Kigezi and its People	Paulo Ngologoza
22.	A History of Bunyoro-Kitara	A.R. Dunbur
23.	Contesting Catholics: Benedicto Kiwanuka and the Birth of Postcolonial Uganda	Jonathon L. Earle & J.J. Carney
24.	Rwanda before the Genocide: Catholic Politics and Ethnic Discourse in Late Colonial Era	J.J. Carney
25.	The Genocide against the Tutsi, and the Rwandan Churches: Between Grief and Denial	Philippe Denis

www.ingramcontent.com/pod-product-compliance
Lightning Source LLC
Chambersburg PA
CBHW052056300426
44117CB00013B/2150

The Definitive Diva

ALSO BY JOHN LOUIS DIGAETANI
AND FROM MCFARLAND

An Invitation to the Opera, Revised Edition (2016)

*Carlo Gozzi: A Life in the 18th Century Venetian Theater,
an Afterlife in Opera* (2000; paperback 2014)

Richard Wagner: New Light on a Musical Life (2014)

*Wagner Outside the Ring: Essays on the Operas,
Their Performance and Their Connections with Other Arts* (2009)

*Stages of Struggle: Modern Playwrights
and Their Psychological Inspirations* (2008)

Inside the Ring: Essays on Wagner's Opera Cycle (2006)

Wagner and Suicide (2003)

The Definitive Diva
The Life and Career of Maria Callas

JOHN LOUIS DiGAETANI

McFarland & Company, Inc., Publishers
Jefferson, North Carolina

All photographs are provided by Photofest, New York. All rights reserved.

Library of Congress Cataloguing-in-Publication Data

Names: DiGaetani, John Louis, 1943– author.
Title: The definitive diva : the life and career of Maria Callas / John Louis DiGaetani.
Description: Jefferson, North Carolina : McFarland & Company, 2021. |
Includes bibliographical references and index.
Identifiers: LCCN 2021032380 | ISBN 9781476662633 (paperback : acid free paper) ∞
ISBN 9781476643403 (ebook)
Subjects: LCSH: Callas, Maria, 1923-1977. | Sopranos (Singers)—Biography. |
BISAC: MUSIC / Genres & Styles / Opera | BIOGRAPHY &
AUTOBIOGRAPHY / Entertainment & Performing Arts
Classification: LCC ML420.C18 D46 2021 | DDC 782.1092 [B]—dc23
LC record available at https://lccn.loc.gov/2021032380

British Library cataloguing data are available
ISBN (print) 978-1-4766-6263-3
ISBN (ebook) 978-1-4766-4340-3

© 2021 John Louis DiGaetani. All rights reserved

No part of this book may be reproduced or transmitted in any form or by any means, electronic or mechanical, including photocopying or recording, or by any information storage and retrieval system, without permission in writing from the publisher.

Front cover image: The newly-slender and glamourized opera singer, Maria Callas, in her chic maisonette apartment in Milan, 1957 (Photofest).

Printed in the United States of America

*McFarland & Company, Inc., Publishers
Box 611, Jefferson, North Carolina 28640
www.mcfarlandpub.com*

For Silvia Montemurro

Acknowledgments

I would like to thank Hofstra University for the sabbatical leave and travel funds it granted me, in order to research and write this book. I would like to give special thanks to Craig Rustici and to Silvia Montemurro at Hofstra for their help and encouragement. Also, grateful thanks to the Hofstra librarians for their tireless help throughout my research; Nick Patterson of the Wiener Music Library at Columbia University, and Tom Lisanti at the New York Public Library for the Performing Arts, Lincoln Center. I would like to thank Howard Mandelbaum of Photofest for his valuable help in assembling the photographic collection contained herein, and Gregory Moore for his expert editing of this book.

I am greatly indebted to the previous biographies of Maria Callas, especially those by her mother, sister and other family members. Those Greeks knew her very well and understood the Greek part of her personality. Her recordings have also been intensely studied, especially by musicologists and opera experts like John Ardoin. I have learned from all these previous studies of her life and career—for example, the ones by her husband Giovanni Battista Meneghini and others, which give us new insight into her complex personality and her fascinating stage performances. For the valuable information contained in these previous studies of the life and career of Maria Callas, I am most grateful.

Table of Contents

Acknowledgments vi
Preface 1
Introduction 3

1. Birth in New York 7
2. Athens and World War II 20
3. Back to New York 32
4. Verona and the Arena 41
5. Conquering Italy and South America 57
6. Titta, Marriage and Meteoric Ascent 66
7. La Scala at Last 75
8. Back to La Scala—Conquering America 83
9. Enter Onassis, and Addio, Titta 104
10. 1959 and the Affair with Onassis 118
11. Free of Battista and Pursuing Aristo 127
12. Loving Onassis 132
13. Enter Jacqueline Kennedy 140
14. Vocal Problems: "The Wobble" 150
15. The Return of Onassis 158
16. Teaching in New York, Directing in Turin 162
17. The Final Tour with Di Stefano 169
18. Death in Paris 184
19. The Aftermath and the Callas Legacy 192

Bibliography 203
Index 207

Preface

As the centenary of the 1923 birth of Maria Callas approaches, worldwide interest in her singing career, her singularly charismatic personality and her highly dramatic life—both on- and off-stage—seems to continue to grow, in spite of the fact that it is approaching 50 years since her untimely passing. Re-masterings and re-releases of her recordings and videos of her television performances keep appearing. She is also a lively presence on the Internet, with "views" and "likes" of Maria Callas–related videos numbering in the multi-millions. Maria Callas, "The Woman, The Artist," has taken on mythic status, most especially in the opera music world.

But hers was a life lived on the world stage—and her fame (some would say infamy) extended to the entire "public consciousness" of many parts of the world. Thanks to her recordings, her singing and acting continue to thrill new generations of opera fans. We can still experience her art, if not the subtle complexities of her live performances, not to mention her luminescent personality.

This book will take a new look at her life, her family, her problems and her stellar career. She began life in a troubled, unhappy family of Greek immigrants in New York City, and went on to become the most famous, glamorous opera singer of the 20th century—and beyond.

Maria Callas was only 53 when she died in Paris on November 18, 1977.

Introduction

Maria Callas was born in 1923—and in light of the centenary of her birth, new generations (and old) have been given an opportunity to take a concentrated look ("a deep dive," in the current parlance) into the storied life and career of this enigmatic, supremely talented American artist (yes, she was born in Manhattan, to Greek émigré parents). Especially in this era of advanced technology, we have a limitless resource of knowledge, as well as access to virtually every known recording and/or video of *La Divina* (as she is commonly known amongst her millions of fans to this very day). There is no other *La Divina*. She is it.

Interest in Callas has never waned in the 40+ years since her death in 1977. Quite the opposite. The joy of discovering her other-worldly, exquisite singing has been experienced by several new generations in the years since her passing. There have been several films about her life and career, including Franco Zeffirelli's *Callas Forever* (2004) and the Tom Volf documentary *Maria by Callas* (2018). She became the most important opera singer of the 20th century, even though her career as a singer was shorter than it could have been. She recorded at the beginning of the long-playing record era with Cetra in Italy, and then with Angel/EMI in Britain. Some of her performances, or parts of the performances, were broadcast on the radio, or televised, as were some of her concerts and recitals at the end of her career. Callas' voice, career and her charisma have endured into the 21st century. Surely, that indicates that we need a new biography of her very eventful and turbulent life.

A unique artist, Callas influenced many others in her art. She drew great attention to herself during her career, and by the late 1950s, all the major opera houses of the world were vying to get her to perform for their audiences. By the end of her life, she had become a popular icon so that even people who were not interested in opera were talking about her. She sang primarily at Milan's Teatro alla Scala, Covent Garden and the Metropolitan Opera, but also at opera theaters in Naples, Rome, Palermo, Venice, Paris, Chicago and Dallas. She gave recitals which were routinely sold out and she made many recordings of both complete operas and recitals. She became the most-recorded opera singer of her time, and thank goodness she made those recordings so that we have some permanent record of her voice and singing career. She was recorded in her major roles, especially the title roles in *Lucia di Lammermoor*, *Norma* and *Tosca*, her three most famous parts.

However, aside from her singing, her life also fascinated the world at large. She was born in New York City in 1923 into an immigrant family from Greece. She received most of her vocal training from a singer of Italian opera in Athens, the Spanish soprano Elvira de Hidalgo. She began her career in Verona, Italy—and within five years she was singing at all the most famous opera houses in the world. She was on the cover of *Time* magazine in 1956, right before her Met debut, but the article within was really a personal attack since it discussed primarily her family feuds, especially with her mother and sister, with whom she was then not speaking. She had also become notorious for feuding with various opera companies. She made the headlines when she was presented with court papers by a bailiff after a performance of *Madama Butterfly* at Chicago's Lyric Opera. In stage makeup and in costume, she screamed at the bailiffs and majestically announced that she would never sing in Chicago again—regally punishing the whole city. She and her husband Gian Battista Meneghini insisted that she be paid more than any other opera singer, paid in cash, and treated with greater consideration. She also became famous for feuding with many general managers of famous opera companies—and even feuding with the Pope.

Still, she kept insisting that she was only interested in producing great art. More and more people were interested in her, repelled and yet fascinated by her prima donna tactics. "Who does she think she is?" the public wondered. Was she worth all the fuss she created, all the fights she was having with various opera companies and opera company directors and various singers?

Rumors were flying around her and paparazzi were also flashing cameras around her. She got press coverage just for getting on a boat or off a plane. She also became notorious for rumors about her alerting the press when she would arrive in a city and on what flight—to ensure that her arrival was covered by press representatives and their photographers. She became a master of promoting herself and her career, though she also became famous for cancelling performances. She even spread silly rumors about how she lost a hundred pounds and turned herself from a very fat soprano to a thin and glamorous woman in the style of the svelte movie star Audrey Hepburn. She remained fascinated by American movies and their stars.

What were the facts behind the rumors? Was she really as narcissistic and self-obsessed as she appeared to some cynics at the time? Was she as great a singer and actor as some reviewers asserted? Was she really the greatest diva of the 20th century? How was she unique as an artist and why did her performances attract so much attention in the opera world? How did her career and her life evolve once she became famous all over Italy for her performances at La Scala in Milan, La Fenice in Venice, the San Carlo Opera House in Naples, and all the other major (and some minor) opera houses in Italy? In addition, why did she become notorious for cancelling performances so frequently toward the end of her career?

Her sudden death in 1977 made headlines around the world and was reported on most television stations. She was cremated within four days of her death under mysterious circumstances. The ashes of the world's most famous opera singer were later scattered over the seas around a country that wasn't her birthplace.

She was constantly in the headlines during her career—exactly where she wanted to be. She generated as much publicity as she could get in the media since she believed that there was no such thing as bad publicity, even when that involved problems within her own family. She pretended to hate being followed by those annoying *paparazzi* (a new Italian word which appeared in the 1950s)—but she actually loved all the attention. She was especially fond of television, and loved doing TV interviews.

It was within her own family that her personal problems began. Sigmund Freud was certainly right about our personalities being the results of our connections since infancy with our own families and the problems that begin there, with our parents, especially our mothers, who would influence and in some cases control us for the rest of our lives (Freud 370–80). Certainly this was the case with Callas, and she had difficult relationships with members of her family: in particular, her complex, demanding and sometimes rejecting mother certainly had a profound effect on her throughout her life. When Callas became a famous opera singer in her 20s, she rather melodramatically cut herself off from her mother and never spoke to her again; but her mother, father and sister remained profoundly influential on her life and her behavior. Her mother, father and sister never left her inner life even after she terminated contact with them. It is sad that she could never reconcile with the woman who knew her best, her mother, who helped her to survive World War II. It was ironic that the people who inherited Callas' estate were exactly the people she most hated: her mother Evangelia, her sister Jackie and her husband Gian Battista Meneghini.

Callas' discipline, her musical genius, her acting abilities, her ability to understand and memorize an operatic score—the greatest irony was that these were the things which made so much of her life unhappy and ultimately tragic. The skills that made her such a successful acting singer on stage blinded her to the complex realities of life around her. She was rarely able to see situations as they were; instead, her imagination turned human confrontations into surreal perceptions that caused her so much misery.

Still, she was one of the truly great performers, in terms of operatic singing and acting. Some of the sopranos who followed in her tradition were Gwyneth Jones, Elena Suliotis, Raina Kabavanska, Magda Olivero and Sondra Radvanovsky. Her tradition in many ways goes back to the beginnings of opera in 17th-century Venice when the castrati made the new art form popular throughout Europe. Now no city that considers itself sophisticated and cultivated in the arts and an international center can be without its own opera company.

Callas and her ability to generate headlines attracted people, not only to her performances, but also to the art form of opera itself—a traditionally artificial, other-worldly combination of theater and music that can create onstage magic. Combining music with drama remains difficult, but Callas had a genius for doing exactly that. While drama and music remain in many ways natural enemies, with a great composer, these conflicting elements can be combined to create probing insights and unique pleasures. In addition, a great singer and actor can make those dramatic insights come alive on stage before you.

Callas' achievements still fascinate those who are interested in opera, the soprano voice in opera, and opera's great vocal tradition. An artist who garnered much attention, she has left a recorded legacy that is still being enjoyed and examined. She also wanted to become a popular icon, and she succeeded here too. She has remained in the public consciousness as a tragic but fascinating and unforgettable artist. *The Oxford Dictionary of Opera* said of Callas: "She was one of the century's greatest singing actresses, and an artist who touched every role she sang with her genius."

1

Birth in New York

What is now the Terence Cardinal Cooke Medical Center on New York's Fifth Avenue at 106th Street used to be Flower Hospital, and it was there that Maria Callas was born on December 2, 1923. There is a plaque in white marble in the lobby to commemorate the event. Her mother Evangelia always claimed that the date was actually December 4, but the hospital medical records are accurate. Claiming that the day of Maria's birth was actually two days later became a way Evangelia attempted to maintain her control over her daughter with a mother's alleged superior knowledge and wisdom. Mother Callas (called "Litza" at home) wanted to dramatize everything in her family to keep herself the center of attention—a lesson her daughter would quickly learn and mimic.

The mystery of Maria's birth date became the first of many complications in her complex and difficult relationship with her mother, a woman whom she eventually shunned. She inherited from her mother a personality that was quick to make enemies and quick to distrust people as traitors, especially people in her own family (Stone 3–13).

Maria was three before she was baptized, though Greek Orthodox families normally baptize a child within six months after birth. Maria's family came from Greece, and the name on both her birth and baptismal certificates was given as Cecilia Sophia Anna Maria Kalogeropoulos, which most Americans would find unpronounceable and vaguely comical—the reason that her father George eventually Americanized it to Callas. The baby girl weighed 12½ pounds at birth, according to Leonidas Lantzounis, a physician friend of George's, who attended the birth and became the baby's godfather. At home, she was called Mary. It would take six days before the mother would hold and nurse the baby (Bret 3 ff.).

In the days following Maria's difficult delivery, Evangelia grew despondent, so fixated had she been on delivering another boy. She agonizingly recalled her first son Vasily, who had died back in Greece after living for only three years. She had been praying for a replacement son—not another daughter. Today, a mother exhibiting Evangelia's post-childbirth behavior would be diagnosed with post-partum depression, but that term did not exist in 1923 (Galatopoulos 12–15).

After the family moved to New York in 1923, Maria's father soon came to like America, especially New York, and wanted to become a citizen. His

The newly renamed Callas family in New York City in 1924: Maria as a chubby infant, on the lap of her father George, with her sister Jackie and her mother Evangelia.

1. Birth in New York

wife had a problematical relationship with the city and eventually decided to return to Athens with her daughters in 1937—just in time for World War II and the Fascist and Nazi invasions of Athens in 1941, followed by the Greek Civil War. Maria's father, George Callas, became very fearful of returning to Greece since there clearly was another world war looming, thanks to Adolf Hitler and Benito Mussolini. From 1936 to 1939, the Spanish Civil War was waged; historians often called it a dress rehearsal for World War II, in which over 50 million people died (Levey 798 ff.).

Maria spent the first 13 years of her life in New York and usually thought of herself as a native New Yorker, though the family moved around often. Her parents were born in Greece; her mother was born and raised in Athens, and originally Maria's parents settled in Meligala, a town in the Peloponnese Region, where her father had been born and where her new husband wanted to start a pharmacy—since he had gone to school in Athens to become a pharmacist. Evangelia always loved living in Athens, which she considered her home. Evangelia and George were married in a Greek Orthodox church in Athens on August 7, 1916. She was only 18 when she married him, and he was 12 years older. Women in Greece at the time had little say in important family matters, which were usually decided by the men in the family. The couple had planned to stay in Meligala, where their pharmacy did well, but there were a series of traumas that encouraged the family, or at least George, to immigrate to America (Edwards 4–11).

The first problem became the marriage itself. Evangelia was quite young when the couple married, and within a year, the marriage had serious conflicts. Evangelia asserts in her 1960 memoir about her relationship with Maria that Evangelia's father, Peter, begged her not to marry George, arguing that he would be a terrible husband and that he would be unfaithful. Evangelia wrote that she was a young woman in love with a very handsome man, and he eventually wore down any resolve on her part. Her father finally agreed to the marriage, but died before the troths were pledged. He had been wounded while fighting in the Greek Army during World War I.

George, a pharmacist with an interest in science and healing, found his new wife difficult to live with. She was always feuding with members of her own family—not talking for periods of time with her own mother and other family members. Evangelia seemed to have what Freud would call a hysteric personality (Freud 70–94), always turning minor problems into major confrontations in which she was always the victim of diabolical forces and people within her own family (Wirth-Caution 4–80). She tended to see conflicts with other people as attempts to murder her. There was clearly a paranoid and melodramatic side to her personality. She tended to see any new person as her best friend; then, after a minor disagreement, she turned her former friend into a "traitor" who had always been plotting her death. Psychologists now call this behavior "splitting," seeing people as either completely wonderful or totally evil (Yeomans 19 ff).

Most people can see the many different facets that comprise all of humanity, but those who have been diagnosed with what is now known as borderline personality disorder see people as either totally good (themselves) or totally bad (most other people). The term "borderline" did not enter general psychological terminology until the last years of the 20th century and was not in general usage during Callas' lifetime, and during her life she was certainly never diagnosed as such. But Evangelia most certainly exhibited this behavior, and it had a profound influence on her children.

George and Evangelia, between their frequent arguments, yearned for a son. Very soon in the marriage, the father got tired of all the drama caused by his wife. She seemed to have the personality of an operatic diva with none of the musical talent—always excitable, easily roused to fury by imagined slights, always feuding with one or another of her relatives or neighbors. She also accused George of being unfaithful with other women, which he denied. George wanted peace and quiet and soon found out that he would never get that with Evangelia.

Evangelia Dimitriadis came from a family that had long had artistic aspirations. Her father Peter was named after *his* father Peter (Petros), a career officer in the Greek military. He was remembered in his native village and Athens for his singing, and he enjoyed performing in public. Evangelia dreamed of a career in theater, or singing in opera, but at that time, her family felt that no respectable daughter from a respectable middle-class Greek family should ever appear in on stage, in public, as any sort of "entertainer." So instead, Evangelia generated much excitement and theatrics within her family. She had fostered virtually no friendships, outside of her family. She seemed to have an ability to antagonize people, resulting in their avoiding her. She had great difficulty making friends and assumed that everybody else was jealous of her exotic blonde beauty (especially other women) and her superior intelligence.

She tended to be narcissistic, convinced that she was the brightest and most beautiful woman in the world—but surrounded by envious people who did not recognize her genius. Now she was a married woman living in a small town in the Peloponnese, Meligala—which was reasonably proximate the nation's capital, Athens, but might as well have been a continent away.

Within a year of the marriage, Evangelia produced a daughter, Iakinthy, eventually called "Jackie" in New York. Born in Greece on June 4, 1917, Jackie seemed to be a "golden child." In 1920, Evangelia produced the longed-for son Vasily, who was much adored by his parents in male-centric

1. Birth in New York

Greece. When he was just three, Vasily came down with typhoid fever and soon died. His grieving parents were nearly inconsolable (Bret 10 ff.).

Within a year, perhaps as a way of dramatically changing his immediate scene, George decided to move to America. He sold his pharmacy and bought one-way ship's passage for the entire family. He had several friends already living in New York City and decided to take a shot at "the American Dream" there. One of his best friends, Dr. Leonidas Lantzounis, was a highly successful surgeon in New York and promised to help George (Stassinopoulos 18–30). In her memoir, Evangelia said her husband told her they were leaving Greece only the day before they all boarded the boat and left for New York. He, of course, denied this. The true story may never be known (Callas, Evangelia 5–20). One rumor in the family was that George, who was notorious for his flirtatious behavior around pretty women, had impregnated the teenage daughter of Meligala's mayor, and so had to leave the town immediately to avoid prosecution or an even worse fate.

While Evangelia always told her daughters how wonderful it was to live in sunny Greece, their father had unpleasant memories of life in their homeland. In fact, the years between 1913 and 1923 are often called "Years of the Great Catastrophe" by Greek historians. When World War I began in 1914, Greece's King Constantine I wanted Greece to be on the side of Germany, primarily because his wife was the sister of the German Kaiser, Wilhelm II. But several of Greece's prime ministers, especially Ileftherios Venizelos and General Ioannis Metaxas, favored entering the war on the side of the British and the French. When Greece entered the war allied with the British and French, this division continued. The situation became more complicated when the Turkish general Ataturk invaded Smyrna, then a Greek city, and massacred thousands of Greeks and Armenians and made Smyrna part of the new Turkey. Thousands of Greeks, Armenians and Jews had to flee to Greece to avoid slaughter by the Turks. During this time, another Greek, who would become a major part of the Callas story, suffered travails of his own. Aristotle Onassis and his family survived, but had to flee Smyrna and lost everything they had. Clearly the years between 1913 and 1923 were catastrophic for Greece, because of World War I and the five-year civil war in Greece after the war's end. Evangelia's father Petros had been wounded as a result of fighting in that war. Surely, George Callas must have wanted to protect his family from all the wars and upheavals in Greece during this period. One historian commented:

> It is not known how many Christians—Greeks and Armenians—lost their lives in and around Smyrna and in other parts of Anatolia between 1921 and 1923. The number is generally reckoned to run into the hundreds of thousands. Even this huge toll reflects only one part of the total losses, on all sides, during the twelve-year "War of the Ottoman Succession" that was only now coming to an

end. It has been estimated that by 1923 the total population that had been living within the borders of the [Ottoman] empire in 1911, Muslim and Christian combined, had fallen by some 20 percent. In the annals of the modern Republic of Turkey, which would be formally inaugurated just over a year later, the taking of Izmir (Smyrna) marked the crowning victory of the nation's "war of independence." For Greeks, the destruction of the city and the mass killings and deportations that followed are remembered as the horrific climax of the "Asia-Minor Catastrophe," often shortened to just "The Catastrophe." (Beaton 225–26).

As the Catastrophe was ending, the Kalogeropoulos family arrived by ship in New York on August 2, 1923, and the young couple found all the flags in New York Harbor at half-mast due to the sudden death of President Warren Harding by heart attack. The superstitious Evangelia immediately considered this a bad omen for their American venture (DeCeccatty 35 ff.).

The early years of the 20th century brought millions of Europeans to America. As mentioned above, Greeks were fleeing from Greece as a result of World War I and the Greek Civil War—and war with Turkey after that. The same thing tragically occurred in Greece right after World War II. The New World had brought comparative wealth and happiness to millions of other Greeks, so why not to the Kalogeropoulos family. To cross the Aegean, the Mediterranean and the Atlantic was bound to separate them from their unhappiness and all the warfare in Greece and bring them some new happiness or at least some new adventures. They did not think the streets were paved with gold, but they had heard of friends or relatives leading comfortable, middle-class, peaceful lives in America, and they both wanted to escape their own families. The Callas family was not like the millions of poor Europeans who were moving to America during this period; George and Litza were not destitute, illiterate peasants from the provinces, and they did not want people to think of them as such. The family did not travel in steerage but had their own cabin, and Evangelia did not want people to conclude that they were impoverished Greek farmers like most of the other Greeks onboard the ship.

Evangelia tried everything she knew to become a center of attention on the trip from Greece to New York. She boasted that she had to travel with her pet canaries, all of whom were wonderful singers—according to Evangelia, all credit to her. As she paraded around the boat with her cages of canaries, some of the passengers assumed she was some narcissistic minor "entertainer." She behaved like the wealthy society matrons who had to have a lap dog or two around them at all times. Her husband found her theatrics embarrassing, but to keep the peace, he usually let her antics go unchecked.

Evangelia made clear to her husband that she bitterly resented this

1. Birth in New York

move since they were not Greek farmers but prosperous middle-class professionals. But she felt she had no choice but to obey her husband, given her situation. When the family lived in Greece, Evangelia had a few servants to help her around the house, but she must have realized that this would not be possible in New York. George, on the other hand, was eager to avoid all the wars and economic upheavals in Greece at the time. Dr. Lantzounis had rented an apartment for them in Astoria, Queens—then as now, home to many Greek immigrants. However, the Callas family soon moved to Washington Heights in upper Manhattan, near where the George Washington Bridge would soon rise (the bridge was not finished until 1931). Washington Heights, much like Astoria, was then full of recent Greek immigrants. In such a neighborhood, Evangelia could converse with shopkeepers in her native Greek, at shops owned by her countrymen, rather than in American English, which she found troublesome. South of Washington Heights is Morningside Heights, which was (and is) anchored by Columbia University. In 1927, Casa Italiana opened on Amsterdam Avenue and 116th Street, the home of Columbia University's Italian Department. The Casa Italiana also had the Paterno Library, home to a collection of books on Italian literature and culture, and a small theater for concerts of Italian music, especially opera scenes, and for lectures on Italian theater and opera, as well as Italian culture and literature (Dolkart 190–92). Did the Callas family ever go to any of the operatic events? We cannot be sure, but they certainly lived nearby.

By 1902, Manhattan's subway system was in place and the #1 Line had stations on Broadway on the west side, which made it very easy for the Callas family to get from Washington Heights to Morningside Heights. There is another proximate connection with opera in Upper Manhattan, since the first professor of Italian at Columbia was Lorenzo Da Ponte, the librettist for Mozart's operas *The Marriage of Figaro*, *Don Giovanni* and *Così Fan Tutte*. Da Ponte arrived in New York about 100 years before Maria Callas, and he became the first professor of Italian at Columbia University from 1826 to 1837. He helped Manuel Garcia stage the first performances of Italian opera in New York in 1825, and co-founded an Italian opera house in New York in 1833. Da Ponte died in 1838 and was buried in a Queens cemetery (Rosenthal 317). Maria, as a child student, could have been taken on field trips to the Casa Italiana, though there is no evidence that she did visit this home of Italian culture.

Serious financial distress soon developed. George failed to pass all the tests needed to become a pharmacist in New York. So he instead became a pharmacist's assistant, who helped in dealing with Greek patients. In Midtown Manhattan, George opened his own pharmacy, the Splendid Pharmacy at 39th Street and 8th Avenue—near the old Metropolitan Opera House. It did well. Evangelia, who was used to living in Athens, missed her family there and all of Athens' cultural opportunities. There were many cultural opportunities in New York but most of them came in English, a language Evangelia never spoke easily. (Even George was still struggling with English.) Washington Heights with its large Greek immigrant community became comfortable for the Callas family, though they frequently changed apartments due to Evangelia's quarrels with landlords and neighbors (Bret 2–25).

It was five years before George was certified as a pharmacist. In that era, pharmacists functioned more like doctors in his native Greece and even more so among the Greek community in New York. Many poor Greek immigrants in New York could not afford to go to a doctor when they or their children were sick, so they first went to their pharmacist. He would consider their symptoms and recommend a medicine—either something sold over the counter or something he'd concoct, such as a cough syrup, a salve for a painful muscle or medicine for an earache. If these medications did not work, the patients would only then go to a more expensive physician—with great fear since they thought they must really be sick if they had to go to a doctor.

Most Greek families, along with the population in general, had to bury a few of their children because of the many dread illness like diphtheria, typhoid fever, measles and whooping cough. Today's mothers and fathers could not imagine raising children without inoculations and antibiotics, but they were not generally available until after World War II. An English scientist, Alexander Fleming, discovered penicillin in 1928, but it needed more development. During World War II penicillin was used primarily for wounded soldiers—and was considered a miracle drug, which it was. Penicillin became available to the general public in 1945, after the war ended (Levey 651).

Dr. Lantzounis had described New York as a wealthy city that needed more pharmacies, and with large communities of Greeks in several of the five boroughs. He himself was not married at the time and had no family, so he was also happy for a substitute family and for the company they provided. He was a very good godfather to Maria, helping her frequently throughout her difficult and tempestuous lifetime. Her godfather was one of the few people from her early life with whom Maria remained close.

Maria's father had not liked living in crowded Athens, surrounded by his wife's family, a family full of difficult members who were always screaming at each other or not talking to each other. George's family got along much better and without all the hysteria and drama. Evangelia's family was full of accusations of attempted murders and character assassinations, which George found laughable. The suicide of one of Evangelia's brothers added to the family angst. (Evangelia attempted suicide, by drug overdose,

1. Birth in New York

in 1937, and was admitted to New York's Bellevue Hospital.) It soon became apparent that Maria was parroting the behavior of her mother, though she would be loath to admit that fact (Stassinopoulos 60–90). Evangelia was not capable of being a very effective mother. The two children, Jackie and Maria, needed a lot of attention; but in many ways Evangelia remained a child herself, capable of understanding only her own needs and seeing her children as "competitors" rather than as dependents. She tended to get angry when her children voiced their wants and needs—typical of children everywhere. Evangelia seemed to bond most easily with her oldest child, her daughter Jackie, and Jackie was soon seen as the pretty, talented child—tall, slender and graceful—and Mama's clear favorite, unlike the chubby, ungainly Maria. Evangelia tended to see Jackie as the star of the family and Maria as more of an also-ran. Maria often felt neglected and unwanted as a child, even though her mother insisted that she loved *both* of her daughters equally.

According to family lore, it took a week before Evangelia would nurse Maria, since she had so wanted a son to replace Vasily. In her memoir, Evangelia claimed that she received helpful messages from both her dead father and her dead son to help guide her through life. Evangelia often told her daughters how much she missed her beloved Vasily. Her daughters both felt that their brother remained the only *truly* beloved child in the family.

After the prosperous 1920s came the Great Depression, during which George lost his pharmacy in New York and became a traveling pharmaceutical salesman. Now the family experienced what real poverty was like. They moved often, primarily to avoid paying their rent. George may have taken the job to be away from his wife and family as much as possible since divorce was not then an option for most people of modest means in the U.S. and Greece. One had to be very wealthy to get a divorce, and it was a big social scandal as well. George yearned for the peace and quiet that he rarely found in a house full of theatrical women, most notably his melodramatic wife.

Evangelia soon decided that her daughters must also possess dramatic and musical talent, and arranged piano and singing lessons for them. She decided that Jackie was the one who should be trained for a career on the stage, as an actress or opera singer. Maria was near-sighted and had to wear thick eyeglasses from age five, and this overweight, unpretty child reminded Evangelia of herself and her own problems with weight. But the voice, acting and dancing teachers were soon telling the mother that Maria was also talented, not just Jackie. Several teachers even suggested that Maria was the more musically talented and the more disciplined of the two, though Evangelia had seen things quite differently. Evangelia now became the stereotypical stage mother, desperately trying to get her daughters on the stage—rather like the mother in the Broadway musical *Gypsy*. Mother Callas often took Jackie and Maria to auditions for child actors or child singers, which the girls soon began to resent (Kesting 90–98).

In her 1990 memoir *Sisters: A Revealing Portrait of the World's Most Famous Diva*, Jackie wrote that she had always felt that Evangelia much preferred Maria (Callas, Jackie 5–25). Clearly both girls felt insecure about maternal affection.

In July 1929 when Maria was five, she was hit by a car on Broadway in Washington Heights and was in a coma in a hospital for six days. Her mother always felt that that trauma damaged Maria: that Maria's personality changed after she awoke, and that she was much more difficult and quick-to-anger than before. Soon after this, Maria began taking her singing and piano lessons more seriously, and her musical talents began to blossom; her mother encouraged Maria and told her she had a unique voice and a singular musical gift and could become a great opera singer. Evangelia was the first person to tell her that she was a major talent and could have a great opera career if she worked hard enough. Finally, Maria got the loving attention she yearned for from her mother so she did not feel like the fat, ugly, untalented sister, as she had been before. As long as she was serious with her piano and singing lessons, Maria's mother had more time for her and less for Jackie.

The young Maria Callas was forced to play the unwanted role of ugly duckling, disappearing in the shadow of her slim, glamorous older sister. But Maria now assumed the role of the much more talented and disciplined of the two, at least during piano and vocal lessons. Despite the family's poverty during the Depression, the mother insisted that her daughters continue their music lessons. She got Maria to appear on *Major Bowes Amateur Hour*, a nationally broadcast radio show for talented children. Maria's voice was on the radio, a fact that Evangelia was quick to tell any neighbor who would listen. In her later years, Maria told interviewers that children with musical talent are often denied a normal childhood by their ambitious mothers (Tosi 12–18).

In 1931, the Metropolitan Opera began its famous Saturday afternoon radio broadcasts, airing live Saturday matinee performances on nationwide radio, and Evangelia and her two daughters became faithful listeners. They could hear a complete opera from the Met—and at no cost. Maria became a great fan of Italian-American diva Rosa Ponselle and her soprano voice in Verdi's operas. Along with diva Geraldine Farrar, the huge-voiced, legendary Ponselle was the very first of the "American-born opera stars."

Maria was enrolled in the local grade school, New York Public School #189 in Washington Heights when she was six years old, and she remained there until she graduated in 1937. A successful student, she took her studies very seriously. She did not have many friends, but she was liked by several of her teachers. Evangelia did not encourage either her or Jackie to invite their friends to her home, since she felt that the neighborhood children were intellectually and socially inferior to her daughters. She inculcated in her girls the idea that they were superior to the neighborhood's lower-class immigrant Greek children.

Maria's graduation signaled the completion of her formal education. Despite her successes at school, she still felt like an orphan since she had so few friends and feared that her parents did not really love her. Evangelia and Jackie liked to kid Maria about her weight, though they considered it more "light-hearted teasing" than the devastating rebuke Maria took it to be. Evangelia insisted that *both* her daughters prepare for professional careers in the arts, something she herself had long dreamed of having. George instead suggested secretarial school and training on the still somewhat novel machine, the typewriter, which had become a symbol of female liberation in Ibsen's *A Doll's House*. He also talked about finding his daughters suitable husbands—the typical path for Greek girls (and most American girls) at the time.

Evangelia made the dresses for her daughters. Jackie got the lovely, fitted, feminine dresses, the bulkier Maria got homely, shapeless dresses. Their mother did not seem to realize that the world of opera was full of large women who were enjoying highly successful international careers, in spite of their size. During the 1920s and '30s, divas Luisa Tetrazzini, Ernestine Schumann-Heink, Kirsten Flagstad and Helen Traubel had great opera stage success despite their sometimes cumbersome frames. Adding to Maria's unattractiveness was the fact that she required thick eyeglasses all her life. So she manifested her frustration through over-eating. She also sought love from her teachers. The teachers, especially the voice teachers, provided her with the love and the praise she felt she did not receive at home. In her memoir, Evangelia insisted that she loved both her daughters equally and never understood why Maria felt unloved and unwanted.

Maria made no effort to avoid her singing lessons; rather, she seemed as determined as her mother to develop her musical talents. In 1937, for her 8th grade graduation ceremony, she was chosen to make her singing "debut" in the school's "operetta," a Gilbert & Sullivan pastiche.

The Great Depression lingered on. George struggled to support his family (in both New York and Greece) without his own pharmacy. His career was essentially that of a traveling salesman, as he was a representative of several drug companies. He had to do all this in his broken English and while working out of his car, driving around New York State and New England, trying to make a living for himself and the three women in his family.

Evangelia capriciously concluded that, moving forward, the best musical education Maria could get would be in Athens, since her family had contacts with some of the classical music establishments there. New York City most certainly had better musical opportunities, most notably the world-famous Metropolitan Opera Company and the New York Philharmonic Orchestra at Carnegie Hall. Arturo Toscanini and Gustav Mahler shared the Met's conductor's podium at that time, while Puccini was still living and composing. But Evangelia's continued inability to grasp the English language made her long to return to her native Athens.

In 1937, not long after her failed suicide bid, Evangelia insisted on buying ship's passage for three, for a return to Athens, despite the Depression and the tense political situation in Europe, with both an extreme nationalist party and a large party of communists. Evangelia remained determined and even threatened her husband with another suicide attempt if he tried to stop her. She sent Jackie ahead and then booked two tickets for herself and Maria, leaving her husband alone in New York, which was where he preferred to be, though he promised to send money to his wife to support them. After almost 20 years of marriage to Evangelia, George was probably alarmed to see his wife and daughters returning to Athens, but on some level, he must have been glad to be rid of them. He now had a part-time job in a pharmacy in New York, had his regular customers there, and was glad to be free of all the chaotic drama that his wife brought into his life. As a man of science and a man of peace, he wanted to remain in America—a safer spot to survive the coming conflagration. Once his wife and daughters were in Greece, George quietly began an affair with Alexandra Papajohn, daughter of one of his wife's few friends and a neighbor in their building. She eventually became his second wife, and this marriage proved much happier than his first (Edwards 57–62).

Neither Maria nor Jackie was fluent in Greek, being much more comfortable speaking in American English. Both were familiar with conversational Greek, which they had grown up hearing spoken at home and on the streets of Morningside and Washington Heights. Maria's best written and spoken language was decidedly English.

Any sentient person would most certainly have been aware by 1937 that another war was threatening in Europe—and, indeed, the entire world. Newspapers, radio stations and Pathé newsreels in movie theaters were reporting the political conflicts in Europe. Why would Evangelia want to return to Athens? She missed her family, though she was usually feuding with them. In the late 1930s, Athens had only a third-rate, provincial opera company. George kept insisting that Maria could get a fine vocal education right there in Manhattan; besides, he argued, given the global economy and the Depression, couldn't Maria and her mother be more practical about what Maria could do? George was undoubtedly aware of the political conflicts that were brewing right in Greece—and that this was not a good time to be repatriating to Greece. On some level, Evangelia may have felt that if there was going to be another world war, she would want to be in it—since she loved being the center of any drama.

So, at this early point in her life, Maria was forced to ask herself: Was she really an American or was she Greek? Or somewhere in between? This enigma would become a recurrent question in her life. She often told her friends that her blood was all Greek, but was she really as Greek as she thought she was?

Given Evangelia's love of drama, maybe that is exactly what drove her to drag her daughters back to a Europe on the brink of annihilation. If there was about to be another Greek conflict, she was determined to craft herself a featured role in it. It was a role she knew very well.

2

Athens and World War II

Evangelia felt trapped in an unhappy marriage and poor in a foreign country during the Depression. She also found it increasingly difficult to cope with being a mother to her two daughters. She missed her own country, her own language, and her own family very much, and she was happy to be back. She was hoping her family could help her raise her daughters. Jackie had been sent to Athens a few months before, and now the three of them were reunited in Athens (Callas, Evangelia 3–13).

George had warned her that the international situation was becoming worse, with Mussolini in power in Italy, Hitler in power in Germany, and the Spanish Civil War continuing. Things were tense in Greece as well, with extremist parties of the right and left (especially Greece's communist party) at each other's throats (Iatrides 368–72, 555–560).

Evangelia felt that her daughters could get better educations in Athens—the drama conservatory for Jackie, and the music conservatory for Maria. (Maria told friends that she really wanted to become a dentist.) Both women decided that the mouth would be the center of Maria's career. Now that the movies had the talkies, Evangelia envisioned both her daughters as Hollywood stars.

Evangelia was delighted to be back in her native city and not having to struggle with her English to communicate. She and Maria were greeted at the Athens railroad station by Jackie and other members of the family; it was the spring of 1937 and her family owned a house in the center of Athens. They all seemed mostly happy to have Evangelia back. The season was spring, a particularly nice time to visit Greece—before the terrible heat of the Grecian summer. Evangelia reassured both girls that they could become movie stars in Greece (Edwards 16 ff.). Maria had never been to Greece before. In New York, she was Mary Callas, but in Athens she suddenly became Maria Kalogeropoulos. She could speak Greek because of her speaking the language at home, but she was not fluent in it and had little experience in writing Greek. She was happy to rejoin Jackie and happy to meet her mother's family. Here, Maria could improve her knowledge of the Greek language and, her mother hoped, lose most of her English. For Maria, it was an exciting adventure to live in a new country she had never seen before, but she must have soon realized that her mother's family was not as rich or as prominent as her mother had insisted. The family house was not as enormous as Evangelia had said—and the girls must have also sensed after a few weeks they were not as welcome as their mother had predicted. In Athens, Maria had to improve her knowledge of Greek because she had to know enough of it to communicate with her new family and neighbors, who certainly did not know English. Once the Callas family had all arrived in Greece and were living in their mother's parental house, the realities of the situation soon turned very unpleasant. Evangelia was visiting all her relatives, whom she had not seen in 15 years, and showing off her daughters to them. Both girls had to sing before their new Greek relatives. According to some family members, the Greek relatives soon grew tired of hearing Jackie and Maria singing "La Paloma" over and over again, and then being expected to gush over the girls' musical genius. Both sisters kept calling American opera singer Rosa Ponselle the greatest opera singer alive, though the Greek family had never heard of her (Linakis 1–10). Resentments started to mount on both sides, and Evangelia stopped talking to her own mother and some of her other relatives.

It soon became apparent that Evangelia and her daughters would have to find their own place to live since their presence in the house was causing tensions to mount. She found a large apartment for them in Athens at 61 Patission Street, off Concord Square, in the old part of town. Once the women moved into their new apartment, Evangelia bought a few canaries and some furniture. Soon after that, financial problems developed since the money coming from George was being spent quickly, despite the relative strength of the American dollar against the Greek currency, the drachma (Galatopoulos 26–28). Once the Italian Fascists invaded Greece in 1940, the Italian occupying forces would confiscate any money sent from America. How were the women to survive in Athens during the occupation of the city—first by the Italian Fascists, and then the German Nazis in 1941? Being in an occupied country would be frightening to the people living there; the Greek government had to flee to Alexandria, Egypt, and become a government in exile. The period of 1941–42 was later called the Great Greek Famine because of the shortages of food and the warfare; Evangelia and her daughters were there the whole time and struggling to survive with gun and tank battles going on outside their apartment windows (Taylor 524–32). At least a half million Greeks died of hunger during the Nazi occupation of Greece (Hastings 342).

Athens, in 1937, was already a grim place, a city in the grip of the Great Depression, but much smaller than New York, with a population of less than a million people. Greece itself was divided politically with an extreme-right Monarchist party and an extreme-left Communist party. The king and the Royal Family fled Greece in 1940 as Mussolini's Fascists approached. Some felt that Greece itself might devolve into civil war given its political conflicts and its economic problems. Could Greece become another Spain, divided in two by civil war? Into such a tense national and international political situation, Evangelia brought her two daughters for musical and dramatic training—an idea that must have seemed ludicrous to most members of her family given the economic and political realities around them.

But Maria and Evangelia seemed utterly unaware of the catastrophe about to fall on them, in spite of the repeated warnings of George back in New York. He promised to send money every month to support them—and the American dollar went far in Athens in the grip of the global Depression. Evangelia was delighted to be back in her own family's home in the center of Athens, surrounded by her feuding but sometimes loving family. It was spring now in Greece and the aroma of the blooming flowers and trees took Evangelia back to her self-idealized youth in her homeland.

Evangelia used all her family contacts to get Maria into the Conservatory of Music in Athens, one of the country's most prestigious vocal academy. Maria, now 14, was too young to be accepted by any of Athens' musical conservatories, so Evangelia started to lie about Maria's age. Evangelia succeeded, and Maria began to study voice privately with Maria Trivella, a Greek singer who was on the voice faculty at the Athens Music Conservatory. The school did not accept Maria as a regular student, because she was too young, but they said she could study with Trivella, who was immediately taken by Maria's talents and potential for a professional career. Trivella had had a professional career as an opera singer in Greece. Maria must have had an impressive voice even back then, though without much training, since the voice faculty heard her sing and felt that she had the potential to become an opera singer. Maria (like her mother) was determined and very disciplined when it came to her vocal studies, though not so disciplined when it came to her eating. She had lost some weight, but put it back on again within a year. Her mother encouraged her to practice on the piano and on her voice lessons since Maria was the more determined and more disciplined of the two girls. She studied hard to learn the language of music and could soon read a score. She tended to fall a bit in love with her teachers—probably because she was looking for a loving parental figure, which she did not feel she could get from her parents. Maria would not see her father for eight years; her teenage years were spent in Athens, while Evangelia remained aloof and emotionally unavailable.

Maria was now becoming fluent in Greek and began even to think in Greek, though her English was still far better. Many years later, when she sang at the Metropolitan Opera, she said during an interview that she thought in Greek but counted in English (Mayer 232 ff.). Italian and German remained the main languages for opera, Verdi and Wagner being the most influential and important opera composers, then as now.

After a year, Trivella suggested that Maria switch teachers and begin studying with Elvira de Hidalgo, then the most famous teacher on the Conservatory of Music's voice faculty. The Spanish-born diva had had an international career as a coloratura soprano, singing in Italy, Paris, London, Buenos Aires and even the Metropolitan Opera, where she became especially admired for her performances as a coloratura soprano in roles like Rosina in Rossini's *The Barber of Seville*, sometimes with the tenor Enrico Caruso. This very difficult coloratura role was originally written for the mezzo-soprano Maria Malibran, but the opera became so famous and so popular that sopranos wanted to sing the role as well. So it was transposed up into the coloratura soprano range, where it became even more vocally dazzling for the audience. Rossini had a special fondness for sopranos and mezzo-sopranos, in part because his wife Isabella Colbran was a famous soprano; but very soon these roles were transposed up or down so either sopranos or mezzo-sopranos could sing Rossini's coloratura, *bel canto* roles.

De Hidalgo came to Athens as a guest professor at the Athens Music Conservatory, and was trapped there as a result of the international political situation, especially the Spanish Civil War and World War II. She was afraid to return to her native Spain, because of the Spanish conflict. After the war, de Hidalgo tried to remain in Greece, but

Elvira de Hidalgo (1891–1980), a noted Spanish coloratura soprano, circa late 1920s. Maria Callas credited her as her most steadfast friend and vocal mentor throughout her career.

ultimately moved to Ankara, Turkey, where she also taught voice. She later moved to Milan and taught voice. She had a brother there, Luis de Hidalgo, who worked in the wardrobe department for La Scala (where she spent her final years, until her death in 1980).

De Hidalgo stated in an interview how her first impression upon meeting Maria was that of a fat, homely, acne-scarred, poorly attired American girl, peering at the world through thick glasses. When de Hidalgo first heard Maria sing, she heard something unique in that voice. Her large voice had a dramatic ability, an ability to sing the words clearly and to create drama with both music and text. Even at such an early age, Maria had a preternaturally large voice, with a three-and-a-half

De Hidalgo as Rosina in Rossini's *Il Barbiere di Siviglia* at the Metropolitan Opera in 1926.

octave range. She also had the beginnings of the vocal flexibility required for the bel canto repertoire. De Hidalgo felt that Maria Kalogeropoulos (as she was called then) had a lot of talent and operatic potential. De Hidalgo first heard Callas when she was just 15 years old, and offered her free voice lessons, since she knew Callas was from a poor family. Her unique voice needed more control and training, but had tremendous potential. Callas also developed the capability to sing both dramatic and coloratura roles. Though she did not have a conventionally "pretty" voice, she was possessed of an arresting presence and sound (Tosi 50–66).

De Hidalgo felt that, with proper training, Maria could sing both bel canto and dramatic soprano roles, with one of the most unusual of vocal *fachs* (vocal-range classifications). De Hidalgo also felt that Maria could sing both soprano and mezzo-soprano roles—a rare and coveted type of vocal flexibility. She further sensed a desperation in Maria to find a mother figure, since she quickly saw for herself that Maria's relationship with

2. Athens and World War II

Evangelia was problem-fraught. De Hidalgo soon discovered that this teenage girl had the discipline, the determination and the musical intelligence to develop into a professional opera singer. She had the unique timbre of a born diva. De Hidalgo also soon discovered that Maria could sight-read a score and quickly memorize it (Petsalis-Diomidis 178–80). In some ways, Maria's voice and musical intelligence reminded de Hidalgo of her own voice and skills.

De Hidalgo herself did not have a traditionally lovely voice, but she had enthralled many worshipful fans with her wonderful technique and control that could draw thunderous applause from audiences. She was the most famous singer on the voice faculty at the Athens Conservatory, and the fact that she was willing to give Maria free lessons indicated something about her regard for Maria's talent and potential. De Hidalgo had also become an advisor to the local professional opera company in Athens, so she was in a unique position to help Maria develop her career. There were rumors among the students that de Hidalgo was a lesbian, but they were just rumors.

Maria fell deeply under the spell of Elvira de Hidalgo, even more than she had with Trivella. She would spend the whole day in her teacher's voice studio, attending the lessons of all her other students. Maria became her teacher's personal assistant, attending all her teacher's lessons with other voice students. The other students soon saw Maria as a teacher's pet, a favorite. Maria ate lunch with Elvira, talked with her, planned her career with her, and loved her (Wisneski 4–10). De Hidalgo became the loving, supportive mother Maria felt she never really had—and, in some ways, Maria became the loving daughter that Elvira never had.

De Hidalgo had had the kind of operatic career Maria dreamed of—a famous soprano who sang at all the most famous opera houses and became an international diva. That is exactly what Maria wanted, despite the political and economic chaos in Greece and all over Europe. The bloody Spanish Civil War finally ended in the spring of 1939. Generalissimo Francisco Franco boasted that he had ended the war, in spite of the fact that he was the one who had started it in the first place. Later that same year, an even worse conflict would begin with the outbreak of World War II—the bloodiest war in human history. In October 1939, Hitler invaded Poland, and England declared war on Germany (Hastings 118 ff.).

Were Evangelia and Maria not reading the newspapers or listening to the radio at the time? While they were blithely planning for Maria's career in opera and Jackie's in theater and the movies, Hitler was invading Czechoslovakia, and then making plans to invade France and England. Evangelia should have gathered as many family members as she could and taken the next boat to New York to rejoin George. There were plenty of voice teachers and music schools in New York, thanks to the popularity of the Metropolitan Opera. Instead, she was taking her daughters to voice teachers and agents in Athens. Maria was still a teenager and hardly prepared at this point for a career in opera, but Evangelia became convinced that Maria had the next great voice in opera and had to be able to sing professionally in Athens when her training was complete. Evangelia, like most stage mothers, was not going to let a little thing like World War II stop her and her daughter's career in opera—not to mention her plans for Jackie's acting ambitions.

Maria was doing particularly well with de Hidalgo's guidance. Elvira taught her all she knew about singing. She emphasized that *bel canto* method was the basis of all good operatic singing—Richard Wagner, among others, was a fervent proponent of *bel canto*. De Hidalgo emphasized breath control, diaphragm control, and *solfeggio*—those vocal exercises in various musical scales within the soprano range. She also emphasized excellent diction and making the words come dramatically alive and intelligible to the audience—intelligent singing, which made the drama in the score come alive for the audience. She said that the composer put all he wanted in the score, and that it was the singer's job to study the score to understand a given composer's intention, using the music and language to make the score come dramatically alive for the audience.

Maria did have some problems with her singing: Her three vocal ranges did not move smoothly and easily from the top to the bottom of her range. Her highest notes were also often insecure, and those notes could easily wobble. Fellow voice students were known to tease Maria about her vocal wobble, which infuriated her, since she never took any criticism easily, unless it was coming from de Hidalgo.

Maria was also surprised that many of the other vocal students were fascinated with a new kind of American music called jazz. They asked her if she knew of a place called Harlem in New York. She told them that Harlem was in a part of northern Manhattan, right next to her neighborhood, Washington Heights. Jazz music was heard on European radio and had become very popular with young people there, and she confessed that she herself liked to dance to it, though not to sing it, since it was a completely different vocal regimen than the *bel canto solfeggio* she'd made her key discipline.

Elvira felt that, with practice, Maria's vocal problems could be overcome and turned into assets. Elvira assured Maria that with proper training and hard work, she could overcome her technical problems and become a truly great singer and have an international career. As Maria was diligently practicing her *solfeggio* exercises and imagining conquering the world's opera houses, the world (and its opera houses) were about to become

2. Athens and World War II

unattainable to her—and to most of Europe. Italy invaded Greece in 1940. The Italian Fascist invasion of Greece was soon followed by the Nazis in 1941. Athens fell under the control of the Nazis, with an endless cacophony of screaming sirens and falling bombs. The city was not liberated until 1945. The bloody civil war that broke out in Greece (Communists vs. Republicans) did not end until 1950 (Hastings 646). The Allied forces did not want Greece to become part of the Soviet Union but instead remain part of capitalistic and democratic Western Europe. So Churchill and Truman made sure, with their armies, that Greece remained part of the West, no matter what the Greek people wanted.

Evangelia and her daughters were still living in their Patission Street apartment, in the heart of the old part of Athens. During the occupation, Evangelia reportedly took in two English soldiers, thereby risking all their lives. The apartment included a room for Evangelia's canaries, and there she hid the two English soldiers until they could be smuggled out of the country. Did this nice story really happen or was it fabricated by the Callas women? They survived in several ways, but one way was thanks to Jackie's rich boyfriend Milton Embirikos, who was nominally her fiancé, though in reality, Jackie was more of a "kept woman," using the parlance of that time. Essentially, in the absence of George Callas' support checks (which rarely arrived, due to the peripatetic nature of Greece's postal system), it was prostitution that enabled all three women to survive, thanks to Milton's generosity in sending the women food and money. The women also sold anything they could, including jewelry and family furniture. Maria also got some singing fees, and the little money she earned enabled them to eat while Athens was under Italian, and then German occupation. Often Maria was paid for her entertaining the troops in salamis and chocolates, which helped the three women to survive the occupation of Athens. Some 60,000 of their fellow Athenians did not (Stassinopoulos 50–55).

During those terrible war years of Nazi occupation in Athens, called the "Years of Famine" in Greece, Maria finished her musical studies and wanted to start her career as an opera singer. And, in spite of the incredible odds against her, she succeeded, and Elvira de Hidalgo told her she now needed practical on-stage experience. At this point, de Hidalgo became Maria's agent and used her contacts at the Athens Conservatory and with the local Athens Opera Company to get Maria leading roles in local opera productions.

Maria was first allowed to sing major roles (at the age of 15) with her musical conservatory in its student productions. At Athens' Music Conservatory, she gave a concert of songs and arias on April 11, 1938, at Parnassus Hall. On April 2, 9 and 16, 1939, she sang Santuzza in Mascagni's *Cavalleria Rusticana* at the National Conservatory at the Olympia Theatre. She also gave a concert on May 22, 1939, in the Parnassus Hall, and on May 23 she gave another concert of a few arias with other students. Yet another of her student performances occurred on June 25, 1939. She also participated in a concert at the Athens Conservatory on February 23, 1940, and an April 3 concert of duets which was broadcast on Athens Radio. On June 16, she sang the title role of Angelica in a student performance of Puccini's *Suor Angelica* (as part of Puccini's *Il Trittico*).

In the fall of 1940, Maria made her professional debut in Shakespeare's *The Merchant of Venice*, singing incidental music that German composer Engelbert Humperdinck had written for this play, in a production by the Greek National Opera in Athens. In the spring of 1941, Callas sang the role of Beatrice in the opera *Boccaccio* (by Franz von Suppé) with the Athens Opera in Pallas Hall. She also sang in this opera in July of the same year. In 1942, in a portent to the importance that this opera would have upon her life, she sang the title role in Giacomo Puccini's *Tosca* in August and September, also with the Athens Opera. Her performances were garnering good reviews in the local Athenian press (when an edition of the paper could be printed). In October 1942, she gave a recital of Rossini arias and duets with other singers at the Cinema Pallas in Salonika. The concert, celebrating the 150th anniversary of Rossini's birth in Pesaro in 1792, was organized by the Italian military authorities.

During this period, Maria developed a friendship with an Italian officer in Mussolini's Fascist Army, Major DiStasio. He was a fan of opera and went to performances at La Scala before the war. Maria found him fascinating. A portly, middle-aged man, he was in a position to help Maria's career and help to support her family. Did this man become Maria's lover? Was this the reason that he was so helpful and so generous? He also helped to arrange concert appearances for her with the Italian occupying forces (Edwards 42–46).

In 1943, Callas was even busier singing in Athens, despite the Nazi occupation and World War II. In February and March 1943, she sang again with the Athens Opera at the National Theater in the modern opera *Ho Protomastoras* (*The Master-Builder*) by Manolis Kalomiris, a modern Greek composer, based on Ibsen's play. This would be the first and last time Callas ever sang a new opera. In April 1943, she sang in Pergolesi's *Stabat Mater* at the Italian Institute of Culture in Athens, thanks to Major DiStasio. In July 1943, she again sang *Tosca* with the Athens Opera and had a success in the title role, getting good reviews. She gave another concert of Rossini's music in Salonika, and a lieder concert in Salonika the next day. In December 1943, she sang arias from German operas in Athens.

She sang again with the Athens Opera in April of 1944, in performances of Eugen D'Albert's *Tiefland*. She sang the main soprano role of

2. Athens and World War II

Marta. Again with the Athens Opera in May 1944, she sang Santuzza in several performances of Piero Mascagni's *Cavalleria Rusticana*. In July and August 1944, she performed the role of Smaragda in Kalomiris' *The Master-Builder* with the Athens Opera. More importantly, Maria sang the role of Leonore in Beethoven's *Fidelio* with the Athens Opera in August and September 1944, at the Herodes Atticus Theatre in Athens. Most of the people who applauded her were Nazi officers and soldiers. In October, she gave another concert for the Italian troops in Salonica, thanks to the shadowy Major DiStasio. Evangelia was not averse to fostering an affair between the middle-aged Italian major and her young daughter. Maria undoubtedly enjoyed the attention and his praising of her opera singing and encouraging her desire for an opera career.

In early March 1945, she again sang the leading female role of Marta in *Tiefland* for the German soldiers, with the Athens Opera at the city's Olympia Theatre. On March 20, 1945, she sang a concert of English songs for the British troops. Also for the Athens Opera, she sang the role of Laura in *The Beggar Student* (*Der Bettelstudent* by Karl Millöcker) in September 1945 (Wisneski 6–10).

She got a job with another local opera company, singing Santuzza in *Cavalleria Rusticana* and the leading role of Tosca. The city was flooded with German and Italian soldiers who had money to spend for opera performances—unlike most of the local citizens. So Maria sang in *Tiefland* for the Nazis, and for the Italian Fascists she sang the leading soprano roles in *Cavalleria Rusticana* and *Tosca* and got some good reviews (mostly in German military newspapers). As Maria sang the leading soprano role of Leonora in *Fidelio*, one wonders if the Nazis and Fascists in her audience saw any connection between the tyrannical Don Pizzaro and his attempts to murder Florestan with what the Axis soldiers and officers in the audience were doing to the people of Greece.

The reviewers immediately noted Callas' dramatic approach, and her lack of a particularly gorgeous voice. She appeared immediately in major roles despite the fact that she was still a teenager just out of the musical conservatory. She never sang what are called *comprimaria* roles—very small solo female roles—thanks to her musical avatar and voice teacher, Elvira de Hidalgo, who got Maria major roles in Athens' only professional opera company—an amazing feat given that Maria was still a teenager.

Maria began to be seen derisively by locals as a young artist entertaining the occupiers of their country. Was she literally in bed with the enemies of Greece? These rumors earned Maria many enemies among the native Greeks—over a million of whom died during World War II and the Fascist and Nazi occupations of their country.

Maria also began a lifelong pattern by making enemies at the Athens

Opera, and she was not invited back for another year. She became very competitive with other singers and was known to have contentious relationships with them. She could be charismatic on stage, but backstage, she had the reverse of charisma and developed a knack for making lifelong enemies. She had quickly become the stereotypical, narcissistic soprano, even though she was just starting her career and was only 19. Whenever anyone mentioned another soprano or mezzo-soprano in the company, Maria retorted that that singer always sang flat, or some other disparaging remarks. She seemed to feel that she was the only genuine and truly artistic female singer in the Athens opera company, and that the perceived hatred of some of her colleagues was nothing but jealousy. Her insecurities about her own voice drove her to attack other singers, especially other, more conventional sopranos with prettier voices. Maria was also remembered during this period as the fat girl who would gorge herself on any food she could find—including raw tomatoes and cabbage, and sausages and chocolate bars when she could get them. This memory of wartime deprivation and hunger adds a desperation to Maria and her determination to have a career as an opera singer—and she was ready to take down anyone who stood in her way. At one *Tosca* performance, she had to fight and push another soprano in the company to get to the stage. These were desperate times in Athens (Edwards 30–50).

After the Germans and Italians were forced out of Greece—primarily by the British and American Allied Forces, but also by Greek partisans—other singers were accusing Callas of being a collaborator; that she had been more than willing to sing German and Italian operas in Athens made her suspect to many Greeks. Maria defended herself by insisting that she was a young singer trying to develop an opera career in an occupied country, which some Greeks understood but others did not, and many did not forgive her. Maria's mother insisted that the family would have starved to death without the money and food Maria's singing (and other activities) provided (Callas, Evangelia 30–60). These, after all, were the years of hunger and death in Athens (Beaton 268–305).

By the end of the war years in Greece, Maria felt that she had to get out of the country to start her operatic career, since she had made so many professional enemies there. Italy had been badly bombed, and opera was not at the top of the list of priorities in the postwar recovery effort. So New York City and her father, whom she had not seen in almost ten years, seemed like the logical choice and a safe haven.

Maria left Greece with great hatred for her mother, whom Maria felt had turned her and Jackie into prostitutes so that the family could survive. Jackie's Greek "fiancé" never did marry her after the war. He undoubtedly wanted an honorable virgin, not a former mistress. Jackie, in her own book, says that Milton also grew to hate Evangelia. What Evangelia had done with

2. Athens and World War II

her daughters was typical of the desperation of Athens and, indeed, most of Europe during wartime. But Maria never forgave her mother for this. Should she have forgiven her? Maria, Jackie and Evangelia had all survived the war. This was primarily thanks to Evangelia—although she was also the one who had brought them all to Athens just in time for World War II. The three women even survived the Greek Famine in the final years of World War II. Perhaps as testament to her will to survive, Maria remained quite obese during this very lean period.

After these several years of wartime privation, Maria developed a yearning to return to New York City and try to reconnect with her father, whom she had not seen in almost ten years. How would her father receive her after all this time? Could she even *find* him? Was he still living in their last apartment in Washington Heights? Was her father living somewhere else with another woman and another family? Was he even still *alive*? Maria was clearly angry with her mother for moving her to Athens in 1937, though it was thanks to her mother that Maria got her vocal lessons and training, as well as surviving the war when millions had perished

New York City still had its famous Metropolitan Opera, as well as a new, more progressive company called the New York City Opera. During the Depression, the arts had suffered greatly and the Metropolitan Opera teetered on the verge of bankruptcy. But right after the war, the victorious U.S. would surely experience an artistic revival. Unlike Europe, America had never been occupied or bombed. New York seemed like the logical choice for Maria. She managed to persuade her godfather back in New York to wire her enough money to afford one-way ship's passage to the city of her birth. After all, she was still an American citizen. Sick of her long and unpronounceable Greek name, she even wanted to go back to her American name of Maria Callas. When she left Athens in 1945, she never wanted to see Greece again.

3

Back to New York

Right after World War II ended in the spring of 1945, once both Nazi Germany and Fascist Italy were defeated, a brutal civil war broke out in Greece that would last five years. Bombs were still dropping and fighting was still going on in Athens—not a good time to stage opera in the city.

Maria must have considered herself lucky to have survived the global holocaust that was World War II, even starting her fledgling professional opera career in Athens. She now had several operatic roles under her belt, and left Greece with a packet of some very good reviews from local newspapers (as well as from some Nazi publications, from during the Nazi occupation of Athens). The Athens Opera had seen what she had to offer, and seemed unimpressed. Her penchant for collegial animosity flowered early and virulently. She was clearly not seen as a "team player."

Callas boarded a ship called *The Stockholm* (part of the Swedish-American Line) in Piraeus, the port near Athens, and arrived three weeks later in New York. She still had nightmares about gunshots and bombs going off on her block in Athens. She'd often dreamed of returning to the comparatively placid confines of upper Manhattan. She still had her American citizenship, so she had no trouble entering the country—arriving home in New York in September 1945. She had written a letter from Athens to her father, telling him when she was arriving—but got no response. Would he recognize her? Would he even remember her? Did he not receive her letter? He had not seen her for almost ten years, since she was just entering her teen years after graduating from P.S. 189.

When she arrived in New York, George Callas was waiting at the dock. He had randomly spotted her name on a passenger list in a Greek newspaper printed in New York for the local immigrant community (Stassinopoulos 55–65). The current civil war in Greece, plus an earthquake on several islands in Greece, had caused thousands more Greeks to emigrate to America during the late 1940s and '50s. George looked dapper and eager to see her, though ten years older, and she kissed him and took photos with him.

3. Back to New York

Would he still love her as she loved him? In fact, *did* she still love him, after all she had been through in war-torn Athens?

George offered her a bedroom in his apartment, and the refrigerator was full of food. She was delighted in New York, where there was no rationing, where nothing was unavailable in the stores. For a girl coming from war-torn Europe, this must have seemed like Paradise (Levey 931 ff.). Perhaps life would be better, now that she was home in the city of her birth, and with her father. Could she begin a career in Manhattan, now that she had reconnected with her father? Who could help her?

Soon after her arrival in New York, Maria contacted her wealthy godfather, Dr. Lantzounis, and pleaded with him for some financial assistance, so that she could continue her voice lessons. She also needed money for decent new clothes, so that she could "dress the part" of the would-be operatic diva. She was startled to discover that her godfather had married a woman named Sallie, who was as young as Maria was. Dr. Lantzounis gave her money and sent her to shop for her clothes with Sallie, whom she came to like. After all, Maria reminded them, she was already an opera star in Athens and she had the positive reviews to prove it. However, the New York agents she approached must have made it abundantly clear to her that a success at the opera house in provincial Athens, during the worst years of World War II, did not count for much in New York's operatic community.

George suggested that Maria be on the lookout for a nice Greek boy so that she could marry and start a family. Given her own experiences with family life, Maria was not remotely interested in marrying a nice Greek boy (or any boy, for that matter), let alone starting her own family. (Neither Maria nor Jackie ever bore children, despite the hopes of their father.) She remained determined to launch her career in America as an opera singer. George's repeated entreaties for Maria to receive secretarial school training were met with resentment.

The New York that Maria returned to was a bustling postwar boom town. Her favorite shops were still in Washington Heights, her favorite movie theaters still showing the American films she always loved. She found that most young Americans still liked jazz music and the jazz big bands. But money was required to indulge in the frequent shopping and eating junkets Maria enjoyed.

As the months passed and no offers for her singing appeared, she became desperate. She had not sung in any of the major opera houses in Europe, so her résumé and collection of good reviews (all in Greek or German) did not seemingly impress anyone. The fact that her only "professional" American singing appearance had been on *Major Bowes Amateur Hour*, when she was a child, did little to impress anyone. She discovered that talent agents did not even want to represent her. It was difficult even to get an audition. She kept her sights set on the Metropolitan Opera—and couldn't imagine settling for anything less than that.

Maria could eat to her heart's content, and that is exactly what she did. As a child, she had contented and comforted herself with food, especially her favorite American candies such as Hershey's chocolate bars and Snickers bars. She comforted herself with food, since her mother had long treated her like an unloved and unwanted child, the ugly younger sister, the fat ugly duckling to her sister, Jackie's thin, glamorous swan. She had lost significant weight in the past, but the weight always came back.

One of her New York voice teachers was Louise Caselotti, who herself was a promising new soprano. Caselotti also wanted to have an opera career and had a promising voice—though Maria was convinced that her own voice and training were far better. Maria was forever grateful for the training she had gotten for free, thanks to Elvira de Hidalgo. It was still very difficult for Maria to praise any other singer, least of all another soprano. Her friends in Greece noticed that any time they mentioned any other singers, Maria would quickly dismiss them as always singing flat rather than singing accurately. It was really almost impossible for her to say anything nice about any other soprano since she was so insecure about her own singing and so competitive.

Fate then led her to cross paths with Giovanni Martinelli, a famous Italian tenor who was singing at the Met. She sang for him, and he told her she had a lovely voice but she needed many more lessons to become a singer at the Met. She felt she already had become a professional opera singer in Athens and did not need any more lessons. Clearly, Signore Martinelli did not understand that he was in the presence of a great opera star. That was Maria's "take-away" from this audition.

She *had* to insist that she remained the greatest soprano in opera at this point in her career. Other people found this somewhat delusional, but Maria insisted upon this point. This line of thinking remained a constant, throughout her career. She never was able to develop a long friendship with any other soprano or mezzo-soprano though she would sing with so many of them. Beneath all of her bravado lurked the very insecure woman that Maria always was, an aspect of her she revealed to very few people. She was, at heart, so deeply insecure about her own singing that she desperately needed constant reassurance about her voice and her performances (Zeffirelli 150 ff.).

Maria soon learned that Louise Caselotti's husband, Edward Richard Bagarozy, was trying to form a new opera company in Chicago: the United States Opera Company. Bagarozy, a slim, dashing young Italian-American, promised that he would cast her in both *Turandot* and in *La Gioconda* in the title soprano roles in his new opera company. Maria may have had a

3. Back to New York

brief affair with him during this time, since their surviving letters have a somewhat overly familiar and flirtatious tone. She always wrote to him as "Eddie," not as "Mr. Bagarozy." She was certainly physically attracted to him. He praised her voice extravagantly, which added greatly to his appeal for her. That he was married to another singer and, in fact, to her vocal teacher, made him even more tempting to her, since she fantasized about stealing him from his own wife and possessing him herself. Both of them believed in her star quality and her great potential as an opera singer (Galatopoulos 47 ff.).

Maria began to suspect that her father was having a clandestine affair with one of their neighbors, Alexandra Papajohn, a kindly widow whom her mother had once considered a friend. This suspicion about her father's affair infuriated Maria, since she had the ridiculous fantasy of her parents being somehow happily reunited in Manhattan while, in fact, neither one wanted to see the other at all. George felt that his marriage to Evangelia was over, and considered himself free to openly pursue other women.

Maria continued to struggle to get an audition at the Metropolitan Opera. The story she told her friends at the time was certainly sunnier than the reality. She maintained that she was offered some roles, which she haughtily refused, convinced that the Met's general manager, Edward Johnson, was trying to sabotage her career by offering her uninteresting, supporting roles, sung in English, that would forever tarnish her reputation. It was here that she began a long series of feuds with operatic general managers. Even when the heads of various opera companies offered her plum roles, Maria almost always saw them as "out to get her." This sounded like paranoia to most people. There were thousands of young sopranos who were desperate to be offered a role—any role—at the Met, but Maria prided herself on rejecting them first—before somehow giving them a chance to reject her. According to Maria, Johnson offered her a *Fidelio* and a Mozart opera sung in English, but she was convinced he was somehow trying to trick and trap her. Naturally, she would resolutely refuse such unworthy assignments.

Did such an offer come from the Met? If so, there is no evidence of it in the Met Archives, and it does seem incredible that the Met would offer starring roles to a singer with such limited credentials. Years later, Johnson said he had "tentatively" offered her some roles, to be sung in Philadelphia or Brooklyn, rather than on the Met's main stage in Manhattan. The evidence seems to indicate that Callas fabricated this story to prove to her friends what a great prima donna she already was before singing anywhere other than in Greece. She would repeatedly do this—fabricate stories which could not be confirmed. She seemed to believe in these stories that elevated her status in the world of opera, even when people suspected they were not true. Still she could not tolerate being criticized, except by a few voice teachers, such as Elvira de Hidalgo or, later, by important conductors.

She also auditioned for the director of the San Francisco Opera Company, America's other major opera company at the time, and here, too, she became very haughty. The director and founder of this company, Gaetano Merola, said she should sing first in Europe, and then maybe San Francisco would offer her a role. She supposedly responded that if she succeeded in Europe, she would not need to sing in San Francisco, and would not need San Francisco's opera company, and, indeed, she never sang there. She rather melodramatically told this story to many of her friends, and never did she voice any gratitude for the advice. Was this another one of her narcissistic fabrications to over-inflate her value in the world of opera? She obviously had a great deal of narcissism, even at such an early stage of her operatic career. Did she know she was lying in this case or was she delusional on the topic of her own career? Of course, performing artists need a great deal of narcissism to endure all the auditions and refusals they face early in their careers, but Callas had even more narcissism than most young singers. People were also beginning to wonder if she could tell the difference between real life and the lies she was telling about her singing prowess.

If she had accepted the roles that were offered to her at the Met, her career could have begun in her native country and she could have first succeeded and developed there. From those successes, she could have then started singing in Italy and elsewhere in Europe, once the opera houses had recovered from World War II. But that is not how Maria Callas saw those first offers from the Met (Mayer 231 ff.). If she did not become so paranoid and hostile around authority figures, her career might have been easier but not so dramatic, but her personality necessitated drama. She liked to create drama, especially when she was at the center of the drama—very much like her mother. Callas developed an ability to draw attention to herself and her career. She quickly decided that there was no such thing as bad publicity, and she clearly loved all the attention she could get.

Meanwhile, she continued to be enchanted by Eddie Bagarozy and Louise Caselotti, and their venture to start a new opera company in Chicago—a city then without one. The city had a long history of opera performances, but primarily through traveling opera companies. For a time, Mary Garden performed for a Chicago opera company and became its general director (or "Directa," to use her self-invented title). That company did not last very long. Samuel Insull tried to establish his own Chicago opera company by installing an opera house at the bottom of his new skyscraper; his rationale was that the rents from the office building would help subsidize the opera company, but the opera company he founded went bankrupt as a result of the Depression. His new opera house-office building was completed in 1928, just in time for the Stock Market Crash of 1929. Insull was accused of theft and grand larceny (and was ultimately found not guilty in court) but his opera company did not survive his economic collapse caused by the Depression. Right after World War II, there was a movement in Chicago to start an opera company, not just dependent upon touring companies, to satisfy the city's musical and operatic needs. A few years later, in the early 1950s, the Lyric Opera of Chicago was started, thanks to Carol Fox and some of her wealthy friends (Marsh 30 ff.). This small group created Chicago's Lyric Opera company, which—ironically—was first put on the map by the appearances there of one Maria Callas—and is now considered one of America's premier opera companies.

Eddie Bagarozy's opera venture in Chicago was *not* a success—it folded after just a few rehearsals—but not before Maria signed a contract with him to be her representative in all her opera engagements for the next ten years. She would come to regret signing that contract, but she did sign it and corresponded with him in the intervening years. Those letters were very compromising. He promised to represent her and develop her career, and she promised to give him ten percent of her earnings (Galatopoulos 55–60).

While Maria was busy in New York trying to start her career, Aristotle Onassis and his wife Athina "Tina" Livanos Onassis also lived in New York; their first child, Alexander, was born there in 1948. The Onassis family and Maria certainly would not have crossed paths during this time, since Aristotle was already a wealthy man and Callas was a totally unknown woman of very humble station. Aristotle Onassis did not even like opera.

Once Eddie's Chicago venture failed, Maria found an impresario looking for singers for the Verona Opera Festival in Italy. This was the retired tenor Giovanni Zenatello, who had been the original Pinkerton at the 1904 premiere of Puccini's *Madama Butterfly* at La Scala. The opera's premiere had been a great flop, but the opera was extensively revised by Puccini and became one of his most successful works. Now, the retired Zenatello returned to his native Verona and was helping to run the Verona Opera Festival in the old Roman coliseum, called the Arena. Zenatello himself had been born in Verona in 1876. This festival started in 1913 and was quickly expanded and funded by Mussolini because he liked its connection with ancient, imperial Rome. The festival had to cease performances during the two world wars, because of allied bombing of Verona and other parts of northern Italy.

But just two years after the war, 1947, the opera festival began again and the company wanted to stage Ponchielli's *La Gioconda*; Maria Callas had sung its most famous aria, "Suicidio," in Athens. Zenatello auditioned Callas in New York, was very impressed with her singing and signed her to sing some performances of this dramatic soprano role. Zenatello noted that Callas had a very large and interesting voice, and the opera festival in Verona needed very large voices to fill its enormous Arena, an old Roman amphitheater. The acoustics in this Roman amphitheater remained so good that amplification was not needed, provided the voices were large enough. Zenatello had sung in the Arena with great success.

This was the opportunity Maria had been longing for—a major role in one of Europe's leading opera festivals. Now all she had to do was get to Verona (the setting for Shakespeare's *Romeo and Juliet*) and turn the role of the title character of Ponchielli's *La Gioconda* into a star vehicle for herself. She would find operatic success—and even love—in Verona (Galatopoulos 55 ff).

Maria had to be in Verona for rehearsals two months before the grand opening, and the festival did not provide funds for this travel. Her beneficent godfather, Dr. Lantzounis, came through with money so that she could follow her dream to the legendary city. She booked passage on a ship to Naples, and then went by train to Verona. She was offered very little money from the company and she had very little money herself but thanks to continued support from Lantzounis, she was able to put on the front of being a "woman of means." If she succeeded in Verona during the summer opera festival there, she could really launch an international career since that summer opera festival's performances were reviewed by some of the international musical press.

Maria had to improve her Italian since, though she could sing in that language, she was certainly not fluent in spoken Italian. She missed her teacher back in Athens, Elvira de Hidalgo, who could coach her and prepare her for a role like *La Gioconda*, a tragic opera by Amilcare Ponchielli. The title and the title character, La Gioconda, is clearly meant ironically since she is a very sad character who commits suicide in the final scene. She is hardly the happy, cheerful woman that her name suggests. Callas identified with this tragic character, who had a difficult bond with her mother, and Callas would sing this role successfully and with great conviction. Maria was drawn to this part and sang it in several opera houses, and she later recorded it as well. Elvira de Hidalgo had repeatedly emphasized that Italy was the proper place for Maria to begin her career. And now, Callas had a contract to make her Italian debut in a starring role. She also knew that she needed some kind of over-arching "benefactor"—a wealthy older person with a knowledge of opera and a lot of money, who could help her launch her career.

Maria's father did not have enough money to support Maria until she established her own career—something Maria never forgave him for. George had never made much money, but he had survived in New York during the Great Depression, and he was able to support his family while they were in New York with him.

In the meantime Maria was going to her singing lessons in New York, doing her solfeggio exercises at home at her piano, as her teacher Elvira de Hidalgo had recommended, and going to anyone who would hear her sing for auditions. Callas also practiced vocal exercises on her trills, *portamento*, *crescendo*, *diminuendo* and other bel canto vocal decorations. Louise Caselotti had also suggested that she was really a mezzo-soprano since her low notes were more impressive and seemed to come more easily to her. Maria was also very musical and was also a good pianist who could read and play from vocal/piano opera scores. Unlike some singers, she could read music and accompany herself on the piano, which was the way she taught herself a role. She had also learned in Athens that she could memorize a role in opera within a week. She clearly had all the necessary skills to be a great opera singer. She wondered when the rest of the world would recognize this undeniable fact.

She also seemed able to sing both coloratura soprano roles and dramatic soprano roles—a most unusual versatility, found in very few female singers. She felt she was really a "dramatic coloratura" soprano, as Elvira de Hidalgo had called her. She had an unusually large voice, a voice that could fill large international opera houses like the Met or La Scala or London's Covent Garden Opera House—and even Verona's enormous Arena. But just beneath the surface, this narcissistic young opera singer was a fat, insecure girl who could barely see without her glasses. But then, opera was full of plus-sized women. As the baseball player Yogi Berra (himself an opera fan) said on several occasions, "It isn't over until the fat lady sings." Callas was not trying to be a model or a Hollywood movie star (yet), but her insecurities remained constant companions to her, throughout her career and beyond.

Maria would be traveling to Italy with Louise Caselotti, who would get ten percent of her fee since she acted as Maria's agent, in the stead of her husband. Neither Eddie nor his wife were wealthy people who could afford to subsidize Maria as she was beginning her career in Italy. However, Maria was happy to have the company of Louise on this long sea voyage to Europe.

Springtime in Italy, she was told, was an enchanting time to be there, before the heat of the Italian summer set in. But after living in both Athens and Manhattan, she was not to be intimidated by the heat of a Mediterranean summer. In fact, she liked the heat—even the heat of the pressures of a career in opera; and like her mother, she hated cold weather. So she boarded the ship *Rossia* in New York on her first trip to Italy—the ancestral home of opera and, in fact, the very birthplace of opera. She was about to assay a starring role, in a legendary venue, but could she manage to succeed there? Sometimes she was confident and hopeful, and other times she was fearful and even frantic, but she was not about to turn down a golden opportunity to make her Italian operatic debut. Legions of other young singers would jump at this proverbial "golden opportunity," if she didn't. Why should she help another soprano? No, Maria would go to Verona and sing there if it killed her—or Louise Caselotti. Maria bought a new dress, thanks to her generous godfather, brought along her score of *La Gioconda*, and prayed to both the ancient Greek gods and more modern Christian God of Greece for success in Verona. Maria boarded the S.S. *Rossia* on June 13, 1947, for the two-week trip from New York City to Naples with just one piece of cheap luggage, a large purse, and her score of Ponchielli's opera (Stassinopoulos 55 ff.). She prayed that the forces of her destiny were urging her to make that journey to her future greatness as an opera star. As she was leaving New York, her mother Litza had arrived there a few months earlier—determined to somehow resuscitate her marriage, Maria could hear her parents arguing in their apartment as she left for Italy, where she hoped to find a new life in opera—and a new family as well.

4

Verona and the Arena

Maria Callas was back on a ship crossing the Atlantic again in June 1947. She was traveling with her very good friend and teacher, Louise Caselotti. At the time, Louise and her husband, Eddie, seemed like the loving parental unit she had always sought in vain. Maria and Louise arrived on June 27, 1947, in the lovely bay of Naples with Mt. Vesuvius smoking in the background. Maria in any case, she was glad to get away from her home, in Manhattan, where her parents were reunited after the war but still battling with each other in their small, stuffy Washington Heights apartment.

Maria's voice teacher in Athens, Elvira de Hidalgo, said her career would blossom in Italy and then the Met would beg her to sing in New York in any role she wanted. That was the way to international stardom in opera, according to her famous teacher, who had herself once been a star in both Europe and the Americas, exactly what Callas was dreaming of doing herself. Maria also saw that Elvira had helped her so much in her voice lessons, and to find her way into the labyrinth that was the professional opera world. Maria found out that to develop a career, a wealthy older mentor to sponsor and support you is essential, especially if one is penniless, which she felt she nearly was. She needed a benefactor, and soon.

Italy was then still repairing all the damage it had suffered during the war—a war started by the lunatic Benito Mussolini and his Fascists. That dictator was now dead, and a financially devastated Italy was trying to recuperate. From 1943 to 1945, Italy had become the battleground of Europe as the British and American armies fought their way from Sicily up the Italian peninsula, driving the Nazi army back into Germany (Hastings 446 ff.). Naples had been devastated by bombings. (One of its daughters, Sophia Loren, was trying to establish a career in acting during this same postwar period.) A major earthquake had occurred in Naples and its environs in 1944, with Vesuvius erupting that year as well, adding to the horrors Naples had to endure during this time. One way of surviving was by reviving the summer opera festival in Verona, reigniting one of Italy's major sources of revenue, tourism.

Maria had to go to the railroad station and get a train ticket from Naples to Verona. As she saw Mount Vesuvius in the distance, Maria rejoiced to be, at last, in Italy, the home of opera. The lovely islands of Capri and Ischia and the Amalfi Coast were visible to them, but she and Louise had no time (or money) to do any sightseeing. The women would have also noticed the bombed-out and burned shells of buildings along the city's Mediterranean coast.

During her voyage, Maria had been practicing the breathing exercises and *solfeggio* scales that Elvira gave her. She would find her roles through performance, Elvira emphasized, and that would lead her to international stardom. Callas arrived in Naples with one piece of cardboard luggage and a handbag full of makeup. A representative of the festival met her at the Verona train station and brought her to a hotel with a restaurant.

A diva emerges: Maria Callas in Verona, Italy, in 1949.

This excellent hotel, the Accademia, was (and is) situated very near the Arena, where the festival performances were staged—and where they are still held every summer. The huge amphitheater seats about 30,000 people and has ample room for a large stage, which lends itself to huge and elaborate productions of popular operas that attract opera fans and tourists from around the world. The festival closed down due to World War II, but the Arena itself, on the Piazza Bra, had not been bombed or damaged. The small but beautiful city, on the banks of the Adige River, needed the revenue the opera festival brought to the town. Most hotels, pensions and restaurants in Verona filled up quickly during the opera festival in June, July and August. The amphitheater had been there since the Romans built it in about 100 A.D. The summer opera festival was greatly expanded by order of Mussolini with performances of Wagner's *Die Walküre* in the 1920s—the Fascist dictator being a great admirer of German culture and its composers and of Italy's past as the center of the Roman Empire. The Verona city fathers soon realized that an expanded summer opera festival would encourage thousands of tourists to come there every summer. Given the enormous size of the Arena and the number of people it could contain, this was not a place for intimate chamber operas. Large, elaborate, colorful productions were needed at the Arena with major singers with large voices. Verdi's *Aida* was often staged there, and this grand opera needs a grand production. The opera stage was set up at one end of the circular amphitheater's seating area, with the audience surrounding the rest of the Arena's seating area or sitting on chairs set up on the floor of the amphitheater. Such a seating arrangement seemed to work best for both sight lines and acoustics. When Callas first saw the famous Arena, she must have been very fearful and wondered if her voice would be heard by every member of the audience.

A new young American tenor named Richard Tucker was also heading to Verona and hoping that success there would lead to an international career and a contract with the Met. Tucker would become one of the most famous American tenors of his generation and became a star tenor at the Met who sometimes sang with Callas, though they never really became friends (Mayer 210 ff.). Callas rarely developed friendships with other singers because she herself was so competitive that she saw other singers as rivals rather than as colleagues to befriend. The Italian-Russian bass Nicola Rossi-Lemeni, whom Maria met in New York, would also be singing at the Arena that summer. Another new Italian soprano, young Renata Tebaldi, would also be making her Verona debut that same year.

Maria was approached by one of the festival's most important administrators, Giovanni Battista Meneghini, a great fan of singers, especially sopranos. He was also one of the wealthiest men in Verona, and quickly becoming even wealthier. He was in his 50s and living in the hotel during the festival. She was in her early 20s and desperate, but very ambitious. He was sharing a hotel room with another man, and there were rumors that both men were gay. However, the hotel shortages in Italy right after World War II were likely a quite credible reason for having had to share his room with a friend. The Meneghini family business was construction, with a specialty in brickwork and masonry. Their services were in great demand in postwar Italy, and their coffers were full to overflowing (Meneghini 12 ff.).

Even though Meneghini was the first son and head of the family business, he was still a bachelor—one of the city's most desirable bachelors. He was a rich man and much more interested in opera than in his brick and construction business. He was the oldest son in a family of six children, and so, according to Italian tradition, he was in charge of his family and the family's business, but he was doing this grudgingly. He dreamed of being in the world of opera, though he did not have a singing voice or any great musical talent. However, he had become a good administrator, was knowledgeable about voices, and remained very helpful to Verona's summer opera festival in its ancient Arena.

One of Meneghini's musical friends was Tullio Serafin, one of the festival's guiding spirits. A world-renowned conductor, he was still conducting there over 30 years after he inaugurated the festival in 1913. As a young man, Serafin began as an assistant to the legendary Arturo Toscanini, and by 1947 he had conducted at most of the world's greatest opera houses, including La Scala, the San Carlo in Naples, the Met and Covent Garden, in addition to all of the major opera houses in Italy. He was considered the greatest living conductor of bel canto operas at the time.

Well-connected and wealthy, Meneghini could be of great use to a budding and ambitious young opera singer trying to establish a career in Italy. Maria Callas was in need of a *benefattore* in Italy, to establish her career. Is it any wonder that Callas and Meneghini were immediately attracted to one another? (Meneghini 50–70).

Verona is one of the most beautiful cities in northern Italy, with the homes and palaces and churches built during the medieval and Renaissance periods by its ruling family, the Scaligere. Smiling equestrian statues of the Scaligere generals and dukes dot the town. It also became famous as the site for the legendary love story of Romeo and Juliet, made famous by William Shakespeare and by Bellini's opera *I Montechi e I Capuletti*. Charles Gounod composed an operatic version of the famous love story in 1867, *Romeo et Juliette*, and there have been numerous film versions of the story, including one by Franco Zeffirelli in 1968. The town's *Centro Storico* (historical center) remains gorgeous, with lovely medieval and Renaissance buildings, and with the beautiful Adige River, which is as blue as the Veronese sky even during the hot summer, with a series of ancient, picturesque bridges spanning it. In this romantic city, Maria Callas fell in love and married—and also had her first major success as an opera singer. All of her operatic dreams began to materialize in fair Verona.

In many ways, Gian Battista Meneghini became a mentor and the loving father figure she always dreamed she would have, and never got, in her own father. Gian Battista, or "Titta," as his friends called him, was passionately interested in opera and opera singers, unlike her own father, who was bored with opera. Battista was also in the business of opera and engaging opera singers for the festival, so he knew opera directors and agents and the very best voice teachers, vocal coaches and opera conductors in Italy. He was also very knowledgeable about the singing voice, so he could help her in ways that her real father could not. In addition, Meneghini (again, unlike George Callas) could afford to hire people to help her in her career—money would not be a problem for Maria, thanks to him, and he believed

4. Verona and the Arena

in her voice, her unique talent and the development of her career. The baritone Enzo Sordello (and others) called Meneghini "The Pygmalion of Callas," the person who created her (Sordello 20–40).

Maria and Meneghini first met at a ristorante, Padavena, and shared a meal there. As he welcomed her to his hometown of Verona, he also wished her success in her Italian debut. As they gradually got acquainted, Callas struck him as a lonely and desperately ambitious young woman who needed help. He offered to give her a tour of his favorite Italian city, Venice, which he knew and loved. While in Venice, he stopped at the Church of the Frari and pointed out "The Assumption of the Virgin," a famous Titian painting that inspired Richard Wagner to write Isolde's Liebestod at the end of *Tristan und Isolde*. As Meneghini got to know Maria and hear her sing, he became more and more impressed with her (Meneghini 12–30).

Is it any wonder they fell in love? She wanted a career as an opera singer and he wanted to manage an opera singer's career and become a part of the world of international opera. Here was the rich mentor she'd dreamed of finding, a man with valuable connections. From Maria's point of view, this was a match made in heaven.

One of the first things Meneghini did was to drive her several times to the floating city of Venice. He became her Cicerone (her tour guide) and showed her all its wonderful and unique sights. He pointed out that *La Gioconda* was set in Venice and reflected some of its history and political conflicts. He hired a gondola and showed her the city's unique Byzantine architecture. He also pointed out to her one of the most beautiful opera houses in the world, Venice's La Fenice (the Phoenix). He showed her the Palazzo Vendramin-Calergi, along the Grand Canal, where Richard Wagner died in 1883. In that Palazzo, in the rooms where Wagner died, there is now a Wagner museum. Meneghini also showed her the busts of Verdi and Wagner in the city's Giardino Publico. He even took her for cappuccino and pastries at Café Florian on the Piazza San Marco. He pointed out that both Verdi and Wagner had dined there in the 19th century. He did not urge her to avoid the creamy Italian pastries at Florian's, as her mother and sister would have. Venice would figure significantly in her future opera career, he told Maria (Meneghini 51–65).

He even offered to pay for an expert vocal coach in Verona (a friend of his) to help her with her role. Ferruccio Cusinati, the chorus master of the festival, went over the title role of La Gioconda with Callas, making many useful suggestions regarding the high notes and the pronunciation of some of the Italian words. Cusinati told Meneghini that Callas had an impressive vocal talent but still needed some vocal polishing. Once the rehearsals started, the conductor Tullio Serafin told his friend Meneghini that Maria had a real talent and could become a great soprano but needed more refining of her talent. Serafin was also impressed with Callas' sense of drama and the unique quality of her vocal timbre (Meneghini 64 ff.).

In the meantime, she had to succeed in the title role in *La Gioconda* ("The Smiling Woman" based on the legend of the Mona Lisa) in her debut at the Arena, which took place on August 3, 1947. She twisted her ankle during the dress rehearsal, but she was determined that that accident would not prevent her from making her Italian debut. Tullio Serafin, the conductor of this performance, had an avuncular interest in her. He had conducted many times in Verona and all over the opera world, on both sides of the Atlantic. Callas obviously had a great opportunity here. If she was a flop, it would probably have ended her career in Italy. She had to prove that she was a major talent who deserved much praise.

The titular soprano character in *La Gioconda* sings her greatest aria at the beginning of the last act: "Suicidio," suicide, which is what she is considering by this point. (She does commit suicide at the end.) This is the role that first made Callas famous—she sang the role six times in Verona, and at other opera houses in Italy. She was considered a huge success in that role and she recorded the opera as well.

Maria garnered some very good (but not great) reviews for her theatrical approach to the role, as well as for her singing. The reviews described her as a very promising young American singer with an interesting voice and real acting ability. One critic noted that she had a large voice with "a timbre of a most moving and individual quality." Finally, Callas had success in a major role at one of the world's most famous opera festivals.

Maria twisting her ankle during the dress rehearsal was the first known instance in which she created backstage drama by claiming she had a major injury—but, due to her professionalism and fortitude, she soldiered on. It would not be the last.

In his memoirs about his life with Maria, Meneghini reported that she brought out the father in him. She looked so sad and poor and lonely and needy when he first saw her at the restaurant that he wanted to help her. She was all by herself with no family (or man) to help her, so near-sighted that she was always staring at him. He also found her uniquely talented. Maria brought out the paternal in him, and he wanted to use his resources to help her. His family, however, especially his brothers and sisters, were immediately suspicious of Maria. They thought she was an opportunist who would use the family's money to further her career, and dump him once he was no longer useful to her. They warned him about her, and as it turned out, they were completely right about Maria though Meneghini did not believe this at the time. He was a man in love with a young opera diva who had immense talent. He felt it was his duty to "take her under his wing."

It was Meneghini who introduced Callas to Tullio Serafin, arguably

4. Verona and the Arena

the most important conductor of Italian opera at the time. Arturo Toscanini was more famous, but he did not conduct in Italy very often since he and his family lived at their Wave Hill estate in the Bronx. He was now conducting primarily in the United States and recording in New York. Toscanini was in his 80s by this time and did not have enough energy to conduct whole operas. Meneghini later also introduced Callas to Biki, one of the most famous designers of women's clothing in elegant Milan, and a relative of the composer Giacomo Puccini. Biki dressed her elegantly and urged her to lose weight so that she looked better both on the street and on the stage (Meneghini 10 ff.). She would prove to be one of the most influential style mentors of Maria's life.

It was probably Biki who told Maria about the expensive Swiss clinics that help wealthy women and movie stars lose weight, often with wonderful new drugs coming from America to increase the metabolism and quell one's appetite. The wonder drug was Dexedrine, which was just beginning to be used as a drug to help people lose weight. Think how wonderful Maria would look on stage! Just imagine how much more believable Maria would be if she became the gorgeous woman Biki insisted she could be.

Callas thought seriously about this, though she suspected this was a fantasy since she had always been fat, even as a baby. She had lost weight in the past, but it always came back. She felt that it was her destiny to be fat, and the art form of opera had many fat singers performing on the great stages. As Callas became more famous, Italian newspapers and tabloids began to report on her career, and she hated seeing the accompanying photos. She felt they made her look fatter than she really was, but she knew she was very overweight and hated how she looked.

In an *Oggi* magazine interview, Callas said that she fell in love with Meneghini within ten minutes of meeting him, and that what was most important in her life was her marriage and her love for him. She also said that she would gladly give up her opera career if her husband asked her to do so. She revealed that what she wanted more than anything else was to have Meneghini's baby. That comment must have given her friends quite a laugh since they knew that what was most important in her life was her career in opera. Motherhood had never been very attractive to her given her own sad experiences with family life and with her own mother.

Callas very clearly knew what Italians wanted to hear about the role of women in Italy right after World War II. So she presented herself in that guise to improve her image. She also told reporters that she was very religious and prayed for God to guide her, another comment that would have amused her friends. She loved publicity and seeing herself in newspapers and magazines. She read the very glossy magazines and shared their readers' interest in the lives of the rich and famous, especially American movie stars.

While living in Italy, she became fluent in the Italian language, though with a Veronese accent. She had studied the language with her voice teachers Maria Trivella and Elvira de Hidalgo back in Greece to help her memorize the roles in Italian opera that she most wanted to sing. Her teachers convinced her that her voice was most suitable for the bel canto roles of Rossini, Bellini and Donizetti. Elvira also told Callas that her voice was big enough and her technique solid enough to sing some dramatic soprano roles in the early operas of Verdi. She really was a borderline soprano; she could sing some high mezzo-soprano roles in addition to the soprano roles in these operas. Opera reviewers were beginning to call her the new Maria Malibran, a great soprano of the bel canto period for whom Rossini wrote some of his greatest roles. Malibran became more famous for her acting in opera than for her singing and could perform with great success both tragedy and comedy.

Callas was uniquely equipped for a singing career because of her ability with languages and her ability to memorize long operatic roles (both words and music) with amazing rapidity. She was also a natural actress, something unusual in opera; but she was not the first opera singer who could act. Throughout its history, opera always had a few singers who were also terrific actors. Stars like Malibran and Wilhelmine Schroeder-Devrient are examples of this kind of singer in the 19th century. Malibran had inspired Rossini just as Schroeder-Devrient had inspired Richard Wagner. The drama was in the music so audiences did not expect much drama in the acting on stage, but Callas wanted to change that.

In the '50s, Lily Pons was a small, thin, lovely soprano famous for her fine acting and her lovely coloratura soprano voice. At the suggestion of Giovanni Zenatello, her main voice teacher, Pons became a starring singer at the Met from the '30s to the '50s and was often heard on the Met's radio broadcasts and appeared on American television. Anna Moffo became famous in the '50s for her gorgeous voice plus her acting ability and her thin and lovely figure. Callas eventually became renowned for her acting ability more than the beauty of her voice. She was especially adept at using the Italian language and Italian music to create a unique dramatic excitement on stage and on her many recordings. She also knew how to change the timbre of her voice and her body language for each of her different roles. These were ways to keep an audience fascinated with her during her performances. She clearly also had what the French called *presence d'etage*—stage presence. When she was on stage, the audience would remain focused on her despite all the other performers and tons of scenery (De Ceccatty 165 ff.).

After her performances as La Gioconda in Verona, Tullio Serafin began to recommend that she get more voice lessons so that she could then sing in opera houses where he conducted in Venice, Milan, Rome and

4. Verona and the Arena

Florence. Maria continued to work with vocal coach Ferruccio Cusinati in Verona, and he helped her with the technical control of her voice (Meneghini 32 ff.). Since Serafin was such a famous opera conductor, he could significantly improve her career by asking opera companies to hire her. His wife Elena Rakowska had been a Wagnerian soprano herself and could help Callas with her breathing and pronunciation. Both Meneghini and Callas felt that since Serafin believed in her voice and her musical ability, he was in a unique position to help her develop a career, and this Serafin did as he became her trusted mentor and advisor.

Now Maria had her Titta (Meneghini), who became not only a friend but protector and agent as well as a father figure. She trusted him and she wanted more from him. She wanted him for her husband since she fell madly in love with him and wanted him around her constantly. She was not a woman who liked traveling and living alone.

They were living together now but that raised eyebrows in Italy; in fact, it was against the law for two people of the opposite sex to share a room unless they were related. If he was her husband, they could share one double room and save a lot of money in hotel expenses, and she was always very concerned with money. Speaking of money, she also trusted him with her money, now that she was earning some. She liked having him as her agent and representative who could drive a hard bargain and get her top dollar for her performances. She was paid very badly for her first performances in Verona, and she wanted to change that quickly. She dreamed of being the most highly paid opera singer in the world, a goal she would achieve thanks primarily to her husband.

After Maria's promising Verona premiere, Meneghini took over her career, sent her to the best voice teachers and vocal coaches in Verona, and tried to get her bookings to perform for smaller opera companies in Italy. If she succeeded there, then he had contacts at La Scala and could offer them someone who had succeeded at all the country's second-tier opera theaters. Titta worked very hard with agents to convince them to book her, and he pleaded with Serafin to hire his wife anywhere he was conducting. Maria would have been embarrassed to do all this for herself and was very thankful to have such a helpful agent in her husband. All this pressure paid off for Maria, since her voice had steadily improved thanks to some new teachers (especially Serafin's wife and Ferruccio Cusinati) and Serafin's coaching. So Serafin started to hire her where he himself was conducting and their collaboration was getting them both good reviews.

Callas made successful debuts at opera companies in Naples, Venice, Florence and Rome. Serafin decided he wanted her to sing Wagner, one of his favorite composers. Like Toscanini, Serafin loved to conduct both Wagner and Italian opera composers. So in Venice she sang Brünnhilde in *Die*

Walküre, Isolde in *Tristan und Isolde* and Kundry in *Parsifal*—singing in Italian rather than in German and in shortened versions of these operas. (Both of these approaches were then traditional in staging Wagner's operas in Italy.) Maria became a Wagnerian soprano, something she never thought she would become, though she had sung Leonore in Beethoven's *Fidelio* during the war in Athens. Her main voice teacher de Hidalgo told her she could sing both dramatic and coloratura roles, if she was careful, though she never imagined Maria singing a major role in a Wagnerian opera.

Venice's Teatro la Fenice had a long tradition of staging Wagnerian opera. Wagner was very fond of Venice and visited the lovely city several times during his life. He liked to go to Italy in the winter to avoid the harsh winters in Germany, especially toward the end of his life when he developed a heart condition which ultimately caused his fatal heart attack in Venice on February 13, 1883 (Newman, IV, 697 ff.).

During a run of Wagner's *Die Walküre* in Venice in 1951, the coloratura soprano Margherita Carosio, who was supposed to sing Elvira in Bellini's *I Puritani*, got very sick with the flu and had to cancel. Serafin asked Callas to come to his hotel room (she was staying in the same hotel) and proposed that she also sing Elvira between her already scheduled performances of Brunnhilda in *Die Walküre*. She said she did not know the part and had never sung it, but she did know one of Elvira's arias, which she sang for Serafin. He told her he would teach her the rest of the role and she would sing it in public in five days. He told her she could pull this off, and Meneghini also assured her she could do this. She thought that if these two great men had so much confidence in her abilities, then she would have to agree to do it, and she did. Clearly, beneath all her insecurities, Callas had a firm belief in her own power and greatness as a singer.

To understand the challenge that Callas faced, one must realize that Brunnhilda in *Die Walküre* is a dramatic soprano role, a Wagnerian soprano part, and a very difficult one. Elvira in *I Puritani* remains a very high and difficult coloratura soprano role. That Callas could succeed in both roles indicates the breadth of her vocal range of three octaves and her mastery of both the dramatic soprano's range and the coloratura soprano's breath and vocal agility and flexibility. Her success in both these very difficult roles within a week attracted her first really great reviews and the beginning of her international reputation. This tour de force occurred in Venice's La Fenice during the 1951 season.

Maria's feat created headlines throughout Italy, and it was also reported in other parts of Europe. Suddenly, she was seen as a wonderful and unique new soprano who could sing both dramatic Wagnerian soprano roles plus very difficult coloratura parts like Elvira in *I Puritani*. This was even reported in North America and South America, which had many opera fans and opera companies, especially in Argentina and Mexico. So Callas' career was really taking off now. She began to realize that Serafin and especially her dear friend and agent (and future husband) Gian Battista were creating all these opportunities for her to perform and impress opera audiences. Also, Meneghini could pay for her travels and her studies with voice teachers and vocal coaches.

After a whirlwind romance, Callas and Meneghini married in Verona in 1949 despite the fact that she was not an Italian citizen and not a Roman Catholic but an American and Greek Orthodox. Callas was not a churchgoer, but she was not an atheist either and did believe in some kind of God who was protecting her and furthering her opera career. She seemed to believe in the ancient, pre–Christian Greek belief in fate—that she was destined to succeed or fail by the gods. Several of her friends, especially her sister-in-law Pia Lomazzi, laughingly called her a pagan believing in her own primitive gods and pagan beliefs and not a Christian at all (Tosi 140 ff.).

Maria brought out the father in Meneghini and even the lover in him despite the fact that he was 30 years older. He was old enough to be her father, and he became the fatherly advisor and mentor who would direct her career. She brought excitement to his life and he loved the idea of

Maria Callas and her husband, Giovanni Battista Meneghini, in 1949.

managing the career of a great diva and traveling all around Italy and the world to represent and support her. She needed a lot of encouragement and support, and he was happy to do this for her in spades (Kesting 126–40).

Very quickly, however, members of his family came to dislike Callas. In part, they wanted him to continue to direct the various family construction businesses, and in part they felt that she was using him for his money and his contacts in the opera world to further her own career. They warned him that he had become the Don Pasquale to her Norina, as in Donizetti's comedy *Don Pasquale,* an old man being abused in marriage by a very shrewd young woman who wanted his money and who would ultimately leave him. But Callas swore that she would love to be his wife and would always be faithful to him—though within ten years she would indeed dump him for another short old man who was even richer.

Maria's fantasy was that she would get rave reviews after her performances in Verona's Arena, and then La Scala and all the other opera houses in Italy would beg her to sing for their audiences. That is not the way things turned out. Though she did succeed at her Italian premiere in Verona, she got mixed reviews and then a terrible silence and no offers followed from other opera houses. Clearly, she needed more training and better representation to further her career, and here Meneghini's help and his wealth were invaluable to Maria.

First, he found the best voice teachers in Verona and Milan to improve her singing, and then he also found the best vocal coaches to improve her range and vocal and dramatic performances. Meneghini also had to go to the agencies that hired singers or represented opera singers to plead with them to promote his wife's career and get her contracts to sing at other opera houses in Italy. Meneghini became a man with a mission—to turn Maria's success in Verona into an international career in opera. This is something Maria could never have done for herself because she did not have the operatic connections her husband did, and she did not know the Italian language nor its operatic culture or the business side of opera performance.

On December 30, 1947, Callas made her debut in Teatro la Fenice in Venice singing the role of Isolde in Wagner's *Tristan und Isolde* with Serafin as her conductor. Fedora Barbieri sang Brangane, the tenor Fiorenzo Tasso was Tristan, and Boris Christoff sang King Marke. Callas sang three more performances as Isolde in January 1948, all with Serafin conducting. Her Isolde got better and better and got positive reviews, all the reviewers commenting on her ability to get through such a long and difficult part. By the end of January 1948, she was singing the title part in Puccini's *Turandot;* her conductor here was Nino Sanzogno and her director was Mario Frigerio (who would also direct her at La Scala). The La Fenice audience applauded

4. Verona and the Arena

her, but in Venice she got mixed reviews, some commenting on her difficulty with the highest notes in this very difficult role. Wagnerian sopranos often sang the part of Turandot, but Callas had just sung Isolde so she felt confident.

Callas next went to the Teatro Puccini in Udine to sing Turandot. Here Jose Soler sang Calaf, and Liu was sung by Delores Ottani. The conductor was Olivero De Fabritiis, and Callas' director was again Augusto Cardi. She sang two performances of the great composer's *Turandot* on March 1948. This was one of Italy's minor opera houses, though they paid well. The next month, Callas was singing Verdi's *La Forza del Destino* in Trieste's Politeama Rossetti; she was their Leonora. Her conductor was Mario Parenti. Her amazing ability to learn a difficult and long role came to her aid here.

She was back with Serafin the next month at the Teatro Grattacielo (Skyscraper Theater) in Genoa. She sang Isolde again in Genoa and succeeded again in this very difficult and long role. Her Tristan this time was Max Lorenz, a very famous Tristan at the time. Elena Nicolai sang Bangene and Nicola Rossi-Lemeni sang King Marke. Next she sang at the Terme di Caracalla, Rome's famous summer opera festival at the ruins of the Baths of Caracalla. Here she sang Turandot again. Her Calaf was Galliano Massini, and Vera Montanari sang Liu. Oliviero DeFabritiis was again her conductor and thus she made her debuts in Rome on July 4, 6 and 11 of 1948.

At the end of the month, she was back at the Arena di Verona to sing the title role in Puccini's *Turandot*, this time with conductor Antonino Votto. Here she was directed by Calvini, in a production designed by Pino Casarini. Her Calaf was Calareza and her Liu was Razzieri. She sang Turandot in Verona on July 27 and August 1, 5 and 9, and this time she was well paid for her singing thanks to Meneghini. She then rushed to Genoa's Carlo Felice Theater to sing Turandot there with Mario Del Monaco as Calaf and Montenari as Liu. Callas sang there on August 11 and 14, 1948. Maria had been in Italy for only one year but was already singing in some of its important opera theaters.

The next month, Callas went to Turin to sing at the Teatro Lirico. She made her debut there in the title part of Verdi's *Aïda*, with Serafin conducting. The next month she was at the Teatro Sociale in Rovigo, also to sing *Aïda* with conductor Umberto Berrettoni and director Augusto Cardi. She again sang *Aïda* in Rovigo, with each production adding nuance and confidence to her performance in this long and difficult role. Callas then went to Florence to sing Norma at the more important Teatro Communale. She sang her first Normas under Tullio Serafin there. His help was invaluable to her. Norma would become one of her signature parts and one of her most successful roles (Galatopoulos 520 ff.). Serafin was also pleased that her voice did not wear out by the final act. Callas never had to sing small, comprimaria roles like most new sopranos—thanks again to Meneghini.

Meneghini arranged for their hasty marriage. He got all the required paperwork and dispensations needed for their marriage in a small Verona church, the Church of the Filippini, on April 21, 1949. Most of Titta's family did not attend. Nor did Maria's family members, though her mother sent her a congratulatory telegram—and in it, she added, "Remember that your art must always come first." But Maria hardly needed this reminder about the primary importance of her commitment to her career as a singer and artist. Maria's first commitment would always be to her career in opera since she loved both the attention it gave her as well as the large sums of money that were now starting to come to her. She dreamed of being rich and famous, and her dreams were beginning to come true in Italy, just as her teacher Elvira had predicted.

Soon afterwards Maria had to rush to South America where she was contracted (thanks to her husband) to sing in Buenos Aires, Argentina and Mexico—the main opera houses in South America. As a result of her successes first in Verona and then elsewhere in Italy, and the good reviews she got for these performances, South American audiences were eager to hear this exciting new coloratura soprano who could also sing dramatic soprano as well as coloratura roles. Meneghini was having the kind of life he always dreamed of: the manager of a major new diva in the colorful and fascinating and bloodthirsty world of international opera.

Now Maria Callas did not feel so alone. Now she had a life partner, and a rich and supportive one at that, a man who believed in her unique talent and the greatness of her artistry and her career—just what she needed. She needed someone to manage her career, someone who believed in her and her talent unconditionally and would help her.

Maria had quickly conquered Italy. She was singing at some of the important opera companies in Florence, Venice, Naples, Palermo, Rome, etc. But of course she dreamed of singing at Milan's Teatro alla Scala, Italy's most famous opera house and opera company. She hoped to conquer the wealthy Milanese public and the international opera-going public.

Some international critics started saying that this brilliant "new" soprano had single-handedly turned opera performances into actual dramatic and theatrical events. In reality, throughout the history of opera, from its founding early in 17th-century Florence to its development into a public art form in late 17th-century Venice, opera singers have fallen into two categories: the ravishing voices and the good actors with less than ravishing voices. Callas fell into the latter category, but Meneghini became convinced that she could have an international career—plus he was rich and well-connected in the opera world. He and Maria were both careerists.

4. Verona and the Arena

In the meantime, she was yet again crossing the Atlantic from Italy to Buenos Aires, Argentina, to sing at the most famous opera house in South America. This became the third time she was crossing the Atlantic in three years, but this was the last time she was crossing it by ship. Thereafter she would fly across the Atlantic and save three weeks of time—despite the high cost of flying. Money was not an object as long as her husband was there to help her. She was determined to have a big success in South America in some of opera's greatest roles. While most of the European opera houses closed in the heat of summer, in South America those same months were winter there and some of Italy's greatest singers (people like Enrico Caruso) had gone to South America's greatest opera houses and had success. These singers also made a lot of money there.

Now Maria was about to make her Argentinian debut in Buenos Aires' Colon opera house, South America's most famous opera company. If she succeeded there, the major opera companies would want her. For a poor American girl from Washington Heights, she was making amazingly speedy progress. With her great musical and dramatic talents and her ambition and Meneghini's financial resources, the sky was her limit and the sun was clearly shining on her parade. That parade was beginning to march through two continents. However, she was no longer talking to or writing to Louise Caselotti or her husband Eddie Bagarozy. They were a part of her past that Maria did not want to think about now that she was on her way to international stardom. Maria also did not want to pay Eddie the commissions which she had agreed to pay him in their contract that she had so eagerly signed in New York. However, Eddie had not forgotten that contract and wanted the commissions legally due to him. Some ugly conflict between them was becoming inevitable.

By the end of the '40s, the bloody Greek civil war was slowly coming to an end. As one historian summarized this period:

> The decade of violence and bloodshed was over. A six-year civil war, beginning in 1943, had lasted almost twice as long as the foreign occupation that had triggered it. What followed was a victors' peace. There was to be no accommodation with the losing side. The Communist Party of Greece had been declared an illegal organization at the end of 1947. It would remain banned for the best part of thirty years. Thousands of communist supporters now lived in exile behind the Iron Curtain—many of them concentrated, by the will of the Soviet authorities, in faraway Tashkent. In Greece, those who emerged from prison during the 1950s continued to be subject to surveillance and harassment. Former collaborators with the Nazis found themselves easily rehabilitated, often rewarded with positions of trust and pensions. No such forgiveness would be extended to those who had fought against them, until the 1980s. The impact of American intervention had a decisive effect on the future shape of the Greek economy. A year after the Truman Doctrine came the Marshall Plan, a four-year program of massive

economic aid to the stricken countries of Europe to help reconstruction after the Second World War. During that period, more than one billion dollars were disbursed in aid to Greece, the poorest country in Europe at the time. The sudden influx of American affluence changed the landscape and many aspects of Greek society (Beaton 306–07).

Callas was certainly glad the Greek civil war was over and that her immediate family remained safely in New York City. Her extended family in Athens had mostly survived and remained there. Maria did not want to see any of them ever again.

5

Conquering Italy and South America

Titta promised Maria that he would turn her into the most famous and best-paid soprano of her time, and he did, despite all the postwar reconstruction going on in Italy. The good reviews Callas was getting for her performances in Italy were now being publicized by her husband. She was being interviewed in the Italian press—and those articles were read by the huge numbers of Italians who had emigrated to South America. Those Italians, plus other opera fans in those countries, now wanted to hear Callas, live, in South America. Meneghini followed up these reviews with inquiries to opera companies in South America and offers started pouring in.

Maria set sail from Italy for Buenos Aires the very day after she and Meneghini were married. She spent the time studying the three roles she was contracted to sing (Turandot, Norma and Aida), plus a planned concert of arias from these three operas (DeCeccatty 138–80). When Callas arrived in Buenos Aires, she was all by herself. She keenly felt the lonely melancholy of being a new bride, separated from her new husband. She and Titta did not even have a honeymoon because of her engagements in South America and Mexico. She was constantly writing and telephoning her husband back in Verona, telling him how lonely and sad she was without him. She knew that his business concerns in Verona prevented him from accompanying her on such an extended voyage. Her "anchor" for this engagement was her beloved Tullio Serafin, who would be conducting all her performances—and that certainly was a comfort (Kesting 103–23).

The first role she sang in South America was, once again, the title role in Puccini's *Turandot*, on May 20, 1949, at the exquisite Teatro Colon in Buenos Aires. The Pantheon-worthy tenor, Mario Del Monaco, sang Calaf, Helena Arizmendi was Liu, and the Timur was sung by Nicola Rossi-Lemeni. The production was generally well-reviewed, though some critics were not so enamored of Callas' Turandot.

This opera was repeated in May 29, June 11 and June 22, 1949, at the

Colon, and the audiences seemed to get fonder of Callas in the title role. Hers was not the most beautiful voice, but the audiences were noticing her fine acting and the drama she generated in the role, as well as her impressive vocal technique. Callas continued her pattern of regularly clashing with colleagues. She saw herself as a dedicated and disciplined artist surrounded by mostly jealous and hateful colleagues, though some of those colleagues felt that the reality was the exact opposite—that she was the jealous and hateful one. Clearly, Callas needed someone around her to side with her, encourage her and protect her—her husband Meneghini.

On June 17, 1949, she sang Bellini's *Norma* at the Colon, and here, Callas got a much more favorable reception, as more and more fans became aware of her captivating acting in this famously difficult title role, as well as her faultless coloratura technique. Fedora Barbieri was equally memorable as Adalgisa, and their duets were much-appreciated by the audience. Antonio Vela was the Pollione and Nicola Rossi-Lemeni sang Oroveso. Under the baton of her trusted Serafin, Maria drew sustenance and confidence whenever he smiled at Maria from the podium. *Norma* was repeated in June of that year and Maria grew quite fond of Buenos Aires. With each ensuing performance, her commitment, confidence and vocal acrobatics combined to create what would become her signature role (De Ceccatty 140–50).

On July 2, 1949, Callas had one performance of Verdi's *Aïda*, singing the title role at the Colon, and that, too, was well-received. On July 9, also at the Colon, she sang in a concert performance featuring excerpts from *Norma* and *Turandot*. The concert was sold-out and was very well-reviewed. She then immediately flew back to Italy—a journey that took two days instead of three weeks—and was finally reunited with her new husband. They could finally have a well-deserved honeymoon in Verona—the city for lovers, the city of Romeo and Juliet. She quickly developed a love of flying, rather than the time-consuming crossing by ship. She remembered that her father George was always talking about Charles Lindbergh, who had flown from Long Island, New York, to Paris in 1927. George had been amazed at this feat, as had the rest of the world, and now his own daughter was flying across the Atlantic.

Maria's next public appearance was in September, in the Church of San Pietro in Perugia, Italy, singing the soprano solo in Stradella's oratorio *San Giovanni Battista*. It was written in commemoration of St. John the Baptist, which was also the Christian name of her husband. She sang this Stradella oratorio primarily as a gift for her new husband. He appreciated her gesture, as did her audience.

She was now free to vacation with her husband until December, when she performed her final engagement of the year at Naples' Teatro San

5. Conquering Italy and South America

Carlo: three performances in Verdi's *Nabucco*, singing the very difficult role of Abigaille—a part sung first by Giuseppina Strepponi, who eventually became Verdi's second wife. Verdi composed the role for a soprano who had wonderful technique. The traditional vocal "beauty" was not necessarily Abigaille's key element, since the character becomes one of the villains of the opera. The Teatro San Carlo was then Italy's second-most-important opera company, and Callas was monumentally successful in the role.

Meneghini kept hard at work, trying to find future engagements for his wife in Italy's other opera houses. The agents started asking questions like, is Maria Callas Greek or American? Will she become an Italian citizen soon? What is her background? Press agents and opera house administrators also wanted to know these things. Since she married Meneghini, was she now an Italian citizen or still an American citizen? Meneghini assured her that she was a unique combination of all three cultures and to stop worrying about this legal enigma. However, Maria remained full of insecurities and always needed someone around who believed in her—even though she tended to turn on those very people and reject them after they had helped her.

Meneghini continued to pour money into Callas' voice and career as an opera singer. As her career continued to catapult toward world renown, Callas demanded all of him—that he leave his family, his hometown and his business career, to dedicate himself wholly—*wholly*—to her and her career. Defying the resentments of his Veronese family, Meneghini finally realized that his first obligation would have to be to make his wife both successful and happy, and that necessitated that step backward from his family's thriving construction business. His first allegiance had to be to his wife.

All Italian opera singers dream of singing at La Scala, Italy's most famous

Maria Callas, in costume for Verdi's *Il Trovatore*, on the hallowed stage of La Scala in Milano in 1953.

and prestigious opera house. Meneghini felt she was not quite ready for this, especially after an unsuccessful audition with Mario Labroca, La Scala's artistic director (Meneghini 32–40). Thrillingly for both Mr. and Mrs. Meneghini, it became undeniable that a "buzz" was building, worldwide, and that Maria was being talked about as *the* new dramatic soprano to watch.

While Serafin and his wife Elena recognized that Callas had the potential to become a great singer, both of them also heard problems with Maria's voice. Firstly, it was not a beautiful voice, but it was a large and interesting voice with a singularly unique timbre. Callas' voice was not seamless, up and down the scale. Her top notes could tend to sound strained and tentative. Even this early in her career, one could detect a wide-ish quaver, especially on extended high notes. Her three vocal registers did not connect well; instead they seemed to be three different voices coming out of the same soprano. She had trouble with her *passaggios*, the transitional notes between the three registers, and her voice did not move smoothly from her head register to her chest register. While she used her voice intelligently, it did not always flow evenly from top to bottom.

This Maria Callas publicity portrait (from the early 1950s) shows the beginning of Callas' astonishing metamorphosis into the slim, glamorous diva who soon conquered the opera world.

Serafin's contacts with Venice's main opera company resulted in her being offered Wagnerian roles there, such as Brunnhilde, Isolde and Kundry. Most of these performances would occur at Teatro la Fenice in Venice. She had not been trained as a Wagnerian soprano, but Meneghini had spent enough time around singers and opera companies, especially at Verona, to know how to help guide a young singer to develop an appropriate repertoire, and Maria was more than willing to listen to him—and certainly benefited from his suggestions and his use of his operatic contacts. Her new husband had already become her own personal miracle man.

5. Conquering Italy and South America

Many opera houses in Italy had been bombed—especially Milan's Teatro alla Scala—and had to be rebuilt. In many cases, their costumes and sets had also been destroyed in warehouse bombings, so the companies had to mount new productions and engage new artists to attract new audiences at a time when most Italians were struggling to rebuild their own houses and lives after the horrible destruction of World War II. So much of the war had occurred in Italy, and the American, British, German and Italian armies had all fought each other on Italian soil between 1943 and 1945 (Hastings 427 ff.).

As Maria was going to voice teachers and vocal coaches, owing to Meneghini's seemingly limitless wealth (something she could never have afforded on her own), Titta was starting to work miracles. The fact that Callas could sing both Elvira in *I Puritani* and Brunhilda in *La Valkyria* (in Italian) within a week soon made headlines all over Italy and elsewhere in Europe. Quite a "hat trick" of vocal versatility, one that hadn't been successfully accomplished by any other major soprano in recent memory. She could sing both a very difficult coloratura role plus a very weighty dramatic role in Wagner's *Ring Cycle*.

As both Luchino Visconti and Franco Zeffirelli said at the time: "*Madonna!*" At first Zeffirelli was skeptical about what Callas could do, but his mentor, the director Luchino Visconti, told him that she was the greatest diva alive (Zeffirelli 85–95). Visconti asserted that Maria was the reincarnation of the great Italian actress Eleanora Duse, and he wanted to work with her and direct her.

Maria was now becoming famous—and Meneghini used his formidable public relations skills to spread this information all around Italy. She soon realized that publicity, any publicity, could do great things for a rising young opera singer. At first, Maria loved seeing her name and photos in the Italian newspapers, tabloids and magazines. Berlin, Munich, Dresden, Vienna, Milan, Florence and Turin all had had their famous opera houses bombed. Milan's Teatro alla Scala finally reopened in 1946 for concerts and for opera in 1948. Toscanini conducted at the official reopening concert of La Scala in 1946. The old, wealthy and aristocratic families in Milan had always attended the opera and sat in their boxes—but things were changing now. Many newly middle-class people, thanks to a heated new economy after the war, also wanted to go to the opera and wanted people to know they could afford to go to the opera.

The year 1950 became one of the most important years in Callas' career both in Italy and South America. On January 13, 15, and 19, she sang *Norma* at Teatro La Fenice in Venice. Her Pollione was Gino Penno, Elena Nicolai was her Adalgisa, and Tancredi Pasero sang Oroveso. Her conductor was Antonino Votto, and she succeeded here too, even though she was not singing with Tullio Serafin. She found that she could succeed in this very role, even without her mentor conducting her performance.

She was at the Teatro Grande in Brescia, to sing Aïda on February 2 and 7, 1950. Mario Del Monaco was again her Radames. The opera-going citizens of Brescia liked her highly dramatic approach to Aïda. She then traveled to Rome to sing Isolde in Wagner's *Tristan und Isolde* with Rome Opera. The German tenor, August Seider, sang Tristan (in Italian). The five performances in Rome were all conducted by Serafin, and the production was directed by Mario Frigerio and designed by the famous Emil Pretorius. Pretorius was becoming one of the revolutionaries in the modern, postwar productions of Wagner's operas. His modern style of simplified, minimalist sets and subtle lighting had a profound impact on Wieland Wagner, the grandson of Richard Wagner, who used this same approach at the Bayreuth Festival in Germany.

While in Rome, Maria sang Bellini's *Norma*. She was becoming more and more famous for singing and acting this most challenging of bel canto soprano roles. Galliano Masini was her Pollione, Ebe Stignani sang Adalgisa, and Giulio Neri was the Oroveso for most of the performances. Serafin again conducted her. She sang five performances of *Norma* in Rome in February and March 1950. She then went to Turin to sing arias for RAI radio. The performance was heard all over Italy.

In March 1950, she was in Catania, Sicily—Bellini's birthplace—to sing his *Norma*. Though the production was thought to be less than optimal, Callas' interpretation of Bellini's Druid priestess continued to develop and evolve, to the point where some reviewers called her an "ideal" Norma. But this Sicilian Norma was a mere appetizer for what was coming up.

In April 1950, Callas finally made her debut performance at Milan's famous Teatro alla Scala, Italy's most famous opera house, then as now. She had first sung in Italy in Verona in 1947, and within three years she had now reached the pinnacle of Italian opera, La Scala. She was there owing to the illness of Renata Tebaldi, who was supposed to sing Aïda. Thanks to Tebaldi's illness, Callas sang three performances of Aïda: April 12, 15 and 18, 1950. She was well-reviewed, but it bothered her that she was a guest artist, substituting for Tebaldi. The Milanese seemed to like Callas … but their love had been, historically, saved for Tebaldi. Some in the audience were left wondering whether or not this role was a good one for Callas. Didn't Aida call for a more traditionally beautiful voice than Callas had? Many in her ever-growing throng of fans preferred her in the bel canto repertoire, especially *Norma*. Her long-awaited La Scala debut had been a qualified success, since she had been a replacement artist.

By the end of April 1950, Callas was back in Naples' Teatro di San Carlo, where she was becoming a frequent and favorite singer. Here, she

5. Conquering Italy and South America

again sang the title role in Verdi's *Aïda*, with Serafin at the podium. The tenor, Mirto Picchi, was once again her Radames, the now-legendary mezzo-soprano, Ebe Stignani, sang Amneris, and Ugo Savarese sang Amonasro. Maria sang Aïda four times in Naples that spring. Most of the audience liked her performances, and she got more ovations in Naples than she had gotten in Milan—something she certainly appreciated.

Maria then got on a plane—she sat in first-class, while her husband sat in economy class. She had become one of the earliest proponents of the "jet-set" lifestyle, her arrivals and departures increasingly becoming a tangle of *paparazzi*. She was making her debut in Mexico City at the main opera theater there, the Palaccio di Bellas Artes, and she sang in four operas: *Norma*, *Aïda*, *Tosca* and *Il Trovatore*. Callas' appearances were greeted with rapture by the very enthusiastic Mexicans. Certain well-informed opera lovers came from the United States to hear her. Her fame was spreading around the globe.

For her debut there, she performed the role of Norma, which was an enormous success with the audience. Maria then sang three performances of Verdi's *Aida*. Kurt Baum was her Radames, Giulietta Simionato sang Amneris, and Robert Weede sang Amonasro. The audience nearly went berserk over her several interpolated high Cs in her Aïda, which are not in Verdi's score. These *Aida* performances were further additions to her diadem of achievements in the year 1950, which is viewed in retrospect as her "miracle year."

Also in Mexico City, Callas gave two performances of *Tosca*. Mario Filippeschi sang Cavaradossi and Robert Weede sang Scarpia. Callas ended her highly successful visit to Mexico City with three performances of Verdi's *Il Trovatore* with a world-class cast, including Kurt Baum singing Manrico, the great mezzo-soprano Giulietta Simionato singing Azucena, and the American baritone Leonard Warren singing Count Di Luna. The Mexican audience vigorously showed their approval of these performances, which received positive reviews and were reported as "special events" in the U.S., where more and more people were clamoring to hear this new operatic phenomenon. Leonard Warren's performance in this *Il Trovatore* also got audience approval. Ten years later, on March 4, 1960, he died of a heart attack onstage at the Met during a performance of *La Forza del Destino*.

Maria and Meneghini took a well-earned break: After flying back to their home in Verona, they rested for the remainder of the summer. They were back on the road in September, going to Salsomaggiore where on September 22 she sang Puccini's *Tosca* for just one performance. It was a rather provincial opera company, but it paid well. Two days later, Callas was at the Teatro Duse in Bologna to give one performance of *Tosca*. The Bolognese seemed to like the performance and all the singers were applauded. Some of the critics called Callas "the new Eleanora Duse of opera" because of her mesmerizing acting in the role of Tosca. She had also developed a reputation for changing the color of her voice for each of the roles she sang, which was noted admiringly by the critics. On October 2, she was back at Rome Opera to sing one performance of *Aïda*. Maria then took the train to Pisa to sing at its Teatro Verdi. There she gave two performances of Puccini's *Tosca*.

She then went to Rome's Teatro Eliseo to sing in Rossini's comic opera *Il Turco in Italia*. She had never sung a comic role before, but she relished the experience. While this is not one of the great Rossini operas, in the right hands, it can be a comic triumph—which was the case here. She sang the role of Fiorilla four times in Rome that October. The reviewers were amazed to discover that Callas could easily navigate between operatic comedy and tragedy and were rhapsodic in their praise.

Callas was still in Rome to sing Kundry in Wagner's epic *Parsifal* for the Italian Radio's RAI station. Due to the opera's length (four and a quarter hours of music), the opera was split into two successive nights. She sang Act I on November 20 and Acts II and III on November 21. And thus ended Callas' "miracle year" of 1950, a year in which she finally sang at the Pantheon of opera, La Scala. She acknowledged that her unparalleled success that year was largely due to her husband. She had reached the pinnacle of operatic success. How could she top such a year?

The next year, 1951, would turn out to be even busier than 1950. Maria felt that she was living in a fantastic world and singing at all the famous opera house in Italy, where the art form of opera began with the Count Bardi circle in Florence in the 17th century (Smith 3 ff.). She began the year again being conducted by her mentor Serafin at the Communale in Florence in her first performance of Verdi's Violetta in *La Traviata*, which would eventually become one of her greatest and most successful roles. Her three performances received mixed reviews, some critics disliking her approach to this revered Verdi masterwork.

Her life became frantic and exciting as she moved from one opera house to another, getting primarily rave reviews and pleasing larger and larger audiences. More and more Italian opera companies were contacting Meneghini to engage Maria. Meneghini knew how to drive a hard bargain and get his wife top dollar for her appearances.

Could she conquer the world with her singing and acting? Could she make her dream come true and become the greatest operatic diva of her time? With the help of her Veronese husband, she was realizing that the dream was becoming a reality, and it was happening quickly—all within four years of her Italian premiere at the Verona Arena.

Some of the second-tier opera companies in Italy offered her starring roles—places like Palermo, Rome Opera and San Carlo in Naples, as well

5. Conquering Italy and South America

as the opera theaters in Florence and Venice—as audiences became interested in this new Greek-American singer who could do amazing things on the operatic stage. The beautiful opera house in Venice (Teatro la Fenice) had come to Callas' rescue with offers of major roles, thanks again to Serafin. What new stages were there left for her to conquer as she looked toward her exciting and successful future? She had succeeded almost beyond her wildest dreams, and not yet even 30 years old. But the triumphs had only just begun.

6

Titta, Marriage and Meteoric Ascent

Maria hoped that 1951 would be even more successful than 1950, and her wonderful Titta arranged an exciting series of performances for her. She was beginning to feel like a gypsy, living out of suitcases and going from opera house to opera house—and she loved this life, as long as she had her new husband by her side, since she dreaded being alone. In January 1951, she was in Florence's Communale to sing three performances of her Violetta in *La Traviata*. Her Alfredo was Francesco Albanese, and Enzo Mascherini sang father Germont. Serafin conducted this score admirably, and the production was directed by Gianni Vagnetti. Maria succeeded with her audience in Florence, and Violetta soon became one of her favorite and most acclaimed roles. However, she always worried about her breathing and her vocal cords and whether they could endure all she was demanding of them. After all, her whole career as a singer depended on those two little muscles in her throat, and they had to be able to project her voice to thousands of people in the audience without any amplification. This scared her, but Ferruccio Cusinati—now her only voice teacher—gave her more confidence in her vocal cords, her breathing and her vocal technique.

Callas and her husband then flew to Trieste, to the Teatro Giuseppe Verdi, to participate in a concert. She then flew to the Communale in Florence to sing a new role that she had been studying, Elena in Verdi's *I Vespri Siciliani*. Giorgio Bardi-Kokolios sang Arrigo, Enzo Mascherini sang Monforte, and Boris Christoff sang Procida. The famous Erich Kleiber conducted. Her director was Herbert Graf and the set and costume designer was Giani Vagnetti. The four performances were on May 26, 30 and June 2 and 5, 1951, and they convinced her that she could sing this difficult role with success and please her public.

She and her husband then took the train to Florence, and she participated in a real rarity, a production of Haydn's *Orfeo ed Euridice* which had

6. Titta, Marriage and Meteoric Ascent

never been staged before. Callas was not wild about this Haydn opera and chose never to sing it again.

While in Florence, she also sang a concert at the Grand Hotel. Her piano accompanist was a young Bruno Bartoletti, who would eventually become one of her favorite conductors. She included arias from *Norma, Dinorah, Aida, Mignon* and *La Traviata*. She missed having an orchestra with her, but she did like Bartoletti's expert piano accompaniment.

She then got on a plane to cross the Atlantic once again to sing at the Palacio des Bellas Artes in Mexico City, where she had built a slavish band of opera fanatics via her previous performance there. She sang three performances of *Aida* in July 1951, as she had the year before. Del Monaco was again her Radames. Just days after her triumphal Aïda, she again sang at the Palacio des Bellas Artes four performances as Violetta in *La Traviata*. The new young tenor, Cesare Valletti, was her mellifluous Alfredo.

Immediately afterward, she flew from Mexico City to São Paulo, Brazil, to make her Brazilian debut at the Municipal Opera House on September 7. She sang just one performance of *Norma*. Mirto Picchi was again her Pollione, the great mezzo Fedora Barbieri sang Adalgisa, and Nicola Rossi-Lemeni sang Oroveso. Two days later, still at the Municipal, she gave one performance of *La Traviata*, this time with her beloved Serafin. Giuseppe Di Stefano was her Alfredo, thus beginning their long and complicated professional and personal relationship. The Germont was Tito Gobbi, another great artist whose life would intertwine with Maria's.

The next day, Maria flew to Rio de Janeiro to make her debut in Brazil's most beautiful and famous city, but things did not go so well. She sang Norma with Antonino Votto as her conductor instead of Serafin. Mirto Picchi was again the Pollione, the mezzo-soprano Elena Nicolai was the Adalgisa, and Boris Christoff was the very reliable Oroveso. But the director of the company, Barretto Pinto, was clearly not pleased with her performance. Between the two *Norma* performances, on September 14, 1951, she sang as part of a concert which Pinto thoroughly disliked.

She then brought her ever-evolving Tosca to Rio. She was then supposed to sing two performances of *La Traviata* at the same theater. She sang the first one with Gianni Poggi as Alfredo and Antonio Salsedo as Germont, Nino Gaioni conducting. But director Barretto Pinto would not allow her to sing the second performance. She insisted on being paid for the second performance because of her contract, but had trouble collecting the money. Pinto again harshly criticized her singing—and she said she grabbed an object on his desk and threw it at his head, grabbed her check and left Rio. She also said, in her best prima donna manner, that she would never sing in Rio again. Pinto later denied that any of this had occurred, but said he did dislike her singing and felt that it was his responsibility to prevent "his" audiences from hearing such a second-rate performance.

Callas grabbed her husband, stormed out of Brazil and flew back to Italy in a huff. She and her husband then flew to Catania, Sicily, and Maria sang her first Norma there—at the Massimo Bellini.

Also at the Massimo Bellini, she sang four performances of Elvira in *I Puritani* in November 1951. She then flew back to Milan for seven performances of Elena in *I Vespri Siciliani*. She was again hired by Antonio Ghirighelli at La Scala, but as a temporary singer for seven performances of this opera—in December 1951 and January 1952. Maria had had an audition with Mario Labroca at La Scala many months ago, but it did not go well, and clearly La Scala had changed its mind about Maria's singing (Meneghini 32 ff.). This time her appearances were a major success for her, and the La Scala audience liked her very much in this role. It was a wonderful production, and her cast was very good. Eugene Conley sang Arrigo, Enzo Mascherini was Monforte, and Boris Christoff was the Procida. Now the director of La Scala, Antonio Ghiringhelli, said he wanted Callas to sing more often at La Scala and become one of their regular sopranos. So she had much to celebrate: becoming a permanent soloist at the most prestigious opera house in Italy.

She then took the train to Parma's Teatro Regio, famous for its exceedingly critical audience, for one performance of *La Traviata*. The performance was generously received by the critics; the rhapsodic audience called Maria back for multiple curtain calls. Callas and her husband had a lot to celebrate that New Year's Eve given her increasing success on both sides of the Atlantic, and scoring a major success with the Milanese subscribers at La Scala. She was contracted to sing in three productions at La Scala the next year. At their New Year's celebration, she and Titta drank champagne in their new house on Milan's fashionable Via Buonarotti. She was now becoming one of the most famous singers of her generation, and she said she owed all her success to her loving husband.

Other singers of the period were married to their agents and representatives, or even their conductors. Joan Sutherland's husband, Richard Bonynge, advised her, accompanied her on the piano, and managed her professional appearances in addition to being a fine bel canto conductor who often conducted her opera performances. Marilyn Horne was married to Henry Lewis, a conductor who sometimes conducted her, and certainly advised her on her choice of roles. Horne was once asked how she handled a difficult conductor, and she said she would divorce him. Callas had such a relationship with Meneghini, and though he was not a conductor, he encouraged her to practice her scales every day and advised her on the roles she should sing. He believed in her great talent and guided her career, and

6. Titta, Marriage and Meteoric Ascent

in the beginning she loved him for this, though ultimately she got to hate him for the very same reasons. He also provided her with the praise she desperately needed since she was filled with insecurities.

Once she became obsessed with what was then called *café society*—the very wealthy people who flew around the world for parties or for particular opera, musical or theater performances—it was impossible for Maria to turn back to living in her former style, that of deprivation and second-class travel. Maria was very demanding of her husband, which caused him anxiety, since he was in charge of his large family and his many family business concerns. These he had to sacrifice to help his needy wife.

Meneghini liked being her agent, the *presence grise*, as the French say, behind her stardom. Some asserted that he was her Pygmalion. He would soon be photographed with her in the most glamorous opera houses and hotels and restaurants, and those photos were appearing all around the world, and Meneghini liked all this glamour and attention, brought to him thanks to his marriage to Callas. He was photographed with some of the most famous and wealthy people in the world—people like Marlene Dietrich and Noël Coward—thanks to his wife. She was living her dream of becoming an internationally famous opera singer, but her husband Titta was also living his dream of being a part of international opera by representing her.

Meneghini was uncomfortable with foreign languages and could speak only Italian with any degree of comfort. His wife, however, was now more confident and she told the press that she wanted only to cook her husband's favorite meals. She also said she wanted to be the mother of his children. What Maria most wanted remained to have her husband with her when she was performing, since he knew how to comfort and reassure her. He was always with her backstage and throughout her performances. With her Titta nearby, she usually gave her best operatic performances.

What was their sex life like? We can never know with certainty, but he was 53 when they were married and she was only 23. The 30 years between them must have had some effect, though Callas was clearly attracted to older men, especially if they were rich. Certainly in the beginning of their marriage, they seemed well-matched and very happy together.

When Callas was interviewed for newspapers and magazines during these early years, she often said that her greatest wish was to be a good wife and especially to become a mother. Why didn't this ever happen? According to Meneghini, Callas could not get pregnant due to a gynecological problem. One rumor is that they were not having sex. Another rumor circulated that Maria and her husband were practicing birth control when having sex to insure that she would not get pregnant, and that when she repeated that she wanted more than anything else to have his child, this was only to fit into the popular image of European and American women in the 1950s. Callas clearly had become very savvy about telling the press exactly what she sensed her public wanted to hear.

Maria soon developed an instinct for generating good publicity for herself, a canny ability to provide just what interviewers wanted to hear from her about her career and her goals. She gave interviews to popular Italian celebrity magazines like *Oggi* and *Epoca* at a time when most opera singers did not want to appear in such silly (if popular) magazines. She loved being the center of attention in the press, radio and television. Television became increasingly popular in the years after World War II and Maria wanted to see herself on this new medium. However, she sensed that the popular magazines and TV stations were most interested in movie stars, not opera stars. The tabloid magazines were filled with celebrity gossip and astrological forecasts. Maria herself read these magazines, including their astrological columns, and she became a great believer in astrological signs and their interpretations. She became a great believer in astrology, read her horoscope religiously and often described herself as a typical Pisces.

She also had a small Madonna painting, given to her by Meneghini, and it became her good-luck charm. Yet she was not a churchgoer. She told the press she could not sing without her Madonna. Before one performance in Vienna, she sent her sister-in-law Pia back home to Verona to get the portrait of the Madonna, which Maria had forgotten to bring with her (Stassinopoulos 154 ff.). With her Madonna painting, Maria had a great success in Vienna's Staatsoper. Callas also began to like having her sister-in-law Pia with her, using her as her personal assistant, to wash her clothes and tackle an endless series of errands.

Along with Maria's growing worldwide fame as a great new opera star came a reputation for being "difficult." It was around this time that she began her tabloid-fueled feud with another great diva, Renata Tebaldi, whom Maria quickly sized-up as her "enemy," from the time both sopranos were appearing on the roster of Teatro Colón in 1949. Her rivalry with Tebaldi, added to her appearances in the press, kept her performances well-attended and reviewed. Callas hated seeing how fat she appeared in her press photos. Tebaldi seemed so much slimmer (Edwards 96–119).

While some audience members found Maria fascinating onstage, others criticized her voice for not being as traditionally beautiful as Renata Tebaldi's—which, alas, was true. Thus developed the famous rivalry between Callas and Tebaldi, and Callas, if not Tebaldi, soon realized how valuable such a rivalry became to her in generating press coverage and publicity.

A feud between two singers, especially two sopranos, was beloved by the press, and it had a long tradition in opera. Meneghini encouraged

6. Titta, Marriage and Meteoric Ascent

Callas' rude behavior, since it helped him to market her. As early as the 18th century in London, Handel realized that two feuding singers attracted press coverage and sold tickets. The famous war between Faustina Bordoni and Francesca Cuzzoni, two of Handel's starring sopranos, resulted in an on-stage fistfight between them—which was later parodied in John Gay's comic *The Beggar's Opera*. There was also a composers' feud in 18th-century opera between Handel and Giovanni Bononcini, and feuds between two castrati who pretended to hate each other, though in some cases they actually did hate each other. These feuds helped to sell tickets! In the 18th century in Italy, France and elsewhere, feuding castrati also attracted press coverage and sold more tickets than merely fine singing and acting. These singers' feuds could turn an opera performance into an *event*—something people wanted to witness for themselves. They wanted to be at an *event*, even if they did not particularly like opera. Tebaldi already was a star, and Callas was the newcomer. Arturo Toscanini had said that Tebaldi had the voice of an angel. When Callas replaced the ailing Tebaldi at La Scala, it certainly set the stage for a full-fledged diva feud. Tebaldi hated this rivalry and resented Callas' use of it to generate publicity for herself, but what could Tebaldi do other than pretend to ignore it? (Edwards 110–12). Both Tebaldi and her mother Giuseppina came to hate Maria. Maria stated publicly about Tebaldi, "The public got bored with her singing," and that what she needed was a husband—implying that Tebaldi might be a lesbian.

Even at this early stage in her singing career, Maria was already developing a reputation as an exciting but wildly uneven performer who sounded wonderful some nights and wobbly and off-key on other nights. She did not get universally wonderful reviews, and some opera directors disliked her voice and certainly did not appreciate her high-handed attitude, both on- and off-stage.

Callas soon became known for what the French call *presence d'etage*—stage presence—which even her non-admirers couldn't deny. She dominated a stage by her mere force of character. She was usually the tallest female singer on stage, and often the widest. But Callas was determined to go right to the top as a diva in opera, though she also realized that her large size was hampering her abilities as an actress. She now wanted to become a popular star, in addition to being a successful opera singer. But at this point in her career, this was merely a fantasy on her part. The general public was much more interested in movie stars than overweight opera singers.

By 1952 she desperately wanted to lose 100 pounds, but how on earth would she achieve such a goal? She would go on diets and lose some weight, but then she'd swiftly gain it back. According to her sister-in-law Pia, Maria went to a clinic in Switzerland to help her lose all that weight. Swiss clinics often helped wealthy women get fashionably thin. Wallis Simpson, who was oft-quoted as saying, "One can never be too rich or too thin," was a frequent habitué of "the Swiss Cure." The Swiss clinic undoubtedly put Maria on a strict diet and a rigorous exercise regime—and with time, her weight started to drop. But more importantly, the clinics also gave her diet pills, especially Dexedrine, which then was just becoming legal and popular among the wealthy in America and Europe. "Uppers" like Dexedrine seemed to increase Callas' metabolism, along with eliminating her appetite. (Doctors did not yet know how dangerous this new drug was for the heart.) Maria was undoubtedly taking amphetamines.

Over the next five years, she lost all her excess weight and became the svelte woman she had always dreamed of being. The weight loss from her face altered her appearance considerably. She suddenly found lines and bones in her face and neck that she did not know she had. Her dramatic facial features seemed suddenly oversized—her mouth, her eyes, her nose, her newly angular jawline. But onstage, with operatic lighting and makeup, she now had a fierce, almost overly severe new look. Her body was no longer an embarrassment and her face appeared even more striking and even beautiful.

To help her lose weight, she started to smoke, which had been so glamourized in films. The movies often showed thin, glamorous people smoking and drinking cocktails (these plugs were paid for by the alcohol and tobacco lobbies). So Callas started smoking to help her lose weight, and it did help to curb her appetite and appear more glamorous—just as Audrey Hepburn smoked in her movies and in public. It was not uncommon for opera singers to smoke cigarettes, sometimes to excess. The damage that can be caused by smoking tobacco was not yet established by the medical community. Later, she even suggested that she had swallowed a tapeworm, sometimes saying it was a living tape worm, other times saying it was dead, and always laughing when she told the story, blithely stating she washed it down with a glass of French champagne.

And where was Evangelia during Maria's whirlwind of worldwide success and self-transformation? When Maria was performing in Mexico City in June 1950, she flew her mother down to meet her there. Maria put Evangelia in a wonderful hotel and had her room filled with flowers. She even gifted her mother with a mink stole. Evangelia was most grateful for the chance to dress the part of the proud "mother of the diva." When Maria left Mexico City, she gave her mother other gifts, a big kiss and a large, generous check—and then never spoke to her or saw her again for the rest of her life.

Maria's estrangement from her mother (and, later, from her sister Jackie) produced all sorts of negative publicity. But now her sole determination was to become a star at La Scala. Her hatred for her mother became

6. Titta, Marriage and Meteoric Ascent

pathological and unceasing, and she could not credit her mother for doing one good thing for her. Maria felt that Evangelia had abused her and exploited her talents. So she rejected her Greek family and focused solely on her husband and, more importantly, her career. Out of desperation for money, Evangelia wrote a scurrilous autobiography, *My Daughter, Maria Callas*, in 1960. It registered briefly in the public consciousness, resulting in negative publicity for Maria, who was portrayed as a selfish, thankless daughter. That book enraged Maria and provided her with a concrete reason to exile permanently her own mother from her life.

Teatro alla Scala is still considered the greatest opera house in Italy (and, arguably, in the world) and all great singers want to sing there. Maria was no exception. Now that she had had successes in Italy, the only Italian opera house where she had not sung regularly was La Scala. Antonio Ghiringhelli, its managing director, did not seem impressed by Maria. However, he was getting interested in her performing at his theater, especially now that Toscanini specifically requested that she sing Lady Macbeth in his envisioned new production of this great Verdi opera. He had repeatedly said that Renata Tebaldi had the voice of an angel—and Verdi had written that a soprano with an ugly voice should sing the role of Lady Macbeth. Toscanini said he wanted his Lady Macbeth to be Maria Callas. Verdi had a weakness for dramatic sopranos with *voci brutte* (literally, "ugly voices"), and he even married one: Giuseppina Strepponi, who had been his original Abigaille in the premiere of his *Nabucco* at La Scala in 1842. She was a striking, dramatic opera singer with an ugly but memorable voice.

Maria met with Toscanini and with Ghiringhelli and they discussed the possibility of her singing that role there, with the great Toscanini at the helm. Toscanini's daughter Wally, who lived in Milan, had become a Callas fan and facilitated his meeting with Maria (Kesting 244). Ultimately, this proposed dream-pairing of Callas and Toscanini never came to pass, and Callas always blamed Ghiringhelli for this.

In retrospect, Maria's years spent with Meneghini were, professionally speaking, the greatest, most successful years as an opera singer that she would ever have. He also turned her into the highest paid opera singer of her time.

Maria was horrified to discover that a pasta company, Pastificio Pantanella (owned at that time by a relative of the current pope, Pius XII) was running ads claiming that Callas' dramatic weight loss was due to her eating their pasta! Outraged that her name was being used without her consent, she sued and eventually won the case. This conflict with the Pope's relative's pasta company frequently appeared in the Italian press, resulting in more free publicity for them. Such silly coverage of a silly issue helped turn Callas and her husband into international celebrities and helped to increase her performance fees, thanks to the expert management and marketing of Meneghini. Ultimately, Callas got an undisclosed financial settlement from the pasta company for the illegal use of her name (Stassinopoulos 149 ff.).

But such tabloid fodder was merely a distraction from what remained Callas' all-consuming goal: to be anointed by Italy's most prestigious opera house as their *prima donna assoluta*.

7

La Scala at Last

As Maria's career skyrocketed, it seemed inevitable that La Scala would want to bring her back for a "proper debut." (Her substitution Aïda performances there in 1950 were far too inauspicious to be considered a true "debut" for an artist of her increasing prestige.) One of the reasons Maria wanted to sing at La Scala, aside from the fact that it remained the most famous and best-paying opera house in Italy, was that her beloved mentor, Elvira de Hidalgo, had performed there. Elvira had predicted that Maria would one day sing there as well.

Maria began 1952 by returning to Florence's Comunale to sing Elvira in Bellini's *I Puritani*. In spite of her enormous success there, for Maria, it was a mere "warm-up" for what was to come next.

Callas then immediately went by train to Milan to start rehearsals for *Norma* at La Scala. She sang eight performances of *Norma* at La Scala on January 16, 19, 23, 27 and 29 and February 2, 7 and 10, 1952. Franco Ghione conducted, and the lovely production was directed by Mario Frigerio, with sets designed by Giuseppe Marchioro. Gino Penno sang Pollione, Ebe Stignani sang Adalgisa, and Nicola Rossi-Lemeni sang Oroveso. These performances went over very well and she loved the thunderous applause at La Scala, and the many ovations and curtain calls she got. She had clearly impressed the La Scala audience and had an enormous success, both as a singer and as an actress (Meneghini 160–67).

In March, back at the Massimo Bellini Theater in Catania to sing *La Traviata*, she gave four performances to great acclaim. The Sicilians were wildly receptive to her Violetta, though her critical reviews were decidedly mixed. Maria returned to La Scala by the end of March and prepared for her next role there, Constanze in Mozart's *The Abduction from the Seraglio*. She sang four performance of this opera and left no doubts that she certainly had the coloratura agility to sing Constanza's very difficult, florid arias. It was the first and last time she sang in one of Mozart's operas. She told colleagues she found his operas dull, albeit with some lovely arias, so she would never become a Mozart singer. Clearly, Callas was indicating that drama was central to opera as she understood the medium—and by that, she meant drama in operas by Italian composers.

In the middle of April, Callas was back at Florence's Teatro Comunale to sing the title role in Rossini's *Armida*. This is not one of Rossini's greatest operas but there are some wonderful moments. Set during the medieval crusades in the Holy Land, it requires five tenors, so it is rarely staged. Callas gave three performances of this opera and she certainly impressed with her skilled technique in negotiating this very difficult role. Her coloratura technique was on display in this role, and she was rapturously received by discerning audiences.

She next boarded a plane to Mexico City to begin rehearsals for another *I Puritani* at the Palacio de las Bellas Artes. She sang two performances there in May 1952, and had another huge personal success. Callas liked singing in Mexico City because audiences were especially demonstrative of their adoration for her. She was now being treated as a revered diva there, and enjoyed it very much. The newspapers, magazines and TV stations interviewed her and she loved the attention—and even her knowledge of Spanish was improving. While in Mexico City, she sang two performances of *La Traviata*, again with Giuseppe Di Stefano as Alfredo. Her next Mexico City triumph was three performances of Lucia in *Lucia di Lammermoor*. Callas debuted yet another new role in her hugely successful Mexico City run: Gilda in Verdi's *Rigoletto*. Giuseppe Di Stefano sang the Duke and Piero Campolonghi was the Rigoletto. Finally, on June 28 and July 1, 1952, Callas brought her Tosca to Mexico City, adding an additional jewel to her diadem. Di Stefano was the very ardent and moving Cavaradossi and Piero Campolonghi sang Scarpia. Personalities aside, Maria always worked well onstage with Di Stefano.

After her Mexican successes, she flew back home to Verona to sing at the Arena's summer opera festival. She felt nostalgic about the site of her Italian debut and was loyal to this festival. She was again performing *La Gioconda* at the Arena, the opera she sang when she made her 1947 debut there. On July 19 and 23, 1952, she sang Gioconda, opposite Gianni Poggi as Enzo. She also sang Violetta in *La Traviata* at the Arena that summer. She sang four performances of *La Traviata* in August 1952. Giuseppe Campora was her Alfredo, Enzo Mascherini sang Germont and Francesco Molinari-Pradelli conducted. Callas was now completely confident in her voice's ability to project well into this very large outdoor venue.

Callas spent that summer in their beautiful new home in Sirmione on Lake Garda, with much of her attention spent on further study of the score of *Norma*, in preparation for her upcoming Covent Garden debut in the title role. In November, she sang Norma at the Royal Opera, Covent Garden. Her Pollione was Mirto Picchi, Ebe Stignani sang Adalgisa wonderfully, Giacomo Vaghi sang Oroveso—and a young Joan Sutherland sang the small comprimaria role of Clothilde. The Royal Opera paid very well, and its public was clearly enthralled by this dynamic new diva: All of her performances were sold-out. Norman Lebrecht said of her first Norma in London:

> On opening night, Callas' first big duet with the mezzo-soprano, Ebe Stignani, earned her an ovation and was, against house rules, encored. When she delivered "Casta diva," the house erupted. If ever a star was born, this was the moment. What made Callas so compelling was her reckless passion in performance, risks that she took, half-knowing that they could damage or destroy her voice. Joan Sutherland, as Clothilde, sidled up to Callas in the wings and whispered shyly that she would like one day to sing Norma. "Why not?" said the diva. "It means a lot of work, but why not?" (Lebrecht 153–54)

Sutherland would take on the role of Norma a few years later, but she sang much more cautiously, with an emphasis on purity of tone (along with her much-criticized, indistinct diction). Another great soprano of this period was Monserrat Caballé, who sang both coloratura roles and some dramatic soprano roles. Her acting remained rudimentary, and she fought a long but futile battle with her weight, but her singing, especially her soft singing, was consistently ravishing. Her career lasted 20 years longer than Callas' and she sang at all the major opera houses in Europe and America. Mirella Freni also began singing in the early 1950s, was very careful with the roles she picked, and her career also lasted 20 years longer than Callas'.

On the heels of her thrilling London success, Callas returned to her "home company," La Scala, for a new production of Verdi's *Macbeth*. She received glowing notices. This was the production in which Maria was to have worked with the great Arturo Toscanini, who was now in his 80s and having memory lapses (he died just five years later). Also that month, she brought her Gioconda to La Scala, with Giuseppe Di Stefano as Enzo. Callas had finally become a La Scala diva and loved it.

Maria was becoming more and more famous for her moving Violetta in *La Traviata*. She took a train from Milan to Venice's gorgeous Teatro La Fenice to sing *La Traviata* there (two performances) on January 8 and 10, 1953. She then rode the rails to Florence and its Comunale theater to sing her first (of four) performances as Lucia di Lammermoor, conducted by Franco Ghione. Maria held the Florentine opera-going public in the palm of her hand, and they eagerly joined the ever-growing "Maria Callas fan club."

She returned to La Scala for five performances of Verdi's *Il Trovatore* in February and March. She truly savored being a regular member of the La Scala company, but she also sang with other companies while under contract to La Scala. Renata Tebaldi had largely moved her base of operations to the Metropolitan Opera. Callas regularly denied any friction between the two divas, but her denials seemed disingenuous.

Rome Opera very much wanted Maria back, and she returned on April 9 for four performances of *Norma*. Cast as Pollione opposite Maria's Norma was a thrilling new tenor, Franco Corelli. He went on to become one of the most revered operatic tenors in history, and a dual-bill of Callas and Corelli became a surefire-sell-out. Reviewers had to consult their thesauruses to come up with new superlatives. In a rare display of warmth, Callas expressed admiration for the matinee-idol–handsome young Italian, and they continued their onstage partnership until the end of her operatic career.

She then returned to Catania and the Massimo Bellini Theater for two performances of *Lucia di Lammermoor*, for which Callas got very good reviews. Critic Francesco Pastura, in the *Giornale dell'Isola,* commented on Callas' success in several Bellini operas:

> Maria Callas has repeated the feat, not unusual in former times, but today, almost astonishing, of interpreting two Bellini operas which require two different types of sopranos. Thanks to the enormous range of her voice and the precious technical devices which allow her to sing with absolute ease of emission, this exceptional soprano demonstrated last evening, in the difficult part of Elvira, the marvelous vocal resources at her disposal (Wisneski 55).

Reviews like these encouraged interest in staging the Donizetti and Bellini operas, and not just *Norma*. Callas' success in these bel canto roles created a wave of renewed interest in this formerly "rarified" niche of opera.

Callas returned to the Teatro Comunale in Florence for a revival of an opera she was interested in but had never sung: *Medea* by Cherubini—originally written in French, though now sung in Italian (in Italy). *Medea* was not a very popular opera, but the role of Medea fascinated Callas because the plot was similar to Bellini's *Norma*. She sang three performances of *Medea* and succeeded in this most challenging of roles. Though the opera has very few memorable arias, its recitatives remain dramatic and mesmerizing—at least when sung and acted by Maria Callas.

In May, Callas was in Rome for three performances of *Lucia di Lammermoor*. Then in June 1953, she was at London's Royal Opera for three performances of *Aïda*. The revered Sir John Barbirolli conducted. The British public warmly welcomed her back to London, where Maria was firmly enshrined as their favorite operatic soprano. Later that month, she sang four performances of *Norma* at the Royal Opera. She rounded out her month-long residency at Covent Garden with three performances of *Il Trovatore*.

Maria flew from London to Verona to sing Aïda in the Arena in July

7. La Scala at Last 79

and August. Mario Del Monaco sang Radames. Maria's anchor conductor, Tullio Serafin, conducted in a *molto grande* new production, directed by famed Austrian film director G.W. Pabst. Verona's enormous Arena is a venue particularly suited to a grand opera like *Aïda,* with its demands for lavish and enormous sets and legions of chorus singers, dancers, supernumeraries (extras) and live animals.

Callas and Meneghini enjoyed the splendor of their Lake Garda home, preparing for her upcoming autumn and winter performances. In September, she was at Berlin's Staadlische Oper to sing Lucia, but these two performances were with the La Scala company, which was on a visit to Berlin in September-October 1953. This very important *Lucia* was both conducted and directed by young musical supernova Herbert Von Karajan, an Austrian conductor who was quickly becoming very famous.

In the 21st century, it's hard to imagine international opera singers being a subject for the daily tabloids, but this certainly was the case in the 1950s. The "feud" between Callas and Tebaldi increasingly became the story the press wanted to cover. Some members of the press were now calling Callas "The Tigress," an appellation that she certainly didn't object to. Tigresses, generally speaking, win in conflicts with other animals, like rival sopranos. Callas told an interviewer that comparing her to Tebaldi was like comparing champagne to Coca-Cola; Callas' nasty comment was printed and reprinted (Meneghini 150 ff). Her husband encouraged her to say provocative things about Tebaldi. But, at La Scala, Tebaldi had one advantage: its director Antonio Ghiringhelli did not like Maria. But Callas was garnering more and more excellent reviews and press coverage for her performances all over Italy—especially in Venice, Florence, Naples and Rome—and Ghiringhelli realized that he had to hire Callas despite his personal dislike for her singing, not to mention her pushy husband.

Ghiringhelli was also now dealing with Giancarlo Menotti over the premiere of his new opera *The Consul,* which La Scala had agreed to stage. Ghiringhelli was not happy when Menotti said he wanted Callas to sing the main role. Menotti insisted and he personally offered the main role to Callas, which she ultimately rejected; she said she found contemporary music uncomfortable to sing (Strassinopoulos 96–97). She had sung a contemporary opera while in Athens during World War II and felt it was not her *oeuvre.* Ghiringhelli gave her more new productions during her 12 years at La Scala than any other singer, though Callas was always convinced that he was really trying to trick her and destroy her career (Meneghini 142 ff.). Gratitude was never her strong suit.

Maria turned her penetrating gaze westward, feeling she was now ready to perform in her native city, at the Metropolitan Opera (still in its original location, at 39th and Broadway). She had not yet professionally sung anywhere in the U.S., and she missed New York and her American roots. She did not have many friends in the city of her birth, though her generous godfather Leonidas Lantzounis still lived there with his wife Sallie. Callas' mother and sister were also in New York, but she had no desire to see them.

Maria recorded extensively at La Scala for Angel/EMI Records during the 1950s. She had previously recorded for the Italian company Cetra, but Angel/EMI offered her worldwide sales and a much more generous contract. Angel's recordings were also technically superior, especially now that the new long-playing 33 1/3 format was popular. The head of Angel's Classical Music division was Walter Legge, a Britisher who was married to Austrian soprano Elisabeth Schwarzkopf. They were both impressed with Callas' La Scala performances and felt that they should be preserved through recordings. Meneghini made sure that his wife was well-paid for the recordings, which he predicted would sell very well—and, of course, they did.

Anywhere she sang, Maria's performances quickly sold-out. Movie stars and people in the popular press, like Elsa Maxwell, Grace Kelly, Noël Coward and Marlene Dietrich, were coming to her performances and then visiting her backstage and posing with her for photos. Maria's narcissism was gratified during this period, though some opera fans were wondering why she encouraged such publicity. Did opera singers really want to be like popular Italian movie stars such as Sophia Loren and Gina Lollobrigida, and Hollywood starlets like Marilyn Monroe? Callas certainly did.

Callas' "rather startling physical transformation" into a svelte woman with Audrey Hepburn's figure and wide eyebrows did not go unnoticed in the press. She had also acquired the ultimate "diva prop," a toy poodle that she named Toy. She loved being photographed with her newly slender silhouette, in a Biki-designed dress—not unlike her mother and her canaries. She had turned herself from a fat, homely woman into a proverbial swan.

As for the Metropolitan Opera, Maria still stood by her story that she had already turned down Edward Johnson, its director, when he had offered her several roles there in the immediate postwar years. She also claimed to have turned down the director of the San Francisco opera, though this was never confirmed. She certainly never sang with that company. She had a way of becoming paranoid and sadistic around authority figures—reminiscent of her difficult relationships with her father and mother. She now had her husband to run interference for her and act as her agent, and he was certainly not paranoid about authority figures. In fact, he was one himself, at least within his own family in Verona, especially given his age and status as the oldest son. Meneghini did not want to return to his family in Verona to sell bricks; he loved arguing with Ghiringhelli for more money for his wife to sing more frequently at La Scala.

7. La Scala at Last

In the early '50s, La Scala began using what became known as the Piccola Scala, a small theater within its main building, to stage unusual or very intimate operas. *Il Turco in Italia*, a Rossini comedy that had not been staged very often, was being put into production, directed by a young Italian dynamo, Franco Zeffirelli. He had specifically requested that Maria be cast in the main soprano role of Fiorilla. He recognized her dramatic intelligence and musical sensitivity. *Il Turco in Italia* was a comedy and he felt Callas did not really have a very keen sense of humor, but he was convinced that she could be funny in this role with his help (Zeffirelli 126 ff.). He was right, since his production became a big hit. Now that Callas was a hit at the Piccola Scala, surely she should sing more often in the main theater, Teatro alla Scala.

It is interesting to note that Callas even became famous at La Scala in a comic role, Fiorilla in *Il Turco in Italia*. A few years after that, she played Rosina in Rossini's *Barber of Seville*, also at La Scala. These were the only times that she sang Rossini's comic roles. She must have felt, perhaps because of her husband and director Margarete Wallmann, that she was much more suited and much more successful in tragic roles. There, she certainly succeeded, especially the bel canto roles of Norma and Lucia di Lammermoor, though Puccini's Tosca became a frequently performed role for her as well; that was a role much shorter and easier for her than Norma or Lucia. By the late '50s, she was performing Tosca more often because it was a short opera and not as demanding vocally as Norma or Lucia.

Callas wanted to sing everything: bel canto roles, Wagner, Verdi, Puccini, Rossini, Bellini, Donizetti and even more obscure composers like Ponchielli and Gluck. She did this in the beginning to be able to sing at all—flexible artists were offered more roles and got more publicity, and Tullio Serafin and Meneghini encouraged this, so that Callas could establish her career in Italy. Callas also had her remarkable facility with languages and could memorize her role (both words and music) in an opera score within one week. But even Serafin warned her to limit herself carefully, once she became famous and could pick and choose what roles she would sing. Callas did not heed this advice. Of course, this added to her star-power: She could sing any soprano roles, and even some high mezzo-soprano roles, because her voice and her training enabled her to sing anything in her wide vocal range. By the end of her career, she was recording *Carmen*, in part because it was a mezzo-soprano role, and she could avoid exposing her wobbly high notes. She never sang the role onstage because she said she felt that, even after her stunning weight loss, she still retained the stout ankles of a heavy woman. Thanks to her svelte figure, Maria became a pop icon. She had conquered Italy and South America, but could she also conquer the world of opera in her native country, the U.S.?

In the meantime, Tebaldi was having great success at the Met and greatly pleasing audiences there. Surely Tebaldi did not want Callas to start appearing at the Met, though the fact that Tebaldi was a starring diva at the Met would naturally have made Callas want to sing there herself, if only to attempt to outshine Tebaldi.

It is the nature of narcissists to make enemies. When Meneghini, or close friends, tried to talk to Maria about this and indicate how she could improve her behavior toward her colleagues, she became enraged. She could not endure *any* criticism from other singers. There were very few people whose constructive criticism she would allow, let alone take to heart. She had a tendency to see new friends as wonderful, and then become enraged when they did something she did not like. Her borderline personality disorder would hound her for the rest of her life. She argued that she was only interested in *art*, the art of operatic theater.

As she became more of a glamorous woman, she was desired all over the world, especially now that she had become the *prima donna assoluta* at La Scala and was known as "La Regina della Scala." It was time at last for her to perform in the city of her birth: New York.

8

Back to La Scala—Conquering America

As the year 1954 began, Callas was again singing at what she now considered her home theater, La Scala. She spent most of January and early February singing Lucia di Lammermoor there. Her conductor was again Herbert von Karajan, who also directed the new production. This opera remains Donizetti's most-popular work, and certainly his most-performed opera. Callas enjoyed working with von Karajan, who was rapidly becoming one of the major new conductors. Karajan had presumably softened his stance regarding "never wanting to work with Callas ever again."

Callas was back at La Scala by the middle of March 1954 to star in a new production of Gluck's *Alceste*, a role she had never sung before, in one of Gluck's "reform operas," with one great aria and a lot of exciting recitatives. Carlo Maria Giulini, then a promising new international conductor, commanded the podium. Maria finally got to work on a new production with director Margarete Wallmann, who had already proven to be one of her true allies at La Scala. Wallmann expertly directed Maria's acting style, coaxing a remarkable performance out of her, in the style of the great French tragediennes of 18th-century Paris.

Prior to the latter half of the 20th century, *Don Carlo* had not been considered one of the great Verdi operas, and this brilliant, epic new production surely went a long way toward burnishing its classic status. This production, designed and directed by Nicola Benois, emphasized the complexity of both the opera's characters and the situations, as well as the complexities of Spanish politics at the time. Audiences were compelled to reconsider *Don Carlo* and see it as another of Verdi's masterpieces. The essentially passive nature of the character, Elisabetta, did not suit Callas very well, and she was not eager to sing this role again. She felt she did better portraying wildcats than lambs (Edwards 108–109).

It was also in 1954 that Meneghini sold his business to his brother so that he was free to dedicate himself full-time to managing and negotiating

Maria's increasingly complex international career (Edwards 108 ff.). Maria rested with Meneghini for a few months at their lakeside retreat before returning to the Arena di Verona for a new role: Margherita in Boito's *Mefistofele*. Maria was well-received (and well-reviewed), but she was not especially fond of the relatively brief role of Margherita—though she continued to feature Margherita's dramatic main aria, "L'altra note," in recitals and concerts. Next on her schedule was another *Lucia di Lammermoor*, at Teatro Donizetti in Bergamo. Francesco Molinari-Pradelli conducted her two performances with skill and sensitivity. She was well-paid for these two performances and liked being able to visit this lovely town in Lombardy where Gaetano Donizetti was born on November 29, 1797, and where he died, hopelessly insane, on April 8, 1848.

At the forefront of Maria's mind was her next "major event": her American debut. It would not be at the Met but in America's "Second City," Chicago (November 1 and 5, 1954, at the newly formed, very well-funded Lyric Opera of Chicago). Created by Carol Fox, Lawrence Kelly and conductor Nicola Rescigno, the Lyric Opera first came to prominence in the early 1950s and thrives to this day. Callas was contracted to sing two performances of what was already considered one of her signature roles, Bellini's Norma—along with two other showcase roles. Rescigno conducted all three operas and became her favorite new conductor. She also sang two performances of *La Traviata*. Leopold Simoneau sang Alfredo and Tito Gobbi sang Germont. She capped off her Chicago debut triumvirate with *Lucia di Lammermoor*. Her stolid La Scala tenor co-star, Giuseppe Di Stefano, performed opposite her Lucia as Edgardo. Callas' brilliant success put Chicago's Lyric Opera on the international map of important opera companies. Claudia Cassidy, the *Chicago Tribune*'s music and theater critic, kept giving Callas rave reviews, and this helped the new opera company to get established and thrive (Davis 229 ff.).

Maria's regular recording company, Angel/EMI Records, told her that if she performed in America, her record sales could exceed what she was already making from her European record sales. The American record market had become much larger than that of any European country, though opera recordings were (and still are) considered to be a niche market compared to the market for popular music. In the 1950s, the records of Frank Sinatra, Patti Page, Doris Day, etc., became much more popular than Callas' recordings. With the invention of the long playing record, a golden age of recording of classical music began, and there was a lot of money to be made in opera recordings. Callas' records sold quite well. Complete opera recordings could now be made on three or four long-playing plastic discs. Before then, 78 rpm recordings of complete operas required dozens of discs.

The Lyric Opera could pay more than the Metropolitan Opera because

8. Back to La Scala—Conquering America

of its wealthy backers, though singing at the Met had far more prestige. But the Met was not pursuing her. The Lyric Opera's Carol Fox *was* pursuing Callas, and with large amounts of money. So Callas decided to sing three of her greatest and most popular roles there: Norma, Lucia di Lammermoor and Tosca, during the 1954 season. Her Chicago performances became *events*. By this time, Callas' newly slim figure added to her star quality and allure for the opera-going public. Chicago was Maria's kind of town, to paraphrase the popular song. So much so, she decided to return there the following season.

A buzz was sweeping through the American opera-loving community about this exotic Greek-American diva, whose powerhouse reputation made them demand to see her for themselves. Chicago audiences were especially impressed by the fact that Callas had been born and raised in America. In the middle of the 20th century, there was still an unspoken bias against American-born opera singers (with a few prominent exceptions being Rosa Ponselle, Grace Moore and Risë Stevens). The autocratic Rudolf Bing, Viennese-born general manager of the Met, refused to take Americans as seriously as their European counterparts. Enormously popular, Brooklyn-born Beverly Sills, for instance, famously never sang at the Met until Bing retired. Sadly, her actual years singing at the Met were of limited duration, since by 1975 when the new management brought her onto their roster, she had entered a period of vocal decline. She channeled her rage at Bing's dismissal of her by becoming America's Diva, with her sparkling personality and wit, and highly telegenic personality, at the New York City Opera—which was initially based at the enormous City Center Auditorium in midtown Manhattan, before relocating directly next door to the Met at Lincoln Center. After her retirement in 1979, she took the helm of the NYCO, becoming the company's general manager and taking the company to new levels of quality and popularity. (She went on to become chairman of the board of the Met before her final major engagement, which was chairman of the board of Lincoln Center. In his memoir, Bing goes out of his way to point out that not hiring Sills during her prime was "a mistake.")

After her performances in Chicago, Maria was back at La Scala in December 1954 to star in a new production of Spontini's *La Vestale* (The Vestal Virgin). She was reunited with the now hugely popular, Roman-coin-handsome tenor idol, Franco Corelli, who sang Licinio opposite her Giulia. Antonino Votto again conducted her, in a production directed by the man who would become one of Maria's fiercest admirers and protectors, the great Italian director Luchino Visconti. This opera gives the tenor more to sing than the soprano, yet Callas hardly stood dimly in his shadow. She sang five performances of *La Vestale* in the final weeks of

1954. She loved working with Visconti, and the public and the critics loved her in the role, though they did not all love Spontini's opera.

During these performances, she developed an antipathy toward the baritone, Enzo Sordello, with whom she would perform again in New York. The rest of the cast wondered what Sordello had done to be singled out for the wrath of the prickly *La Callas*. Her reputation for being a "colleague-eater" was growing with every new engagement. Some colleagues only hoped to survive their experience with Callas relatively unscathed. Her wrathful repute now preceded her everywhere.

Maria ushered in the year 1955 back home at La Scala. She sang Maddalena in Umberto Giordano's *Andrea Chenier*. The reliable tenor Mario Del Monaco sang the title role of Andrea Chenier. Chenier was an actual historical figure—a young poet guillotined during France's 18th-century Reign of Terror.

In the midst of this run of performances, Callas somehow shoehorned-in three performances of her *Medea* at Rome Opera. Margarete Wallmann again directed. Wallmann said she liked working with Callas, in spite of the inevitable backstage drama, due to the intensity of Callas' performances. According to Wallmann, Callas' portrayal of Medea was particularly riveting:

> She identified with the role. She, herself, was torn between America, Greece and Italy—like Medea, a wanderer without a real home. And, like Medea, when it was necessary, she found the strength to cut long-held ties in order to go on and survive. She was still a very young woman, and married to a much older man. ... I am sure that certain sexual frustrations found an outlet in her work—unfulfilled passions were released in her singing and acting (Edwards 118).

Callas returned to La Scala in March and April to appear in Luchino Visconti's new production of Bellini's *La Sonnambula*. Callas sang the title role of Amina, "the sleepwalker." The brilliant young American phenomenon, Leonard Bernstein, conducted, and the production was a huge success for Callas and Bernstein; the ten performances quickly sold out. Bernstein repeatedly called Callas' performances "pure electricity," and Visconti's balletic production gave the whole opera the atmosphere of the ballet *Giselle*. Callas' newly svelte silhouette made her a wraithlike, ethereal and sympathetic figure on stage in this new balletic production.

Callas had another major success with Rossini's *Il Turco in Italia* at the Piccola Scala, the small, experimental theater next to Scala's main theater. Franco Zeffirelli once again directed Callas. Enormously successful, it was considered the comic success of the season. Callas was not a natural comic actress, but Zeffirelli worked with her to make her performance subtly comical, and the audience loved the result (Zeffirelli 133 ff.).

Callas remained at La Scala in May and June of '55, to perform

8. Back to La Scala—Conquering America

Rehearsal discussion for *La Sonnambula* (La Scala, Milan, 1955). Left to right: Maria Callas, tenor Cesare Valletti, director Luchino Visconti and American conductor-composer Leonard Bernstein.

once again her much-admired Violetta in *La Traviata*, with Giuseppe Di Stefano as Alfredo and Ettore Bastanini as Germont. Director Luchino Visconti lifted Callas to yet another career highpoint. Critics and audiences praised this new production, calling Callas the finest Violetta of her generation. Visconti helped Callas to make Verdi's Violetta a moving, sympathetic and tragic victim of her society, as well as her terminal illness. Especially in the last act, Callas made her Violetta truly human and devastatingly real, during her protracted death scene.

By this point, Callas had become borderline-obsessed with Visconti, especially after he gave her a personal tour of his home, Palazzo Visconti in Milan. He was the son and heir of one of the wealthiest and most aristocratic families in Milan. He impressed her with his palazzo, his learning and his sophisticated knowledge of theater, opera and film. That he was also gay did not seem to be a barrier for Maria, since she was used to dealing with gay and bisexual men in the theater. She even sometimes wondered if her husband was bisexual, yet, at least for now, they were happy together. Visconti was much more urbane and sophisticated than her husband (Edwards 106 ff.). Maria seemed to be falling in love with the handsome and charismatic Visconti.

That September, her next appearance with La Scala took place at Berlin's Stadtische Oper while on tour, with Herbert von Karajan leading two performances of *Lucia di Lammermoor*. Von Karajan had his Waterloo with Maria Callas during these Berlin *Lucia*s but they continued to work together a bit longer.

That November, Callas was lured back to Chicago to sing three more blockbuster soprano roles: Norma, Lucia and Butterfly. She had a firm grip on the first two roles; the third was a new one for her, and was, according to Maria, not a proper fit for her voice and temperament. She performed Cio-Cio-San only three times in Chicago and then dropped it from her repertoire, finding the role very tiring and not that fulfilling. She was not comfortable or entirely credible playing such a passive victim like Cio-Cio-San. She was also required to be onstage for nearly the entirety of *Butterfly*.

On November 17, after her final performance, a sheriff tried to present her with legal papers. She responded with fury while still in her Cio-Cio-San costume and makeup, and in front of many press photographers. These photos of her as a humble Japanese geisha-turned-virago were seen in newspapers around the world and even appeared on some television stations. She vowed to never again sing with the Lyric Opera, and she kept her word, try as they did to bring her back.

The legal papers served upon Callas were the result of a suit pressed by her old friend and agent Eddie Bagarozy, who asserted that she owed him his agent's fees for the past ten years. Callas, playing the unfairly wronged *artiste*, dismissed him as a liar and a thief, and argued that the Lyric Opera Company should have protected her from this criminal and his criminal wife. Company director Carol Fox argued that she and the company had no idea that anyone was trying to present Callas with legal papers, but Callas remained convinced that Carol had engineered the whole scandal to generate more publicity for her new opera company (Marsh 140–45). The press photos of her Cio-Cio-San screaming at a sheriff seemed comic to most people. She was not at all embarrassed by the photos of herself in the international press. She made a melodramatic exit from Chicago, vowing never to sing there again, and flew back to Milan with her husband. (She and Battista now had a chic house on the fashionable Via Buonarroti.)

The public was left to ask: Was Eddie Bagarozy really a thief? Had she really signed a contract giving him ten percent of her fees? Had the Lyric Opera failed to protect her? Callas resolutely proclaimed her innocence, to anyone who would listen—whereas the reality of the situation remained a bit more complicated. Court papers indicated that she *had* signed a contract with Bagarozy granting him ten percent of her earnings for ten years, and there were also very compromising, flirtatious letters from her to him that raised a few eyebrows. The letters even suggested that she may have

8. Back to La Scala—Conquering America

The shot seen 'round the world. This 1955 photograph, taken backstage at Chicago's Lyric Opera, where Callas (still in costume as the delicate Cio-Cio San in Puccini's *Madama Butterfly*) was served with legal papers. U.S. Marshal Stanley Pringle is in the foreground. This photograph did more to cement her image in the international public consciousness as a tempestuous diva than perhaps any other single image. The unnamed process server was clearly abashed by her oversized outrage. Callas never sang with that company again, owing to this incident.

been the married Bagarozy's lover for a while. Ultimately, Meneghini and his lawyers read these letters and documents and had to pay a large amount to settle the affair quietly (Stassinopoulos 174 ff.). Soon after that, Bagarozy died in an automobile accident. Who was the real victim here, Callas or Bagarozy? Bagarozy was able to provide the legal contract they'd both signed in 1947. In fact, Maria's mother later argued that Callas owed much to Bagarozy's encouragement (Callas, Evangelia 5–70). He helped Maria and offered to represent her at a time when she was not getting offers. His tragic early death left Maria with no feelings, other than a bitter *schadenfreude* over the dismal fate of one of her perceived enemies.

Now that she'd essentially burned her own bridge to her American "home base" company (and with the Met still cagily avoiding Battista's entreaties on her behalf), Maria and her husband chose to "follow the money"—and there was an oil-money–funded company being formed in Dallas, Texas, that told them to name their price. Her two key allies at Lyric Opera, Nicola Rescigno and Lawrence Kelly, eagerly encouraged her to follow them to Texas, hoping she'd have the same effect on the nascent Dallas Opera that she'd had on Lyric Opera. They even promised Callas a new production of one of her favorite opera roles, Cherubini's Medea. A famous Greek director, Alexis Minotis, had been signed to direct this new production.

Maria liked singing this role of a mother who murders her two sons to get revenge on her faithless husband. She appeared in this production in the newly formed Dallas Civic Opera Company in November 1958, and here, too, she flew into a rage with her director, and left vowing never to perform in Dallas—thereby punishing the whole city, or so she thought. Her rages and dramatic exits and her feuds with opera company directors were beginning to seem pathological and even comic. One wondered where she would rage next and by the late '50s some were wondering about her sanity (and then, the declining condition of her voice). Yes, she was difficult to deal with, but new American opera companies like the ones in Chicago and Dallas realized that she was great for generating publicity, which was wonderful for them since it helped put them on the map. There is no such thing as bad publicity, as PR people always say—at least to each other and their clients.

Callas' performances were becoming *events*, and even people who did not like opera wanted to be at one of her *events*. (Some of these people even began to like opera.) During this period, she developed a reputation for her ability to revive interest in 18th- and early–19th-century operas that had fallen out of favor. She could make these bel canto operas come alive due to her wonderful singing and acting. She started as a Wagnerian soprano after World War II, but she clearly felt more comfortable in the bel canto roles. (Plus, right after World War II, there weren't many performances of Wagnerian opera because Hitler loved Wagner's operas and used them for Nazi propaganda.) Of course, Wagner died in 1883, 50 years before the start of the Nazi regime in Germany, and Wagner's anti–Semitism reflected the 19th century and not the 20th.

Maria returned to La Scala at the end of 1955 to sing in a new

8. Back to La Scala—Conquering America

production of *Norma* with Mario Del Monaco as Pollione. Antonino Votto again conducted these performances and Margarete Wallmann directed. Wallmann emphasized all the internal conflicts within Norma and her reactions to the demands of the chorus.

Nineteen fifty-five became one of Callas' most successful years at La Scala and elsewhere on the international opera circuit. She had become the Norma of her generation of singers, and her performances of this opera continue to astound audiences—since, fortunately, she also recorded this opera for Angel/EMI. Her friend Margarete Wallmann had an even more eventful life: She became a famous modern dancer, was driven out of Germany by the Nazis, moved to Vienna to dance, and was then forced out of Austria. She went to Hollywood, could not get hired by the movie studios, and then went to the Colon Opera in Buenos Aires to run their dance program. She returned to Vienna after the war, came down with polio and could no longer dance, and then turned herself into an opera director (with braces on her legs) and directed at La Scala and all over the world.

In January 1956, Maria appeared at La Scala to once again sing Violetta in *La Traviata*, in the now-famous Luchino Visconti production. La Scala got its money's worth from Visconti's successful new production of Verdi's *La Traviata*, presenting Maria's Violetta in 17 performances throughout the first five months of 1956. Maria relished working with Visconti on this production, and his insights into the character of Violetta added to Callas' effectiveness in the part. It was around this time that Callas' obsession with the gay Visconti came to the fore. She seemed to want to marry this genius, even feeling that she could "cure" him of his homosexuality (Stassinopoulos 133 ff.).

Callas appeared in another comic opera, a new La Scala production of Rossini's *Il Barbiere di Siviglia*. This did not please the public as much as her previous bravura performances, and it was not critically well-received. There were not as many performances of this *Barbiere*—in fact, only five. She certainly disliked the fact that Tito Gobbi's notable Figaro got most of the applause, especially at the final curtain calls.

In May 1956, Callas appeared in a new La Scala production of Giordano's *Fedora*, an opera about the Romanov royal family in Russia before the Communist revolution. The tenor role of Loris was sung by the now very-popular Franco Corelli. The reliable Nicola Benois designed the gorgeous elaborate sets and historically authentic costumes to reflect the final years of the Romanov dynasty. Though Callas undoubtedly felt that *Fedora* lacked musical sophistication, she succeeded in her portrayal of the main character, Fedora, and her tormented love of a nihilist, and both the audience and the critics approved of this new production.

In June 1956, Callas was again singing Lucia di Lammermoor for La

Scala. Herbert von Karajan was again conducting his own production. But these performances by La Scala were being given at the Staatsoper in Vienna, Austria. Von Karajan again both conducted and directed this production for La Scala. There were three performances on June 12, 14, and

Maria Callas in costume for the role of Violetta in Verdi's *La Traviata* at La Scala, Milan, 1955. That year was one of her "miracle years," her very zenith.

8. Back to La Scala—Conquering America

16, 1956, and the Viennese public certainly enjoyed them. Von Karajan was now developing an international reputation as a man who could both conduct and direct striking opera productions. Callas and Meneghini took the rest of the summer off to enjoy their home at Sirmione and to prepare for Callas' debut at the Metropolitan Opera in the fall.

Like most ambitious sopranos, Callas had long dreamed of singing at the most important opera house in America, the Met. It did not pay its singers as much as the Lyric Opera, but it had greater visibility—and their Saturday matinee radio broadcasts went across the country. Maria listened to those opera broadcasts when she was a child living in New York. After her repeated successes in Chicago and her "*Butterfly* scandal," it became imperative that the Met hire her, and Met director Rudolf Bing eventually called on her and offered her some roles. Bing, Callas and Meneghini all came to an agreement and she made her Met debut in Bellini's *Norma*, which was already viewed as perhaps her finest role, on October 29, 1956, repeating the role on November 3, 7, 10 and 22. Mario Del Monaco (or Kurt Baum) sang Pollione, Fedora Barbieri sang Adalgisa, and Cesare Siepi (or Nicola Moscona) sang Oroveso. Fausto Cleva conducted, since Maria had stopped talking to Tullio Serafin over some imagined slight. The production (not new) was originally directed by Dinos Yannopoulos, but now re-directed by Charles Elson. The reviews were mixed—some critics loving Callas' Norma, others hating it. This was predictable, since artists with as singular a sound and style are not always beloved by all.

Right before Maria's debut, she was on the cover of *Time* magazine, which thrilled her—but, reading the article inside, she was enraged that it was a hatchet piece. It focused on her refusal to talk to her own mother and other family members, and even quoted from some of her meanest letters to her mother (provided, of course, by an eager Evangelia) as well as her nastiest comments about Renata Tebaldi. Callas was painted as a dramatic contrast to Tebaldi, who reported that she found it difficult to perform without her mother in the audience. It is amazing how often Callas and Tebaldi's careers intersected. Tebaldi had left La Scala once Callas began to sing there, and Tebaldi was dismayed to learn that Callas had followed her to the Met. At this point, Tebaldi did not want to be anywhere near Callas.

Callas then sang Tosca at the Met for two performances, November 15 and 19, 1956. She next appeared on CBS-TV in New York in excerpts from Act II of *Tosca* with the elegant baritone George London as Scarpia. Both singers showed their ability to sing and act and generate dramatic excitement on stage. It is one of the best extant examples of Callas at her zenith.

Maria was interviewed on American TV by Edward R. Murrow, then one of *the* most TV personalities. She presented herself as a sweet, naïve American girl, born in Manhattan; this was one of her finest examples of

Maria Callas at the Metropolitan Opera, at last, performing what became (arguably) her signature role, that of Floria Tosca in Puccini's *Tosca*. Shown here with legendary basso, Tito Gobbi (photograph from a later Metropolitan Opera pairing in their roles, in 1965) who was her frequent co-star throughout her career.

her skills in acting. When Murrow confronted her with the accusations that she was always fighting with other singers and directors and even with family members, she smiled innocently and said she did not know where such silly gossip originated.

Maria also sang one performance of *Norma* with the Metropolitan

8. Back to La Scala—Conquering America

Opera, at the Academy of Music in Philadelphia. She then sang Lucia in *Lucia di Lammermoor* at the Met in December 1956. There the tenor lead was sung either by Giuseppe Campora or Richard Tucker (whom she had sung with at her premiere in *La Gioconda* in Verona back in 1947). Fausto Cleva conducted these *Lucia* performances. After one of them, Callas had a big argument with the baritone Enzo Sordello over some minor issue. He tried to give her roses at the airport while she left New York, but she refused them. Of course, someone had alerted the press, whose photographers were there to capture the scene. Both Callas and Sordello seemed to enjoy the grim confrontation at the airport, and they were on the same flight back to Europe. The Met had expected some off-stage drama with Callas and was pleased that there was only this one scene at the airport.

Maria Callas as Violetta in Giuseppe Verdi's *La Traviata*, London, 1958. It's considered to be one of her signature roles; she frequently performed it around the world, to enormous acclaim.

In his memoirs, Sordello remained quite bitter about Callas' efforts to destroy his career at both the Met and La Scala (Sordello 77 ff.). Though she did not succeed, she made enemies of Sordello and other singers, like Gobbi and Tebaldi, with her attacks on them. Sordello felt that Callas' biggest victim was her husband Meneghini (Sordello 91–92).

Her final U.S. appearance that year occurred on December 17, when she gave a recital of arias from Italian opera at the Italian Embassy in Washington, D.C. Clearly, 1956 had been one of the most successful years in her now very busy career, including her debut (at last) at New York's Metropolitan Opera, America's most famous and most prestigious opera company.

In his memoir *A Knight at the Opera*, Rudolf Bing wrote of having to deal with both Callas and Meneghini. He had been warned about the difficulties of dealing with them by La Scala's Antonio Ghiringhelli. But by then she had become an international sensation and New York opera audiences were demanding to hear her at the Met, so he began negotiations with them. Bing writes about how impressed he was by her performances, especially in *Norma*, and he found both her singing and acting mesmerizing (Bing 100 ff.). In that era, $1000 was the top fee at the Met for any single performance, but Meneghini wanted more. Bing had other superstars to deal with—Renata Tebaldi, Jussi Björling, Antonietta Stella, Franco Corelli, Anna Moffo, Birgit Nilsson, to name a few—so he was reluctant to offer only Callas higher fees, but Meneghini insisted, since he knew his wife could sell out the enormous opera house, something not many other singers could singly do (Bing 100 ff.). All the publicity was having a good effect on his wife's career. Even her appearance on the cover of *Time* magazine added to her notoriety. The most gossiped-about quote in the *Time* article came from one of Maria's letters, saying that if her mother was having financial problems she should "throw herself out of a window." Clearly Callas' mother and sister were living in poverty in Athens, and most people felt that Callas should have helped them, now that she was a very wealthy woman.

Maria Callas performs yet another role for which she's often been upheld as the paradigmatic interpreter: Lucia in Donizetti's *Lucia di Lammermoor.*

She began 1957 with a concert at the Civic Opera House in Chicago. At this concert, sponsored by Sol Hurok Management, she sang excerpts of some of her most famous roles while she was singing with Chicago's Lyric Opera. It is interesting that on January 26, 1957, Francis Poulenc's new opera *Les Dialogues des Carmelites* had its successful premiere at La Scala and went on to become one of the great operas of the 20th century. Callas had been offered a role in the new opera directed by Margarete Wallmann but declined because of her antipathy to modern music.

At London's Covent Garden, Maria sang two performances of *Norma* in February 1957. Many in the Royal Opera's audience had now become fans of Callas. It was around this time that she started attracting an adoring, slavishly dedicated following among gay men. The term "opera queen" certainly has a pejorative tone in today's more "enlightened times," but in the late 1950s, there was a much more fervid gay following of opera than there is today, and they themselves used the term. Young gay men would

Ecco il baccio di Tosca! (Here is Tosca's kiss). Maria Callas rehearses *Tosca*, Covent Garden, London, 1964.

camp on the streets, sometimes for days, to be in line when tickets went on sale, to whichever opera performance they deemed a "must-see." Across the globe, Maria Callas soon became the focus of their adoration.

Callas rehearsed at La Scala for a new production of Donizetti's *Anna Bolena* with her beloved director, Luchino Visconti. The production was much-admired, though Callas' outsized stage presence was almost dwarfed by Nicola Benois' enormous Tudor sets. Maria played a vulnerable woman becoming a victim of the bloodthirsty King Henry VIII and his neurotic jealousy.

Maria made a triumphal return to Greece that summer, performing a recital at Athens' ancient Herodes Atticus Theatre—an ancient open-air theater on the side of the Acropolis. This was her first appearance in Greece since the war and she wondered if she would be welcomed back. She certainly was, in spite of the collective memory of her performing for Greece's enemies during the war. In August 1957, she trekked to Edinburgh, Scotland with the La Scala Company to sing four performances of Bellini's *La Sonnambula* in Visconti's now famous production. The company begged her to stay in Edinburgh to sing one more performance, but she refused, causing yet another scandal. The press insisted that Callas had reneged on a promise, but Callas vehemently insisted that she had been contracted to sing only four performances and she sang only these performances. Her understudy Renata Scotto sang the final performance and later described in her memoir the difficulties of working around Callas' ego (Scotto 49 ff.).

Callas began 1958 with what was supposed to be a gala performance of *Norma* at Rome Opera. The president of Italy, Giovanni Gronchi, attended this January 2 performance. Maria's "tenor of favor" Franco Corelli sang Pollione and Gabriele Santini conducted. But what promised to be a brilliant success soon devolved into a shocking international scandal, when Callas withdrew after singing just one act, claiming that she was ill. (She began the opera by telling the director of the company that she was feeling well.) Her singing was problematical during that first act, after which she announced that she could not continue. There was no cover for her, so the performance had to end. While leaving via Rome Opera's stage door, a chorus of boos rained down upon her. The next morning, tabloids around the world (especially in Italy) described this "*disgrazia*." Most of the scurrilous coverage framed her "walk-out" as a personal affront to President Gronchi. She and her husband held a press conference which enraged the public even more. She claimed she had bronchitis and that is what forced her to cancel the performance, but she did not look or sound sick or even hoarse. She was dramatically costumed in a black dress and black hat, with a black veil around her face. She did not look ill, but in fact looked pleased with

8. Back to La Scala—Conquering America

The transformation is complete. The newly slender and glamorized Maria Callas in her chic maisonette apartment in Milan, 1957.

herself for causing all the ruckus. This added to Callas' press coverage, and she undoubtedly enjoyed that.

Callas began to draw a distinction in her life between "Maria" and "Callas"—the first, a woman; the second, the great artist. She repeated this in several of her interviews during this period. Such a dichotomy suggests that she lacked a clear sense of identity, wondering whether there was an essential difference between herself and her brilliant stage persona—or even whether these two women could co-exist peacefully.

She left Rome for her home in Milan and then soon afterward flew to Chicago for a January 22 concert of arias with Nicola Rescigno at the Civic Opera House. During this highly successful concert, she sang a series of arias and sounded excellent and well-rested. By the end of January, she was in New York to perform again with the Metropolitan Opera: She gave two performances of *La Traviata* with Fausto Cleva conducting. She hated this production and did not like being conducted by Cleva; she asked Rudolf Bing for a new production of *La Traviata* with Luchino Visconti, now her favorite director. She then sang in three performances of an old production of *Lucia di Lammermoor* at the Met, again with Cleva conducting. She also suggested to Bing that he should give her a new production of *Lucia*, though this never happened. She ended her performances at the Met in 1958 with two performances of *Tosca*, opposite Richard Tucker as Cavaradossi. The performances were very well-received, though Callas told Bing the Met needed a new *Tosca* production as well. She was used to getting exciting new productions at La Scala and annoyed that she had to appear in dreary old productions at the Met. Then Bing offered her a new production of Verdi's *Macbeth* for the next season. They agreed on the dates, and she signed the contract. However, she ultimately withdrew from this new production before its premiere. Leonie Rysanek sang the role of Lady Macbeth, without great success.

Callas traveled by train to the Sao Carlos Opera in Lisbon, Portugal, to sing two performances of *La Traviata*. Alfredo Kraus sang a flawlessly executed Alfredo. But Callas' performances (on March 27 and 30, 1958) did not go well. In his 1989 play *The Lisbon Traviata*, Terrence McNally cleverly portrayed the many gay men who were becoming obsessed with Callas and her singing and acting, with the plot revolving around the rare, mightily flawed bootleg recording of one of her Violettas in Lisbon.

She was back at La Scala in April 1958 to sing in Visconti's *Anna Bolena*. Her performances were sometimes booed at La Scala and other opera companies, and her performances began to be inconsistent. Callas was being contrasted with Anna Moffo, another slim and glamorous singer who could act very well. Moffo had the kind of gorgeous, creamy voice that Callas lacked. The American soprano, Roberta Peters, remained one of Rudolf Bing's stalwart "house sopranos," due to her professionalism, reliability and relative lack of temperament.

In the late 1950s, Callas always posed as the model wife whose life revolved around the wishes of her husband. She also said her greatest wish was to have a child, though her husband (in his memoirs) insisted that this was never a possibility for them due to problems with her body's

8. Back to La Scala—Conquering America

reproductive system. Callas knew that such pronouncements were catnip to the press. She was becoming known for alerting the press on her arrival and departure dates, along with flight numbers, thus insuring that she would be met by a phalanx of reporters and photographers. Callas then could look annoyed at all the press attention she had arranged. Tebaldi did not engage in such self-promotional "games."

Maria had a shrewd instinct for generating publicity and how to capitalize on it. She gave interviews to certain newspapers and magazines which ran favorable articles on her, along with photos of her looking slim and glamorous. Her records were selling very well for Angel Records/EMI, a company famous for its fine recordings of classical music and opera. During this period, she was not only recording complete operas but also recital discs.

In the summer of 1958, Maria's father George Callas, was very sick and could not pay his medical bills. A hospital in New York wrote to Callas, asking her to pay his bill. She resolutely refused. Her sister Jackie wrote to Maria that their father had returned to Greece and he was probably dying—something also confirmed by Dr. Lantzounis, who recommended that she visit her dying father. Again, she refused to be moved. For a woman like Maria Callas, who had experienced such deprivation during World War II in Athens, this must have been very gratifying. Maria was still angry with her father for allowing Evangelia to spirit her and Jackie away to Greece, at such a dangerous, volatile time, and she had come to the conclusion that this "betrayal" by her father was grounds for permanently severing all ties with him. When he eventually died in Athens, she did not attend the funeral. Maria had isolated herself from all the members of her immediate family, people whom she now described to her friends as evil and parasitic, trying to exploit her and her fame and steal her money. Maria was especially annoyed by family entreaties for financial assistance. However, in later moments of reflection, Maria was somewhat regretful over her abandonment of her dying father (Edwards 302 ff.).

By this time, Meneghini's sister Pia had assumed the role of Maria's personal assistant, helping her prepare for performances and helping manage Maria's ceaseless schedule. This relationship, too, turned sour. Maria treated her sister-in-law like a personal maid, sending her off on errands, like getting some soup for her, or mending one of her costumes. Pia became resentful over Maria's condescending attitude toward her, and could not forgive her for severing her ties to members of her own family. When Pia suggested that Maria contact her mother in Greece, Maria flew into a rage and refused to speak to Pia ever again (Tosi 102 ff.). Callas was prone to ending close relationships, without ever looking back or offering anyone a "second chance." She had done this with her own family for years, and now she was doing this same thing with the few members of Meneghini's family that she actually spoke to. Maria had to be right about everything now that she was the great diva. She was becoming the tyrant in the family—right about everything and everyone, and no one was allowed to contradict her. After all, she was the star in the family.

Maria eventually stopped speaking to nearly everyone, accusing each person of being stupid and/or trying to kill her and her career. Many former friends saw her as the stereotype of the opera diva: narcissistic and arrogant, always fighting with colleagues. These antics also attracted some people to her who wanted to be around her, to worship the great diva. One of her friends from Milan, Gina Malozzi, began to feel that Maria was becoming schizophrenic—friendly with her one minute, but transforming into Callas the Diva the moment she entered the theater (Tosi 102–175). Callas' behavior became increasingly hard for some people to endure. She often appeared angry with the world and everyone in it, especially her husband.

By the end of the 1950s, she could no longer hide the fact that she was developing vocal problems, and that she was no longer enamored of Gian Battista Meneghini, though she had vowed to love him forever and insisted that she yearned to be the mother of his children. Beneath her argumentative nature, she was also a very insecure and needy woman who, despite her great fame, feared for her career and feared being abandoned by both her friends and her fans. Most singers go through a period of vocal problems that they can sometimes cure … and sometimes can't.

She undoubtedly knew that her wobble was getting worse and at La Scala, she had sometimes been booed. This enraged her, but she must have also known that she was not singing as well as she once had. Once while having dinner with Angel Records head Walter Legge and his soprano wife Elisabeth Schwarzkopf, Maria confided to Schwarzkopf that she was still having problems with her high notes. Schwarzkopf laughed and gave her another impromptu singing lesson on hitting those difficult high notes. Callas never forgave her for that little laugh during that casual lesson on hitting high notes. There was even a photographer present to photograph the incident, which Callas later found embarrassing (Stassinopoulos 100 ff.).

Her cancellations of performances became more frequent. Memories of the Rome Opera "*scandalo*" kept recurring in Maria's mind. At this point, she was becoming more famous for her cancellations than for her actual performances. Nevertheless, she continued to perform at La Scala and elsewhere, including the Royal Opera at Covent Garden. But she was feeling more and more pressure and anxiety before her performances. She wanted her performances to be major events, and she realized that would be so if they were rarer—not to mention, this would lessen the strain on her declining vocal resources. She had to sing much more carefully now, and her singing lost the exciting, youthful spontaneity she had at the beginning of her career (Edwards 245–248 ff.). She was still in her 30s and her voice should have been in better shape. Could she survive her vocal crisis and save her own career?

9

Enter Onassis, and Addio, Titta

Maria Callas had become an international sensation by the spring of 1959 (a year which proved to be a pivotal year) and she was enjoying all the attention—and all the money. The gossip magazines had been covering her for the last seven years and she had given them plenty of exciting stories. She was posing for many press photos and was rarely disinclined to be interviewed, as she seemed to enjoy the *faux contretemps* while being covered by these tabloids. She was undoubtedly paid for granting many of those interviews, but she must have realized that those glossy fan magazines were helping her career and selling tickets to her performances.

She also appeared on television for interviews both in Europe and the U.S. She was always perfectly turned-out whenever she appeared in public, in carefully crafted ensembles, almost all of which were custom couture, designed for her by Biki's fashion house in Milan.

She was still taking amphetamines to help her lose weight and *keep* the weight off. In Switzerland, she learned that Hollywood stars like Judy Garland and Ginger Rogers had been taking amphetamines—both uppers and downers—since the 1930s to help them maintain their svelte figures when they appeared in the movies. We now know that amphetamines can cause heart attacks and strokes, and they were taken off the market in most countries by the late 1970s. They remained legal in some countries.

During this period, the mezzo-soprano, Christa Ludwig, did some recording with Callas, and was suspicious of all the silly rumors Callas was spreading about how she had lost all that weight. She commented in her memoir:

> A singer has to eat and drink well to calm the stomach and also the nerves. Eating well also keeps the mucous membranes moist and oily, and forms a protective layer on top of them. But, of course, one then risks gaining weight, and this worries many singers. Maria Callas wanted to lose a lot of weight and took

9. Enter Onassis, and Addio, Titta

medications to do it, which made her extremely nervous. The subject of medication, tranquilizers and stimulants could fill a long chapter. When a singer is fine vocally, he or she doesn't need to take anything. But the time always comes when "the voice" causes singers to become more nervous, and then they get a lot of different advice. I concluded after many years that nothing really helps when one is very nervous (Ludwig 206).

Starting in the late 1950s, after she lost all that weight, Callas and Meneghini began visiting the French Riviera and Monaco, the central gathering spot of café society—a group of very wealthy and glamorous celebrities whose only "job," it appeared, was getting on and off enormous yachts in St. Tropez and Monte Carlo. While in Monaco, she met two people who would become very important to her: Elsa Maxwell and Aristotle Onassis. Prince Rainier of Monaco and his wife, former movie star Grace Kelly, came to Maria's performances in Europe and invited her and Meneghini to dine at their famous palace in Monaco. The royal family of Grimaldi in Monaco had been struggling for control of Monaco and its finances with Aristotle Onassis, now considered one of the wealthiest and most powerful men in Europe. There Maria got to see the lifestyle of the super-rich

The merging of two of Greece's greatest shipping dynasties: the 1946 wedding of Aristotle Socrates Onassis (in the tuxedo, second from the right) and Athina "Tina" Livanos (next to him, third from the right). The other attendees pictured here are unidentified.

society and the international jet-set—people with billions of dollars who could fly around the world to see her perform, who lived in palaces and had homes or apartments in Monaco to avoid taxes. Maria liked what she saw. She and her husband were now wealthy themselves, thanks to her earning

Aristotle Onassis and his family aboard his world-class yacht, *The Christina*, in the 1950s. Left to right: Tina Onassis, Alexander Onassis, Christina Onassis and Aristotle Socrates Onassis. There were rough waters in their not-too-distant future.

9. Enter Onassis, and Addio, Titta

power, though Meneghini himself came from one of the wealthiest families in Verona. To all the world, they appeared to be an operatic "power couple."

They had never seen the lavish wealth that they now witnessed in Monaco. These people lived like royalty and nobility (and some of them *were* royals). Two of the first people they met seemed to be the de facto "leaders of the pack," Aristotle Onassis and his wife Tina. He was now a billionaire, with an international fleet of ships that delivered oil to all the wealthiest countries.

It was Elsa Maxwell who introduced Maria to Onassis. Elsa wrote newspaper columns, primarily about movie stars and celebrities, but was also an occasional opera reviewer. She was an outspoken fan of Renata Tebaldi's, but Callas was sure she could win her over to her side through the famous Callas glamour and charm, which she could turn on when she was determined to. Callas could be very flirtatious around Elsa when she wanted to use her, as some of their photos indicate. Certainly Callas would have heard the rampant rumors that Elsa was a lesbian, and that Maxwell's interest in her might have been in a more intimate way than Maria was comfortable with—though the elderly, trollish columnist's school-girlish adoration of Maria didn't seem to pose an immediate threat. And if Elsa covered her career for the international press, this would surely help Callas's career and reputation (Stassinopoulos 168 ff.). Callas could be very winning and agreeable around people who could help her—people like Meneghini, who near–single-handedly had helped her to skyrocket to stardom.

But now, Maria was beginning to view her husband as a liability and an embarrassment. He was 30 years older than she was, short, fat, and not very interesting, especially compared with the legendarily vibrant Onassis.

When they were first introduced by Elsa, Aristotle Onassis and Maria were both married to other people, but they fell in love, and adultery added to the excitement of their clandestine relationship. Maria had always presented herself to the public as dedicated to her husband and longing for children. She also talked to the press about her joy in cooking for her husband, and what her husband's favorite dishes were. However, now that she was appearing in photos in a bikini (designed by Biki di Milano) alongside Aristotle Onassis, rather than her own husband—they both kept insisting to the press they were just good friends (Edwards 150–170).

Maria had also become convinced that Meneghini was stealing her money. She wanted her own money separated from his money, and she asserted control of her increasingly large performance fees and royalties from her many recordings. She sensed that her husband was not really comfortable with her new rich friends, people like Prince Rainier and Grace Kelly, Winston and Clementine Churchill and Ari and Tina Onassis. She began to find him an embarrassment, especially in Monaco

Callas (right) with the soon-to-be-ex–Mrs. Aristotle Onassis in 1959. One can almost viscerally feel the brittle tension between the two.

and on the Rivieras (Edwards 186 ff). He did not own a yacht, unlike the billionaire Onassis, who kept one of the world's most luxurious private yachts, *The Christina* (named for his young daughter) harbored in Monaco. She increasingly found her decidedly *un*sophisticated husband an encumbrance.

She had developed into an international icon of glamour in the

9. Enter Onassis, and Addio, Titta

popular culture of the day. All her battles with other singers and with directors of opera companies, like Antonio Ghiringhelli at La Scala and Rudolf Bing at the Met, added to her reputation as an exciting performer and even more exciting personality. As she sang less and less frequently, her few performances were usually sold-out well in advance. Her decreasing number of performances made tickets to Callas' performances even more coveted. She liked being a singer whose appearance could become an "international event." By 1959, she had transitioned more into the concert arena, since she

Maria Callas and Aristotle Onassis, at sea aboard his yacht in 1967.

found concerts to be less vocally demanding than operatic roles. As stated above, the main reason she was singing fewer performances is that she could no longer ignore the vocal problems that had started plaguing her.

The critics were noticing it as well, and mentioning it in their reviews. She had always had an unusually prominent *vibrato*, even when she was a student at Athens' music conservatory. Part of the problem was that she had been singing professionally for at least 15 years by this point. More often than not, a steadily-working female singer cannot sustain a career of 20-years singing professionally much longer than that. In addition, she had abused her voice in many ways—singing roles that were too dramatic or too high or too long for her. Once she became the "hot" soprano, she was lured by the prestige and by the enormous fees, to agree to do more performances than were, perhaps, prudent, which is also very damaging to a singer's voice. She was known to sing in full voice at all her rehearsals, unlike most other singers who "marked" during rehearsals (avoiding all the high notes and using little volume) and sang out, full-voiced, only during performances. Some critics have suggested that her considerable weight loss had badly affected her voice and her breathing, which compromised her vocal support.

In New York in October 1959, Maria Callas confronted the paparazzi amidst revelations of her scandalous, adulterous affair with Aristotle Onassis.

Callas' last La Scala performances were in a new production of Cherubini's *Medea*, based on a famous Greek tragedy by Euripides. She excelled in the role, but more for her acting than her singing. She sang this role in January 1961 and later when the opera was revived in June 1962. The new young and dashing American conductor, Thomas Schippers, conducted this new production very effectively, and Callas liked working with him. La Scala brought in a Greek team to direct this opera. Alexis Minotis directed the very exciting production, with sets and costumes by Yannis Tsarouchia.

9. Enter Onassis, and Addio, Titta

They used a modernistic and primitive approach to this opera about one of the most appalling characters in Greek tragedy, a mother who murders her two sons to get revenge on her husband Jason who has abandoned her for a younger woman. The new, young Canadian tenor, Jon Vickers, sang the role of Giasone, and Giulietta Simioniato sang the role of Neris. This opera was carefully picked for Callas because it was a short opera, written with many recitatives, a format which Callas could still manage with her diminishing vocal resources, but still-incandescent acting ability.

But by 1961 and 1962, Callas was spending less time singing in the opera house and more time with Onassis in nightclubs. She seemed to lose

Aristotle Onassis and Maria Callas host their illustrious guest, Sir Winston Churchill, as they arrive into New York Harbor aboard *The Christina* in 1961.

her focus in opera and was tired of all the vocal practice needed to sustain her usual technical control of her voice. She now, for the first time, reveled in café society and the life of endless parties. For her, the homely, unpopular girl in the thick spectacles was now the belle of the ball, and she liked it very much.

Onassis' marriage to Tina was merely "in name only" by this point. Tina spent most of her time with their children in Paris or London and she did not enjoy cruising on the Mediterranean on her husband's famous yacht—whereas Maria loved yachting with Onassis and his international cadre of celebrities, most notably Winston Churchill and his wife and the prince and princess of Monaco. That Churchill was now in his 80s and suffering from a gradual descent into dementia did not diminish his star quality as the great victor of World War II. When he and his entourage were aboard *The Christina*, the press was always nearby; they were now often collectively referred to as "the *paparazzi*," an Italian slang term for photographers who hound celebrities (Stassinopoulos 223 ff). Titta was rich, but Ari was far richer. Actually, Meneghini and Onassis were about the same weight, with the same "height deficit"—and were, in fact, less than ten years apart in age (though Meneghini seemed far older than Onassis, who had a striking, charismatic personality). Who could resist the legendary charms of a man such as this? Not Callas.

Poor Titta thought he was a happily married man and he was proud of his wife and happy to be managing her wonderful career. One night on the *Christina*, Tina confided in him: "You have lost your wife and I have lost my husband now." All of a sudden, Callas came out of Onassis' bedroom and abruptly told Meneghini that she wanted a divorce so she could be free to marry Onassis. The blatantly cuckolded Meneghini never recovered from this rejection, as he made clear in his memoir. He was the biggest casualty in this new arrangement. He felt he had dedicated himself to Callas' career and helped to make her the most famous diva in opera. Now she accused him of exploiting her, stealing her money and no longer enough of a man to satisfy her. Ari, in fact, had no concrete matrimonial plans for Callas—though he did want to have her for his mistress and cruising companion (Edwards 210–224). As Meneghini told a friend during this period, "Maria thinks she is entering a golden throne now but she is really entering a golden coffin." He sensed that Onassis would ruin Maria's singing career and turn her into a society dilettante—which is, perhaps, what she really now wanted to be. She had been a slave to her art for so many years, as Franco Zeffirelli commented at the time, but now she had become a rich society beauty and that was what "the new Maria" wanted (Zeffirelli 143 ff). It's important to remember, she was not an educated woman who relished reading at night or listening to classical music. She was now in her late 30s, she wanted to relax and look beautiful and be with the rich and beautiful

9. Enter Onassis, and Addio, Titta

people. Callas also told Zeffirelli that Ari was the sexiest man she had ever met and much more exciting in bed than her old, sexually disinterested husband. She now called her husband "that mean old man," in a contemptible tone of dismissal. (Edwards 233 ff.).

At first, Meneghini thought Callas must be losing her mind. He had sacrificed his own life and his own business career for her and her career, and now he was being dumped for a man with no interest in the arts—rather, only an interest in money and status. Meneghini described being onboard *The Christina* and seeing Onassis sunbathing in the nude—and describes him as "looking like a hairy, grotesque, sleeping ape." Meneghini must have realized that Onassis' money was the big attraction, and that Maria loved not having to practice her scales but instead cruising onboard the luxurious *The Christina*. Callas also loved being in bed with Onassis, whom she found more fun and sexually adventurous than her own husband (Meneghini 225–255). All the publicity their affair engendered made the Callas-Onassis pairing a major item in the popular press. Both Callas and Onassis craved this kind of worldwide attention and publicity, though they kept insisting that they were "just good friends." Meneghini, however, found this whole Riviera scene vulgar, materialistic and totally mindless, and he publicly

Aristotle Onassis awaits a post-performance Maria near the La Scala stage door.

Maria Callas and Aristotle Onassis, shamelessly in love in Naples, Italy (September 7, 1960).

9. Enter Onassis, and Addio, Titta

accused his wife and Onassis of adultery. He grew to despise Onassis, whom he accused of being a predatory and traitorous host who seduced other men's wives.

Maria, it seemed to Meneghini, was betraying her vocation as an artist and her dedication to maintaining the discipline her art demanded. She was also betraying him and their marriage vows. He was embarrassed by the way she flaunted her adultery before the press. While she and Onassis kept repeating that their friendship was platonic, their body language betrayed them and the truth of their sexual relationship was plain to see.

Maria was doing precisely what Meneghini's brothers had predicted she would do, which further compounded his humiliation. Did she really want to humiliate him so publicly, making no effort to avoid being photographed in the arms of Onassis? In short, yes, she did. She grew, at this point in her life, very angry with her husband and enjoyed humiliating him. He was now a *cornudo* (cuckold). Titta predicted that Callas would destroy her voice and career, thanks to Onassis, and then *he* would dump *her*—all of which happened sooner than anyone could have predicted. But, for now at least, she was enjoying the very public role of adulteress.

Both the Greek Aristotle Onassis and the Greek Maria Callas were careerists whose previous marriages were, in part, motivated by developing a career. Onassis' wife Tina was born Athina Livanos, a member of the family that had become his major rival in the Greek shipping business. By marrying into that family, Onassis was able to form a partnership with one of the wealthiest families in the Greek shipping industry (Evans 30 ff.). This was a classic manifestation of Maria's "borderline" characteristic—of only seeing others as totally wonderful or totally evil.

When Maria and Aristotle met, they were already famous people—the two most famous Greeks in the world. Given what they had achieved and what they could do for each other, they were naturally attracted. They found, according to Franco Zeffirelli, a powerful sexual attraction to each other—and when that was added to their fame and wealth, they fell madly in love. Onassis felt that he had a trophy mistress in Maria Callas. Maria undoubtedly felt that her new lover became a trophy lover, since he was one of the wealthiest men in the world. At one point in their Mediterranean cruising, they stopped on a Greek island and a bishop blessed them both, seemingly sanctifying their illicit relationship. He could not marry them, of course, since they were both married to other people, but still he blessed them. Greek men of that generation did not marry their mistresses, and their mistresses didn't expect them to—that was part of the social code of the period. But Maria hardly viewed herself as anyone's "mistress." She wanted Ari to marry her.

Maria wanted and intended to continue her opera career. But since she was a teenager, she had been practicing and training her voice, and now she

Aristotle Onassis proudly escorts his glamorous opera star through the town he "owned" (Monte Carlo, Monaco) in 1959.

wanted other pleasures like food and drink and Aegean seas. Zeffirelli compared her to a "nun who was sick of her vocation" (Zeffirelli 50–80). Being a singer involved constant discipline and practice, which she had been doing for so many years; it was now more fun to spend the day in her swimsuit

9. Enter Onassis, and Addio, Titta

ordering the many servants on board to fetch whatever she wanted. *La dolce vita!* This really was the sweet life, and she could not resist Onassis' many attractions, especially the lifestyle his wealth and outsized personality could offer her. He introduced her to a new set of friends, who happened to be the richest and most glamorous people in the world—people like the Aga Khan and Prince and Princess Lee Radziwill (sister of Jacqueline Kennedy). He seemed to know Lee Radziwill particularly well. Onassis suggested that Callas retire from the stage and spend all her time with him, but she missed all the attention and excitement of performing opera.

On one of her cruises with Aristotle, she stopped in Athens to get together with Jackie for a pre-arranged meeting and trial reconciliation. Maria enjoyed showing off the yacht to her sister, implying that she was a great success and a great and wealthy lady, now that she was sleeping with the owner of such a luxurious ship—unlike Jackie. She even publicly called her older sister "an old woman." There clearly remained a great deal of sibling rivalry still between the two sisters, especially on Maria's part, since she wanted her sister to know about all her successes, which she knew Jackie would then relate to their mother. Jackie and Evangelia were living in near-poverty in Athens.

The occasion for this attempted reconciliation with Jackie (but not her mother) was Maria's 1961 performance of Cherbini's *Medea* at the ancient Greek amphitheater at Epidaurus. Aristotle wanted Maria to reconcile with her family since he was so fond of his own family (his mother had died when he was a small child), but this reconciliation was not to be.

The first scheduled performance had to be cancelled due to a rainstorm. However, the second performance did occur and got wonderful reviews. Maria was finally successful in Greece, where she had begun her career in opera and where she lived during the worst years of World War II and the civil war in Athens (Stassinopoulos 235 ff.). But Callas had no desire to live in Greece now.

Surveying her life at this time, Callas felt as if she had finally reached her zenith, achieving goals beyond her dreams. However, she wanted more; she wanted to be Mrs. Aristotle Onassis.

She also still wanted to practice her art and sing opera. She still had a contract at La Scala, and other opera directors at the Met and London's Covent Garden were begging her to perform in their theaters, in roles of her choosing. It was around this time that Maria underwent an official name change. After she married Meneghini, she'd changed her name to Maria Meneghini Callas. Now she wanted to be known to her public and in her performances and recordings only as "Maria Callas." She also hoped that she would soon become "Maria Callas Onassis."

10

1959 and the Affair with Onassis

Aristotle Onassis now claimed to love opera—though by this, he generally meant about a half-hour of opera arias, not opera for an entire evening. What he most liked about opera was that it was considered classy, and he now wanted to be considered classy and to socialize with classy people. Both he and Maria were narcissistic, and they both craved celebrity, and so they fed each other's needs. He loved having the most famous opera singer in the world in a bikini on his yacht as his public mistress, and she loved being loved by the richest man in the world and being on board the most luxurious yacht in the world. She also loved that Ari found her so sexy and irresistible in bed (Gage 20–50). She often reminded people that her astrological sign was Pisces, the sign of the fish, so she loved sailing and bathing in the sun. That Maria and Aristotle were both Greek and could converse easily together in that language naturally added to their fascination and obsession with each other.

The paparazzi besieged them every time they docked somewhere and got off *The Christina,* adding to the excitement of it all. They loved the attention and loved seeing themselves in all the newspapers, magazines and tabloids. That they were both married to someone else added to the fun, though not for their spouses. That they had to call the paparazzi to ensure that they would be met with flashing bulbs when their yacht docked did not diminish their fun much. Onassis and Callas would soon use this phrase *la dolce vita* (the sweet life) to describe their glamorous lifestyle. Onassis was a billionaire, while Meneghini remained a mere millionaire. Who could ask for anything more than life with Ari? (Evans 130–50).

While she loved to talk to the press about being dedicated to her art and having to pressure her colleagues in the opera to be up to her high standard, she also wanted to be a very wealthy woman, hounded by the press and jetting from location to location for parties or performances. Such a lifestyle certainly connected with the narcissistic part

10. 1959 and the Affair with Onassis

of her personality—being the center of attention and hounded by the paparazzi.

Onassis' soon-to-be–ex-wife Tina was often angry with him for being more interested in celebrity than interested in her, their son Alexander and their daughter Christina. Meneghini was horrified to see the wife he loved, proudly going to Onassis' bedroom every night on board his famous yacht while he was still onboard. That she would have the nerve to humiliate him so publicly infuriated Meneghini. He got off the yacht as soon as it returned to Monaco. Maria insisted on staying on board to be with Onassis. Meneghini's betrayal by his wife was absolute.

Maria now seemed to her husband like a teenage girl infatuated with a new boyfriend, instead of the 35-year-old married woman she was. He was horrified and tried to talk to his wife and turn her back into the woman he knew and loved, but instead, she avoided him and sidled up to Onassis before her husband's eyes.

For Maria, Giovanni Battista Meneghini had become the enemy, a man who meant her harm—her "jailer," as she now called him, who had been stealing her money. She now viewed Ari as the perfect man: rich, powerful, sexy, and in love with her. That he happened to be married to someone else did not seem to bother her in any way. He was perfection, and she felt that she *deserved* perfection! The lifestyle she had read about in her movie magazines was now being offered to her, thanks to Onassis. In her mind, she was "trading up"—which she certainly felt was her due.

If she had had some education, if she had had some psychotherapy, things might have played out differently for her, and she might have saved herself and the people around her much grief. She might have been able to see the world and the people in it more realistically. But she was who she was, and even now, it is very difficult for psychiatrists to do much for borderline personality types. If she was willing to admit that maybe she was being hasty, maybe she was not being fair to Meneghini—a man who had created her and guided her career for the last ten years—things might have been different. A psychiatrist might have been able to show her that she was seeing people as either good or bad, while, in fact, "perception" of a person's self, in relation to others, is certainly a multi-faceted thing. But she was not able to see beyond her own needs and desires. Her narcissism precluded the possibility that her view of the world may be as short-sighted as she was, without her eyeglasses.

Meneghini recounts in his book on his wife:

> My housekeeper, Emma Brutti, who was with me even when I was living with Maria, remembered the following incidents very clearly. When Maria learned that one of our friends had been unfaithful to his wife, from whom he was now separated, she no longer wished to see him. Once Emma admitted someone into

the home who had often come to visit us and who now had left his wife, Maria made a scene and refused to speak with him. "Now that he has left his wife, he is no longer our friend," she declared.

Ingrid Bergman and my wife were good friends. One day we ran into Ingrid, who had just been separated from Roberto Rossellini. Ingrid greeted us with her usual warmth, while Maria was rather cool. Later, as we chatted, the subject of the recent separation came up. My wife reproached Bergman and said that from that moment, they could no longer be friends in the way they once were. Maria judged people who cultivated her friendship with that uncompromising, intransigent attitude (Meneghini, *My Wife*, 184–85).

Needless to say, Maria's attitude suddenly changed now that she was in bed with Onassis.

The institution of marriage itself has become much more of a transitory vow than it was in the late 1950s and early 1960s. When one looks at the current statistics for marriage in most countries, the findings remain grim. Fully 50 percent of marriages in both America and Britain end in divorce. Many people, it seems, may have been traumatized by their own divorce(s), or their parents' divorce(s), and today some people see marriage as a painful and dated institution. Or perhaps Callas and Onassis were just responding to the *zeitgeist* of the 1960s, when human freedom, free love and breaking barriers were being normalized by the young.

Onassis' wife was from the very powerful Livanos family, so this adultery was a snub to them as well as to Meneghini. The effect on the two Onassis children would also be very traumatic—children are always the biggest victims in a divorce: They usually don't understand why their family is being torn apart, and they tend to blame themselves for the catastrophe. Alexander was 12 years and Christina was nine years old when their parents divorced. These two

Maria Callas, at the very peak of her career in 1957. She had good reason to appear so buoyant, since that year she had triumph after triumph.

10. 1959 and the Affair with Onassis

children immediately blamed Maria Callas for the destruction of their family and never got over their hatred of her—the narcissistic diva, the mistress who had destroyed their happy family life.

Their affair would prove fatal to Callas' marriage, and to Onassis' as well. Onassis urged her to give up her singing career and, instead, cruise with him on the Mediterranean. Ari liked to call himself Odysseus (or Ulysses) and he liked to call Maria his new Penelope.

And what did Maria Callas offer to Aristotle Onassis? Onassis liked being connected with the world's most famous opera singer, and enjoyed being seen at gala premieres and performances at top opera theaters (if they did not last too long), and he liked the attention he got when he was with Maria. Maria felt the same way about Onassis. He was now giving her fabulous jewelry from famous stores like Cartier and Tiffany

In 1959, Maria arrives at New York International Airport (now called John F. Kennedy International Airport) with her requisite "diva prop," her toy poodle, who was rather unimaginatively named "Toy."

In the aftermath of the calamitous 1959 cruise, Meneghini undoubtedly dreaded returning to Verona and seeing his family's knowing looks and hearing their remarks. His family had warned him from the beginning about Maria. Now, much to Meneghini's embarrassment, his family was proven right; Titta was also a devout member of the Roman Catholic Church and took his marriage vows very seriously (Meneghini 306).

While Meneghini was horrified by his new situation, he contacted Tina Onassis to learn her reaction to the situation. Would they join forces to try to make their spouses go back to their marital duties? Or would they agree to divorces and not get in the way of the lovers? As Meneghini knew, divorce was then illegal in Italy, and he had no intention of cooperating with any kind of a legal separation or a divorce granted by another country. He always claimed to be the injured party since he had not committed adultery and remained a practicing Catholic in a Catholic country. He

Aristotle Onassis with his only son, Alexander Socrates Onassis in October 1968. Both were dead within six years' time.

had vowed to be Maria's faithful and loving husband until he died, and he did not plan to alter this. She did, however, meet with him and Onassis in Milan and announced her love affair with Onassis, and they both asked him to grant Callas a divorce or a legal separation. Meneghini refused. Onassis offered him $1 million if he would cooperate. Tina Onassis, on the other hand, told Meneghini that she was quite willing to divorce Onassis, provided she and their two children were well provided for. She knew Aristotle would agree to this (DeCeccatty 216–236).

Battista did not have to worry about facing poverty, and his family certainly wanted him to "return to the fold" and resume running the construction business. He was the oldest of six children, and they still looked up to him as a big brother and father figure who was so good at running the now-expanding family business in Verona. Gian Battista Meneghini had managed it very well before Callas, so why could he not go back to it now that the Callas whirlwind was finally over—*finalmente! Basta!* But actually he did not want to go back to the rather prosaic construction business; the world of international opera remained much more exciting and fascinating for him.

Callas wanted to continue her singing career, despite the emotional upset all around her. On September 17, 1959, she appeared at the Coliseo Albia in Bilbao, Spain, along with her current favorite conductor, Nicola

10. 1959 and the Affair with Onassis

Aristotle Onassis with his only daughter Christina, at his 1968 wedding to Jacqueline Kennedy—presumably an event that Christina did not attend gleefully. She was Onassis' primary heir upon his death in 1974.

Rescigno, to sing a concert of arias from Verdi's *Don Carlo* and *Ernani*, Thomas' *Hamlet* and Bellini's *Il Pirata*. Seven days later, September 23, 1959, she was at London's Royal Festival Hall singing arias from *Don Carlo*, *Hamlet*, *Macbeth* and the final scene from *Il Pirata*. This program was well-received, though some critics noted vocal problems.

At London's Wood Green Empire Theatre, she was to sing a concert of arias, with Sir Malcom Sargent accompanying her. The BBC televised it on

October 7, 1959. On October 23, she appeared at the Titania Palast in Berlin, again with Rescigno conducting, to sing a program of her most popular arias.

She then flew to Kansas City, Missouri, to sing at Loew's Midland Theater. On October 28, 1959, she sang a concert of arias, again with Nicola Rescigno. Rescigno recalled in interviews that he and Callas had a special rapport and worked well together in either complete operas or recitals. He also knew how to help her when her vocal insecurities developed (Kesting 153–193).

In early November 1959, she flew to Dallas, Texas, for two performances of *Lucia di Lammermoor*. This Dallas production was borrowed from London's Royal Opera at Covent Garden, now staged by the Dallas Civic Opera in the State Fair Music Hall in Dallas. Also in Dallas, she sang two performances of Cherubini's *Medea* on November 19 and 21. Jon Vickers was again her Jason. Callas kept saying how wonderful it was to work with Vickers, calling him "a tenor who could actually act" (Williams 89 ff.). Vickers reported being very happy to be performing with Callas.

Callas went back to Italy to get a legal separation from Titta. They both appeared in a courtroom in Brescia, Italy, and on November 14, 1959, an Italian judge granted them a legal separation and their assets were divided. Divorce was not legal in Italy then so they could not be legally divorced, and because of this, Meneghini eventually inherited half of Callas' estate after her death since, legally, he was still her husband—Callas' mother and sister got the remainder of Maria's estate. This is highly ironic, in that she was not speaking to any of these people at the time of her death. Her paranoia and arrogance got worse as she aged. She accused people of wanting to use her, though the truth (at least according to her mother) was the exact opposite (Callas, Evangelia 70–80). But this is certainly not how Maria viewed herself.

After her November opera performances, Callas flew to France to be with Onassis. All the rich and beautiful people in the world, it seemed, were drawn into Ari's orbit and were more than eager to be aboard his yacht. He loved being surrounded by celebrities (the "classy" people, as he called them) and he had both the money and the personality to attract them. For a poor girl raised in Washington Heights, this new environment must have been dazzling. Maria felt that she had reached the top echelon of society—the beautiful people who were rich and could live wherever they wanted, had multiple residences, and enjoyed the most luxurious of lifestyles. The utter opulence of *The Christina* was mind-boggling, then as now (when viewed on film or photographs). The yacht was filled with priceless art and luxurious accommodations. The faucets were gold-plated, if only to serve as a reminder to everyone on board of Onassis' wealth. The onboard swimming pool could be converted into a dance floor at the flick of a switch.

Sir Winston Churchill was a frequent guest on *The Christina*, as well as other English and French celebrities. Photos of the yacht and its passengers were often in the international press, and Maria Callas liked the attention—especially at a time when her voice was giving her problems and her reviews were getting less favorable. But she could still be obstinate; several times, Churchill asked her to sing for them, and she always refused, which annoyed Ari. He was sometimes embarrassed by her in situations like this, and the fact that she refused to speak to her own mother embarrassed him as well. Aristotle himself loved his now-dead parents, especially his mother, who died when he was only four years old, and he was still very close to his sister Eugenia and visited her whenever he was in Greece.

Callas had long harbored deep, hidden insecurities about her singing, and needed to be reassured. Meneghini was always willing and happy to do this, but Onassis was getting impatient with her need to be the center of attention. (Edwards 198 ff.). Also, because of her need for his undivided attention, Callas grew to resent, and even hate Aristotle's two children and suggested he avoid them and stop inviting them onto *The Christina*. To Maria, the yacht was now her domain—even though it was named for the very daughter she resented.

Onassis tired of Maria's need to make scenes. It was not at all unusual for her to storm out of rooms, ending any discussion she found annoying. Meneghini was willing to put up with these tantrums, but Onassis found them embarrassing. He wanted to socialize with the most famous people, people like Churchill and the Kennedys, and did not want to be embarrassed by Maria's inability to deal with any kind of criticism or disagreement. He still loved her, though he certainly did not want to marry her (Edwards 203).

Some earlier biographers, such as Nicholas Gage, have reported that Maria got pregnant on board *The Christina*, and nine months later had a son who died within a few days. Some have also claimed that, acceding to a demand by Onassis, Callas had an abortion.

During this period (1959–1960), Maria and Meneghini were consulting their lawyers to see what legal options they had. Callas wanted to make sure that Meneghini no longer controlled any of her money—though most of their money was already in separate bank accounts, and there was now a sizable amount of money to fight over, millions of U.S. dollars. Meneghini had made sure that she was the highest-paid singer on the opera stage, and he negotiated very generous contracts for her live performances, as well as for her recordings with EMI.

Perhaps to avoid the personal and legal mess she was now facing, she wanted to go back to performing. She was still being offered contracts to perform in any role she wished to appear in on the most famous opera stages. All the press coverage Maria got as a result of her affair with Onassis made her operatic appearances box-office dynamite. Even people who did not like opera wanted to see and hear this woman who was being painted in the press as some kind of operatic hellcat. Metropolitan Opera director Rudolf Bing was especially eager to negotiate her return to his theater, now that Meneghini was out of the picture (Bing 248 ff.). She could still captivate an audience with her acting, if not always with her singing.

Eventually, Maria shared both Onassis' yacht *and* his lavish apartment in Monaco. She often asked Ari why he also kept a fully functional apartment in New York; he insisted he needed it for business reasons.

But as they sailed ahead, storm clouds were gathering on the horizon.

11

Free of Battista and Pursuing Aristo

In 1960, Callas celebrated the fact that (in her mind, at least) she was finally a free woman, free of her husband, Meneghini. The Catholic Church, as well as the rule of Italian law, would likely have disagreed with her.

Some have suggested, most notably Franco Zeffirelli, that Maria was attracted to Aristotle primarily because of the sex (Zeffirelli 140–50). She discovered sexual passion with Onassis; he was a wild and sex-driven man. He was clearly interested in her mostly as a woman and less as an opera singer—which, seemingly, is exactly what she wanted most at that time in her life. She was also now going through menopause, which causes hormonal changes that can affect the voice in detrimental ways. And she, who had always talked about the sacredness of her marriage, was now cruising around the Mediterranean in a blatant adulterous affair. Ari had no trouble getting a quick-and-quiet divorce from his wife Tina, who was happy to cooperate provided she got a good financial settlement for herself and the two children.

Solfeggio exercises and breathing exercises had kept Maria's vocal problems under control, but now she was getting tired of doing all those exercises and practicing the piano to help her stay on pitch. Increasingly, she was letting her fingernails grow long, which made playing the piano well almost impossible. She decided that she was tired of practicing her voice and playing the piano but would instead have glamorously long, painted fingernails. She now wanted to be thin, elegantly coiffed and dressed like a rich society woman rather than an opera singer who kept practicing her musical scales to keep her voice under her technical control (Edwards 163–76).

When they stopped and disembarked from Onassis' yacht to shop in Capri, Ischia or Taormina, Callas was fascinated by how rich people shop. She was used to looking at the price tags and haggling with shopkeepers to lower the price if she could. That is not how the wealthy shop, she soon discovered. They did not look at the price tags but just bought the item if they wanted it. No wonder shopkeepers were so happy to see Onassis and his friends enter their shops. For Callas, this was a revelation since she remembers haggling over prices from her experiences shopping with her mother in New York and in Athens before and during the war. And she still liked to haggle over prices (Zeffirelli 143 ff.).

It grew increasingly evident that Onassis' children hated Maria and wished their father to return to their mother—as most children in this situation would want. Ari's children saw Maria as the whore who had destroyed their parents' happy marriage and their happy family, though there had been problems in the marriage before Maria arrived on the scene. Still, their antipathy toward this interloper, whom they viewed as the sole cause of their father's departure, continued to enrage them. And things would get worse, rather than better.

By 1961, once both Maria and Onassis were putatively free of their respective spouses, Aristotle was very happy to leave things as they were, and he was enjoying his freedom. But Maria wanted to make her relationship with Ari a legally recognized one. Once she was detached from her husband, she was not particularly discreet about their affair and enjoyed posing for photos on board *The Christina* in a revealing bikini bathing suit and on Onassis' arm. She did not want to be secretive about their adulterous affair, but instead wanted to flaunt it.

During this period, Winston Churchill became an increasingly frequent guest aboard *The Christina*. He enjoyed reminiscing, in a rather stage-y dramatic way, about his leadership during World War II. Winston liked flashing his famous "V for Victory" sign to the paparazzi and the onlookers, as he did during World War II when he was the prime minster of Britain, winning a world war against the Nazis and the Axis powers of Germany and Italy. Having been the head of the victorious Allies during the bloodiest world war in the history of humanity became the high point of his political career. Though he was already in his late 60s during World War II, his flashing his victory sign became an iconic figure of resistance to both the Nazis and the Fascists. He had led Britain and the Allies to victory in Europe in the spring of 1945—when the Japanese finally surrendered, Germany having surrendered earlier the same year (Hastings 630 ff.). Onassis reveled in Churchill's stentorian wartime reminiscences, but they left Maria bored. She, too, had wartime memories, though she was loath to share the tales of desperate poverty and prostitution among her new café society "friends." She had moved on, and that chapter had forever closed.

Not only was Onassis unwilling to wed Maria at this time, he continued in his lifelong pattern of infidelity. He had a brief affair with

11. Free of Battista and Pursuing Aristo

Princess Lee Radziwill, in part to get away from Callas and her demands (Edwards 257–62). She was the sister of Jacqueline Kennedy, wife of the current American president. Onassis found that he liked the Kennedy aura of discreet wealth and awesome political power. Lee and Jacqueline did not make scenes in public, and Onassis admired that quality. They seemed to Onassis more "high-class" than his current mistress, Maria. Maria eventually detected that Onassis was beginning to avoid her and spend time with other women. Her invitations from Onassis were becoming less frequent, which scared her. He did not want her on board all of his cruises, and he began to feel that she was demanding too much of his time. He stopped inviting Maria onboard his ship when Winston Churchill was aboard, since she liked baiting the elder statesman into arguments—arguments in which the now elderly Churchill couldn't always adequately defend himself in. She pressured Ari to marry her, but he liked his freedom.

She was singing fewer performances every year. Between her performance fees and her royalty fees from her many recordings, she had become a millionaire but that seemed like poverty when she was aboard *The Christina* with people like Prince Rainier and Grace Kelly, Noël Coward and Lord Harewood, the director of London's Royal Opera Company, who was always begging her to return to Covent Garden.

In the mid–1960s, Maria was still continuing her full-court-press to get Ari to marry her, but Onassis felt like Hercules unchained after breaking free of the bonds of his marriage to Tina, and seemed disinclined to enter into another marriage.

Despite Maria's intelligence, especially her musical intelligence, not to mention her dramatic intelligence as an actress, she could see people only as black or white—totally good or totally evil. She was not capable of seeing the human complexities in people, and least of all in herself. The narcissistic part of her personality became more of an embarrassment for Onassis.

Despite all the luxury in her new life with Onassis, she still missed the excitement of performing. She missed being the prima donna in an opera house and getting ovations. Surely she could still excite an audience with her acting and singing and her commitment to the art of opera. If she could no longer sing an entire opera, a recital where she could pick and choose what music she would sing would be much easier, and would draw thousands of people. She wondered if she still had the stamina—and would her audience still be waiting to hear her? Some operas, of course, were shorter than others, so maybe if she chose wisely, she could still sing a complete opera. Surely there were still opera companies and opera directors who wanted to work with her, even in her vocal decline. Rudolf Bing and other opera company directors were writing to her to suggest roles she could sing with their companies (Bing, A Knight, 95–105).

The inextricable tie that Maria and Onassis shared was their prominently Greek world image. She told reporters, "Seven years of my career were spent in Greece. The blood in my veins, my character, my thoughts are all Greek" (Gage 218). Onassis expressed similar assertions about Greece: "Like Callas, Onassis the Anatolian professed a deeply felt essential Greekness. In fact, he considered Hellenes of the diaspora, like him, to be more Greek than those born and raised in the country. 'We are all like orphans who were deprived of their real mother and long for her embrace,' he once said." (Gage 218). Both Ari and Callas knew what the local press wanted to hear and would print. Onassis had been born in Turkey and Callas was born in New York City, and neither of them had spent much time in Greece during their lives—though those facts were largely swept from their public "bios." The truth was that Callas still had nightmares about her adolescence in Athens during World War II and had no desire to live in Athens again. Still, their romance was widely viewed by the public as the union of the two most prominent avatars of all things Greek.

Soon after her divorce from Onassis was finalized, Athina married the English Marquess of Blandford and moved to England, remaining married to him for ten years. Then she married Nicholas Niarchos, Onassis' lifelong business rival and the widower of Onassis' sister Eugenia (who had apparently died by suicide). One historian commented:

> The second half of the 18th century and the first years of the 19th saw a huge increase in seaward shipping in the Aegean. Most of the trade was carried on in small ships that covered relatively short distances. Control of long-distant routes came to be concentrated-upon three very small islands: Hydra and Spetses, both close to the northeast coast of the Peloponnese, and Psara in the eastern Aegean. Ships were locally built and owned by small businesses based on the extended family, patronage and the sharing of risk. It was a business model that, astonishingly, survives, more or less intact today, and would go on to generate the vast wealth of such legendary shipping dynasties as Onassis, Niarchos, and many others (Beaton 25).

In December 1961 (and then May and June of 1962), Callas sang at La Scala in Alexis Motiotis's colorful production of Cherubini's *Medea*, with impressively bright sets and costumes by Nicola Benois. Jon Vickers was her Giasone, and Giulietta Simoniato was Neris. Nicolai Ghiaurov sang Creonte with great success. (Years later he would marry the wonderful soprano Mirella Freni, with whom he frequently sang at La Scala.) Callas heard some booing at the final curtain calls, which she considered a total betrayal, an unforgiveable sin.

11. Free of Battista and Pursuing Aristo

Those performances of *Medea* in the 1961-62 season proved to be her final performances of opera at La Scala, and also in all of Italy. Because of Meneghini and Italy's non-divorce laws, Callas would come to dislike the country and no longer relished singing there. Italy had been the golden land that had given her the start of her legendary career. But now, Italy became the hated country where her evil husband lived. Maria, as had been her lifelong pattern, sealed shut her "Italian chapter."

12

Loving Onassis

When Maria got a legal separation from Meneghini in November 1959, she finally had total control of her own money; Meneghini was no longer receiving any of her performance fees. In his memoir, Rudolf Bing reported that Meneghini wanted cash in advance, before Callas' performances at the Met (Bing, *5000 Nights*, 237 ff.). Bing also reported that one night he paid Meneghini in $5 bills to embarrass him, though Titta did not seem embarrassed (Bing 237). Meneghini had also continued to receive hefty royalty checks from Angel/EMI Records—and Maria's records were selling well. But now, Callas was in charge of her own money and wanted all royalty checks sent only to her. Maria told her friends that Meneghini had fleeced her and left her penniless, but Meneghini denied that this had ever happened. In her public appearances, Maria did not look like a fleeced lamb, so few believed her tales of poverty.

When she had decided to divorce Meneghini, she discovered through her French lawyers that if she renounced her American citizenship and became a Greek citizen, she was not legally married to Meneghini, because they had not been married in a Greek Orthodox Church. She discovered that in Greece she was not legally married—in fact, she was still considered a virgin, at least legally. Now, she hoped, her Greek lover Onassis could marry her in Greece, and this would be legal there, and she would finally be married to the man she loved. Callas very publicly renounced her American citizenship and legally became a Greek citizen, which she was able to do since both her parents had been born in Greece. She knew that the public considered her the cause of the destruction of Onassis' marriage, with two small children as "collateral damage" (Alexander was 12 and Christina was nine at the time of the divorce).

The directors she worked with (especially Visconti and Zeffirelli), who had helped to make her such a success on the operatic stage, were increasingly being confined to the category of "traitors," because of some minor disagreement with her. She could not tolerate disagreement or criticism. Her constant insecurities about her voice, her acting and her talent

12. Loving Onassis

created a very dependent and insecure woman behind all her public assertions about her dedication to *art*—far above that of any other singer, she argued. She often accused her colleagues of being materialistic and lazy and not willing to work as hard as she did on their roles, which of course offended them (Edwards 228 ff.). Maria's need for attention and emotional support was also driving Onassis away from her. He sensed that his friends did not like being around her—she was too much like a jealous child who had to be the center of attention in any social situation or she became silent and angry. Since, as a child, she felt that she did not get enough attention from her parents, she remained, in many ways, like a needy and envious child.

As Callas' vocal devolution continued, fewer and fewer of the major opera companies were willing to put up with her demands on them. Both the director of La Scala, Antonio Ghiringhelli, and the director of the Met, Rudolf Bing, fired her and dropped her from their roster of singers. Still, some great and important opera companies still wanted her, and she had developed a group of fans who were more in love with her star quality than her actual singing. These super-fans wanted to see and hear her performances because she had become a world superstar. Now she was more of a pop icon, rather than a great opera singer. Norman Lebrecht and several other critics now argued that Maria had a large following among gay men, owing to her larger-than-life persona (Lebrecht 177 ff.).

Walter Legge was telling friends at Angel/EMI Records that Callas' wobble was making him seasick. While he had been one of her biggest fans and arranged for her to record complete operas and recitals for his company, he was getting tired of dealing with her narcissism now that her singing had become so problematical. He felt that her voice should no longer be recorded by Angel/EMI Records, but that company was still making good money on her past recordings. In the early 60s, the company's executives decided to continue recording her—either complete operas or recital discs. She was famous for agreeing to record an opera or recital album for Angel, and then, when the company sent her a contract, she would not sign and return it. Legge would then have to visit her at one of her homes in Italy, with flowers and plants, and beg her to sign the contract she had already verbally agreed to. There was clearly a sadistic part of Maria that enjoyed torturing people who wanted her to perform or record for them (Meneghini 303 ff).

Rudolf Bing recalled in his memoir that his hair turned gray, waiting for her to sign and return contracts for future performances, which she had already agreed to do for the Met. Her prima donna antics had made an enemy of him, especially now that her vocal problems were getting worse. Bing reported that she would agree in his office to sing certain roles in certain operas and on certain dates, and then when the contract arrived at her home in Italy, Maria would suddenly play "hard to get." Endless phone calls and pleading by Bing would prolong the ordeal (Bing 237–50). Callas has complained that the Met never gave her any new productions—so Bing dangled the prospect of a new production of Verdi's *Macbeth* before her, and she agreed with the dates of her performances, and then withdrew at the last minute. She had done the same thing with Antonio Ghiringhelli at La Scala. Passive-aggressive behavior like this made her many enemies in the world of opera, and her behavior in this regard actually got worse as her vocal problems got worse (Stassinopoulos 158 ff.). And yet Maria always saw herself as an innocent victim (and great artist) in these situations.

Ari's children often complained that they rarely saw their father since he was usually on his yacht, sailing the world for both business and pleasure. They sensed that she disliked them, and she did not want them on board *The Christina* while she was on board. When Callas tried to make peace with Ari's children and gave them elaborate gifts, they would not open them—passive-aggressive behavior they probably learned from Callas herself (Kesting 240–60).

Maria was a good sailor and did not get seasick but actually enjoyed when the ride got a bit bumpy. She was, after all, a Pisces, as she told her friends, a person who loved being on water. She loved monopolizing Onassis' attention, and preferred when they were the only passengers onboard the yacht. He had also just bought a Greek Island, Skorpios, and said he would build a house there for just the two of them. But now that Callas so desperately wanted to marry Aristo, she felt him slipping away from her. The harder she clutched his hand, the more she felt him slipping through her fingers.

Maria did not want to perform at the Met, since it was so far from her and Onassis' centers of operation (Monte Carlo, Paris, etc.). She seemed to naturally gravitate to Paris (which, eventually, became her final home). In love with Paris, she eventually lived in an apartment there, in the highly fashionable 16th Arrondissement, at 36 Avenue Georges-Mandel, not far from the Arc de Triomphe. She sang a series of recitals at the Paris Opera, the first of which was televised live all over Europe, and became the most important event of the opera season in Paris. While in Paris, she made a famous recording of *Carmen* with George Pretre, then considered the most important new opera conductor in France. When Pretre talked about working with her on the role of Carmen, he found that she worked differently from most singers: For Callas, the word was primary. She was most concerned with the lyrics she was singing and their dramatic meaning at a given point in an opera. Her work on *Carmen* produced a very successful recording of the complete opera; Pretre was very pleased with it, as was she.

12. Loving Onassis

She was using part of her voice, her lower voice, her mezzo-soprano range. She had not used these lower notes much before, and she was much more comfortable singing these lower notes since her vocal wobble was less evident on lower-pitched notes. Franco Zeffirelli liked this recording so much that he wanted to make a film based on it; he told Callas all she would to do was act the part and lip-synch the singing, since she had already made a wonderful recording of the opera. Callas seemed to agree, and then she changed her mind when the contract from Zeffirelli arrived.

Some voice teachers have argued that Callas was *always* really a mezzo-soprano, as her low notes were her most comfortable and reliable notes. Maybe she should have turned herself into a mezzo-soprano at this point in her career, so she could avoid her high notes where her voice was now so insecure. But could she find a teacher in Paris who could completely retrain her as a mezzo-soprano? Should she go back to Elvira de Hidalgo to be retrained as a mezzo? She did, in fact, contact de Hidalgo, who was now living in Milan, and flew her to Paris so they could both work on her voice, especially her lower range (Edwards 299 ff.). But Callas was used to being a prima donna—and prima donnas were sopranos, not mezzo-sopranos.

Regina Resnick, another singer of Callas' generation, had started as a soprano and then transitioned into the mezzo-soprano *fach* in the middle of her career, when she had difficulty with her upper register. Resnick had great success in her transformation into a mezzo-soprano and singing mezzo roles (Mayer 284 ff). She even had success in the title role in Bizet's *Carmen*. Maria certainly must have considered this option.

Maria continued to escalate her demonization of the man she now considered to be very much her *ex*-husband, Giovanni Battista Meneghini, and now fully considered herself a resident of France. She was now vowing never again to set foot in Italy, a country that had betrayed her. She kept remembering the booing she had received from members of the La Scala audience and concluded that all the people in Milan—and indeed in all of Italy—had been rude to her. After all she had *done* for them. Now Callas considered herself a Parisian woman—*une Parisienne*.

Maria was becoming less thrilled to be Onassis' mistress, and yearned to be his wife. She was at the height of her fame, and the affair with Onassis made her even more famous. During this period, she gave a short television interview in which the journalist asked if it was true that she had renounced her American citizenship. She said that she had, and that she was now a Greek citizen, and according to Greek law, she was not a married woman at all, since she had not been married by a Greek Orthodox priest in a Greek Orthodox Church, and that would mean that she was now free to marry Onassis in Greece. She clearly indicated that she had renounced her American citizenship and assumed Greek citizenship so that she could marry Onassis. But did he want to marry *her*?

Zeffirelli wrote about the difficulty of being around the demanding Maria Callas:

> Tragically, I had not realized that Maria's behavior was a cry for help. I must also admit that I was not blameless. I was having a run of success and could not bear the thought of wasting an evening rehashing the past. Unaware of the seriousness of her condition, I didn't realize how painful for her my refusals were. Her failure to turn up at rehearsals or at my premieres I put down to pique, and, heaven knows, I had enough reason to believe that this must be the case; great performer though she was, Maria was incredibly petty in private. An evening with Maria was an evening talking about Maria: how good she looked, how nice her hair, her dress, how she really must make a comeback, etc., etc., etc. Frankly, it was frequently very boring and only my memories of *La Divina* on stage, when she was transformed by her art, were enough to get me through it" (Zeffirelli 296).

Behind all Maria's need for attention was also the Greek concept of fate. It occurs in ancient Greek literature, especially the tragic plays of Aeschylus, Sophocles and Euripides. In the ancient Greek religion, before Greece became a Christian country, lurked the pre–Christian Greek gods Zeus, Hera and Aphrodite with their powers to control and determine human destiny. Human effort and human resistance were futile in the face of fate and the power of the gods on Mount Olympus, and they had total control of human destiny. Oedipus and Hippolytus tried to avoid their fate, but fate would always prevail in the end. Some contemporary Greeks still believe in this ancient fatalism, as do other people around the world, though fate was not a part of Christian belief. Some Greek philosophers argued that character was destiny, which certainly applied to Maria and her life.

Callas and Onassis believed in this concept of fate, though they both claimed to be Christians. But neither one of them (both of them, nominally members of the Greek Orthodox religion) were church-goers, and they were now seen by their co-religionists as public adulterers. All she seemed to believe in was her own career, and she remained at heart a careerist (Stassinopoulos 27 ff.).

Inevitably, cracks appeared in their perfect idyll. Onassis' infidelities were becoming ever more frequent. He was also discovering there were easier things in life than trying to co-exist in the orbit of a legendarily temperamental, difficult woman such as Maria. In spite of his short stature and somewhat startlingly intense face, he had his pick of any one of dozens of women who'd be happy to be his "silent partner." One woman who was very attracted to Aristo was Princess Lee Radziwill, sister of Jacqueline Kennedy.

12. Loving Onassis

The two sisters had a very troubled relationship and they had always been neurotically competitive with each other, especially on Lee's part, since she felt that Jackie always had the richer and more famous husband. They were both obsessed with money and its power, primarily because of their mother, who was now Mrs. Hugh Auchincloss. She had married Auchincloss after divorcing John "Black Jack" Bouvier (father of Jackie and Lee), due to his alcoholism and financial failures.

By nearly all accounts, Onassis truly did love Maria, in his own fashion. Yes, he loved Maria, and in a way, he always would—but not *only* her, and not for the rest of his life. He was sure he had many more years to enjoy his wealth and his virility—or so he thought. But did he want to spend the last of those years with Maria Callas, the great diva both on and off the stage? That question would answer itself soon enough.

Callas began 1962 with a February 27 concert at Royal Festival Hall in London, conducted by George Pretre. She sang arias from *Don Carlo, Le Cid, Cenerentola, Anna Bolena* and *Macbeth*. In March 1962, she gave a series of concerts in Germany, where she maintained a fiercely loyal following. Her program included arias from *Le Cid, Cenerentola, Carmen* and *Ernani*. Pretre was again her accompanist. She appeared at the Deutsches Museum in Munich on March 12, 1962 and at the Musikhalle in Hamburg on March 16. She sang at the Stadtische Saalbau in Essen on March 19, and in Bonn at the Beethovenhalle on March 23. Each of these German appearances was met with sold-out, wildly cheering and ecstatic crowds (and a packet of mixed reviews).

In April 1962, she learned via the newspapers that her mother had attempted suicide in New York City. Maria was staying in the Dorchester Hotel in London at the time and was warned by the director of the hotel that a large group of journalists and photographers were waiting in the lobby to interview her. She was frantic at the thought of all this bad publicity, and was silently disappointed that her mother's suicide attempt had not succeeded. She avoided the photographers and journalists and tried to reach her ever-reliable godfather in New York, Dr. Lantzounis. She also had to wire him thousands of dollars to pay her mother's large medical bills and to try to hush up the public scandal (Edwards 242 ff.). But she did not fly to New York and did not want to see her mother during this crisis. As always, Evangelia also knew how to create drama.

Maria jetted to the U.S. to perform on May 19, 1962, at a Madison Square Garden concert. It was a gala to celebrate the 45th birthday of President John F. Kennedy, and he was there with close friends, his brother Robert and his elegant wife Jacqueline. Callas sang two arias from *Carmen* with the pianist Charles Wilson, but she was completely upstaged by the performance of Marilyn Monroe, who appeared practically nude (actually in a sheer, spangled, skin-tight dress) to sing "Happy Birthday, Mr. President." Marilyn Monroe, it's been widely rumored, was having a clandestine affair with Kennedy at the time. Callas was upstaged by a woman who could not really sing (Monroe) but was well-paid for her appearance (Edwards 242 ff.).

After taking the summer off to be with Onassis, Callas sang at a concert in London's Royal Opera, Covent Garden, again with Georges Pretre conducting. This concert was broadcast on television as part of the *Golden Hour* series of BBC concerts. Thus ended Callas' performance agenda for 1962.

She started 1963 with a concert in Germany (again with Pretre), singing *Norma, Nabucco, La Boheme, Madama Butterfly* and *Gianni Schicchi* arias. She sang this concert at the Deutsche Oper in Berlin on May 17 and then repeated this concert at the Rheinhalle in Dusseldorf later that month.

On June 5, 1963, Maria sang a concert of opera arias at the Théâtre des Champs-Elysées with Pretre accompanying her. She sang arias from *Semiramide, Cenerentola, Werther, Manon, Nabucco, La Boheme, Madama Butterfly* and *Gianni Schicchi*. Clearly, she was singing more French arias to please her Parisian audiences. Her French audiences responded with standing ovations to each of her performances. In the fall of 1963, she got a letter from her godfather, Dr. Lantzounis, telling her that Evangelia had recovered from her suicide attempt. At this time, Maria wrote to a friend in New York that she had to bear two crosses in her life, her insane mother and her greedy husband who had stolen most of her money. However, she still had her Aristo and his yacht.

In 1964, she performed even less. She was scheduled to sing six performances of *Tosca* at Covent Garden. Seemingly back in her good graces, Franco Zeffirelli directed the production. Tito Gobbi sang Scarpia with a simmering ferocity. Act II of one of these performances was televised on BBC from the Royal Opera. Callas cancelled some of her Tosca performances (replaced by Marie Collier) but sang most of them (Lebrecht 255 ff.).

She sang *Norma* at the Paris Opera with Charles Craig or Franco Corelli as Pollione, Fiorenza Cossotto as Adalgisa, and Ivo Vinco as Oroveso. Her conductor for these performances was Pretre. She was back under the guiding hand of director Zeffirelli. These performances were Callas' only performances in 1964. She was now finding the very demanding role of Norma too much for her current stamina and vocal resources, though she was still receiving regular, near-hysterical standing ovations.

She was a bit busier in 1965, singing *Tosca* at the Paris Opera, which was housed at the legendary opera house, Palais Garnier (it was becoming her favorite venue). This was the production that Zeffirelli had produced

12. Loving Onassis

for Covent Garden, now moved across the English Channel to Paris. There were nine performances of this *Tosca*. Either Franco Corelli or Renato Cioni sang Cavaradossi, and Tito Gobbi again sang Scarpia. Pretre or Nicola Rescigno conducted these performances.

Callas flew to New York for two performances of *Tosca* at the Met on March 19 and 25, 1965. Titto Gobbi sang Scarpia and either Richard Tucker or Franco Corelli sang Cavaradossi. Fausto Cleva conducted. These turned out to be her final Metropolitan Opera performances. Bing tried to lure her back with offers like the soprano role in Poulenc's *La Voix Humaine*; Callas promised Bing she would study the score, but ultimately rejected the idea (Bing, *5000 Nights*, 241–60). She appeared at the Paris Opera for her final five performances of *Norma* in May 1965. The final performance (May 29) did not include the last scene because Callas became too ill to continue.

Callas was back in London on July 5, 1965, for one performance of *Tosca* with Renato Cioni as Cavaradossi and Tito Gobbi as Scarpia, again in Zeffirelli's hugely popular production. She was scheduled to sing four other performances of her Tosca but performed only one very uneven performance (Lebrecht 255–57).

Maria did not perform at all in 1966, 1967, 1968 or 1969. She was clearly approaching the end of her singing career.

13

Enter Jacqueline Kennedy

When Maria saw the TV coverage of the November 22, 1963, assassination of President John Kennedy in Dallas, she could never have imagined that this horrible event would affect her life in any way. She sang at his 45th birthday party at Madison Square Garden the previous spring, and he and his wife seemed so young and so happy and successful. Frank Sinatra produced, performed and emceed the gargantuan "cavalcade of stars" who also performed that night—but so overwhelmingly "cheeky" was Monroe's soft-porn rendition of "Happy Birthday" that history would have us think that Monroe was the sole performer that night. To study the photos is to see two mega-watt superstars at their zeniths. They don't really interact in the photos. Their smiles seem particularly practiced in most of them, and each woman seems to be sort of levitating in her own world. To consider Callas' own later connection to the Kennedys, an entirely separate layer of fascination is added, especially in light of the fact that Monroe was found dead, under mysterious circumstances, less than three months after this meeting of two of the most glamorous women in the world.

Maria had sung in Dallas several times in the last few years. In fact, it was one of her most lucrative "bread-and-butter gigs" (as they are called by musicians: high-paying engagements in the provinces). Onassis told her he was a friend of the Kennedys, so he flew out to Washington, D.C., to offer his condolences, and remained there for several weeks with the Kennedy family. Maria was aware that he had had a friendship with Jacqueline Kennedy's sister, Princess Lee Radziwill, and her husband. Maria also suspected that Aristo had had an affair with Lee Radziwill—and she was right. Maria offered to go with him to Washington and help to comfort Kennedy's widow, but Aristotle told her he did not think this was a good idea and he went alone. He called Maria several times from Washington and New York, telling her how distraught the Kennedys; he said that Jacqueline, along with her two small children, was especially frantic, and he felt he had to try to help her. She seemed like a person traumatized by a war, having witnessed the murder of her husband sitting next to her in the backseat of a car. His blood and brain matter were on her dress when she left that car.

The Kennedy assassination was one of the single most traumatic events in U.S. history. He and Jackie were viewed as the glamorous young couple who would take America into a new Camelot. They were young, highly educated and from two of the wealthiest and most distinguished families in the East: "the Harvards," as Vice-President Lyndon Johnson called them. Kennedy was, of course, from the famous Kennedy family and he was injured during World War II but survived and soon became a Massachusetts Senator. His older brother Joseph had been a famously heroic World War II pilot; he died in Europe in 1944, in a spectacular plane crash. His sister Kathleen died in a plane crash in England in 1948.

Jacqueline Bouvier (born in 1929) was from a wealthy family from Hammersmith Farm in Newport, Rhode Island. (It is considered one of the marquis Gilded Age mansions, in one of the most optimal locations. It is now open to slack-jawed tourists.). She also had family on Long Island and in New York City, where her father John "Black Jack" Bouvier lived after his divorce from his wife Janet. Life for the young Jacqueline Bouvier was something not dissimilar to a Jane Austen novel, where a young woman was trained to be on the lookout for a rich man to marry, since she could not make money herself, and wealth and money were all. As Austen wrote in the famous opening line of *Pride and Prejudice*, "It is a truth universally acknowledged that a young man in possession of a fortune must be in need of a wife." Jacqueline's mother Janet reflected that mentality and passed it on to Jacqueline and Lee. She warned them to wed carefully, to look out for a very rich man who could provide them with financial security and luxury as well. Both girls, like their mother, wanted a luxurious lifestyle and not middle-class respectability, or worse, genteel poverty (Taraborelli 20–50). In America in the '40s and '50s, there were not many other options for fairly wealthy young women—this was before the women's liberation movement. Neither daughter saw herself as a career woman; they wanted to be the pampered wives of rich, preferably very rich, men. These attitudes were very typical of the period.

"Good fortune" led to her crossing paths with John Fitzgerald Kennedy. After a very public whirlwind romance, they married at Hammersmith in 1953. By nearly all accounts, it truly was a love match—at least at first. The proverbial "elephant in the room" with their marriage was his shameless womanizing. There were times in their marriage when divorce was discussed. However, politician Kennedy was canny enough to know that in that era, divorce would torpedo his presidential ambitions. Jacqueline did not want to divorce him either, even though she knew about his numerous infidelities, as she had grown accustomed to the perquisites of being a Senator's wife (Leaming 75 ff.). They were also both Roman Catholics, at a time when religion was very important in America. Kennedy's father, Joseph Kennedy, had established the family's wealth and went on to be President Franklin Roosevelt's choice to be the American ambassador to Great Britain in the 1930s—quite an accomplishment for someone from a poor Irish immigrant background. Joseph Kennedy harbored a dream that one of his sons would one day become the country's first Catholic president. Like his father, John Kennedy had posed as a devout Roman Catholic, which had worked well for his political campaigns in Massachusetts. It also added to his glamour and allure at the time—though we now know that his Catholicism was more of a cynical political tool that he could brandish when needed. His sexual infidelities and his irregular attendance at Sunday masses certainly contradicted his public image as a faithful Catholic, despite his appearances with local bishops and cardinals in the upper hierarchy of the church. There were rumors that Joseph Kennedy offered Jackie one million dollar to remain married to his philandering son. After all, Joseph Kennedy, Sr., had had a notorious affair with Hollywood movie star Gloria Swanson; his wife never divorced him, in spite of the fact that he and Swanson carried on their affair over many years. Jacqueline's mother had divorced her first husband, Jack Bouvier, for doing the same kind of thing, and also for squandering nearly all of his inheritance during the Great Depression. Her marriage to Hugh Auchincloss was much happier and much more stable—and he was much wealthier than her first husband (Leaming 70–90).

When Jacqueline was a child, she witnessed the outcome of the marriage of her parents. It gradually dawned on her as a young teenager that her father was not faithful to her mother, though her mother had put up with it. Jackie also began to realize that her father Bouvier was an alcoholic and that women had to put up with things, especially if they wanted to be part of society's wealthy upper crust (Leaming 50–70). The most important factors in her life, behind her coquettish façade, were the acquisition of money and social prominence. She was trained by her mother to accept the societal norm that a woman had to endure affronts in marriage. Jacqueline was only 11 when her parents divorced. She would not inherit a great deal of wealth when her father died, so she soon realized that she would have to marry someone quite rich if she wanted to maintain the lovely affluent lifestyle she was raised in. Jacqueline was particularly competitive with her sister Caroline (who was called "Lee" at home), who later married well and became known as Princess Lee Radziwill, a name she kept even after her marriage to Prince Stanisław Radziwill ended in divorce. She actually insisted on being called Princess Lee, seemingly unaware of, or unconcerned about, the pomposity of it. Her husband was a distant relation of the Radziwills, the royal family in Poland until deposed in the 17th century. Her pretentious behavior earned her a parody by Gilda Radner on TV's *Saturday Night Live*. Princess Lee also acted in a TV drama during this time, a condensed version of the classic 1944 noir classic, *Laura*, and got terrible reviews. The Bouvier family also had some embarrassing cousins on Long Island in a decrepit Hamptons mansion called Grey Gardens. *Grey Gardens* eventually became a documentary film about the lunatic Long Island branch of the Bouvier-Kennedy family. It was turned into a very successful Broadway musical with the same title (Kashner 205–31).

When Jacqueline married John Kennedy in 1953 at the Auchincloss family mansion in Newport, he appeared to be a prime choice as far as husband material went. The first son of a very wealthy and prominent Irish-American family, he had important political connections and presidential aspirations. Marrying such a son could propel Jacqueline into the White House, as indeed it did (Leaming 50–80).

With Kennedy's murder in 1963, he became a martyred American saint and Jacqueline became the world's most famous widow. The Kennedys were undoubtedly aware of Aristotle Onassis, owing to his "friendship" with Princess Lee. Now, however, with Jacqueline's husband dead, Jacqueline dedicated her life to raising her two children, Caroline and John Jr., and surviving in the sometimes hostile environment of the large Kennedy family in New York, Boston and the family's summer compound in Hyannis Port, Massachusetts. She remained very fond of Robert Kennedy, her husband's brother, and she greatly admired civil rights leader Martin Luther King. His assassination in Memphis in 1968 triggered all the horrible memories Jacqueline had of her own husband's assassination five years earlier. Jacqueline attended King's funeral at the request of his wife Coretta. Two months later, on June 6, 1968, Robert Kennedy was assassinated in Los Angeles.

The buffer of anonymity that New York City usually grants upon celebrities did not apply to Mrs. Kennedy, and a pack of paparazzi tended to shadow and record her every public move. The flashing bulbs of photographers always reminded her of Dallas in 1963. She sued photographer Ron Galella in 1969 for stalking her and making her afraid to leave her apartment at 1040 Fifth Avenue, on Manhattan's very fashionable Upper East Side (Leaming 260–91).

One of the first people to comfort Jacqueline in the immediate aftermath of the murder of her husband was Aristotle Onassis, who flew to Washington to be with her and her family. He had business connections in America and, in fact, had had legal problems over his American shipping enterprises. Having a friend in the White House was always a valuable asset for a businessman, especially a billionaire like Onassis.

Jacqueline proclaimed that her sole duty now was to raise her children. As the years went on, she began to see various men more seriously and with thoughts of marriage, but both she and her sister had been brought up to marry for money and status first, not for love.

When Robert Kennedy was assassinated in 1968 while running for president, she became repelled by anything American, a country she began to see as dominated by political lunatics and the easy availability of guns, thanks to the powerful gun lobby. Who would be the next victim? Ted Kennedy, the only surviving son of the Kennedy family? Or her and her children? Now living on Fifth Avenue across from Central Park and near the Metropolitan Museum of Art, she was hounded by the paparazzi. If she was being hounded by the pests from the tabloid press, who else was hounding her? Perhaps some lunatic eager to kill her and her children to get the same press coverage Lee Harvey Oswald had received. She became increasingly afraid to live in America and tired of being hounded by photographers. America had become a frightening country in which to raise young children.

One of the men Jacqueline dated during this period was Lord Harlech (David Ormsby-Gore); one of her late husband's closest friends, he had been the British ambassador to the U.S. Jacqueline met David in Cambodia and loved traveling with him to exotic places. He was a wonderful tour guide, a kind man, and had some money. He proposed to her several times. A number of her letters to him was put on the auction block by his grandson, and in one of them she wrote, "If I ever can find some healing and some comfort—it has to be with somebody who is not part of all my world of past and pain. I can find that now—if the world will let us" (*New York Times*, "Jackie Kennedy's Letters to the Man She Told No," February 9, 2017, pp. 1, 8). She felt that she had to make a break from her past and from friends who had connections with her first husband, and that included Lord Harlech. Why didn't she marry Lord Harlech, an English aristocrat? Most probably, he did not have enough money for her preferred lifestyle, despite his title.

Lord Harlech wrote to Jacqueline after her marriage to Onassis:

> All the pathetic plans I had brought with me for visits to Cyrenaica, holidays near one another and a whole variety of solutions to our marriage problems, including one for a secret marriage this summer—plans which I saw us eagerly discussing, calmly and with complete frankness as we did at the Cape and in Cambodia for the next wonderful ten days—all had become irrelevant trash to be thrown away within a few hours of my landing in New York. ... As for your photograph I weep when I look at it. Why do such agonizing things have to happen? Where was the need for it?

The marriage of Jacqueline Bouvier Kennedy and Aristotle Socrates Onassis occurred on his island of Skorpios, on October 20, 1968. It

13. Enter Jacqueline Kennedy

Aristotle and Jacqueline Onassis in Teheran, Iran, not long after their wedding at Skorpios.

became an international event, though Jacqueline tried to keep it secret. Onassis had bought his Greek island several years before and had a lovely house built on it. The island was beautifully landscaped—at the time, he said the house was for Maria Callas. The paparazzi found out about his marriage to Jacqueline and were there in droves. Aristotle himself may have tipped them off, since he wanted to see himself and Jacqueline, the most desirable and classiest widow in the world, on the front pages of all the newspapers, and on all the television news shows. He agreed with Maria Callas that there was no such thing as bad publicity. Their marriage pictures were soon seen in newspapers and on TV, to Ari's delight. Onassis offered her great wealth and social stability after all the turmoil of her years in the Kennedy orbit. Onassis also owned a house in Monaco, one of her favorite spots in southern France, as well as an apartment in Paris, her favorite city in Europe.

Onassis had a lot to offer Jacqueline Kennedy, including wealth and social prominence. Jackie's son John Jr. developed a close relationship with Onassis, who liked the little boy. However, the two children were not fluent in either Greek or French, and they missed their aunts and uncles (especially Uncle Teddy) and all their cousins.

Jackie's marriage to Onassis soon turned unpleasant. He liked living

Jacqueline Kennedy Onassis seemed to step into Maria's role as "hostess" aboard *The Christina* with ease. She is seen here with her new husband, Aristotle Onassis, on the Isle of Capri in 1969. The others in the photo are unidentified.

on his yacht and moving around the Mediterranean, stopping at any port where he had business or personal interests, but she was concerned about her children and their nannies and schools. Neither Jacqueline nor her two children wanted to live on a boat, even a very luxurious one. Aristotle wanted her to be his wife on his floating mansion, but Jacqueline would get seasick on these voyages and only really enjoyed herself when they came into a port where she could shop. She especially liked shopping in Monte Carlo, the French Riviera and Paris. She loved to shop in small boutiques for clothes or to decorate or redecorate their gorgeous houses with authentic antiques (Kashner 244 ff.).

"Ari and Jackie O," as they were quickly dubbed by the world tabloids. They remained on the front pages of the "scandal press" for decades, even long after his death.

Jacqueline was soon making her new husband angry with her spending binges. She loved going to the boutiques in Paris and spending thousands of dollars on clothes and gifts for her husband and children and even her stepchildren Christina and Alexander. But Aristotle wanted her with him, and being sexually available to him. She sensed a lot of hostility from Alexander and Christina, both of whom seemed to dislike their new stepmother even more than they disliked Maria Callas. Jackie knew that Christina called her "the black widow spider" behind her back.

Maria was certainly traumatized by the 1968 marriage of Onassis and Jacqueline. Aristo had given her no warning that he was going to leave her and marry Jacqueline. On the day of the marriage, Maria commented to a TV interviewer, "I wish them both every happiness, but only one of them deserves it." This enigmatic answer was broadcast around the world and caused much comment. Maria felt nothing but betrayal. Or did Callas feel that Jacqueline had seduced her lover, Ari?

Within one year of his second marriage, Ari was back in Paris, courting Maria, and she eventually welcomed him back into her life and her bed. Certainly the marriage caused Maria much anger and depression since she so desperately wanted to marry Aristo herself. She visited many of

Maria, still looking radiantly chic at 45 in 1968, with *Vogue* journalist Sandy Bertrand.

her friends at the time, expressing her anger at being betrayed by Onassis. During this time, she often quoted from one of her favorite roles and favorite arias, Tosca's "Vissi d'arte." As Tosca sings, "I have lived for art and for love and never done any harm to anyone." The aria is a moving one, sung by a woman being threatened by a sadistic villain, Baron Scarpia. But the aria can also be seen as the thoughts of a narcissistic soprano (and Puccini knew many of them). She presents herself as a perfect person who lives only for art and love and has no faults and does not deserve Scarpia's terrible treatment of her. In one way, the aria is about a narcissistic diva, but in another way it questions the suffering of the innocent in the hands of an indifferent God. This is certainly one of the great Puccini arias, and in it, he questions the very existence of God.

In Callas' case, she was not a perfect person or a totally innocent victim. While she bewailed her fate of being dropped by Onassis, she herself had just as unceremoniously dumped Meneghini. At the time of Onassis' marriage to Jacqueline, Callas told friends that he had forced her to have an abortion of their child. She also told friends that she had had a son by Onassis but he had died within a few days. Maria did all she could to demonize Onassis, just as she demonized Meneghini after she left him. People were, for her, either angels or devils—nothing in between—and most of the people she knew began (in her mind) as angels—though all eventually became devils. She saw herself as quite perfect and really a singing angel.

The sad fact is that Maria was not deluded about her vocal decline, most especially, her now *very* prominent "wobble." Still, she felt that she could continue to have a career and to once again be the greatest *prima donna assoluta* in opera.

14

Vocal Problems: "The Wobble"

In the wake of her sudden, unexpected "dismissal" by Onassis, Maria was forced to face the fact that she was now alone, and she now had to face a reckoning of what she had left of her life. As had been the case throughout her life, she turned to her singing. Elvira de Hidalgo had long advised her most famous student: Don't overburden your vocal cords. They are very delicate and they will not last forever. As the Austrian soprano Leonie Rysanek said, "…a voice is like a wurst, a sausage, and there are only so many slices in it."

Tullio Serfin had convinced Maria that she could sing Elvira in Bellini's *I Puritani* and then, five days later, she could sing Brünnhilde in *Die Walküre*. Such a feat got her international press attention, but she had not been trained to sing these very difficult Wagnerian roles. Serafin also wanted her to do roles like Turandot, Leonora in *Il Trovatore* and Tosca—and once again Callas knew that her voice teacher had been quietly appalled at her "over-reach" with these various styles of soprano singing. Callas was trying to develop a career and she needed all the attention and all the work she could get.

Callas had always possessed an unusually large, dramatic voice, but with problems all along—problems that had considerably advanced with age. Her three vocal registers had never moved particularly smoothly from head voice to chest voice. Her lowest notes were exciting, but they seemed to come from a different voice altogether, since the timbre of those low notes was not the same at the rest of her voice. She could not move smoothly through the tricky *passaggio* from one vocal register to another. She could not maintain a consistent vocal tone through her entire voice, and her highest notes could sometimes wobble out of control. Later in her career, her high notes were no longer reliable. As she got older, her voice lost some of its volume and vocal quality.

Some of her Italian detractors called her *la caprina*, "the little goat,"

14. Vocal Problems: "The Wobble"

because of that animal's famous wobbling bleat. Numerous fans and critics considered her a kind of borderline soprano, who had an impressive bottom voice and could sing mezzo-soprano roles as well—and she was also a borderline soprano in the sense that she could sing both coloratura roles and dramatic soprano roles. But could she really do anything vocally without permanently damaging her voice?

When Onassis wed Jacqueline Kennedy, Maria was 45 years old—which is "mature" for a female opera singer, though many prominent examples of other singers who somehow maintained their vocal resources well beyond that age. Some vocal coaches argue that once a wobble is heard in a voice, there is really no way to get rid of it. The singer must learn how to still sing effectively, in spite of a wobble, by avoiding certain notes, especially high notes, which can amplify the wobble. An occasional wobble is sometimes forgivable, but a constant wobble on the same notes annoys audiences since it indicates a singer's inability to control his or her voice—not a good thing in a professional opera singer. Some singers have had major careers despite a wobble—Dame Gwyneth Jones and Anja Silja, to name two (Macy 240 ff.). Maria's wobble was not heard in all of her performances; some nights she was blessedly free of this vocal imperfection. But it was appearing more frequently in her performances in the early '60s and beyond. It was also heard on her recordings, since the recording engineers could not eliminate it with any of their clever editing. There were also surgical techniques to attempt to treat a wobble, but these came with terrible risk, leaving the singer unable to sing or even speak.

Some critics have argued that she was really a mezzo-soprano, since her lower notes were so impressive—and that she should only be singing mezzo-soprano roles; that the basic color and timbre of her voice was most comfortable in the mezzo range. Yet for years, she was heralded for her clarion-like high notes. As she began to age, her highest notes became more unreliable, and at some performances, she spectacularly cracked on some of her high notes. She had been booed after a La Scala performance, as a result of missing those high notes, and she was traumatized by this incident. Callas blamed the rudeness of the Milanese, but other audiences noticed this problem as well (Edwards 245–50).

Callas could not have been so self-unaware as to ignore or deny all these factors, but she did not want to give up on her professional career, since her ego needed all the spotlights and attention she could get. Most singers adjust to the realities of time, and the limited time of any singer's career, but this was very difficult for Maria, to realize that the gift of vocal ability, like physical beauty, was only a transitory gift. She was also surrounded by people who were telling her she was singing better than ever. Such flattering friends and conductors knew they were telling her what she wanted to hear. The tenor Giuseppe Di Stefano assured her that she was not in vocal decline, she was still the greatest soprano alive, and that she should continue singing professionally. He felt that as she got older, she lost her confidence in her ability to sing. Since she herself was a perfectionist, she heard all the vocal flaws that were appearing in her singing and she winced at them. She did not allow most of her taped performances to become recordings because of the flaws she could hear. Naturally, all singers have good days and bad days; in addition, as she aged, Maria began to sing more carefully while at the beginning of her career she was always famous for her fearlessness and apparent effortless and abandon when she sang.

Did her great weight loss cause her these problems? That seems to be the accepted "common wisdom" amongst opera fanatics, seeking a singular reason for her seemingly rapid vocal decline—though that theory seems to be debunked, merely by listening to many of her greatest recordings, which were made well after her chrysalis-like transformation into a slim, glamorous fashion plate. Could menopause have been partially to blame for her vocal problems? Different experts have different theories. As long as she had had Meneghini to advise her and encourage her, she could control her fears of singing in public, but now Maria had no husband to help and protect her.

During the mid–1960s, when she was developing these vocal problems, she was also developing legal problems. One of Onassis' oldest friends, Panaghis Vergottis, was not only in the shipping business but also a great fan of opera. When Vergottis and Onassis were joining in a partnership to buy a new ship, Onassis suggested including Maria in the deal and making her part owner of the ship. Maria added some money and the three celebrated being partners in the ownership of an oil tanker with some champagne. They signed the partnership in 1964, but within three years they were all in litigation. Maria felt that she had been fleeced by Vergottis, and he felt that Maria and Aristotle had fleeced *him*. By the time the conflict was settled in a British court five years later, all three had become enemies (Edwards 270 ff.).

Callas was becoming increasingly paranoid. In one of her conversations with music critic John Ardoin, she asserted that every La Scala opera house employee, from the director to the ushers, wanted her to fail with the audience (Ardoin 50–80). How could she believe this? How could she have felt she made so many enemies in the opera house's staff? Could every employee backstage and in front of the stage have been hoping for her failure in her roles? She did have a knack for making enemies, but could *an entire company* be wishing for her to flop during a performance?

Here, Callas makes an interesting contrast with Joan Sutherland. In

14. Vocal Problems: "The Wobble"

her autobiography, she comments about 1951 as her beginning year at the Royal Opera, Covent Garden:

> The great day of initiation arrived and five days later I had my first production call in the foyer with Christopher West and the young conductor, John Pritchard. This was the beginning of a long association with John, and I think Christopher (who was the Resident Producer with the Company) immediately wanted to help me as much as his busy schedule permitted. I found all the other members of the Company very helpful and there was always a good deal of fun at rehearsals, as well as the serious business of the day. I cannot say that I have ever worked with a spiteful or unkind colleague in all my forty-odd years, except for one or two conductors. One had always read of jealousies and rivalries and I expected to find this at "the Garden." But the friendly acceptance of myself and the encouragement I was given by them all, throughout the House, was very heartwarming and a great lesson for me in the future, when I began to meet the younger generation of singers who seemed to hold me in such awe" (Sutherland 26).

Sutherland's experience with colleagues was very different from Callas'—especially now that Callas was approaching the end of her career.

Other friends suggested other things Maria could do if she felt that she could no longer sing. Some former Met stars, like Rosa Ponselle and Lauritz Melchior, had moved to Hollywood and made some films, some very successful. Melchior even appeared in 1947 in a film with Esther Williams called *This Time for Keeps*, though he did not swim with her. Clearly, retirement is a trauma for most singers, but it did not have to become a tragedy. Given Callas' background as a child during World War II, and her tremendous need for attention, she often felt that her opera career was all she had—especially now that she no longer had a husband, or even a "significant other." So she especially dreaded the end of that career which was so central to her sense of self-worth. One of Callas' options, since she was so famous as an actress, was for her to act on stage or on film and avoid having to sing at all. Her acting on stage remained one of her most exciting assets as an opera performer.

In what Maria must have considered some kind of divine intervention, Italian director Pier Paolo Pasolini approached her with a tantalizing proposal. He was making a film of an ancient Greek play, Euripides' *Medea*, and he wanted her to play Medea—*not* singing the operatic role in the opera by Cherubini, but appearing as a speaking character. This she eventually did in 1969. The film was not really a success but it's still worth seeing for Maria Callas fans, and her firebrand acting and fierce presence remain impressive. Pasolini wanted her to wear exotic, primitive costumes and to act only with her face and her body. He did not give her many lines to speak since he found her face and her gestures and body movements so expressive. He also found her spoken Italian highly accented since she was not a native speaker of Italian. Pasolini was undoubtedly also aware that her presence in the film would generate much-needed publicity for the project (Siciliano 332 ff.). Pasolini was not an opera fan, but he knew that Callas had become known as a remarkable actress on the opera stage. Could she act in film, he wondered? He became convinced that under his direction, she could. Callas, of course, became very excited by the prospect of making her film acting debut, hoping that this would be the first of many films. She met Pasolini and liked both him and his *Medea* project, and agreed to make the film.

It's possible that Callas was simply getting tired of singing. To sing professionally, she had to practice every day to keep her vocal muscles and breathing muscles toned. Her ex-husband (and now enemy) Meneghini had always encouraged her to practice her scales, to keep her voice under control, but after she left him, there was no one to prod her to do so. Ari, on the other hand, had urged her to retire from professional singing. She was a very wealthy woman by the end of the '50s, so maybe she felt at times that she had had enough of the difficult and disciplined life of a professional singer (Zeffirelli 159–99).

Studio portrait of Maria Callas in Pier Paolo Pasolini's Italian-French-West German film *Medea* (1969).

On the other hand, she loved performing in opera, despite all the attendant anxiety involved; it had essentially been her entire identity for the past 25 years. She loved the perquisites of being the *prima donna assoluta* of a major opera company. Agents and managers were still approaching her with proposals and offering her contracts. Perhaps she was also thinking that she really should retire now, before she was booed off the stage.

Another theory, presented by Italian physician Mario Giacovazzo (and critics Franco Fussi and Nico Paolillo), argued that toward the end of her singing career,

14. Vocal Problems: "The Wobble"

Maria Callas in the film *Medea*. Though considered something of a *succès d'estime*, it was not a box office favorite and did little to advance Maria's dreams of becoming a film star.

Callas developed dermatomyositis, a disease that causes a degeneration of all the muscles in the body, including the vocal muscles. It would cause a worsening of her vocal wobble. Dr. Giacovazzo said that he examined her and diagnosed this disease in 1975, two years before her death. He also said that this disease had started in Maria years earlier. Perhaps this very grim diagnosis added to the depression she was experiencing in the last years of her life. Facing a future in which all the muscles in her body were deteriorating must have been very frightening. This doctor claimed that he also told her that the disease could have been in her muscles five years before it could be diagnosed (Aversano 250–350). In 1979, a similar fate befell Elinor Ross, a very promising new dramatic soprano at the Met. She was singing Aïda there when suddenly she lost control of her facial muscles. Her doctor informed her that she had come down with Bell's palsy, a terrible affliction that causes the paralysis of the facial muscles. It sometimes goes away as quickly as it had appeared; in other cases, it can become chronic and incurable.

In spite of her ignominious, mortifying abandonment by Onassis, Callas yearned to be reunited with him. She stopped singing completely between 1969 and 1971—in part because of her grief over losing him. Jacqueline was spending more and more time in New York City to be with her two children and to supervise their education. In a rare show of self-abasement, Callas stepped forward to fill the void.

Callas was living in her exquisite apartment in Paris; why not just enjoy living in the most beautiful and cosmopolitan city in the world and have some fun? Because she was not able to remain content with that. She was growing increasingly isolated as she dropped one friend after another for alleged slights. By this point in her life, in her middle forties, she could not tolerate any disagreement with her point of view. She could have learned from the people around her, but her narcissism made that impossible. She was isolating herself, and what she seemed to enjoy most was soaking in her tub in her beautiful marble bathroom, listening only to her own recordings. Diva Regine Crespin said at the time, "Callas should listen to other singers' recordings," as most other singers did, and not just to her own. But Callas' increasing narcissism made her want to be alone, want to listen only to her own voice in her best recordings. Narcissism personified. She wore out her recordings and had to ask Angel Records for new copies. She claimed that she loved only her two French poodles.

Callas continued to pin her hopes on Onassis, that he would one day return to her and resume their affair and marry her at last. Could this happen? She had done everything she could to please him, but he had left her and married Jacqueline Kennedy—how could she forgive that? Onassis did eventually return to Maria, but he certainly did not want to marry her.

Franco Zeffirelli suggested a film version of *La Traviata*, based on her recording of the role; or, alternately, a film version of her *Carmen*, which she had also recorded; all she would have to do was act since she had already made a complete recording of the opera. All she had to do was lip sync and physically reenact a role she was already well-familiar with. Zeffirelli begged her to do this and tried to line up the backers and the money

14. Vocal Problems: "The Wobble"

for this project. In the initial stages, Maria enthusiastically agreed, before ultimately rejecting the idea. She gave Zeffirelli starter money for this project, but then inscrutably backed out. When she demanded her money back, Zeffirelli reminded her that he had spent the money lining up equipment and film locations. Callas was enraged. So, of course, she stopped talking to him. He eventually filmed *La Traviata* with Teresa Stratas, who was also having vocal problems and personal problems, but Zeffirelli's film of Verdi's *La Traviata* was made and is still very moving and Stratas succeeded in the role in that film (Zeffirelli 211 ff.). (Zeffirelli later directed a film called *Callas Forever* with Fanny Ardent, Jeremy Irons and Joan Plowright, an interesting window into the world of the twilight years of Maria's life.)

It was repeatedly suggested that Callas should write a memoir, after which she could tour bookstores and sign copies, basking in the acclaim. But she refused to even consider divulging the painful details of her life's story to *anyone*, least of all the public in general. There were far too many skeletons in her closet to consider seriously a truthful and candid recounting.

As the release date for Pasolini's *Medea* approached, Callas relished the adulation and attention. There was a gala premiere at a film festival in Sicily, followed by a more prominent premiere at the Paris Opera on January 28, 1970. The film got mixed reviews. Callas could tell that, despite her grandiose entrance with Pier Paolo Pasolini at its Paris premiere, that the audience did not really love the film, and was often bored by it. It followed the general plot of the opera but tried to provide more background on the primitive, non–European background of Medea, and it ended with a Wagnerian immolation scene. This was not considered to be one of the greatest of Pasolini's films (Stassinopoulos 300–02).

Pasolini was seen in Italy as a "saint" who loved Marx but hated Italy's Communist party, then the country's second-largest political party. Also, Pasolini's openly homosexual lifestyle made many Italians uneasy. Maria had been very comfortable working with gay men, and some of her most famous directors (people like Luchino Visconti and Franco Zeffirelli) were gay.

With Pasolini's passing went Maria's hopes for a continuing, nurturing relationship with him, continuing to make films together, providing her with her next chapter as a performer. It was not meant to be.

15

The Return of Onassis

With her marriage to Aristotle Onassis, Jacqueline Bouvier Kennedy Onassis toppled from her throne as America's First Lady Emeritus. She was widely reviled and proclaimed a gold-digger and even "anti–American" for marrying this mysterious Greek tycoon. Many Americans saw the marriage as Jacqueline's rejection of America—which, in a way, it was. As outlined in Chapter 13, she had become completely disheartened with America, where in her mind every potential assassin could get a gun and murder public figures—and with no effective gun control laws, unlike most of Europe, where there were (and are) strict gun control laws. Jacqueline had longed to live in Europe, where she felt she and her two children would be safer. She became convinced that with both her husband and brother-in-law assassinated, if "there was an open season on murdering Kennedys," she and her children were prime targets.

Jacqueline had known about Onassis' long affair with Maria Callas, but it gave her little concern. She also knew about his earlier affair with her sister, Princess Lee Radziwill. Ari, as she called him, assured her that his affair with Maria was over and that she had never meant much to him—he did not even like opera, he assured her. As a young man in Buenos Aires, Onassis had had an affair with the soprano Claudia Muzio so he had a weakness for prima donnas—but that was in his distant past. Jacqueline could live in Greece, on Ari's island of Skorpios, could shop in Paris or Monaco, visit London and Italy, and lead a wonderful life there, away from her fishbowl existence in America. Her two children would be raised at boarding schools near them, and they could now spread their wings as "international citizens."

In the beginning of the marriage, Jacqueline and her new husband felt an almost dream-like satisfaction—that they had both gotten what they wanted. Onassis had his own private security force to protect them all. Their photos were often in magazines like *Life* and *Look* and in the tabloids, and they came to expect all the attention, especially Onassis. Now she wanted her privacy so she could enjoy her new husband and her wealthy

15. The Return of Onassis

lifestyle. The flashing bulbs of the international paparazzi traumatized her still since they reminded her of the Kennedy assassination (Leaming 126–50).

But things did not work out as well as Jacqueline had planned. After about two years, she and Ari began to avoid each other. Certainly, the interests of her two children were of paramount importance to her—and both children had made their dislike of European life known to her. They did not want to learn either Greek or French, and they missed their American cousins, relatives and friends. Jacqueline had always liked living in New York, especially the Upper East Side, which is a haven of great museums and great wealth. She had been a millionaire's wife already, but being married to a billionaire sounded even more enticing to her.

By 1970, Ari was getting sick of dealing with Jacqueline, even though he had been married to her only for a few years. He was particularly fond of Jacqueline's son John, and the feeling was mutual (Gillon 101 ff.). By 1971, however, Aristotle was spending less time with his new wife and family and beginning to miss Maria Callas. Within a year of his marriage to Jacqueline, he was making quiet, secretive phone calls to Callas in Paris. In spite of her reputation for volcanic temperament, Callas relented to Onassis' renewed "courting" and allowed Ari back to her bedroom, even though she vowed that she would never do such a thing. Ari was able to woo Maria back by proclaiming that his marriage to Jacqueline had been a terrible mistake. Onassis had come to the conclusion that he had made a costly mistake and wanted out of this foolish marriage. His new "trophy wife" had become, to him, anything but an asset. As her unbridled spending continued unabated, he began to see her as a decided liability. Ari's friend, Helene Rochas, acted as a "go-between" with Ari and Maria, inviting them both to one of her large dinner parties to help engineer a reconciliation (Edwards 292 ff.).

Ari's children clearly did not like Jacqueline Kennedy Onassis, as she now called herself. Alexander thought of her as an American fortune-hunter who was attracted to his father's enormous wealth, and Christina saw her as an Atalanta figure who brought bad luck and death to anyone around her. There was no love lost between the Kennedy children and the Onassis children, either. John Jr. and Caroline missed their former apartment in New York and their summers in New England with their Kennedy relatives and their schools in Manhattan (Leaming 250–60).

Things were clearly getting tense and ugly on Skorpios and on Onassis' yacht. Jacqueline was not that fond of being on board the yacht because that reminded her of Aristo's affair with her sister Lee and also Maria Callas, both of whom loved the yacht. Ari liked the status and glamour of being married to Jacqueline Kennedy more than he liked the reality of her and her family of haughty New Englanders.

In flagrante delicto? A Parisian paparazzo snapped Aristotle Onassis and Maria Callas in a very candid moment together, in the early 1970s—not long after his marriage to Jacqueline unraveled.

15. The Return of Onassis

Onassis was not usually a superstitious man but he was beginning to listen to his daughter Christina, who was insistent that Jacqueline would bring bad luck and death to the family. While the father was famous for boating and yachting around the world, essentially a sailor like Homer's Odysseus, his son Alexander wanted to be a more modern man, become a pilot and fly around the world. Aristotle eventually encouraged the idea by allowing his son to learn to fly with one of the pilots at Olympic Airways. He was taking pride in his son's young adventures, and after all he now owned Olympic Airlines, Greece's national airline.

Maria was happy to have Ari back in her life, though she still considered him a *traditore*, a traitor, for betraying her and marrying Jackie. But no one else had taken his place and she was lonely. She also missed her sex life with Onassis; Ari really liked having sex with her, too, more than having sex with his frosty new wife (Edwards 236 ff.). Maria simply wanted Aristotle back in her life, whatever the terms. Or the cost, as it turned out.

16

Teaching in New York, Directing in Turin

Maria received an unexpected and intriguing offer in 1971: The director of New York's famous Juilliard School, Peter Mennin, implored her to give a series of master classes there. Peter felt that her classes would be beneficial for both the school and for Maria. So she flew to New York City in the fall of 1971, and again in the winter of 1972, to teach these classes, which were very well-attended by both voice students and opera singers, as well as members of the opera-going public in New York. This could have been the beginning of a wonderful and rewarding new career for her. She had tried teaching the year before at the Curtis Institute in Philadelphia, but that experience had not worked out very well. Mennin offered her a suite at the hotel of her choice while she was teaching at this prestigious academy of the arts at Lincoln Center. Maria's master classes sold out soon after they were announced. Juilliard would certainly have loved to have Callas, now a world-famous and iconic figure, on their staff as a voice teacher; just about every music school in the world would have considered her a premium "marquee" name to add to their faculty roster. But could she teach? Would she enjoy teaching? Could she be an effective voice teacher for young music students who wanted opera careers?

She could have also settled on performing smaller, suitably showy roles in opera. Some opera singers, like Hans Hotter (a renowned Wotan) and Astrid Varnay (a legendary Brünnhilde), sang smaller, non-starring roles at the end of their careers, when they could no longer sing the major roles due to their aging voices. But would Maria Callas be willing to consent to this? She did not start her singing career with those small parts, like most other opera singers, and she did not want to end her career that way, either. She was accustomed to being *the prima donna* (the first lady) and wanted to remain so, even as her voice was betraying her in the roles she had become famous for singing.

Maria had a hidden agenda: She trusted Mennin, and she knew the

16. Teaching in New York, Directing in Turin

conservatory had a smaller-sized opera theater with good acoustics. She wanted to sing in it and restart her singing career. She wanted to arrange a private "audition" for Mennin, to assess the current state of her vocal abilities. Mennin promised to do everything to facilitate this secret audition. She sang some arias in the Juilliard theater with a pianist (Alberta Masiello, a coach at the Met) and asked Peter's honest opinion. After listening to a few of the arias she'd prepared, he paused a moment and then said she should now retire from opera singing. He suggested she retire immediately and start teaching at Juilliard. He obviously felt her singing was no longer on a professional level and that she should not ruin her legacy with some calamitous performances or concerts. This enraged her, though with curt politesse, said she would think over his advice. She had implored him to be candid, and he was. And she never spoke to him again (Edwards 298 ff.).

Maria Callas, leading her now-legendary "master classes" at the Juilliard School in New York City in 1971.

Those who were present at Callas' Juilliard master classes insisted that she was consistently supportive and tried not to be intimidating to the students or to the audience. Beautifully made-up and well-coiffed and -attired during those classes, she made many perceptive and supportive comments to the students and the audience. (She had personally chosen the students in advance of the classes.) She had long, polished fingernails and she appeared with understated elegance as the wealthy and socially prominent star that she was.

She sometimes used her own singing voice to illustrate some bel canto techniques, and some members of the audience reported being impressed with the sound of her singing during those lessons, though of course she was only singing fragments from arias. She certainly maintained her distinctive timbre and dramatic use of language, but she also avoided any high notes. Her teaching emphasized the need to study and analyze the musical score to hear what the composer was telling the singer, and she also emphasized coloring the words in the libretto to emphasize the drama in both the language and the music. She kept saying that all a singer had to do was study the score, to know the score, and there the composer tells the singer exactly what he wants.

She also kept saying that a pretty voice was not enough to be a great singer. As the classes continued, it became apparent to many in her audience that what she heard in the score was not what most people heard. She had a unique ability to color her voice in a dramatic way to create a character on stage; most other singers did not have this insight and did not read the same directions in the score. She emphasized the need to vary the sound of each role, to be sure no two roles sounded the same. She also indicated how her acting and her body language helped to create a distinctive character for each of the arias she analyzed. She seemed to do this automatically, even unconsciously. Callas was basically repeating to her Juilliard students what Elvira de Hidalgo had told her about how to approach an operatic role and make it interesting for an audience. Callas also emphasized proper breathing to support the singing voice to the audience. However, she also implied that what she was doing with the score was correct, and any other way was incorrect, though that seemed overly rigid. Surely there was more than one approach and one interpretation of an aria and of a character.

The Callas master classes were audio-recorded and can be found on the Internet. To study them is a window into the mind of a woman who could be kind, considerate and encouraging to new young singers, in spite of her almost feral reputation. She certainly was kinder to them than to her own colleagues. She really sounds positive and encouraging to the Juilliard students. John Ardoin produced a very good written version of Callas' critiques of the arias that the Juilliard students sang for her classes, a book entitled *Callas at Juilliard: The Master Classes* (New York: Knopf, 1987). He wrote in his book, "More than any other singer of this century, Maria Callas (1923–1977) exerted a dominant influence on the Italian operatic repertory and style of performance in our time" (Ardoin xv).

Callas' method of teaching involved hearing a student sing an aria of the student's choosing. Callas then went over the aria with the student, word by word and note by note, suggesting changes in the quality of the singing and the enunciation of the words. She emphasized clarity of diction and making sure that the musical emphases reflected what appeared in the score and the drama of the character singing the aria and the character's particular dramatic situation at that point in the opera. Callas also emphasized knowing who the aria was addressed to—another character on stage?

16. Teaching in New York, Directing in Turin

Or to the audience directly? Callas' suggestions to the singer for improving the performance made sense and seemed quite helpful. She also emphasized the need for proper breathing while singing, to support the notes. Callas sometimes sang some of the notes and words herself. The students indicated that Callas's suggestions helped them (Ardoin, *Callas at Juilliard* 20–50).

Callas' suggestions clarified the complexity and added to the mystery of the operatic voice and operatic careers. Why do some promising singers go on to major careers while most do not make it? What is that ineffable quality that creates an "opera star"? Part of it is just plain luck. There clearly remains much mystery about what it takes and how it happens that a major career develops in opera—or in *any* of the arts. Part of that equation is having the financial support of a benefactor, a patron of the arts—someone who is able to underwrite a young talent at the beginning of their career. Part of it is an innate sense of superior musical ability: sometimes even genius. Another decided asset that is needed to maintain a major career as an opera singer is a kind of single-minded narcissism; an ability to defend one's self in a sometimes brutally competitive realm. But, in the end, being possessed of preternatural vocal and dramatic talent remains the most important component. and those kinds of singers sometimes only come along once or twice in a generation.

Maria was wined and dined while she was in New York—about a month in the fall of 1971, and for a month the following winter. Here she was, back in the town of her birth—yet she had long ago shed any remaining friends or relatives, so she found herself with virtually no one from her "old life" to greet her triumphant return. She was often lonely in her suite at the plush Plaza Hotel. Her generous old godfather and patron, Dr. Lantzounis, who helped her in her youth, used to live there with his wife Sallie, and Callas always saw him while she was in Manhattan. However, he was living in retirement in Greece by the time of her return. With his departure went Maria's final real tie to her past life. At one point during her stay in New York, she phoned her maid in Paris and asked her to ship her favorite poodle to her, since she felt so lonely (Stassinopoulos 310–330).

In retrospect, Callas' vocal decline was somewhat predictable. She had started singing professionally in Athens in 1938—and it was now 34 years later, 1972, when she completed her Juilliard master classes. Love her or hate her, it was undeniable that she had had a spectacularly successful career, always sung at full-tilt. But public adulation is like a drug that some performers cannot resist. American soprano Beverly Sills, for instance, was shrewd about when she retired, so that an audience never heard her sound embarrassing. Callas was not so shrewd.

In the end, Callas' master classes were considered enormous successes, both for her as well as for the Juilliard School. This new role as Juilliard "Meistersinger" should have led to a career as a voice teacher—but it did not. Though the experience was somewhat fulfilling to Callas, she viewed it as a disappointment—one that was hardly as personally fulfilling as her glamorous career before the footlights had been.

Offers for Callas' singing services continued to arrive. Callas was developing a plan to star in a road show series of dual recitals., joined by a "duet tenor" and a pianist rather than an orchestra. This tenor could do some solos so that all the singing would not be completely her responsibility, and a pianist would be much less expensive than trying to tour with an entire orchestra or trying to assemble an entire orchestra in each tour location. Having to pay just three people would make the whole venture economically viable. So that is exactly what she decided to do as the next phase of her career as a singer.

Maria was horrified to learn of a January 1973 plane crash that killed Onassis' 25-year-old son Alexander. While she herself was never particularly fond of the young man, she knew what his death would mean for his father and mother. Onassis and his daughter were totally distraught at Alexander's funeral in Athens, a funeral which Callas did not attend. By all accounts, Onassis was forever darkened by the death of his only son. The death of a child is every parent's worst nightmare, and that very nightmare happened to Aristotle Onassis. All the power and wealth in the world could not help him.

Maria was very sorry for the whole Onassis family and still dreamed of reuniting with Ari and continuing her fantastic career as a prima donna. Sadly, neither dream would come true.

The Torino Opera Company had rebuilt its badly bombed famous old opera house (the Teatro Regio) and was finally reopening it in the spring of 1973, and the company and its director wanted to make an international splash. The company invited Maria to direct the opening production of Verdi's *I Vespri Siciliani* (Stassinopoulos 322 ff.). Callas herself had sung Aïda in Turin in 1948, in the Teatro Lirico (the company's temporary home after the war). Callas had also sung Elena in *I Vespri Siciliani* at both Florence's Teatro Comunale and Milan's Teatro alla Scala in 1950. She told Turin's opera company that she was willing to direct the new production with the proviso that her friend and frequent co-star, Giuseppe Di Stefano, could co-direct. She had never directed an opera performance before, though she certainly knew the opera inside out. Di Stefano liked the idea, and the Turin Opera agreed.

The cast was impressive. It included Raina Kabavanska, a new soprano already becoming famous for her acting ability in opera—more so than for the beauty of her voice. Was she "the new Callas" as some critics were proclaiming her to be? It was certainly a situation ripe with potential volatility,

16. Teaching in New York, Directing in Turin

In 1974 Monaco, a devastated Aristotle Onassis arrives at the funeral of his son Alexander, accompanied by his "in name only" wife, Jacqueline Kennedy Onassis.

owing to Maria's career-long antipathy toward most fellow singers. But rather than resent Kabavanska, Callas decided to try to direct her.

Maria and Di Stefano worked with each of the soloists and briefly with the chorus, but their directorial debut was not a great success. They were especially at a loss when dealing with the chorus, and of course it is the chorus that intrinsically makes an opera different from a play. Callas and Di Stefano had never really given much thought to an opera chorus before. Kabavanska rehearsed with Callas and found much of her advice useful, as she told various interviewers. She went on to have a major opera career, singing all over Europe and at the Met. However, the rest of the cast of soloists refrained from talking about their co-directors to the press—not a good sign. The production itself, which opened on April 10, 1973, was poorly reviewed, and the Callas–Di Stefano co-direction itself also got few favorable notices. This experience became, like her film of *Medea* with Pasolini, just one more dead end. Some might even say it was a failure, and it certainly did not lead to a new career for her as an opera director. Right before the premiere, Callas was feeling desperate and called Franco Zeffirelli to ask for his help. He felt that Callas and Di Stefano were not really fit to be directors (Zeffirelli 269–70). His opinion was that she remained a uniquely great artist but had no real insight into the job of the opera director. Instead of finding directing an opera fulfilling, Maria found is exasperating and vowed to never again direct an opera—a vow that she kept.

In the spring of 1973, Callas returned to her luxurious Parisian *maison* at Rue George Mandel 26, where she was greeted by her two domestic servants, Bruna and Ferrucio, along with her two toy French poodles. Onassis visited her on occasion and even shared her bed there, though he made clear that though his marriage to Jacqueline was "in name only," he did not intend to divorce her and marry Maria. He remained consumed by the terrible loss of his son Alexander. Maria had to content herself with being his "primary mistress," which she both enjoyed and bitterly resented.

Onassis' health rapidly declined in the aftermath of Alexander's death and his stays at the American Hospital in Paris grew lengthier, with an increasing battery of ailments. He consulted with the ruthless, reptilian American lawyer, Roy Cohn, about divorcing Jacqueline. In the end, though, he never did pursue this option, in spite of Cohn's advice on how to get out of his marriage without being fleeced. (After being disbarred for his criminally corrupt activities, Cohn died of AIDS on August 2, 1986. Some 40 years later, his name returned to the news when it was revealed that he had been the key mentor to a protégé, one Donald Trump.)

Alexander's death would continue to haunt his father, his mother and his sister—and his de facto "stepmother," Maria Callas. His demise acted almost as a harbinger of tragedies to come in the lives of Callas and Onassis—as if scripted by Sophocles himself, in one of his "Greek tragedies." Maria had not enjoyed teaching at the Juilliard School in New York, and she felt she had failed as a director of *I Vespri Siciliani* in Turin. But she somehow convinced herself: She could still sing.

17

The Final Tour with Di Stefano

Maria Callas and Giuseppe Di Stefano proceeded with their plans for a 1973 recital tour that would circle the globe. Maria was living alone in Paris, yearning for Aristotle Onassis, a very sick and grieving man who did not want to see her very often. Maria's father George had died the year previously, but she did not attend his funeral, nor did she ever visit him while he was dying. Maria and Giuseppe had had a brief affair, but Giuseppe was now a happily married man, and he was deeply worried about his daughter Luisa, who was dying from a type of brain cancer (Edwards 299 ff.).

Aristotle Onassis never did get over the death of his son, and never came to terms with the guilt he felt over his shortcomings as a father. He had been a hard and demanding father to his children, especially to his son, not really spending much time with them. Partially, he blamed Callas for her urging him not to invite his own children on board *The Christina*. In catering to Maria's demands and her narcissism, he was neglecting his own children. He also blamed himself for allowing his irresponsible son to take flying lessons.

Onassis came down with a series of gruesome neurological problems, including one in which his eyelids would not close so he could not sleep. He received the dire diagnosis of myasthenia gravis—if untreated, a severe and potentially fatal neurological illness with no known cure. For the last two years of his life, he was slowly dying—in great pain and great guilt. Maria tried to visit him in the hospital, and did visit him once, but daughter Christina tried to keep Maria away.

Maria was lonely in her spacious, luxurious apartment. She was relying more and more on Bruna, her maid, and Ferruccio, her chauffeur and general factotum. She was also drawing closer to Vasso Devetzi, a Greek pianist whose husband was a lawyer and financial planner; they could handle some of Maria's financial and contractual obligations. Maria did not want to see anyone else, since she had decided that all her family, what was left of it, and all her previous friends were not to be trusted. She could count on her two faithful servants—as long as she continued to pay them, of course. They undoubtedly did not dare to disagree with their boss, lest they lose their jobs.

As time progressed, Maria became less the haughty diva and more like a dependent child who did not want these two people—her maid and her chauffeur—to leave her, even when they had a rare day off. In her passive-aggressive way, she sometimes "forgot" to pay them when their salaries were due until they had to beg her for the money. At the time of Callas' death, they were both left with large sums still owed to them.

Maria always found Giuseppe Di Stefano (or "Pippo," as she called him) fairly reliable—though they had had their quarrels. She refused to talk to him for a while, when he refused to appear at all their rehearsals at the Lyric Opera in Chicago. They would have some dramatic reconciliation—which meant that Pippo could do something for Maria. Franco Zeffirelli's film *Callas Forever* presented Maria in the final year of her life—avoiding everyone, taking too many pills, becoming suicidal, withdrawing from projects she had agreed to do, and remaining wildly passive-aggressive.

Di Stefano envisioned a worldwide tour beginning in Europe and moving east to America and then the Far East. Japan and South Korea had a burgeoning fan base for Western opera, so they decided that it would be a good place to end their tour. They were international superstars in opera, he reminded her, and fans can be very forgiving of their favorite singers. He also argued that many of their fans would not even notice an occasional wrong note (DeCeccatty 304 ff.).

Pippo soon tired of Maria's well-known narcissism—the idea that she was the only singer alive who was dedicated to art, and as a result had to whip her materialistic colleagues (especially Pippo) into rehearsing endlessly to achieve the best artistic results. While she liked the rehearsal process before a performance, Pippo got bored and annoyed during a rehearsal, especially when Callas was making one of her *scenas*. (Di Stefano even joked that Callas could actually talk to Donizetti, Verdi, Bellini and Puccini.) Di Stefano felt that too many rehearsals could ruin the spontaneity and excitement of a live performance, and he especially resented rehearsing roles like Alfredo in *La Traviata*, a role he had actually recorded, as well as sung countless times (Edwards 134 ff.).

Fortunately for them, they still had many fans who would be willing to pack their recital halls to capacity, even though they were both in vocal decline. Both singers were in their early 50s (Maria turned 50 in 1973) but he felt that with some rehearsals and a wise choice of repertoire, they could still sing effectively. If they were both shrewd in what they picked to sing, Di

17. The Final Tour with Di Stefano

Stefano argued, they could still impress and entertain an audience and even some critics. Di Stefano felt that what Callas lacked was self-confidence in herself and her voice, which was certainly never true of the sometimes cartoonishly pompous Di Stefano. She seemed too reliant on other people's opinions, he felt, and she should just sing confidently and entertain the paying public. Callas, on the other hand, felt that Di Stefano remained too confident of his singing, which had clearly declined since their "golden years" together at La Scala (and beyond).

Callas suddenly got an offer to give a master class in Osaka, Japan, of all places. The Japanese had become very interested in Italian opera, and they offered Callas an all-expenses-paid trip to Japan, in addition to her fee for the classes themselves. She talked to Di Stefano about this, and he offered to go with her, since he knew she hated to travel alone and hated being alone in general. They flew to Japan and, on May 20, they gave a master class at the Festival Hall in Osaka. They both concluded that the master class succeeded well, and the Japanese sponsors of this endeavor told both singers they handled the Japanese students beautifully, and also entertained the audience attending the class. This experience convinced Callas that she could now work with Di Stefano, and when they got back to Paris, she contacted her agent, Sander Gorlinsky, to continue detailed planning for their worldwide series of recitals. He suggested the fall of 1973 and all of the following year, 1974. That tour, they both hoped, would keep them prosperous and keep Callas free of her depression (Edwards 298 ff.). Gorlinsky, their agent, assured them that the tour should be very profitable.

Callas and Di Stefano were both well-prepared when their tour began in Germany in 1973. Maria had wanted the tour to include an orchestra, though she was eventually convinced of the financial infeasibility of such an undertaking—and agreed that a piano accompaniment would work fine. They had both previously worked with the pianist, Ivor Newton. A second (understudy) pianist and page turner would be required, too, and Newton suggested Robert Sutherland, a much younger man. Ivor was in his eighties, and though a great accompanist, had now become an old and sometimes enfeebled man. Sutherland eventually wrote a book on his experiences on this tour. Sutherland, many years later, was interviewed for an illuminating article in *Opera* magazine (September 2017, to coincide with the 30th anniversary of Callas' death) about his final visit to Callas in her Paris apartment in 1977, a few months before her death. Sutherland reported that at his final meeting, she told him how much she enjoyed rehearsing with him, and how much she appreciated his support (Sutherland 15–35).

Maria's chic Parisian apartment had a fine piano, and she invited Di Stefano and his wife over for dinner to hammer out a final program for

Poster art for 1974's "An Evening with Maria Callas and Giuseppe Di Stefano."

their tour. Both Callas and Di Stefano were still names to be reckoned with, and they had often performed together, as well as making some magnificent Angel Records/EMI recordings together (among them, their complete *Lucia di Lammermoor,* under conductor Tullio Serafin). Their joint recordings had become popular and had been heard by many people who would want to hear them live. Angel/EMI suggested that they release a joint recording of part of their planned program to attract audiences. Callas and

17. The Final Tour with Di Stefano

Callas makes an appearance at New York's famed Carnegie Hall in 1974, flanked by singer Giuseppe Di Stefano (left) and pianist Robert Sutherland (right).

Di Stefano recorded some of their planned program together for EMI, but she refused to release the disc when she heard the results. She remained a perfectionist and was horrified by what she heard on this disc, though Di Stefano was not. This was not a good omen for the tour (Stassinopoulos 324 ff.).

Something else that was troubling for Di Stefano was Callas' increasing dependence on pills. She still took diet pills to keep slim, and sleeping pills to allow her to sleep at night. She also needed other pills to get her up in the morning. In addition, she suffered from worsening depression and needed anti-depression pills as well. Sometimes she forgot what pills she took and would accidentally double her allotted dosages or forget to take her pills altogether. Especially before a performance, Callas became so nervous that she also needed anti-anxiety pills to appear on stage. Di Stefano was worried about the prospect of touring with the anxious and pill-popping Callas, who was most-panicky when she had to perform. Even her maid, Bruna, dreaded having to accompany her on a performance tour since she saw first-hand how anxious Callas became, especially now that she was so unsure of her voice and her technique. Despite the general misgivings, Callas went to Milan that spring to see Biki, her favorite couture designer, and asked her to make some striking performance gowns for her. Callas loved playing the role of the prima donna, the performing artist at the center of a large stage before a live audience (DeCeccatty 298 ff.). She took comfort in knowing that she would once again be performing the role she knew best: *Prima Donna Assoluta*.

As Luciano Pavarotti once said, "The greatest satisfaction an artist can have is reducing thousands of well-dressed and well-educated people into screaming, happy animals." Pavarotti, as a young performer, also once said that the tenor he most admired was Giuseppe Di Stefano. Rudolf Bing had complimented Di Stefano while he was singing at the Met on his amazing ability to sing a high C with a seemingly effortless diminuendo while on the note. While Di Stefano could no longer accomplish that feat, he still had an operatic voice worth hearing, even though he was no longer in his prime (Bing, *5000 Nights*, 231 ff.). Di Stefano maintained his tremendous self-confidence as a singer, something that Maria now lacked, and she was plagued with fears and doubts (Stassinopoulos 324). Maria's wobble had gotten even more pronounced, and she sometimes sang flat, in spite of her best efforts. Giuseppe's high notes were not very reliable any more, either. He also tended to sing everything very loudly, which would drown Callas out. Clearly, he was no longer able to sing softly or with much subtlety. Her voice had always been large enough to fill the largest opera houses, but now it was losing both its size and its quality of tone. In a recording studio, they could repeat passages and certain notes until they sounded good—in most cases—but at a live recital, they did not want to sound flat or wobbly and embarrass themselves. Callas' voice sometimes lost its power and normal volume and, at times, required concentrated effort to remain audible.

Before their tour, both singers again entered EMI's recording studios in London and made a joint recording to generate some advanced publicity. When Callas heard the resultant tapes, she would not allow them to be released, though Di Stefano certainly was willing to do this. He was not as fussy and demanding as she was about his recordings and was very forgiving of a few mistakes, which he was sure the recording engineers could correct. Callas was not so cavalier; she had always been a perfectionist and dreaded that all her vocal imperfections would be saved. And she would not have that.

The dual recital tour is remembered by history as a sad spectacle, but it was not altogether devoid of artistry. Callas became especially fond of Robert Sutherland, the "standby accompanist" who became her sole accompanist, as Ivor Newton grew increasingly unreliable and had to be replaced. During the tour, Callas even had to call her friend Vasso Devetzi in Paris and fly to her in, to play at one of their recitals because Di Stefano had cancelled the day before (Stasinopoulos 269 ff.).

They finally agreed on what they would be singing. Maria would sing the following arias: "Pleurez, mes yeux" (*Le Cid*), "Habañera" (*Carmen*), "Suicidio" (*Gioconda*), "L'altra notte" (*Mefistofele*), "Non Pianger, mia compagna" (*Don Carlo*), "Tu che la vanita" (*Don Carlo*), "O mio babbino caro"

17. The Final Tour with Di Stefano

Maria Callas and Giuseppe Di Stefano gladly accept their ovations, bouquets and requests for yet more encores. In moments of reflection, they almost certainly knew that these laurels were for their past performances, not for their present, sometimes ragged vocal states.

(*Gianni Schicchi*) and "Quando me'n vo" (*La Boheme*). The duets: "Laissez—moi" (*Faust*), "C'est toi, c'est moi" (*Carmen*), "Una parola, o Adina" (*Elisir d'amore*), "Ah! per sempre" (*Forza del Destino*), "Io vengo a domandar" (*Don Carlo*), "Tu qui Santuzza?" (*Cavalleria Rusticana*) and "Quale, o prode" (*I Vespri Siciliani*).

Di Stefano had his own list of arias he would sing. The two singers would never perform all of this music at any one recital; instead, the audience would see this list in their programs, and the two singers would decide which selections they would sing that particular evening.

The tour began at the Congress Centrum in Hamburg, Germany, on October 25, 1973. Though the singers did not get very good reviews, the public seemed to love them, and the recital was sold out. Early in the tour, their voices both sounded fairly good on most evenings. The singers gave the same recital at the enormous Philharmonie in Berlin on October 29, and here, too, they both felt that they had succeeded though they were not always audible in the rear seats. A few days later, Callas, Di Stefano and their pianist moved to the Rheinhalle in Dusseldorf and sang there on November 2 to genuine acclaim. Callas and Di Stefano took the train to Munich and sang at the Deutches Museum. They got lots of applause and flowers there, though, once again, the reviewers were more restrained. The critics pointed out all the vocal problems but often said that the artistry of the two singers remained intact. On November 9, the singers appeared in Jahrhundert Hall Hochst in Frankfurt and got a fairly good ovation there. On November 12, they performed at the National Theater in Mannheim. They were both worn out and did not sing their best, but the audience was forgiving and applauded them. Di Stefano and Callas knew how to make a good entrance onto the stage and smiled often, which pleased their German audiences. Callas, especially, had not sung very often in Germany, but she had her fans there. As had been the case at most of their concerts in Germany, Callas and Di Stefano got much applause and even flowers at the end (DeCeccatty 302 ff.). Aristo was still alive at this point but fading rapidly—and he never sent her any backstage flowers, as he had so often done earlier in their relationship.

After their successes in Germany, they proceeded to Spain, where their accompanist was now Robert Sutherland. Newton, enraged at being replaced by Sutherland, never spoke to the young pianist again (Sutherland 20–50). In Spain, the two singers appeared first in Madrid, at the Palacio Nacional de Congresos y Expriciones. Their Spanish fans appeared in force and applauded and cheered vigorously.

The singers and Sutherland flew to London, appearing at the Royal Festival Hall on November 26 and December 2, and again the response was very positive. Though the critics complained about their vocal decline, the recitals played to mostly sold-out houses and got standing ovations from their fans, who were clearly there to applaud the two singers for their earlier triumphs, rather than for the actual performances they'd just heard.

A 1974 photograph of the quarrelsome duo, Giuseppe Di Stefano and Maria Callas.

The two singers, their accompanist and their various entourages then flew to Paris, and they gave their recital at the Theatre des Champs-Elysée. The Parisians loved Callas and Di Stefano and they received lots of applause and flowers.

17. The Final Tour with Di Stefano

Four days later, on December 11, they were all in Amsterdam at the famed Concertgebouw, and here, their success was much more muted. The Dutch performance was not sold out and the audience did not seem as uncritically positive about Callas and Di Stefano's singing. The applause at the end was more polite than enthusiastic.

The two singers then had a break of about two months and decided to separate and go home for the Christmas holidays. While they were not performing, Callas decided to add some new pieces for the coming year, 1974. Callas remained fearful and insecure about her voice and very anxious about her singing. The new pieces she added for their joint recitals were "Voi lo sapete" from *Cavalleria Rusticana*, "Sola, perduta, abbandonata" from *Manon Lescaut*, "Air des lettres" from *Werther*, "Vissi d'arte" from *Tosca*, "Adieu, notre petite table" from *Manon* and "Mi chiamano Mimi" from *La Boheme*.

For the 1974 tour, Robert Sutherland would be their sole accompanist. Callas and Di Stefano began the tour on January 20, 1974, singing at Milan's National Cancer Institute, really a hospital, and their audience largely consisted of doctors and patients. This was a charity event, and the recital was warmly received. Among the patients was Giuseppe Di Stefano's daughter Luisa, who died the following year. This was to be their only appearance in Italy, but Maria had not forgotten being booed at La Scala and refused to sing anywhere else in evil Italy.

Problems soon developed between Callas and Di Stefano's wife Maria, who knew that Callas and her husband were once lovers, felt threatened by the recital tour and insisted on joining them. The two women soon developed a real dislike for each other, and their joint dinners became very tense and unpleasant for everyone around. Callas could become very clingy and needy around Pippo, and this offended Mrs. Di Stefano, who felt that Maria did not recognize normal social boundaries.

They all flew to Stuttgart, Germany, for a January 23, 1974, performance at the Liederhalle. Right before the recital, Di Stefano suddenly got sick and cancelled. Callas performed and the pianist Sutherland filled in with some piano pieces, but Di Stefano's cancellation upset Callas greatly. Then they all boarded a flight to Philadelphia for the North American leg of their tour. On February 11, they gave a recital at Philadelphia's Academy of Music. All went pretty well here, and the sold-out audience seemed to enjoy the performers and applauded vigorously. The local music critics were not as charitable, pointing out the vocal problems with both singers and Di Stefano's tendency to sing everything loudly. He sometimes drowned out Callas during their duets, which angered the ever-suspicious—and competitive—Maria Callas. The performers flew to Toronto for a Massey Hall recital on February 21, then to Washington, D.C., for a Constitution

Hall performance on February 24. Callas' singing was becoming more insecure and tentative. Still, one could be transported by her sheer artistry and larger-than-life presence, when performing an aria that suited the "reduced circumstances" of her vocal reserves.

They then flew to Boston for a February 27 performance in the city's famous Symphony Hall. Callas had to sing alone, since Di Stefano again cancelled due to illness. Callas was becoming more frantic because of Di Stefano's increasing number of cancellations. She was the one who had become famous for cancelling performances, but now Di Stefano was cancelling regularly. She phoned her agent and told him she was not talking to Di Stefano anymore and that she wanted to cancel the rest of their recitals. The agent informed her that such a cancellation would cost her about a million dollars in cancellation fees. Confronted by this financial reality, Callas decided to rethink her silent treatment of Di Stefano.

The quarrelsome team then flew to Chicago for a March 2 recital at the city's Civic Opera House. Most of the audience seemed pleased. The singers were not singing under the aegis of Chicago's Lyric Opera Company, since Callas still nursed her grudges against Carol Fox and her company. The team then flew to New York City for a March 5 concert at Carnegie Hall. The ticket sales were surprisingly soft, so the hall had to be "papered" with free tickets given to music students and retired people. Things did not go smoothly, and there was only tepid applause after the recital. The team then had to fly to Detroit for a recital on March 9. The killing pace was beginning to make all the team members edgy, especially Callas. With only a few days between performances and jet lag to deal with, Callas and Di Stefano were becoming exhausted and frazzled. The Detroit recital on March 9 included only Callas, since Di Stefano again cancelled; the concert pianist Ralph Votapek agreed to fill in at the last moment with his fine piano playing. Being left with all the evening's vocal responsibilities seemed to have somewhat unnerved Maria, though the audience was receptive, and her reviews were respectable enough. Just three days later, the small troupe was in Dallas, a city filled with memories of great operatic triumphs—as well as ghosts of Kennedys, past and present. Maria was furious when Di Stefano once again cancelled, then gamely faced the audience alone at the enormous, barn-like State Fair Music Hall. Pianist Earl Wild played to fill in the program. The hall was not full.

The Callas–Di Stefano team then flew to Miami, where they had several days to recuperate in Florida's warm weather. On March 21, soprano and tenor sang at the Miami Beach Auditorium and were both in comparatively good voice. They continued their tour at a similar breakneck pace, performing at some lesser, regional venues. On April 15, Callas and Di Stefano were back at Carnegie Hall, where ticket sales were once again disappointing. Some critics pointed out that neither singer had much voice left, but praised their artistry. Rumors about their weak vocalizing had spread throughout the "opera community." They performed several more regional concerts in the U.S. and Canada and Di Stefano was present for all.

On the first of October, after completing their North American tour, they boarded a flight to Seoul, South Korea, for two concerts there, followed by two concerts in Tokyo, and further regional appearances throughout Japan. On November 11, 1974, at Sapporo's Hokkaido Koseinenkin Kaikan Auditorium, Callas and Di Stefano made their final appearance in Japan together. In spite of their somewhat tired-sounding voices, both were warmly and respectfully greeted. As it would turn out, this was not simply Callas' final performance with Di Stefano, this would be Callas' final public performance of her singing career.

All flew back to Europe, and Callas and Di Stefano parted ways—and never saw each other again. Both parties were glad to be returning to their separate corners, to nurse their various wounds from what had been a taxing tour. Both ended up making large sums of money—but by the end of what must have been a grueling series of humiliations, Callas never wanted to see the tenor or his wife ever again (Stassinopoulos 325 ff.).

While Callas never performed again, Di Stefano continued to sing, though in smaller and smaller comprimario roles. He obviously loved performing in public so much that he could not bear to leave the stage. His final performance was as the Emperor, playing a very small but prominent role in Puccini's *Turandot* in July 1992. Toward the end of his life, he and his wife became fascinated with Africa and bought a villa in Nairobi, Nigeria, and enjoyed spending time there each year. Then both were badly beaten and robbed during a terrifying home invasion robbery in 2007; Maria Di Stefano died as a result of the injuries she sustained, and Giuseppe needed emergency surgery in Nairobi before being flown back to Italy. He received further emergency surgery in Milan but never really recovered. In 2008, Giuseppe died at home in Santa Maria Hoe in Lombardy at age 86. (During this same period, Italian diva Renata Scotto permanently removed her entire family from Italy after she and her family were tied up by home invaders who cleaned out their villa's valuables. Scotto moved the family to a suburb of New York City.)

Callas and Di Stefano's final tour (between 1973 and 1974) triggered conflicting reactions from their public and the music critics. Many who remembered them in their primes found these concerts a travesty, since both singers were in advanced vocal decline. They both had occasional moments when they sounded fairly good, but these were only moments. The few existing videotapes of these concerts make for sad viewing, though there are a few surprisingly transcendental moments as well. Some of these concerts were televised, especially in Japan. But both singers also often got standing ovations and flowers from kind people who remembered them from better days, or from those who did not know enough about the operatic voice to notice how relatively poor they both sounded at this late date. But there were more than a few attendees who walked out during the performances, horrified by what they heard coming from these famous throats. For historical accuracy, it must be pointed out that on some nights and with some arias, the singing was brilliant enough from both Callas and Di Stefano that the audience could turn back the clock and hear shimmering reminders of the greatness that once was both of these singularly great (but now compromised) artists.

Callas received many bouquets of flowers, as well as other tokens from her countless faithful fans at the end of these recitals. That can become very addictive, since she loved the adulation. Many performers get used to that and do not know when to stop performing. To know when to retire involves a real awareness and wisdom; some stay too long, and that is what Callas and Di Stefano did—to the damage of their legacies. Di Stefano argued that the cheering and the flowers proved that their tour had been a success; but for Callas, the tour was starkly sobering, and she could no longer fool herself into thinking that she still had the required voice and stamina. When she heard the tapes of their performances, she could no longer deny the truth: that the voice she'd essentially abandoned for several years had now abandoned *her*.

One of the few people who could offer Maria criticism, and get away with it, was her now-beloved accompanist, Robert Sutherland. In his book on the tour, he recalled that Callas would accept his constructive criticism when it was combined with helpful suggestions on how to improve her performances. Sutherland recounted in his 2007 interview with *Opera* magazine about the last time he saw her in her apartment in Paris in 1977. She seemed so happy to be rehearsing with him again, and gladly accepted his tactful suggestions.

After the tour ended in Japan, Di Stefano said on television that they had made thousands of their fans happy. He argued that Callas' vocal concerns were primarily in her own head and a product of her own insecurity. Their mutual friend, Tito Gobbi, said that after a rest, they should organize a tour to cities they had missed in their first tour. Callas, however, wouldn't even consider such a prospect. As a lifelong perfectionist (not to mention an incomparable artist), she must have been horrified to hear how out-of-control her voice had become. She had long been able to deny "inconvenient truths" in her life, but listening to the recital tour recordings must have been torturous for her. She was known to study her old records, reliving her greatest moments as a great and greatly beloved diva. Now, one

17. The Final Tour with Di Stefano

can only imagine the feelings of loss—and loss of control—that were so evident on these recordings. Callas had existed in a "reality" of her own imagination most of her life, but she had never lied to herself about her singing. These tapes were merciless proof that her former friends, Peter Mennin of Juilliard and critic John Ardoin, had both been correct when they had offered their honest assessments of her current vocal resources. She'd scornfully rejected their "impertinence" and opted to cut off contact with both, rather than even consider they might be correct. They had told her that she should no longer be performing. She finally realized: They were right.

When listening to the recordings from that tour, one is struck by how, on certain arias, it's like listening to two different singers. She could still sound powerful in some of her high-noted sections—but when a composer then led her from that range into her lower register, it was as if "never the twain shall meet." She had lost what is called in opera the *mezza di voce*, the middle range of a singer's voice, which acts as a passageway (or *passaggio*) between high and low notes. One aria she frequently performed on the tour, "O, mio babbino caro" (Puccini, *Gianni Schicchi*), was a poor choice for her, at this stage of her career. With its frequent leaps between high and low notes, it viciously exposes the no-man's land that was now her *mezza di voce* (middle voice). It is interesting to compare Maria's final recital tour

A candid rehearsal photograph of Callas and Di Stefano, before they embarked on their somewhat star-crossed international tour in 1974.

with the final recital tour of her most-noted rival, Renata Tebaldi. Tebaldi's tour was with Maria's frequent former co-star, the legendary matinee idol tenor Franco Corelli, around the same year as Callas' final tour with Di Stefano. Tebaldi and Corelli never sounded particularly "off," or "embarrassing."

When Maria was on the plane back to Paris, she must have wanted to weep at her foolishness and what she had allowed herself to be talked into. What would she do with all the free time she now had? She often thought of Aristo Onassis, but at this point, he had lapsed into a coma at the American Hospital in Paris. She remembered an old Greek proverb that said "The years fly but the days drag, especially the last days." Though she longed to be by Onassis' hospital bedside, she had no "right" to be there, since he was, in fact, still married to Jacqueline. And, essentially, Maria's role in his life (at least in the public consciousness) was defined as "Onassis' mistress." Not even that—his *ex*-mistress.

To get her mind off her increasingly frequent bouts with melancholia, she flew to Florida to visit a friend. While there, on March 15, 1975, she learned of the death of Aristotle Onassis in Paris after emergency surgery. The cause of death was given as complications of *myesthenia gravis*. Maria now felt truly alone since she had reconciled with Ari and looked forward to his visits to her in Paris. Now that he was gone, she felt that she had lost the only great love in her life, though he, too, had betrayed her. How

Rarely did Callas (and Di Stefano) get a more fervent reception than the one they got at Paris' Théâtre des Champs-Élysées in 1974.

17. The Final Tour with Di Stefano

could she go on without him and his love for her? How long could she last? Was he even worth grieving over, she wondered, when she remembered his marriage to Jacqueline Kennedy? Had Ari really loved her, she wondered, or was he simply another betrayer, just like everyone else in her life?

Maria had been able to have one final bedside visit with Aristo, though he had already lapsed into a coma at that time. When he died, Maria felt that a part of her had also died. She still loved him and missed him terribly, but she also hated him for refusing to marry her and keeping her so long as his mistress rather than as his wife. He had provided so much drama in her life. Her happiest memories with Aristo involved the two of them on board *The Christina*, and now she missed all that nautical luxury and excitement. Maria still had her faithful *domestiques*, Bruna and Ferruccio—but, to Maria, she was utterly alone. Consequently, she began ignoring her personal appearance, and began eating more and more candy, especially *maron glacée*, one of her favorite treats. How much time did she really have left, she wondered? As it turned out, she did not have much time left at all.

18

Death in Paris

Maria was now alone in a world where she was no longer one of its most singularly talented and glamorous eminences. True, she was now a very wealthy woman—but a big bank account balance was no substitute for having a man who loved her, by her side. Ever since Onassis abandoned her, for Jacqueline Kennedy, the idealized image of him in Maria's mind rendered null the idea of finding a man to replace him. Who *could* replace the legendary Aristotle Onassis? Bringing further grief into her life: Four days after Onassis' death, on March 19, 1975, Luisa Di Stefano, daughter of Giuseppe Di Stefano, died after much suffering. Callas felt very sorry for Pippo, and even set aside her loathing of Di Stefano's wife, since she knew of the trauma they'd endured during their daughter's lengthy illness (DeCeccatty 308 ff.).

On November 2, 1975, Maria was watching the TV news when she was horrified to learn that one of her dearest friends (and her cinematic mentor), Pier Paolo Pasolini, had been murdered—beaten, run over by his own car, tortured and then set afire, on the beach at Ostia, Italy. The following day, the TV news reported that the murderer had been apprehended: Pino Pelosi, an underage Italian street prostitute. Maria had starred in Pasolini's film *Medea* and loved working with him. She even loved *him*—and he was absolutely besotted by Maria Callas in return, and hoped that they could do another film together. The grisliness of Pasolini's murder shook her to her core. Yet one more important link to her past, gone forever.

About a year after Pasolini's murder, on November 17, 1976, Luchino Visconti died suddenly in Italy of a stroke. Her favorite operatic director, Visconti, 69, had directed her in some of her most famous roles, including Violetta in *La Traviata*. He had directed her in five new productions at La Scala, and all the productions had been impressive and enormously successful. She had learned much from him. At La Scala, Visconti had directed her in *La Vestale* (1954), *La Sonnambula* (1955), *La Traviata* (1955), *Anna Bolena* (1957) and *Iphegenie en Tauride* (1957). During this period, Visconti called her "the most important actress since Sarah Bernhardt and Eleanora Duse," and she had loved him and had never stopped hoping that he would, against all odds, suddenly become sexually attracted to women. He had often invited her to his family's palace in Milan. guiding her through its gorgeous rooms. Toward the end, he had lived with his final partner, Austrian actor Helmut Berger, with whom he had made several films, including *The Damned* (1969) and *Ludwig* (1973). Visconti had always been obsessed with Wagner and his operas—in fact, his very first exposure to Maria Callas occurred when she was singing Kundry in Wagner's *Parsifal*. Visconti had also directed *Death in Venice*, his wonderful film version of Thomas Mann's famous story.

It surely bothered her that two of the very few people she trusted at this point were her employees. It's not difficult to imagine that at this austere, reflective time in Callas' life, she may have re-examined some of the relationships she'd deliberately severed, and considered her own culpability. Other people had family and friends that they trusted—why not her? Could it be that all the personal conflicts in her life were all her fault? At least in part? (Zanarini 64–70). In her less-narcissistic moments of self-reflection, she must have suspected that she herself might be the problem.

Seeing people as either wonderful or terrible, with no one in between those extremes, had isolated her from the very people who were most concerned for her wellbeing (Silver 3–10). She had developed a nice relationship with Nadia Stancioff, a journalist from Rome who had been her understudy in her film *Medea*, and Maria used to call her and invite her to visit her in Paris. But now she would not call Nadia or respond to her calls, and Nadia could not understand why. Maria may have concluded that Nadia was planning to write a book about her—which was, in fact, true in this instance. Stancioff's book was published after Callas' death.

Franco Zeffirelli called her when he was in Paris,

Sola, perduta, abbandonata. A revealing candid of Maria Callas in 1971, as she faced life on her own for the very first time.

but at this point, Maria would rarely answer her phone. Her maid, Bruna, would answer Franco's call, take the message, and tell him that the signora would call him back. But Maria would not. She certainly knew how to nurse a grudge. She could understand only her own point of view and no one else's. She did trust her friend Vasso Devetzi (on most days) and continued to see her and allowed her to work on her (Maria's) legal papers. Vasso told Maria that her husband was a lawyer and would never charge her. And Maria could never resist a bargain.

Maria complained to Giuseppe Di Stefano during a phone call that each day she got through was one day less, which suggested that she must have been suicidally depressed. She also became convinced now that people were all trying to use her because of her fame, which made her sound increasingly paranoid. Such borderline behavior was isolating her at a time when she really needed family and friends. Her generous godfather, Leonard Lantzounis, was now living in retirement in Athens. Callas probably had also suspected that he, too, had betrayed her, since both her mother and sister were also living in Athens and were in contact with him. She imagined all three of them plotting to betray her.

Thus we have the tragic effects of her neuroses on her already difficult personality. She was trapped on the border between neurosis and psychosis. People in this condition can have neurotic and also psychotic episodes, like hearing voices ordering them to do horrible things, or imagining that they see long-dead friends on the streets (Zanarini 64–70). Ironically, each year Maria became more like her mother, the woman she despised above all others.

Perhaps if Ari had lived, things might have been better for her, but inevitably she would have come to hate him too. She hardly had a pattern of stability in terms of the intimate relationships in her life. Borderline personality disorder is very hard to treat, and impossible to treat with a patient who refuses to seek treatment. The problem was *certainly* not Maria Callas, since she was a musical genius and generally above all others. The problem remained the fault of the world itself and its terrible people, who kept lying to her and betraying her.

Maria was taking more and more pills—perhaps in a conscious (or subconscious) attempt to end her own life. She had been warned by her doctor that taking some of her medications, like Mandrax, were considered dangerous and could result in fatal outcomes, but she got the medication in Athens, surprisingly, thanks to her sister Jackie, with whom Maria had forged a rapprochement of convenience. Maria had used Mandrax (a highly addictive sedative) for years; it helped her to sleep at night. At the time, one did not need a prescription for Mandrax in Greece. Jackie was financially rewarded for her pharmaceutical interventions (Silver 3–30).

18. Death in Paris

Religion might have provided some solace for Maria, but by this point she was even suspicious of God, who had put her in such a terrible world. She was increasingly also guilty of *misandry*—the belief that men would always abuse women since that was the nature of the beast. Because of her problematic relationship with her father, she tended to be simultaneously desperate for male companionship and protection and also suspicious of men as exploiters of successful, brilliant, wealthy women, which she now was. She had a fortune of almost $20 million U.S., which should have enabled her to create some happiness for her. But for Maria Callas, it was not to be.

In early 1977, Franco Zeffirelli encountered Maria one last time and described that final meeting. John Tooley, then the new director of the Royal Opera, Covent Garden, wanted Zeffirelli to direct a new production of *The Merry Widow* and Callas to sing the lead role. Callas found the idea of singing in an operetta ridiculous. According to Zeffirelli:

An early '70s vision of Maria Callas, as she briefly tried to re-brand herself as something of an "elder stateswoman" of the opera world.

> I told her that, far from being easy, the role of the Widow is very demanding and needs a damn good voice, and I emphasized how wonderful she would look in the Belle Epoque costumes. She was definitely attracted to the idea, but she was already preparing her excuses to reject the offer. Yes, she would consider it, but she was so busy; however, she would be in touch. I began to get a little irritated and told her she should trust her friends and stop wasting her time and talent. Perhaps I ought to have seen what was happening to her and realized that she was beyond such pleading. I had noticed that her once beautiful hands now looked transparent; you could see the veins below the skin. Then, as I walked her back to her apartment after lunch, I was appalled to realize that she was actually afraid. She kept close to me, terrified that she would come into contact with passersby; she hesitated at crossings, looking wildly about her

until I led her firmly forward. This was partly due to her usual problem of being unable to see without her spectacles, but now it went deeper. She kept on talking about how dangerous the world had become, that terrorists were everywhere and she would never go back to Italy because of all the kidnappings. From time to time, she gave a little involuntary shiver. It was beyond any normal distress at the present state of the world, it was paranoia. Though I could see this evidence of her mental state, I was unaware of just how far her physical decline had gone. When I left her at her apartment, she had recovered her poise sufficiently to promise to consider John Tooley's offer, but I think I knew in my heart that it would never come about (Zeffirelli 298–99).

And it never did. Increasingly Maria was signing papers and turning over her life to Vasso Devetzi, her pianist/accountant friend—a woman fluent in French, Greek and English, whose husband was a lawyer, and who offered to serve her without a fee. Vasso and her husband were now getting power of attorney and handling Maria's finances. It's possible that Maria's judgment could have been clouded by her increasing use of drugs, and not knowing exactly what it was that she was signing.

Maria's long-suffering ex-husband Meneghini was still living in his native Verona. After Onassis' death, he had made subtle overtures to mutual friends suggesting he'd like to mend their fractured marriage and resume their life together. He still owned their home in Sirmione, in the Italian lake district, a place she always said she loved but had not returned to. However, by this point, she hated Meneghini and had convinced herself that he was evil personified.

This kind of narcissistic behavior caused a bitter recounting from Renata Scotto in her memoir. She herself was a victim of Callas's narcissistic behavior, back when she began performing at La Scala, singing some of the roles that Callas herself had been celebrated (starring roles in *Lucia di Lammermoor* and *La Sonnambula*). Some Callas fans booed Scotto when she sang roles that Callas had sung at La Scala. As Scotto acridly recalled in her autobiography:

> Opera was not born with Maria Callas, and it did not die with her death. Opera did not die with the death of Malibran or Ponselle. It will not die when I am gone. It lives on, as it must, in new voices. Callas may well be a beautiful memory against which many great sopranos will be measured, but each artist has her time. Callas had hers then, before mine. The competition and polemics were imagined and perpetuated by sick fanatics. (Scotto 109).

Scotto was sick of being compared to Callas, and annoyed by stories of Callas leaving Scotto's own performances early and looking disgusted. Scotto began by understudying Callas and taking over her roles when Maria was ill. Covering for other singers is how many singers begin their opera careers. As Scotto elaborated: "I remember how Callas had to face

18. Death in Paris

horrible fans in the same theater, and how she left La Scala in terrible disappointment. It is disillusioning and unfair. If it were not for my family it would hurt so much more, but 'Vissi d'arte' is not my song. I have a life outside the theater, so my love for it is only one aspect of my love for life. And that I will never lose." (Scotto 113 ff)

Some biographers have made the claim that Maria was the starring player of a classic Greek tragedy, whose denouement was set in motion by the death of her one true love, Aristotle Onassis; that once Onassis died, she lost the will to live any longer. Is this "sentimentality," or is it the truth? *Was* he the great love of her life and *was* she his victim? Some of her friends, like clothing designer Biki, felt that he had ruined her career and life. He did not want to marry her, even after his marriage to Jacqueline Kennedy disintegrated. Given Maria's narcissism, it is hard to imagine her really loving anyone for very long. By the end, was she pining for Onassis or was she angry with him for using her? The second explanation seems more likely, though it's possible that both were true. She could love pets and paid servants like Bruna and Ferruccio, people who did not dare disagree with her, lest she fire them. But she could not deal with real people who also had problems to endure.

Maria was only 53 in 1977. Better death than being told by an audience that they no longer wanted her. Better death than singing small comprimaria parts next to people who could sing the major roles and get all the applause. Better death than no longer being the *prima donna*—the star of the show in the major female roles of Lucia, Norma, Anna Bolena, Tosca and Carmen. If her whole life was being a prima donna, a diva, how could she live if she could no longer do that?

She now had no resources, other than her fairly sizable wealth. Had she been better educated, she could have done more reading or taken courses at Paris universities. She could have lectured on opera's history and performance practices. She had often said that she envied people who had had an education. Why did she not get one herself, now that she was retired and had plenty of time on her hands? If she was too embarrassed to do this, she could easily have hired private tutors. If she had seen a psychiatrist, she could have talked to someone about her loneliness and depression and she could have been helped. She had so many options, especially as the millionairess that she was. She could have returned to Greece and tried to reconnect with her family. She could have contacted Battista Meneghini, who was still her husband (at least in Italy), and most probably he would have taken her back.

On the morning of September 16, 1977, Maria was sipping a cup of coffee when she suddenly fell over on the floor, and her servants ran to her. They did not call for an ambulance, instead phoning her doctor, whose waiting room was full of patients. He told them to call an ambulance immediately. Why did Ferruccio and Bruna fail to do such an obvious thing? Why did Ferruccio instead call another doctor of a friend of his? Did the servants fear that a medical examiner would call the death a suicide or even a homicide? Did they fear that a toxicology report would show that she had become a frequent user of illegal drugs?

The news of Maria's untimely death flashed around the globe via television and radio news. She had been the most famous opera singer of her generation, and her death was reported in bold-faced, front-page headlines in all of the international press, which would doubtlessly have pleased her.

Because she did not leave a valid will (or, at least, one that survived), the vultures almost instantly circled around her corpse. A time-worn legal aphorism states, "Where there's a will, there's a relative." Maria's husband Meneghini did possess a will she wrote when she had just begun her career in the early 1950s, and a French judge declared it her only authentic will so she did not die intestate (Meneghini 3–26).

Maria was cremated after a hasty funeral arranged at the local Greek Orthodox Church in Paris. That same day, her friend Nadia Stancioff arranged a memorial service at a Greek Orthodox church in Rome, attended by Nadia and her friends. Why had Callas' body been reduced to ashes so quickly? She had never told friends that she wanted to be cremated, at least according to Giuseppe Di Stefano. Cremation was not the normal practice in the Greek Orthodox religion, and suicide was considered a mortal sin. Callas' ashes were interred at the most famous cemetery in Paris, Père Lachaise. After a year, her ashes were mysteriously stolen but then, just as mysteriously, found.

Taking the lead on all things post-mortem Maria Callas was her Greek "friend" and sometimes "financial manager," Vasso Devetzi, who took charge of the situation by announcing that she was Maria's best friend and head of the Maria Callas Foundation, by the order of Maria herself. There was much mystery and many questions to be answered in the aftermath of Callas' death. She was only 53 when she died, and of course a very famous and wealthy woman. Devetzi had ingratiated herself to Callas and eventually managed clandestinely to gain control of her estate and reward herself mightily in the process.

Why such haste to incinerate Callas' remains? Did that come from Maria's written request or was this Vasso Devetzi's? The enigmatic Vasso Devetzi was ordering people around under the guise of being the director of the mysterious Maria Callas Foundation, which had never legally existed, and which this woman would use to grab millions of Maria's dollars for herself rather than for any educational or philanthropic purposes. Vasso took over after Maria's death and waved around wills and powers of attorney and other legal documents, to assert her own power. Were all these signed documents legal or fraudulent? Knowing Callas' lifelong propensity for creating drama, is it possible that she herself had planned and executed her own suicide and the subsequent confusion?

In his memoir, Rudolf Bing wrote, "Maria Callas was the superstar of stars. She not only had a glorious voice, she was musical and had an enormous stage personality and good looks. There was nothing missing." Of her death, he wrote, "Alas, she did not keep her voice long. Her end was tragic and, although I have nothing to support my view, I felt that she herself ended her life. It may well have been unbearable for her, to sink from the top of the world to her total loneliness in Paris" (Bing, A Knight, 95–96).

19

The Aftermath and the Callas Legacy

On June 14, 1978, an auction was held in Paris, to disperse the contents of Maria Callas' apartment. Most of the articles up for auction were bought by Giovanni Battista Meneghini and sent to his home in Sirmione. He told the press that he was planning to establish a museum dedicated to his wife. Much of the artwork at the auction had been, in fact, originally purchased by him, as gifts to Maria. He even bought their matrimonial bed. He said he wanted the museum to be in Italy—a country he was well-aware that Maria had grown to despise.

But it was not to be: Meneghini died on January 21, 1981, and everything was willed to his second wife, his former housekeeper, Emma Brutti, who sold some or all some of the Callas estate. Perhaps some of this Callas material is still sitting in some warehouse in and around Sirmione or Verona—a tragic irony for the setting of the story of Romeo and Juliet in Shakespeare's telling of the tale. A Maria Callas museum in Verona, where Callas had had her first major success, and where her husband had lived, would have been a wonderful addition to the city's small collection of museums.

In the spring of 1979, Maria's ashes were disinterred and put on a boat to Greece. On June 3, they were scattered over the Aegean Sea by Dimitris Nianias, Greece's Minister of Culture (Hanine-Roussel 317).

Director Federico Fellini made a film called *E La Nave Va* (*And the Ship Sails On*), based on Maria's funeral. It appeared in 1983, five years after Maria's death and three years after the scattering of her ashes. So, clearly, Fellini and the cinema-going public remained fascinated by the death and burial at sea of this famous diva.

What happened to the millions of dollars left in her estate, and the royalties from Angel/EMI that her recordings are still earning? There was talk of a Maria Callas Foundation, which would offer scholarships to young singers, and a reference to the establishment of a Maria Callas museum. Vasso Devetzi was declaring that she was in charge of the Maria Callas

19. The Aftermath and the Callas Legacy

Foundation and was giving orders based on Maria's wishes, but no such foundation ever existed. As for Callas' royalties, it was later revealed that they were being sent to a Maria Callas Foundation run by Devetzi (who did send some token "hush money" to Callas' mother and sister). Devetzi and her husband ultimately used up most of the money and then Vasso died in 1987, before anyone caught up with the fraud being committed in the name of Maria Callas. Much later, an official Maria Callas Foundation was established in Athens, though not much money was provided for it (it is still extant). There is a plaque to Maria Callas in Père Lachaise cemetery in Paris, and Callas fans pay their respects there regularly. The block where she lived in Paris is now officially renamed *Allée Maria Callas*.

By the time of a legal settlement in a French court, several years after Callas' death, the French judge based it on a will found by Meneghini which she had signed early in her career. This will gave all she had to her husband. The court declared all other wills null and void. A French judge decided that half of her money should go to her mother and sister and half to her still-legal husband Meneghini—the very people that Callas hated the most. How ironic and how tragic, given the good that all that money could have done, especially toward helping new young singers in need of financial support to begin their opera careers—just as Maria Callas had needed, some 35 years earlier. Perhaps that French judge understood Maria only too well and realized that her money should be divided and given to the people who had most loved her and were most responsible for her fantastic success. Callas' mother and sister were still living in poverty in Athens when Maria died. Their circumstances improved dramatically after the death of their Maria.

Callas was outlived by her most important teacher, Elvira de Hidalgo. She died in Milan in 1980, after many years as a voice teacher there. Even before that, on December 16, 1977, the brilliant young conductor Thomas Schippers died of cancer at age 47; he had conducted her in *Medea* in both Greece and at La Scala, and they had grown close through these associations.

Remarkably quickly after Maria's death, the rumor mills started churning out "theories" as to how she had actually died. There was (and still is) a good deal of speculation that Maria took her own life. This possibility cannot be ruled out. It must have added to her depression that she was gradually losing control of all the muscles in her body, including her vocal cords. If she had lived much longer, she would not have even been able to talk. The official cause of death was listed on her death certificate as heart attack. Determining Callas' "official cause of death" became an impossibility after her remains were so quickly cremated, so there's still a good deal of mystery surrounding it. Friends like Franco Zeffirelli, as well as her husband,

Elvira de Hidalgo, who reveled in her image as the "teacher of Maria Callas," in her Milan studio in the mid-1970s. She outlived her famous student by three years.

opined that Maria was actually *poisoned* by Vasso Devetzi (Meneghini 320 ff.). Some (notably Nicholas Gage) have suggested that once Aristotle Onassis died, she lost all will to live. Are truly narcissistic people even capable of such a profound love of someone other than themselves?

Did she pine in the end for her former lover, Onassis? Zeffirelli wrote that, in his last visit with her, she seemed very paranoid, convinced that all her friends were trying to use her, and she was still convinced that her own family had betrayed her. She also told him that she feared terrorism all around her in Paris.

After Vasso Devetzi revealed herself to be a duplicitous swindler *par excellence*, Gian Battista Meneghini did not want her to go unchecked in her obvious "deathbed power-grab," and had his lawyer investigate. The lawyers were told that the Maria Callas Foundation was handling all the details. Meneghini was entitled to half of her estate as her husband, according to Italian law, but not according to French law. Meneghini asserted that he did find Maria's will among his possessions, which a French judge ultimately found legitimate. Callas wrote this will in 1954 while she was

19. The Aftermath and the Callas Legacy

still happily married to Meneghini. Into this legal imbroglio entered the enigmatic Vasso Devetzi. Before a full accounting and reckoning could be arranged by the French courts, Devetzi died in 1987, after squandering millions on herself and her husband.

After Maria's death, her mother and sister moved to Paris, but ultimately returned to their native Greece. Little did they know that Vasso Devetzi—a woman they had grown to trust—was robbing them blind. A legal battle for Callas' estate was developing with her mother and her sister and her husband all beginning to take legal action and hiring French lawyers. All the lawyers involved were doubtless making a fortune out of all this international litigation.

After Aristotle Onassis' death, Christina Onassis inherited the bulk of her father's enormous estate, but she only survived her father by 13 years, dying in Buenos Aires on November 19, 1988, at age 37. The cause of death was listed as heart attack. She had been married and divorced four times during her short life. Her French-Swiss ex, Thierry Roussel, whom she eventually grew to despise, raised their daughter in Switzerland after Christina's death, and that girl (Athina, named for her grandmother) inherited what remained of the Onassis fortune, about $400 million. Her Swiss father made sure she studied the Greek language as part of her education. In the "through-line" of many accountings of the "tragic life" of Maria Callas, Christina Onassis' brief, sad life is also added to the litany of "tragedies" that touched Callas.

Jacqueline Kennedy Onassis lived for many years after the death of her husband Aristotle, but she never married again. She lived at 1040 Fifth Avenue in Manhattan, and saw her daughter Caroline married in 1986. Toward the end of her life, her "frequent companion" was a wealthy New Yorker, Maurice Tempelsman. But she contracted a particularly virulent cancer (non–Hodgkin's lymphoma) and died very quickly after her diagnosis, in 1994, at the age of 64. Soon after her death, her son John started taking flying lessons, now that his mother was no longer there to stop him. He died, like several Kennedys and like his stepbrother Alexander Onassis, in a plane crash, on July 16, 1999, at the age of 38. Occurring off the coast of Cape Cod, the crash also killed his young wife and her sister. His ashes were spread over the Atlantic Ocean, off the coast of Cape Cod. His wife's family ultimately sued the Kennedy estate for the loss of both their children (Carolyn and Lauren Bessette), due to John's negligence as a pilot. (He ignored warnings that the terrible weather that night made it unsafe to fly a private plane.) The Bessette family received a $20 million settlement from the Kennedy clan. As of this writing, John's sister Caroline Kennedy Schlossberg is the "last one standing" of John Fitzgerald Kennedy's direct family. She lives with her husband Edwin Schlossberg in New York City.

The Definitive Diva

Gian Battista Meneghini died in 1981 in his late 80s, in his home in northern Italy. His wife Emma Brutti died a few years later, and whatever Maria Callas possessions she still had were randomly dispersed. They're now likely to forever remain in "private hands" (or lost).

Renata Tebaldi, whom Callas turned into a great rival and personal enemy, died at 82 on December 19, 2004. Her final years were very pleasant and productive for Tebaldi: After her retirement from the opera stage, she taught master classes in Busetto, Italy, Chicago, Milan and Paris. She saw individual singers for private lessons, especially soprano Aprile Millo. Tebaldi also received numerous awards from Italy, France, and Great Britain for her career in opera. She maintained friendships with her personal friends and many of her colleagues, especially Franco Corelli, Tito Gobbi and Carlo Bergonzi. Tebaldi became a frequent guest on Italian television, talking about her career and the art form of opera. She also commented positively about new young opera singers and their performances on TV or in opera houses. She especially enjoyed talking with young singers on TV about opera's future in Italy and elsewhere.

Rudolf Bing, who had both hired and fired Callas, had a very sad ending. After his wife Nina died in 1983, he became increasingly irrational, and married Carroll Douglass, a mental patient. They wandered around the world until Bing's money ran out. They became a recurring sideshow in New York's daily tabloids, who were happy to report the latest antics of the profoundly unstable "Lady Bing." Ultimately,

Momentary détente for the cameras. Maria Callas seemingly "buried the hatchet" with her long-time soprano rival, Renata Tebaldi, when they "warmly" embraced at the Metropolitan Opera House in New York after Tebaldi's performance in *Adriana Lecouvreur* in 1968. At least as far as Maria was concerned, this public show of affection between the two was only for show, and she carried her animus for Tebaldi to the grave.

19. The Aftermath and the Callas Legacy

this second marriage was annulled by a New York court, and he was declared unfit to handle his own affairs, owing to rapidly advancing Alzheimer's disease. Thanks to Roberta Peters and Teresa Stratas, retired Met sopranos, Bing was placed in the Hebrew Home for the Aged in the Bronx, where he died in 1997 at age 94.

Maria Callas has certainly left a legacy, more than any other singer of the 20th century. During her 25-year career, she was prodigiously documented, on records and (to a lesser extent) film. Warner CD/Angel/EMI has reissued all of her commercial recordings on remastered CDs, and the sound is much-improved. This collection of over 30 CDs gives us a complete record of her commercial records. She can also be heard on pirate recordings of some of her performances—though, naturally, she never agreed to the release of these covert, sometimes very poor-quality recordings. She remains a major presence on the Internet and YouTube, and there are many photos of her on the Internet as well. (Callas' recorded output is now well-represented online, on streaming audio sites such as Spotify *et al.*) Many of her TV interviews and performances also appear on YouTube—and in several languages. The Callas legacy burns brighter than ever in the 21st century, as her centenary approaches. Digital transfers of her many interviews (with people like Edward R. Murrow and Barbara Walters) can be easily found on YouTube, and there one can examine her personality, as well as her larger-than-life glamour. In her remastered CDs, we have a complete history of her recorded voice—from the strong, secure recordings of her youth, to the more insecure, wobbly recordings at the end of her professional career. One can hear her startlingly distinctive timbre, her wide range, from very high, even above high C, to her lowest voice and her exciting low chest-notes. We can also hear her ability to control her dynamics, so that she can sing beautifully both at high volume and quietly and softly. One can also hear the unevenness of her voice, since her three ranges do not move smoothly from the highest head tones to her middle range and then to her lowest chest-tones. One can also hear her usually fine and clear Italian diction; she had an instinct for emphasizing the drama in the text of her role. She does not simply sing beautifully, but she does sing dramatically, and her diction, her ability to color her voice to create great drama in the text and characterize each role she sings, and her use of volume clearly serves to make the role she is singing come alive.

One feels that Callas never just sang beautifully, but always sang theatrically and dramatically. On YouTube, one can view filmed records of Callas during parts of performances and recitals, which reveal how she used her movements, her body and her facial gestures to create characters as she sang. Her genius at making opera truly dramatic can be seen during these videotaped performances. She could act effectively even when she was not singing but reacting to other singers onstage; her acting does not appear unconvincing or mannered.

Perhaps the best documentary overview of Callas' life and art is found in Tom Volf's fascinating *Maria by Callas*. Released to theaters in the fall of 2018, it got excellent reviews in *The New York Times* and many other noted publications. Maria herself is the film's de facto narrator (though there is no "narration," per se), as the story is told "in her own words," often through letters and quotes from Maria, as interpreted by noted opera singer–teacher Joyce DiDonato, a Callas devotee. Previously unseen video footage was unearthed by Volf, including an illuminating one-on-one interview with British journalist David Frost, long been thought to be lost. Callas is unusually frank (in her own way) and seems fairly relaxed and candid, even discussing her relationship with Onassis—and, by extension, Jacqueline Kennedy Onassis. Much of the old footage in *Maria by Callas* was colorized, giving the modern viewer an idea of how she might have appeared in the old days, "in living color."

La Divina in a late 1960s "character study," her famous allure still tangibly alive.

Maria's influence continues in the revival of the bel canto repertory, which has lasted into the 21st century; those operas are still performed: the three Tudor operas of Donizetti, *Anna Bolena*, *Maria Stuarda* and *Roberto Devereux*, in addition to Bellini's *Norma* and *La Sonnambula* and Rossini's serious operas *Mose in Egitto*, *Tancredi* and *Semiramide*, and his eternally wonderful comedies *The Barber of Seville* and *L'Italiana in Algeri*. Also, the Donizetti comedies *L'elisir d'amore*, *Don Pasquale* and *La Fille du Regiment* appear frequently in opera houses.

Callas has also had a profound effect on drama and film. Zeffirelli's *Callas Forever* continues to fascinate opera fans. Fanny Ardent plays Callas, lip-syncing to Callas recordings to recreate her performances on stage, and Jeremy Irons gives a fine performance *as* Zeffirelli. It's like watching

19. The Aftermath and the Callas Legacy

Callas returned to life. Pier Paolo Pasolini's *Medea*, with Callas in the title role, gives us an example of her ability to create drama even without singing—instead using body language and facial gestures. These films and several televised performances have been reissued on DVD.

Playwright Terrence McNally wrote two plays about her and her legacy, specifically *The Lisbon Traviata* (1989) and *Master Class* (1995). Staged around the world, they further the legend and the artistry of Maria Callas. *The Lisbon Traviata* presents examples of gay men ("opera queens," as they were once dismissively known) obsessed with Callas' career and recordings, even enjoying bad pirated recordings like her *Traviata* in Lisbon, recorded illegally and then distributed in a sub rosa network, from fan to fan. *Master Class* shows Callas teaching at the Juilliard School. That play features a vivid and sympathetic depiction of Callas. Zoe Caldwell, Tyne Daly and Faye Dunaway (among others) have played Callas in this play in both New York and London. Dunaway optioned the rights, to create a film adaptation, and for several years announce that it was in development. It is said that she still owns the rights and still hopes to see the film project to completion—though as she approaches her 80s, she is nearly 30 years older than Callas was when she taught at Juilliard, making Dunaway's "dream project" increasingly unlikely (at least with Dunaway in the lead).

Opera houses in Europe are called theaters—Teatro all Scala, for example—and opera is considered a branch of theater, not a recital in a concert hall. Callas' recordings show us how a singer can color and shape a note to emphasize the dramatic quality of a word, a part of the drama onstage. This, too, is part of the Callas legacy and helps to continue her influence on contemporary singers and audiences—and even orchestra players, who also can use their instruments to add to the drama on stage. This is part of the Wagnerian concept of the *Gesamptkunstwerk*, that in opera, the experience must be music, drama, and all the elements on stage must contribute to the drama on stage. Richard Wagner emphasized that the singers must not just produce beautiful sounds, but also create theatrical excitement in front of the audience. Callas sang several Wagnerian roles at the beginning of her career, especially Brünnhilde, Isolde and Kundry, and it is unfortunate that she left this repertory so quickly in her career. She might even have become a great Wagnerian *Heldensopran*, had her career trajectory gone differently.

Singers who have followed in Callas' footsteps include Magda Oliveiro, Elena Suliotis, Gwyneth Jones, Renata Scotto, Raina Kabavanska, Joyce DiDonato and Sondra Radvanovsky. All of these sopranos became famous for their acting talent and their ability to make the words and the drama in an opera become of primary importance. Jones, despite a persistent wobble, was able to make opera exciting for audiences because of her commitment to the text and drama in a particular opera, especially Wagner and Strauss operas. Jones made a very interesting recording of *Medea* early in her career, which indicates her debt to Callas, since that opera had been frequently performed by Callas. Jones performed a memorable Brünnhilde in the centennial *Ring Cycle* in Bayreuth in 1976, and sang both Venus and Elisabeth in Wagner's *Tannhäuser* at Bayreuth to powerful dramatic effect.

Several cities have plaques on their streets, dedicated to the memory of Maria Callas: in New York, in the lobby of the hospital where she was born, now called the Terence Cardinal Cooke Medical Center; in Paris, at Père Lachaise Cemetery; in Milan, Athens, London and elsewhere. As the 50th anniversary of Callas' death approaches, her name is still widely recognized, even by those who've never listened to an opera.

Only now, in the 21st century, can we see her life and her legacy in a more even-handed way and from a more impartial perspective. She suffered much during her life, thanks primarily to her own neuroses, but she got to enjoy one of the most illustrious and fabled of careers in opera, thanks to her ability to mesmerize audiences with her sheer charisma, talent and force of will. Modern technology has enabled us to continue to enjoy her singular artistry.

Completing the circle that was Maria Callas' life and career: A new opera based upon her life was commissioned by the Bayerische Staatsoper in Munich (a co-production in conjunction with the Paris Opera, Berlin Opera, Maggio Musicale Fiorentino and the Greek National Opera). *The Seven Deaths of Maria Callas* was scheduled to world-premiere in the fall of 2020, until the Coronavirus pandemic made itself felt. Doubtlessly, it will eventually have a series of

Still the quintessence of international glamour, Callas poses for a candid photograph in the late 1960s.

19. The Aftermath and the Callas Legacy

Maria Callas in her signature opera, *Tosca*, at London's Covent Garden in 1964. Her performance in the title role remains the standard by which all ensuing Toscas have been measured. Her Tosca remains one for the ages.

major premieres and, based upon its success, could enter the repertories of opera companies worldwide.

And there is—finally—an official Maria Callas Foundation in Athens, established with funding from the Greek government. Greece has fully claimed its most famous opera singer, though she had not actually become a citizen of that country until late in her life. While an official Maria Callas Museum remains but a dream, in 2017 there was a hugely popular museum exhibition in Athens called "Maria Callas—The Myth Lives On."

History has largely forgotten that Maria Callas was actually born in America, in New York City, as Cecilia Sophia Anna Maria Kalogeropoulos. But with her passing, she became a virtual citizen of the world—and, inarguably, "one for the ages." The impact she made upon the opera world—indeed, upon the world itself—is inestimable.

Bibliography

I have used all these sources and have depended on them for previous works on Callas' life, performances, and legacy. An asterisk marks the sources that have been especially helpful to me.

Addison, Paul. *Churchill on the Home Front—1900–1955*. London: Pimlico, 1993.

Allegri, Renzo. *Maria Callas: Lettere d'amore*. Milan: Mondadori, 2008. *

Allegri, Renzo, and Roberto Allegri. *Callas by Callas: The Secret Writings of Maria*. New York: Universe, 1997.

American Psychiatric Association, *The Diagnostic and Statistical Manual of Mental Disorders* (DSM 5). Washington, D.C.: American Psychiatric Association, 2013.*

Ardoin, John. *Callas: The Art and the Life*. New York: Holt, Rinehart and Winston, 1974. *

Ardoin, John. *Callas at Juilliard: The Master Classes*. New York: Knopf, 1987. *

Ardoin, John. *The Callas Legacy: The Biography of a Career*. New York: Holt, Rinehart and Winston, 1982.

Atkinson, Rick. *The Day of Battle: The War in Sicily and Italy, 1943–44*. New York: Henry Holt, 2007.

Atkinson, Rick. *The Guns at Last Light: The War in Western Europe, 1944–1945*. New York: Henry Holt, 2014.

Aversano, Luca, and Jacopo Pellegrini, eds. *Mille e una Callas: Voci e Studi*. Macerata: Quodlibet, 2016. *

Bailey, Kate, ed. *Opera: Passion, Power, and Politics*. London: Victoria and Albert Publishing, 2017.

Beaton, Roderick. *Greece, Biography of a Modern Nation*. Chicago: University of Chicago Press, 2019. *

Bing, Rudolf. *5000 Nights at the Opera*. New York: Doubleday, 1972. *

Bing, Rudolf. *A Knight at the Opera*. New York: Putnam, 1981. *

Bret, David. *Maria Callas: The Tigress and the Lamb*. London: Robson Books, 1997.

Burton, Deborah, Susan Vandiver Nicassio, and Agostino Zino, eds. *Tosca's Prism: Three Moments of Western Cultural History*. Boston: Northeastern University Press, 2004.

Burton, Humphrey. *Leonard Bernstein*. New York: Doubleday, 1994.

Callas, Evangelia. *My Daughter Maria Callas*. New York: Fleet Publishing, 1960. *

Callas, Jackie. *Sisters*. London: St. Martin's Press, 1989. *

Cannon, John, ed. *The Oxford Companion to British History*. New York: Oxford University Press, 1997.

Capella, Massimiliano. *Maria Callas: The Exhibition*. Verona: Arthemisia, 2015.

Casanova, Carlamaria. *Renata Tebaldi: The Voice of an Angel*. Translated and edited by Connie Mandracchia DeCarlo. Dallas: Baskerville Press, 1995. *

Chiarelli, Cristina Gastel. *Maria Callas: Vita, Imagini, Parole, Musica*. Venice: Marsilio, 1981.

Davis, Ronald L. *Opera in Chicago*. New York: Appleton-Century, 1966.

DeCeccatty, Rene. *Maria Callas*. Paris: Gallimard, 2009. *

Dolkart, Andrew S. *Morningside Heights: A History of its Architecture and Development*. New York: Columbia University Press, 1998.

Edwards, Anne. *Maria Callas: An Intimate Biography*. New York: St. Martin's Griffin, 2001. *

Erlanger, Steven. "Jackie Kennedy's Letters

to the Man She Told No." *New York Times*, February 9, 2017, pp. 1a ff.

Evans, Peter. *Ari: The Life and Times of Aristotle Socrates Onassis*. New York: Summit Books, 1986.

Freud, Sigmund. *On Metapsychology*. Translated by James Strachey. Edited by Angela Richards. London: Penguin Books, 1984. *

Gage, Nicholas. *Greek Fire: The Story of Maria Callas and Aristotle Onassis*. New York: Knopf, 2000. *

Galatopoulos, Stelios. *Callas: Prima Donna Assoluta*. London: W. H. Allen, 1976.

Galatopoulos, Stelios. *Callas, La Divina: Art That Conceals Art*. New York: London House Maxwell, 1970.

Galatopoulos, Stelios. *Maria Callas: Sacred Monster*. New York: Simon & Schuster, 1998. *

Gillon, Steven M. *The Life of John F. Kennedy, Jr.—America's Reluctant Prince*. New York: Dutton, 2019. *

Ginsborg, Paul. *A History of Contemporary Italy: Society and Politics, 1943–1988*. New York: Palgrave Macmillan, 2003.

Hanine-Roussel, Jean Jacques. *Callas Unica*. Paris: Editions Carnot, 2002.

Hastings, Max. *Inferno: The World at War, 1939–1945*. New York: Vintage Books, 2012.

Hoffman, Perry. *Beyond Borderline: True Stories of Recovery from Borderline Personality Disorder*. Oakland, CA: New Harbinger Press, 2016.

Hutcheon, Linda, and Michael Hutcheon. *Opera: The Art of Dying*. Cambridge, MA: Harvard University Press, 2004.

Iatrides, John O., ed. *Ambassador MacVeagh Reports: Greece 1933–1947*. Princeton, N.J.: Princeton University Press, 1980.

Jellinek, George. *Callas: Portrait of a Prima Donna*. New York: Ziff-Davis Publishing, 1960. *

Kashner, Sam, and Nancy Schoenberger. *The Fabulous Bouvier Sisters: The Tragic and Glamorous Lives of Jackie and Lee*. New York: Harper Collins, 2018.

Kesting, Jürgen. *Maria Callas*. Berlin: Ullstein, 2018.*

Kesting, Jürgen. *Maria Callas*. Translated by John Hunt. Boston: Northeastern University Press, 1992.

Lauterbach, Iris. *Der Central Collecting Point in München*. Munich: Deutsche Kunstverlag, 2015.

Leaming, Barbara. *Jacqueline Bouvier Kennedy Onassis, The Untold Story*. New York: St. Martin's Press, 2014. *

Lebrecht, Norman. *Covent Garden: The Untold Story—Dispatches from the English Culture War, 1945–2000*. London: Simon & Schuster UK, 2000.

Levey, Judith, and Agnes Greenhall. *The Concise Columbia Encyclopedia*. New York: Columbia University Press, 1983,

Linakis, Steven. *Diva: The Life and Death of Maria Callas*. Englewood Cliffs, N.J.: Prentice-Hall, 1980.

Linehan, Marsha M. *Cognitive-Behavioral Treatment of Borderline Personality Disorder*. New York: The Guilford Press, 1993.

Lorcey, Jacques. *Maria Callas*. Paris: Pac, 1977.

Lorcey, Jacques. *Maria Callas: D'art et D'amour*. Paris: Pac, 1983.

Lowe, David A. *Callas as They Saw Her*. New York: Unger, 1986.

Ludwig, Christa. *In My Own Voice, Memoirs*. Translated by Regina Domeraski. New York: Limelight, 1999.

Macfadam, Alta. *Blue Guide: Northern Italy from the Alps to Rome*. New York: W. W. Norton, 1991.

Macy, Laura, ed. *The Grove Book of Opera Singers*. New York: Oxford University Press, 2008.

Marsh, Robert C. *150 Years of Opera in Chicago*. Dekalb: Northern Illinois University Press, 2006.

Mayer, Martin. *The Met: One Hundred Years of Grand Opera*. New York: Simon & Schuster, 1983.

Meneghini, Giovanni Battista. *My Wife Maria Callas*. Translated by Henry Wisneski. New York: Farrar Strauss Giroux, 1982. *

Michelin: Italy, Green Guide. Paris: Michelin, 1983.

Morbio, Vittoria Crespi. *Maria Callas: The La Scala Years. A Catalogue to an Exhibit at the La Scala Museum*. Milan: Umberto Allemandi, 2007.

Nardacci, Federica. "Vissi d'arte, On the 40th Anniversary of Maria Callas' Death, Federica Nardacci Talks to Robert Sutherland, One of Her Final Accompanists." *Opera*, September 2017, pp. 1138–41.

Nilsson, Birgit. *La Nilsson: My Life in*

Opera. Translated by Doris Jung Popper. Boston: Northeastern University Press, 2007. *

Pasi, Mario. *Maria Callas—la Donna, la Voce, la Diva*. Milan: IMI Press, 1981.

Petsalis-Diomidis, Nicholas. *The Unknown Callas: The Greek Years*. Portland: Amadeus Press, 2001.

Porr, Valerie. *Overcoming Borderline Personality Disorder: A Family Guide for Healing and Change*. New York: Oxford University Press, 2010.

Remy, Pierre-Jean. *Maria Callas: A Tribute*. Translated by Catherine Atthill. New York: St. Martin's Press, 1978.

Rosenthal, Harold, and John Warrack. *The Concise Oxford Dictionary of Opera*. London: Oxford University Press, 1974.

Sachs, Harvey. *Toscanini: Musician of Conscience*. New York: Liveright, 2017. *

Scott, Michael. *Maria Meneghini Callas*. Boston: Northeastern University Press, 1991.

Scotto, Renata, and Octavio Roca. *Scotto: More Than a Diva*. New York: Doubleday, 1984. *

Scruton, Roger. *Death-Devoted Heart: Sex and the Sacred in Wagner's Tristan und Isolde*. New York: Oxford University Press, 2004.

Segalini, Sergio. *Callas: Portrait of a Diva*. London: Hutchinson, 1981.

Siciliano, Enzo. *Pasolini: A Biography*. Translated by John Shepley. New York: Random House, 1982.

Simon, Carly. *My Friendship with Jackie*. New York: Farrar, Straus & Giroux, 2019.

Smith, Patrick J. *The Tenth Muse: A Historical Study of the Opera Libretto*. New York: Knopf, 1970.

Sordello, Enzo. *Autobiografica—Verita di un Baritono: Il "Fattaccio" Callas-Sordello-Metropolitan*. Mareve, Italy: Mario Astagiano Editore, 2000.

Stancioff, Nadia. *Maria Callas Remembered*. New York: E. P. Dutton, 1987. *

Stargardt, Nicholas. *The German War: A Nation Under Arms, 1939-1945*. New York: Basic Books, 2015.

Stassinopoulos, Arianna. *Maria Callas: The Woman Behind the Legend*. New York: Simon & Schuster, 1981. *

Stathopolou-Kalogeropoulos, Yacinthy (Jackie Callas). *Sisters*. London: St. Martin's Press, 1989. *

Stone, Michael. *The Fate of Borderline Patients—Successful Outcome and Psychiatric Practice*. New York: Guilford Press, 1990.

Sutherland, Joan. *A Prima Donna's Progress: The Autobiography of Joan Sutherland*. Washington, D.C.: Regnery Publishing, 1997. *

Sutherland, Robert. *Maria Callas: Diaries of a Friendship*. London: Constable, 1999. *

Taraborrelli, J. Randy. *Jackie, Janet & Lee: The Secret Lives of Janet Auchincloss and Her Daughters, Jacqueline Kennedy Onassis and Lee Radziwill*. New York: St. Martin's Press, 2018.*

Taylor, A. J. P. *English History: 1914-1945*. New York: Oxford University Press, 1985.

Tosi, Bruno, ed. *The Young Maria Callas*. Toronto: Guernica, 2010. *

van Zoggel, Karl. *The Definitive Maria Callas: The Life of a Diva in Unseen Pictures*. Dublin: Roads Press, 2016.

Vaughan, Roger. *Herbert von Karajan—A Biographical Portrait*. New York: Norton, 1986.

Voigt, Deborah. *Call Me Debbie—True Confessions of a Down-to-Earth Diva*. New York: Harper, 2015.

Warrack, John, and Ewan West. *The Oxford Dictionary of Opera*. Oxford: Oxford University Press, 1982.

Williams, Jeannie. *Jon Vickers: A Hero's Life*. Boston: Northeastern University Press, 1999.

Wirth-Cauchon, Janet. *Women and Borderline Personality Disorder*. New Brunswick, N.J.: Rutgers University Press. 2001.

Wisneski, Henry. *Maria Callas: The Art Behind the Legend*. New York: Doubleday, 1975. *

Yeomans, Frank, Michael Selzer, and John Clarkin. *Treating the Borderline Patient, a Contract-Based Approach*. New York: Basic Books, 1992.

Zanarini, Mary, ed. *Borderline Personality Disorder*. New York: Taylor & Francis, 2005.

Zeffirelli, Franco. *The Autobiography of Franco Zeffirelli*. New York: Weidenfeld & Nicolson, 1986. *

Television Interviews:

BBC, David Holmes TV interview, November 29, 1973.

David Frost, TV Interview, Dec. 10, 1970.
Edward R. Morrow, TV Interview, January 24, 1958.
Maria Callas, South Bank Show, LWT, London, 1987.
Maria Callas, "Life and Art," Kultur TV.
Mike Wallace, CBS-TV *60 Minutes,* February 3, 1974.
Today Show, NBC-TV interview with Barbara Walters, April 15, 1974.

Index

Aida (Verdi) 43, 53, 57, 58, 62–64, 67, 75, 78, 79, 156, 166
Andrea Chenier (Giordano) 86–87
Angel/ EMI Recordings 101, 102, 156, 172
Ardoin, John 152, 164, 181
Athens 4, 9, 10, 13–41, 50, 56, 79, 96, 98, 101, 116–17, 128, 130, 165–66, 186, 193, 200–201

Bagarozy, Richard Edward 34–36, 37, 55, 88–89
Bartoletti, Bruno 67
Bavarian State Opera, Munich 200
BBC 123ff., 138, 205
Bergman, Ingrid 120
Bernstein, Leonard 86–88, 203
Bertrand, Sandy 148
Bessette, Carolyn 195
Biki, Madame 47, 80, 107, 173, 189
Bing, Rudolf 85, 93–96, 100, 109, 126, 129, 130, 132, 133–34, 139, 174, 196–97
Bonynge, Richard 68
Bordoni, Faustina 71
Brutti, Emma 119ff., 192, 196

Callas, Evangelia 7, 8, 15ff, 22ff, 72–73, 117, 121, 124, 137
Callas, George 8, 9, 18–21, 32, 38, 101ff
Callas, Jackie (Iakinthy) 10ff, 30ff, 117, 120ff
Callas, Maria vii
Callas, Vasily 7, 10, 11, 115
Carmen (Bizet) 81, 134–37, 156, 174, 175, 189
Carnegie Hall 18, 173, 178
Caselotti, Louise 34–36, 39, 40, 41, 55
Cassidy, Claudia 84
Cavalleria Rusticana 27, 29, 175, 177
Chistoff, Boris 52, 66–68
The Christina (yacht) 106, 108, 111–18, 124–29, 146, 169, 206
Churchill, Clementine 27, 107, 111, 112, 125, 128, 203
Churchill, Winston 27, 107, 111, 112, 125, 128, 203
Cleva, Fausto 93–95, 100, 139
Colon Opera (Buenos Aires, Argentina) 55–58, 70, 91

Corelli, Franco 91, 96, 98, 138–39, 182, 196
Count Bardi Circle 64
Coward, Noel 69, 80, 129
Cusinati, Ferruccio (voice teacher) 45ff
Cusinati, Ferruccio (Callas' chauffeur) 169ff
Cuzzoni, Francesca 71

Dallas Civic Opera 90, 124
De Hidalgo, Elvira 4, 23–29, 34–38, 41, 48, 50, 75, 135, 150, 164, 193, 194
Del Monaco, Mario 53, 57, 62, 76, 79, 86, 91, 93
Devetzi, Vasso 169, 174, 186, 188, 190–95
Les Dialogues des Carmelites (Poulenc) 96, 206
DiDonato, Joyce 198–99
Dietrich, Marlene 69, 80
Di Stefano, Giuseppe 67, 76–77, 84, 87, 152, 166–69, 178–90
Don Carlo (Verdi) 83, 123, 137, 174, 175
Don Pasquale (Donizetti) 52, 198
Duse, Eleonora 61, 63, 64, 184

Epoca 70

Fate 11, 34, 51ff, 90, 136ff, 149, 156
Fedora (Giordano) 91ff
Fellini, Federico 192
Flagstad, Kirsten 17
Fleming, Alexander 14
Fox, Carol 37, 84–88, 178
Franco, Francisco 25ff
Freud, Sigmund 5, 9, 204

Ghiringhelli, Antonio 68, 73, 79, 80, 95, 109, 133, 134
Giacovazzo, Mario 154, 155
Gilbert & Sullivan 17
La Gioconda (Ponchielli) 34, 37–46, 76, 95
Gobbi, Tito 67, 91, 94, 139, 180, 196
Great Depression 15–18, 20–22, 31–39, 142
Greek Civil Wars 11–12
Gronchi, Giovanni 98ff

Harding, Warren 12
Haydn, Joseph 66

207

Index

Horne, Marilyn 68
Hotter, Hans 162

Irons, Jeremy 157, 198
Italian Fascists 21–29

Japan 170–80
Jazz music 26, 33
Jones, Gwyneth 6, 151, 199, 206
The Juilliard School 162–68, 199

Kabavanska, Raina 6, 166–68, 199
Karajan, Herbert von 79, 83–88, 92, 93, 204
Kelly, Grace 80, 105, 107, 108, 129
Kennedy, Caroline 159, 195
Kennedy, Jacqueline Onassis 117, 123–36, 140–55, 159, 167, 183–89, 195–98, 205
Kennedy, Pres. John F. 121ff, 137ff, 204
Kennedy, John, Jr. 159ff
Kennedy, Joseph 141ff
Kennedy, Robert 143–44

Labroca, Mario 60, 68
Lantzounis, Leonidas 7, 11–14, 33, 38, 80, 101, 137–38, 165, 186
Legge, Walter 80, 102, 133
Lindbergh, Charles 58
Lisbon Opera Co. 100, 199
Lomazzi, Pia 51
London, George 93
Lord Harlech 144ff
Loren, Sophia 41, 80
Lucia di Lammermoor (Donizetti) 4, 76–78, 81–88, 91, 95–96, 100, 124, 172, 188
Ludwig, Christa 104ff
Lupoli, Bruna (Callas' maid) 169ff
Lyric Opera of Chicago 4, 36–37, 84–85

Macbeth (Verdi) 73, 77, 100, 123, 34, 137
Madama Butterfly (Puccini) 4, 37, 88–89, 100, 138
Major Bowles Amateur Hour 33
Malibran, Maria 23, 48
Malozzi, Gina 102
Mandrex 186ff
Mann, Thomas 185
Marquess of Blandford 130
The Master-Builder (Kalomiras) 29
Maxwell, Elsa 80, 105–107ff
McNally, Terrence 100, 199
Medea (Cherubini) 78, 86, 90, 110, 117, 124, 130, 131, 193
Medea (Pasolini) 153–57, 168, 184, 185, 199, 200
Meneghini, Giovanni Battista 43–59, 69, 75–89, 107, 112–22, 132–35, 192–93
Mennin, Peter 162ff, 181
Menotti, Gian Carlo 79
Metropolitan Opera 3, 13, 16–18, 23–35, 78–84, 93–95, 100, 126, 139, 196

Misandry 187
Moffo, Anna 48, 96, 100
Monroe, Marilyn 80, 137, 138
Murrow, Edward R. 93, 197
Mussolini, Benito 8, 20, 37, 41–42

Nabucco (Verdi) 59, 73, 138
Nazis 21, 25–29, 55, 91, 128
New York City 1, 4, 8–11, 18, 30–31, 40, 56, 85, 130, 137, 141–43, 156, 162–63, 178–79, 195, 200
Nianias, Dimitris 192
Norma (Bellini) 4, 53, 57–58, 61–68, 75–88, 91–98, 138–39, 189, 198

Oggi 47, 70
Onassis, Alexander 106, 111–23, 159, 161, 166–67, 195
Onassis, Aristotle Socrates 37, 105–118, 132–43, 156–184, 189, 194–95, 204
Onassis, Christina 106, 120, 159, 195
Onassis, Tina (Athina) 106–112, 121, 206

Papajohn, Alexandra 18, 35
Parsifal (Wagner) 50, 64, 185
Pasolini, Pier Paolo 153–157, 168, 184, 206
Pastificio Pantanella 73
Pavarotti, Luciano 174
Piazza Bra (Verona) 42ff
Pinto, Barretto 67ff
Pons, Lily 48
Pope Pius XII 73
Pretre, George 134, 137
Pringle, Stanley 89
Puccini, Giacomo 28, 37, 47, 52–57, 63, 64, 81, 89, 94, 179
I Puritani 50, 61, 68, 75, 76, 150
Pygmalion 45, 69

Radvanovsky, Sondra 6, 199
Radziwill, Princess Lee 117, 129, 136, 140–42, 158
Rainier, Prince 105–108, 129
Resnick, Regina 135
Rochas, Helene 159
Roosevelt, Pres. Franklin 142
Rossi-Lemeni, Nicola 42–58, 67, 75
Rossini, Gioacchino 23–24, 28, 48, 64, 76, 81, 86, 91, 198
Roussel, Thierry 195
Royal Opera, Covent Garden, London 76–78, 102, 124, 129, 138, 153, 187
Rysanek, Leonie 100, 150

Schippers, Thomas 110, 193
Schroeder-Devrient, Wilhelmine 48
Schumann-Heink, Ernestine 17
Schwarzkopf, Elisabeth 80, 102
Scotto, Renata 98, 179, 188–89, 199
Serafin, Tullio 44–48, 53, 57, 62, 78, 81, 93, 172

The Seven Deaths of Maria Callas 200
Silja, Anja 151
Sills, Beverly 85, 165
Sirmione, Italy 76, 93, 188, 192
Sordello, Enzo 45, 86, 95
South Korea 170, 179
Splendid Pharmacy 13
Stancioff, Nadia 185, 190
Stignani, Ebe 62, 63, 75–77
Strepponi, Giuseppina Verdi 59, 73
Sutherland, Joan 68, 77ff, 152, 205
Sutherland, Robert 171–178, 180, 204

Teatro alla Scala (Milan) 3, 54, 59–62, 73ff, 83, 102, 110, 130, 166
Teatro la Fenice (Venice) 50–52, 60, 65, 77
Teatro San Carlo (Naples) 44, 59
Tebaldi, Renata 43, 62, 70–74, 77–79, 82, 93, 96, 182, 196, 203
Terence Cardinal Cooke Medical Center 7, 200
Tetrazzini, Luisa 17
Time 4, 93, 96
Tosca (Puccini) 4, 28, 30, 63–67, 76, 81, 85, 93–96, 100, 138–39, 149, 150, 177, 189, 201
Toscanini, Arturo 18, 44, 47–49, 61, 71, 73, 77, 205
Traubel, Helen 17
La Traviata (Verdi) 6–68, 76–77, 84–87, 92–95, 100, 156–57, 170, 184

Tristan und Isolde (Wagner) 44–45, 50–52, 62, 205
Tucker, Richard 43, 95, 100, 139
Turin Opera Co. 166ff.
Turkey 11–12, 24, 130
Toy (poodle) 80, 121, 168
Trivella, Maria 22ff, 48
Il Trovatore (Verdi) 59, 63, 77, 78, 150
Turandot (Puccini) 52, 53, 57, 58, 150, 179

Varnay, Astrid 162
Venice 3, 4, 6, 28, 45, 48, 50, 52–54, 60, 65, 79, 185
Vergottis, Panaghis 152
Verona Opera Festival 37, 38, 41–43
I Vespri Siciliani (Verdi) 66, 68, 166, 168, 175
La Vestale (Spontini) 85, 184
Vickers, Jon 111, 124, 130, 205
Visconti, Luchino 60, 61, 85, 86, 87, 91, 98, 100, 132, 157, 184
Volf, Tom 3, 198
Votto, Antonino 53, 61, 67, 85, 91

Die Walkure (Wagner) 42, 50, 150
Washington Heights 13, 14, 16, 18, 26, 31–33, 41, 55, 124

Zeffirelli, Franco 3, 44, 61, 81, 86, 127ff, 132, 135–39, 154, 156, 157, 168, 185, 186, 193, 205
Zenatello, Giovanni 37, 48

www.ingramcontent.com/pod-product-compliance
Lightning Source LLC
Chambersburg PA
CBHW052059300426
44117CB00013B/2210